Poli Sci

850

LONG SHADOWS

BY THE SAME AUTHOR

Jews: An Account of Their Experience in Canada

Stepfamilies: Making Them Work

Unhealed Wounds: France and the Klaus Barbie Affair

The Garden and the Gun: A Journey inside Israel

The End of Days: A Story of Tolerance, Tyranny, and the Expulsion of the Jews from Spain

LONG SHADOWS

TRUTH, LIES AND HISTORY

ERNA PARIS

BLOOMSBURY

Published by Bloomsbury, New York and London.
Distributed to the trade by Holtzbrinck Publishers

Library of Congress Cataloging-in Publication Data

Paris, Erna,
Long Shadows : truth, lies, and history / Erna Paris
p. cm.
Includes bibliographical references and index.
ISBN 1-58234-210-5 (alk. paper)
1. Holocaust, Jewish (1939-1945)—Moral and ethical aspects. 2. History, Modern—Historiography. 3. Genocide. 4. Ethnicity. 5. Nationalism—History—20th century. 6. National socialism—Psychological aspects. 7. Holocaust, Jewish (1939-1945)—Errors, inventions, etc. I. Title.

D804.348 .P38 2001
2001018455

First published in hardcover in the United States by Bloomsbury in 2001.
This paperback edition published in 2002.
10 9 8 7 6 5 4 3 2 1

Printed in Great Britain by Clays Limited, St Ives plc

For Roland

The arc of the moral universe is long,
but it bends towards justice.

– THEODORE PARKER, anti-slavery abolitionist

Contents

Acknowledgements

THIS BOOK would have been impossible to research and write were it not for the help of dozens of people around the world. Some provided me with important introductions to those who became central to my story. Others put aside the necessary time to be interviewed at length, discuss ideas and direct me to written sources or to places they thought I should visit. The unqualified support I received on this journey over four continents reconfirmed for me a truth I first absorbed as a student living in Paris: beyond the superficial differences of language and culture that divide us, most human beings share a deep commitment about what is just, in both their personal and their political lives; and, second, that it is often possible to communicate at a profound level with just the rudiments of a common language (or through the intermediary of a translator).

I wish to thank all those whose conversation and experiences became part of this book for agreeing to meet me; those who briefed me on the situation in their countries; those who interpreted from one language to another; and the dozens of complete strangers who assisted me at every turn. Thanks to the wonder of the Internet and e-mail, I was able to set up interviews across continents with the press of a button. I could send queries to people I had never met, who were experts in a particular field and, more often than not, get an almost immediate response. The Internet also turned out to be an invaluable tool in other ways: it offered me the chance to participate in several high-level discussion groups, including International Justice Watch, that kept me in touch with events long after I had left the country in question, and provided a facility for reading international newspapers on a regular basis. To name all those who assisted me would be impossible, but without their vast contribution I could not have completed this work in just over three years.

Besides those who are mentioned by name in the text and are therefore part of the story, I would like to express special thanks to the following people for assistance related to specific chapters.

Germany: Joel J. Levy, Thomas Frankl, Rabbi Gunther Plaut, Gerda Freberg, Rabbi Haskel Besser (Ronald S. Lauder Foundation, New York), Bernie Farber, Klaus Schütz, Daniel Mogües, Annegret Ehmann, Michael Bouteiller, Pastor Günter Harig

France: Michelle Lapautre, Lucie Aubrac, Raymond Aubrac, David Assouline

Japan: Joseph Wong, Catherine Bergman, Katherine Ashenberg, Brian Burke-Gaffney, Katsukuni Tanaka, Noboru Tasaki, Yukiko Matsuda, Akitsugo and Saori Taki, and Masamichi Sugihara and Kazuo Tanaka of the Japan Foundation, Toronto

United States: Maxine Sidran, Mark Potoc, Penny Weaver, Rep. Alvin Holmes, Joshua Washington, and the students and teachers at Septima P. Clark Corporate Academy, Charleston, South Carolina

South Africa: Marq de Villiers, Thom Rose, Vernon Seymour, Aggrey Klaaste, Bandi Mvovo, Robert S. Kriger, Brandon Hamber, André du Toit, Mary Burton, Stephen Friedman, Hermann Giliomee, Mossie Van Der Burg, Sam Hutamo

Belgrade and Sarajevo: Amela Simić, Duško Vidak, Bora Kuzmanović, P. Vlahović, Nemanja Krajčinović, Slavo Šantić, Sead Fetahagić, Kemal Kurspahić, Mladen Pandurević

The Hague: Minouche Mangnus, Patricia Sellers, Catherine Sissé

I am greatly indebted to several people who were kind enough to read draft material during the writing of the book, although I hasten to say that all errors in fact and interpretation are mine alone. They are R. John Pritchard, director of the Robert M. W. Kempner Collegium, Programmes and Publications on the History and Jurisprudence of International Criminal Law and International Human Rights, in London, who read the chapters on Nuremberg and Japan; Yoshiyuki Masaki, human rights activist and professor of English at Fukuoka, Kyushu, who read the chapter on Japan; Andras Riedlmayer, Fine Arts division of Harvard Library, who read the chapter on Bosnia and Serbia; Raphael de Kadt, professor of political science at the University of Durban, who read the chapter on South Africa; Thomas Lutz, director of the Memorial Museums department of the Topography of Terror Foundation in Berlin, who read the chapter on Germany; and David Lewis Stein, who read the chapter on the Holocaust. Lynn Cunningham offered useful suggestions on the first drafts of several chapters, and Don Obe edited an early version of the Japan chapter as part of my residency at the Banff Centre for the Arts in July 1996. Special thanks are due as well to Myrna Kostash, Phyllis Grosskurth, Alberto Manguel, Eric Miller, Ruth Miller, Tony Miller, Ian Montagnes, Maurus Pacher, Gail Singer, Victor Solnicki and my nephew, Adam Newman, for help that ranged from advice on subject matter to providing me with contacts and documentation.

Louise Dennys, the publisher of Knopf Canada, personally edited the manuscript with her renowned skill. I consider it a special privilege to have worked with her, as well as others in the Knopf team with whom I have been involved—Michael Mouland, Noelle Zitzer and Nikki Barrett—and freelance copyeditors Beverley Beetham Endersby and Alison Reid. My enthusiastic agents, Bruce Westwood, head of Westwood Creative Artists in Toronto, and his colleagues Jennifer Barclay, Samantha Haywood and Hilary Stanley never failed to bolster my spirits when my energy ebbed. I owe thanks as well to my editors at Bloomsbury for their commitment to this book: Bill Swainson in London and Colin Dickerman in New York; and to Derek Johns at A.P. Watt Literary Agency, London.

On the practical side, I am profoundly grateful to the Canada Council for the Arts for financial assistance with necessarily onerous travel expenses; to the Japan Foundation in Toronto, for financing part of my trip within Japan; and to the Cultural Journalism and Creative Non-Fiction program at the Banff Centre for the Arts for the productive 1996 summer fellowship.

As ever, my deepest thanks go to my immediate family for their generosity in putting up with a wife, mother and daughter who has been away, buried at her desk or generally preoccupied for several years. My father, Jules Newman, who died in January 1998 during the writing of this book, was a man who "[drank] life to the lees," in the lovely words of Alfred Lord Tennyson. His intelligent curiosity about people, places and ideas never flagged. It was he who first opened my eyes to the world. My mother, Chris Newman, has supported my interests for a lifetime. It was she who directed me, by example, to read a daily newspaper—a habit that taught me early in life that the most dramatic human stories can be found, unadulterated, in the real world. My daughter, Michelle Paris, has, for years, performed feats of technical wizardry with my ever-failing computers and been willing to listen to me read sections of my work aloud—for content, rhythm and tone. Our trip together to Yad Vashem in Jerusalem was an experience neither of us will forget. My son, Roland Paris, an assistant professor of political science and international affairs at the University of Colorado in Boulder, made an inestimable contribution to the research on this book. He supplied me with information about hundreds of relevant new journal articles, for the study of post-conflict justice and reconciliation is currently emerging as an important topic of academic investigation. Whenever possible, we talked together about the issues, which also interest him in a professional capacity. *Long Shadows* is dedicated to him, with love and gratitude.

Finally, my thanks are due, as always, to my husband, Tom Robinson, without whose devotion and unfaltering love not one of my books would have been written.

Long Shadows

Prelude

A Journey to the Stricken Lands

In his landmark work, *Nineteen Eighty-Four*, George Orwell reminds us of what the powerful have always known: "He who controls the present controls the past. He who controls the past controls the future." Although I first read Orwell's novel as a adolescent, I was well into university before I thought about what he might have meant. In fact, I vividly remember the occasion: it was a class in philosophy, and the professor was talking about the ways that those happenings we call history can be shaped by selection or manipulation. Since I had unthinkingly looked upon the known past as a circumscribed collection of facts that had been dutifully recorded by a tribe of faithful scribes, the idea that "history" might be vulnerable to interpretation—possibly *malevolent* interpretation—stirred my imagination. Perhaps learning happens when we are startled out of prejudices we are barely aware of.

Looking back, I may have taken the first step towards writing this book in that long-ago classroom, but the driving force came from my years living in France, during the 1960s, when I first encountered the grisly reality of the Second World War and the Holocaust by inadvertently stumbling across Natzweiler-Struthof, a Nazi death camp in the Vosges mountains, during a carefree weekend outing with school friends. A guide led us around the site. We were alone; there was no one else in that remote place. Trailing behind him, we entered a small building. Inside were two rooms, one of which was a gas chamber. We gaped while he explained that a Jewish mother and her adolescent daughter were the first to die there. I grew taut with dread, overcome by the instant crush of my imagination: that mother became my mother, I was her terrified child. We shuffled numbly next door—to the "dissection room." In the centre was a large table with channels for run-off blood. It was an oversize version of my mother's silver well-and-tree platter.

Nothing in my earlier life had prepared me for that encounter—I barely knew about the mass murder of the European Jews—and the shock affected me in lasting ways, creating a puzzle in my mind about remembrance. Because what was striking about my French friends and neighbours in those days was not so much what they said about the war as what they did not say. My questions were usually met with evasive replies or claims of wartime heroism on the part of the French Resistance. And there was complete silence about the fate of the French Jews, who seemed to have been left out of the story altogether. It was 1983 before the many-faceted pieces of that youthful experience began to fit together: that was the year fugitive war criminal Klaus Barbie was captured in Bolivia and transported back to France, where he eventually stood trial for his wartime role as head of the Gestapo in Lyons.

From the moment I heard about Barbie's arrest, there was no question in my mind that I would write a book about him—about his connection to France and France's connection to him. I sensed immediately that his story might allow me to explore the mysterious lacunae I had felt when I lived in the country, because, from the first announcement of his arrest, people began to talk as though their words had been bottled up under pressure and had just been uncorked. Barbie's return to French soil occasioned a virtual explosion of talk—and opened the door to a passionate national debate about the Vichy Collaboration. By the time I finished that work, I was hooked on the ambiguities of history: I could imagine nothing more compelling than to hunt down the ways that the past is managed to suit the perception of our present needs.

The question is, Whose perception and whose needs? Who gets to decide what happened yesterday, then to tell the tale?

As we begin the twenty-first century, many nations are wrestling with their unassimilated history. South Africa has held its extraordinary "truth and reconciliation" hearings, in the hope that the confession of crimes committed during the apartheid era might help heal the wounds of oppression and lay the foundations for a democracy that includes a full recognition of human rights. Since the end of the Second World War, Germany has paid more than 104 billion Deutschmarks in reparations to more than 500,000 survivors of the Holocaust and is still struggling over how to cope with the memory of that terrible time. France since the 1980s has been trying to come to grips with its legacy of anti-semitism and wartime deportations, and in 1995, the government finally apologized to the country's Jewish citizens. But the 1997–98 trial of Maurice Papon, the Vichy civil servant who was responsible for "Jewish Questions" in the Bordeaux region during the Occupation, made it clear that the national wound inflicted by questionable actions fifty years ago still festers. In Japan, there is increasing pressure to apologize to wartime victims: the so-called comfort women, who were sex slaves to soldiers; Allied prisoners of war; survivors of the 1937 Rape of Nanking, an event that is once again attracting public attention in the West; and anyone who escaped from, or survived, the Japanese medical installations in China and elsewhere, where experiments were performed on living subjects to develop tools of biological warfare. On the other side of the Pacific, Americans continue to struggle with the corrosive legacy of their slave past. In Chile, after almost thirty years of privileged licence, General Augusto Pinochet was indicted, under international law, for his crimes; and it now seems inevitable that Argentines who were responsible for the "disappearance" of thousands will also see their immunity dissolve. Finally, two international United Nations courts—one in The Hague, the other in Arusha, Tanzania—are trying people for crimes against humanity committed throughout the former Yugoslavia and in Rwanda in the 1990s. Other tribunals may be established for Cambodia and East Timor.

This unprecedented assault upon the impunity of the powerful, and the attempt to impose some form of justice (whether or not successful), are emerging as new benchmarks of international human rights at the cusp of the new century—along with growing pressure on governments to acknowledge past wrongdoing in the hope of creating a more just future.

I began this book almost by chance in the spring of 1996, while on a trip to Japan that had been organized for other reasons. Since I was there, I decided to visit Hiroshima and Nagasaki, both wellsprings of twentieth-century history and imagination. I was curious to know how the nuclear bombings of civilians were remembered by the Japanese themselves. The Canadian embassy in Tokyo kindly put me in touch with a number of key people, who led me to individuals such as Hitoshi Motoshima, the former mayor of Nagasaki, who was shot at for daring to suggest that Emperor Hirohito carried responsibility for Japanese warcrimes. But when I boarded the train for the south, I did not know that I was embarking upon the first stage of a three-year journey around the world and a personal encounter with the unsettled history of several nations, or that I was about to meet countless unforgettable people whose experiences would affect me deeply and shape my view of the past.

I became quickly aware that what I was learning in Hiroshima and Nagasaki meshed effortlessly with my long interest in the way collective memory develops and what happens to people who find themselves excluded from the narrative, and I began to wonder where else a carefully restructured, or selective, view of history might have patterned the present, especially after calamitous events. There were, I realized, dozens of situations in the world to choose from: the Troubles of Northern Ireland; the still-unresolved partition between India and Pakistan; the transition in Iran from autocracy under the shah to theocracy under the imans; the (certainly temporary) power vacuum in post-Soviet Russia; unassimilated Nazi memory in Austria; the long, unfinished lurch from Maoism to capitalism in China; and the human anguish brought about by Argentina's *punto final* amnesty for the perpetrators of the Dirty War . . . to name just a few. Above all, I wanted to explore the way that certain critical events have been remembered—or deliberately *not* remembered, as the case may be—and the effects on ordinary people whose experiences may, or may not, have been included in the official narratives of their nations.

The storyline of the book presented itself to me in a natural way: I decided to embark on a journey to explore first-hand the underpinnings of national remembrance. My subject would be the effects of war and its approximations—civil conflict, repression and mythmaking—seen from different angles. In addition to the usual library research, my sources would be my own experience as a writer fascinated by how, and why, societies redirect their course over time, and the people I would meet.

My first questions were, How to proceed? How not to become overwhelmed by the magnitude of the subject? I had deliberately chosen the most direct path, and the most intimate, which was to place myself alongside other curious travellers who have, over the centuries, explored the world through encounter with their fellows as well as by study, hoping that my long involvement with some of the issues would cast light on experience. I knew that in these voyages I would always be the outsider, always looking in, and from the start I was aware that I might be seen as an intruder. I could only hope that empathy and my genuine desire to understand the often bewildering patterns of national memory, with its fabrications, justices and injustices, would give me the access I needed.

The outsider enters the scene from a peculiar angle, which is why I have not included my own country, Canada—although, when it comes to historical memory, we have no shortage of material—from the endemic mating dance of Quebec and "the rest of Canada" to my country's shameful treatment of its native peoples, which is only now being addressed in small ways. At home, I am always a potential actor in events: either actively, if I participate in the ongoing national discussion, or passively if I do not, in the sense that to abdicate in a democracy is itself a political act. Although all of us carry our baggage of personal biases with us wherever we go, the view from outside appears to present a less cluttered perspective with fewer starting prejudices.

I decided too that I would travel alone, since tandem travel is better suited to tourism, in my experience, and solo travel would, I hoped, allow me to focus on the people I met, without mediation or distraction. But en route I did make occasional mistakes in judgment, as when I found myself in a dangerous situation in the destroyed village of Ahmići near Sarajevo.

Having settled on my mode of exploration, I then laid out my historical itinerary. First, because it is inescapably the most powerful legacy of the twentieth century, my starting point would be the unsettled history of the Second World War, a period I was especially drawn to. Japan, France and Germany have not yet overcome the fallout from that crisis, now so long ago, although each has tried to manage its history of defeat in its own way: by denial, in the case of Japan; by mythmaking, in the case of France; and by a painful complex of different approaches, in the case of Germany. In each instance I asked myself, How has remembrance been shaped, and what is preventing reconciliation after so many decades? Then I moved on to another theme of our time—a subject that lives at the heart of *fin-de-siècle* consciousness: the continuing conflict between the white and black races. In the West, this clash has lethally afflicted two nations: the United States, which has not recovered from the tragedy of having instituted chattel slavery on its democratic soil, and South Africa, which has tried to confront its apartheid past more directly. As the third motif of my historical journey, I chose to explore the way war can be used as a catalyst for national identity, and I picked the Jews and the Serbs as examples: the Jews have made the remembrance of a historical tragedy a central focus of their contemporary religious identity, though not without internal conflict, while Serb intellectuals and politicians consciously manipulated their national stories to serve deadly ends, victimizing their own people as well as millions of others.

Finally, I set out to probe the role justice can play in pacifying unreconciled historical memory—by visiting two geographical places of tribunals and judicial accountability for international crimes. Like so much else in my intellectual and emotional life, I date my interest in the post-war Nuremberg Tribunal, and the questions that were raised there about what constitutes apt punishment for deeds that penetrate to the core of our humanity, to that long-ago day when I happened upon Natzweiler-Struthof. I was determined to investigate the rebirth of "Nuremberg" in the new United Nations courts that were created as a response to war crimes committed in Bosnia, Croatia, Rwanda and, later, Kosovo—and to confront questions about collective guilt, forgiveness and forgetting that have troubled me for years.

As I researched and wrote *Long Shadows*, the subject grew ever larger in my mind. I was touched by the openness of people to a foreign writer they had never met—and by their willingness to try to articulate the connections between their individual experiences and the complicated histories of their nations. Because a rare kind of intimacy seemed to occur in many of these encounters, the book gradually became even more personal than I had originally intended it to be. It has become a diary and a journal, as well as the story of several countries and a reflection on the way history is made and remembered.

A Word about Sources

I read voraciously in preparation for each of my trips, and the titles of the books I found most helpful can be found in the chapter notes, but the following sole-authored works also deserve a prominent mention.

They are *Between Vengeance and Forgiveness* by Martha Minow; *Imagined Communities: Reflections on the Origins and Spread of Nationalism*, by Benedict Anderson; *Blood and Belonging: Journeys into the New Nationalism*, by Michael Ignatieff; *The Faces of Injustice*, by the late Judith N. Shklar; *Mass Atrocity, Collective Memory, and the Law*, by Mark Osiel; *Moral Responsibility in the Holocaust: A Study in the Ethics of Character*, by David H. Jones; *The Wages of Guilt: Memories of War in Germany and Japan*, by Ian Buruma; *The Unmasterable Past*, by Charles S. Maier; the brilliantly argued *Not All Black and White: Affirmative Action, Race, and American Values* by Christopher Edley Jr.; and an insightful book that I have returned to often over recent years, *The Roots of Evil: The Origins of Genocide and Other Group Violence*, by Ervin Staub. Every one of these works, and many others that I have noted in the text, were crucial to my understanding of individual countries and to the concept of memory. My only regret is that Peter Novick's fine book *The Holocaust in American Life* appeared too late for me to incorporate it into my research on that topic. I have also alluded to, and occasionally quoted from, my own earlier works on the theme of history, politics and memory, especially *The Garden and the Gun: A Journey inside Israel*; *Unhealed Wounds: France and the Klaus Barbie Affair*; *The End of Days: A Story of Tolerance, Tyranny, and the Expulsion of the Jews from Spain*; and an article titled "Pulling the Threads Together," published in *Beyond Imagination: Canadians Write about the Holocaust*, edited by Jerry S. Grafstein.

Memory and the Second World War

I

The Stone of Sisyphus

Germany

What is past is not dead, it is not even past.
We cut ourselves off from it, we pretend to be strangers.
– CHRISTA WOLF, *A Model Childhood*

A STENCH of sewage pollutes the streets of East Berlin; exposed wires dangle ominously; uncollected garbage spills into sunless, dilapidated courtyards. The graffiti scrawled across walls speaks of uneasy transition—layer upon layer of a still-stratified past. "Nazi lives here!" accuses one notice painted on an apartment building. "Attack fascism!" orders another. "Defend squatters' rights!" commands a third. The developers from the West are moving in, juxtaposing restored nineteenth-century facades and modern cubes of steel and glass with the decrepit cinderblock construction of the German Democratic Republic. Some of the residents are angry.

But the development frenzy cannot silence the airy whisperings of unquiet ghosts that can be heard, should one care to listen, in the hundreds of empty spaces that pockmark the city: in memory holes that have never been plugged, either by choice, in order to mark the terror of the Nazi era, or by default, as in the East, where the continuing presence of bombed-out structures and vacant lots was for decades useful antifascist propaganda.

It is these whisperings I have come to hear, these memory holes I have come to explore. And finally, after months of planning, I have arrived in the country that has for years been a source of personal uneasiness. Ever since I first realized the magnitude of the Holocaust and understood my own life as part of a swell of survival—I am the daughter of Canadian-born Jewish parents—Germany has felt forbidding and ominous. In the 1960s, when I was inexperienced and ignorant of history, I crossed the border from France into Germany several times to visit Freiburg, in the region of the Black Forest—a city that charmed me. That was before I visited Natzweiler-Struthof, the Nazi death camp in the nearby Vosges mountains; in any case, I was young enough then to feel closer to the Brothers Grimm than to Auschwitz. And I had not been back in the country since.

Now it is 1997, and I have learned over the years, in excruciating detail, what happened here between 1933 and 1945 and struggled to understand how and why. Part of this exploration has been about memory—about how calamitous events, such as the Holocaust, are shaped in the collective story of perpetrator nations, how ordinary people remember and what they tell their children. I have come here with the understanding of one who has studied the facts and now seeks deeper answers.

My plan is to start in Berlin—in East Berlin, to be precise, where the old Jewish community of the city used to live—and then to travel in search of the memories and the whisperings. Here in Germany, as elsewhere, some of my itinerary is planned and some is not. People tell me things. Or I just follow my nose.

Memory: the pre-war Jews of Berlin—once the centre of German-Jewish life—were deported long ago, but in an indefinable way their vibrant world remains both occult and palpably evident. Thanks to Joel Levy, a former American diplomat who now heads the German branch of the Ronald E. Lauder Foundation, which funds the reconstruction of Jewish life in Europe, I am staying in a partially rebuilt, once-famous building, the Neue Synagoge on Oranienburger Strasse in the erstwhile East, that feels to me like the epicentre of that peculiar ambiguity. When Levy invited me to stay here, in one of two or three available guest rooms, I accepted with alacrity: I thought—rightly, as it turns out—that I would not get much closer to the past than in a place that housed so many ghosts.

The Neue Synagoge was built in 1866, with thirty-two hundred seats, and for seventy years this stately palace-like synagogue embodied the excitement and bourgeois pride of the new Jewish Reform movement, which had embraced the modernity of the Enlightenment by casting off the embarrassing, outmoded forms of orthodoxy that differentiated Jews from their fellow Germans. In the Neue Synagoge, Jews practised their religion just as their compatriots, who happened to be Lutherans, practised theirs. They were proud Germans of the Jewish persuasion. But the synagogue was destroyed by bombs in the Second World War, and for the next fifty years, the charred ruins were left untouched by the East German government (along with other destroyed buildings), as presumed evidence of Western, fascist brutality: until 1988, that is, when the German Democratic Republic (GDR) entered its final death throes. That was the year Communist Party chief Erich Honecker promised to help finance the reconstruction of the famous landmark. (Since he was about to leave for a visit to the United States, he might have been hoping the gesture would help him overseas.) The government in Bonn also contributed funds, and the building's foundations were redone. Then, on November 9, 1988, on the fiftieth anniversary of Kristallnacht—the night the yellow-red flames of burning Jewish homes and businesses illuminated the Berlin night sky—a commemoration was held at the partially reassembled site.

That the reconstruction was merely partial seems deliberate and symbolic—like a Japanese haiku that forces the reader, or in this case the visitor, to imagine the rest. Half recalled, blurred, wispy, irretrievable, the building is here yet not quite here; it exists, and parts of it are once again in use, but it is now manifestly a museum and a pointer to the past. There is also a notable police presence, which unintentionally evokes both past and present. Every time I leave or re-enter the building, I pass through a metal detector and show my passport to the same suspicious-looking guards, who seem never to recognize me. A plaque to Kristallnacht on the outside wall attracts a steady stream of passers-by: they stop to read with looks of consternation on their faces. Before the Berlin Wall came down in 1989, few West Germans knew this place.

For an entire week, I seem to be the only person rattling around the upstairs halls—but nighttime is the worst: it is unnerving to be alone in a museum of missing people. I grow addicted to watching television and channel surfing. One evening I happen upon a U.S.-made documentary about unapprehended war criminals living in Canada.[1] Is this one of the first features on this subject to be shown to the citizens of the former

East Germany? I wonder. I sit ramrod straight on my chair, as the nation that invented Nazism is informed that *my* country has one of the worst records in the Western world for permitting the immigration of thousands of escaping Nazis and their East European collaborators after the war.[2] Of course, Canada is not the only country to have its shameful record belatedly confronted: evidence of iniquity has surfaced over the last decade in a dozen new places, as the terrible effects of the Holocaust ripple anew across the world. Even bland Switzerland has had to struggle publicly with its hidden legacy of appropriated Nazi gold.

Alone in my silent museum, I imagine the thousands of empty seats looming in the darkness just down the hall. They have been replaced just where they used to be—wordlessly memorializing their missing occupants. Inside these new-old walls, the past already feels too close for comfort.

In the streets that surround the synagogue are empty spaces containing nothing but remembered forms. Inexplicably, my guide and I peer into such places and talk about what used to be. She is Lara Dämmig, an East Berliner in her early thirties, who works for Joel Levy, and she knows this part of the city well, because, as a Jew who has "returned" to the faith since communism evaporated, she has spent a lot of time exploring such evocative sites. We walk together to a vacant lot, where the internationally renowned artist Christian Boltanski has created a conceptual work titled *Missing House*. Plaques engraved with the names of all those who lived in the vanished apartment house until 1945, and their dates of residence, have been hung on the outer walls of the buildings on either side of the emptiness: Jewish residencies ended in 1942.

We walk up the street, across a block, where one of the buildings once housed a day-care centre for Jewish children, then down the next street to a still-extant building with a memorial plaque to the Enlightenment philosopher Moses Mendelssohn and the Jewish school he founded there in the late eighteenth century. During his lifetime, Mendelssohn was held up as a model by liberal Christians who admired what they saw as his attempt to help his fellow Jews "Germanize" themselves and assimilate. But Mendelssohn rejected the idea of total assimilation as culturally impossible—and undesirable—in that it condoned the disappearance of Jewish identity. For him, the ideal of equality, which was inherent in the emancipation of the Jews, meant the right of the minority to continue its practices within an environment of liberal pluralism. What mattered was the willingness of people to live together with reason as the yardstick of the worthy life.

This was not to be, even during his own lifetime. Mendelssohn engaged in a searing public dispute with his friend Johann Lavater, a theologian who had challenged him to convert to Christianity. Afterwards, he suffered a nervous breakdown, and one can only speculate that part of his despair might have come from Lavater's suggestion that he would never be a "real" German as long as he remained a Jew.

From 1829 until 1945, the empty space next door to the one-time school was occupied by a Jewish home for the aged; then during the Nazi era (and before it was bombed), the now-invisible building was utilized by the Gestapo as a holding depot for neighbourhood Jews awaiting deportation to Auschwitz. The apartment dwelling immediately adjacent survived the war. At such close proximity, it is impossible to believe that the tenants neither saw nor heard what was happening to fifty-five thousand of their neighbours, which is the number of people dispatched from these premises. At least ten storeys of multiple windows look down on the spot.

Next to the vanished home for the aged is the largest of the disappeared places: the oldest Jewish cemetery in Berlin, in use from 1672 until 1827. Mendelssohn was buried here, along with many of his contemporaries, but these dead "died" twice. The graveyard was levelled by order of the Gestapo in 1943, and now it is a featureless expanse of land shaded by trees. Complete oblivion—with one exception: the site of Mendelssohn's grave was remembered and restored. On the crushed, levelled earth there stands a single memorial stone inscribed with the name and life dates of the man who once personified the dream of integration.

But while the vanished Jews of Berlin whisper to me of their fate by seeming to inhabit the shadowy empty spaces, the architecture of what remains of the recent Communist era openly proclaims its inherent fakery. Lara and I hail a taxi on Oranienburger Strasse and get out at Husemannstrasse, a thoroughfare that was rebuilt in the 1980s. It is just one outwardly restored street, large enough for the leader of the people to parade along, but the restoration was surface only. A decade later, the underlying decay has eaten through the cracks of the flimsy facades, and the roofs along the show street are in an advanced state of collapse. We continue to the famous Brandenburg Gate, where history and memory are on sale for a mark or two. Once, Adolf Hitler rode between these imperial columns as emperor of the Thousand-Year Reich; now Turkish pedlars hawk kitsch: GDR police caps (someone has patched on the red star insignia for added effect), Russian fur hats and Russian nesting dolls. A niche inside the Gate houses yet another piece of the unprocessed past: in tribute to the 1989 reunification of the two Germanys, an earnest lady presides over a non-denominational "Room of Silence," inviting all who pass by to reflect on universal peace.

Down the road, defaced and as ruined as Shelley's statue of Ozymandias, sits the former parliament of Erich Honecker. From here emanated the orders to shoot would-be fugitives scaling the Berlin Wall; from here the Stasi secret police kept tabs on everyone, with the help of everyone. Now graffiti sprout over abandoned stones.

Just over the Wall, the municipality of West Berlin had constructed a large, ultra-modern glass building facing east. Its message was obvious enough: enslaved people, look and see what *we* have! The Honecker government responded by erecting apartments that blocked the view and by designing maps for schoolchildren that showed East Berlin—and white space where the Western part of the city ought to have been.

The Nazis and the GDR, memory holes and histories overlapping. Fraternal ghosts of the twentieth century, still disconnected, still unabsorbed.

Lara has embraced Judaism, but without most of the trappings of organized religion, and she has *not* revived the wishful hopes of Moses Mendelssohn. Unlike the great philosopher, she describes herself as a "Jew living in Germany"—not as a "German Jew," an identity she adamantly rejects. In 1989, she avoided the joyful reunification celebrations because, in her words, the event was "too German." It made her uncomfortable.

"But you *are* German," I say.

She looks unhappy. "Well, yes, of course . . . No, that's not right! I am a Jew living in Germany."

"Do others feel as you do?"

"Yes. There are the Germans and there are the Jews, but even the *Germans* don't like to be German. They call themselves 'Europeans' or I don't know what. To be German is very hard."

"Do you have 'German' friends?"

"Of course! Lots!" She looks at me as though I have asked something impossibly stupid. "I was born here!"

I learn that Lara's ambivalence is not unique when she takes me to meet her friend Eva Nickel, who is the daughter of a Holocaust survivor whose first husband and two small children, age five and seven, were deported to Auschwitz. After the war, Eva's mother married the son of the brave Catholic family that had rescued her and tried to save her daughters. That young man was Eva's father, and he had insisted that she be raised as a Jew.

Eva's apartment is not far from the Neue Synagoge, where she works in community administration. And an extraordinary apartment it is, with a colourful history. The building was constructed by her great-grandfather in 1865, with money that had come into the family in an unusual way: an ancestor had purportedly saved the life of Frederick the Great of Prussia, in the mid-eighteenth century. According to what Eva calls "the family legend," the king fell off his horse one day during the Seven Years' War (1756–63) and was lying, injured, surrounded by his enemies, when Eva's ancestor—a soldier named Moses Isarch—rushed to the scene and lifted the monarch onto an ox cart. Isarch covered him with dry grass so he would not be seen and slowly walked off the field, with the king hidden under the camouflage. Isarch was well-known in Berlin Jewish circles—he was, says Eva, a friend of Moses Mendelssohn's; and Frederick, like Mendelssohn, was a leading exponent of the liberal ideas of the Enlightenment. In fact, his insistence on religious toleration widely affected the intellectual currents of his age. So the king was intent on recompensing the Jew who had saved him, and he paid Isarch very well—enough to allow him to establish a "foundation" of sorts. When Isarch died, he stipulated in his will that the boys of the family were to receive an inheritance, in order to establish themselves in a profession, and the girls were to receive money for a dowry—but only if they married Jewish men. "He could see what was happening," says Eva. "All the Jews were going to Church and becoming baptized. So he said the girls had to continue the Jewish line."

A charming story—whether true or not—that reminds me, as I listen, of the long, complex past of Jews in Germany. Frederick the Great—an "enlightened despot"—set the contemporary standard for religious tolerance. Eventually, reflecting the new ideals of rationality that were sweeping across Europe after the French Revolution, German Jews were emancipated into full citizenship towards the end of the eighteenth century. But there was also a particularly brutal history of anti-semitism in Germany that stretched back to the Middle Ages:[3] some of the worst massacres of so-called well-poisoners (during the plague years of the fourteenth century, Jews were accused of infecting the water supplies) took place in this community. On an icy February day in 1349, nine hundred Jews were hurled into bonfires in the city of Strasbourg alone. The blood libel (according to which, Jews were accused either of killing a Christian child in order to mock the Passion of Jesus, or of desecrating the consecrated host), though actively bruited about in many European countries, was nowhere more volatile than in Germany, where indelible images of "murderous Jews" cleaved to memory and folklore. Emancipation allowed German Jews to enter the modern world, where they prospered in the liberal professions and in business, but their very success raised philosophical problems for many people, as well as the usual jealousies. The social philosopher Hannah Arendt put it best when she wrote that "the breakdown of the feudal order [gave] rise to the new revolutionary concept of equality, according to which a 'nation within a nation' could no longer be tolerated."[4] Although many of the Jews rushed to convert to Christianity (a reality that Eva's great-grandfather had tried to counter in his own family), baptism was not obligatory, creating the difficult contradiction Arendt attempted to analyse. It was hardly a wonder that Moses Mendelssohn had had a nervous breakdown after his debate with Johann Lavater.

They were a middle-class family. Before the war, Eva's mother was a milliner, and her husband owned a transport company, but when the persecutions began in the 1930s, after the election of Adolf Hitler, they tried to leave for Argentina, sending their rugs and furniture to London in preparation for the sea voyage. But their passports were "not right," says Eva, and the money they had paid for them was stolen. So they stayed in Berlin.

In February 1942, her mother's husband was rounded up by the Gestapo at his workplace and deported. In desperation, Eva's mother asked a Catholic family—friends—for help. They agreed and took the two little girls to their country house forty kilometres outside Berlin. Eva's mother stayed in the city, cleaning the houses of loyal, tight-lipped friends to pay the children's board; then, when the situation became too dangerous for her to continue living in the Jewish neighbourhood, she moved in with another gentile friend: this woman's son became her future husband, Eva's father.

Every weekend, she put herself at risk by removing the yellow star that identified her as a Jew and taking the train to see her daughters, until the day in 1944 when she found them missing. They had been denounced to the Gestapo by someone who had seen them playing and was suspicious.

The apartment had somehow escaped both the bombings and appropriation by the Nazis, and, once again it became the locus of family life—although the family was now reconfigured. Eva was born in 1948, and she tells me that during her years at school, no one, including her teachers, ever talked to her about what had happened to her family. "Here in East Germany, everyone was considered a victim of fascism, but some of us had more status than others," she says with an ironic smile. "The Communist fighters were the most important and Jews were the least." I had been reading about this: the state-run war museums had glorified the anti-fascist struggle led by the Party, but the deportation and murder of civilians was barely acknowledged. It was the mid-1980s before a stone commemorating Jewish victims was added to the memorial at the Ravensbrück concentration camp. "East Germans never thought much about what happened during the Nazi era, except that it was fascist and now we were socialist," she continues. "We lived in a new world, and everything from the past was pushed away. This is what we were taught, and people from my generation heard and believed the same messages as their parents. But in their hearts they knew, we all knew. What happened during the Nazi time drew a line between Germans and Jews, and this is still true today."

She is as fully integrated into her society as any other East German; in fact, she used to teach socialist economics to high school students. But remembering my earlier conversation with Lara, I'm burning to ask a question: "Are you a German?" I ask her.

She shrugs and laughs. "I guess I am whether I like it or not; this is my language and my culture. But really, I live in two worlds. Even today Germans are very uncomfortable about Jews. They are very interested, and things that seem Jewish are fashionable right now, but obviously they have never met any. I was at a birthday party in Kiel recently, and when I told people I am now the director of the Jewish Centre in Oranienburger Strasse in Berlin, there was a long silence. Everyone looked down into their glasses. I find I have to learn to read faces, because when people hear I am Jewish, they are very careful about what they say, and it isn't natural anymore. This is typical. There is a chasm between Germans and Jews in spite of all the fake interest in Jewish culture. Between us lies the Holocaust."

It was 1992 before Eva could put her past to rest. Her mother never spoke about what had happened during the war, but for the rest of her life she talked obsessively about her two lost daughters. And she screamed at night. "Mother was very ill in the last six months of her life in 1987. She was always thinking they were coming back. She kept calling for them—Ruth! Gittel! Her last words were their names. From that point, I had to find them, and find peace for them, and for me. I went to Auschwitz. It was terrible. I stood in the gas chamber and beside the oven, but it was not good for me. Then I decided to go to Israel—to Yad Vashem, where they have all the names of the victims. By then we were allowed to travel, so I went, and I found their names. The man there was so nice to me. He said, 'You must go into the memory garden for children.' And I said, 'Okay, I will go.' I went inside the garden, and I felt very peaceful there—still and peaceful—for the first time. And from this moment I felt they were finally at peace, and so was I. I had found their resting place."

I finish my cup of tea in near silence, so heavy are the shared feelings in the room. It is not until we have said goodbye and I am walking down the stairs to the ground floor of the building that I allow the sadness to wash over me: sadness for Eva, for her suffering mother, for the lost children. I tune my ear to the whispering voices of the dead and think about the layers of history in this ancient sector of the city.

Although no one seems able to explain to me exactly why, the moneyed chic that has invaded East Berlin since reunification includes *Jewish* chic, and it is fashionable to approximate, or more realistically perhaps, appropriate, "Jewishness." This is true all over the country, but nowhere more so than in the eastern sector of the capital. In a land where few people under the age of fifty-five have ever met a Jew, Jewishness is the latest fad.

On Oranienburger Strasse, one can dine in the Café Mendelssohn, or the Café Zilberstein (someone researched the restaurants' original pre-war names); and there are dozens of klezmer bands composed entirely of German Christians playing to audiences of German Christians. Lara had told me she found all this disconcerting. "They are swallowing Jewish culture without any understanding or real interest," she complained. The apparent fascination with things Jewish does have a strange feel to it. On my first evening in Berlin, I had attended a concert at the cultural centre attached to the Neue Synagoge that included

Maurice Ravel's famous *Kaddish*, the Jewish prayer of mourning. The audience was mostly gentile Berliners, and they looked visibly stricken as they listened.

"Many Germans try to attend every Jewish event," said Joel Levy of the Ronald E. Lauder Foundation, when I questioned him after the event. "They send their children to parochial Jewish schools and Jewish summer camps. They come to the synagogue and the centre whenever they can. They can't seem to get close enough."

"But the Neue Synagoge is a *museum*," I said, feeling perplexed.

"That tells its own story, doesn't it?" replied Levy. "I don't claim to understand, but they seem to be looking for comfort."

One evening, curious to observe post-Holocaust religious life, I attend a synagogue service in West Berlin, and, since the environment is Orthodox, I am banished with the rest of the women to the back of the room, behind a latticed screen. One person there seems more devout than the rest: she wears a headscarf, is praying intensely and seems to be alone. I approach her after the service, and she tells me this is her first visit to a synagogue. I ask why she has come, and she replies that she recently had a dream in which it was revealed that part of her family had been Jewish, and through which she understood that she personally carries the guilt for the deeds of her gentile relatives. Since then she has prayed constantly to God to forgive her family and studied Judaism. Now it is time to participate in Jewish religious services. "I feel the guilt of my family and I know I must make things right again," she says earnestly.

"Do you think some of the Jews will eventually accept Jesus Christ?" she asks me.

"Highly unlikely," I reply.

"I just feel things in my bones," she sighs with a sad little smile.

This confused, passionate appropriation of Judaism is, it seems, not unusual. Several people tell me about the case of a convert to Judaism who had been taking a university degree in Jewish studies. The woman grew more and more agitated at the makeup of the class—her teachers and fellow students were all gentile—and the secular, historical slant of the course, until one day she exploded and shot her professor. "No gentile should be allowed to teach the Talmud," she declared self-righteously to the police.

The woman who has been running the Jewish adult education and culture program in Berlin for ten years, and is in a position to know about such things, thinks gentile interest in things Jewish is on the increase. "Germans queue up for three hours to get into our Hebrew classes!" Nicola Galliner tells me incredulously when I meet her at the Jewish Centre. "They say they want to read the Hebrew press in the original or that they're considering a trip to Israel. We've planned other events for a hall that holds six hundred and had more than a thousand people turn up. They are well-meaning people; most of them are middle class and educated, but the interest really does seem disproportionate. The smallest event in our tiny Jewish community—for example, hiring a new rabbi—often gets on the front page of the larger circulation newspapers in the city and across the country.

"You know, a lot of Germans are looking to Jews for answers, but this is not the right place to look. They need to go into themselves, to look at what their parents or their grandparents did. Sometimes I think they are searching for peace of mind, but you can't ask the people you tried to kill to deal with problems you might have because you tried to kill them!"

Her dismissive attitude seems to confirm Lara's rejection of her German identity. Neither of these women wants a close connection with "Germans," nor do they want "Germans," who may be feeling guilty and needing comfort, to come to them.

But Hermann Simon and Chana Schütz, respectively director and curator of the Neue Synagoge and the attached centre, understand the surge of interest differently. "In Germany we commemorate the concentration camps, and every school child sees terrible photos," Schütz tells me. "The Holocaust seems to be everywhere, all the time, on television, in the newspapers, but there is a still a mysterious prejudice because most people have never seen a living Jew. So they come to us with very odd questions about *kashrut* [kosher-ness] and circumcision and just about everything else."

Chana uses the word *they*, but her name was Christiane before her conversion to Judaism. Born in 1956, she was, unlike most Germans, the daughter of a family that had had a great deal of contact with Jews: her father, Klaus Schütz, was mayor of Berlin from 1967 to 1977 and Germany's ambassador to Israel from 1977 to 1981.[5]

"People see the centre and the synagogue as living memorials," says Hermann Simon. "They bring us things—boxes of photographs documenting their lives—because they think our archives are the right place for them. People come from America asking us to find out what happened to their relatives—yes, even after all this time. We have two researchers working on tracing, but of course it is twenty-five years too late for most of this work. Just yesterday a woman who was born in Berlin in 1935 came in looking for her real mother, who was Jewish. It's sad. Sometimes we get people who are embarrassed, who say, 'I had a neighbour, and I've always wondered what happened to him, so now I'm retired and I have more time . . .' I suppose this is a place where it is relatively comfortable for people to come and speak about the past. We keep learning more about how people acted and lived during the Nazi period."

"Until we arrived on the scene in 1995, only philo-semitic gentiles and the churches provided information about the Jewish experience. Now the Jewish perspective is being heard for the first time," Chana adds.

The Neue Synagoge and the attached centre have been open to the public for just two years, but already 350,000 people have come to the half-reconstructed building on Oranienburger Strasse to seek information or to see the permanent exhibition called *Teach Them to Remember*.

"Has anyone come here to confess?" I ask.

"No," snaps Simon. "We don't want those people. Never. Never. This is a problem."

"But how would you react if it happened?"

"This is *not* the right place," he repeats, closing the lid on the subject.

Germans and "Jews living in Germany." No reconciliation, as far as I can see. More than fifty years after the war, the new generations are shadowboxing with memories that seem unassimilable to both Jews and gentiles, and the standoff appears to be deepening, as repentant Germans try, in growing numbers, to atone for the deeds of their parents and grandparents, and Jews become increasingly uncomfortable with their entreaties and their appropriation of "Jewish space." I think about this as I leave Chana and Hermann's office. Is it ever possible for the living to "forgive" on behalf of the dead? Is it right that they even be asked? The moral dilemma is searing, for without "forgiveness," how will future generations conduct themselves? On the other hand, some lines cannot be transgressed. As Hermann Simon implied, certain absolutions cannot—will not—be made.

Remembrance of the Holocaust is multi-layered, and the restoration of memory has been long and slow, but there is, at least, movement now—unlike during the post-war decades, when the Nazi experience was rarely talked about. After 1945, Germans put away the past; it was the start of a new era, time to move on, to democratize with the help of the victorious Allies, to develop a viable economy, to approach the rest of Europe as a partner rather than as an antagonist. The Cold War was in high gear, and some former Nazis were welcome anti-Communist collaborators. Furthermore, although some Germans dismissed the Nuremberg war crimes trials of 1945–46 as "victors' justice," the international tribunal could also be viewed as a means of catharsis. Hitler and his henchmen were dead or duly punished: it was possible to pretend that the slate had been wiped clean, as the French did after the war. History could start anew.

But with whom? The post-war Federal Republic of Germany (FRG), under its first chancellor, Konrad Adenauer, needed a judiciary, but most judges had served the Nazi cause. They had condoned atrocities, sentenced prisoners who had been kidnapped and deported from occupied countries to death, tolerated the systematic murder of the infirm and backed the notorious Nuremberg Laws that deprived Jews of civil rights and citizenship. The Nazi judiciary had actually run its own concentration camps in the Emsland region and in Hamburg-Fuhlsbuttel, but after the war they were the only game in town.

The FRG also needed experienced bureaucrats, but having performed their appalling duties with efficiency and expertise, they, too, were tainted. The same was true for the diplomatic corps and the military: almost everyone had an unsavoury past. So, for practical reasons (few who had lived through the Hitler years in Germany would have escaped indoctrination), and because historical amnesia was a painless and easy option, so-called de-nazification was (at best) half-hearted, and people sentenced to jail were released as soon as possible in order to reassume their duties. In the immediate post-war years, the working infrastructure of the new FRG relied almost entirely on men and women whose personal histories included perpetrating injustice, and sometimes genocide.

Because this was a well-understood (if little-discussed) fact of life, West Germany also protected itself *from* itself with a new constitution called the Basic Law. The Law, first promulgated in 1949, opened with a statement of unconditional individual rights. It sought to curtail the possibility of unlimited, overly centralized power through division and control, somewhat along American lines—and it rejected isolationism born of nationalism by setting rules for a co-operative foreign policy. Recognizing that the war had been waged against the Jews of Europe, the new FRG also adopted the principle of reparations for survivors.

The new constitution became a bible for millions of Germans who were afraid their country might repeat its history (just as the new postwar constitution of Japan is a bible for pacifists in that country who fear a new rise of militarism), and it remains the point of reference for public intellectuals whenever there is a hint of crisis. But the learning from history that produced Germany's Basic Law seemed mostly institutional, because, at a popular level, the past continued to be suppressed. Although schoolchildren had general information about their country's recent past, many young Germans were ignorant of their parents' involvement with Nazism. At the family level, a deep silence reigned.

Sometimes the ambiguities of memory and forgetfulness bordered on the grotesque. The crematorium at Dachau was opened in the late 1940s—as a bar—and there were few memorials at any of the former concentration camps beyond anodyne, generalized inscriptions reading: "To the Dead: 1933–45," or "In Memory of the Victims of National Socialist Tyranny." Such bloodless dedications meant little, for as Thomas Lutz, the director of the Memorial Museums department of the Topography of Terror Foundation has pointed out, "Citizens probably tended to associate [such] monuments with the fallen soldiers from their town."

It took two decades before the first blows against silence were struck, and not surprisingly they came from the young. The anti-establishment "revolution" of the late 1960s in Germany was a part of the same movement that swept across other Western countries, as young people rejected the values of their parents, adult society and national institutions, believing that they could wipe out the past and kick-start history anew. But in Germany, the so-called generation gap had a special edge. Young people demanded to know what their fathers had done in the name of the führer; and when they found out, or (as was often the case) when their parents refused to answer, many families splintered apart. In schools and universities, some members of the traumatized second generation tried to redefine German identity in new ways. They rejected guilt in the absolute sense: born after the war, they had committed no act for which they could be condemned. In their idealism, they attempted to outline a new character for German society. If xenophobia and racism had led to the unimaginable, they would shun the values that had historically defined German "nationhood."

Some of them committed themselves to personal reparation, often through their churches. The Aktion Sühnezeichen Friedensdienste (Action reconciliation service for peace) campaign encouraged "atonement" in Germany, Poland and Israel by working with Holocaust survivors, restoring Jewish cemeteries and building synagogues, as well as caring for the handicapped—another group that had been targeted by Hitler's regime. Others were literally unable to remain on German soil. Years before this visit to Germany, I had encountered a woman in New York City who had left Germany with her brother after they discovered their father was an unrepentant Nazi. The brother had immigrated to Israel. She worked for *Aufbau*, a German-language Jewish newspaper. And then there was Beate Klarsfeld who, with her French husband, Serge, became one of the world's most notable Nazi hunters. I had met both of them in Paris in the mid-1980s, when I was researching my book on the Nazi war criminal Klaus Barbie, whose capture in Bolivia and return to France they had planned and carried out. Beate was born in Berlin in 1939 to a conventional family who expected little of their daughter; in fact, she dropped out of school to become a secretary. But in 1960, she decided to take a year off to study in Paris, where she met Serge in a café. He was a Holocaust survivor, whose father had been ripped from the family in September 1943; she was a callow student who knew nothing about her country's murderous history and was shocked to the core to learn.

She had never minimized responsibility by saying "it" could have happened anywhere; instead, she internalized the guilt of her parents' generation and committed herself "to restore my country's honour," as she put it to me when we met. Arguing that it is impossible to turn a page of history until those responsible for monstrous crimes have been brought to account, she furiously attacked former Nazis who occupied important positions in Germany during the 1960s and 1970s—including then-chancellor Kurt-Georg Kiesinger, who had worked for Josef Goebbels as deputy director of radio propaganda for foreign countries. On November 7, 1968, she attended the Congress of Christian Democrats in Berlin. Conservatively dressed as a prim secretary with a notepad, she approached the podium just as the chancellor was about to give a speech. "Nazi! Nazi!" she screamed, publicly slapping his face. The congress dissolved in pandemonium, and Klarsfeld was sentenced to a term in jail. But the publicity was worldwide.

In 1970, Beate and Serge blocked the appointment of Ernst Achenbach, a member of the West German parliament, as the German representative to the European Commission in Brussels. Achenbach had lobbied to stop war crimes trials in Germany, with good reason: the Klarsfelds had unearthed documents proving that between 1940 and 1943, he had been engaged in the persecution and deportation of French Jews.

Beate and Serge Klarsfeld were responsible for dozens of dramatic actions over the years, but in Germany Beate's passion was best understood by the angry young: by the late 1960s, thousands had joined the anti-Nazi crusade. The price she paid was family: her father was dead, but her mother was ashamed of her notorious daughter. "Everything I have done is as a German who is not a Jew," Beate has made a point of saying.[6]

It was not until the '68ers (as the younger generation called themselves) moved into positions of prominence that the process of restoring memory of the Nazi years began in earnest. The education curriculum was reformed: teaching about the Nazi era now included student visits to former concentration camps, and major memorials were created at sites of incarceration where atrocities occurred, many of them finally naming the Jews as uniquely targeted victims. Slowly, and against considerable conservative opposition, a reluctant acknowledgment of the depth and reach of Nazi collaboration within German society began to emerge, until by the 1980s the old view that the "monsters" of Hitler had been duly taken care of at Nuremberg, and that everyone else was a victim of National Socialism, had lost considerable ground. Karl Jaspers's famous distinction of four decades earlier—that there is a difference between "guilt," for which there is only individual culpability, and "communal responsibility," for crimes that could not have been committed without a collective looking-away, shifted back into focus. On the other hand, as Lara Dämmig put it so bluntly, none of this made it any easier to be a German.

The foreign passengers on the open-air bus tour are snickering: "Beautiful Berlin" is a gigantic construction site. Cranes wave menacingly over rubble, men in hard hats shout above the din of machinery and the dust from a million crushed building stones clogs the air. The speculators have arrived in force, "building for the future" as Germany prepares to turn yet another page in its history. Bonn is about to relinquish its role as the seat of the federal government, and for the first time since the Third Reich, Berlin will once again become the capital of Germany: the principal city of central Europe, straddling east and west, a strategic bridge between cultures.

Not everyone is comfortable with this return to the geography of a dubious past. Following unification, the great writer Günter Grass (who has been called "the conscience of the nation") declared himself "alarmed" at the potential for a return to nationalism and angered conservatives by daring to say that Germany united would be an inherently dangerous entity. There is, in truth, something discomfiting about the massive excavations and hovering cranes, the digging-up and the filling-in, that are a prelude to new construction. What lies buried underneath? The entire Berlin terrain is replete with unquarried war memories—and nowhere more so than next door to the old Reichstag parliament itself, at the enormous intersection of Potzdamer Platz. Now known as the largest construction site in Europe, Potzdamer Platz resonates with the screech of drills and machine whine; but at the heart of its vast circumference lies a no-man's land of grasses and mounds cordoned off with barbed wire: Hitler's bunker lies deep under this ground like an unexploded land mine; in fact, the entire area looks like an unexcavated archeological site. No decision has been reached about what to do with this embarrassing reminder, except to ensure a visible police presence on the grounds. One of the city's biggest fears is that skinheads and neo-Nazis will openly venerate the locale.

A few short blocks away lies another terrain of layered memory, the district bounded by the former Prinz-Albrecht-Strasse, Wilhelmstrasse and Anhalter Strasse. From 1933 to 1945, this small sector housed the most important institutions of Nazi terror: the headquarters of the SS and the Gestapo, the Security Service of the SS (SD) and the Reich Security Main Office (RSMO). Heinrich Himmler, Reinhard Heydrich and Ernst Kaltenbrunner all had their head offices here. At this site, the genocide of the Jews and the Gypsies was prepared and co-ordinated and the fate of the Nazi-occupied countries decided upon.

The Reichstag stands in all its nineteenth-century majesty (it was rebuilt in the 1960s) about to be reinhabited, in spite of Günter Grass, and so do the remnants of the Berlin Wall. The Wall, which was erected in 1961 to divide the Communist East from the "fascist" West, now attracts thousands of gawking visitors. Tour operators proudly point out the narrow passage from east to west once known as Checkpoint Charlie, and the emotionally disarming, one-word question someone once scrawled across the concrete in red paint: "WHY?" As many as a thousand people died trying to flee from East to West.

There was no response to that painful question. Instead, local politicians furiously reinvented street names to reflect changing realities. After 1945, Prinz-Albrecht-Strasse, which then belonged to the Soviet sector, was renamed Niederkirchnerstrasse, after Käthe Niederkirchner, a German Communist heroine who was murdered in Ravensbrück in September 1944. After the Wall came down in 1989, it was suggested that the street become Prinz-Albrecht-Strasse once again, but the proposal failed: too reminiscent of the Nazi era. Eventually, the matter was decided by the Berlin Post Office: they decided to keep the name Niederkirchnerstrasse and give the road its own separate postal code. "This is how Germans deal with history," laughs Thomas Lutz, a thoughtful man of about forty who has dedicated his career to the recovery of public memory.

I meet him in his office in the centre of Berlin, not far from the Bahnhof Zoo, the huge railway and metro station at the heart of the city: a place that speaks more to the present than the past, with dozens of destitute-looking young drug addicts and their dealers openly trading in the halls and on the sidewalk outside. Unemployment is high in reunified Germany, especially in the former East, and the marginalized are drifting to the capital in large numbers. The police are there, too—just watching.

Thomas Lutz directs the Memorial Museums department of the Topography of Terror Foundation. In Berlin, a permanent exhibition with this name documents the workings of the Nazi police agencies, but in addition to this, Lutz has since 1984 co-ordinated the work of a growing number of memorial museums located throughout Germany. There are sixty of these now, running the gamut from large, on-site concentration camps, such as Buchenwald and Sachsenhausen, to smaller places run by volunteers. And there are markers at several of the early *Arbeitserziehungslager* (educational work camps), which were used by the Gestapo to discipline national and foreign slave labourers. Memorials have been raised to homosexuals, the handicapped, resistance fighters and Gypsies, all of whom were until recently, says Lutz, "forgotten persecutees." Some exhibitions also document the involvement of professionals, such as doctors, psychiatrists and the judiciary, in escalating Nazi persecutions. Lutz estimates that approximately three million people visit these places every year.

The Topography of Terror Foundation offices occupy an entire floor in a high-rise office building, which leads me to reflect on the irony of bureaucracy and bureaucrats. During the Nazi era, men toiled at desks in the service of genocide; now, their stricken children, and sometimes their grandchildren, toil at desks in order to memorialize the victims. Lutz himself is a serious-looking, wholly committed member of the generation that has devoted itself to atonement. He tells me that as a high school student in the mid-1970s, he spent ten volunteer days studying and working at the Auschwitz memorial—and that this searing experience changed his life, catapulting him into the study of history and politics and the pledge to do peace work. "Commemoration is essential to the development of democracy in Germany, but the *way* we present information is important," he explains. "We help visitors empathize with the victims of the Nazis, but we discourage facile emotional identification. Since the vast majority of Germans were not victims, emotionality without context contributes little to their understanding. We see our task as giving people the tools they need to integrate the events of the Third Reich into an understanding of history."

He says he starts from the belief that acknowledging the murdered Jews of Europe is Germany's most important task. "Virtually all the larger memorial museums in reunited Germany now refer to the fate of the Jews, and although the treatment of the subject in the GDR [East Germany] left much to be desired, there have been improvements there. All our memorials strive to reconstruct the links that existed between the central terror agencies here in Germany and the murder sites that were located outside—in Poland, for example." We make a date to meet the following day at the *Topography of Terror* exhibition: it is at the heart of the old memory terrain around the Reichstag—attached to the excavated foundations of the former Gestapo headquarters.

The complete name of the exhibition is *Topography of Terror: Gestapo SS and Reich Security Main Office*. Its location—next to the Gestapo and immediately adjacent to the Wall—is deliberately ironic. When it first opened in 1987, in conjunction with the 750th-anniversary celebrations of Berlin, the presentation was meant to be temporary, but it became so popular with the German public that it was continued on a permanent basis. Ten years later, between 100,000 and 150,000 people still visit annually. "It is far more difficult to erect a monument when you are the perpetrator and not the victim," Lutz explains as we stand outside. "*Topography of Terror* is our attempt to invite the German public in."

We look at the foundations of the Gestapo building: it was destroyed by Allied bombing, but the old prison cells in the basement have been exposed. I try to imagine the innards of this place as it was then—try to imagine the men, whose very names frighten me, at their desks, poring over their charts of occupied Europe, studying their daily dispatches from the Einsatzgruppen (the SS-led killing squads that followed in the army's wake) on the Eastern front: from Ukraine, for example, where members of my own family were murdered in 1941. Here, more than anywhere so far, the apprehension I have brought with me into Germany feels the strongest: simply to stand in this place of memory fills me with dread.

Lutz leaves, and I enter the exhibition. It is a straight-arrow, no-nonsense mix of information and photographs about the bureaucracy of Nazi terror. First, the SS and the Jews, starting with the application of the Nuremberg Laws, through the deportations and concluding with the role of the police in the death camps. The photograph of an elderly Berlin Jew in topcoat and formal hat waiting apprehensively with others at the train station needs no caption: this was a thoroughly assimilated, middle-class German citizen being expelled, we viewers know, to his certain death. The exhibition documents the deportation of Gypsies and nationals from other countries; the fate of political prisoners, some of whom were held in the Gestapo cellars just next door; and the last days of the war, when this central core of the city was devastated by bombs. There are official portraits of the men who sat at the top of the Nazi police hierarchy, including evocative and deliberately provocative portraits of SS cadres who died peacefully of old age in the post-war FRG.

I am struck by the psychology of killing as captured by the uncensored camera lens. On one wall hangs a framed photograph that was taken seconds before a multiple murder. We are somewhere in Latvia in 1941. Three anonymous men kneel at the edge of a pit as three SS members of the Einsatzgruppen stand over them, holding guns to their necks. The gunner closest to the camera grins with excitement. I have seen similar scenes in other museums. This is always what disturbs me most. The indisputable pleasure that spreads over the murderer's face.

I walk around the building and order tea at an outdoor café on the cobblestone terrace of the Martin-Gropius-Bau building: a lovely nineteenth-century structure that was rebuilt at the end of the 1970s, when it was restored to its original use as a museum and exhibition hall. The shadows of late afternoon grow long and languid, but at the outside edges of tranquility the scars of war still jar the senses: fifty years later, machine-gun holes from heavy fighting in the last days of the war still pockmark the Martin-Gropius-Bau walls. Eighteen months of saturation bombing destroyed most of the buildings in this sector, starting in November 1943, and the half-obliterated hulks and empty, bombed-out spaces surely helped promote amnesia at the same time as they called attention to the past. Because after the defeat, most Berliners preferred to ignore the ignominious locale, in spite of occasional, mostly desultory talk about "coming to terms with the past." They spurned the site for decades, "pretending to be strangers," as the writer Christa Wolf put it. What remained of the core buildings was blown up after the war, followed by rubble clearing and razing, until the physical terrain of Nazi memory was a flattened, empty space.

I glance at some of the voluminous documentation Thomas Lutz gave me on his work and the history of German memorials, and learn that after ten years the city of Berlin announced plans for an international urban renewal contest "to fashion the center in such a way that it will become a visible expression of Germany's capital and that of a modern metropolis."[7] However, the erection of the Berlin Wall at the heart of the former Nazi capital summarily ended these schemes to bury the past under a new "modern" present. The Wall further eroded the memory of Nazi days: Who cared to reflect on what had happened on this spot when the symbol of a divided city, a divided country and a divided world assaulted sensibilities on a daily basis?

It was the late 1970s before the beginning of a public discussion ensued. What should be done with the space? Someone proposed a plan for a road reconstruction, which elicited an open letter from the International League for the Rights of Man to the Senator of Internal Affairs, reminding him that "the brown terror once held sway on Prinz-Albrecht-Strasse" and demanding that a dignified memorial be incorporated into the plans. In 1983, then-mayor Richard von Weizsäcker sponsored a competition. "For better or for worse, Berlin is the custodian of German history," he said, announcing the event: "It is not only as a sponsor that I take a lively interest in this remarkable contest."[8] True enough, his interest was far from academic: von Weizsäcker, too, was a son of the Nazi past. From 1938 to 1943, Ernst von Weizsäcker, his father, was the leading civil servant at the Foreign Office of the Third Reich, and in 1946, young Richard had defended him before the tribunal at Nuremberg.

The contest rules stated that the successful applicant would "reconcile the historic depth of the location" with practical functions. People submitted proposals. Someone won. Then in 1984, the Senate resolved not to proceed.

The ostensible reason for the cancellation was a decision to wait for the 750-year celebration of the city of Berlin, a festive occasion that would, it was hoped, overshadow the gloomy necessity to remember "the historic depth of the location." But it was already too late for such official transparencies. In early May 1985, just days before the fortieth anniversary of the Nazi defeat, an organization calling itself Aktives Museum Faschismus und Widerstand in Berlin (Active museum of fascism and resistance in Berlin) sent out an appeal for a "symbolic dig" at the site of the former Gestapo headquarters. "At 11 A.M. on Sunday, May 5, we will try to draw attention to the history of the terrain at Prinz-Albrecht-Palais," the organizers wrote. "The approach of May 8, the anniversary of liberation from Nazi Fascism, prompts us to commemorate the resistance fighters who at immense sacrifice offered opposition to the Nazi regime. . . . Furthermore, we demand that in future days, a 'site of contemplation' be built on the spot where the terror headquarters of German Fascism once stood. This way the experiences and insights gained from history will be passed on so that fascism and war shall never again spring from German soil."[9]

On May 8, a small group of young people arrived at the site of the Gestapo, carrying signs that read "Dig Where You Stand," and before a crowd of astonished onlookers, they began to hack at the earth, to dig into the history of the place, so to speak—to excavate the foundations of a taboo past.

"It was a turning point," Thomas Lutz tells me when I call to talk about his literature.

Then, in December 1985, a group called Citizens Concerned with the History and Future of the Gestapo Terrain wrote to the new mayor of Berlin, Eberhard Diepgen. They reminded him that the Nazi site had international significance and informed him that the disposition of the site no longer fell under his unique jurisdiction. "Neither politicians, special administrative bodies, nor single individuals are competent by themselves to determine the terrain's future appearance, or to safeguard the still remaining traces of the state's former terror headquarters. This is simply not possible after a process of repression that has lasted forty years," they said.[10]

Was it their courage and their boldness? Where officialdom had stalled and prevaricated, ordinary people—young people—had taken over, and this time the municipality of Berlin caved in. Excavations began, the still-intact basement walls of the Gestapo building and the layout of former cells were uncovered: the ghostly architecture of a buried past, reassembling itself at last.

Richard von Weizsäcker was by then president of the Federal Republic, and on May 8, 1985, on the fortieth anniversary of the Nazi defeat, he delivered a speech to the Bundestag about the past and present of his nation, thus becoming the highest-ranking German politician to speak openly about the victims of Nazi crimes and the need to keep memory alive. His words about historical blindness have become so famous that they now risk being dismissed as cliché—wisdom so encapsulated can be easily jeopardized—but I doubt they can be too often repeated. He paid tribute to "the endless army of the dead [and the] mountains of human suffering," and to those who were sterilized, raped or forced to labour under inhuman conditions. He called attention to the special suffering of women in all the occupied nations and to the fact that mentally disturbed persons, Gypsies and homosexuals also were murdered under the Third Reich. He recalled the price paid by those who had tried to resist Hitler. "At the root of the tyranny," said von Weizsäcker, "was Hitler's immeasurable hatred against our Jewish compatriots. . . . The genocide of the Jews is . . . unparalleled in history. The forefathers [of our younger generation] have left them a grave legacy. . . . Anyone who closes his eyes to the past is blind to the present. Whoever refuses to remember the inhumanity is prone to new risks of infection."[11]

There had been other high-level gestures: in 1970, Willy Brandt fell to his knees before the Warsaw ghetto memorial in a breathtaking act of repentance. Nonetheless, Richard von Weizsäcker's speech to parliament was the most important moral statement made by a prominent German in the post-Nazi period, and it marked a point of change. "Before von Weizsäcker spoke in 1985, it was difficult to get a politician to speak at one of the former Nazi sites in Berlin," Thomas Lutz said. "By the fiftieth anniversary in 1995, they had to sign up on a list."

Signing up on a list indicated that efforts to teach and to reconcile had become mainstream. But I am carrying in my files statistical evidence of other attitudes towards the past: a survey carried out by the American Jewish Committee's Institute of Human Relations in 1994. The study, called "Current German Attitudes Towards Jews and Other Minorities," was conducted by interviewing 1,434 respondents (992 from the former West Germany, and 442 from the former East). The findings, which were considered to be an accurate sample of the population, according to age, gender, region, political orientation and education, were fascinating—especially given the concern for, and identification with, Jews. Twenty per cent thought Jews had "too much influence" in German society; 31 per cent said Jews "exert too much influence on world events"; 39 per cent thought "Jews are exploiting the Holocaust for their own purposes"; 40 per cent believed that "the Holocaust is not relevant today"; and a whopping 56 per cent (in the former West) endorsed this statement: "In the aftermath of German unification, we should not talk so much about the Holocaust, but should draw a line under the past." These negative attitudes existed in spite of high levels of factual knowledge, since 87 per cent could accurately define the Holocaust, and 92 per cent knew that Auschwitz, Dachau and Treblinka were concentration camps.

Sixty per cent of the Germans polled did want to preserve the memory of the Holocaust; in other words, they approved of the work of Thomas Lutz and the others. But the negative numbers were disturbingly high. That they were even higher for other minorities, such as Gypsies, Turks, Vietnamese, Africans, Poles and Arabs, only increased worries about xenophobia.[12]

There is, I have learned, in a place called Friedrichstadt—a small town in Schleswig-Holstein, near the North Sea—a man who has recreated the entire history of the Jews of his community. No one knows quite who he is or why he has done this. I am intrigued; and after several dead-end leads, starting in Toronto, where I first heard about him from a German-born survivor of the Holocaust, I find him. His name is Karl Michelsohn.

After eight days in Berlin, I leave the city on a fast trans-European train headed for Hamburg, where I change for a local "milk train" travelling north. We chug past circling windmills, people on bicycles pedalling along tree-lined dirt lanes and fallow fields where cows and sheep graze. We pass tiny village clusters of red-brick houses topped with steep, sloping roofs with red shingles, although more than a few are thatched in the centuries-old way. Intimations of a bucolic, tranquil life.

Friedrichstadt, population twenty-seven hundred, is a tiny jewel set in a serene landscape: a seventeenth-century town originally settled by Dutch merchants from Amsterdam. A miniature canal cuts through the *Altstadt*, or old city. Like so much of what appears to remain of prewar German architecture, this "ancient" *Altstadt* was faithfully reconstructed down to its artificially weathered gables, stone bridge and cobblestones. But unlike the Neue Synagoge in Berlin, which was only partially rebuilt in order to stimulate memory, or the ruins of East Berlin and the area around the Reichstag, which were left in their razed state, the Friedrichstadt *Altstadt* has been duplicated as though there never was a war. A plaque outside the town hall reads "Friedrichstadt, City of Tolerance," with a reference to the Mennonites. Tolerance seems to be the town's historical claim to fame. On the other hand, there had been Jews here since 1675; that much I know. And now there are none.

Karl Michelsohn is a fit, youthful-looking man in his seventies, a retired accountant who lives in a little house bordering the fairy-tale canal. He is, he tells me, an amateur historian, a member of the local history society. In 1971, while researching old stories about the town, including stories about the Jews, he began to ask questions. There were just forty Jews in Friedrichstadt when the war broke out (over the decades, most of the community had moved to Hamburg), but Michelsohn had gone to school with Jewish children and he wanted to know their fate. There was a pogrom in Friedrichstadt on Kristallnacht, in November 1938. That was the last time he saw any of them.

He is surprised that I have come from faraway Berlin to meet him, since as far as he is concerned, what he has done is of local interest only. I reply that I have been determined to find him, because I think that on the contrary, his work of reclaiming history is of deep importance—that in trying to trace those who fell into a void of oblivion, he is restoring dignity to their lives, as well as retrieving the lost pieces of his town's history. He looks pleased and tells me that what began as a hobby has finished as an obsession. At first his friends and neighbours were discouraging: they said he wouldn't find records of the Jewish presence, but he has proved them wrong. From the town archives, he has dug out birth certificates, school report cards, passports, handwritten business ledgers, personal correspondence and greeting cards that had been stashed away indifferently after the Nazi pogrom: the minutiae of a community that had apparently vanished without a trace. He has tracked the paths of their deportations (many went first to Theresienstadt, then to Auschwitz), and the deeper he has probed, the more involved he has become. Almost three decades have passed since he began, but his work is not yet complete.

We walk along the little canal and stop before a building that used to be the synagogue. It was built in 1845, and it was also the Jewish school and the rabbi's home, he says, but it was mostly destroyed by the Nazis, then later reconstructed as a house. There is a plaque on the wall. It reads: "Let us live together in tolerance and remain vigilant."

"Who wrote this?" I ask him.

"I did," he replies shyly.

We continue through the tiny streets to the town archives: another miniature space, with glass cabinets filled with the medieval seals and emblems of the city. A small room has been allotted for his research, an area crammed with filing drawers and display cases. "This is my book of remembrance," he says softly, pointing to a large portfolio under glass. One page has been assigned to each of Friedrichstadt's Jews.

He pulls down a few of the blue loose-leaf folders stacked neatly on shelves and opens the first one at random: it is the archive of the Kurt Heyman family, containing a school report card from 1920, a visiting card, Heyman's official permission to practise a profession (he sold horses), an application for a passport stamped with a large *J* (for *Jude*) in red ink, and, in 1938, an official confirmation that the name *Israel* had been added to Heyman's official file, according to the law.

Michelsohn waves his hand over his face and laughs incredulously. "It's so hard to understand, so totally crazy!" Our translator, Britta Willrodt, looks shocked. Although she is thirty-eight years old and a schoolteacher, she didn't know this detail of the lexicon of Nazi humiliation: that all Jewish men were forced to add the name Israel, and all Jewish women the name Sarah. "When I was in school my teachers told us to go and ask our parents what happened during the war, but in my family no one really wanted to talk, so I just didn't push things," she says. "Now it is too late to go further. My father died." She is blushing fiercely, as though she personally had done something shameful. "It's a problem, it's a problem," she murmurs, looking away.

Karl Michelsohn joined the Hitler Youth like the other young people in his town, but he insists that with the exception of one teacher, who grabbed his friend Rolf Meyer's ear and said to the class, "This is what a Jew looks like!" there was little or no anti-semitism in Friedrichstadt. Even though there were many Nazis. "Nazis who weren't anti-semites?" I ask him.

"Yes," he insists. "The Gestapo was in the nearby towns of Kiel and Flensburg, and it was the people from those places who effected the pogroms, not locals."

Friedrichstadt once had a long history of fine intercommunity relations. He shows me records indicating that Jews contributed to the rebuilding of the Lutheran church in 1762, and when we visit the church an hour or so later, I note a plaque on the wall that marks the participation of Jewish soldiers from Friedrichstadt in the war of 1848–50. But that was centuries ago. Still, he is resolute: "Before 1930, there were Jews in our municipal government," he says firmly.

He served with the Wehrmacht on the Russian front, and he tells me the war was over before he learned what happened to the Jews. ("I had to believe it, even though I did not want to. It was a terrible disappointment. I always thought Germans were good people," he says sorrowfully.) But the men of the former Wehrmacht are currently experiencing difficult times: a travelling exhibition called *Extermination War: Crimes of the Wehrmacht 1941–44* is touring the country and causing an uproar. The exhibition documents the killing of Jews, Gypsies and prisoners of war by the regular German army in the Soviet Union and the Balkans—not the Einsatzgruppen but the army. There are pictures of civilians being shot and letters and diaries written by ordinary Wehrmacht soldiers telling of mass killings. The curator, Hannes Heer, has been quoted as saying that he does not wish to suggest that every army unit committed atrocities, but that what happened needs to be known. Neo-Nazis have been demonstrating in cities hosting the exhibition with signs that read: "Our fathers were not criminals and we are proud of them," and anti-immigrant banners that say: "Jobs for Germans First."

Karl Michelsohn has heard about the exhibition, and he is shocked. "*Nothing* like that happened in my unit!" he says.

Building block by building block, he has reconstituted an archive of three hundred years of Jewish life in Friedrichstadt, from the mid-seventeenth to the mid-twentieth century. He raised funds to restore the synagogue. Friedrichstadt survivors and their sons and daughters sent him documents for his archives, and every year someone from somewhere in the world arrives on a pilgrimage to the town of their, or their parents', ancestors. He is, just now, about to receive visitors from the United States and Paraguay. He always takes them to the archives and brings down their family book. "They sit at this table and they weep," he says quietly, indicating the place.

"We are ashamed, all of us," he adds, looking out the window. "With my work I am trying to make peace."

Some attempts at memorializing are more successful than others. And at the opposite end of the spectrum, in the category of "absolutely appalling," is a monument in the western sector of Berlin, which I am taken to see by Nicola Galliner, of the Jewish adult education program, when I return to the city after leaving Friedrichstadt. It is a large mirror slab on which had been written the names of deported neighbourhood Jews, and it stands in a small square that hosts an outdoor food market several times a week. On the day I visit, the shiny mirror surface reflects two farmers' trucks parked alongside and a large stack of broccoli. When the market stalls closes, I watch several vendors peer through the names of the dead to apply their lipstick before leaving for home.

By contrast, the artists Renata Stih and Frieder Schnock have created what is unquestionably one of the most original memorials in the world—by turning the Bayerische Viertel neighbourhood of Berlin into a living remembrance of the Jews who once lived there. In June 1993, they hung eighty brightly painted signs from lampposts all over the district, each backed with one of the anti-Jewish regulations passed between 1933 and 1944. One of the notices reads: "All local government offices in Berlin must immediately suspend Jewish teachers in public schools: April 1, 1933." The coloured icon on the other side of the sign is a stylized drawing indicating the elementary school teacher's trade: "2+." "Jews may no longer purchase soap and shaving cream: June 26, 1941," proclaims another, backed by a drawing of a red razor. The anti-Jewish laws embraced a range of activities, from the most minute detail of everyday life to notices of catastrophic import: "The emigration of Jews is forbidden: October 23, 1941." A single black rectangle backs these fateful words.

I have asked the artists to meet me here, in the district, so we can walk "their" streets together. They arrive, but before we begin our tour,

Renata Stih delivers a tirade. She is angry at her country, intent on resuscitating the memory of the Nazi era and furious that what she calls "a remake of what took place in Germany" has happened in Bosnia. "We did this memorial when the war in ex-Yugoslavia started, because you can't help the dead, you can only help the living and the future generations. There were concentrations camps in Bosnia, and it took the West so long to do anything, even though they had the information. They *knew* the Serbs were raping women, and they did nothing about it, and to this day, no one is caring for these women. So what kind of world do we live in? Any one who watches television and sees that people are being killed and does not think to do something about it is no better than a Nazi. I mean that if you see that somebody needs help, you have to help; otherwise, we are not human beings. That is the meaning of morality—not memorializing something fifty years after it happens." Her partner Frieder smiles and looks slightly uncomfortable.

I suppose that passion this deep must underscore the desire to create a work of this nature—one that is, necessarily, so public. Like the *Topography of Terror* exhibition, their installation began on a temporary basis, then was assigned permanent status, meaning that the residents of the Bayerische Viertel neighbourhood were, and are, confronted with a reminder of the Nazi past every time they look out their windows or leave their homes. One man shouted, "Get out, dirty Jews," as the artists mounted their work, but the local response was mostly positive, they say. And now thousands of tourists come to walk these streets.

"A friend of ours from Paris told us that although similar things happened there, you could *never* raise such a monument in the heart of the city," says Stih, as the three of us set out to see the rest of their creation. "There is somehow an eagerness to face history in Germany that is still not the case elsewhere." But their own experience suggests that there is also ambivalence. Before installing their work, they questioned people in the street, using a hidden microphone.

"Do you know what group of people used to live here?" they asked an elderly lady of about eighty who was out walking her poodles.

"I think they were Jewish citizens," she replied.

"Do you know where they are now?" asked the artists.

The woman thought for a moment. "Well, they are not here. I think they left for Israel," she said.

"Did you know about the deportations?"

"There *were* no deportations here," the woman stated firmly. "They all survived and now they live in Israel."

"It's not ignorance and it's not lying," says Stih after recounting this story. "People just do not want to get too close, and if we tell ourselves something enough times, we will start to believe it. This woman didn't want to have to care, and people like her still don't, because that would bring discord into their lives in one way or another."

The lamppost signs are linked to corresponding contemporary places. One hangs in front of a bakery; it announces a law forbidding Jews to buy cakes. Another hangs outside a butcher shop; it forbids Jews to purchase rationed meat. Another, at the entrance to a small park, restricts neighbourhood Jews to the use of the yellow benches.

Renata and Frieder think that ambiguities about the past continue in these streets. They point out that Jewish-sounding street names that were changed during the Hitler era have never been restored, or have been only half restored, so that some streets now have more than one posted name; and that the plaque in front of the house of Albert Einstein says only that he lived there from 1918 to 1933, without indicating why the great man might have left both home and country.

I wonder whether they are being too critical—perhaps asking too much. I put the question gently, and the answer is a firm no. Neither of them is a Jew. They belong, rather, to the school of Thomas Lutz: to that group of relatively young Germans who are determined to sustain memory both directly and obliquely. They hate the circus-like political debate swirling around a proposed monument of gigantic proportions that is to be built to the memory of Holocaust victims (the eventual choice was a graveyard-like labyrinth of two thousand concrete pillars by the U.S. architect Peter Eisenman.) "What *we* do is social sculpture that interacts with people's lives," says Frieder. "It forces you to think about the circumstances." "And also to think about *today*," adds Renata angrily. "We want people to be aware that when they go to Weimar and think about German culture, and Goethe, and the Bauhaus, and Nietzsche, they should also know that the former Buchenwald concentration camp is very close by."

(On January 27, 2000, on the fifty-fifth anniversary of the liberation of Auschwitz, the site of the Eisenman memorial was dedicated at a space beside the Brandenburg Gate in Berlin—a place pregnant with memory. Wolfgang Thierse, the speaker of parliament, explained that Germany had decided to commemorate the attempted genocide of European

Jewry in central Berlin because modern German identity was inextricably linked to the recognition of the horror of the Nazi era. The Holocaust survivor and Nobel Peace laureate Elie Wiesel, who had come to Germany for the occasion, said, "No people ever inflicted such suffering as your people on mine in such a short period. Until the end of time, Auschwitz is part of your history and mine." But Eberhard Diepgen, Berlin's Christian Democratic mayor, was pointedly absent. He had repeatedly claimed that the Eisenman monument was too immense and too unsubtle; and his resistance mirrored a universe of private ambiguity.)

An exhibition called *Vision of the Inferno*, featuring the paintings of the Auschwitz survivor Adolf Frankl, is about to open at the German National Museum in Nuremberg. I had been told about this before I left Canada and had contacted the organizer, Thomas Frankl, the artist's son. He mailed me a formal, embossed invitation to the opening. Given the widespread interest in the Holocaust, I was surprised to learn that this was the first time Germany's largest gallery of art and culture had addressed the subject.

So I leave Berlin for Nuremberg—a lovely ancient city that, like Weimar, shoulders the burden of history. The infamous Nuremberg race laws stripping Jews of their civil rights and citizenship were proclaimed here in 1935, and the rallies featuring a sea of human ciphers raising their voices in blind loyalty to the leader also were held in this city. Nuremberg was home to Julius Streicher, the editor of *Der Stürmer*, a Nazi broadsheet that promulgated a racial hatred so deep that it can still astonish half a century later. Nuremberg was the site of the postwar International Military Tribunal that first defined "crimes against humanity" in international law.

Hitler personally loved this ancient city; in fact, I am staying in his favourite hotel, the Deutscher Hof, overlooking the canal. The management looks aghast when I ask to visit the rooms that used to be reserved for the führer (double-suite 104 and 105 is not exactly marked as a tourist attraction). The hotel was partially destroyed during the war, but since it reopened in 1949, it has tried to position itself as a traditional guest house with conference facilities: any reference to its earlier history is deeply unwelcome.

The German National Museum is just steps away from the Deutscher Hof. It displays the strong architectural presence of a mid-nineteenth-century structure designed to demonstrate the importance of culture.

But there is something jarring: alongside the building is an installation, built in 1993, in honour of the Rights of Man, that consists of dozens of huge columns that soar towards the sky. They are instantly reminiscent of Nazi architecture: all those monumental, neo-classical designs by Albert Speer meant to represent Hitler's would-be Thousand-Year Reich. I mention this to Dr. G. Ulrich Grossmann, the director of the museum, whom I meet before the opening of the Frankl exhibition, and he laughs a little embarrassedly. "Some contemporary artists are using these big columns. Personally, I don't like them. I think these columns are artistically empty, without historical sense or content." I gently disagree that they lack "historical sense" and am intrigued to learn that the artist is an Israeli living in Paris. It's just a guess, of course, but the fact that a Jew has transformed Hitler's symbolic architecture into a tribute to human rights here in Nuremberg, where the Nazi order gained strength, does not strike me as accidental.

The auditorium of the museum is filled to capacity with about two hundred people, including local and international dignitaries, such as Dr. Heinz Fischer, the president of the Austrian parliament in Vienna, and Michal Kovac, then president of the Slovakian Republic. (Mr. Frankl was deported from the Slovakian city of Bratislava.) After the introductions, Dr. Fischer clears his throat and acknowledges that National Socialism was effectively born in Austria, since Hitler was a citizen, then announces that the city of Vienna has recently established a foundation for Holocaust survivors. Mr. Kovaç comes to the microphone: he says he is profoundly ashamed of the record of his country, and he now places his faith in the culture of human rights and democracy that characterizes the new Europe; (months later, he is voted out of office in favour of a right-wing opponent). An art historian praises Adolf Frankl's work, and Dr. Grossmann says how happy he is to host this exhibition on behalf of the German National Museum. Everyone looks pleased.

Then an unkempt-looking young historian from Berlin saunters to the podium. (He was invited, but no one expected him to come without a *tie*, I am told later.) "It is extremely important that this exhibition is happening here in Nuremberg," Guido Baudach lectures the dignitaries of the city. "For it all started here, *as you know*! And furthermore, the people of this city were not merely bystanders. They were willing executioners!"

Hitler's Willing Executioners, the controversial book on the eager complicity of ordinary Germans in the murder of Jews, by the American scholar Daniel Goldhagen, had caused a sensation when it was published in Germany in August 1996, a little more than a year before this event. The first printing of *Hitlers willige Vollstrecker* sold out immediately, and 130,000 more copies were shipped to bookstores across the country. When Goldhagen toured Germany, six hundred people came to hear his first talk, in Hamburg, and by the time he reached Munich, the last destination on his book tour, his publicists had to move the event to a symphony hall with twenty-five hundred seats. I remember reading that it had been impossible to scan a newspaper or turn on the television or radio without being assaulted by passionate arguments attacking or defending Goldhagen. The entire phenomenon—and phenomenon it was—had more than any other recent event demonstrated just how alive and raw the memory of the Holocaust remains. Now, a member of the younger generation is standing on a stage accusing his elders—at a Holocaust event, no less; in Nuremberg, no less—of aiding and abetting Hitler in the genocide of the Jews. A deep-throated protest rolls through the audience at this unwelcome intrusion.

Following the speeches, I join the small group that is gathering around Mr. Baudach in the museum lobby. The anger is palpable; the generation gap has widened into a veritable chasm. "Why is your hair so dirty?" one angry matron demands to know. Baudach snorts audibly and laughs.

The late Adolf Frankl created more than two hundred portraits from Auschwitz, both of the victims and their brutal overlords, and his style is reminiscent of pre-war German Expressionism: layers of thick paint in garish blues, reds, yellows and greens applied with emphatic brush strokes. Most of his subjects are faceless: they are depersonalized agents of degradation, depersonalized receptacles of pain.

Except for a few brilliantly executed pieces, I suspect Frankl's work is unlikely to survive as High Art; however, this exhibition at Germany's most prestigious cultural gallery is clearly intended to fill other purposes: it allows the National Museum to make its first public statement about the Holocaust. Perhaps even more important, Frankl's paintings will serve as a powerful tool for educating schoolchildren—something the German government is intent on doing.

On the day after the opening, a class of twenty students gathers in the gallery where these disturbing works hang. They look about sixteen or seventeen years old and pitifully ill at ease as they perch on their chairs under the anguished stares and silent screams of the artist's victims and the leers of his murderous guards, any one of whom might conceivably have been a relative. All German children are required by law to study the Nazi period, so there is no escaping the discomfort, but until this exhibition none of them has had to endure the searing pain captured in paintings such as these.

The first speaker on the program is an elderly woman named Renate Zusman, with a horrifying story. In January 1945, she was stripped naked, shaved and already inside the Auschwitz gas chamber when a rumour that the Soviet Red Army was nearby swept through the camp. In the ensuing commotion, she escaped—and survived.

An eerie silence fills the gallery. The children's faces register shock; even the museum guards at their stations look stricken. After a few moments, an earnest-looking blond boy waves his hand: "How can we comfort older Jewish people like you who survived?" he asks Mrs. Zusman hopefully.

"You can't," she replies, not unkindly.

The child looks taken aback, but what else could Renate Zusman have said? What "comfort" could possibly reach the people who carry within them the torment that Adolf Frankl tried to paint? Authenticity has demanded the transparent reply. Tidy endings belong in fairy tales.

I feel as though I need a short rest from the pursuit of memory in this, Europe's most haunted nation, and Rothenburg ob der Tauber—a reputedly charming little metropolis not far from Nuremberg—looks like a natural place. Having escaped bombing during the war, the town on the famous Romantic Road about fifty kilometres south of Würzburg is praised in my guidebook as a medieval museum piece. And it truly is an architectural delight, with ancient churches and gabled houses made of old wood beams. The town is packed with visitors—a constant state of affairs, I am told—most of whom have crowded into the ancient market square in front of the *Rathaus* to watch "shepherds" and "shepherdesses" in lederhosen and dirndls dance a jig to the accompaniment of an oom-pah-pah band. On the hour, the windows bordering the old councillors' chambers just under the sundial open and little wooden figures emerge, to everyone's delight. It is fairy-tale time in ye olde Germany—all cuckoo clocks and innocence.

But when I read that the state museum, housed in a thirteenth-century Dominican nunnery, has an intriguing-sounding "Jewish Section," my desire for rest evaporates: I can't resist. I have read that the town was home to large numbers of Jews in the Middle Ages and that many were destroyed in massacres when rumours of ritual murder swept across the country, but Rothenburg ob der Tauber is known to have maintained a strong Jewish community until the Second World War.

The museum has a few ordinary pieces on display: seder plates from the annual Passover remembrance of the Exodus and a prayer book from the 1930s, but a strange-looking scene at the back of the room catches my eye: it is a reconstruction of a Jewish cemetery, replete with authentic gravestones engraved with Hebrew words. I find it hard to imagine disturbing a cemetery in order to display funeral stones in a museum, until I remember that there are few Jewish graveyards left in Germany and that the entirety of Jewish life can be considered a museum piece. Stranger still, a wall case claiming to depict the "Holocaust" turns out to be a description of one of the medieval pogroms. Nowhere is there a mention of more recent happenings in Rothenburg ob der Tauber.

I mention this lacuna to the pleasant-looking, elderly ticket seller at the entrance, who, given her age, almost certainly has personal knowledge of more recent events. "Oh, yes," she says, "I think there is a paragraph on that subject in this book." From under her desk, she pulls out a tome on the history of the Jews of Rothenburg and leafs through it carefully. Still nothing. She flips to the cover. Ah! The book is a history of the Jews of *medieval* Rothenburg.

"Well," she says, a little embarrassed, "this is what happened. In 1938, the mayor declared Rothenburg *Judenrein* [free of Jews], so the Jews went away to the countryside."

"To the countryside? Are you sure?" I ask.

"Yes, they weren't allowed to be in the city, so they went to live in the countryside. All of them decided to live in the countryside."

"And then what happened to them?"

"I don't know. Maybe they are still there. But I will tell the director what you said. You are not the first person to mention a problem with our exhibit."

How benign and pleasant, I think—like the defiantly innocent woman walking her poodles in Berlin. Amnesia of this kind is no longer tolerated in many places in Germany, but in rural Rothenburg ob der Tauber, the truth about the recent past remains taboo, even in the Jewish Section of the state museum.

It is time to leave. The fakery of this town sticks in my craw like a fishbone.

The next stop on my itinerary is the Protestant Academy in the town of Bad Boll, near Stuttgart, where I have a date with the director, Gotlind Bigalke. The person with whom I corresponded before deciding to come here explained to me in a letter that "the Protestant Academies [there are about twenty of them] were founded as a reaction of Christians and the churches to the collapse of civilization during the Nazi period."[13] Naturally, I was interested in learning more about their work.

The sprawling, low-slung buildings of the academy are located in a beautiful rural setting: modern and ultra-clean, in an environment that feels conducive to relaxation and meditation. Gotlind Bigalke is an informal friendly woman in her early fifties, a member of the generation of '68 that changed Germany. Her presence here is the direct outcome of her personal commitment to peace and national restoration. We sit on a couch in her sunny office and talk about the German Lutheran Church, and she tells me about the breakdown—about how not all, but most, of the leadership accepted the Nazi demand to expel converted Jews. "They wanted to be good citizens—good, obedient, law-abiding members of the state; that is the Lutheran tradition. So they kicked them out because of their Jewish origin. They said, 'You can't speak to God any longer.'" She is still angry about this.

After the war, there was shame. A young pastor, Eberhard Müller, convinced the bishop of Württemberg to invite Protestant "men of economics and law" to think about how they could contribute to a new democratic Germany. That was the beginning. At a Church conference in 1945, the German Church leaders confessed that they had done wrong, but Gotlind, who is unforgiving when it comes to halfway repentance, says their confession was "soft." "Today, we would say they did not go far enough. They did not regret that they did not help the Jews, or Protestants whose families once had been Jews. They even spoke in the comparative. They said, 'We did not love *enough*, or protest *enough*,' when they did neither of these things." She is convinced that no one "regretted" in a serious way right after the war. "People said they were forced to do what they did. Even in my own family, they talked this way. Of course, it was true in a way but only half true."

There were a few people in the Lutheran Church who had resisted, and Gotlind had joined the Church because one of them—a man who was, she says, clear and trustworthy—had held out a beacon for her, illuminating a path through the "moral fudging." "I was in my teens in the early 1960s, and I was desperate not to repeat the lies. I was looking for people to trust, and I found them here in the Church." Eventually, she became a pastor, but to be German-born was something inescapable, she soon realized—even though no one in her generation was personally responsible for what had happened. The first time she was invited to visit Oslo, Norway, with a group from her Church, she refused to go, fearing rejection. The second time the opportunity arose, several years later, she went; however, when she was invited to the home of a Norwegian colleague, she felt obliged to say to him, "I do understand that it is quite a thing for you to invite me to your house." He replied, "You are welcome here, but it is true: there have not been many Germans before you." When a later exchange was organized with the Dutch Reformed Church in Holland, Gotlind told her congregants not to expect to be welcomed by everyone they met in the Netherlands. "Some people resisted this: they said, 'Why? We have not done anything!' I had to tell them, 'Think about their experience with Germans. They may have to deal with us on an economic level, but they don't love us. Be aware of that.'"

Today, the Protestant Academies are an independent platform for what their explanatory brochure calls dialogue and "civilized argument." They hold conferences on topics of social change, interreligious tolerance and ecumenical issues and invite people from all over the world to join in the discussions. There is a group here from India, who have just participated in a "Whither India" seminar: a Christian bishop from Kerala, a Muslim who founded an institute in Bombay to promote interreligious understanding, a professor and an artist. When we finish our conversation, Gotlind happens to mention an event taking place this very evening in the nearby village of Jebenhausen. It is a klezmer concert, organized by a group of local people with a particular interest in Jewish history, and she thinks I may be interested. They have even founded a "memorial museum."

Before the war, she explains, Jebenhausen was home to a large Jewish community. (The king had invited them to settle this remote area on the border of the Swabian Alps in the nineteenth century, and their arrival had doubled the population.) They lived on the slope of the hill and were "townish." Urbanized. More sophisticated than the peasants who lived in the village proper. One night in 1943, they were pulled from their beds and taken away. Their homes were looted, but religious artifacts and other mementos considered worthless at the time were left lying around on the ground, until they were collected by their gentile neighbours and stored in an ancient Protestant church that was also more or less abandoned. That is how a museum of Jewish life came to Jebenhausen.

"It all started when the people here saw that play, you know, about a fiddler on a roof? So they decided to organize events to learn about the Jewish tradition of this place," says Gotlind. "There is some sort of an association, and they are sponsoring the concert tonight."

We all go together: the bishop from Kerala, the Muslim from Bombay, the professor, the artist, Gotlind and I.

The Protestant church is a small gem, with an eighteenth-century retable and several well-executed paintings of the saints. The Jewish museum is at the back: it professes to explain the history of the local community. A gravestone with an inscription in Hebrew stands propped up against a wall (it once marked the tomb of an exemplary *Frau* whose every act "had brought honour to her husband.") Nearby hangs a sign for a former guest house called The King David: a large metal sculpture of the biblical ruler playing his harp. Glass cases display a seder plate, under which one can read a detailed curatorial explanation of the meaning of the Passover service, a prayer book, a Jewish calendar (with another scholarly explanation), a pedagogic description of the origin of Jewish names, a mezuzah (parchment scroll) from someone's door post, a death certificate and a memento from a bar mitzvah.

As in Rothenburg ob der Tauber, "found objects" were collected to make a museum about people who had been neighbours for centuries.

I ask myself what is the purpose of this archeological excavation at a destroyed site. Are the good citizens of this place trying to understand their murdered neighbours after the fact? To rescue them from a second death by oblivion? Or is this an attempt to protect themselves from the silent accusations that emanate from the little houses that still line the road up the hill? Although these homes were cleaned up long ago and are occupied by others, everyone knows their truth.

The small church is already filled to capacity with middle-aged men and women (hardly anyone looks younger than forty). We are all waiting to hear the blond *Fräulein* and her partner, a young American from New Jersey, sing to them in Yiddish. Speaking in a strong American accent, the man tries to explain the Yiddish world of Eastern Europe where klezmer music originated. He exaggerates gestures and intonations; he and the *Fräulein* tap their feet and belt out the music. "How many of you understand Yiddish?" he calls out. A murmur of embarrassed laughter ripples through the room.

Yiddish? Their Jewish neighbours spoke only German, and proudly so. In supreme, unconscious irony, a large portrait of the one-time cantor of this community hangs on the wall, just beside the stage: a most Germanic-looking burgher of the Jewish persuasion, named Heinrich Sontheim. Formerly known as "king of the tenors," Herr Sontheim looks well fed, proud and self-satisfied. *He* would not have identified with the Eastern European music being performed here this evening—even less with the proletarian accents of the Yiddish language. The very thought of it! Herr Sontheim and the other happily assimilated Jews of nineteenth- and early twentieth-century Germany would shudder in their graves to witness this scene being played out in their names.

Is it easier for this audience to listen to the voices of the dead in Yiddish rather than German, the language of their own most intimate thoughts? Herr Sontheim dreamed in German, just as they do.

The performers are teaching the audience Yiddish words. Repeat after me. Let's sing in unison. The audience warbles along happily. *Oy, Oy, Oy*, he instructs. *Oy, Oy, Oy*, they chirrup back, smiling sheepishly at one another. Since most of them were born after the war, this young man from New Jersey may be the first Jew they have even seen. He is a living incarnation of their museum.

Now the singers are performing a sad, emotional song—a Yiddish mother croons to her son: "Study the Torah and work hard, my little one, but most of all, grow up to be a good man." I look around me: Yiddish is so close to German that most of them get the gist of it. Some people in the audience have hung their heads; others are openly blinking back tears. There is a sound of muffled sniffling. The child in question never did grow up, and this room brims with that knowledge.

The tormented children of the killers are weeping—and so am I: from grief for the dead, from compassion for the living and from anger.

In old Maori culture, the warrior ate his enemy in order to absorb his strength and courage. Here, a new generation of Germans eagerly imbibes a caricature of the culture their parents destroyed, identifying with Eastern European Jews, if only for a moment. *Oy, oy, oy.* But the poor dead Jews of Jebenhausen are still not ordinary *Volk*—still not Germans like themselves; no longer the target of hatred, they have become objects of unhealthy veneration.

"Do you know who your audience is?" I ask the New Jerseyite after the concert.

"I've often wondered," he says, looking vaguely bewildered. "They're mostly middle-aged and they seem to idealize Jews. Once a woman came up to me and said, 'Now I know you are the Chosen People!'"

I think about Thomas Lutz's concern that the memorials he supervises encourage understanding and not a neurotic identification with the victims, about his desire to teach in a context where useful learning might take place. Gotlind Bigalke seems to agree. "They do these things over and over again, but there is never any relief," she says sadly as we leave the church.

By the 1990s, all Adolf Hitler's categories of subhumans (*Untermenschen*) had been acknowledged and memorialized in one way or another by the German government. But there was one class of sufferers the führer had never imagined: the children and grandchildren of his loyal foot-soldiers who would bear the burden of their parents' deeds. None have struggled more than the sons and daughters of the men who masterminded the Third Reich or supported it in public ways; and the confusion, bitterness, grief and rage that spills from some of these people is nothing short of awesome. Gottfried Wagner, for example, great-grandson of the illustrious Richard. He is the Princess Diana of German musical royalty, telling all in the transparent hope of destroying his family's internationally famous Bayreuth Festival. Wagner travels the country shouting his hatred of his father and grandmother, whom he calls liars and protectors of the Nazi faith.

I heard him speak at the German National Museum in Nuremberg, the day after the opening of the Adolf Frankl exhibition, and noted that although he was born more than a century after his detested ancestor, Gottfried was noticeably like Richard, both physically and otherwise:

he is large-boned, impulsive and bombastic, with a flair for the large gesture. And as I listened to him speak to a rather unfriendly audience (he was promoting a book in which he exposed his family, and they were shifting uncomfortably in their seats), I found my mind wandering back to Richard Wagner's ecstatic romance with the German nation: "I am Revolution, I am the ever-fashioning Life. . . . I proclaim to all the world the new Gospel of Happiness," the composer wrote, transported by mystical fervour.[14] Gottfried, it seemed to me, had turned his great-grandfather inside out: he hated the ideal of "the German nation" with the same overweening passion. But the similarities between the two men appeared almost greater than their ideological differences.

Few would have wanted to quarrel with his depiction of Richard Wagner as a rabid anti-semite. In 1850, Wagner published *The Jews in Music*, in which he repudiated the liberalism that underpinned Enlightenment values and dehumanized Jews in a style that would be honed to perfection in the years to come. "If emancipation from the yoke of Judaism appears to us the greatest of necessities, we must hold it crucial above all to assemble our forces for this war of liberation. . . . Then we can rout the demon from the field . . . where he has sheltered under a twilit darkness," he wrote. But the German National Museum happened to border Richard Wagner Platz, and the opera house was opening its new season with a Wagnerian megawork. The magic of Wagner's music was as powerful as it had ever been: Gottfried would face an uphill battle in his struggle to discredit his famous family.

He had been an opera director and musicologist—the first in his family since Richard—but thanks to the lobbying of his father, Wolfgang, and grandmother Winifred, both of whom had disowned him, he had been effectively blackballed in Germany and now lived in Milan, Italy. These familial counterattacks did not dissuade him from his self-appointed task. His rage ran too deep.

From the stage, he told the audience that the beginning of his life had corresponded with the post-war revival of the Bayreuth Festival, which became, in his words, "the absolute centre of family life." To have been born a Wagner, he said, was to accept the famous heritage: to find oneself enmeshed in a certain vision of Germany that was sanctified by the family.

He was fourteen years old when history intruded into his life in 1961. Without any advance preparation, his schoolteacher showed the class an American-made movie about Nazi Germany that included scenes from the liberation of the concentration camps. To his surprise, the swelling music that accompanied the film was Richard Wagner's.

"I asked my father what it all meant, and he told me I was too young to understand," he said. "I asked my grandmother why there were concentration camps, and she said, 'Those are the lies of the New York Jews.'"

Not long afterwards, he discovered an old box in the family attic with a stash of films inside. Secretly, he examined them with a magnifying glass. They were images of his uncle Wieland and his grandmother Winifred with Hitler.

"That's when I put it together for the first time," he told the audience. "The movie I saw at school, the concentration camps, the Nazi rallies, my family. I hid the films in my room, and from then on I was an outsider. I tried to find out as much as I could by pretending I didn't care."

The technique worked, after a fashion. Wolfgang Wagner proudly told his son that Hitler had visited him when he was wounded in Poland. And that Hitler had once said that when the world was rid of Jewish Bolsheviks, he, Wolfgang, would control the world of theatre in the east, while his brother, Wieland, would command the west.

In 1990, he was invited to Tel Aviv, as a musicologist, but his very name created a scandal. Journalists asked his opinion on Richard Wagner's tract, *The Jews in Music*, and whether Wagner's music ought to be played in Israel. His appearance at the university was preceded by death threats. Four hundred people came to hear him speak, but no one would sit in the front row.

"That trip was a turning point in my life, because I realized I had been trying to excuse Richard Wagner by concentrating all the blame on the family. But the ideology of proto-Nazism informs all of Wagner's work, including his music. There is a unity between the music, the libretto and the thinking of Richard Wagner."

This was an audience of Wagner lovers who had come to defend the composer. They whispered loudly, waiting impatiently for question time.

"Why do you call Richard Wagner a Nazi?" asked one woman angrily. "There *were* no Nazis then!"

Gottfried looked primed for a fight. "You are excusing him," he retorted in a raised voice. "Richard Wagner was a *fierce* anti-semite!"

"Everyone knows he was an anti-semite," countered another woman, jumping to her feet. "What are you trying to accomplish?"

Now Gottfried turned positively furious. "There are ten thousand deliberately unpublished letters from Richard Wagner being held by my family. There are love letters between my grandmother and Hitler. She actually sent him the paper to write *Mein Kampf* while he was in jail. This is a scandal in a democratic country."

"What has any of this to do with his music?" asked someone else.

"If we understand him, we can change the way the music of Richard Wagner is interpreted," said Gottfried. "We can, and must, introduce program notes so people will understand the relationship between his appalling nationalist thinking and the way he composed music."

His anger was so palpable—so huge, so distended—that I wanted to talk to him personally, so I introduced myself and invited him to have lunch with me the next day. He chose a restaurant beside the canal that was filled with businessmen quaffing beer. The raucous music was so loud it was almost impossible to speak. "I'd kill the Bayreuth Festival if I could, but at the very least I would like to see Wagner's music accompanied by a historical text to clarify the themes in his music and his librettos," he shouted above the din. Offstage, he had lost none of his intensity: his fury filled all the emotional spaces.

He told me that since his critical visit to Israel, he had found solace in the company of Jews, and that his first-ever experience of warmth and acceptance had come from the Jewish community in New York. (Given his grandmother's remark about the concentration camps, it was, I thought, no accident that he chose New York Jews as his friends.) He was active in Holocaust education and had established personal relationships with the directors of Holocaust memorial museums in the United States.

"Do you know what *yichus* means?" he asked me, waving his salad-filled fork dangerously in the air. "Well, that's what I experience when I'm with my friends in New York. Pride. Pride in my adopted family."

It has been said that the common theme of Richard Wagner's mature works is the romantic conceit of "redemption through love." Richard's great-grandson Gottfried also sought redemption through love: the love of those whom his relatives, both immediate and distant, had chosen to hate with a violent shared passion. His answer to his nation's—and his family's—past was rage.

My travels are carrying me ever closer to the soft nerve centre of pain and memory from which no one in Germany can easily escape. They cannot ignore it in the way of the Japanese, by displacing the bad parts and focusing on what was done to *them*, as in Hiroshima and Nagasaki; nor can they make up a rousing story of nationwide resistance, as the French did during the post-war decades. Now I am about to meet the son of the man who was head of the Nazi Party chancellery and second in power to Hitler himself: a man who has been saddled for life with the name Martin Bormann Jr. I had first learned of him though the work of Israeli psychologist Dan Bar-On, who is the first professional to have explored the effects of the Holocaust on the children of Nazi perpetrators.[15] Bar-On has run workshops for the children of survivors and of perpetrators—first individually, then, with greater difficulty, together. I had made contact with Bormann Jr. from Canada, and he had agreed to meet me in his home town of Hagen, near Dortmund.

The train travels north from Stuttgart along the banks of the wide Rhine River, past the fairy-tale castles that dominate the hill peaks between Bingen and Koblenz. These delightful fantasies made real carry me back to childhood picture books, to early innocence. I stop for a day in Cologne, looking for the respite I didn't find in Rothenburg ob der Tauber. The centre of the city contains wonders: the famous cathedral beside the railway station—a masterpiece of Gothic art that was started in the thirteenth century and not completed until the nineteenth—and the nearby Römisch-Germanisches Museum with its perfect mosaic floor from the Roman occupation of Germania. But once again, the masses of young people milling in front of the train station speak of more modern concerns: unemployment, drugs and marginalization.

I board the train again, heading north, and when I descend in Dortmund, Martin Bormann Jr. is there to meet me.

He is sixty-seven years old, tall, lanky, even shy, a mild-looking man who seems slightly ill at ease in his own skin, as he bends awkwardly to pick up my suitcase. We drive to a small hotel outside Hagen, where he has booked me a bed for the night. When I have unpacked, we meet in a room the management has provided for our talk. He has thoughtfully planned everything in advance.

Although he has devoted his own life to teaching Holocaust education in German schools, Martin Bormann Jr. remembers his father as a "loving family man." And he tells me he never heard an anti-semitic word in his home, despite the fact that both Bormann and his wife,

Gerda, were known as fanatical anti-semites. Bormann *père* also promoted "war" between the German churches on grounds that Christianity was a threat to Nazi ideology, and he was fiercely hostile to Slavs: "In so far as we do not need them, they [ought to] die," he wrote in August 1942.

To honour the memory of a father who happens to have been a mastermind of murder is no small feat: Bormann Jr. accomplished this by becoming a Catholic priest.

But this is to skip too far ahead in an absorbing human tale, for the love we feel for our parents can transcend all else.

He was born in 1930, the eldest in a family of eight surviving children (his mother was rewarded for her fecundity with a gold medal from Hitler), and he spent his early years in Munich, where the family lived in a protected compound for NSDAP—National Socialist German Workers' Party, or Nazi Party—cadres. Life in this guarded environment was carefree and comfortable. Martin Bormann Sr. went to work in the morning and came home at night, and his young son was unaware of the violence beyond the compound gates.

The real world intruded in 1940 when Martin Jr. was sent to the Reichsschule der NSDAP, a school for the children of party members at Starnberg, south of Munich. The aim of this school was to prepare a professional elite for the new Reich; the atmosphere was military in the style of the Hitler Youth. Because discipline promoted obedience and submission to the state, the students were punished with beatings and face slappings; because Nazi culture idealized the muscular male body, physical training occupied a large part of the day. Only the strong could repel the enemy.

The school's academic program centred on Hitler's *Mein Kampf*. "We studied it as a Bible," Bormann Jr. tells me. "Hatred was our creed." I remember having read that hate, defiance and passion were defined as the "genuine" qualities of the German *Volk* by Alfred Baeumler, professor of philosophy at the University of Berlin and one of the leading theoreticians of the Third Reich, and that the children of the Party elite were subject to special indoctrination.

"At school, we were shielded from reality, just as in the home compound. We knew there were concentration camps, but they told us they were to reeducate criminals and teach them how to work so they could be worthwhile members of society. We were taught that was good.

There was a company of prisoners from Dachau building additions to our school under the supervision of the SS, but we never saw anyone mistreat anyone else. Not in front of us."

He remembers April 23, 1945, as if it were yesterday: that was the day his class of fifteen-year-olds were dressed in SS uniforms and sent to the southern front in Italy to battle the Americans—without any guns. There were no passable bridges, and the roads were blown out. "For a week we drove around just trying our best not to meet the enemy. Then, on April 30, we learned that Hitler was dead: they told us he died fighting for his people. I was totally devastated. I truly thought the world had come to an end."

Eight of the adults in their small group shot themselves on the spot. The boys were ordered home to their families.

Families? "I did not know where my mother was. I believed my father was dead because I knew he was in the bunker with Hitler. I was devastated, just devastated. I began to run, sort of at random, until I found a farm on the German side of the Austrian border. I told the farmer my name was Martin Bregman, because they had told us at school never to say who we were. He gave me shelter and accepted me as a member of his family, without ever asking questions."

The farmer subscribed to a Stuttgart newspaper, and one evening, after the family had gone to sleep, young Martin learned about the war crimes trials taking place in Nuremberg. Sitting at a table in the "good room" of the farmer's house, reading by gaslight, he saw the first photos of the liberation of Bergen-Belsen and read the testimony of the prosecution.

"That was when I discovered that my father had been convicted *in absentia*. I felt crushed, completely destroyed." He pauses and swallows. "I loved him."

His voice cracks and his eyes glisten, even after fifty years, and the room is silent as I wait for him to regain his composure. "I also learned they had not found his body," he continues. "For a long time I thought there was a possibility he was still alive. Until 1973, when they traced the remains of his body outside Hitler's bunker. He had taken cyanide."[16]

"What went through your mind when you read the accusations against your father?"

"I felt terrified, but I never believed that this was a lie of our enemies. The documentation was clear and unemotional. I knew it was true."

"Martin Bregman" could not speak to anyone about what he had read, but the farmer noticed he was upset. "What faith are you?" he asked the boy one day. Bormann, Jr. lied and said "Protestant," although his family had converted long ago to the semi-pagan Nazi religion. Although the farmer was a devout Catholic, he sent his daughter to buy a Protestant Bible, thinking it might help.

"Reading it changed my life," he says now, "because I saw that a person who was lost and desperate could be saved by the grace of Christ, and that even criminals could be saved. This gave me hope for myself and for my father. I prayed that if he were alive, he might find religion and be pardoned."

In May 1947, Martin Bormann Jr. converted to Catholicism. In August, as he and the farmer worked together in a mountain meadow, the seventeen-year-old boy revealed his true identity to the man who had saved his life, a man who happened to have fought in the anti-Nazi resistance. The farmer had only one response: "Don't tell the women."

Bormann Jr. resumed using his real name. In 1958, he took his vows as a Catholic priest. During the 1960s, he worked as a missionary in the former Belgian Congo, until illness forced him to return to Europe. Later he taught religion in the schools. Only once was he rejected because of his notorious name—in a small town in Bavaria.

"Bormann! Certainly not! We'll be in all the papers," objected a member of the school board when his candidacy was raised.

"Did you go through a period of hating your father?" I ask him as we sit quietly together.

"Never. I felt only crushing grief and pain."

"Do you hold him responsible for what he did?"

"Yes, I do. He was responsible because he gave all his strength to propagating a terrible ideology. My father committed an error, but a human being has a right to err. None of us is without error."

He had saved himself from a lifetime of torment when he adopted Catholicism, for religion allowed him to forgive without qualification. To this he had added a dollop of pop psychology: he now thought his father was probably a victim of Hitler. Martin Bormann Sr. ran away from his own brutal family in 1914, when he was fourteen, worked on a farm and never went to school. When he met Adolf Hitler in 1926, he was immediately hooked. "I think Hitler gave meaning to my father's empty life. He literally gave himself to the führer," says his son. "I once asked him what National Socialism meant and he said, 'National Socialism is the incarnation of the will of Hitler.'"

Bormann Jr. also thinks Hitler may have been a victim. "Hitler was prey to ideology when he was a young boy in Vienna, although afterwards he was responsible for what he did with that way of thinking. I believe that both Hitler and my father were victims before they became war criminals."

Poor, traumatized Martin Bormann Sr. and his victimized pal Adolf. "I'm sorry to push you on this," I say, "but fifty-five *million* people died in the war your father perpetrated hand in hand with Hitler, including millions of Jews whose entire civilization in Europe was wiped out."

"Yes," acknowledges the son. "The responsibility for all of that started with human fallibility."

"Has your faith allowed you to forgive what your father did?"

"It is not my duty to forgive. Only God in his mercy can decide."

"Some people might find that answer exculpatory and insufficient."

"In his political role, [my father] is fully responsible for the consequences of his actions."

"Can you accept that and still feel love for him?"

"Yes. I accept that he is responsible only before God."

I retreat into silence. Theology has allowed him to transform pain and grief over a criminal father into a bland, bloodless paste.

The Austrian journalist Peter Sichrovsky was the first writer to conduct interviews with the children and grandchildren of prominent Nazis, and when his work hit the German bookstores in 1987, it created a sensation. The title, *Born Guilty: Children of Nazi Families*, said it all: people born into a legacy of love, hate, defiance and shame; people suffering from anger and depression.

The adolescent grandchild of a major Nazi war criminal lashed out about how fed up he was with all those exasperating classes about the Holocaust. "Say what you will about the Nazis, at least they looked good in their uniforms! It must have been exciting, with all those parades and rallies. Tell me where you can find something like that today!" One day the boy expressed his thoughts to his high school class. "It was like a dam that burst," he told Sichrovsky. "Everyone started to scream, and the teacher said, 'What else would we expect from you, with a grandfather who was executed as a war criminal!'"

A young man named Rudolf thought he ought really to be in jail since he was clearly guilty of something in the eyes of the world. "Who knows what evil I carry within me," he added sadly. Another said he was obsessed with Jews and read everything he could find about the concentration camps. He called it "reverse prejudice" and said his relationship with the victims was "almost erotic." A young girl had dropped out of school. "I'm alive—isn't that enough?" she challenged the interviewer. "There's nothing interesting now. When I look at the old pictures of my family, they all looked so great in their uniforms. We were somebody then. They had a chauffeur and there was excitement. Not like now, living in three rooms. Anyway, I can never get any answers out of anyone. When I ask about my grandfather all I hear is 'He was an evil man.' Who was he? A sorcerer? I don't know. Maybe I'm too stupid to understand any of it."

In the preface to his book, Peter Sichrovsky wrote: "[After the war] the parents saw themselves as victims, and when they were young the children accepted that view. However, once they became old enough to learn something about the actual role their parents played during the war, the children themselves often became victims—the victims of their parents . . . victims of a mentality which, even though the war was lost, fostered a fascistic attitude in the home. The external setting had changed; Germany and Austria had long become democratic states. But the National Socialist ideology was deeply embedded in the minds of the perpetrators . . . and so the postwar generation found itself confronted by democratic structures on the outside and fascistic structures at home."[17]

With exceptions such as Wolf Hess, who has never stopped defending his father, Rudolf, who hanged himself on August 17, 1987, in Spandau prison, and Edda Goering, the daughter of Hermann, who in 1995 proudly informed a reporter for the French newspaper *Le Monde* that her father was still "popular" in Germany,[18] few children of Nazis were able to establish a positive identification with their parents or grandparents.

I continue by train from Dortmund to Hamburg, where I have a date with Niklas Frank, son of Hans, the erstwhile governor general of Nazi-occupied Poland. I am curious about Frank, for he is the author of one of the most crushing books I have ever read: *Der Vater* (in English, *In the Shadow Of The Reich*), which also was published in 1987, and also caused a sensation. When it was translated into English four years later, the American publishers insisted on bowdlerizing one of the most psychologically violent scenes, and for this, Niklas has not forgiven them. In his mind, the fact that he celebrates each and every anniversary of his father's execution at Nuremberg by masturbating to orgasm while fantasizing his father's last moments is central to his purpose. "I felt I could hurt my father the most by including this. Besides, it is absolutely true," he tells me in his office at *Stern* magazine, where he has worked as a foreign correspondent since the late 1970s. "You can well imagine that October 16 was always a holy time for our family and friends. Our father died again and again, year after year. So I marked that great moment in my way. The nauseating bastard."

In his book, he writes, "As a boy I absorbed, and was absorbed, by your death; I made it a part of me. I had to do that because I wanted to live. Do you understand that—do you hear me? And I made it; I'm the one who is alive! And I'm older now than you were able to get to be. That is something I aimed for. That is something I swore I would accomplish, even as a child. Even if it would be only one moment older than you were at your death."[19]

He is a portly, balding man of fifty-eight with a ready, cynical laugh. He and his older brother are the only surviving members of their family. "I'm sure my sisters and my brother died because of father," he says, sniggering contemptuously. "One sister always said, 'I don't ever want to be older than our father,' and she died of cancer when she was forty-six, exactly his age. My other sister also died; she went to South Africa during the wonderful days of apartheid, and she defended my father all the time. My brother started to drink milk—almost thirteen litres a day. He got fatter and fatter, then died of problems in his kidneys and his lungs and I don't know what else. He also defended my father all the time—said he was innocent and a victim of the Allies and rubbish like that. None of them could find their own life. I'm not sure I found my own life, either. But I survived." He grins.

Der Vater is shot through with anguished questions. *Why, Father,* did you choose that life when you had so many other options? You were a gifted lawyer, a fine musician; you were sensitive, cultivated, easy to like. *Why, Father,* did you lie to everyone, and especially to me, your son who hates you but wanted to love you? *Why, Father,* were you so cowardly that you actually retracted your only truthful statement—the one you made at your trial about the enormity of the crimes you dedicated your life to? *Why, Father,* did you sully my life by keeping me with you, a spoiled baby princelet, when Jewish children my age were being smashed against the walls just two kilometres away?

A possible clue lay in the personality of Hans Frank. In his definitive work on the Holocaust, the historian Raul Hilberg calls Hans Frank "a moody autocrat who displayed sentimentality and brutality. . . . In his castle in Krakow, [he] behaved like a cultured ruler who entertained guests by playing Chopin's piano music, [but] in the conference room, he was one of the principal architects of the destruction process in Poland. Powerful but vain . . . [he was] referred to as *Koenig* [King] Frank."[20]

Niklas is convinced that his father was a craven opportunist—no more, no less—and, if joining the Nazi cause and espousing the necessary rhetoric was the way to fulfil his personal ambitions, then he would make whatever adjustments were demanded. Like Martin Bormann Jr., Niklas was unable to recall any anti-semitic talk in his family, an impression he confirmed later by questioning his siblings and his aunts. "If Hitler had said, 'Kill all the Austrians, or the Chinese, or the French,' my father would have carried out his orders with the same cruelty. He wasn't interested in ideology or racism; he didn't give a shit about anyone except Hitler. He longed for the love of Hitler, I think sexually. What mattered to my father was presiding over his 'kingdom' from our royal castle. Personal power. Oh yes, and uniforms and jewels."

In early 1945, with the Red Army at the Polish border, the Franks escaped back to Upper Bavaria ("Father made sure he grabbed whatever he could carry from the hoard of loot he had acquired"). At the beginning of May, Hans Frank was arrested by the Americans. Niklas, who had just begun school, was aware that his father was in prison and would probably be hanged. "Everybody in our village was talking about it, and besides, there were the newspapers. I couldn't read yet, but there were lots of pictures, the pictures from the concentration camps. I knew they were from Poland. I saw pictures of children just like me and I was sick with shame. They died and I was going to live. So I taught myself to read very quickly and that is how I learned I was a member of a criminal family.

> Mother must have been eternally grateful to Hitler and Himmler for the ghettos, those first supermarkets with discount prices—special for the Frank family. Ghettos had to be created so that Mother could have all her tailors in one place. . . . With what consuming greed she would set out on a shopping spree in her Mercedes,

accompanied by an SS escort. I was also permitted to accompany her there, hand in hand with nursemaid Hilde. . . . Someone picks me up to look through a peephole. The man says, "See the wicked, wicked witch sitting in there?" I see only a woman seated near a wall. She doesn't look our way, but only stares at the floor. I begin to cry. "She won't hurt you," the man consoles me. "She'll be dead soon anyway. . . ."[21]

Father, whenever I hear the word "fur" I see Mother pawing through gigantic heaps of fur coats stolen from Jewish women before they were taken off to be gassed. . . .

I carry unspeakable images around in my head, Father. . . . I also know that one can never get rid of them. . . . Did you never pause, never stop, never weep from the sheer horror of being you, and of what you did?[22]

While he was in prison, Hans Frank wrote a self-pitying memoir called *Face to Face with the Gallows*, a book of "disgusting vanity," according to his son. "Sentimental crap, enough to make a pig puke," he says, referring to his father's literary opus. The Russians have arrived in Poland and King Frank is about to escape from his castle:

"Farewell, farewell forever, you people of Poland and you land of Poland! God be with you and grant you happiness!" writes the sovereign as he reflects on this tragic moment. It is this strangely delusionary, romantic self-aggrandizement that repels Niklas the most—and his father's apparent inability to speak the truth. At his trial Hans Frank suggested fleetingly that he had changed. The man who once said, "We must annihilate the vermin Jews wherever we find them," now told the court: "A thousand years would not suffice to erase the guilt brought upon our people because of Hitler's conduct in this war."[23] Niklas rejoiced when he learned about that statement, but he soon felt crushed again: his father retracted his words in a final statement to the court, when he said, "Every possible guilt incurred by our nation has been completely wiped out, not only by the conduct of our wartime enemies toward our nation . . . but also by the tremendous mass crimes of the most frightful sort, which . . . have been and still are being committed against Germans by Russians, Poles, and Czechs. . . . Who shall ever judge these crimes against the German people?"[24]

"In his book he never said a word about his years in Poland. Not a word. He never said, This is what I have done. It was published in 1951, so I was twelve when I started to read it. It made me want to vomit because I could feel that this guy was lying to me again."

Niklas's mother supported the family from this book, sending letters to every susceptible Nazi in Germany; they all bought as many copies as they could. They also wrote her sad letters about the unwarranted death of Hans and their beloved führer. Winifred Wagner helped out with her supply of acquaintances who remained faithful to Hitler's memory; she wrote to say she found Hans Frank's book "the best character study of Hitler that I have ever read." As a teenager hiking around Germany in the early 1950s, Niklas found that the very mention of the name Frank could be counted on to elicit sympathy for poor Hans and his fatherless children, from just about everyone who picked him up on the road.

He delights in telling the audiences who come to hear him speak about *Der Vater*, "Sorry, I do not trust Germans." This does not go over well, he says, but he doesn't care. "I hope I'm wrong, but all the killers who survived the Third Reich did build up families," he tells me. "And *you* tell *me* what sorts of things they have been teaching their children over Sunday lunch."

"Are you suggesting that German democracy does not have real roots?" I ask him.

"Exactly. We have built up a democracy only because we were closely observed by other countries. For sure, we like it. It doesn't hurt. But how do we deal with all the labourers we asked to come here? This shows me that under the white sheet we have spread over ourselves, there is still a lot of typical German behaviour, and I fear the day when it will break out again. That's why I am in favour of a united Europe. It will keep us from getting too strong again."

He is twiddling a pencil between his fingers as he talks—excitedly, nervously, angrily. As I listen, I think about the telling poll of German attitudes that was carried out by the American Jewish Committee just three years before. Some people dismiss Frank as "obsessed" and "nuts"—I've been told that—but the AJC study suggests he isn't entirely off the mark.

"I understand the Germans," he continues. "What happened is really hard to live with, and our schools have done a pretty good job. But it is like having a constant pain. You can't be like other people who have a history full of *ordinary* crimes. Before 1933 we were a normal criminal people, like all the other nations with terrible things in their past. But not now. People say, 'It was our grandfathers, so we don't care.' But they do care. They can't escape it, and sometimes this makes them really angry. Outside our country we Germans will always be stigmatized."

"You talk as though Germans carry some genetic character defect."

"No, no, it's not genetic." He laughs. "Just tradition."

His office at *Stern* magazine faces the famous port of Hamburg, where a large plaque commemorates the fate of the passengers of the *Exodus 1947*, the ship filled with four thousand Jewish survivors that set sail for Palestine, then was eventually forced by the British to return to Hamburg, to this very spot. The *St. Louis* had also shipped out from this harbour, in 1939, with almost a thousand hopeful Jewish escapees on board. That relief effort also failed. But Niklas Frank doesn't need such public memorials. His private torment is constant and everlasting.

"If my brain is working, there is no chance of forgetting. I think of my father every day. Every day I must ask him, 'Why, why did you do it?'"

"You said he was a coward and a liar, that he was in love with Hitler, that he was intrinsically obedient. What else do you need to know?" I ask as gently as I can.

"Maybe I keep asking because I fear I may have his character," replies the son. "To prevent what he became from happening to me."

He reminds me of the novelist Günter Grass, and both men summon up Sisyphus, the ancient king of Corinth, who was condemned forever to roll a huge stone up the hill, only to have it slide down again—the difference being that Frank and Grass sustain their ordeal willingly. In Greek mythology, Sisyphus was punished for cheating Death, which is what Frank and Grass each have done in symbolic ways. As payment for having survived in a state of "sin"—that is, as Germans after the Holocaust—they both have fashioned lives of private and public expiation.

Grass, like Frank, never loses an opportunity to tell his fellow countrymen that he fears them, and by implication himself. In 1997, he called his compatriots "closet racists"; in their behaviour toward would-be immigrants, Germans were accomplices in a "war of extermination," he said, choosing his words for maximum shock value, and adding, "It is probable that we have all become passive witnesses, once again, to a barbaric act—this time a barbaric act backed by democracy."

Günter Grass hated talk about the "unmastered" past. "As if we could ever 'master' the past," he harrumphed in 1997 in a documentary made for French television.[25] History exposed continuities that could be diverted only by extreme vigilance; Grass and Niklas Frank had assigned themselves to the watch.

In some quarters, the fierce anger of "the children" has never abated; it flares up every time anyone in high position insensitively congratulates himself on having been lucky enough to have been "born late," in the unfortunate words of the former chancellor Helmut Kohl, now in disgrace for accepting suspicious campaign financing. The ambivalence resurfaces every time intellectuals—in particular, historians—revisit the mined terrain of the past; all attempts to "regularize" the historical record are pounced upon as sacrilege. In the mid-1980s, to cite the effort known as the *Historikerstreit*, or historian's debate, Ernst Nolte, one of Germany's most prominent historians, tried to integrate the Nazi period into an explainable, partly "normal" past—a past that may have contained murder but not senseless, uncontextualized murder. Nolte implied that with few exceptions, every major nation has had its "Hitler era," thereby diminishing the exceptional nature of Hitler's genocidal regime and at the same time recalling Hans Frank's final speech to the Nuremberg court, in which he stated that crimes committed against Germany by other nations not only mitigated Germany's guilt (Nolte's point) but completely erased the stain. Nolte suggested that Stalin's gulags, in which millions of so-called enemies of the state perished, were "more original" than Hitler's designs for racial extermination. He asked, "Is there not some justification for resisting the demand constantly to lament the Nazi past?" He resurrected old canards blaming David Ben-Gurion and "the Zionists" for sacrificing their coreligionists for the sake of the new Jewish state, and most egregiously he suggested that "talk about 'the guilt of the Germans' all too wilfully overlooks the resemblance to talk about 'the guilt of the Jews,' which was a major Nazi argument."[26] As if the problematic discussion over ongoing national responsibility for real transgressions paralleled confabulated Nazi propaganda about the Jews.

Nolte was a professional historian with what looked like an apologist agenda: a troublesome fusion of ideas that revived memories of the Nazi era, when many of his colleagues had degraded their profession by propagandizing ideology. But there was nothing particularly new about his apparently exculpatory approach: at approximately the same time, the French press was vigorously debating the return of the Nazi war criminal Klaus Barbie with similar relativizing arguments about the many massacres that had occurred in the world since Barbie's lead role on the stage of occupied France.

The difference was this: Nolte was a German, and he was probing a still-festering wound. Mastering the past? Forty years after the war, the Nazi era was an undefused bomb in the country that can neither consolidate nor disgorge its awful history. An uproar ensued. Beyond the widespread fear that Nolte's work confirmed a trend to the nationalist right in German public opinion and a desire to launder the past, many thought the famous historian was seeking to divert attention from the only question that mattered: How did it happen that ordinary people with doctoral degrees and professional careers, including the life-affirming practice of medicine, came to participate in such things? And how did the Nazi catastrophe emerge in the middle of an everyday mid-twentieth-century European society?

Nolte found himself in angry confrontation with heavyweight opponents such as the social philosopher Jürgen Habermas, another ever-vigilant foe of German nationalism. Habermas's questions went straight to the heart of the national dilemma: Do those born afterwards still bear responsibility? he asked. His own answer was a blunt yes. "The simple fact is that even those born later have grown up in a context of life in which *that* was possible," he writes. "None of us can escape that milieu, because our identity as individuals and as Germans is indissolubly woven into it."[27]

Habermas argued that the memory of the Holocaust is as important for contemporary German national identity as it is for Israel. "Can one claim to be the legal heir of the German Reich, can one continue the traditions of German culture, without taking historical responsibility for the interconnected origins of those crimes, with which our own existence is historically woven, in any other way than by means of a solardistic memory of what is now irreparable; in any other way than by means of a reflective, critical attitude vis-à-vis the traditions that endow our identity?" he asks in a famous essay.[28] The language may be convoluted, but the message is stark: look at yourselves, you who were born from the loins of Nazis.

Niklas Frank, Günter Grass, Jürgen Habermas, Beate Klarsfeld, Thomas Lutz—all struggling to found a narrative of German historical understanding about the Nazi period, all self-appointed guardians of truth.

But the infection just under the skin never dissipates, never disappears, and soon there were other voices in other quarters. In 1998, more than a decade after the Ernst Nolte debacle, the German novelist Martin Walser was presented with the annual Peace Prize by the German Association of Publishers and Booksellers for "reintroducing Germans to their country and Germany to the rest of the world." This could hardly have been more ironic, given what he said in his acceptance speech. Walser, who was in his seventies, had started his career by pleading for a recognition of collective responsibility, *à la* Jürgen Habermas, but he had been shifting into another sphere. In 1988, he had supported Germany's reunification, leading to accusations of incipient nationalism, but in 1998, he went much further—lamenting (in the style of Nolte) that German guilt was a "moral stick" used to beat the German people and condemning what he called the "instrumentalization" of Auschwitz as "a permanent exhibition of our shame." He received a standing ovation, seemingly for having the courage to say the unmentionable in public (he had introduced his remarks by saying he was about to make a statement that made him "tremble" at his own audacity). Only the late Ignatz Bubis, then head of Germany's Jewish community, and his wife remained seated.

But Walser was not Ernst Nolte, who was widely viewed as having an agenda; he was a man long associated with the moral centre. That's what made his public comments so unusual. Walser said aloud what approximately half the population thought, according to the 1997 poll of the American Jewish Committee: he said that the burden of shame and guilt had become too heavy. "Why not let bygones be bygones?" was the meaning of his plea.

This was understandable; the torment of having to drag an active remembrance of the Nazi past into the twenty-first century was unbearable to many good people. But his entreaty was also historically meaningless—and dangerous—a reality the former president Richard von Weizsäcker alluded to, a few days later, in the *Frankfurter Allgemeine Zeitung*, when he accused Walser of "cutting provocation." The burden of the perpetrator nation would not dissolve simply because millions of Germans were angered and encumbered by their collective past.[29]

Is "reconciliation" a meaningful concept when it comes to the Holocaust, or even possible? Certainly, some attempts were ludicrous. Take the comic-opera absurdity of May 1985, for example, when, to mark the fortieth anniversary of the Nazi defeat and the liberation of the concentration camps, Ronald Reagan, president of the United States, planned a diplomatic visit to a military cemetery at Bitburg, a German town near the border of Luxembourg. Reagan wanted to promote "reconciliation": for him, May 1985 marked not the end of war but the beginning of peace, a stance that initially led him to reject Chancellor Helmut Kohl's suggestion that he include Dachau in his itinerary. "I want to put that history behind me," he said at a White House news conference. "None of them [the German people] who were adults and participating in any way [in the Second World War] are still alive, and very few . . . even remember the war. . . . They have a guilt feeling that's been imposed upon them, and I just think it's unnecessary."[30]

These ahistorical, stunningly ignorant remarks were only the beginning. In April, a month before the planned visit, news reports revealed that forty-nine Waffen-SS soldiers were also buried in the Bitburg grounds: they had been members of the Second SS Panzer Division, "Das Reich," which had massacred 642 villagers at Oradour-sur-Glane, France, in 1942. The French were outraged; the Holocaust survivor Elie Wiesel urged President Reagan to cancel, telling him, "That place, Mr. President, is not your place. Your place is with the victims of the SS"; and, in a massive 390 to 26 vote, the U.S. House of Representatives asked the American president to reconsider.

Within days, in a reverse, mirror-image vote of 398 to 24, the West German Bundestag defeated a motion from the Green Party asking the Kohl government to eliminate Bitburg from President Reagan's itinerary. Helmut Kohl responded by thanking Ronald Reagan for his "noble gesture" in not cancelling. "Reconciliation is when we are capable of grieving over people without caring what nationality they are," he stated.

Buoyed by their apparent rehabilitation, veterans of the Waffen-SS Death's Head Division gathered at a ski resort near Nesselwang and proclaimed, "We were soldiers too, just like the others."

On May 5, President Reagan laid a wreath at Bitburg and visited the Bergen-Belsen concentration camp memorial museum. On May 8, President Richard von Weizsäcker made his famous speech to the Bundestag about memory and responsibility. And on May 11, veterans of the SS Panzer Corps held *their* first reunion, also at Nesselwang.

The moral confusion that characterized the Bitburg fiasco exposed the unreconciled past that lived just below the surface of everyday life, always ready to erupt when the circumstances were right. Stupidity was a likely trigger: in seeking to brush aside the complexities of "collective guilt" without a trace of subtlety or understanding, Ronald Reagan had enveloped the Third Reich in what Raul Hilberg later called "a nebulous, collective innocence."[31] The results were predictable. At Bitburg, the American president unearthed the very skeletons he thought he would lay to rest. Renate Zusman, the elderly woman who had narrowly escaped the gas chamber in Auschwitz, said it best: there was no facile comfort for the survivors of the Hitler era. Not for those who had been its target, or their children, or their grandchildren. Nor was there easy resolution for the perpetrators' children.

But as the twenty-first century appeared on the horizon, there were glimmerings of new ways, premised on the understanding that however well-intended, building memorials, weeping over klezmer music, mounting bizarre Jewish museums with "artifacts," or frantically studying Hebrew would not dispel the awful spectre of Nazi deeds. Psychiatric in their origin, the new approaches tried to pick apart fear and collective grief to "work through," rather than to "master," the past.

Dan Bar-On, of the Hebrew University in Jerusalem, was studying what effect the post-war silence about Hitler's attempted genocide had had on Germany's children, and he was learning, in the process, that the children themselves were often willing co-conspirators, so to speak, in that they sensed the need to turn their eyes from something hidden and appalling—they knew not what—for the good of their families. The workshops he established in Germany for the children of perpetrators offered a new kind of relief. For Martin Bormann Jr., Gottfried Wagner and Dirk Kuhl, whose father, an SS commandant, was hanged as a war criminal for having headed a slave-labour camp, these meetings were the first time they had talked to others who suffered like themselves. (Niklas Frank was contacted, but he did not participate.) Hilde Schramm, the daughter of Albert Speer, had already dedicated herself to a crusade against racism. One man had married an Israeli. ("The grandchildren of my father are Jews!" he announced triumphantly.) Another reported that his sister had killed herself because she was convinced she had "poisoned blood."[32]

Eventually Bar-On arranged for the children of Holocaust survivors, who were mostly Americans, and the children of the Nazi perpetrators to meet. There was great trepidation. Julie Goschalk, the daughter of Holocaust-survivor parents whose entire families had been exterminated, said she was physically afraid to set foot on German soil and had nightmares for weeks before the encounter. The first person she met from the other group was Martin Bormann Jr., whose very name froze her blood.[33] Bormann Jr. told me he felt overwhelming "shame" at this coming together. Initially hesitant, they were eventually able to talk together. And finally to cry. A German participant asked whether he was personally complicit if he continued to love his mother and father. He sobbed when the son of a Holocaust survivor took his hand and told him he had the right to love his parents.

I am back in Berlin, at the end of my journey, when an acquaintance tells me that a therapist named Hanni Lewerenz has picked up the Bar-On idea and expanded it to the larger population. I learn that she and a partner run psychotherapy workshops for young Germans, as well as for the children of Jewish survivors. I ask to meet her, and the acquaintance arranges a meeting.

It is the morning of my last day in Germany. We meet in a small café; she is warm, direct and immensely likeable.

"We are not interested in cheap reconciliation. We're interested in honest confrontation and getting to know one another," she says. "In psychological terms, the mass murder of Jews has not yet been integrated in this country. Most Germans have never met a Jew and there is a tremendous amount of projection on both sides."

She tells me that because young Germans are ashamed, they fantasize that the Jews in the group will see them as "Nazis," while the Jews, on the other hand, are afraid of being used as all-forgiving "salon Jews" by the Germans. "The Jews also feel shame," she says, "the shame at being the child of a victim. Abuse produces shame."

Her groups are composed of about sixteen people, 75 per cent of them the children of perpetrators. "We ask everyone why they have come. The Germans often do not express their motives as clearly; they say they are students of this or that, but they do not say what always comes out sooner or later—that what they really want to know is how their grandfather influenced their father, and how their father has influenced them. Deep down they fear they may have criminal tendencies.

We still have this blood thing in Germany. We call it *Abstammung*, meaning from which stem you come. So people come here with a conscious, or subconscious, idea of genetic culpability. It's pure fantasy, but it can be powerful and disabling."

She says that part of the fear results from a confusion between natural aggression, which all people display on occasion, and cruelty, and a worry that normal, less-elevated behaviour is an expression of innate "evil." "Some people in the generation of '68 reacted by going to extremes at the other end of the political spectrum, with left-wing revolution and terrorism. They knew where their anger came from. Their children are softer but more depressed and self-destructive, without knowing why. The connection is further away, even for the self-selected, motivated people who come to us for help. I think these post-war generations are paying the price their Nazi parents and grandparents never paid."

I think about Niklas Frank and his veiled fear that he might be "like" his father. He had mobilized his life to distance himself from what he called his "criminal family"—and by extension the residue of Nazism in present-day Germany. The people in Hanni Lewerenz's groups feared experiencing the shock Frank and Martin Bormann Jr. had felt, though not on the same level. "They may have lived with the illusion of parents and grandparents as good people," she says. "Suddenly they must recognize them as murderers."

Since 1993, only one person from the former East Germany has signed up for her groups, and she thinks this is significant. First, East Germans saw themselves as victims of "Western fascism"; now they see themselves as the victims of German unification, which has not fulfilled its promise of prosperity. Complicity and guilt over the Nazi era are not their concern. Not yet.

"What happens when it becomes clear that simple reconciliation is not really possible?" I ask her, thinking about Lara Dämmig, who refuses to call herself a German, on the one hand, and the sad, wishful, guilt-ridden gentile woman in the synagogue, on the other.

"It is a hard, liberating moment for everyone. A wake-up. We cannot change reality, but we try not to flatten it either; we can only help each other to deal with it and recognize each other as innocents. We are neither perpetrators nor victims. We are the children and the grandchildren. We can try to rid ourselves of the projections and the fantasies about genetic guilt and have compassion for ourselves, after all the hardness we have inherited, because accepting ourselves after what our families did is the most difficult thing of all."

To my surprise Hanni is crying. "It's very touching to see people learn to confront themselves and their conflicts with such courage," she whispers. I reach across the table and take her hand. She is German, not Jewish. I understand with a slight shock that in helping others, she is trying to heal herself.

Beyond the battles and the endless debates, there are places without words that speak only of truth. One of these is the Weissensee cemetery in Berlin, founded in 1880—the largest Jewish graveyard in Europe. Somehow it escaped destruction, unlike that other desolate place of the dead, where only the tomb of the great Moses Mendelssohn breaks the flat contours of razed earth.

Lara and I have come here together. Autumn leaves blanket cobblestone alleyways, and ivy-covered plane trees lean over the walks. Dozens of paths beckon in different directions through thick brush and ferns. The cemetery is mysterious, vastly overgrown, forsaken. There are too few to tend the graves.

Like an ancient narrator, Weissensee tells the story of its one hundred years. Some paths lead to ornate family mausoleums from the optimistic nineteenth century that contain not a sign that their occupants were Jews. These were the emancipated hopefuls of their era, living at a time when elements of society were already turning against them as outcasts who would never assume the mystical splendour of *Volk*, but who steadfastly maintained their "Germanness" to the end. A half century later, hunted Berlin Jews hid with the dead in these monumental crypts.

An entire section honours the fallen of 1914–18 with rows of little white headstones lined up with perfect military precision. Their occupants were musketeers, grenadiers, telegraphists and officers. The date is 1927. Time is running out, but it is still possible to honour German Jews for having died as patriots for the Fatherland.

I stop before the gravestones from the late 1930s that are marked as suicides. The Nuremberg Laws were in effect. People were stripped of the right to earn a living, the right to school their children, the right to buy food when they need to—stripped of everything except the right to remain alive.

Then, finally, the stones that mark the end of a long era. Two of these read:

The Zadek Family: Murdered 1942–43
Wilhelm, 53; Erna, 51; Siegfried, 54; Hulda, 47;
Hanna, 19; Ruth, 19

The Schafer Family: Murdered 1942–43
Edgar, 74; Elise, 72; Martin, 46; Lotte, 42; Ilse, 19
"children and grandchildren"

The Weissensee cemetery holds a hundred years of history for those who care to read its open book. Between its haunted spaces of memory and neglect lies Germany's unmasterable past.

2

Through a Glass Darkly

France

One owes respect to the living;
but to the dead one owes nothing but the truth.

– VOLTAIRE, *Lettres sur Oedipe*

I'VE MADE A POINT of leaving Berlin in time to attend the opening of the trial of Maurice Papon in Bordeaux, but there has been a bureaucratic mix-up—my ticket for the courthouse has not come through—and I shall have to wait a week or two. I don't mind; I have rented a small apartment in Paris as a base for my travels, and having to spend a few extra days in my favourite city is not a hardship. So I am back in the fourteenth arrondissement, where I usually land, enjoying the familiar sights. "My" café at the corner sells fresh Arcachon oysters from straw trays stuffed with ice and seaweed, just outside its front door. Down the street, the delicious odour of freshly baked croissants wafts from the local *boulangerie*, and the cakes and *tartes* in their window look exquisite. My greengrocer is Algerian—I've known him for many years—and we talk about the weather and the quality of his produce this week. Not far away is the market of the rue Daguerre, a place of utter sensual delight. The open-air fish market is a marvel; one Christmas they had live sea horses on display, and I watched the discerning Parisian matrons examine them, with an eye to dinner, without a hint of surprise at the preposterous offering. That same year, in the window of a nearby *charcuterie*, I saw a pie with the heads of several (dead) blackbirds poking out of the crust, presumably in honour of the "four and twenty blackbirds baked in a pie" of nursery-rhyme lore. In France, everything edible is a pretext for a meal that may be remembered, and talked about, for years.

I love France, and I've been coming here regularly since I was barely past childhood; I'm even a citizen, of sorts—as a result of a youthful first marriage. It was in France that I first confronted the reality of the Holocaust, where I first felt the compulsion to explore memory, but where I also discovered beauty of a kind I had never dreamed of. The French are profoundly artistic; the way they create something as "ordinary" as the Christmas decorations at the Rond Point on the Champs Elysées can take my breath away.

I returned here in the mid-1980s for a year or so, to document the return of the Nazi war criminal Klaus Barbie to French soil, after he was discovered by Serge and Beate Klarsfeld in his Bolivian hideout and brought back, with much fanfare, to be tried. Barbie, like Maurice Papon, was accused under the rubric of crimes against humanity, a charge that came into French law in December 1964 as a ratification of the Nuremberg precedent. Under the French penal code, all crimes are automatically "prescribed," or exempt from prosecution, ten years after they were committed. But crimes against humanity carry no such statute of limitations, and they were enacted into French law in order to prevent Nazis like Barbie from claiming legal immunity. Barbie, known as the "Butcher of Lyons," had been the chief of the Gestapo in that southern city, and his cruelty was still legend forty years after the war. He kicked heads, injected acid into his victims's bladders and hung almost lifeless people from ceiling hooks without apparent concern. When he took a break from his duties, he liked to play little love songs on the piano (his favourite was "*Parlez-moi d'amour*"). But his main wartime tasks were the destruction of the French Resistance, whose centre of activity was in Lyons, as well as the obligatory rounding-up and deporting of Jews; and as the destroyer of Jean Moulin, the hero *par excellence* and mythologized symbol of the Resistance, he was seen as the enemy of all that is most noble in the French spirit. After his forced return to France in 1983, he had made it clear that he would be happy—*very* happy—to talk at his trial about all the French people who had helped him in his wartime duties, slyly telling one of his interviewers that the only things he remembered from those halcyon days of youth and power were the names of these former friends. In the years between his return to France and the opening of his trial in 1987, many people—and most of the media—worried incessantly about what the former SS *Hauptsturmführer* might say, and whether he might disrupt the uneasy calm that had pervaded the country on the subject of the Collaboration since the purges immediately after the war. There were also rumours of vengeful attack and counterattack. When I went to Paris to promote the French-language publication of my Barbie book in the fall of 1985,[1] I was warned by an officer of the Canadian embassy not to sleep in the same bed two nights in succession.

Barbie's trial was a theatrical production in the French style, complete with melodrama and lawyer's histrionics (his attorney, Jacques Vergès, tried to link the Resistance and the Collaboration with the horrors of the colonial war in Algeria, with some success); and questions about who was, and was not, a *résistant* were raised, causing chaos outside the courtroom. None of this ultimately helped the defendant. Klaus Barbie was convicted and sentenced to jail for life. In September 1991, he died of leukemia, at the age of seventy-eight.[2]

Since I cannot be present at the opening of Maurice Papon's trial on October 8, 1997, I ensconce myself in front of my television set and watch, like millions of others. The scene is appropriately dramatic: fourteen police wagons line the cobblestone street leading from the ancient cathedral of Bordeaux to the eighteenth-century yellow limestone Palace of Justice, and the discreet driveway behind the courthouse is crowded with jostling photographers and officials. They are waiting impatiently for the paddywagon with the tinted windows, the one carrying Papon, the former deputy prefect of Bordeaux in charge of "Jewish Questions" under the German occupation; then, after the war, a highly placed civil servant in Algeria, chief of police in Paris and a politician under successive governments of the Fourth and Fifth Republics. Papon now stands accused of complicity in crimes against humanity, under the same Nuremberg legislation that was applied to Klaus Barbie, for the deportation of 1,560 French and refugee Jews from his region of southwestern France between 1942 and 1944. During his years in Bordeaux, it was Papon's job to identify who was Jewish, by researching affiliations, baptismal records and the rest; seize Jewish property for "aryanization"; make arrests, either individually or en masse; and arrange for the transfer of prisoners to Mérignac, the closest Vichy-established concentration camp, then to Drancy, site of a holding camp in a northeast suburb of Paris. Drancy was an antechamber to Auschwitz; the trains left regularly for what was euphemistically called "the East." Papon was, in other words, a principal *French* actor in the process leading to the Final Solution.

In his pre-trial defence, he had claimed that his post was "secondary and obscure" and that he had merely been following orders, insisting that he did not know the final destination of the convoys of men, women and children he dispatched to Drancy. Did he ever visit Drancy, I wonder, as I watch the media circus begin to unfold in Bordeaux. In 1984, when I was researching the Klaus Barbie story, I had been taken there by members of the former Jewish Resistance. The prisoners' barracks were still intact, and so was the barbed wire: Drancy was not a secret—anyone driving along the road would have known it was there. The camp was also conveniently located near the railway station. Maurice Papon had sent mothers and tiny children there in sealed airless freight cars, and when they arrived, they huddled together on dirty straw, without food or sanitary facilities. The mothers were often sent on to Auschwitz immediately, the children left behind—temporarily. Some of the children arrived in Drancy alone, and I will never forget reading the post-war account of a prisoner named Odette Daltroff-Baticle. She writes: "The children arrived in sealed freight cars, ninety to a car with one woman in charge. They ranged in age from fifteen months to thirteen years. . . . They all belonged in the infirmary, but this was impossible since they were to leave for an unknown destination. . . . They show us their most precious possessions: the pictures of their mothers and fathers which their mothers gave them when they parted. . . . We try to make a list of their names and are surprised by a tragic fact. The littlest ones do not know their names. A small boy repeats endlessly, 'I am Pierre's brother.' Opposite their names on the deportation lists is a question mark."[3]

Another question mark—one that will loom over the jury in Bordeaux fifty years later. What *is* the moral responsibility of a government functionary? And at what point, if ever, ought conscience to assume precedence over a pledge of duty? Back in 1949, at the trial of René Bousquet, the chief of police under the collaborationist Vichy regime, the subject had been quickly passed over, even though the Nuremberg Tribunal had reached its own conclusions just three years before: by sentencing twelve senior Nazis to death, the court had set a legal precedent in rejecting the plea that the defendant was merely carrying out superior orders. That judgment, which had entered the body of international law, meant that no one is legally free to breach fundamental human rights, even if commanded to do so.

There was one other prosecution in the decade since France began a belated investigation of its past with the trial of Klaus Barbie: the case of Paul Touvier, in 1994. But the Barbie and Touvier cases were not comparable. Barbie was a German Nazi, meaning people could view him as a foreign import who had wreaked terrible damage on an innocent, occupied people. Touvier, although French, had been a member of the Milice, a paramilitary force of indigenous fascists modelled on the SS: he, too, was a Nazi, though homegrown. But Maurice Papon is different: he was not an obvious subscriber to any identifiable creed, except to the ideal of public service, and he was a loyal functionary who had carried out his duties with diligence and expertise. In his defence, he has gone beyond pleading that he was following orders and was ignorant of the intended outcome for the Jews he deported to cast himself as a victim of an international conspiracy hatched by outsiders from "New York" who want to destroy him and France. He has claimed that he was really a member of the French Resistance, playing a double game, and to the surprise of just about everyone, including his supporters, compared himself to Alfred Dreyfus, France's Jewish archetype of false incrimination. Papon had never marched about in jackboots or cracked whips, and he may never have waved a Vichy flag with patriotic ardour; yet, fifty years later, he is as defiant and self-justifying as Klaus Barbie himself.

The French are as fascinated and troubled by this exceptional trial as they were by the earlier Barbie *affaire*. The Papon investigation has been in the works for sixteen years, having been strategically delayed by the canny François Mitterrand and only recently agreed to by President Jacques Chirac, in a laudable act of political courage. This trial might once again shine a light into a hidden universe of buried deeds, perhaps implicating other stalwart citizens in the process; once again, the ideological roots of the post-war nation may be called into public account, an outcome that has been studiously avoided for the past half century. The Barbie trial had opened the door to these memories, but had not begun to reconcile them. Since Papon is eighty-seven, and most of his colleagues are dead, his trial may be the last chance to revisit this dark corner of history: the collaboration of the puppet Vichy regime that governed the unoccupied zone of the country with the Nazis, and the deportation of the Jews.

I cannot watch the media wait expectantly for the prisoner in the paddy-wagon without remembering how brilliantly Maurice Papon survived the Nazi defeat—by leaping directly from "Jewish Affairs" to the bureaucracy of national reconstruction under the hero-sublime of the French Resistance, Charles de Gaulle, and thinking that this very individual act, which was mirrored in different ways by different people, exposes the implausibility of the official post-war history in which the entire population was touted as having heroically resisted the Germans. This dearly beloved fiction of all-encompassing resistance was invented by General de Gaulle because he believed it was in the best interests of the nation, but the truth, as it later turned out, was quite the contrary. Historians currently estimate that only 1 per cent of the French population actively fought in the Resistance, while another 1 per cent actively participated in pro-Nazi activities; the remaining 98 per cent openly or passively supported the Vichy leader, Marshal Henri Philippe Pétain, and his collaborationist policies.

At an undefined level, many people have recognized the resistance myth as a fairy tale that they and their compatriots willingly promoted because at war's end it was necessary to convert to a new republican present. But as the decades passed, and the inherently false story became progressively harder to uphold, a new problem emerged: to reject what was in effect a lie about French history, as some longed to do, was to risk undermining the conceptual underpinnings of the post-war republics. The trials of Klaus Barbie and Paul Touvier had caused an uproar by initiating this process, and now the prosecution of one of France's top civil servants for complicity in crimes against humanity is threatening once again to illuminate ambiguities some prefer to leave slumbering in the shadows. But opinion is changing: a recent poll has indicated that 67 per cent of the population thinks the prosecution will help the country understand its recent past, and 77 per cent believe that public servants like Papon should be held responsible for the deportation of the Jews.

"I think everyone has lied to me since I was a child. If I had known, I would have asked questions a long time ago," Bertrand Poirot-Delpech of the Académie Française tells his psychiatrist in a distraught spoof called "*Marianne au divan*" (France on the [analyst's] couch) published in *Le Monde*.[4] He was right to view the national angst in a Freudian light. The daddies and mommies in France, as in Germany, had some belated explaining to do.

The French have a term for the fake history they adopted long ago and were teaching their children; they call it *la boue* (the mud), and anyone who tries to "stir it up" is publicly pounced upon. Buried within "the mud" are a tiny handful of undisputed facts about France's wartime experience. They include the following:

- On June 14, 1940, the victorious German army marched triumphantly into Paris after the collapse of the vaunted Maginot Line of defence. They were met with no open resistance.
- On June 16, 1940, the Third Republic government of Paul Reynaud fell, and 569 of France's 649 deputies and senators voted in favour of giving Marshal Henri Philippe Pétain what amounted to dictatorial powers—to save the honour of the nation.
- On June 17, 1940, Marshal Pétain announced the French surrender and the intended collaboration of his new government. "I offer to France the gift of my person that I may ease her sorrow," he began his famous address. "It is with a heavy heart that I tell you we must halt the combat. Last night I asked the adversary whether he is ready to seek with us, in honour, some way to put an end to the hostilities."[5]
- Under the terms of the armistice, the Germans occupied three-fifths of France, including the northern sector and the Atlantic coast, and a quasi-independent French government was established under Pétain in the spa town of Vichy. The laws of the Vichy regime were valid for both the occupied and the unoccupied zones, provided they did not counteract German regulations. In the occupied zone, German orders were enforced by the French administration. Hence the wartime career of Maurice Papon in occupied Bordeaux.

What happened during the next four years has been subject to dispute for half a century, although the fact that collaboration was warmly embraced by a majority of the French has recently gained chagrined acceptance. In fact, the French adored Philippe Pétain: as a hero of the

First World War and a symbol of hope for his compatriots, he came as close to being revered as a saint as a living person could. Ordinary men and women wept for joy when he passed, and the French Catholic Church supported him without question, at least at the beginning when the language surrounding him was deliberately religious in tone. At the start of a visit to Lyons in November 1940, Pétain was welcomed by the local archbishop, Pierre Cardinal Gerlier, with these sanctifying words: "France needed a leader to conduct her toward her eternal destiny [and] God allowed you to be there."[6]

The myth that France had been victorious over Germany and that resistance was universal sprouted on June 14, 1944, the day General Charles de Gaulle landed at Bayeux, Normandy, where he was greeted by a crowd of thousands shouting, "*Vive de Gaulle*" and "*Vive la République*." *Vive la République*? Having noted the changed direction of the wind, many of the celebrants had only just reconverted to republicanism after years of offering their support to an authoritarian pro-Nazi regime. The people who waved the tricolour and shouted republican slogans as they welcomed their new saviour home had already forgotten yesterday, and the myth that defined France for three generations took shape in the interstices of their opportune transformation. They were delighted to swallow the fiction that "France" had resided in London with de Gaulle, where the general claimed to have led a government in exile, as though the millions who remained on the Continent (themselves included) had been severed from the physical and historical nation. Although as crushed as any of its continental neighbours, and demonstrably more compliant with the occupier, France now had the rich opportunity to identify itself with the winning side. Charles de Gaulle returned from London unblemished by collaboration—as a triumphant victor, a *French* victor, who had fought with the Allies.

The pretense worked well; after all, the novel idea that citizens can effectively wipe out the past and start history anew with an equivalent of "Year One" had already been tried in France at the time of the 1789 Revolution. And in the immediate aftermath of occupation, an *épuration*, or purge, tried to divorce the discredited past from the republican present, just as the excesses of the post-revolutionary Terror were intended to destroy the old and give birth to the new. After 1945, about 300,000 of the most visible pro-Nazi collaborators were summarily tried and pilloried: more than 7,000 were sentenced to death, and, outside any trial procedure, some 9,000 were lawlessly executed by vengeful enemies.

But nothing symbolized the reshaping of the past more visibly than the prosecution of Philippe Pétain himself. The marshal was condemned to death on August 15, 1945 (although reprieved by Charles de Gaulle three days later). Some of his chief deputies were indeed executed—Pierre Laval, prime minister of Vichy France, for one, and Joseph Darnand, head of the SS-style Milice. On the other hand, René Bousquet, the police chief who had personally negotiated the delivery of 30,000 Jews to the Gestapo, was immediately exonerated after being sentenced to five years of "National Indignity"—because he was deemed to have helped the Resistance. Bousquet and thousands of other collaborationist officials, civil servants, businessmen, journalists and the like were considered necessary to the success of post-war society, which meant they had to be rendered respectable—transformed, that is, into *résistants*. The tool was the useful device the French called the "double game," which held that these men and women had only pretended to serve the Nazis while they were actually operating as double agents: as Resistance fighters.

In August 1953, the French National Assembly passed a general amnesty law that dispatched the entire embarrassing business of 1940–44 into a national attic of forgetfulness. Then a deep amnesia took hold. The same oblivion had seized post-war Germany, the difference being that while some Germans were happy to relativize the Nazi horror, it wasn't so easy to opt for outright denial. French historical memory was infinitely more flexible. De Gaulle's France had been on the side of the Allies. "France" had *won* the war.

For decades, a taboo subject was the wartime fate of France's 330,000 Jews, a peculiar memory lapse that became evident (if an absence can be so described) during the trial of René Bousquet. Although he had negotiated the deportation of thousands of Jewish civilians with the head of the SS in France—arrests and deportations that were effected by French police and could not have happened without them—that aspect of his biography was summarily passed over. Bousquet's defence in 1949 was identical to that of Maurice Papon in 1997: he was obeying orders, he had no real authority, his overly zealous subordinates had exceeded their mandate. The court, at the time, was sympathetic.

I remember this eerie lacuna from my first years in the country in the 1960s. "Deportees" were members of the Resistance, never Jewish civilians—in fact, Jews seemed not to exist. There was, all the same, much anti-semitism. I shall never forget seeing "*A mort les juifs*" (death to the Jews) on the walls of the Paris Métro, and the "friend" who said in a shocked voice, "But he's a Jew!" when I mentioned the name of a physician I had just visited. One day, I inadvertently found myself in a small shop in the old Jewish quarter of the city, and as I paid for whatever it was I was buying, I told the owner who I was. "Ah, Canada," he said to me in a soft voice, "How is it for us there?" I had never thought collectively; I did not know, then, what he had lived through. Years passed before I understood the full meaning of his words.

The Jewish genocide was not an issue for anyone in those days, including the Jews themselves, as I later learned. Before 1940, French Jews had thought of themselves as purely and uniquely French, which translated into stunned disbelief when the Vichy government passed strict anti-Jewish measures on October 3 of that year. Since France had been a haven for thousands of refugees since the time of the czarist pogroms in Russia and Ukraine at the end of the nineteenth century, and since it had been the first country in Europe to emancipate its Jewish minority, the betrayal was staggering. Decades later, in the 1980s, I came across a moving instance of the sense of abandonment experienced by one individual. He was Raymond-Raoul Lambert, head of the French Jewish Council in the southern, unoccupied zone until he and his family were deported to Auschwitz. His cultural and historic points of reference were all French; thus, he was unable to assimilate the "impossible" fact of a rejection by his own nation.

When he read that the Vichy government was about to announce new anti-Jewish laws, Lambert wrote in his diary: "It is possible that within a few days I shall be diminished as a citizen, and that my sons, who are French by birth, by culture, and by faith will be cruelly cast outside the French community. . . . Is this possible? I can't believe it. France is no longer France."[7]

After the war, the French government sent out death certificates to the surviving family members of Jews who had perished in Auschwitz. They all said the same thing: "Died at Drancy," with the date of deportation and the strange inscription "*Mort pour la France*." But patriotism had somehow remained constant: French Jews identified their personal tragedies with the collective national sacrifice, and many willingly accepted the lie of the official death certificate. There are gravestones in the Père Lachaise cemetery in Paris where the families of those who never returned from the camps have described their loved ones in exactly these words: "*Mort pour la France*"—not as having died *par la France*, not *by* the hand of their nation, which was the reality, but *for* the nation.

But the most powerful myths are eventually exposed, just as deep silences are ultimately shattered. By the late 1960s, there were signs of change. Pierre Nora, France's foremost historian of memory, dates this shift to the Six-Day War in 1967. As the possibility of another Jewish destruction loomed, young people found themselves face-to-face with a half-suppressed genocide only two decades old, and they were horrified. Left-wing thinking characterized this generation, including the intelligentsia. Jean-Paul Sartre and Simone de Beauvoir were battling for Algerian independence, helping to end France's colonial empire, and identity awareness was emerging as a worldwide phenomenon: women reinvented feminism, minorities flexed new muscles, and the young hived themselves off from the adult collectivity. The Jews of France, by then the largest Jewish community of Europe, were little different. The ranks of the concentration-camp returnees had been augmented by a massive immigration of Moroccans and Algerians, who were closer to their Jewish roots than their assimilated co-religionists who had lived on French soil for centuries. All were gripped by a renewed self-awareness that led in a direct line back to the events of Vichy France.

The recovery of repressed Jewish memory was vivid and painful. Before long, some of the stones over the empty graves at Père Lachaise were recast to read "Murdered at Auschwitz."

I remember the day I saw *The Sorrow and the Pity*, Marcel Ophüls's seminal documentary film on the occupation and the collaboration. It premiered in France's cinemas in 1969, because the state-run television network refused broadcasting rights, but I watched it in my living room in Toronto—on Canadian television—and it stunned me. With every scene and every interview, the mysterious war-related memory holes I had stumbled into during my years in France reassembled themselves into newly comprehensible historical shapes, and the visit to Natzweiler-Struthof assumed greater meaning. The French, too, were shocked by Ophüls's film, and a bitter debate followed. But argue as they might over recorded images, the story of Vichy France and the Jews would soon be exposed in irrefutable detail. In retrospect, it is hardly surprising that the initial historians of Vichy were not French at all: they were nosy foreigners, like the American scholar Robert O. Paxton, whose 1973 book, *Vichy France: Old Guard and New Order*, was the first to unmask the hidden history. In 1981, Paxton published another influential work with Michael Marrus, a younger Canadian colleague.[8] Both books documented unpalatable truths, including crucial evidence that the notorious anti-Jewish legislation of the Pétain regime—168 laws that approximated the Nuremberg decrees, and in some cases went further—was not commanded by the Germans, as had been publicized and widely believed, but initiated without prompting by the ministers of Vichy. The Vichy regime registered all Jews living in unoccupied France, excluded them from jobs and professions and pushed many of foreign birth (who had escaped to France as refugees) into twenty-one internment camps, where thousands died of malnutrition and disease before they were sent to Drancy by men like Maurice Papon. France, it turned out, was the only occupied Western European country to have enacted its own anti-Jewish legislation. Thanks to the willing assistance of the French, the Germans had needed only twenty-five hundred Gestapo police for the entire occupied territory. On the other side of the demarcation line, Vichy France was the only Western European territory to hand over Jews to the Nazis from areas that were not under German occupation.

These disclosures were a frontal assault on the stock explanation for Pétain's connivance with Hitler: that by offering help to the enemy in certain areas, the marshal had preserved French autonomy in others—collaboration as the ultimate patriotic act.

The publication of these books launched an intense public debate over what might actually have happened between 1940 and 1944, and what it all meant, a controversy that has continued without stop for almost three decades. Although dozens of corroborating works have appeared, exploring every aspect of the collaboration, still the commotion rages. When I lived in France in the mid-1980s, it was virtually impossible to watch television or listen to the radio without hearing an impassioned quarrel on the subject. Dark shadows gathered over the reputations of men and women in high places, including previously unassailable, *genuine* members of the French Resistance who now found themselves accused of having been double agents who worked for the Nazis. (This charge resembled the claim of thousands of collaborators like Papon, who insisted that they were double agents working for the Resistance.)

New allegations against certain high-profile members of the Resistance had first came to light in the 1980s, during the lead-up to the trial of Klaus Barbie, and had much to do with the settiing of old scores left unattended since the war. Such accusations were probably inevitable as the veil that had hung across the past for forty years began to lift, but some were stranger than others. François Mitterrand, for example. In 1994, Mitterrand, president of the Republic, and for almost thirty years leader of the self-mythologized "People of the Left," spilled the beans—on himself. His biography[9] turned out to be more colourful than even his enemies might have imagined: from his teens in the 1930s (when he opted to support Franco, and not the Spanish republicans, during Spain's civil war) until well past his thirtieth birthday, young François was aligned with France's conservative faction. After the defeat in 1940, he chose Philippe Pétain. And he always remained on friendly terms with René Bousquet: until the mid 1980s, Bousquet was a frequent guest at the presidential Elysée palace.

Was this the same François Mitterrand who had been an icon of the glorious French Resistance for half a century? The answer was yes. In post-war France, everyone was a self-declared graduate of the Resistance.

Before he died, Mitterrand avowed publicly what the French had "known" for fifty years: that the lines between the Resistance and the Collaboration were often fluid and that some people remained philosophically loyal to both sides. He himself had joined the Resistance late—in 1943—then distinguished himself in action; at the same time, he had continued his connection with his ultra-rightist friends from Vichy.

"I was the product of my family milieu," he said in self-justification. "My family was bourgeois, provincial, conservative, Catholic, patriotic and perhaps conformist. They were not anti-semites. They were moderates."[10] The Socialist president of the Republic explained that it was natural for an ambitious young man from his background to attach himself to Marshal Pétain. After three years he had changed his mind—after much personal reflection. In the meantime, he had gathered intelligence on Communists, Gaullists and other "anti-nationals" and participated in anti-foreigner rallies. Maurice Papon had walked farther along the same collaborationist road. And he too had waited until 1943 before joining the Resistance. The two men had shared a common trajectory that was intimately understood by the generation that lived through the war. Such were the perplexing ambiguities of French political life.

During his famous televised interview of September 12, 1994, President Mitterrand alluded to the old historical divisions of France: to the "eternal civil war," as he called it, of the "left" and "right" that had divided his countrymen long before the German occupation and continued through it. So opposed were these rival visions concerning the essence of the French nation, these competing myths that had shaped political discourse ever since the Revolution, that by the twentieth century the historian Ernest Lavisse was able to write about "*les deux France*" and be understood by everyone. The two perspectives on the nation were like the two faces of Janus: the first was pre-Revolutionary, prizing order and firm rule; the other was post-Revolutionary, valuing justice and the modern nation-state. The 1789 Revolution and Vichy France were archetypal components of *les deux France*, and the long road from one to the other had been marked by periods of intense conflict that sometimes approximated civil war. (As late as 1960, Grenoble schoolchildren were asked in a poll, "Was the Revolution of 1789 a good or an evil?" Fifty-five per cent said good, 30 per cent said evil.) One might even suggest that in the 1990s, "Revolutionary" France had put its opposite number on trial, in the person of one Maurice Papon.

The images on the television screen have shifted: Papon has arrived, entered the courthouse, surrounded by a phalanx of security police, and seated himself behind a bulletproof plastic shield on the right-hand side of the trial chambers. The courtroom is packed with lawyers, relatives of the victims and journalists (only half get seats, and the overflow is shunted into a larger room with a video camera trained on the proceedings). Today will be given over to introductory formalities, like jury selection. The defendant identifies himself, as requested by the judge, in as few words as possible: "Papon, Maurice, eighty-seven, retired," he says in a firm, ringing voice.

The long-awaited trial has begun.

My entry ticket is dated two weeks hence, but there is plenty to watch in Paris: the city is vibrating with news and comment from Bordeaux being broadcast from every newspaper, radio station and television screen. Although they have naturally mutated over the years, the country's long-standing ideological divisions are much in evidence. At the extreme of the political spectrum are small groups of reactionaries who continue to look back two hundred years to the halcyon days that preceded so-called modernity. Some of these are monarchists who hold a yearly mass on the anniversary of Marie Antoinette's death—an event that illuminates the origins of that deeply rooted strand of French historical memory that led to Vichy France, Pétain and Papon.

So on October 16, 1997, along with about 150 men and women, I file into the twelfth-century Basilica of St-Denis in Paris, where the tombs in the crypt below once held the bodies of the kings and queens of France. In each pew is a letter from the duke of Bauffremont lauding tradition and the "ancestral principles" of French survival (before pleading for donations to keep the "Memorial of France" alive). The female royalists are wearing feathered hats and Chanel suits; the men sit ramrod straight, chins high, in the way of the French upper classes, and wear dark green overcoats, a class badge in the wealthy sixteenth district of the capital. An organ and choir blast the notes of the Dies Irae through the Gothic chamber.

Standing before an altar decorated with gold fleurs-de-lis, a priest talks about the tragedy of the queen's death, especially about her indisputable love for her children—and with every impassioned phrase he edges closer to his evident wish that Marie Antoinette be named a saint of the Catholic Church.

"They had no *proof* of her treason!" he calls out in a tremulous, grief-stricken voice. "She was judged on political grounds only. And by *revolutionaries*!" The awful contours of this last accursed word fill the cathedral.

"Let us pray for France, for those who gave their lives for the *patrie*, for Marie, queen of France," he concludes. The mourners cross themselves and pray for a certain idea of *La France*, one that survived 1789, and the later revolution of 1848, as well as the commune of 1870, one that survived the apparent victory of the "traitor" Alfred Dreyfus in 1899 and the disgrace of Marshal Philippe Pétain, who once governed in their name. An idea of France that has survived all the left-wing governments this country has ever known.

Carrying candles, we descend in silence to the crypt. Yellow flame spots illuminate the darkness. A choir sings; the others recite the Lord's Prayer; then we press our noses against the grille and stare at the empty marble tomb of the guillotined queen.

Outside the basilica, the monarchist movement France Royaliste distributes flyers decorated with the fleur-de-lis, a cross and a heart; and *Action française hebdo*, a paper named after the early-twentieth-century anti-Republican movement of the same name, sells its two hundred-year-memorial issue (from 1993) on the death of Marie Antoinette. I turn to the editorial; it is a diatribe about the dangers of democracy.

For those who have come here to remember, nothing of lasting good has happened in their beloved land since the day the rabble stormed the Bastille. Now one of theirs, an elderly man who once carried out the lawful ordinances of Philippe Pétain, is on trial in Bordeaux. They have come to remember a past that has been submerged, perhaps only temporarily. Because in this country, one ought never to say subdued.

The mainstream of the French Catholic Church, which no longer reflects the royalists at the memorial service in the Basilica of St-Denis in the way it used to, is tending its own difficult memories during these early days of the Papon trial. Until very recently, the Church was firmly identified with anti-modernism. In the mid-nineteenth century, the papal *Syllabus of Errors* (1864) attempted to counteract developing liberal trends, both inside and outside the Church: all societal freedoms were denounced—freedom of the press, freedom of speech for non-Catholics and freedom of worship for non-Catholics. Other "errors" included the false belief that the Church ought to reconcile its teachings with progress and modern civilization. Up to and including the Nazi occupation and the creation of Vichy France, the French Catholic Church was a bedrock of nationalist ideology: as an institution, it was delighted with Philippe Pétain, since the stated values of the new regime—Work, Family, Native Land—complemented its teachings. "These three words are our own," applauded Cardinal Gerlier the day of Pétain's first visit to Lyons. "France is Pétain and Pétain is France."

According to the historian Etienne Fouilloux, the French episcopate reacted to the defeat of 1940 in the same way as the majority of the population; that is, "We have lost the war and we must now do our best under the circumstances." Fouilloux was not suggesting that the French Catholic Church was pro-Nazi, for it was not: it was, however, "patriotic" in its support for a government that thought collaboration with the Nazis was in the national interest. Many collaborators had joined in because they hated democracy and communism and because they were anti-semitic—attributes that also characterized important elements within the Church. In my research on Klaus Barbie, I came across a statement by a man who put this thinking perfectly: "I joined the Collaboration because I was anti-communist, and because I wanted to defend France and the old continent against the new Asian barbarians," he explained. To accomplish this he was prepared "to overcome my scruples and join the ranks of the new crusaders."[11] The religious language was deliberate—and common. Millions of people who wrote letters denouncing their neighbours to the Gestapo often signed their notes with self-congratulatory chauvinism, such as: "A good Frenchman, a good Catholic and a war veteran,"[12] or "A patriot serving his country."[13] The Catholic Church—in its role as the preserver of "Christian civilization"—was a foundation of the Vichy collaboration in the early years of the war.

But the historical pendulum has a habit of swinging in France. In 1791, the new republic became the first country in Europe to emancipate its Jewish minority into full civil rights, but one hundred years later, the pendulum swung to the right again, with the notorious Dreyfus Affair that imperiled the very stability of the nation and is still a loaded subject at some French dinner tables. In retrospect, Alfred Dreyfus the man was the least of it: he was an unremarkable Jewish army officer from an old Alsatian family who was falsely accused and convicted of treason, then eventually reinstated when the calumny was exposed. But the uproar surrounding his case sharply delineated the old political divisions. At a time of fast industrialization and disconcerting modernization, Dreyfus the Jew—that is, Dreyfus a member of the non-Catholic minority—became the focus for the discontents of his age, and leaders from both camps—the pro and the anti—entered politics. On the right was the anti-democratic Action Française movement, featuring ultranationalism and anti-semitism as its mainstays; on the left was the future prime minister Georges Clémenceau, who articulated the values of Republican France when he wrote regarding Dreyfus: "There can be no patriotism without justice." In the short term, the potent philosophy of Action Française marked the path that led from the Dreyfus Affair to Vichy France and the Nazi collaboration. Prejudice against "foreigners" deepened in the intervening years: a culture of "Frenchness" was defined in opposition to the foreign, menacing, supposedly "rootless" Jew. Anti-semitism sprang, elemental and whole, from a collage that swept together the anti-Judaic heritage of traditional Christianity, the racism of the emerging anthropological sciences and populist anti-capitalism. And sitting at the centre of the Christian right wing was the French Catholic Church.

So it was that when Philippe Pétain independently passed anti-Jewish legislation in October 1940, he knew he was reaching out to a generally receptive population. This was the world in which the ambitious young Maurice Papon felt at home and prospered. In 1942, when he authorized the transportation of Jewish civilians to Drancy, he was probably no more or less anti-semitic than any of his contemporaries. The patriotic vision of the day was of a France that was Catholic and ethnically pure—a France that did not include the Jews, although they may have been loyal citizens for two hundred years. On this side of *les deux France*, a minority could be sacrificed in order to preserve the organic nation that excluded them by definition; in this France, an important leader of the Catholic Church could welcome Philippe Pétain as having been sent by God to rescue the nation.

With the exception of a tiny handful of courageous bishops, the French Catholic Church did not react in October 1940 when the anti-Jewish laws were passed; nor did it protest when further discriminatory legislation was carried out in 1941. No one knew that the Final Solution was around the corner; nonetheless, the human rights of non-Catholic civilians were of little concern. By contrast, the Protestant parishes of France were far more attentive, and their outrage paid off: strong leadership from the head of the French Protestant Church, Marc Boegner, galvanized entire communities into uniting to save Jewish fugitives from the Nazis and from the men of Vichy, such as Papon.

The turning point came in July 1942. On July 16, Parisians awoke to screams as Jews were assaulted with blows from rifle butts and dragged from their homes. By the following afternoon, 12,884 men, women and children had been interned at the Vélodrome d'Hiver, a large stadium where no provision had been made for food or toilet facilities. There was hardly a German uniform in sight. Only the French police.

The French Catholic hierarchy was shocked into belated protest: under the signature of the archbishop of Paris,[14] a letter was dispatched to Pétain representing the cardinals and bishops of France. When round-ups took place in the southern unoccupied zone the following month, Cardinal Gerlier—the same man who had welcomed Pétain as heaven-sent—also wrote. Then Gerlier then did something unprecedented: he personally rescued eighty-four children who were passing through Lyons on their way to Drancy and placed them under the protection of the Church.

The revolt of the senior clergy was a serious blow to the regime, for the Church was the bedrock of nationalist ideology and government support. Vichy-authorized roundups of Jews were cancelled, and the number of people deported from Drancy to Auschwitz suddenly dropped so far, and so fast, that Adolf Eichmann, who was in charge of filling the trains, furiously declared, "This is a matter of prestige!" and warned that France might be dropped from the list of countries to be favoured by the New European Order after Germany had won the war. But public resistance was engaged and spreading. In the end, fewer Jews were deported from France (proportionate to their population) than from any other country in occupied Europe[15]—and much of this was due to the changed direction of the Catholic Church and to the population that began to help.

Since the mid-1970s, the higher ranks of the clergy had been debating difficult questions. Why did the Catholic Church remain silent in the first place? And why did it take so long before its leaders protested injustice of the worst order? Since this has been a matter of intense public interest, I would like to talk to someone about it. I call the office of the archbishop of Paris, Jean-Marie Cardinal Lustiger: we had met in Toronto in 1989 and talked about the French response to the Klaus Barbie affair. Cardinal Lustiger was born Jewish and had converted to Catholicism as an adolescent, a fact that, naturally, did not protect him or his family during the war—his mother never returned from deportation. But he had been rescued by people who hid him, without asking questions, and provided him with forged documents. Lustiger was doing more than any Catholic cleric in the history of France to effect a rapprochement between Christians and Jews.

His "special adviser" faxes a reply: His Eminence is sorry, but he is about to leave the city and "will not be able to further the exchanges started in Toronto in 1989"; however, the Reverend Jean Dujardin will be happy to see me. I call Father Dujardin and arrange an appointment at his office in central Paris for later in the week.

Father Dujardin is an informal man with a passion for French and Jewish history: the walls of his study are lined with books on these subjects. He is the secretary of the Episcopal Committee for Relations with

Judaism and the man responsible, on a day-to-day basis, for his church's dialogue with the Jewish communities of France. He tells me he has been involved in this work since the time of the Klaus Barbie trial.

"After the war, the Church's attitude was that the purge and 'National Reconciliation' were all that we needed," he says. Until 1966, when a work by Jacques Duquesne titled *Les Catholiques français sous l'Occupation* (French Catholics under the Occupation)[16] charged that ordinary Catholics had shown more compassion than their religious leaders. Duquesne's book was controversial and courageous, says Father Dujardin, but it was the Paxton histories that truly galvanized the debate. "That's when the general view of Vichy began to change: the deeply embedded notion that the Pétain regime did the least harm possible under the pressure of the Germans."

The discussions within the French Catholic Church were helped along by changes taking place in Rome, beginning with the Second Vatican Council in the early 1960s, during which Pope John XXIII repudiated those parts of the ancient liturgy that encouraged hatred of Jews and Judaism, including the enduring designation of the Jews as "perfidious." Over the next decades, Vatican research continued to explore the roots of anti-semitism in Christian teachings, and in 1992, in preparation for the fiftieth-anniversary remembrance of the July 1942 Paris roundups that had first roused the French Church to take action, Pope John-Paul II wrote to the French to ask what ought to be done. Father Dujardin, who was asked to reply, published an article suggesting that the Catholic Church, like the French nation itself, ought to examine its conscience.

On September 30, 1997, just three days before the anniversary of the Vichy anti-Jewish legislation, and eight days before the opening of the Maurice Papon trial, the French episcopate held a memorial ceremony at the Drancy concentration camp. The purpose was "repentance" in the face of the silence and acquiescence of the Catholic hierarchy during the Occupation, says Father Dujardin. The declaration was delivered by Monsignor Olivier de Berranger, the archbishop of the diocese that includes Drancy. "Today we confess that silence was a crime," the archbishop read from a prepared text. "We recognize that the Catholic Church in France failed in its mission to educate the conscience of its congregation, and that along with individual Christians, [our Church] carries the responsibility for not having delivered help from the beginning, when protest and protection were necessary and possible. [We avow this] even though there were innumerable individual acts of courage. . . . This failure of responsibility of the Catholic Church of France towards the Jewish people is now a part of our history. We confess this fault. We implore the pardon of God, and we ask the Jewish people to hear these words of repentance."

These were uncommon words at an uncommon time, and the response—from Jews, the media and Catholics in general—was largely positive. All the same, says Father Dujardin, the priests who wrote the Declaration of Repentance were appalled by the virulence of some of the rejoinders that came in the mail. "We received several hundred letters, and a lot of them called us 'treasonous.' Many anti-semites have traditionally enjoyed thinking the Catholic Church was on their side, and now they feel abandoned. But I call tell you that some of the bishops were shocked enough to say that if they had ever doubted the need for such a document, they no longer did. We have tried to make it clear that although we were not personally guilty, the institution was. Our intent was to take a lesson from yesterday so that we can live better today, and in the future, of course. We must grapple honestly with the past in order to understand our lives today, but unfortunately, many Christians do not comprehend the importance of this."

It is no surprise that the declaration was inspired by a letter from Pope John-Paul II. In late 1993, this remarkable pontiff signed a fundamental agreement with Israel, committing the Holy See, with the Jewish state, to combat religious intolerance. In November 1994, he issued a statement saying that the Catholic Church had an obligation to express "profound regret for the weaknesses of her sons and daughters who sullied her face over the centuries." On March 12, 2000, dressed in the purple robe of repentance, he delivered the most expansive papal apology in the history of the Church, repenting for the errors of 2000 years. That same month, he travelled to Israel and the Occupied Territories; in Jerusalem, he stood inside the Holocaust memorial, Yad Vashem, surrounded by Israeli statesmen and religious leaders, and by childhood friends—survivors from his home town of Wadowice, Poland. His extraordinary contributions to Jewish-Christian reconciliation, like those of John XXIII, marked a dramatic change in the history of the Catholic Church.

There was more. Two years before the Declaration of Repentance, on July 16, 1995—the anniversary of the infamous Vélodrome d'Hiver roundups by French police—François Mitterrand's presidential successor, Jacques Chirac, had become the first leader of post-war France to acknowledge the responsibility of the French state for the criminal offences of the Vichy regime—specifically for crimes against the Jews. "The criminal madness of the occupier was seconded by the French, by the French state," he stated. "Those black hours soiled our history forever; they wounded our past and our traditions. France, the land of the Enlightenment, the land of human rights, the land of refuge and asylum. [With these deportations] France committed the irreparable."[17]

Although this speech was made a decade after Richard von Weizsäcker's powerful plea for remembrance in the German parliament, it was the most important sign, to date, that France had begun a process of confronting the past. With this extraordinary declaration, Chirac publicly challenged the national myth that "France" had somehow resided in London during the war, thus making the Vichy regime "illegitimate" and therefore no blot on the subsequent Fourth and Fifth Republics. A storm erupted, but the fateful words had been voiced and could not be recalled. The chief of state had given the Vichy past a name: he called what took place "a collective error."

Chirac implied that France would never put its demons to rest until the Gaullist fairy tale—the notion of "France" in England—was finally and forever dismantled and until the French themselves assumed responsibility for their history, which included the democratically chosen government of Philippe Pétain—a statement that went a long way towards explaining why Maurice Papon found himself in a courtroom just two years later. François Mitterrand had stalled this trial, believing to the end in the usefulness of national reconciliation, pardon and amnesty, all of which were based on denying the obvious and on the "illegitimacy" of Vichy France—a rhetoric that had protected Mitterrand, as well as thousands of others who had flipped allegiances during the war. Although Chirac was a younger man (he was eight years old in 1940), and there was nothing in his personal past to keep him from speaking the truth, his words were politically courageous, without a doubt. More important, he was signalling the possibility of reconciliation between the disparate sites of French historical memory.

I'm on the train heading south to Bordeaux along a route I know well: (my former in-laws live in the southwest, in and around Bayonne, near the border with Spain, and we have stayed in close touch). Bordeaux is the metropolis of the region—famed for its wines, of course, but also for its magnificent traditions of gastronomy, especially the production of foie gras. It is an ancient patrician city that began as a thriving Roman capital; from the twelfth to the fourteenth centuries, it was owned by the English, along with the rest of Aquitaine (the English helped develop viniculture production, stocking the renowned wine cellars of medieval Oxford and Cambridge). The city was home to the illustrious Girondistes of the French Revolution and the birthplace of Montesquieu and Montaigne. It is, in other words, a microcosm of France—glorious, sybaritic France, shot through with great literature, a vivid intellectual life and (most evident of all) jittery politics.

The pendulum clock of history swings back and forth inside the august walls of the Palace of Justice, where Maurice Papon's trial is now entering its third week. I take my seat inside the courtroom—a plain, rectangular space painted lavatory green—near the rows of "civil parties," the men and women in whose names this prosecution is taking place. They are the survivors of the one-way trains to Drancy and the sons and daughters of those who died at the next stop: Auschwitz. If Maurice Papon is in the prisoner's box today, it is because one of them, Michel Slitinsky, spent hours doing research in the musty archives of the region.

On October 19, 1942, the police roundup closed in on the district where Slitinsky and his family lived. The others were arrested and deported, but Slitinsky, then seventeen, escaped by climbing onto his apartment roof. He joined the Resistance, and when he returned to Bordeaux in 1946 to discover that his father, brother and aunt were still missing, he began to ask questions. The rump families of other lost deportees refused to believe that French police had conducted the arrests, but Slitinsky was certain that no Germans had been involved. He proceeded alone in his investigations, never giving up.

Two decades later, acting on a tip from an archivist friend, he discovered hidden files detailing research that was conducted into Jewish families by French police and administrators. But a crucial piece of the puzzle was missing: the name of the person in charge. Many more years passed; then, in 1980, a document containing information on the wartime prefecture of the Gironde turned up at a Bordeaux flea market. The name Slitinsky was looking for was Maurice Papon, general secretary in charge of Jewish affairs.

In May 1981, the investigative satirical weekly *Le Canard enchaîné* published an exposé on the man who was currently budget minister in the government of Raymond Barre.[18] Slitinsky, his childhood friend Maurice-David Mattisson and the Bordeaux lawyer Gérard Boulanger brought charges for complicity in crimes against humanity.

The principals sit at the front, the prosecuting lawyers (in multitude, since, according to French law, civil parties, both individuals and associations, can be represented by separate counsel) are to the left of the trial chambers. Gérard Boulanger has been on the Papon case from its start sixteen years earlier. His personal commitment began in early childhood during the Algerian war of independence, on the day he happened to witness an old Arab deliberately hit on the head with a rock. This act of racial violence stayed in his memory, directed him into the study of law, then propelled him along a path that would eventually cross that of Maurice Papon. To the right of the chamber sits the defence team headed by Jean-Marc Varaut, a distinguished, grave-faced attorney of sixty-five. Varaut is an intellectual of the philosophical right, a monarchist and a devout Catholic, yet also considered a defender of human rights (he has written a book on the Nuremberg Trials). Varaut does not disavow the existence of crimes against humanity: he argues that the state has nabbed the wrong man.

Varaut stands, raises questions about the responsibility of Maurice Papon. Where was Papon in the line of command? Did he know about the final destination of those he deported to the Drancy way station? What were the facts of his membership in the Resistance? The question facing the Papon jury is the same that had confronted the international military tribunal at Nuremberg: Where does duty lie? Is the foot soldier responsible to the general from whom he takes his orders, and is the general responsible to the chief of state? Is the civil servant inextricably tied to the laws enacted by his government and to his oath to carry them out?

Gérard Boulanger has already written two books on the Papon *affaire*, and at regular intervals during the course of the trial he reads aloud, and at length, from one or the other. Jean-Marc Varaut has also published a tome, which he strategically reissued earlier this month, just before the trial began. Trial by literature. Even the defendant finds an opportunity to say his piece inside and outside the courtroom: the BBC broadcasts an interview in which Maurice Papon declares that he is a scapegoat for a regime that belongs to the past. "I have nothing to be ashamed of," he asserts. "The genocide against the Jews has left an indelible mark on the twentieth century, which has been the worst century known by humanity. My heart is filled with sorrow."[19]

Papon sits behind bulletproof glass, beside his counsel, looking every inch a man of cool, unassailable authority. He holds himself perfectly erect in his specially padded chair, his head inclined forward as he studies a sheaf of handwritten notes. His silver hair is flawlessly coiffed; he wears the perfect dark suit with a red handkerchief that edges over the breast pocket. Maurice Papon is altogether French in the impeccable style of his generation, and every visible attribute will be immediately recognizable to his compatriots, an awareness that reaches to the heart of this prosecution. For to have been a high-ranking government functionary was the career of choice for the sons of the well connected. If the French state was the guardian of the national interest, its civil servants were agents of notable power: only recently had the centralizing role of government been called into question as France's creaky economic and social structures faltered in the face of economic globalization. In 1942, Maurice Papon might have been any ambitious son of the bourgeoisie.

Papon was born into a well-to-do middle-class family with a culture of centre-left politics. He studied literature, law and political science—a not-uncommon preparation for public service—served in the army until the defeat of 1940, then obtained his post with the Pétain government through personal connections. In 1942, when he was posted to Bordeaux, he was thirty-two years old and already reputedly loyal. In April 1943, a German report categorized him as a fine collaborator and "accommodating with the German authorities."[20] A second report in July of that year called him "a good negotiator with a courteous manner. In delicate matters, he is often evasive and retires behind his superior, Maurice Sabatier. He co-operates fully with the *Kommandantur*."[21]

Papon negotiated a brilliant career that incarnated the continuities, and ambiguities, of twentieth-century French history—that is, the threads that linked the Vichy regime with the past and the future of the Republic. Such continuities were scandalous only when they became explicit and public—which, in the case of thousands of other Papons, had not happened.

But the public mood has changed, especially since the jarring trial of Klaus Barbie in 1987 and the trial of Paul Touvier in 1994 (Touvier was condemned to a life sentence in April of that year), and Papon has been caught in the shift. His case is sensational because, say what one might about the principle of one individual before the law, this indictment of a high-ranking state functionary calls into question the myths the nation has lived by, including the personal trajectories of many like him, some of whom had the good sense to die before they too were called to sit in a prisoner's dock. Principles aside, Papon incarnates the ghosts of higher-ups who were slated to occupy his place; in particular, Jean Leguay, who was René Bousquet's deputy and chief of the Vichy police in the Nazi-occupied zone before he went on to enjoy a successful business career on three continents. Leguay was arraigned as early as April 1979 but died of cancer in 1989 before he came to trial. Or Bousquet himself. After his pardon in 1949, he, too, had an outstanding career, as an international banker. Bousquet was eventually indicted for crimes against humanity, thanks to the efforts of Serge and Beate Klarsfeld, but he was murdered at the door of his Paris apartment in June 1993, before he could be tried.

Facing the spectators in the courtroom sits a row of red-robed, ermine-collared judges led by Jean-Louis Castagnède, a man known for independence, discretion and intellectual rigour. Earlier on, Castagnède had scandalized the country by liberating Papon for the period of his trial (Papon immediately rented rooms in a five-star hotel and invited the press to join him for champagne), prompting Arno Klarsfeld, one of the prosecuting lawyers, to reveal the judge's family ties with a relative of one of the victims. French trials are never short of drama that not infrequently spills over into posturing, and this one is no exception. Klarsfeld, the son of Serge and Beate, was young, caustic, well prepared and media-savvy. His unkempt shoulder-length hair hung over his face, requiring large, camera-attracting tosses of the head so he might peer through his locks, and he slouched in his chair with Byronic nonchalance. During breaks, he sauntered about the foyer in a black, short-sleeved T-shirt, with a cigarette dangling from the corner of his mouth, looking like James Dean circa 1954 as he searched for a television lens to declaim into. The daily newspaper *Le Monde* affectionately likened him to a "mad dog," and he played the role to perfection. After each session he sped away to his hotel room on Rollerblades.

Klarsfeld has a pedigree when it comes to this prosecution, for if any two people were responsible for the Papon trial *and* the Chirac declaration that had preceded it, they are his parents. Besides ferretting out former Nazis occupying high places in contemporary Germany, such as Chancellor Kurt-Georg Kiesinger, they focused their attention on the men who had operated in France and, after years of lobbying, successfully brought about the precedent-setting trials of three leaders of the Gestapo: Kurt Lischka, head of the Nazi police in Paris from 1940 to 1943; Herbert Hagan, right-hand man to Carl-Albrecht Oberg, head of the SS in France; and Ernst Heinrichsohn, SS officer in charge of the Drancy deportation camp. Until they were exposed by the Klarsfelds, all three had been leading tranquil lives as professional men in Germany. (Heinrichsohn was mayor of his town.) The Klarsfelds battled for the return of Klaus Barbie from Bolivia and also went after Leguay, Bousquet and Papon.

Their tactics were typical of the age: bold, media-attracting stunts that communicated their message to a wide audience. Back in 1976, Serge attended a meeting of neo-Nazis in Munich, intending to draw attention to the revival of the party. "I decided to become the first Jew since the war to be publicly beaten up by the Nazis," he told an interviewer. He was duly beaten up, and the rise of neo-Nazism was dutifully reported. Later, with painstaking research, he compiled a record called *Memorial to the Jews Deported from France*, listing every name that could be tracked down. Men and women who had disappeared in the crematoria of Poland, and babies who were said to have died at Drancy "pour la France," were belatedly recognized in simple lists that exposed the individual fate of each. There were plenty of people who disliked the Klarsfelds and their embarrassing tactics, people who wished they would stop stirring up the proverbial "mud"; but in both Germany and France, this exceptional couple successfully pried open the closed doors of memory and demanded justice for the dead.

Now the legacy of the Klarsfelds' thirty-year campaign to expose the crimes and prevarications of the past is being acted out in a courtroom in Bordeaux. The victims of Maurice Papon—and, by extension, of Vichy France—have waited all their lives for this moment.

From the first days of the trial, the myths of the post-war era have clashed publicly with the newer culture of transparency initiated by Jacques Chirac; the victims and their counsel are seeking nothing less than a radical revision of France's mythologized history. Two-thirds of the jury are forty years old or younger, and their verdict on the innocence or guilt of Maurice Papon may point to which of *les deux France* is likely to carry the future.

As I watch from my coveted seat in the audience, touchstones from the disputed past appear on the courtroom stage as aging politicians and illustrious Resistance fighters are called as witnesses for the defence. The defence? Isn't Maurice Papon on trial as a Pétain collaborator? And weren't these Resistance heroes supposed to have been on the other side? This is the heart of the ambiguity.

Jean Bozzi, seventy-six years old, and a former member of the Corsican parliament, introduces himself as the son of a "pro-Dreyfus" family, thus aligning himself with the liberal camp in the theatre of French politics. Having established his republican credentials, he says that although Monsieur Papon, with whom he worked after the war, is "cold" and "firm," he is also a man of liberal values. Knowing this, Bozzi feels absolutely certain that Papon could not have discerned the fate of the Jews when he signed their deportation orders.

"I hope that this trial will be the last of a kind that can harm France," he pleads. "And that there will be a pardon if necessary!"

"We are here to judge a man vis-à-vis the law, not to discuss pardons," Judge Castagnède reprimands him.

After Dreyfus's brief visit, France's symbolic hero of the Resistance, Jean Moulin, makes an appearance. Moulin's famous name has been ever so slightly besmirched in recent years. He was arrested by the Nazis—by Klaus Barbie, as it happens; that much is known—but there have been recent questions about whether he was betrayed by another member of the Resistance, and whether he might not have been murdered but committed suicide in his cell, as Klaus Barbie had once asserted. Few people believed either Barbie or his histrionic lawyer, Vergès, a man who took mischievous pleasure in disconcerting the populace while defending his notorious client. But the fact that the accusation was made, whether true or not, has cast doubt on a previously inviolate reputation.

Jean Moulin's name is invoked by both the prosecution *and* the defence. Like Papon, Moulin was a local prefect at the beginning of the Vichy era, but as the prosecution reminds the court, he resigned immediately in order to join de Gaulle in London. And paid the ultimate price for his resistance. Maurice Papon, on the other hand, remained in his position and became an accessory to crimes against humanity.

"Jean Moulin also applied the anti-Jewish laws of Vichy until he left in 1940!" retorts the chief of the defence team, jumping to his feet.

Jean-Marc Varaut's response is unfair; the Nazis occupied Paris on June 14, 1940, and Jean Moulin's refusal to co-operate dated from June 17 (for which he was beaten, tortured and imprisoned); furthermore, the exclusionary legislation of Vichy came into effect on October 3, and by November Moulin was already on his way to London. But Moulin's personal itinerary is not really the point, it seems to me: what is remarkable is that a dispute about the Resistance, as personified by its greatest hero, is on the floor of a French courtroom, fifty years after Moulin's death, during the trial of a former colleague who is accused of having been an accessory to the most heinous crime of our century.

Again Judge Castagnède calls the court to order. "This is not the place to talk about Jean Moulin," he reproaches the lawyers. "Jean Moulin did not *deport* anyone."

Poor Jean-Louis Castagnède, trying to keep this symbol-laden trial in focus. Crimes against humanity—defined in 1945 by the international military tribunal in Nuremberg as "murder, extermination, slavery, deportation, or other inhuman acts committed against any civilian population before or during [a] war; or persecution on political, religious and racial grounds . . . whether or not in violation of the domestic law of the country where perpetrated"[22]—were but a part of the drama being acted out in Bordeaux. Try as he may, the judge can only hope to keep the entanglements of his nation's history from assuming centre stage.

The famous men step forward to the witness stand in defence of Maurice Papon. Pierre Messmer, eighty-one, had served with the Free French in London from 1940 and as prime minister of France from 1972 to 1974. In a loud, clear voice, he reiterates the de Gaulle–inspired mythology that had, until the declaration of Jacques Chirac, exonerated the entire nation. "From the moment the government of Vichy signed the armistice, it was illegitimate," he booms. "An illegitimate government does not represent France, nor can it engage France. It is responsible to itself alone and that includes the functionaries and military who chose to obey its rules."

It is not immediately clear to me just how this testimony is supposed to help poor Maurice Papon, sitting so rigid and straight behind his bulletproof glass, since Messmer allows that he did not met Papon until 1960. But he has not come to Bordeaux to talk about the accused. He is here to defend "France" against the new vision of collective responsibility put forward by the current president of the Republic.

"I am totally opposed to the declarations of the highest authorities of our state that impute to France, and thus to all French citizens, responsibility for the crimes of Vichy," he expounds with fervour. "Such words are intolerable to the men and women who joined Free France, General Charles de Gaulle and the Resistance!"

He catches an emotion-filled breath. "As my own death approaches, it seems to me that fifty-five years later, the time has come for French people to stop hating one another and to forgive."

"Are forgiveness and reconciliation possible before a recognition of wrong?" interjects the prosecution lawyer Michel Zaoui. Messmer sails on, choosing to ignore the crucial question. "I would like to say that whatever respect I have for the victims of the war, especially innocent victims, I have greater respect for those who died standing up bearing arms, for it is to them that we owe our liberation," he declares.

The insinuation that the Jews might be taking up too much space at the expense of the Resistance had first emerged during the Klaus Barbie affair. In practice, crimes against humanity have meant crimes committed against the Jews.

"What do you think about the actions of a high functionary who obeys the inhuman orders of an illegitimate government?" asks Arno Klarsfeld, attempting to bring the testimony back to its presumed subject.

Pierre Messmer, witness for the defence, does not hesitate: "People ought to have resigned as soon as acts contrary to their conscience were ordered," he replies before leaving the stand. Not once has Messmer deigned to glance in the direction of the defendant. Maurice Papon sits stony-faced and still.

Other surviving members of the general's post-war regime march up to testify, including Raymond Barre, seventy-three, also a former prime minister of France. Barre met Papon in 1976, and in 1978 he appointed him to the post of budget minister in his cabinet. No, he replies to cross-examination, he did not know of Papon's wartime duties; and no, it had *not* been necessary to verify his new minister's past. "His reputation was excellent," he states categorically.

And what was the source of Maurice Papon's excellent reputation? Olivier Guichard, seventy-six, the so-called baron of Gaullism, met Papon in 1958 when the latter was chief of police in Paris, and he remembers that Charles de Gaulle himself had once said that Papon had "rendered great service" to the man who was de Gaulle's representative in Bordeaux at the time of the Liberation. Guichard is remarkably open about the national myths: "At the Liberation, de Gaulle had a strong desire to unite the country. That's why he invented the story that the Vichy regime did not exist in reality [that it was illegitimate] and the other myth that we won the war," he announces to the court. "De Gaulle was trying to avoid having to try the majority of the French people. His reasoning was that you couldn't incriminate people on behalf of a state that simply did not exist!"

The courtroom falls silent; no one expected to hear such a matter-of-fact appraisal of the inventions that have been taught to every schoolchild as history for half a century. But Olivier Guichard has even more to say: "Of course, *all* the prime ministers under the general[23] were previously in the public service of Vichy. But since Vichy was illegitimate, it was as though it had not been."

Has Alice in Wonderland dropped down the rabbit hole and resurfaced in Bordeaux? I wonder whether any other Western country could boast a hoodwinking exercise quite as sophisticated as that contrived fifty years ago in France.

None of this has much to do with the unfortunate Maurice Papon, except to suggest that other career paths had paralleled his—from officer in charge of arranging for the transport of civilians to Drancy, to late membership in the Resistance, then on to important positions in the post-war Republics. A presumed role in the Resistance was the key to everyone's future, but unlike François Mitterrand's, who had also joined late, Maurice Papon's participation had been less than heroic. After Hitler was defeated at Stalingrad in late 1943, Papon cannily began to take precautions. He invited a Jewish *résistant*, a man he had known before the war, to his home,[24] then publicly refused a promotion within the Vichy system. In May 1944, he gave up his job as head of Jewish affairs, and in June, the war effectively over, he pointedly entertained Gaston Cusin, General de Gaulle's clandestine representative in France, who was looking for a toehold in Bordeaux, then spread word about the meeting. Two days after the liberation of Bordeaux, Papon brought together all the local chiefs of police and redirected them to serve Gaston Cusin, and within days he had resurfaced with a new title. Now he was Maurice Papon, director of the office of Gaston Cusin, commissioner of the Republic and prefect of the Landes region.

As secretary of Jewish affairs, Maurice Papon had carried out the exclusionary anti-semitic laws, his official signature authorizing the deportation of entire families, but in his testimony, he claims he was always compassionate. He rises before the court to protest that he requisitioned blankets to cover the children during their transit to Drancy. He exclaims that he felt deeply for the Jews he had to expel, and that he even tried to save several of them: he once sheltered a Jewish man in his home for a short while. And one Christmas, he and his wife wept with sorrow after a wagonload of children was dispatched during the bitterly cold holy season. The survivors in the audience look incredulous, express their dismay with audible contempt.

Papon's defence is that he did his best while obeying orders. Service to the laws of his country was a patriotic trust, and a loyal civil servant did not consider abandoning his post. Cry over what had to be done, perhaps. Requisition blankets, perhaps. But signing orders was a duty: he was commanded to do so by a superior.

An elderly woman approaches the witness stand. Gillette Chapel is now eighty-three. She is the widow of Jean Chapel, the former deputy to the head of the entire Bordeaux operation, Maurice Sabatier.

Madame Chapel and her husband moved to Bordeaux from Vichy with Sabatier: she is the only witness who knew Maurice Papon when he was on the job. "Maurice didn't order the arrests. Maurice is a man of integrity! The French police ordered the arrests!" she says in a rapid, barely controlled voice. "Maurice ordered the trains, and he really *tried* to get passenger wagons, not the cattle cars! He even gave them blankets, didn't you, Maurice? This trial is just *awful*! Maurice was a great *résistant!*"

She turns to look at her old friend, whom she has not seen for many years. Papon has turned white. In the audience, we lower our heads in embarrassment.

"It was awful, just awful! We were just sick," she continues, oblivious. "When you think that they deported the mothers and left the children! Those poor little ones, then they came and got them afterwards. And the [French] police? Ach, disgusting! Only one of them went to prison, and he was totally Vichy-Vichy. And you know, Monsieur Sabatier's wife was Jewish! So he can't possibly have known what was happening to those people!"

Judge Castagnède looks astonished. "Monsieur Sabatier's wife was Jewish?"

"Yes, that's right." Madame Chapel nods. "That's why he arranged to get out of Vichy. He thought it would be safer for her in Bordeaux."

Small wonder the judge was surprised. In 1981, a commission that examined Maurice Papon's past history established that Sabatier had "assumed entire responsibility for the anti-Jewish repression within his jurisdiction."[25] Sabatier, like Papon, was investigated during the 1980s, but he died before he could be indicted.

"When my husband saw what they were doing to poor Maurice [in 1981], he was just shocked," continues Madame Chapel. "He said, 'This is horrible! They don't understand anything!' And three months later, he [her husband] killed himself. . . ."

She slumps over the witness bar: old, exhausted, defeated.

The cross-examination is gentle. "Madame, since you have such precise memories, can you tell us in what way Maurice Papon was a great *résistant?*

"No, not really," she replies. "I wasn't at that high a level. But you know we have all been called accomplices and murderers. I loved *all* children, Jews and Bretons too. It is painful. Before I came here, my bodily functions all stopped!"

A little snicker travels through the audience. The judge looks stern.

"Judge Castagnède, if you could only bring a little forgiveness and serenity . . ." She stops and hangs her head.

"Madame," answers the judge in a kindly voice, "forgiveness is not within the capacity of this court."

The pendulum swings back to the Vichy era, and wherever it stops is where we, the audience, must live for a few pained moments as men and women step forward to relive their past. Next at the bar on behalf of the defence is Maurice Druon of the Académie Française, also a former member of the Free French Forces and subsequently minister of culture in the cabinet of Pierre Messmer. Druon speaks of the sacrifice, the lack of food, the cold, the separation from one's family and the constant danger of Resistance life, as though it were yesterday. It is clear that for him, as for many others within that brave 1 per cent of the population who actively fought in the French Resistance, nothing before or since could approximate the experience.

He is angry. "This trial is an insult to the memory and the sacrifice of those who died [for France]," he says. "There is something astonishing about seeing a functionary of Vichy, who has been recognized as a *résistant*, stand accused before a jury when another jury of thirty-five million French twice elected a man who was decorated with the Francisque [the medal of Vichy] *and* the medal of the Resistance and deserved them both!" (Druon's suggestion that the population knew about François Mitterrand's Vichy past when he was elected is false, but the point is clear.)

He slides into the standard defence of the Collaboration: "If they [Papon et al.] had known what was happening in the concentration camps and refused to go along, why then things would have been worse! And if the Jews themselves knew, they would not have allowed themselves to go along like sheep to the slaughter!"

A man in the audience jumps to his feet. "We were unarmed!"

"The trials of Vichy finished after the war, but here we are starting them all over again," Druon continues, ignoring the commotion. "We praised everyone who suffered or fought: the deported *résistants*, the hostages, the Jewish *résistants*. And today we are trying to create a special category. As though only the Jews were victims. As though those who died blowing up the trains somehow deserved to die. This is vengeance [wrongly] called justice.

"And just who is this trial in aid of? I will tell you. It is in aid of Germany. Germany is now reunited. Tomorrow it will have regained its power. Only one thing can prevent Germany from being seized by its imperialist demons, and that is the remembrance of its Nazi demons. If we condemn a symbolic Frenchman it will be easy [for the Germans] to say, 'The French were as bad as we were.' Their guilt will be dissipated. There is a certain paradox in seeing the children of the victims becoming allies of the children of the executioners."

"My father was a member of the Jewish Resistance," shouts Francis Jacob, a lawyer for the prosecution. "I will not tolerate this!"

"*I* am French, Catholic, baptized in childhood," retorts Druon, staring Jacob in the face, "but one part of my ancestry is Jewish. *I* will not tolerate having one side of my blood raised against the other!"

"No!" calls out Arno Klarsfeld. "If France today does not condemn the France of yesterday, the civil service of tomorrow could also send Jews to their death."

"On November 11, 1945, when all the victims of the war were honoured, why was there no mention of those who were deported for reasons of their birth alone?" the prosecution lawyer Michel Zaoui demands to know.

"It is certain that in the hearts of many, this was a major breach," intercedes the judge.

"This is a trial against France itself," Druon calls out in a loud voice. "But France didn't conduct itself so badly!"

The free-for-all atmosphere of a French court is disconcerting in itself, but in a short phrase Maurice Druon has managed to expose the murky amalgam of wartime Vichy and the post-war Republic. His audience is meant to understand that this "trial against France" that he speaks of is the trial of the "legitimate" nation, the "real" France, the country of the French Resistance that also happened to include, at its eleventh hour, Vichy collaborators like Maurice Papon who were needed to rebuild society. Just as it had included Resistance heroes like the late president of the Republic, François Mitterrand, who had successfully concealed his personal, clouded past until the very end of his life.

Maurice Papon raises his hand to speak. He rises slowly to his feet and turns to the judge. "For the past several days I have observed that my trial has veered into a trial of General de Gaulle [and the Resistance]," he says in a ringing, sarcastic tone of voice. "I share the outrage of Monsieur Druon that this has happened. With him, I am in good company."

More mind-bending confusion? The man on trial for having collaborated with the Nazis in crimes against humanity is expressing his outrage as a member of the Gaullist Resistance.

Maurice Druon's diatribe, in which he came close to accusing the victims and their children of being enemies of the state, would have sounded familiar to the men and women of his generation in the Bordeaux courtroom, for old-style anti-semitism was the racism of their era. But in the 1990s—and in Germany, as well as in France—the same hatred is more overtly directed against "immigrants," which is in France a code word for Arabs and blacks. In fact, the courtroom web of mixed loyalties and cross-allegiances has been amply reflected outside the Bordeaux tribunal. The leader of France's extreme-right political party, the National Front, has been making statements similar to those of Maurice Druon: Jean-Marie Le Pen has called the Papon trial "judaeocentric" and said it is dishonest to forget that the Second World War caused the deaths of tens of millions of people, and that communism was responsible for the deaths of 150 million more. On two previous occasions, Le Pen has dismissed the Nazi gas chambers as a "detail of history": once in 1987, then again in 1997, while he was in Munich promoting a biography of himself by the right-wing German political leader Franz Schönhuber, a former SS officer.

Le Pen attracts media attention by being "spontaneously" outrageous. In 1988, he called a Jewish government minister, Michel Durafour, "Durafour-Crématoire" (Durafour-Crematory), and said of another minister, Simone Veil, a survivor of the death camps, "When I speak of genocide I always say that they missed old lady Veil." In a 1987 radio interview he asserted, "I don't say that the gas chambers did not exist, but I haven't been able to see any myself and I have not studied the question especially."

Like Germany, France had enacted legislation making it a crime to deny the magnitude of the Holocaust, and in the way of demagogues everywhere, Le Pen enjoys claiming that the mavens of "political correctness" conspire against his right to unfettered freedom of speech. He is frequently charged under this law and fined, a gesture that seems to serve his purposes since his followers applaud each time he opens his mouth to undermine minorities. Le Pen's core constituency is the ultra-conservative face of *les deux France* that has been in and out of prominence since the Revolution, many of whom did indeed keep silent after the defeat of Vichy France in order to save themselves. It also includes former Communists who continue to remain pointedly uninterested in the political centre. That Maurice Druon, a Gaullist minister, a high-ranking member of the Académie Française and indisputably a Resistance hero, has aligned himself with the language of this milieu is an indication of the political and historical intricacies being revealed in the trial of Maurice Papon.

When the weekly paper *L'Action française hebdo* congratulates Druon on his testimony and speaks of the "howling of fanatic Jews," the conflation becomes even more bizarre. "We cannot allow Germany to lighten its guilt by sharing it with France," the writer declaims, quoting Druon. "Monsieur Chirac [was wrong] to implicate Vichy for those so-called crimes that were carried out by the Nazis and a few French accomplices. . . . When all is said and done, the record of Vichy was largely beneficial. . . ."[26] How close this seemed to the standard explanations heard in pre-1968 Germany: only a small number of wrong-headed people did the dirty work. Certainly not "us."

Allowing for inevitable changes in the "enemies-of-the-state" category over half a century, Jean-Marie Le Pen and his National Front were a more or less direct continuation of the deeply conservative thinking that had informed the Action Française movement decades before. Action Française was fascist in a peculiarly French mode: Charles Maurras, the leader, was no murderer, but rather a snob, an aesthete, a masculinist and a worshipper of the ancient world (he admired Plato and dreamed of installing a monarch in France who would enforce the rule of the elite). He was an anti-democrat who rejoiced in France's capitulation to the Germans. "Our worst defeat has had the good result of ridding us of democracy," he once announced.

Although Maurras fell out of favour when Republican France took over after the war, many of his ideas suffered only temporary eclipse. But it was not until the emergence of Jean-Marie Le Pen in the 1970s that a major challenge to the liberal status quo was mounted. Because overt racism and anti-semitism had been socially taboo for decades, the public was surprised to learn in 1983 of an extraordinary meeting taking place in Paris in the context of "French Friendship Day." The identity of the members of the new National Front was intriguing: at Le Pen's side were the executive assistant of the man who had once directed Vichy's radio propaganda, the leader of a right-wing student group called the New Order, a member of the extremist organization that had threatened de Gaulle with a military coup during the Algerian war and writers from a publication titled *Défense de l'Occident* (Defence of the West). Some very familiar ideas seemed to have found new circulation. "Four superpowers are colonizing France: Marxists, Jews, Freemasons and Protestants," proclaimed a pro-family organization in a newly revived evocation of Charles Maurras. The editor of a newspaper announced that "the only community that is not protected is the French community." The author of a contemporary book, *Ce Canaille de Dreyfus* (Dreyfus the scum), said Arab immigrants "breed like rabbits" and that a highly placed government official "looked like a Turk." But the most palpable presence was that of Marshal Philippe Pétain himself, whose picture adorned ashtrays, posters, buttons and plates. The conservative flank of the old schism, so long in eclipse, was emerging from the shadows.

In 1984, the National Front captured 11 per cent of the vote at the European elections, establishing Jean-Marie Le Pen as a central political actor and anchoring his party on the map. He managed to keep it there for more than a decade, winning 15 per cent of the vote in France's presidential elections of 1995.

Le Pen successfully unleashed racism, making religious and ethnic hatred respectable for the first time since the Vichy era, until it was newly acceptable for people to openly state racist convictions and in some cases applaud the murders of Algerian immigrants who were collectively blamed for the economic woes of the country and uncertainty about the future. Disturbingly, Le Pen's popularity had scared the centrist political parties into adopting their own (though lesser) anti-Arab rhetoric and putting forward anti-immigrant legislation, although by the late 1990s, he faced powerful rivals and his personal future, and that of his party, seemed less secure.[27]

This is the fragile political environment in which the trial of Maurice Papon is taking place. Although a large majority approves of the prosecution, many people also seem to believe there is altogether too much talk about the Jews in this affair, a point of view expressed openly by Maurice Druon and the extreme right—and more covertly in other places. (No one has officially measured this reaction, needless to say, but unguarded conversations are there for the hearing, in cafés and at dinner parties where friends meet.)

My allotted time at the trial is up, and I must give up my seat to someone else. I return "home" to Paris, where, I discover, an interesting-sounding meeting called "Is France Disappearing?" is about to take place at the *mairie* (city hall) of my own fourteenth district. On the designated evening, I walk the few blocks to join about two hundred other people who are waiting to hear the speaker. They are mostly middle-aged and working class in appearance and thoroughly white in complexion.

The lecturer, who is about forty and a self-described "specialist in immigration," opens with a tirade against foreigners. Once they were colonized by France, he says, but they are now colonizing the French in their own land. "France" is in danger of disappearing: France, a country of white Christians of European stock who speak French is being swamped by Arabs.

I look around; the audience is listening carefully and some people are nodding agreement. Although his ideas are as old as the first xenophobe, the speaker seems to be working up to his subject carefully: I suppose French laws against hate speech make such tiptoeing necessary. He starts with the alarming spectre of "the revenge of the cradle": foreigners (Arabs) have many children, he says, while the French birth rate is down; foreigners (Arabs) eat strange foods, and their awful cuisine produces unpleasant odours. And their children speak Arabic—one can actually hear the grating un-French sounds in the street. He talks about single mothers and their "broods," about high unemployment among the French, against whom Arabs are competing for jobs.

He is not a racist, he says. He is a man of the "rational centre," a patriot and a defender of French civilization. An assimilationist: in fact, his own grandfather on his mother's side was a foreigner (a titter passes through the audience). However, only people issuing from "the Judaeo-Christian tradition" are amenable to proper assimilation. Certainly not the Arabs. Not unless they are Christians. To assimilate is to abandon one's cultural past and to accept the culture of the new land in its entirety. Muslims are unable to do that, and in their ugly persistence they are colonizing France.

The specialist in immigration sighs. He has no answers, he laments. We can't trust our politicians. No guts. Even if France deported tens of thousands of foreigners, which would be a good first step, the problem would still be there. His forehead crinkles with sorrow, but he has just stated his solution. Deportation.

No one in the room questions the wisdom of—or the human capacity for—the complete abandonment of the cultural self, here described as "assimilation." Total assimilation as a precondition for belonging is an old French ideal, born of cultural universality, an ideal that is currently being challenged across Europe by changing demographics: the French are not the only people troubled about multicultures in their midst. The speaker worries pointedly about the inability of foreigners to "disappear into the population," as he puts it; however, since *foreigners* and *immigrants* are understood code words for blacks and Algerians, he does not have to mention that their colour is an insurmountable barrier to their becoming "French."

At the time of Vichy, Frenchness was defined according to religion (only Catholics need apply), but by the 1990s the criteria had shifted—somewhat. Only somewhat. Because fifty years later, the Jews are, well, the Jews are . . . The speaker seems unsure about what to say next. Even though he supports the "Judaeo-Christian tradition," he may hesitate to speak openly at this sensitive time when a Frenchman is sitting in the prisoner's dock for having effected precisely what he is proposing for Arabs: deportations. His lapse lasts only a moment: "Jews were able to come here and disappear into the population," he picks up quickly. "And we must remember that Judaism is a religion and not a race." The stony-faced audience looks unconvinced. After all, Jean-Marie Le Pen doesn't hesitate to include the Jews in his tirades. Maybe this "specialist" is a sellout.

In any event, assimilation is a red herring, for even if non-whites could "disappear into the population"—and there is nothing in this line of thinking to suggest that might be possible—the supposedly assimilated are never assimilated enough, even though they and their ancestors may have lived in France for centuries. Although he was an officer in the French army and a member of an old Alsatian family, Alfred Dreyfus was not "French" as far as the xenophobes of his day were concerned. Neither was Léon Blum, prime minister; or Pierre Mendès-France, prime minister; or Pierre Masse, jurist and senator, who was deported to Auschwitz in 1942; or Victor Basch, president of the League for the Rights of Man, who was murdered by the French Milice in 1944. As a result of humanistic policies born of the Revolution, France is one of the most mixed nations in Europe; but the French have had difficulty accepting classic pluralism, the notion that religious and otherwise diverse communities might be accepted as they are and protected under the national umbrella. The man on trial in Bordeaux represents an earlier instance of that failure. This meeting in Paris is a new incarnation of the same old rejection.

But liberal France is also mounting an offensive. Is it likewise a coincidence that as the Papon trial unfolds in Bordeaux, the Comédie Française in Paris happens to be performing *Nathan the Wise* by the eighteenth-century German dramatist Gotthold Ephraim Lessing? All Lessing's works reflect his Enlightenment-inspired commitment to tolerance and humanity. The philosopher Moses Mendelssohn was one of Lessing's closest friends (both men attempted to model their lives on truth and reason, the twin principles of their age), and in *Nathan the Wise* Lessing pays open tribute to Mendelssohn, who was known even in his own time as "the German Socrates."

I buy a ticket: how wonderful it is to have an excuse to step inside this magnificent theatre, with its famous bust of Voltaire—an even more famous exponent of the Enlightenment—and the very chair that Molière was sitting in when taken fatally ill on stage in 1673. The didacticism of Lessing's play does feel dated, but its subject—the equality of the three great Western faiths in their ethical foundations and the revelation of mankind's one true religion, love without prejudice in the service of humankind—could not have been more relevant in the troubled atmosphere choking this country at the end of the twentieth century. In *Nathan the Wise*, the main characters discover that they are related to one another (the family of man, presumably), but only the Jew—that is, Moses Mendelssohn himself—lives up to Lessing's ideal through his willingness to speak the truth, even to the most powerful of men.

In my mind's eye I see the gravestone of Moses Mendelssohn standing alone in the desecrated Jewish cemetery in the former East Berlin. And yet he is honoured here in Paris, two hundred years after his death and fifty years after the Nazi outrage. I think to myself that Maurice Papon is on trial because he lacked the courage of which Lessing speaks, as did most of his compatriots when faced with difficult moral choices. I know that such weakness is understandable—and also that it is not excusable. Papon has never acknowledged any wrongdoing—only contrition that he did not know the final destination of his victims.

Others do regret. The Catholic Church, with its Declaration of Repentance. And the main police union of France,[28] which recently asked forgiveness for the role its members played in the roundups, arrests and deportations. In their statement they called their predecessors "accomplices in the deportation of Jews during the Occupation" and judged them harshly: "Those who committed these ignoble [acts] were not a minority," they said. Almost simultaneously, the president of the medical association of France issued his own apology for the anti-semitism of his professional organization, which had imposed strict quotas on Jewish physicians.

The rash of apologies and pleas for forgiveness for a long-ago past are all too much for some people. "VICHY, THE RESISTANCE, THE ALGERIAN WAR . . . FRANCE IS SICK FROM MEMORY," screams the cover of *Le Point* magazine on November 1, 1997. Whatever one's opinions, it is hard to disagree.

Through Lucie Aubrac, one of France's most famous *résistants*, and her husband, Raymond, whom I first met while researching the Klaus Barbie book, I make contact with Danièle Rousselier, a high school history teacher at the Lycée Voltaire. She invites me to meet her class of seventeen- and eighteen-year-olds. The school, in the multi-ethnic eleventh district, has a good academic reputation, and the room is populated with a sprinkling of Algerians, blacks and Jews, as well as children from old French stock, all of whom giggle and elbow each other as they enter, like adolescents everywhere.

I have come to find out what they know about Maurice Papon and what they think about the issues, if they think about them at all; no matter what their elders may be saying in Bordeaux or Paris, these children's ideas count. France is a multicultural nation, in spite of certain pretenses to the contrary. This history class may provide interesting clues to future attitudes.

Yes, they do know who Maurice Papon is, and yes, they know he is on trial "for helping the Nazis." Only seven out of thirty are actively following the proceedings on a day-to-day basis in the newspapers, but most of the others are watching televised news reports. They have strong opinions and are eager to share them.

"Is it too late for your country to hold a trial like this?" I ask.

Only one person thinks it is. "Our grandparents never talked to us. Now they're dead or too old," he says.

The others disagree. "The families of the victims need some resolution, so it's important," offers a girl in the front row. "An individual has to be charged and found guilty or innocent. You can't say it was a faceless hierarchy or something like that. It was people!"

"It *takes* fifty years for stuff like this to ripen," calls out another, "but we're responsible for our actions, always. It's not that it's too late, it's just a pity it's *so* late."

"Mitterrand knew everything, and that's why he held the trial up for so long," says another. "So many people in this country had guilty consciences that they had to wait until most of them were dead!"

"Wait a minute! Not everyone collaborated or took part in a genocide. *My* grandparents were in the Resistance!" interjects a boy who has been silent until now.

"We only think things are bad now, in retrospect," adds another. "During the war, people didn't think collaboration was bad. And we don't know what we would have been like—I mean, we weren't there. When laws are passed today that we don't like, do we do anything about it? No, we don't!"

The discussion returns to the subject of their grandparents, the generation that lived through the Occupation. "In the 1960s, young people in Germany began to ask their parents what they had done during the war. That was thirty years ago. Have you, or as far as you know, your parents, ever actually asked the question, Father, or Grandfather, what did you do?" I inquire.

Silence. "I tried," says one boy eventually, "but my grandparents said I was too young to understand what things were like then. But my grandfather is filled with real hate. He was in a prisoner-of-war camp, and he cannot hear the word *German* without swearing. And he *never* uses bad language. It is striking to me that he has never forgiven."

"What! You think he should forgive those people who killed millions of Jews!" interrupts a girl, jumping to her feet.

For these students, the post-war myths of "France" in London and the "illegitimacy" of Vichy are a hilarious joke. "Whoa, the French did certain things, but 'France' did nothing? I don't get it!" shouts one boy, to general laughter. And they have almost as much contempt for the apology of the Catholic Church. Although most of them think that doing something of a moral nature is better than doing nothing at all, they are relentlessly critical about the wording of the Declaration of Repentance in which the Church has asked forgiveness of God but not of the families whose relatives were deported. "It's right that they ask God's pardon, but they should also have asked forgiveness of mankind," asserts a girl at the back, to a chorus of approval. And the police apology? "They should ask forgiveness every day for what they do to us!" (Applause.)

"Excuse me, when the Church asks forgiveness of God, that leaves me cold, but when the police ask forgiveness of the Jews, as they did, that touches me," someone calls out. "General de Gaulle ought to have spoken about what happened—certainly not hidden it all the way he did."

"Yeah, but they couldn't put *everyone* on trial. The country just had to go forward," retorts another.

We are back on the merry-go-round of French memory, except that being very young, these adolescents are typically pitiless in their assessments. "Will the national discussion over Vichy end with the Papon trial?" I ask.

"No way, it will always return," several of them reply in different ways, talking over one another. "Either you put everyone on trial, or you try to close the situation—those are the only choices. But neither is possible. So it will always return."

A boy of Algerian background who has been slouching over his desk shyly raises his hand. "I think this trial is important because of the

National Front," he says in a soft voice, "because they are using the same language and they would do the same things again."

A black girl who has not yet spoken also raises her hand. "If people thought Vichy was bad, just wait until the National Front gets to power," she warns. "Then everyone will be a target: the Jews, the Arabs, the blacks. Who will be 'pure' French, and who will get to decide?" The class falls silent. They seem collectively afraid of the Front and Jean-Marie Le Pen. "Personally, I don't think the French people will allow that to happen," the girl continues. "I have confidence." A young Parisian woman with black skin who is sanguine about her Frenchness. Eternal optimism renews itself in the very young.

This small sample of French youth has rejected the old myths of nationhood, myths that seem to be unravelling at the trial of Maurice Papon. But they have no confidence that the peculiar perplexities of French historical memory will ever be clarified—in spite of endless talk, in spite of rivers of ink. Although it is never too late to indict and try an individual for crimes against humanity, they think too many of those responsible have died peacefully in their beds for the nation to put away its past. "I'll be eighty and we'll *still* be talking about Vichy!" calls out a boy at the back of the class. His friends laugh and nod vigorously.

Danièle Rousselier always teaches the Vichy era to her students, including the collaboration with the Nazis, but she thinks her priorities may be exceptional. Although dozens of books pour off the presses every year and the topic is formally part of the school curriculum, many teachers somehow don't get around to it. "They finish the course with 1939 and say they don't have time for the rest," she tells me. "Many teachers do not think studying what happened during those years is important for French children today, but I happen to believe that nothing is more important for understanding the present in this country. Of course, the teachers themselves are fairly ignorant since none of them studied the subject. I'm fifty and I never even heard about Vichy France when I was at school."

Guilty. The jury delivered its verdict on April 2, 1998, after the longest trial in French history. Maurice Papon was convicted of complicity in crimes against humanity for arresting and deporting Jews but acquitted of complicity in their subsequent murder. The sentence of the court was ten years in prison, half what the state had requested. The defence immediately filed an appeal.

Many people thought justice had been done and that an important chapter in history had been thoroughly aired. Robert Badinter, once a minister of justice in the government of François Mitterrand, spoke of the "courage [demonstrated by] this great nation, so bound to its history, in facing the dark pages of its past and their consequences." A national association of former Resistance fighters said the responsibility of the French administration during the Occupation had necessarily come to light so that people could distinguish between those who chose the side of refusal, often at the price of their lives, and those who became zealous servants of the machinery of deportation. Most of the victims pronounced themselves satisfied. The sixteen-year wait had been worth it, they said: the murder of parents, children, siblings, aunts and uncles had been recognized and legally condemned.

A few people were disappointed, including two prominent historians: Henri Amouroux, the author of *Pour en finir avec Vichy: les oublis de la mémoire*[29] (Let's finish with Vichy: memory and forgetting), and his younger counterpart, Henry Rousso, author of *Le Syndrome de Vichy: de 1944 à nos jours* (The Vichy syndrome: 1948 to the present).[30] For Rousso, the entire process was "a step backward." He deplored the "trial in the media"; the reopening of the post-war purge; the "commemorative" aspect of the proceedings that were, he said, unsuited to a court of law; and what he called the "vengeance" of the Klarsfeld family, who were "trying to write history as they wanted it written by means of the trial." Rousso also called for an end to "judaeocentrism," thus aligning himself with the language of the National Front.

Henri Amouroux limited his criticisms to what he called an unfortunate "black-and-white" rendering of a complex time, but his objectivity was called into question when he was publicly reminded about his own collaborationist past as a young journalist with the pro-Pétain newspaper, *La Petite Gironde*. In a country as politicized as France, it was inevitable that any commentator with a personal history would find himself exposed.

As for the defendant, he felt "only contempt," according to his lawyer, a sentiment Papon corroborated sixteen months later, when he escaped from his guards on October 11, 1999—on the eve of his appeal—and fled to Switzerland, where he registered in a hotel under the aristocratic name of Monsieur de La Roche-Bernard. He also simultaneously published a book titled *La Vérité n'intéressait personne* (The truth interested no one).[31] "Exile is the only way to preserve honour," he told the daily *Le Sud-Ouest* in a mysterious communiqué, comparing himself to some of "the greatest men of our history" who had done the same—in particular, Victor Hugo. He also accused the court of having been "influenced," without saying by whom. "I refuse to bow my head," he proudly asserted. Papon was discovered ten days later at the fancy Swiss ski resort of Gstaad, having assumed yet another famous surname, this time of literary renown: La Rochefoucauld. The Swiss government extradited him back to France, where he was eventually incarcerated in the redoubtable prison of La Santé, in Paris. Because he had failed to turn up for the hearing, his appeal was automatically voided; but Jean-Marc Varaut, his lawyer, has said he will take the case to the European Human Rights Court at Strasbourg.

Papon's jarring distortions on the subject of "honour," and his remarks about "influence," are a reminder that he never did break faith with the touchstone values of his Vichy years and a further indication of his lack of regret. On the other hand, his trial and the verdict are both striking evidence of how far from that thinking mainstream France has travelled.

In the months before Klaus Barbie was brought to trial in 1987, the French press relished the wishful hope that Barbie's prosecution might serve as a lesson about the Holocaust, about the true role of the French Resistance, about the colonial war in Algeria and about everything else that had long been deliberately obfuscated. Only a few chose to remember that under the law, one man would be tried for the specific crimes he had been charged with and that this was the foundation of justice.

The trial of Maurice Papon was similarly difficult. The defendant repeatedly referred to himself as a scapegoat for the collective actions of a generation now slipping away, and he was partly right: the core of Vichy France—its public administration—was on trial. But his exculpatory suggestion that he was *merely* a "scapegoat" did not follow from this fact. Although the French might have preferred to have had René Bousquet in the prisoner's box, or his colleague Jean Leguay, in the sense that both held higher positions in the hierarchy of Vichy whose orders led to Drancy and Auschwitz, Papon was not thereby innocent of the charges laid against him. Although he had never personally murdered anyone, his signed deportations had resulted in the deaths of more than a thousand people. Although he might not have known his victims were effectively en route to Auschwitz, he did know that the Drancy concentration camp was a place of terror, and he might well have wondered what future old men and little babies had there. The guilty verdict seemed just, given the nature of the charges. The reduced sentence of ten years (rather than life imprisonment) properly reflected his minor status in the Dantesque circles of hell.

Maurice Papon was not Adolf Eichmann, nor was he René Bousquet, the man who first linked the government of his country to Hitler's Final Solution. He was a morally flexible paper-pusher, a technocrat of superior intelligence and matchless ambition who believed, like the majority of his contemporaries, that Nazi Germany would win the war. When that day arrived, Papon wanted to be in line for the treats.

To have reaffirmed the conclusions of Nuremberg in French jurisprudence—that the laws of a duly elected government may be contrary to the precepts of human civilization, and that obeying such laws is not a legal defence—is the most important outcome of the Papon verdict. The decision to convict a government functionary carries special weight. At the very least, no French bureaucrat will ever again blithely obey anti-human decrees without remembering the trial of his hapless predecessor, Maurice Papon, the very epitome of a proper civil servant.

The trial was also a warning bell signalling that impunity had finally been confronted in a French court, for impunity—brought about by the ten-year statute of limitations on prosecutions and facile, politically inspired amnesties—has sunk deep roots into the culture. Under the cozy blanket of amnesty, every collaborator who had not been "purged" was released from the threat of indictment in 1953; General de Gaulle exonerated Carl-Albrecht Oberg, the supreme SS commander in France in 1958; all war crimes from the Algerian conflict were made immune from prosecution in 1962; and the Milice chieftain, Paul Touvier, was initially pardoned by President Georges Pompidou in 1971. But these amnesties produced neither forgetfulness nor brotherhood; on the contrary, they created an environment where crimes were ignored and criminals walked the streets, a culture in which victims and their descendants were denied recourse to justice. At the very least, the trial and conviction of Maurice Papon indicated a shift that the country appears to have welcomed.

Is "Vichy" over? I doubt it, although the gate of memory and future reconciliation has creaked open a little wider. A decade of increasingly bold prosecutions may have offered young people the tools to distance themselves from the historical myths that permeated their society for half a century, and the government has been struggling to reconcile the old dualities, so that the French, as a nation, can take responsibility for what happened in their country between 1940 and 1944. Germany has been trying to do the same, for a much longer time. As the historian Robert Paxton has pointed out, Germany and France are the only major Second World War belligerents to have tried any of their own citizens for crimes against humanity for acts committed during that conflict.[32] But just as Germany's past will remain "unmasterable"—and even unassimilable—until many generations have lived and died, so France will not easily forget, or heal, the memory of having trespassed civilized norms. Of having, in Jacques Chirac's unsparing words, "committed the irreparable."

3

Erasing History

Pretense and Oblivion in Japan

If the nail sticks out, hammer it down.

— JAPANESE PROVERB

I HAVE ALWAYS BEEN INTRIGUED by the traditional architecture of Japan, by those simple wooden houses with wide screened doors that slide open to reveal all, or perhaps just a part, of what is outside. What is "out there" can be framed by these movable screens, according to inclination—so unlike the solid structures of Europe and North America, whose immutable lines dictate how the world is to be viewed. If there is a formal garden attached to the house, as there often is in Japan, one can observe it from different perspectives simply by adjusting the opening of the doors. Before visiting Japan, I had often imagined this experience to be a powerful one, for like a god one contours reality. Metaphysical, too, since the very idea of movable, fluid space raises questions about what is truly there.

And what about the "movable screens" of politics? In France, they were judiciously adjusted after the Second World War by General de Gaulle, in what he presumed to be the general interest. Shifting screens were—and are—an apt metaphor for reshaping nationalism, wherever they exist, and for concerted efforts, like war, which require all to see as one. They can be positioned to conceal the unseemly past when it gets in the way.

Previously, whenever I thought about Japan, I remembered the awful story of Hiroshima. I learned about what happened there many years ago, in a moment I can summon up on a private reel of memory anytime I choose. There is my child-self, curled up in the family "reading chair." The book I am holding in my hand has been selected at random from the volumes on the shelves that line the wall. It is *Hiroshima*, John Hersey's seminal reportage on the calamity that swept the cities of Hiroshima and Nagasaki in August 1945.

Childhood innocence ended that afternoon as Hersey's images imprinted themselves indelibly on my memory: drowning people clogging the Ota River that traversed the city, gasping and clutching at falling debris while the nuclear fire devoured their streets; melted eyes running down faces. And the special horror of the verb Hersey used to describe what was happening to those who survived the initial seconds: their skin, he said, "sloughed" off their bodies.

Many years later I read about other crimes that had been less talked about—for example, the so-called Rape of Nanking, during which hundreds of thousands of Chinese civilians were destroyed by Japanese armed forces loosed on the population, and the aberration of Unit 731, an infamous military group in occupied Manchuria whose medical researchers—there and ultimately elsewhere in greater East Asia—conducted grotesque experiments on living captives in preparation for biological warfare. Many decades after the world learned about Hiroshima, these crimes were only slowly emerging into public view: they had been displaced from the centre stage of Western memory by the horror of the world's first atomic-bomb attacks and by the Holocaust, which had happened closer to home. In Japan, the post-war generations knew even less than Westerners about their country's war. The exquisite screens had been repositioned to shut out that part of the past.

I had always wanted to see Japan, and in 1996 the opportunity arose: my husband, Tom Robinson, was asked to give a series of guest lectures in several universities, and I was invited, too. I was deeply curious about the Japanese remembrance of Hiroshima and intent on exploring my own memory in that city, whose terrifying experience, retold, had corroded my childhood one quiet afternoon so long ago. How was the Second World War recollected, especially those Japanese-authored crimes we seemed to know so little about? I wanted to visit a particular Shinto monument at the heart of Tokyo that is one of the most controversial places in the country. I had read that on any ordinary day, people might be found there worshipping the souls of the dead, including the glorified spirits of convicted war criminals who were hanged following the post-war Tokyo Trials.

The Yasukuni Shrine is more than a century old, having been dedicated to the cult of the imperial ruler of Japan in 1868, after the samurai defeated the Tokugawa shogunate and introduced the Meiji Restoration of the emperor. Psychologically, it functions as the remaining physical locus of a cult at the heart of Japanese culture until the end of the Second World War: a religious, social, cultural and political system of belief that was all-encompassing. And tidy, too, with none of the dangling loose ends typical of messy Western democracies, a cult that venerated the ruler and the soldiers who died in his service, all of whom once occupied the upper echelons of a pyramid that represented the nation itself, with the emperor presiding at the apex. Japan used to be a tightly wrapped cocoon; it was an indivisible, organic body tied to its royal and military chiefs in a perfect hierarchical constellation. According to the earliest myth-history of the country,[1] the holy warrior Jimmu had reigned as the first emperor. Because Jimmu's ancestor was believed to be the sun goddess, Amaterasu—the chief deity of the Land of the Rising Sun—all future emperors had assumed the god mantle, meaning that every royal act, of whatever moral cast, was in perfect harmony with the divine. The god, the god-ruler and his dominion were one.

Within this spiritualized union, which sprang from a mix of Confucian ideals of order with populist Shinto beliefs, what mattered most was obedience. Deference began within a context of unequal relationships that started at the bottom with filial piety and the submission of wife to husband. Every commitment, up to and including each person's loyal covenant with the emperor himself, was born from this archetype. "Heaven remains above and earth remains below" was the oft-quoted poetic explanation.

The Yasukuni Shrine continues to speak to those who come to hear its antiquated message from a time that officially ended with the Second World War, after which an American-imposed democracy took over. It speaks of past unity in the failed war effort—a synthesis strengthened by official propaganda that told the suffering Japanese that their national spirit could, in fact, conquer death itself, by self-discipline. To a population exhausted by bombings and twelve-hour working days, the authorities announced, "The heavier our bodies, the higher our spirit rises above them. . . . The wearier we are, the more splendid the training."[2] To a people with too little to eat and nothing to keep them warm, they prescribed body-heating calisthenics. The religious infrastructure of pre-war Japanese society made such exhortations possible: in a Buddhist-Shintoist country where self-control, meditation and the quest for spiritual enlightenment were an ancient way of life, the transfer of religious values to the political arena was not as big a leap as it might seem.

But the continuing presence of this shrine in downtown Tokyo tells its own story. Unlike Germany, which has excised all reminders of its Nazi past and criminalized the ideology that made it possible, Yasukuni remains an official site of religious-historical memory. It is as though a memorial to Germany's top Nazis still sat at the centre of Berlin.

Tokyo is flashy—choking with millions of people who press relentlessly through the streets—but one step through the Shinto archway and I am inside the park-like grounds of a sacred place. The trees at the entrance have been officially dedicated to the war dead, and little white ribbons flutter from their branches, fabric trimmings representing prayers for lost sons, fathers and husbands. White doves patter about on the footpaths; they are reincarnated souls, now thought to be heroes and "gods."

A group of Second World War veterans and their families who have come here on a pilgrimage are gathered in a small open-air shrine, and two Shinto priests dressed in white officiate at a service. The old soldiers and their bent, aged wives sit together on benches, motionless and in silence.

I am with three graduate students in philosophy from Tokyo University whom I have met through my husband's colleagues in the city. None of them has ever been to this place, and they are visibly uncomfortable. "My grandfather died in the war; he was a Buddhist priest and he died in a POW camp in China," says one in a low voice.

"This is a sensitive place, a sensitive place," repeats another anxiously.

Together we enter the shrine museum. It looks conventional enough: the usual displays of firearms and cannons, dating from the Meiji Restoration, and idealized representations of Emperor Hirohito. Hirohito died in 1989, but he was considered to be a god while he was alive, at least until August 15, 1945, the day of national surrender, when he informed his people in an address that he was, in fact, a human being. Beyond the humiliation of defeat, this awful declaration shocked the emperor's adoring subjects, for with that one phrase he destroyed the ideological underpinnings of their world.

The next room portrays the Manchurian Incident of 1931 (military invasions were frequently minimized as "incidents"), which has been detailed, at least outside of Japan, as Act One in a fourteen-year war of aggression. But museum convention ends here, for these displays hold what are clearly meant to be sacred relics: bits of disintegrating clothing, pictures of smiling, heroic young men and stoical last letters to stalwart mothers. The emphasis is on courage and nobility in the face of death.

The adjoining room introduces Nanking 1937, described as the Chinese Incident. There are more relics and more commemorative displays, but not a word about what actually happened in that city.

Finally, at the centre of a large central rotunda is Yasukuni's *pièce de résistance*: a full-size kamikaze bomber. The kamikaze were a special corps within the air force who were charged with the suicidal mission of crashing into an enemy target, and their very name had religious-national overtones: *kami* means "god," and *kaze* is a reference to the "heaven-sent" wind that, according to legend, once saved Japan from defeat. In this display, the kamikaze bomber is flanked by models of human torpedoes: life-size frogmen walk the bottom of the ocean, carrying poles tipped with bombs to blow up submarines and themselves. The young men who gave their lives for emperor and nation were conditioned to accept this ultimate sacrifice with language expressly designed to help them detach themselves from life: "You are like gods, free from human desires," they were told over and over again. The ideal of a spiritual "family-nation" through which all Japanese were commanded to obey the wishes of their superiors in a hierarchy leading to the emperor also helped them to accept their fate.

Aki, one of my companions, says he is having strange thoughts: he came in anxious and distanced, he admits, but as he reads the letters, the poems and the prayers of these young men, he is feeling more involved—and uncomfortable. He says he is beginning to understand these warriors, who were younger than he is now, and the way they were led to think. He is disturbed by his own response, because he does not *want* to understand these people, or their "sacrifice" for the divine emperor. His friends stifle their emotions with mockery. They say they have never seen anything as ridiculous as this place, with its nonsensical relics and gods.

In a small alcove beside the kamikaze bomber, wartime newsreels on a never-ending loop feature smiling soldiers dropping bombs and a unit in Burma that poses for the camera with their trophy, a terrified-looking British soldier. The soundtrack is the kind of cacophony that typifies stirring patriotic music everywhere. The veterans, who are now touring the museum, huddle on stools and stare mesmerized at the newsreels, lost in remembrance. Watching them, I, too, remember. Once, in Toronto, I attended a screening of Leni Riefenstahl's brilliant propaganda film *Triumph of the Will*, a staged documentary about a Nazi rally at Nuremberg that conveys the hypnotic presence of Adolf Hitler with dazzling immediacy. When the lights went up in the theatre, I was distracted by the audience, whom I had expected to be people interested in either history or film. But these were old men with rheumy eyes and nostalgia on their faces. One of them could not bring himself to leave. I watched him as he slumped in the front row, head bowed, until both he and I were invited to leave the premises.

The Yasukuni Shrine offers no analysis, no explanation and no distance from the events it portrays. For these veterans, now aged and leaning on canes, the past is a remembered land of youth and exploit.

After the war, official visits to Yasukuni by public figures virtually ceased, but thirty years later, conservative factions were once again so influential that Prime Minister Takeo Miki thought it advisable to pay a well-publicized personal visit. Most of his successors followed his lead, insisting that they did so only as private citizens: in August 1990, for example, the year after Emperor Hirohito died, no fewer than fourteen members of the government cabinet participated in ceremonies at the controversial site. The timing was of particular interest: in January of that same year, right-wing extremist thugs tried to kill Nagasaki mayor, Hitoshi Motoshima, because he had said aloud what many people had long thought in silence: that Emperor Hirohito bore personal responsibility for the war. By visiting the Yasukuni Shrine in such numbers, the members of the cabinet indicated where they stood on the question of the emperor. They were adjusting the historical screens. And making wordless declarations in defence of Japan's war record.

The year 1990 was a difficult one; in addition to marking the end of a long era, the death of the emperor underlined cultural uncertainties, and some Japanese were reaching into the past to regain their bearings. But to visit Yasukuni was a brazen act fraught with danger. Japan's wartime history, sanctified in this shrine, was a dark place whose secrets were only beginning to seep into public view.

This is what happened during Japan's war. On the morning of December 13, 1937, four divisions of the Japanese army stormed the ancient Chinese metropolis of Nanking, followed by two Japanese navy fleets that occupied both sides of the Yangtze River. Approximately 600,000 people were in the city that day.

During the next two weeks, Japanese soldiers swept through the streets of the city mowing down civilians. The barbarity of their onslaught remains astonishing: people were stabbed, disembowelled, decapitated, burned and drowned; maddened soldiers punched out eyes with awls, excavated hearts from living bodies, castrated men and jammed poles into the vaginas of female victims. Women of all ages were gang-raped in the streets in broad daylight before they were killed; fathers were forced to rape their daughters, sons to rape their mothers. Those who resisted were slaughtered on the spot.

Killing competitions boosted morale among the troops, and rank-and-file soldiers were encouraged to improve their "efficiency." Two men modestly acknowledged that their rivalry, which resulted in the deaths of hundreds of people, was a mere "friendly wager" and "an amusement." Their killing games were reported by the Osaka newspaper *Mainichi Shinbun*[3] as well as the Tokyo papers *Nichinichi Shinbun* and the English edition of the *Japan Advertiser*.[4]

When the savagery was spent, at least 260,000 people had been killed, 20,000 women had been raped and the city of Nanking lay smouldering.[5] And there was also an archive: the massacre was recorded by the Chinese, by war correspondents and photographers, by Christian missionaries and by the Japanese themselves. An English-language book titled *What War Means: the Japanese Terror in China, a documentary record* was published the following year.[6] But war loomed in Europe, and the latter work went largely unnoticed.

Japan's war with China was in many ways an internal affair, for China was a source of Japan's own very ancient culture. Japanese art was notably Chinese in style, as were the characters of the Japanese language. Buddhism was originally imported from China, as was Confucian philosophy. As always happens, such borrowings were absorbed, assimilated, built upon and transformed in the new environment until something indigenous emerged. Contemporary Japanese society was certainly unique; nonetheless, its roots trailed into the civilization next door.

The same Confucian ideals that glorified order, harmony and obedience within a hierarchy had also promoted beliefs about racial superiority, and for centuries Shintoism, an indigenous populist religion, added to the mix. A famous eighteenth-century scholar, Motoori Norinaga, wrote that the Japanese understanding of good and evil was based on divine revelation emanating from the sun goddess: "Our Imperial Land . . . is superior to the rest of the world in its possession of the correct transmission of the ancient way."[7] But the most important element was the political link to the emperor because, as he was a descendant of the sun goddess, every one of his acts and everything he said was divinely inspired. There was, in other words, no morality outside his word. What this meant in practice was that the military, in conjunction with government ministers, could act with a high degree of autonomy in the ruler's name. As long as the emperor did not publicly disagree (and there is still controversy about how much Hirohito actually knew or condoned, since he was never called upon to testify at the post-war Tokyo Trials), the destruction of "lesser" peoples was acceptable, in principle—*provided* it was carried out in the emperor's name.

This ancient ideology of racial superiority mixed with patriotism and a commitment to the war effort also underpinned the medical experiments carried out on human beings from 1932 to 1945. Unit 731 in occupied Manchuria was headed by a young microbiologist and immunologist named Shirō Ishii; in fact, many of the men responsible for human research into biological warfare were trained physicians. Ishii was brash, brilliant and relentless in pursuit of his ambitions, and as the scion of a well-known family he had useful connections in high places. In the late 1920s, he used his relationship with ultra-nationalists at the war ministry to make the case for biological warfare, and by 1930 his ideas had found favour. He was appointed professor of immunology at the Tokyo Army Medical School.

In 1932, Ishii and three hundred associates arrived in Harbin, Manchuria, with permission to carry out top-secret work and a healthy budget from a clandestine account to finance their activities. His first major facility was known locally as the Zhong Ma Prison Camp, and according to the American historian Sheldon H. Harris,[8] the complex was a half kilometre in area with brick walls three metres high capped with barbed and electrified wire. The Chinese slave labourers who built the compound wore blinkers to prevent them from seeing the magnitude of what they were constructing.

There were two wings: one was administrative; the other contained the prison, the laboratories, the crematorium and a munitions dump. Several hundred prisoners were held there at any given time, mostly men, but also women and children, Han Chinese (the dominant ethnic group in China), Soviet prisoners of war, Europeans accused of spying and Jews resident in Harbin. At first, they were all accused of various crimes and summarily convicted, with or without a show trial, but as time passed "suspicious persons" were simply captured and delivered to the prison, especially when human supplies fell low. Captives were held in tiny body-size cages, but well fed and exercised to maintain maximum health as a baseline for the experiments.

Ishii's first research interests were with anthrax, an often fatal disease of cattle and sheep that can be transmitted to humans; glanders, a contagious equine infection that also can be transferred; and bubonic plague, the disease that ravaged Europe in the fourteenth century. Plague-infested fleas were lifted from mice infected in the laboratory, and a bacterium was injected into the prisoners. Results were positive; in 1939, Ishii was happy to report that plague was "effective" as a biological weapon. As for the research subjects, once their usefulness had ended, they were murdered with an injection of poison, then whisked into an adjoining dissection room for analysis; afterwards, their remains were shovelled into the crematorium.

In 1939, Shirō Ishii had a larger facility prepared. Ping Fang, also top secret, contained more than seventy-five structures, including laboratories, barns for test animals, an entire building for autopsies, three furnaces to consume human and animal remains and a full recreational complex (complete with swimming pool) for Japanese staff. Another section of the complex trained young medical students. To distract curious locals, the conglomerate was called a lumber mill, giving rise to a joke among the researchers who referred to their human subjects as "logs" (*maruta*).

A participant who confessed to American investigators in 1949 acknowledged that "the facility produced up to 300 kilograms of plague bacteria every month, 500–600 kilograms of anthrax germs, 800–900 kilograms of typhoid, paratyphoid, or dysentery germs, and as much as 1,000 kilograms of cholera germs."[9] But the secret of secrets was the experimentation on humans. Tests were carried out to determine which foods and other substances could be used to convey germs and what level of toxin was lethal. "Logs," identified only by number, were hung upside down, to establish how long it takes a human being to choke to death, or subjected to air injections to test the origin of embolisms. None lasted more than a few weeks. They either died from the experiments or were "sacrificed," as the terminology went, because they were no longer useful as material.

Throughout his years of operation, Ishii openly published his findings while hiding the human aspect: "monkeys" were the stated subject of his experiments, in particular "Manchurian monkeys," which amused everyone in the know. In 1949, a Japanese general put forward the figure of three thousand dead, estimating that at least six hundred people were killed in experiments during the four years that he served at Ping Fang,[10] but the numbers are estimated to be ten times as high when deaths from cholera, typhoid and plague cultures that were dropped from airplanes in so-called field tests are counted in.[11]

The scientists of Unit 731 were chosen for their medical and research expertise, and according to post-war investigations, they were neither sadists nor otherwise mentally deranged. On the contrary, they were lucid opportunists hoping to advance their careers—which they did, both during and after the war, when many became presidents of universities, deans of medical schools and heads of public-health agencies. They seem to have been ordinary men who at home during peacetime might have recoiled from causing harm, even by accident. Imbued with a belief in Japanese racial superiority and the manifest destiny of their nation, they were able to ignore whatever qualms threatened to disturb their midnight sleep. The dehumanization of the victims as numbered "logs" helped. When necessary, Ishii told his men that since the "criminals" would have died anyway as prisoners of war, they were lucky to have the opportunity to contribute to the advancement of science.

It is not easy to reverse deeply held beliefs taught to us by respected authorities when we are young. In 1999, fifty-four years after the war, a Unit 731 veteran, Toshimi Mizobuchi, who was interviewed while preparing a reunion of his fellows, said he still thought the victims of human experiments were "logs." "They were logs to me, and logs were not thought to be human. They were either spies or conspirators, and as such they were already dead. So they died a second time. We just executed the death sentence," he declared.[12]

Only the Nazis presented as calculated and monstrous an assault on human values—the medical experiments at Auschwitz are an evident parallel, although, as I would later learn, apartheid South Africa, with its mad scientists scrambling to develop cancer-causing poisons and a pill to "turn whites into blacks" (so that whites could infiltrate the ranks of the enemy), came a close second. And in all three countries, a thorough dehumanization of the designated victims had to precede radical behaviour of this kind. Historically, the dehumanized enemy is usually depicted as a disease-infested creature of the lowest sort—in other words, as non-human—and once that belief takes root, appalling conduct can apparently occur in clear conscience. Unit 731 research inflicted deadly diseases on people who were already marked as racially inconsequential; non-Japanese "logs" were nobody's concern.

The movable screens of memory and forgetting were pushed into place immediately after the war in a triumph of compromise and half-truths carried out with the help of the Americans. The International Military Tribunal for the Far East, known as the Tokyo Trials—the equivalent of the court at Nuremberg—held sessions between May 1946 and November 1948, with justices on the bench from eleven Allied nations.[13] Unlike the Nuremberg Tribunal, which convicted most of the accused of crimes against humanity, including murder, enslavement, deportations and genocide, the Tokyo prosecution focused on the conspiracy to wage aggressive war. The atrocities of Unit 731, were carefully skirted around.

Among the twenty-eight "Class A" military leaders who had been captured and incarcerated in Tokyo's Sugamo prison were General Iwane Matsui, the commander-in-chief of the Central Army in China at the time of the Nanking massacre, and General Hideki Tōjō, premier of Japan between 1941 and 1944. For the Allies, Tōjō was by far the most important and symbolic defendant; he was the man who personified the extremist nationalist militarism that had characterized his country. Beginning in the 1920s, Tōjō had promoted an ideology of "total war."

Tōjō and Matsui were both convicted and hanged in Sugamo prison on the night of December 23, 1948, along with five others, then inducted into the Yasukuni Shrine as martyrs and "gods" by their grieving compatriots. But General Matsui may have been a stand-in for a far more illustrious commander. Matsui was ill with tuberculosis the day the massacre at Nanking began, and the command passed to Prince Yasuhiko

Asaka by order of his blood relative Emperor Hirohito. (When he testified at the Tokyo Trials, Matsui blamed himself for not having given the royal prince and the emperor adequate guidance and proclaimed his willingness to die for them.) But the name of Prince Asaka was not on the defendants' roster at the Tokyo Trials, and neither was that of the emperor, in whose name every act, from the momentous to the trivial, had been carried out. The standard explanation offered by the military occupiers and by Joseph B. Keenan, the chief prosecutor, was that the emperor was a powerless figurehead without a political role, a claim that is more ambiguous today than it once sounded. It is now widely accepted that General Douglas MacArthur, the supreme commander for the Allied powers, made a point of insisting that the one man on whom cultural political stability depended be spared investigation.

General MacArthur was correct: the pre-war hierarchy, with Hirohito at the top of the pyramid, did provide stability after the war, even though a new democracy was on the rise and the emperor was self-admittedly no longer divine. But the Americans were sliding the screens into place for their own political ends. The emperor system was the ancient, ultra-conservative face of Japan, and pre-war leadership cadres had grown powerful in their ruler's shadow; so to preserve the emperor was also to preserve this political and social right wing. America's reason was the Cold War, which was emerging from the embers of battle as the trials took place: the old conservative right wing was going to be important in the fight against communism.

"Recognizing that the former industrial and commercial leaders of Japan are the ablest leaders in the country, that they are the most stable element, that they have the strongest natural ties with the U.S., it should be U.S. policy to remove obstacles to their finding their natural level in Japanese leadership," wrote George Kennan in a 1947 paper. The United States, he said, had a "moral right to intervene" to preserve stability against "stooge groups" of Communists.[14]

Shirō Ishii was never charged, which meant that almost nothing about Unit 731 and biological-warfare research found its way into any of the Tokyo proceedings. Only he had an overview of the work carried out at the Ping Fang station (which he razed to the ground before leaving Manchuria), and his investigations were too valuable to expose. As the Cold War assumed threatening dimensions, the United States craved the information that Ishii had acquired. They also wanted to make sure that they, and not the Soviets, had exclusive access to the technology.

A secret deal was struck with Ishii: immunity from prosecution in return for data—but there were public relations and journalistic hurdles to deal with, and the bargain wasn't easy to negotiate. As early as January 1946, several newspapers, including *The New York Times*, published reports about Shirō Ishii and his "human guinea pigs," but by April, all talk had ceased, and the subject of biological research on human beings vanished from the public domain.[15] The decision to kill the story took place at the highest levels, for just as Shirō Ishii could not have conducted his work without the knowledge of the authorities in Tokyo who approved and paid for his services, so the determination to grant legal immunity to a man known to have experimented on humans also could not have occurred in isolation.

In 1986, Frank James, a former American POW in Manchuria, testified to Congress that he was subjected to frequent blood sampling and that fleas were released in the warehouse where the prisoners slept. Perhaps he survived because he was one of two strong men assigned to lift half-frozen bodies onto the autopsy tables where Japanese doctors removed organs. James affirmed that when he returned to the United States in 1945, he was made to sign a document swearing that he would never talk about his experiences in the camp. He didn't. Not for forty years. Then he decided enough was enough.[16]

Ishii's daughter, Harumi Ishii, put the entire process in perspective during an interview with *The Japan Times* on August 29, 1982: "As far as I know, it is true that a deal was made. But it was the U.S. side which approached my father, not the other way around. . . . What I would like to emphatically say . . . is: Isn't it important that not a single man under my father's command was ever tried as a war criminal? I am really sorry for those who had to live in seclusion to evade possible prosecution, but were it not for my father's courage in making a deal with the occupation authorities . . . you know what I mean. . . ."[17]

The truth about Unit 731 did not emerge in the Tokyo proceedings, but during a trial held by the Soviets in 1949, some of the medical scientists confessed in considerable detail. By then, the Cold War had entered a deep freeze, and the American determination to keep that chapter of the conflict secret led to a deliberate discrediting of the evidence for decades: as late as 1996, in an article on the Tokyo Trials, Robert Barr Smith, retired army colonel, author and professor of law at the University of Oklahoma, scoffed at the suggestion that the Japanese had conducted experiments in biological warfare. "The thrust of the Russian trials, such as they were, concentrated on alleged Japanese 'manufacture and employment' of bacteriological weapons (of which the International Military Tribunal found no evidence at all)," he wrote. "The Japanese had started these preparations as early as 1935, the Russians claimed, bred fleas to carry plague and manufactured shells and bombs to spread contamination. Moreover, said the Russian prosecution, the Japanese had experimented on human guinea pigs and actually used bacteria in China between 1940 and 1942. Naturally, the *zaibatsu* [large-scale businesses] were at the bottom of all these nefarious doings." Such accusations were "sanctimonious claptrap," concluded the professor.[18]

They were accurate. "I have more than one thousand pages of Xeroxed documents from this trial," the historian Sheldon Harris told me in an interview. "It was the only serious attempt to expose the scope of Japanese medical atrocities during the Sino-Japanese conflict."

Preserving the emperor helped sustain the pre-war extremist community within the folds of the new democracy; hiding the story of Unit 731 had the same effect. A comparison between the international tribunals in Germany and Japan illuminates the different way each country dealt with the past. At the end of the dual Nuremberg-Tokyo proceedings, the Nuremberg trials had exposed the most important areas of Nazi crimes and served as a catalyst to the inevitably difficult process of transforming political culture. The Tokyo Trials were far less successful in this regard—with distressing consequences down the road.

Because there were never any Japanese-sponsored war crimes trials during the decades that followed the Tokyo Trials (unlike Germany and, more belatedly, France), it was easy to discredit the judgments of the tribunal as "victors' justice." The Nuremberg trials were also dismissed in some quarters as victors' justice, but the seemingly greater transparency of the international court offset the charge in the minds of many Germans. The Tokyo Trials, on the other hand, played trade-off politics with Shirō Ishii, and fierce nationalists, who were still in high positions, could argue that if the Allies thought Japan had waged an aggressive war in Asia since 1931, well, they had their own views on the subject. The war, they said, quoting Tōjō at his trial, was a self-defensive act in the face of Western colonial imperialism—in fact, the aim of Japan had been to liberate its neighbours from the West. The patriots attacked the democratic liberals for digging up the war dirt, so to speak, and undermining national honour.

For almost twenty-five years, there was some public discussion, though certainly no teaching, about the facts of the war in schools. The massacre of Nanking was mentioned during the trials, and the presumed commander hanged. In the 1950s and 1960s, a few guilt-racked soldiers confessed; and there were anti-war films and writings. But in 1971 a series of investigative articles by the award-winning journalist Katsuichi Honda seriously disturbed Japanese conservatives. Honda's work, titled "The Journey to China," based on interviews with survivors of the massacre, was published in the liberal Tokyo paper, *Asahi Shimbun*, in November 1971. He concluded that Japanese soldiers had killed approximately 300,000 people in Nanking.

Travel to China? Interview people? The campaign of denial started with two immediate rebuttals, the first titled "A Reply to Katsuichi Honda,"[19] the second, an article called "The Phantom of the Nanjing Massacre."[20] The attacks continued for more than a decade, and they included "The Fabrication of the Nanking Massacre" by Tanaka Masaaki (1984). While not actually denying the events of Nanking, others claimed that the "incident" had been grossly "exaggerated." This view was elaborated in a 1986 book (predictably titled *Nanjing Incident*) in which the author argued that the real number killed lay somewhere between thirty-eight and forty-two thousand. Furthermore, the event was in no way a "massacre," he added. This book was adopted as a school history text by Japan's ministry of education.

The campaign to disavow a historical event of such scope was reminiscent of the denial or minimization of the Holocaust by similarly interested neo-Nazis; however, denying the Holocaust was a legal offence in Germany, while in Japan elected politicians freely adopted the revisionist line and schools taught the distortion. By the 1970s, reactionaries whose views had never been officially discredited were fighting back with force. And the politicians had begun to pay court: it was in 1975 that Prime Minister Takeo Miki paid a personal visit to the Yasukuni Shrine.

Although it had taken decades to happen, when young Germans began to demand an accounting from the generation of "the fathers" in the late 1960s, many former Nazis in high places were eventually exposed, and German society was ultimately forced to confront its Nazi past. In Japan, the shift was in the opposite direction: from relative openness to the censorship of memory. General MacArthur had wanted Japanese society to remain acceptably constant, with a democratic constitution as a safeguard, but the price for continuing the old order was public remembrance. No one was ever tried for war crimes by Japanese courts after the Americans left; no one from Unit 731 ever faced charges. Perceived stability (and the correct anti-Communist posture) were grounded at least in part on oblivion.

By the time the post-war occupation ended in 1952, the prevailing conservative view was that the Americans had imposed "un-Japanese" values that needed countering, and school history texts were the weapon of choice. When detailed information about the Nanking massacre, the forced prostitution of an estimated 200,000 enslaved Korean and Philippine "comfort women" (only 40,000 of whom lived through the ordeal), and atrocities related to human biological research began to seep into the country in the 1980s for reasons which will become clear, many decent, now middle-aged, people were devastated. "We were taught *nothing*!" spluttered Shino Gotō, a musician whom I met in Nagasaki. Her husband, Jun, was a professor of philosophy in his early forties. Like millions of others, he and Shino now think they were deceived. The students who accompanied me around the Yasukuni Shrine in Tokyo had joined contempt to outspokenness; they, too, had only recently learned certain facts about their country's war. Yasukuni was funny and embarrassing, but it was the embodiment of an old, yet disturbingly familiar, culture—a culture that had leaked into the post-war present and denied them access to their history.

What people *had* been taught in school was one singular happening: the unleashing of the world's first atomic bombs on the civilian populations of Hiroshima and Nagasaki. This was the central content of the war, as taught to countless numbers of children born after 1945.

The Shinkansen bullet train speeds and rocks along its track, heading south, as the contours of the Japanese landscape float by the window: ugly urban sprawl linking city to city for hundreds of kilometres, followed by intriguing hints of transition. The rice paddy that surrounds a low-lying traditional home with a pagoda-style red-tile roof is sandwiched by fat industrial chimneys belching columns of noxious smoke.

This juxtaposition of ancient rural rice paddies with unregulated post-war growth is a striking metaphor for cultural transition: the old and the new flat up against each other but seemingly without space or perspective. I had the same thought just yesterday in Osaka: on the broad streets of the city were hundreds of identically dressed businessmen—dark suits, white shirts, ties, black shoes—most of whom were carrying cellphones and briefcases. An acquaintance suggested laughingly that they were in effect the new samurai. The old samurai, he explained, were compelled to dress in a costume that denoted their class and their status within the group. Today, the ruling class of businessmen conform to similar expectations.

Just an amusing theory, of course, but old ideas of group conformity have clearly survived the apparent Westernization of the country. Blue-collar workers all wear uniforms indicating their position and company, and the so-called office ladies—young, unmarried women who do clerical work and make tea—wear a female version of the dark suit and white shirt. The schoolchildren are the most interesting and ambiguous: although Japan does not have an official army—the famous Article 9 of its U.S.-imposed Constitution expressly forbids this and is referred to in tones of hushed reverence by liberals and leftists, who continue to mistrust their own country—the legions of students marching through the city streets behind stern-looking teachers barking authoritatively into bullhorns are dressed in what look distinctly like military uniforms—the boys in buttoned-up "army" jackets and the girls in the middy blouses of the navy. State public schools dictate their hair length and what, if any, jewellery can be worn. Such discomfort with minimal diversity is a sharp reminder of Japan's culture of compliance. My friend recited an ancient proverb as explanation: *Deru kui wa utareru:* "If the nail sticks out, hammer it down."

No surprise, perhaps, that so many of the people I am meeting seem absorbed by questions of contemporary national identity. Is Japan a "Western" nation? The country has a constitution and a democratic political system, so surely qualifies in that respect. In spite of an economic climate that has slowed down considerably, it is still one of the richest, most technologically advanced nations on earth. Certainly, no population uses more cellphones, although the vision of a lone businessman smiling broadly and bowing vigorously on an Osaka street corner as he presumably clinched a deal over his phone was hardly a "Western" sight. McDonald's and Burger King recently registered the highest restaurant sales in the country, elbowing out purveyors of sushi, sashimi and tempura. Is this a sign of "Westernization"? In addition, the Japanese consume large amounts of chewing gum, a habit they picked up from the U.S. occupation soldiers, and more than one writer has reminisced nostalgically about the discarded silver wrappers that glittered in the streets of his or her childhood. Perhaps Wrigley's gum once stood for "freedom," or "democracy," as these ideas were understood just after the war or, at the very least, for a new world where people could be independent and need no longer vow to give their lives for the emperor.

The young woman wearing the uniform of Japan Railways carries her tray of goodies up the aisle, then turns to bow deeply and thank us before she leaves the car. *Arigatō, arigatō gozaimasu*—thank you, thank you very much. The forms of the language are deeply courteous. Then an announcement over the system: next stop, Hiroshima.

Feeling jittery at the prospect of entering the place where an almost indescribable horror once occurred, I return to thinking about culture and conformity and how the survivors of that terror saw themselves and were seen by their compatriots. A human being who has been pumped full of gamma rays or whose face has been burned off, was, to say the very least, a living "nail" that could *not* be "hammered down." In the West, the survivors of Hiroshima and Nagasaki had been caught in the amber of memory, but paradoxically they seemed to have receded into amorphous symbolism over the decades. They and their bombed cities had metamorphosed into stand-ins for endgames and a half century of brinkmanship during which Doomsday Clocks ticked off the moments to nuclear disaster and puffed-up leaders strutted across the world stage. From time to time we were informed that the survivors suffered, still, from radiation sickness, into the second generation, but while worldwide movements arose to ban the bomb, the victims themselves seemed eclipsed. Were they bypassed by the emerging story of the Nazi Holocaust, or obscured by the enduring memory of Pearl Harbor, the attack that brought the United States into the fray and justified, according to some, a nuclear attack on civilians? Whatever the reason, those who lived through the inferno seemed to have mutated into abstract symbols of the international anti-nuclear peace movement.

The taxi approaches the famous Ota River, source of myth and death. The Canadian director Robert Lepage once mounted an opera on the theme of this river and the memory of survival (*The Seven Streams of the River Ota*),[21] and others, exploring the aftermath of the bomb in fiction, film or documentary, have featured this river as central to the tale. In real time and space, the Ota is beautiful. It cuts through the centre of the city in its several branches and is surrounded in many places by parks. People sit on the banks, enjoying the late afternoon sun.

Through a contact at the Canadian embassy in Tokyo, I have hired Keiko Ogura as my interpreter, and she arrives at my hotel with a schedule of interviewees. She's a no-nonsense professional, clearly accustomed to ferrying foreign visitors about in her white BMW. Most visitors from abroad come to explore the "Hiroshima spirit," she tells me: the Hiroshima spirit stands for the anti-nuclear movement that has made this city a pilgrimage centre for peace activists all over the world. We drive past the Hiroshima Peace Memorial Park. It is a huge tract of green studded with monuments that have been built around the hypocentre of the explosion. There are hundreds of uniformed schoolchildren on the grounds, along with their megaphoned teachers.

The business of Hiroshima wasn't always peace, although Keiko looks surprised when I ask, and certainly does not wish to dwell on the subject. Hiroshima had been an important military centre from the time of the Meiji Restoration: during the Sino-Japanese War of 1894–95, the Imperial Headquarters, Japan's supreme military command, was moved here to direct operations, and during the Pacific war, the city was a main launching base for attacks. On the day the A-bomb was dropped, there were approximately 350,000 people in the city, including at least 40,000 soldiers, and although the target of the *Enola Gay* was originally meant to be Fukuyama, a city up the coast on the Inland Sea, there seem to have been plenty of military reasons to have chosen Hiroshima.

Until the bomb was released over the city on August 6, 1945, the war-focused community of Hiroshima continued to act as one in the spirit of national service. As usual, neighbours watched neighbours to make sure everyone pulled his or her weight. No one doubted that there would be a successful outcome, for military battle was but an outward expression of the mystical Japanese spirit. Yesterday, the sword of the samurai; today, guns and naval boats.

Early on that August morning, the *Enola Gay* lifted off the runway on Tinian Island in the Pacific. The American B-29 was carrying a ten-thousand-pound (five-thousand-kilogram) atomic bomb preciously named "Little Boy." At 8:15 A.M., the crew of the aircraft released their cargo: the bomb exploded with a brilliant flash, followed by a deafening blast and a powerful shock wave sending radiation in all directions. A fireball roared over ground zero until temperatures approximated those of the sun, and a giant mushroom cloud reached towards the sky. Within seconds, half the population was dead and the city was destroyed.

Fifty-one years later, Mrs. Chiyoko Watanabe extends her hand in the lobby of one of the city's best hotels. White hair floats about her face, and her expression is open and warm. She has dressed for this occasion in a carefully pressed print suit and an amber necklace. A large scar marks her forehead. Today is her seventy-fourth birthday.

One of the survivors whom John Hersey followed when researching his *New Yorker* article, that was later published as the book *Hiroshima*, was a doctor who worked at the Red Cross Hospital, the largest medical facility in the city. Of 150 physicians then practicing in the city, 65 were killed instantly and most of the rest were wounded; of 1,780 nurses, 1,654 were dead or too hurt to work. Chiyoko Watanabe was one of the 126 surviving nurses able to help that day. She, too, worked at the Red Cross Hospital, just 1,650 yards from ground zero.

At twenty-two years old, she was already a widow. Earlier she had answered the national call to write letters to lonely young men at the front, and after several years her correspondent proposed. She accepted, and he came home for their wedding. But he returned to duty and was shot down over China.

At 8:15 A.M. on August 6, Mrs. Watanabe was standing in her office on the second floor of the hospital, while at the next desk a young trainee was writing reports. Suddenly there was a blinding flash, followed by a boom, and what felt like a tornado whipped through the room—in fact, wind travelling at a speed of 440 metres per second had whipped through the city. Mrs. Watanabe was knocked unconscious. When she came to, about fifteen minutes later, her colleague had disappeared—blown away or vaporized—no one ever saw her again.

Glass shards had speared her face, and the biggest one was lodged in her forehead: the blood flowing from her wounds blinded her. She ran to the bandage room, but everything had disappeared. There was a towel in the toilet cabinet. She wrapped it around her head.

The hospital was in chaos. Walls and ceilings had fallen on patients, and the wind that followed the blast had shattered windows. Blood splattered every room. Patients were lying dead or running about screaming. Miraculously, all of Mrs. Watanabe's servicemen had survived. She had been especially proud to be assigned to this group of men; to be a nurse had been her dream since childhood, and to nurse injured soldiers in the service of the emperor was her joyful duty.

The wounded from the streets were crushing the entrance to the hospital—more than ten thousand people would make their way there that day to an institution that had only six hundred beds, almost all of which had been destroyed. People lay on the floor, huddled on the stairs, collapsed at the sidewalk entrance; they vomited, bled, screamed or lay quietly in shock. Some were burned so badly that it was impossible to know whether they were male or female.

Soon the fire that started about an hour after the explosion was a roaring inferno as the city's wooden houses fed the flames. Mrs. Watanabe was now the sole nurse in the hospital; the others had run away. The post office next door caught fire, and it was urgent that patients be moved beyond the possible reach of the flames: those who were mobile helped her move the stricken on canvas stretchers. There was no medical treatment, with the exception of Mercurochrome: several bottles of the antiseptic red liquid had somehow survived.

The hospital did not burn, but by evening the staff of about ten people were exhausted. No one had eaten (emergency hard tack would not arrive until the next day), and dead bodies were beginning to putrefy in the heat. Frighteningly, people who had seemed relatively well earlier in the day were now dreadfully sick; they had radiation sickness, a condition no one knew anything about.

In the foyer, the wounded and the dying pulled at Chiyoko Watanabe's legs as she passed, crying for water. One of them pleaded with her, "Stay with us, stay with us!" For the first time in twelve hours, she felt overcome by hopelessness and desolation.

"We will die here together," she promised him in a whisper. Then she made a place for herself on the floor.

Mrs. Watanabe is deeply engrossed in the telling; her eyes have filled with tears as she remembers, and she waves her hands in the air as she speaks. I, too, am overwhelmed by her experience, and awed by the strength and the courage of this woman who was then a girl of twenty-two. I spontaneously take her hand, an old, gnarled hand that is shaking with emotion.

She says she, too, developed radiation sickness, and her white-blood-cell count fell to half the norm, but she never reported her illness. She is vague about this, but I gather she was too proud—or perhaps she was ashamed. In this, she was not alone; many people felt shame at being among the wounded, especially women. She tells me that during the years that followed the bomb, some never left their houses in daylight so as not to inflict the sight of their burned, disfigured faces on others. She is answering the question I had asked myself about what happened to people who were "different" after the nuclear attack: at least some of them believed they had no right to rejoin the community.

The second most terrible event in her life happened just nine days after the attack: Emperor Hirohito addressed the nation on radio and told his devastated subjects to "bear the unbearable": Japan was surrendering, he said. To a people for whom surrender meant unparalleled humiliation, the emperor's speech was quite simply unthinkable. Mrs. Watanabe says she "lost her will" that day, and that the strength that had carried her through—the idea that the bomb was but a terrible moment in a war that would be eventually be won—seeped out of her and took a long time to return. All these years later she still "adores" the emperor. "He was not the only one at fault, and he was never forced to admit to anything. So why should the Japanese people blame him?" she asks, acknowledging the possibility of his guilt and forgiving him at the same time.

I was to hear this rationale many times again, for Chiyoko Watanabe was offering a universal response to the unresolved question of national war guilt: the crimes committed in the name of an all-embracing leader. Although the truth about Unit 731 and the Nanking massacre had been widely circulated throughout Japan before our meeting, she does not recognize any historical context to her personal story of heroism and suffering: during the fifty years between then and now, she says she has never thought about the bombing of her city in anything but personal or local terms. It was wartime, she tells me, and "it couldn't be helped." This expression, which I was to hear often in Japan, conveyed a deeply ingrained fatalism that defied the logic of cause and effect; in fact, I would learn that many people identified the atomic-bomb attack as one of the innumerable natural disasters Japan has been subject to over the centuries. This was the way Chiyoko Watanabe understood, and still understands, her suffering.

She has lived the rest of her life in a tightly structured society where unmarried, childless women have no identifiable place. She has suffered from a form of blood cancer for fifty years. What, I ask, has saved her from bitterness and despair? She answers softly and without hesitation: "I have lived without a child, but I have been a nurse and I think I have helped others."

She invites me to celebrate her birthday over dinner that night. I am delighted to accept, and we eat in the restaurant of my hotel, accompanied by the young manager, who listens attentively as she animatedly tells him her life story. "How do you stay healthy?" he asks her. This is the Hiroshima question. She orders the most expensive sashimi and tempura meal on the menu with much sake and beer. She looks happy and beautiful.

"She says you have a deep insight into what happened to us here, and she is very moved." Mrs. Watanabe is smiling broadly as he translates. Did I? *Arigatō gozaimasu*, thank you. But I'm not sure. What seems more likely is that today is her seventy-fourth birthday, and a stranger from another country has listened with intense sympathy as she remembers the most difficult days of her life.

Sunao Tsuboi was a twenty-year-old university student on his way to school when he saw the flash and felt his body hurtling through the air. When he recovered consciousness, his sleeves and his trousers were burning, and his shoes had been blown away; he was bleeding from his left shoulder and hip, and his hands and feet were badly burned. Also, he says, the sky had turned black. He began to run wildly, his shirt burning on his back. All around was silence. He was close enough to the hypocentre to experience this strange silence—only at farther distances could sounds be heard.

He remembers that he was running for the river, the river Ota whose floating, dying, human detritus John Hersey was to describe so vividly, and that on the way he saw terrible things that have never left his dreams: a schoolgirl whose right eye had popped out and whose hair was burning; a woman with a three-inch spear of glass in her head, running, like him, towards the river; another who was trying to push her intestines back into her body; an old man, his chest sliced open, with a shard of glass in his lung, so that every time he breathed, Tsuboi saw the lung move.

Then the fire in the city started. A child trapped in a house was screaming for its mother, who was outside, in a panic, unable to help, but Tsuboi felt suddenly cool and collected. "The war is just beginning!" he shouted to the mother heroically. "Have courage, for the sake of the emperor!"

"I was abnormal," he says now, with bitter irony.

Eventually he reached one of the bridges over the river, but it was burning. Exhausted, burned and bleeding, he lay down on the road and with a piece of brick carved "Tsuboi died here" into the pavement. Someone on a truck picked him up and took him to one of the ports, took him because he was a young man who had had military training and might still be useful for the war effort. The old men, women and children were left behind to die.

"Then I was happy to be saved, but I am angry now," he whispers, looking away. "They had no humanity."

He suffers debilitating guilt because he made it through and others did not—just like the still-preoccupied survivors of the Nazi Holocaust. During his thirties and forties he continually asked himself why he lived and by what right, and still, at age seventy-two, he dreams. Always someone is crying for help. He is accused. "Tsuboi!" shout his tormentors. "Why did you not help? Why, when you were chosen for life, did you not plead with your rescuers for the lives of others?"

We are talking across a table at the back of a makeshift storefront operation, on a narrow side street, called the Hiroshima Sufferers' Welfare Organization, which helps survivors with practical advice about medical referrals and how to access the tiny compensation the Japanese government provides. I listen to Tsuboi and think how apt is the name Hiroshima Sufferers. At a partially curtained-off table a short distance away, a hunched, anxious-looking old woman is answering questions from a counsellor while her daughter sits beside her, holding her hand. Tsuboi's physical pain has largely abated, though the scars on his hands, face and arms are terrible to see. Hiroshima survivors speak of "scars of the heart." He has these as well.

In his final moments, he, too, was saved by friendship. The soldiers had left him at one of the ports, along with twenty thousand other wounded men, when he was discovered by a classmate. He is still overcome by the memory of what followed: although his friend also was seriously wounded, he carried Tsuboi to the pier and onto a ship for Ninoshima Island, where medical care was available.

Tsuboi slipped into a coma that lasted forty days, during which all his hair fell out and his skin peeled off. He breathed with difficulty, and for two months the doctor told his mother, who had somehow found him, that he was unlikely to live out the day. When maggots invaded his "dead" flesh, his mother picked them out with tweezers; later, she told him his ears had literally been hanging from his head.

On January 10, 1946, he sat up in bed for the first time, and in 1948 he tentatively resumed his life.

The suffering of the survivors of Hiroshima did not end with partial physical recovery. They lived, and still live, in fear of radiation effects, and, of course, they were "different" in a culture that avoided difference. Parents conducted careful research on their children's prospective mates, and A-bomb survivors were unwelcome. Having been exposed to radiation, they would, it was assumed, die young and leave a widowed spouse, or pass on mutated genes to their offspring.

Tsuboi fell in love, and when his girlfriend's parents refused to accept him, the couple met secretly. But her parents found out and accused Tsuboi of trying to kidnap their daughter. Seven years later they relented, but not before their daughter threatened suicide. Tsuboi and his wife were married more than forty years. She died in 1995.

He suffered from other discrimination. Since it was assumed (rightly, as it happened) that he would spend much of his life in hospitals, he was unable to find work in his field of engineering, so he became a schoolteacher at the junior high level. Although he was promoted only towards the end of his career, he was lucky: between 70 and 80 per cent of people exposed to radiation never worked again, and those who did find employment were paid less than the norm.

Unlike Mrs. Watanabe, he soon fell out of love with Emperor Hirohito and all he stood for, although he says now that he was "confused about everything" for about ten years. "When the emperor abandoned us, I didn't know how to live." Then he began to read history. Now he believes in "democracy and equality" and that "the government should apologize to the Japanese for the years of war it subjected us to and for what happened to us. They should also apologize to the foreign countries we invaded and assaulted."

Oddly, he does not blame the American government for dropping the bomb that altered his life forever; he does not elaborate, but his reluctance may be guilt: he is anxious about the atrocities his country committed during the war, prior to the bomb—and especially about the fact that little is discussed and nothing is recognized. But feeling distressed does not translate into doing or saying anything public, for in Japan to voice an opinion even privately is the height of courage. What Tsuboi *does* do publicly is sanitized and sanctioned; indeed, it is the official "work" of Hiroshima. He is an anti-nuclear peace activist. He has even been on a sponsored peace mission to New York.

He tells me his anti-nuclear work has helped transform his feelings of helplessness, but unlike Chiyoko Watanabe, he is not at peace. Antinuclear activism in the bombed city was detached long ago from a taboo past whose truth seems less disputed than erased; history is screened in unspoken, authorized ways, and the veil has increased his suffering.

The Hiroshima Peace Memorial Museum was created in 1955, three years after the end of the U.S. occupation. It took that long because while they were there the Americans censored all public discourse in Japan about the effects of the atomic bombs, which meant that those of us living in the West knew what had happened—through the auspices of John Hersey and others—a lot sooner than the Japanese themselves. But a Hiroshima professor of geology had been collecting remnants of the disaster, squirreling away pieces of melted iron, torn clothing and broken pottery. His neighbours thought he was insane, but his collection formed the basis for the museum.

The tribes of schoolchildren giggle, push and jostle and are hushed by their teachers; in addition to being a place of physical record, this museum, like Yasukuni in Tokyo, is a holy shrine. The geology professor's collection of twisted bottle caps and burned roof tiles is in evidence: there are glass display cases of burned children's clothing donated by grieving parents and a horrific, life-size wax display of a wounded family staggering forward, their arms raised to alleviate the pain. This is a true portrait of reality in the immediate aftermath of the bomb: thousands of people moving, mostly towards the river, holding up their burned arms. The "skin" of the waxed figures has sloughed off—yes, I realize with a shudder, Hersey had the right word—and is hanging in shreds, but their faces are clean to protect the schoolchildren. No eyes stream out of empty sockets. No one has charred skin.

The unmissable message of the Hiroshima Peace Memorial Museum is contained in the second word of its name: Peace, which means *universal* peace. All the wartime suffering of the Japanese has been swept up and funnelled to this place. Yes, atomic bombs were dropped, and yes, we in Japan were the victims of those bombs, but now we must turn our minds to peace for the sake of all mankind. The inscription at the A-bomb cenotaph reads "Let all souls here rest in peace, for we shall not repeat the evil," but the ambiguous "we" does not refer to the specifics of Japanese war guilt. An explanation is offered: "[The inscription] summons people everywhere to pray for the repose of the souls of the deceased A-bomb victims and to join in the pledge never to repeat the evil of war. It thus expresses the 'heart of Hiroshima,' which, enduring past grief and overcoming hatred, yearns for the realization of world peace."

For all its shock appeal and fine intentions, I find myself surprisingly unmoved by the museum and the inscription, precisely because the noble ideal of "peace" has been abstracted from any context. Where, I wonder, is a precise record of the aggression that preceded this atrocity? It seems insufficient to say that war is a bad, bad thing and we must never, ever do it again. Of course, there was discussion about what would appear in this museum, but the conservatives clearly won out, and their message is that what happened in Hiroshima and Nagasaki is unconnected to the larger history of Japan. Hence the abstractions of universal peace in a vacuum. Hence the happy Japanese consular official on the other end of my telephone after I have returned home, asking if I will write something "light and upbeat" on Hiroshima as a "peace city" for their next newsletter.

Keiko and I drive to another part of the city, to the home of Dr. Kōsō Matsuo. His garden blooms with flowers—gardening is a passion, he tells me. In the way of the culture, his medical office is in his house, complete with an anteroom where he can practice surgery.

He doesn't want to talk about what happened to him on August 6, 1945, except to say he was made sterile and never fathered a child with his wife. Instead he hands me a stapled-together manuscript full of cross-outs and translated by himself into something approximating English. The title is "Too Much Worry Recently."

Dr. Matsuo worries about many things. "Why did the United States not warn Japan about the possible nuclear bombing of human beings?" he asks me, apparently expecting an answer, as we sit together on a couch in his living room. He has met lots of Americans and he thinks they feel guilty about this. "I know Japan did horrible things to others, but then there were the terrible firebomb attacks on Tokyo. Wasn't that reprisal enough? Or did the A-bomb represent some sort of balance of victims? Maybe this bomb was necessary," he says. "Maybe it couldn't be helped."

I am startled to hear it again, this fatalistic idea—"it can't be helped." And the surprising but not uncommon belief that the bomb might have been "necessary" to bring "balance" into the conflict. He agonizes over questions of ethics. Two years have passed since the Japanese government was pressured into acknowledging the fact of Korean "comfort women" who were forced to sexually service Japanese soldiers at the front. He wants the survivors to receive an official apology and payment from government coffers to indicate real remorse on behalf of the Japanese people; he wants to build schools in countries Japan invaded, in which truthful history will be taught; he wishes Japan were a "real democracy" where people were free to think independently and voice their opinions. "We only want to forget," he mourns. He shows his tortured writings to his friends in the Hiroshima Lions Club, but they never say anything except, "Oh, what a fine writer you are. Such excellent style!" As for the younger members of his family, they dismiss him as a silly old man with boring memories of bygone times.

"How important is it to express opinions that conform with other people's?" I ask him. He looks perplexed, and even the fluently bilingual interpreter must look up the word *conform*. I explain: to conform means to act and perhaps think in the same way as others.

"Ah," says Keiko after a moment, and writes down the Japanese word *wa* for my edification. *Wa* means "harmony." *Wa o tōtobu* means "the harmonious whole." She nods vigorously as she explains: "It means, 'Let us discuss things but aim for the harmonious whole. We will *endure* discussion if we must, then we will return to *wa*.'"

"We will *endure* discussion." Here, it seems to me, is a key to the reluctance to debate, let alone resolve, the erasure of wartime atrocities from public memory, and an explanation for the evasive response of Dr. Matsuo's friends in the Lions Club—a glimpse into ancient cultural attitudes that continue to survive behind the veil of Westernization. As the culture of Buddhism and Shintoism made it possible for army propagandists to suggest that spirit can conquer physical death in war, so the religious-cultural ideal of *wa* makes open dissent virtually impossible in many quarters. Beyond the government censorship of history texts lies the culture itself.

One man challenged *wa* and almost paid for it with his life: he is Hitoshi Motoshima, the former mayor of Nagasaki. In December 1988, as Emperor Hirohito lay dying of cancer, Motoshima was asked by a left-wing member of his municipal government whether he thought Hirohito was guilty. "Yes, I do believe the emperor bore responsibility for the war," he replied.

Although Hirohito abandoned his god-descended status and donned a civilian suit, he had remained the embodiment of the nation, especially for the conservative right. In the lexicon of the extremist fringe, Motoshima's words amounted to treason. Sixty-two groups of fanatics from all over Japan descended on Nagasaki in black armoured limousines to cruise the streets and broadcast a call for his death. On January 18, 1990, a lone gunman shot the mayor through the lungs. He survived.

Nagasaki was a rarity in Japan for having a long history of foreign settlement. The Portuguese arrived in the sixteenth century to discover a large natural port, and soon the sailing ships of other trading nations were making regular stops. But the Japanese were so intent on maintaining their isolation that in 1638 foreigners who wanted to stay in the country were confined to an island off the city known as Dejima. The edict remained in place until 1854. Christianity also took root in Nagasaki, and the city still houses the largest Catholic community in the country. But try as they might to keep their peoples apart and racially pure, the Japanese authorities could not prevent the most irrepressible of human contacts. There are more curly-headed people in Nagasaki than anywhere else in Japan, and over the decades such children have been subject to attack in the schoolyard. Even today, Nagasaki families await new births with some degree of anxiety lest someone with a "long nose" be born to them.

I travel there to meet a small, somewhat crumpled man in a messy office. Hitoshi Motoshima—perhaps the only male in Japan without a tie at two o'clock on a weekday afternoon—is wearing large glasses that tend to slip off his nose. He looks tired; he tells me he has never recovered his energy.

His critics do not exactly deny the truth of what he said about the emperor's war guilt. They argue instead that Motoshima does not have "a Japanese mind," meaning that he thinks like a Westerner, which suggests in turn that he probably believes the A-bomb attacks were the outcome of Japanese military aggression. Not having a Japanese mind also puts Motoshima on the side of the Americans and their "victors' justice" at the Tokyo Trials, where reasons of cause and effect helped determine the outcome. Noboru Tasaki, the director of the Peace Museum of Nagasaki, put it this way: "The Japanese do not want to believe that Japan did cruel things. We are living in harmony with other peoples." So it appears that Motoshima committed an "un-Japanese" act by disturbing the harmony of life: he disrupted *wa* by assigning blame to the emperor, the archetypal symbol of Japanese spirit and unity. That is why he was punished.

Furthermore, Motoshima belongs to the Catholic minority, although in this respect he does have some fairly surprising ideas. During our conversation he suggests, following Takashi Nagai, the famous author of *The Bells of Nagasaki*, that the bomb that fell over Nagasaki was "God's will." The nuclear bombing was, he says, an "act of grace" that must be "joyfully accepted." He is a believer in sin, guilt and personal responsibility: these led him to the need for national accountability and in turn to the truth about the emperor. But he is on a collision course with some of his compatriots. Looking out the train window, I had been intrigued by the sight of smokestacks in green rice paddies: the new Japan beside the old. I think to myself that Motoshima represents the "new": he has no tolerance for the "rice paddy"—for those who want to incorporate tradition into contemporary Japanese life. Tradition is *wa*, the stifler of memory and debate; tradition is the ongoing, hierarchical organization of society where ideas and orders emanate from the top; tradition is hammering down any nail that dares to stick out; tradition is a culture that says no one is to blame because "it can't be helped." What he embraces is the openness of Western democracies, the diversity of populations, the freedom to speak one's mind and the search for undoctored fact. What he rejects is conformity.

"How is democracy understood in Japan?" I ask him.

"Well, true democracy is a recognition of human rights and of difference, but in my country difference is not allowed. People dress the same, and they think collective opinion is a good thing. Children are not taught history; they do not ask questions in school, even in the universities." He fiddles with his pencil and looks disgusted. "Democracy is a short person looking up at a tall person and speaking his mind," he adds, glancing at me with a sly smile. I laugh out loud. Hitoshi Motoshima is a short person.

Like Dr. Matsuo, he is conscience-stricken as he struggles with suppressed history, with the need for national resolution and justice, with the substance of democracy and with a possible religious meaning to the devastation that was visited on his home city half a century ago. He is committed to the liberalism supposedly inherent in Western-style democracies, but broke an unspoken code by pushing through cultural limits. He is courageous, tragic and out of step: his anguish feels raw and poignant.

With the exception of Mrs. Watanabe, whose attitude reflects *wa* and is therefore not disturbing to her, the survivors I have met are still suffering physically and morally as the wide-screen view of history they seek to memorialize keeps shifting before their eyes. The facts are there, but the worst of their country's recent past seems ungraspable within the confines of their culture—and dangerous to contemplate. Hitoshi Motoshima dared speak out forty years later and almost died in the attempt.

In 1965, a Tokyo professor of education called Sabūro Ienaga sued the government of Japan for censoring textbooks, including those he had written; he said that the ministry of education was curtailing his constitutional freedom of expression. Ienaga had a guilty conscience: as a high school teacher during the war, he had obediently taught imperial myths about the divine origins and uniqueness of the Japanese, but later he was mortified that he had not protested. "In Japan hardly anyone resisted. We are a nation of conformists," he told his supporters after an appearance in court in 1992. Yes, 1992. For three decades Sabūro Ienaga never let up, appealing defeats and initiating new suits until he finally won several important (though partial) victories. A decade earlier, in 1982, he had forced a change in the school-text description of the Japanese role in Asia: the word *aggression* would henceforth replace *military advance*. In 1993, another court decided that the education ministry had illegitimately "screened" Ienaga's text on the Nanking massacre, a judgment that allowed the subject to be taught in the schools. Then, in August 1997, the Supreme Court of Japan decreed that the government had acted illegally by removing a description of Unit 731 activities in Manchuria from Ienaga's text. That Unit 731 existed and had killed prisoners through live experiments "had been established beyond denial," reported the court in a landmark statement.

In August 1997, Sabūro Ienaga was eighty-three years old. Although he had achieved a major success, much still eluded him, including the right to convey information about the army enslavement of "comfort women." Worse, the Supreme Court still condoned the government's right to continue censoring school history texts.

He also had plenty of enemies. The extremists encircled his home and threatened him (although they did not actually attack), and rival historians mounted an aggressive countercharge. Nobukatsu Fujioka, a professor of education at the prestigious University of Tokyo, argued in the old way that the history Ienaga fought for "was not written with Japanese people in mind. [These writers] present a history hostile to Japan . . . [and] the impact on our children is such that they write in their essay classes that Japan is the worst, most immoral country in the world."

"But don't the textbooks now record the truth?" an interviewer from *Asiaweek* asked him.[22] "Our textbooks have become a tool of international politics, a card sometimes played in the domestic politics of other countries or for foreign governments to secure money from Japan," replied Fujioka. "In international politics, once you apologize it merely confirms in people's minds that you are indeed that bad."

At the core of this rationale lay the idea that feel-good nationalism is preferable to fact. Psychologically, Fujioka's point was understandable: although Germany assiduously teaches its children about the Nazi era and tries to instill the concept of "civil courage," or moral responsibility, in the young, it took two decades for change to begin to happen: in the immediate post-war period, the Nazi-tainted old guard continued to run the professions and the state bureaucracy, and the public was encouraged to think of Germany as a normal state with a long, civilized history that was briefly hijacked by a madman. In France, the subject of the *French* deportations of Jews under the Vichy regime was finally included in school texts after four decades of denial and mythmaking, and there were plenty of conservatives in that country who continued to object.

When challenged by his interviewer, Professor Fujioka distanced his country from official German apologies for the Holocaust by pointing out that Japan had never mounted an intended genocide. "Why is Asia still making an issue over what is a thing of the past?" he wondered.

It is the dilemma facing every nation that has a disturbing history: whether it is better to squarely face old troubles, or to put them aside, adopt a usable line about what happened and concentrate on the future. Japan has done the latter for half a century, but now, all these decades after the war, the past is erupting like the volcanoes that periodically spew lava over the land. The difficulty, or part of it, is that essential elements of the "let's start again" solution have been missing; for example, a public acknowledgement of what actually took place and a minimal gesture of reconciliation with the victims.

As the new century opens, there are tiny glimmerings of change. Until the late 1980s, the living presence of Emperor Hirohito helped maintain old continuities; General MacArthur had seen to that. But as the emperor lay dying, pieces of the past that had been kept under wraps simply by his being there began to break through. Hitoshi Motoshima cracked a taboo when he declared that Hirohito "bore responsibility for the war." There have been others: old soldiers with guilty consciences who have had a lifetime to ponder the war deeds of their youth. And some of them want to confess.

The first to do so was Horie Shinzabūro, who published parts of his boyhood diary in *Asahi Shimbun* in 1984. He said that after more than sixty years, he still woke at night, remembering the day in Nanking, in December 1937, when he thrust his bayonet into the chest of a Chinese infant who was being sheltered by his mother. He said he was obsessed by the memory of having eaten the body of a sixteen-year-old boy, along with other starving soldiers. "We must apologize to China and Korea," he stated, trembling, in an interview with *The New York Times*.[23] A colleague who had served in China with the dreaded military police recalled that he had "no emotion" when the Chinese were killed, but became angry when he was captured at the end of the war and saw other Japanese being executed for stealing. For the first time, he said, he began to sense that "life was universal," but it was only later, when he became the father of two daughters, that he fully understood what he had done.[24]

Then there was Yoshio Shinozuka, once a sixteen-year-old member of the Unit 731 youth squad at Ping Fang whose job it was to culture plague, cholera, typhoid and anthrax bacteria, then test them on living people. He confessed, "I still remember clearly the first live autopsy I participated in. The Chinese individual we dissected was systematically infected with plague germs, and the disease took its toll—his face and body became totally black. Still alive, he was brought on a stretcher by the special security forces to the autopsy room. I methodically excised his organs one by one and put them in a culturing can we had already prepared. In this manner I participated in the cruel murder of five people in not more than two months. . . .

"Late nights, when we took our baths, we had conversations that went like this: 'How many logs did you down today?' 'At my station, we downed two!'"[25]

And finally there was the celebrated case of Shirō Azuma, a young participant in the Nanking massacre who also kept a diary during the carnage. He struggled for decades with his conscience before making his journal public in 1987; then on December 13 of that year—the fiftieth anniversary of the massacre—he went to China and apologized publicly at the Nanking Victims' Memorial Museum.

In a written statement, Azuma asked the questions that had tortured him for a lifetime: "Why did people who were good men at home turn into savages? Was it the militaristic education that made us so inhumane? [Our] education taught racism and contempt for the Chinese, and that punishing them was the right action. It taught that loyalty to the Emperor was the first priority—that our lives were nothing more than a bird feather and [we should] not remain alive as prisoners of war, but rather die as a spiritual protection for our country. But this injunction to die was also a form of slavery. The only justice, we were taught, was victory."[26]

Extraordinary acts of contrition, under the circumstances: with their confessions, all three men were pressuring their government to acknowledge the facts of the Second World War, half a century later.

By this time, additional pressure was coming from Chinese communities outside the mainland, for among the Chinese, as among the Japanese, long decades had passed in which the memory of war crimes was suppressed, even among those who were affected. Although media reports of the Nanking massacre had appeared immediately after the event, China's own tumultuous history in the post-war decades made serious research on the attack next to impossible. The Second World War was followed by civil war, which led to the Communist revolution of Mao Zedong in 1949. In the 1950s, the crackdown on scholarship was relaxed briefly, but in the middle of the 1960s the anti-intellectual Cultural Revolution closed down the possibility of investigation for yet another decade. Not until the death of Mao in 1976, and the subsequent power struggle between his ideological successor, Hua Guofeng, and Hua's ultimately successful rival, Deng Xiaoping, did another opening occur for researchers wishing to explore the worst atrocity committed in China during the conflict.

Scholars from the University of Nanking began initial investigations during the brief spring of the 1950s, and a book was completed in 1962, but the work languished unpublished until the Cultural Revolution came to an end. Then in 1979 it was issued—but as a "classified document," which meant that it could not be freely circulated or discussed in articles or reviews.

The government of China had its own reasons for at least partially suppressing the story of Nanking: one was financial, since the Chinese were deeply dependent on Japanese capital for economic reconstruction; the other was self-protective: China did not wish to call attention to its own human rights abuses, and stories about Nanking were certain to invite counteraccusations. All the same, it was useful to have the story of the famous massacre out there in some attenuated form—such as a "classified" publication that could be controlled from above. As for the victims, they had no recourse whatsoever. After the Chinese leadership signed a treaty with Japan in the 1970s stating that all outstanding Second World War issues were definitively settled, their prospects dimmed even further.

In the West, the story of the Nanking massacre had appeared briefly in 1938, then disappeared: post-war Japan was an ally and a partner—and economically one of the strongest nations in the world. It was time to move on.

What happened next was a sign of the times *and* of the problem future leaders may encounter when they attempt to stifle the past. In 1995 a scholar from mainland China took the 1979 Chinese-authored book with him to the United States and posted parts of it on the Internet under the title *Japanese Imperialism and the Massacre in Nanking*,[27] where it was discovered by a young Canadian from Vancouver, who was doing doctoral studies in modern Chinese history. Robert Gray was astonished by the details of this unknown Second World War story. "I translated portions of it and sent them to a few people, including Mark Selden, a professor of Chinese history at Cornell University, who suggested I finish the translation and publish it as a book," he told me over the telephone. "There had been nothing in English since the 1930s and I wanted to do it, but I had a few problems. The original document was written in the usual Chinese style of the times, with heavy-handed, unfair attacks on the foreigners who had stayed on in Nanking after the massacre, especially the Americans and British,[28] and with harsh, racist descriptions of the Japanese. I couldn't use any of this. The original sources were reliable; they were interviews with survivors and actual pictures of the massacre taken by Japanese soldiers who were later captured by the Chinese. But the authors' interpretations were less useful."

In 1996, Gray went to Nanking, found the main author of the text, Professor Gao Xingzu, and told him about his plans *and* his difficulties with the text. Professor Gao admitted that in the 1950s he had had to include attacks on foreigners in order to make his book publishable; he asked Gray to translate a more recent Chinese work from the 1980s. Gray agreed—on condition that Gao arrange for the declassification of his document (by 1996 this was possible) and give him permission to publish the original text in its entirety, minus the offending passages.

"Everyone in China now knows about the Nanking massacre. It's a huge issue, and they're still waiting for an apology from the Japanese government and maybe even reparations. Some people have also rebelled against the Chinese government's hardball attitudes towards them, but covertly—because if you talk to the survivors, they are as bitter about their own leadership's suppression of the discussion as they are about the Japanese. But I think things are changing. Until 1997, no one could openly lobby for reparations, but Sino-Japanese relations have soured since then, and this has opened the door a little to the survivors."

As for the large Chinese diaspora outside the mainland, almost sixty years passed before they were able to confront the memory of Nanking. "Sometimes people didn't even discuss it with each other," said Joseph Wong, a Canadian physician and community activist whose downtown Toronto office is filled with plaques and mementos honouring his work in support of human rights. "The recent history of the Chinese has made them diffident. They were under foreign occupation, and even their own governments have not acted in their interests, so people left as refugees, but often with the thought that they would eventually return. In North America it took a long time for the Chinese to put down roots and feel confident enough to bring their problems of human rights to public attention."

Wong left Hong Kong in 1968 to study at McGill University in Montreal, and for the first five years he kept his watch on Hong Kong time. (Not until he graduated and married did he change the setting: that was when he decided Canada was home.) He had made many Jewish friends, and as he learned about their history, in particular the history of the Holocaust, about which he knew almost nothing, he began to understand the significance of keeping human rights issues in the public domain. When the Chinese communities throughout North America finally began to rally, the Jewish approach to the Holocaust became their model for action. "I came to realize that if the Holocaust was not memorialized on a yearly basis, it would be forgotten, and how crucially important it was for people from all groups to understand what had happened in a once-civilized country. The Nanking massacre was an important event of the Second World War, but it was almost completely unknown, and we wanted it to assume its place in the history of that period. The other thing I learned from the Jews is that you do not need to be apologetic when what you are doing is right. Justice is justice."

The Chinese diaspora communities began to rally at the time of the Tiananmen Square massacre in 1989. In doing so they forged a cadre of more confident leaders. The first act of the new San Francisco-based Global Alliance for Preserving the History of World War II in Asia was "A Declaration to the Japanese People and the Japanese Government," in which they pointed out that as recently as 1994 a minister of the government of Japan had stated that the Nanking massacre was a Chinese fabrication. They urged Japanese "people of conscience" to press their leaders to apologize, pay reparations and open their archives to assist historians in their research into "Japan's misdeeds." Not surprisingly, the government of Japan did not respond, but that was not the expected outcome of the exercise: the point was lobbying and pressure. Global Alliance was joined by Japanese both inside and outside Japan, of whom the most illustrious was the winner of the Nobel Prize for Literature, Kenzaburo Oe, who wrote an article in *The New York Times Magazine* titled "Denying History Disables Japan."[29]

In December 1997, exactly sixty years after the event, the first full-length, English-language exposé of the Nanking massacre was published. It was authored by Iris Chang, a Chinese American who had spent her childhood listening to family stories around the dinner table.[30] As she grew older and tried to research the event, she was surprised to find nothing in the libraries, and it was not until 1994, at a conference sponsored by the Global Alliance in Cupertino, California, that she finally believed that the "folk myth" of her family, as she put it, was accurate. There were photographs of the massacre on display in the hall that nothing could have prepared her for.

Chang's book *The Rape of Nanking* was well received by historians, including many in Japan, but not by the Japanese government. In April 1998, Kunihiko Saito, Japan's ambassador to the United States, condemned the work as "erroneous" and containing "very inaccurate descriptions," without elaborating on what the errors were. "I would say it is not a happy thing to see the book drawing major attention in the United States," he added, before suggesting that the U.S. House of Representatives not sponsor an exposure of the wartime sexual slavery of "comfort women" by the Japanese military, a move that was currently in the works.

In addition to the Japanese government's evident concern that the Nanking massacre was becoming internationally known, there were other signs that the old strategy of lies and denials might be failing.

Along with Sabūro Ienaga's major (though not total) victory with regard to the history textbooks, two other court cases were proceeding in Japan. One concerned Shirō Azuma: in his diary, he had written that the captain of his division, Mitsuji Hashimoto, had brutally killed Chinese civilians, but Hashimoto had sued for libel and won. Azuma appealed, and the ensuing publicity was helping to keep the story of the Nanking massacre before the eyes of the Japanese public. However, his appeal failed—in January 2000.

Like Ienaga, Azuma had to protect himself from death threats. "I was drafted and fought with my life," he testified at his trial, "and sixty years later I am still fighting those who deny what happened and have accused me. They have said the diary of Shirō Azuma is a fiction, and they must correct that fiction and restore the reputation of the Japanese Army and they must correct the fictional account of the Nanking mass slaughter as now stated in school texts. I am in the final stages of my life, and I have had to fight in the Tokyo Superior Court. Japan was defeated in war, but I think also in ethics."

But the subversive new medium of the Internet was about to play a prominent role in the struggle over the right to know the past. Guo Peiyu, a young Chinese artist who went to Japan in 1989 to study contemporary Japanese art, was, he said, "shocked to notice that Japanese people have extremely poor knowledge of the war and their country's role in it." So he created an exhibition about Nanking: three thousand clay "faces" representing the victims whose "souls did not rest peacefully," then tried to find a locale to display his work. The authorities at Hōsei University, where Guo was studying, refused permission, so he applied to the city of Hiroshima. When the municipal government also refused, Guo opened his "museum" in his small Tokyo apartment and created a Web site, where he posted the entire exhibit. He, too, received death threats.

The Global Alliance for Preserving the History of World War II in Asia also created a Web site with links to additional information about the Nanking massacre and chat rooms in which Japanese and Americans could conduct open conversation. But no one in Japan linked activism with the new world of technology more directly than Yoshiyuki Masaki, a college professor of English in Fukuoka, Kyushu. Masaki used his Web site, in Japanese and English, to call on the government of Japan to acknowledge history. He posted details about the Nanking massacre that included Western media news reports and the confessions of both

Shirō Azuma and Yoshio Shinozuka. He informed his "visitors" about the legal plight of Azuma and called for world help. He described the Memorial Hall of the Victims of the Nanking Massacre located in Nanking, and the activities of the Global Alliance for Preserving the History of World War II in Asia. He posted the writings of what he called "honest" Japanese historians such as Akira Fujiwara of the University of Tokyo (Hitotsubashi), and set up Internet links to other international sites. He e-mailed liberal members of the Diet (parliament), asking them what they "thought about" the Nanking massacre. Takashi Kosugi, a former minister of education, replied. He said, "I think it happened and it should be taught in Japanese textbooks." Masaki was surprised and wrote again, asking if he could post these remarks on his Web page. "Being a minister of education, I am in a delicate situation," replied Kosugi. "I would appreciate it if you did not introduce my opinion."

Another Diet member, Kei Hata, replied that she would like Japan to emulate the positive steps the German government had taken with regard to the Holocaust and gave Masaki permission to post her opinions on his Web page. But she received so much hate mail that she eventually asked him to remove all references to her.

I "met" Yoshiyuki Masaki by e-mailing him at his Web site, and he told me that in just two years, thirty-thousand people had visited his pages.[31] That meant Japanese Internet users had access to up-to-date international research even if their school texts ignored or glossed over the subject and their politicians denied the facts outright.

He said his passion was originally fuelled by not knowing *enough*: he was convinced his government was lying about the "comfort women" and the Nanking massacre, but he didn't have evidence to prove it. Surfing the Net in early 1996, he came across a new American publication titled *The Rape of Nanking: An Undeniable History in Photographs*. The book brought together four hundred shocking pictures that were taken during the six-week attack, as well as archival research. "I was terribly surprised, not by the pictures themselves, but by the fact that this event was authenticated and proven," he wrote me. He ordered the book and videotapes, translated the text into Japanese and sent the file to the author, Shi Young, suggesting that they work together to produce a Japanese-language edition.

Masaki presented his own students with documents that included an interview with Iris Chang, the testimony of Shirō Azuma and articles he had downloaded from *The New York Times*. "They saw how much they had been misled," he told me. "They say they were taught that we Japanese were only victims. At least it helps them have a balanced view of history. I doubt whether any professor or politician living in the Dreamworld will be still able to convince them of falsehoods. So far, the authorities could keep evidence like books and films from coming into Japan, but now, with the Internet, all the evidence from outside Japan is flooding in. It's a relief to me to know that many Japanese have a conscience when they finally see that the truth has been hidden from them by a pack of lies."

In December 1999, a three-day conference called "International Citizens' Forum on War Crimes and Redress: Seeking Reconciliation and Peace for the Twenty-First Century" was held in Tokyo under the auspices of the Japan Organizing Committee, representing groups of concerned Japanese attorneys, scholars, doctors and activists; the Global Alliance; the World Jewish Congress; the Canadian Jewish Congress; and teachers' federations from Hong Kong and Taiwan. The delegates included now-elderly survivors of the Nanking massacre and Unit 731, as well as Hitoshi Motoshima, who was met by his enemies, the right-wing nationalists, with bullhorns. They paraded up and down before the convention hall shouting and waving banners that read: "The Nanjing Massacre Never Took Place," "The Great East-Asia War was *not* an aggressive war," and "The USA should repent before God for Nagasaki and Hiroshima." In the conference hall, Motoshima told participants that too many Japanese, including the survivors of Hiroshima and Nagasaki, see themselves as victims, without acknowledging Japan's own responsibility for war crimes. Also present were lawyers, historians and former prisoners of war who were fighting for redress from the Japanese government. The latter, said Masaki, were deeply disappointed: the lawyers reported that the War Crimes Redress bill before the Diet was unlikely to pass. Delegates drew angry comparisons between Japan's refusal to acknowledge its wartime history and Germany's positive attempts to overcome its Nazi past by nourishing memory and paying reparations.

Marc Weintraub, a Vancouver lawyer representing the Canadian Jewish Congress, spoke of the Jewish experience: "The Jewish commitment to memory is what allowed us to survive," he said. "In educating people regarding war crimes, it is not enough to catalogue acts of infamy: Redress is necessary, in order to extract goodness from evil." The participants were informed that in 1999 the Human Rights Committee of the government of the Philippines had demanded a settlement of the "comfort women" issue, and that a similar bill had been tabled in South Korea. But in Japan, during that same year, a "military-guidelines bill," a "war-preparations bill," and a "national flag-and-anthem bill" had all been passed in the Diet, one after another. "In not assuming responsibility for war crimes and not offering an apology and redress to the victims, the Japanese government is disgracing the dignity of Japan as a nation," the conference participants wrote in their collective final statement.

Were they heard? Well, their enemies had taken notice: immediately after the concluding session, almost one thousand delegates took part in a peaceful procession through the crowded centre of downtown Tokyo, to commemorate the victims of the Nanking massacre on the sixty-second anniversary of the event. They were met by another procession—coming in the opposite direction—that was celebrating the *defeat* of Nanking.

With pressure being exerted from many places, the snail's pace of change in Japan crawls ahead for an instant, then stops or moves backward. In 1994, the Japanese government was forced to admit that there had been "comfort women," but in 1997, Seiroku Kajuyama, chief cabinet secretary, accused several of the former sex slaves, to their faces, of being willing, paid prostitutes. In 1995, Prime Minister Tomiichi Murayama apologized for the suffering of wartime victims, conceding that Japan had taken a path of war that resulted in "tremendous damage and suffering to the people of many countries, particularly to those of Asian nations."[32] However, Murayama had failed to get support in the Diet for an official governmental apology by a margin of almost 2 to 1; a national campaign organized by a former education minister had collected 4.5 million signatures against his resolution. In 1997, after thirty-four years of effort, Sabūro Ienaga finally won his lawsuit over the history texts, a victory that allowed the facts about Unit 731 to enter the Japanese school system. But the previous year, Premier Ryūtaro Hashimoto had visited the controversial Yasukuni Shrine, the first prime minister in a decade to do so. There were other backward steps: in 1999, Yūko Tōjō, the granddaughter of General Tōjō, spoke to *The New York Times* about her campaign to rehabilitate the image of her executed grandfather. "He died for his country. He died to save his people," she declared. "This isn't a private matter. . . . To improve the image of Tōjō is to improve the image of wartime Japan, and that's my aim."[33]

(Her book in defence of Tōjō sold 100,000 copies in Japan.) An adult comic book, *Sensōron*, revived the claim that the main reason for the Second World War was to stop white people from colonizing Asia.[34] In 1999, Tokyo elected as its governor Shintaro Ishihara, a nationalist who called the Rape of Nanking "a lie." And in May 2000, Prime Minister Yoshiro Mori told legislators and Shinto religious leaders that "Japan is a divine country with the emperor at its centre."

In the end, the decades-long denial will be rejected by the young as they gradually come to know what was done in their country's name. It was the young in Germany who pushed open the door to the past. It was the young in France. Already, in a poll taken back in 1994, a massive 4 to 1 majority of Japanese said they disbelieved their government on war crimes and desired an official apology, including paying adequate reparations. Yoshiyuki Masaki said that 90 per cent of his mail supported his lobbying efforts.

What Masaki learned from his Internet research has catapulted him far beyond the old traditions of *wa* and reticence: as far as he knows, he is the first person in his family ever to become involved in politics or human rights. "I think the time is ripe now for the government to acknowledge what happened and apologize from the heart," he wrote to me. "That is the day my efforts will come to an end, and I can leave my country in the hands of the younger generation and sleep in peace."

Until that time of official acknowledgement and possible redress, two famous pictures will remain engraved in the collective memory of those who care about such things: one from Germany, the other from Japan. In the first frame, Chancellor Willy Brandt has fallen to his knees before the memorial to the Warsaw Ghetto. The year is 1971.

In the second frame, Prime Minister Ryūtaro Hashimoto stands in the Yasukuni Shrine where the souls of Japan's war criminals have been sanctified. The year is 1996.

In the stricken lands of unresolved event, the struggle endures.

War, Memory and Race

4

The Shadow of Slavery

The United States

Race—it is America's rawest nerve and most enduring dilemma. From birth to death, race is with us, defining, dividing, distorting.

– SIG GISSLER, Columbia University, 1994

THE IMPOSING MEMORIAL to the Reverend Martin Luther King Jr., the distinguished leader of the American civil-rights movement of the 1950s and 1960s, is located at the heart of a rundown, reputedly dangerous ghetto in the city of Atlanta. I ask directions of an older woman who is sitting on a bench at a subway station near the site. She looks me over, sees a white female of small stature travelling alone, then advises me to wait for the bus and not to walk the short block or two. I opt for the bus, and when it reaches my stop a few minutes later, the driver picks up the warning: "Now you be careful, yuh hear? And jes' don' talk to any strangers," she cautions protectively as I descend.

The monument is huge, which is not surprising. Size matters in America. Food is piled on plates in gigantic portions, causing Europeans to gape with surprise; massive shopping malls devour what once were city blocks; and enormous chain stores with a thousand and more outlets bury the small shops. A great American must be honoured by an outsize memorial, and as a Nobel Peace laureate and one of his country's most heroic twentieth-century leaders, Martin Luther King Jr. receives his due.

I climb the stately stairs from the street to a white marble tomb, set in a deep blue reflecting pool amid playing fountains, then step inside the Memorial Hall to face a display of three shrine-like commemorations: one to King; one to his mentor, Mahatma Gandhi, from whose writings King learned to practise non-violence; and one to Rosa Parks, the Montgomery seamstress whose refusal to give up her bus seat to a white man launched the civil rights movement in 1955. In the room dedicated to King, relics such as shirts, cufflinks, shoes and a bottle of cologne (he wore Aramis) are exhibited in glass cases. In another display, a Coretta Scott King doll about forty centimetres high smiles graciously at visitors. Mrs. King, the doll, is elegantly coiffed and dressed in a burgundy evening gown. The wife of a murdered black preacher who died while daring to challenge the humiliations visited upon his people has been transformed, fantasy-like, into a regal figure ready to sweep across a chandeliered ballroom on the arm of her royal consort, trailing her abject subjects in her wake. Coretta Scott King, queen of the dispossessed.

Among the quotations on the walls from King and other black civil rights activists of the era are two whose shared message I will find repeated as I travel through the South. "We blacks also have a soul!" cried Martin Luther King Jr. in his famous oration that recalled Shylock's celebrated "Hath not a Jew eyes?" speech in *The Merchant of Venice*. The other phrase, often echoed since, was printed in block letters on a banner spread across the chest of a demonstrator in Memphis just one week before King was killed. "I am a man," the wearer asserted.

Rereading the terrible words, I wonder how many others in a nation whose very origins included a fervently defended doctrine of equality still feel the need to protest their elementary humanity. When Martin Luther King Jr. attained prominence in the 1950s, almost one hundred years had passed since slavery officially had come to an end, but the so-called Jim Crow laws that separated the races in the American South into an unequal apartheid regime paralleling that of South Africa were still in effect. What King longed for was a second emancipation: the integration of his people into the ordinary ethnic diversity of twentieth-century America, an event he once described as "a great beacon light of hope to millions of Negro slaves who had been seared in the flames of withering injustice."[1] For daring to act on this brazen dream of equality, he was murdered in Memphis on April 4, 1968.

I was young during the civil rights movement, watching from the country to the north as cities burned and marchers protested, as black students advanced on the firmly closed doors of white schools. Why was rapprochement between the races still so elusive, I wondered then—and still wonder now. What solutions, if any, do ordinary Americans imagine? The questions remain troubling because when it comes to other issues, the American government seems to believe that a public recognition of misdeed is a step towards reconciliation: in 1990, for example, Congress apologized to people affected by nuclear tests in Nevada; in 1993, an apology was offered to native Hawaiians for the role the United States had played in the overthrow of the Kingdom of Hawaii a century before; in 1988, President Ronald Reagan apologized to Japanese Americans interned during the Second World War, explaining that he was moving "to right a grave wrong" and setting up a $1.25 billion trust fund to compensate them; then in 1997, an apology was extended to the surviving victims of government-sponsored syphilis experiments that had taken place a quarter of a century earlier. None of these acknowledgements came easily, but after years of lobbying and negotiation, they did take place. Why, then, does the older tragedy of slavery continue to cast a dark shadow across American society more than a hundred years after the freeing of the slaves?

The first emancipation, at the close of the Civil War, ended the modern world's most pernicious economy: an exploitable labour system that made cotton and rice plantation in the South viable. There was a promise of citizenship rights, but such would-be guarantees could not prevent systemic race hatred or discrimination in the shape of new laws that separated the races in the South; nor could they stop the emergence of unspoken taboos against examining the former slave system from too close a range. A full half century would pass before the first pioneering book on the subject of American chattel slavery was published,[2] then forty more years before the impact of the slave system on society became a topic of major study. In 1956, in his landmark work, *The Peculiar Institution*, Kenneth M. Stampp described slavery as "America's most profound and vexatious social problem [whose] impact upon the whole country was disastrous."[3] The South, he added, still lies in the shadow of real tragedy—the tragedy brought about by slavery; the moral unease that accompanies the enslavement of human beings continues to disturb the foundations of society.

The Peculiar Institution appeared just as the civil rights movement was gaining momentum under the leadership of Martin Luther King Jr., at a time when the social climate made newly welcome an in-depth investigation into the effects of slavery on the American people. The call for social change embedded between the lines of Stampp's work helped awaken a younger generation. Stampp detailed abuses that were, naturally, known in the deepest recesses of many hearts—yet simultaneously "unknown," in that they were largely unacknowledged, for slavery is one of those historical episodes that provoke shame in the perpetrator, or perhaps in the children and grandchildren of the perpetrator, once the values that underscore the system have been surpassed and rejected.

In spite of the copious information that is now available about America's slave past—mountains of books, films, television documentaries, talk shows, university courses in African-American history—I found it startling to turn to Kenneth Stampp's dispassionate prose and to experience again the difficulty of entering a time—not that long ago—when a slave master had absolute control over his chattels, including rights of physical punishment, sale and even life and death. With Stampp as a guide, it is easier to penetrate the thought forms of an era when slaves were considered human only because they were thought to have souls, and to understand that no rights flowed from this. One recalls that ownership always included sexual ownership and that "master's rights" gave birth to a large class of people who were considered black, and therefore slaves, according to the race laws of most Southern states. According to the inner logic of this world, there was nothing to stop an owner from marketing his own mixed-race children like cows or hogs: slavery was often its own self-sustaining business, with certain males chosen to breed with certain females and the offspring disposed of at auction. Though visible, such husbandry was often denied, but in 1856 Frederick Law Olmsted, the landscape architect and author of *A Journey in the Seaboard States*, made the point clearly and for the record: "Most gentlemen of character seem to have a special disinclination to converse on the subject. . . . It appears to me evident, however, from the manner in which I hear the traffic spoken of incidentally, that the cash value of a slave for sale, above the cost of raising it from infancy to the age at which it commands the highest price, is generally considered among the surest elements of a planter's wealth. . . . That a slave woman is commonly esteemed least for her laboring qualities, [and] most for those qualities which give value to a broodmare is also constantly made apparent," he wrote.[4]

The need to deny the dehumanizing effects of the slave system, even as they were occurring, was born from that moral unease Kenneth Stampp alluded to, since the anomaly of owning slaves in the statedly egalitarian American democracy was clearly embarrassing for many from the start. It still is, although today it is the legacy of slavery that is at issue as Americans debate the heritage of the civil rights movement, or ponder the subject of affirmative action programs, which were initially designed to help the underprivileged enter the mainstream. Call it a chasm, an ideological fault line, a hypocrisy at the heart of the national enterprise or simply a breach in the avowed patriotic faith that many Americans quietly choose to accommodate, the initial fissure between ideal and reality can be traced back to the written beginnings of the nation, to the oft-quoted Declaration of Independence drafted by Thomas Jefferson and signed by the thirteen United States of America in 1776: that seminal document in which equality is described as a self-evident truth along with the "unalienable right" to life, liberty and the pursuit of happiness.

France's struggle to reconcile the actions of the collaborationist Vichy-led government during the Second World War is rooted in a similar clash of national values: the liberal creed of the post-Revolutionary enlightenment versus a more authoritarian ethos that goes back to the *ancien régime*; and the ideas that informed the American Declaration of Independence did, as it happens, leap directly across the Atlantic from that revolutionary country, where a careless nobility was busily amusing itself in thoughtless ways, dangerously inattentive to the gathering storm. (One pre-Revolutionary nobleman could think of nothing better to record as an epitaph than the awful boredom of his pampered life: "All that buttoning and unbuttoning," he sighed in posthumous recognition of the wasted hours spent dressing for court.) Soon the tumbrils loaded with dukes and duchesses clattered through the cobblestone streets of Paris to the Place de la Concorde where the guillotine awaited them. Soon radical new ideas swept across the continent and the sea.

That the novel principles of liberty, equality and brotherhood (later dubbed "The American Creed") were adopted in the United States with a moral fervour that reflected the piety of the early colonists—dour Protestants whose values attached ideals of personal liberty to individual conscience, and both of these to religious faith—is well known; but from the start, a worm burrowed at the heart of the noble undertaking, since it was conspicuously the case that those who had been bought and sold in the marketplace since 1619 were not free, or equal, or endowed with the right to seek happiness. When he composed the Declaration of Independence, the Virginia planter Thomas Jefferson personally owned two hundred chattels, and he was not alone: 25 per cent of the white population used slave labour. He also fathered a family with his slave Sally Hemming.[5]

Although economic interests overpowered moral qualms when the Constitution was ratified in September 1787, the record suggests that the choice may have been tinged with ambiguity, for as Benjamin Franklin put it, "When you assemble a number of men to have the advantage of their joint wisdom, you inevitably assemble . . . all their prejudices, their passions, their errors of opinion, their local interests, and their selfish views. . . ."[6] Peter Fontaine, a minister from Virginia, expressed the inevitable rationalizations and ambivalence when he claimed that although slavery was a "sin," it was "morally impossible" to survive in the South without slaves. "It is, to be sure, at our choice whether we buy them or not, so this then is our crime, folly, or whatever you will please to call it," he wrote as early as 1757. ". . . All our taxes are now laid upon slaves and on shippers of tobacco. . . . This is our part of the grievance, but to live in Virginia without slaves is morally impossible. . . . This, of course, draws us all into the original sin and curse . . . of purchasing slaves."[7]

In a not-unfamiliar conflation of self-interest and so-called higher law, "moral responsibility" turned out to be strictly financial. And since the United States had already embraced the philosophical attachment to independent capitalism that continues to define that country today, Peter Fontaine's economic argument was probably irresistible to many. All the same, the glaring contradictions lay exposed.

Before I set out on my own quest to explore the lengthening shadow cast by slavery, I turned to a very old, prescient book I had last looked at in 1967, the year race riots and urban fires blighted the American landscape. In the early nineteenth century, an astute French observer already suspected the young nation across the sea might be headed for trouble. No person took greater interest in the American experiment with democracy than the historian and politician Alexis de Tocqueville, a man of liberal conviction (and aristocratic background) who admired the pro-democracy writings of Jefferson. In 1831, just as the pro- and anti-slavery factions were bringing out their long rhetorical knives, de Tocqueville set off across the sea for an extended nine-month visit to America. His book *Democracy in America* was published in 1835, and although his observations were initially met with no small degree of scepticism (he was, after all, a foreigner), his outsider's perceptions shaped a work that was quickly recognized as a classic. And still is. More than 150 years after its publication, there are at least ten thousand pages dedicated to *Democracy in America* on the Internet, most of them originating in the United States.

De Tocqueville was scathing: "It requires great and constant efforts for men to create lasting ills; but there is one evil which has percolated furtively into the world . . . it was cast like an accursed seed somewhere on the ground; it then nurtured itself, grew without effort, and spread with the society that accepted it; that evil is slavery." He was as pessimistic about the future in the North where, he claimed, freeing slaves and passing laws against their importation had actually increased racial discrimination against blacks, as in the South, where he feared emancipation would end in race war, with millions rising in vengeance against their former masters. He was appalled at the ways of the slavers: "The ancients only knew of fetters and death as a means to maintain slavery; the Americans of the South of the Union have found guarantees of a more intellectual nature to assume the permanence of their power. They have . . . spiritualized despotism and violence. In antiquity men sought to prevent the slave from breaking his bonds; nowadays the attempt is made to stop him from wishing to do so. . . . The Americans of the South . . . have forbidden teaching them to read or write. . . . Not wishing to raise them to their own level, they keep them as close to the beasts as possible."

De Tocqueville may have been familiar with the work of Samuel Cartwright, a Louisiana physician who had recently reported on a previously unknown malady called "Drapetomania, a Disease Causing Negroes to Run Away." The doctor's stern paternalism was typical:

> If the white man attempts to oppose the Deity's will by trying to make the negro anything else than "the submissive knee-bender" (which the Almighty declared he should be), by trying to raise him to a level with himself, or by putting himself on an equality with the negro; or if he abuses the power which God has given him over his fellow-man, by being cruel to him, or punishing him in anger, or by

> neglecting to protect him from the wanton abuses of his fellow-servants and all others, or by denying him the usual comforts and necessaries of life, the negro will run away; but if he keeps him in the position that we learn from the Scriptures he was intended to occupy, that is, the position of submission; and if his master or overseer be kind and gracious in his bearing towards him, without condescension, and at the same time ministers to his physical wants, and protects him from abuses, the negro is spell-bound, and cannot run away.
>
> According to my experience, the "genu flexit"—the awe and reverence—must be exacted from them, or they will despise their masters, become rude and ungovernable, and run away. . . . They have only to be kept in that state and treated like children, with care, kindness, attention and humanity, to prevent and cure them from running away.

The good doctor subsequently discovered a second disease peculiar to black people, which he called "Dysaethesia Aethiopica, or Hebetude of Mind and Obtuse Sensibility of Body—Called by Overseers, 'Rascality'":

> Individuals affected with the complaint are apt to do much mischief, which appears as if intentional, but is mostly owing to the stupidness of mind and insensibility of the nerves induced by the disease. . . . Thus they break, waste and destroy everything they handle, abuse horses and cattle, tear, burn or rend their own clothing, and, paying no attention to the rights of property, steal others, to replace what they have destroyed. . . . They slight their work—cut up corn, cane, cotton or tobacco when hoeing it, as if for pure mischief. They raise disturbances with their overseers and fellow-servants without cause or motive, and seem to be insensible to pain when subjected to punishment. . . . The northern physicians and people . . . ignorantly attribute the symptoms to the debasing influence of slavery on the mind without considering that . . . the disease is the natural offspring of negro liberty—the liberty to be idle, to wallow in filth, and to indulge in improper food and drinks.[8]

The Southern clergy, also zealous defenders of slavery, argued that the gospel was a sure way of "preserving peace and goodwill among the Negroes." The slaves were taught that God demanded that they obey their masters and were told about the terrible punishments for disobedience that awaited them in the hereafter. Special religious services conveniently omitted those parts of the Bible that might suggest equality, and a happy eternity was dangled as a reward for submission to God's divine plan. As tension built in the decades leading up to civil war in the 1860s, Southern defences militarized. Militias emerged—night riders—small groups of men who patrolled the countryside at night, terrorizing the slaves who might have been thinking of escape and hunting down those who had bolted. Later they donned white hoods and named themselves the Ku Klux Klan.

Alexis de Tocqueville ingeniously foretold the future: "Slavery, amid the democratic liberty and enlightenment of our age, is not an institution that can last," he warned. "Either the slave or the master will put an end to it. In either case, great misfortunes are to be anticipated."

Slavery was abolished, but more than a century later, there were signs of increasing distress among the descendants of the slaves. In October 1997, William Julius Wilson, a professor of social policy at the John F. Kennedy School of Government at Harvard University, gave the keynote address at a two-day conference on "Sociology and Public Life." His subject was "Jobless Ghettos: The Impact of the Disappearance of Work in Segregated Neighborhoods."[9] Using the historic "Black Belt" core neighbourhoods of Chicago as an example, Wilson said that in 1950, although the majority of the urban black population was poor, 69 per cent of adult males were working; however, by the 1990s, only 37 per cent of all males sixteen and over held jobs in these three neighbourhoods. There were other signs of worsening conditions: in 1968, a presidential commission into urban unrest, headed by then Illinois governor Otto Kerner, concluded that America was "moving towards two societies, one black, one white, separate and unequal."[10] But in 1998, the Milton S. Eisenhower Foundation, which had been set up to revisit the Kerner Commission's work, reported that the situation had actually deteriorated in the interim: the economic and racial gap was growing wider; neighbourhoods and schools were resegregating in new ways.

The foundation recorded that in spite of the emergence of a larger African-American middle class and improving high school graduation rates, unemployment in the inner cities of America was at Depression-era levels, even though the general economy was improving. The child-poverty level in the United States was four times higher than in

Western Europe, and the rate of incarceration of African-American men was four times higher than it was in apartheid South Africa. A black child born in Washington or Harlem had a lower life expectancy than a child born in Bangladesh. The United States was not the racial cauldron it was in 1968, but race and poverty were still intertwined.

That 70 per cent of all black children were born out of wedlock in 1998 did not help the picture; fatherless families were a carry-over from the ban on slave marriages, and "masters' rights," and there is a direct connection between growing up with a single parent and poverty. But the Milton S. Eisenhower Foundation commissioners agreed with William Julius Wilson: they thought the most important finding in their report was Depression-level unemployment. When a parent lacks work, families fall apart.

In the discussion that followed the release of the report, there was much talk about sexual morality, about liberal versus conservative, about a "white economy" that many blacks no longer even aspire to, and race, and little consensus about what to do. However, the previous year there had been two unprecedented initiatives at the highest level, both of which spoke to the ingrained values of the American Creed. The first idea came from President Bill Clinton himself, in April 1997; the second originated with Tony P. Hall, a Democratic congressman from Dayton, Ohio. Clinton created the President's Initiative on Race, a high-profile advisory board that was mandated to hold town-hall meetings around the country, collect research on race relations over the previous fifty years and make projections and recommendations. Hall proposed a Congressional apology to African Americans for the harm "their ancestors suffered as slaves under the Constitution and laws of the United States until 1865."[11]

I was intrigued by both these initiatives, especially by the idea of an apology for slavery on behalf of the nation itself. Apologies were much in the air: the U.S. was making amends to other groups, and on the international scene, governmental apologies for past misdeeds were creating new history: the British prime minister, Tony Blair, had apologized for the failure of his country to respond adequately to the Irish potato famine of the mid-nineteenth century, during which thousands died; Germany had apologized for the Hitler regime's attempted genocide of the Jews; a Vatican document had issued a "call to penitence" on behalf of the many who were silent in the face of the Holocaust;[12] and in the new South Africa of Nelson Mandela, the Truth and Reconciliation

Commission was tackling the legacy of white-over-black oppression with singular originality—tempting perpetrators, with the carrot of amnesty, to publicly acknowledge crimes committed in the service of apartheid, provided certain conditions were met. The hope in each case was that something approaching reconciliation might follow.

President Clinton broached his concerns about race in January 1997, when he made racial division a central theme of his Inaugural Address: Race hatred, he announced, was "America's constant curse." Two weeks later, in his State of the Union Address, he read aloud the biblical passage on which he had chosen to place his hand when he took the oath of office: "Thou shalt be called the repairer of the breach," he quoted, explaining his commitment to healing the racial divide in his country. Such a religious gesture in support of a coming political initiative was to be expected in the most overtly churchgoing nation in the Western world, a country that had in many ways remained true to its radical Protestant origins. Before the scandals of illicit sexual behaviour in the White House, public lies and impeachment in the House of Representatives permanently altered the record of his presidency, Bill Clinton had evidently hoped that racial reconciliation would be the remembered outcome of his term in the White House.

Clinton had a personal interest in the subject of race relations. He was raised in the South, in Little Rock, Arkansas, where he had watched federal troops forcibly integrate the public schools in 1957; in fact, he had been speaking out against racism since the age of sixteen, when he fought to include civil rights in the platform of his party at the American Legion Boys' Nation outside Washington, D.C. Some people thought the President's Initiative on Race said more about Clinton's hoped-for legacy than any plans he might have had for policy renewal—after all, the president in 1996 struck down welfare provisions that profoundly affected the lives of millions of poor black families, especially women and children. But after a long hiatus during which hope for positive change seemed to have dropped off the national agenda, something, even something largely decorative like the Initiative, was better than nothing at all.

As for Tony Hall, there was no one in the Republican-dominated Congress more appropriate to suggest something as unlikely as an apology for slavery. As a youth he had worked as a volunteer with the Peace Corps. Later, as a member of the Ohio legislature, he had authored election-law reforms and legislation providing tax incentives for urban development. Elected to Congress in 1978, he helped found the Congressional Friends of Human Rights Monitors, and the Congressional Hunger Center, as well as initiating legislation to fight hunger-related diseases in developing nations. For this, and for his proposal that a humanitarian summit be held in the Horn of Africa, he had been honoured by the United Nations.

Few of his elected colleagues supported him, which was perhaps not surprising, given that voters at home might decide to register their disapproval at the ballot box. But what was most disturbing to Hall was the vehemence of the public response. Almost two thousand people wrote or called his office; although many said he was on the right track, they were outnumbered by the enraged. Hall classified about 10 per cent as outright hate mail: "Apologize to American Negroes for slavery?" spluttered a correspondent from Texas. "You communist, socialist bastards have gone more nuts than I thought you could!" The writer thought *he* deserved an apology and reparations from the U.S. government for its having divested his great-grandfather of 435 slaves. "You need help, Tony," someone else wrote from North Carolina. "I would like to see our nation return to slavery." Some people said blacks should be happy they were saved from Africa and were therefore eligible to become Americans. Still others argued that the dead on the battlefields of the Civil War were "apology" enough, and that Abraham Lincoln had personally expressed the nation's remorse in his second inaugural address, in March 1865, when he referred to slavery as an offence against God and to the war itself as God's retribution. Many children of immigrants to the United States called in to say that slavery had nothing to do with them; their ancestors had been oppressed by other people, and *they* weren't demanding apologies. "If I get all these hate calls over a simple apology, we have a problem," said a chastened Hall. He admitted he was "stunned" by the anger and racism. A week after he introduced his resolution, Hall took the floor of the House of Representatives in a counterattack: "Many people have told me that apologizing is an empty, meaningless gesture, but if it was so meaningless, why has the resolution created a firestorm of controversy throughout the nation?" he asked. "We are a nation of immigrants. Those who came as free men went in one direction; those who came from slave ships another; we owe it to our children to clearly mark that the early fork in the road was the wrong one. All of us today, white and black, live in the shadow of our past. We all pay a price for slavery."[13]

Writing in *The New York Times*, the editorialist Brent Staples, author of a memoir called *Parallel Time: Growing Up in Black and White*, called the subject of the slavers and the enslaved "nearly as explosive today as [it was] during the 1860s."[14]

President Clinton did not make any promises when Tony Hall suggested a Congressional apology for slavery, but he did not exclude the possibility. The following year, he said in Mukono, Uganda, "Going back to the time before we were even a nation, European Americans received the fruits of the slave trade. We were wrong in that." During that same trip to Africa he made a point of visiting Goree, off the coast of Senegal, where captured Africans had awaited shipment to the United States, chained to the walls in underground cubicles, where, as in an appraisal of workhorses, men's muscles were examined, women's breasts were measured for their capacity to provide milk for slave progeny and children's teeth were inspected. All were fattened to what was considered to be the best shipping weight; those who failed to meet the standard were thrown into the sea.[15]

A minimal response, perhaps, but by the time he travelled to Africa, Bill Clinton had been well warned about the political dangers of official repentance (his spokesman Mike McCurry had hastened to say that whatever the president did, he would *not* be making a direct apology, because such a gesture would be "extraneous" and because the issue was "not on the minds of Americans"). When Clinton next addressed the subject, Hall's proposal was effectively dead. "Most of my African-American friends and advisers don't believe that we should get into what was essentially a press story about whether there should be an apology for slavery in America," said Clinton. "They think that that's what the Thirteenth, Fourteenth and Fifteenth Amendments were, they think that's what the Civil Rights Amendment was, and they think we need to be looking towards the future."

There was no question that the mere suggestion of an apology had inflamed many in the media, as well as the ordinary folk who told Tony Hall what they thought of his wimpy initiative. And not surprisingly, the response to Hall's proposal split along black-white lines. Back in 1995, before the jury delivered its verdict on the O. J. Simpson murder case, in which Simpson was accused of killing his ex-wife and her friend, a nationwide Harris poll had found that 61 per cent of white Americans thought Simpson was guilty while 68 per cent of black Americans believed he was not; and when Tony Hall suggested a formal apology for slavery, there was a similar divide. Asked in two Gallup polls whether the U.S. government should pass legislation that "officially apologizes to American blacks for the fact that slavery was practiced before the Civil War in this country," 67 per cent of whites were opposed the idea while 65 per cent of blacks were in favour. (The greatest discrepancy occurred in the former slave states of the South, where 73 per cent of whites were solidly opposed to an apology.) These differences closely mirrored the results of other polls in which Americans have been asked about race-related legislative initiatives, such as affirmative action or strengthening civil rights legislation. Whites are largely opposed; blacks are largely in favour.

On the other hand, although many African Americans wrote publicly saying that an apology would help kick-start a long-overdue process of national healing, other prominent blacks opposed the idea with as much zeal as the most stalwart white conservatives. Many thought Hall was naïve and that an apology with teeth had to be tied to financial reparations: "It's just more race entertainment," the Reverend Jesse L. Jackson retorted dismissively. The syndicated black writer Thomas Sowell called the apology idea "insane, mindless mush," and declared it was impossible to apologize for the actions of long-dead people. This point, which was echoed by others—some of whom added that no collectivity (Congress) could officially regret the actions of individuals, and that no individual (the president) could speak for the nation's shared past—reflected a peculiarly American perspective: in the United States the notion of personal responsibility is as germane to the national psyche as the idea of collectivism is foreign. Thomas Sowell also claimed that since slavery was once a worldwide phenomenon, it was unfair to apologize for it in America. "There are islands in the Caribbean that imported more slaves from Africa than the U.S. did, and Brazil imported six times as many. The Islamic countries of the Middle East and North Africa took even more slaves from Africa than the entire Western Hemisphere. Why then is slavery being spoken of as if it were some problem peculiar to America?" he asked. "The idea of inherited racial guilt—a Nazi conception—behind the proposed apology would do nothing to heal the racial divisions in this country today—it would only promote further polarization. What would this apology do for blacks? Is looking backward a way to prepare for the future?"[16]

It was gripping to hear this point of view put forward by a black writer, especially his view about "inherited racial guilt," because I had already experienced the environment of Germany. I thought the problem of collective guilt was much more than a Nazi concept; in fact, it was central to the way many Germans remembered their past. I was also planning to visit South Africa, where Bishop Desmond Tutu was known to be openly ambivalent on the subject of collective responsibility for the abuses of apartheid. The subject seemed to be far less cut and dried than Sowell was making it appear.

To my ears, the most "American" element of Sowell's polemic was the very last sentence in which he questioned the importance of dealing with the past. In the "new" land of the United States, immigrants, regardless of their provenance, absorb the national ideology—a belief in the future. Change will happen tomorrow, or the next day; facing the future rarely entails looking to the past. The rhetoric of equal promise holds that tomorrow will bring better times, even if it never does, and there is no better example of this thinking than Martin Luther King Jr. himself. King did not look at slavery and its aftermath and conclude that racism was so deep as to be ineradicable. On the contrary, in his Washington speech, during which he repeated his now-famous incantation, "I have a dream," he revealed that he believed in the power of the future as passionately as any American; all that was required was an effort of will. Whether he intended it or not, Tony Hall's suggestion that America apologize for its slave past cut to the ambiguity at the heart of this dream. Japanese Americans had received an official apology, but their shabby treatment had occurred in an out-of-the-ordinary wartime situation: like the victims of syphilis experiments, they did not call into question the core of American history. Slavery did—because it contradicted the founding rhetoric of equality and because more than a century later the devastating outcome of race bondage stubbornly refuses to disappear into a happy future.

Within months, Tony Hall's resolution looked moribund, but not because no one cared. The hurricane winds that Congressman Hall's suggestion had unleashed left little doubt that the memory of America's slave past remains razor-sharp and unsettled.

I am growing depressed as I wander through this mausoleum in the still-disconsolate heart of black America: wondering about race wounds, and the faces of hope that decorate the walls, and the dead. I remind myself that Martin Luther King Jr.'s yearning for a second emancipation was a marker point of the American twentieth century and that he personified another stage of freedom: one that changed the legal face of his country. Yet, as I think about the still-raw problems of race, underclass and non-reconciliation, his success seems partial, at best. I find myself wondering whether Tony Hall's generous idea for a Congressional apology would have made any difference.

I leave the memorial and walk quickly, purposefully, to the bus stop. Around me are boarded-up, abandoned buildings; random clusters of windswept papers and other detritus; and tight knots of bored, wary-looking unemployed youth—all of which radiates an unbridgeable remoteness from the massive grassroots social change Dr. King and his friends once imagined. What would it take to overcome this? Mississippi, I decide, is the place to start my journey: the place King once famously described as "sweltering with the heat of injustice."[17] There have been vast changes since he made that observation in 1963, but of all the Southern slave states, Mississippi fought the hardest to retain the old ways. Memory resides there.

The heat in Jackson, Mississippi, is so heavy, so dense, that for a moment I think I have passed too close to a steam laundry whose doors are open. I breathe with effort until my lungs have acclimatized to the thick, moist air. The city seems peculiarly quiet. Although this is a midweek working day, there is scarcely a person to be seen; I guess the smart locals are inside, huddled around their air conditioners. Jackson feels small—more like a town than a state capital. The grass on front lawns has burned brown: it is September and flowering trees still line streets etched with literary and political history. Eudora Welty was born here in 1909; I think about her jewel-like short fiction and the way she exposed the human complexity beneath the stifling conformity of white Southern life. In a collection of autobiographical essays titled *One Writer's Beginnings*, she once described the social conventions of early-century Jackson, where ladies of leisure visited one another every afternoon: "Everybody had calling cards, even certain children; and newborn babies themselves were properly announced by sending out their tiny engraved calling cards attached with a pink or blue bow to those of their parents."[18] The Old South: hard to imagine a tinier, more circumscribed world than that of the privileged white class that had been liberated from all labour; but Welty's penetrating vision extended beyond her own community: her photographs of the people of the region, especially blacks, are among the most revealing of the poverty other Mississippians endured. Her house sits next to the local branch of the American Civil Liberties Union (ACLU), which is flanked by camellias and a centuries-old live oak dripping Spanish moss. In their different ways, she and the Jackson ACLU have illuminated the psychology of this region.

To the northeast of the city lies the town of Oxford, Mississippi, home of William Faulkner, one of myriad Southern authors who loved and was repelled by the legacy of his birthplace. When Faulkner was in his prime, his fellow Mississippians didn't think he was worth reading, but when I was a child, the foreboding just under the surface of his mysterious Mississippi and his portrayal of the languid, inexorable decline of the post-slavery decades illuminated my Canadian world with a spectrum of new colour. Whatever the South might be, Mississippi, I came to believe, was its heart—for better or for worse.

During the civil rights era, in the 1950s and 1960s, it was definitely for worse. The struggle to overthrow the Jim Crow laws that governed every aspect of a black person's life—from which drinking fountain or public toilet a man or woman could use to the way he or she was to address a person of white complexion—found its nadir in this then-backward place. Here, segregationist whites battled hardest against the threat of change; here, lynchings, arson and shootings were carried out with impunity. Byron de la Beckwith, for example, was a racist murderer from Greenwood, in the Mississippi Delta, with an improbable, romantic name. Greenwood was already notorious, even before Beckwith: in 1955, a fourteen-year-old named Emmett Till was murdered there by a posse of white men as punishment for supposedly having looked at a white woman in too forthright a manner. All told, Mississippi had more recorded lynchings than any other state in America.[19]

I had a personal connection to Jackson through my late cousin, Rabbi Perry Nussbaum. In the 1960s, he acquired a reputation as a supporter of civil rights among the "white hoods" of the local Ku Klux Klan, and late one night in 1967, a bomb was lobbed into his house while he and his wife, Arene, were sleeping. Miraculously, they were not injured. According to the U.S. Federal Bureau of Investigation, the Ku Klux Klan Imperial Wizard Sam Bowers, who masterminded the attack, was also responsible for nine murders and three hundred bombings, burnings and beatings. It was he who had contrived and carried out the murder of three civil rights workers in 1964: a young black named James Chaney, and Andrew Goodman and Michael Schwerner, two white college students from New York City who had come down to Mississippi to join the Freedom Marches. Bowers also firebombed the Hattiesburg home of Vernon Dahmer, a respected black businessman who was active in the voter registration drive: Dahmer died of smoke inhalation. Bowers was convicted in the case of the assassinated civil rights workers—but on grounds of usurping their civil rights, since it was impossible to get a white jury (there were no blacks on juries at the time) to convict a white man for murders carried out in the name of white supremacy. His criminal trials ended in acquittal—until 1998, when he was retried in the Vernon Dahmer case and this time convicted.

Before he was arrested for the 1963 murder of the black civil rights leader Medgar Evers, Byron de la Beckwith was open about his violent hatreds. He once asked the Mississippi Congressman Frank Smith to "let me know if I can kill a nigger for you." Just months before the Evers murder, he warned the National Rifle Association of his willing intentions: "Gentlemen," he said, "for the next fifteen years we here in Mississippi are going to have to do a lot of shooting to protect our wives, our children and ourselves."[20] Although police retrieved the murder weapon covered with his fingerprints, Beckwith was released after two trials resulted in hung juries. In each case, the establishment of Greenwood came to his defence with a public collection and high-powered lawyers, including the attorney for the city and a member of the state governor's law firm.

Medgar Evers's career as a political organizer began in November 1954, after he was refused entry into the University of Mississippi Law School on grounds of race. He became the first field secretary of the Mississippi branch of the National Association for the Advancement of Colored People (NAACP), travelling widely and openly—so much so that by June 1963 even his closest friends thought he was a marked man. He went door to door, through towns and villages, organizing voter drives to register black electors, and the prospect of masses of black voters frightened Beckwith and others like him: Evers was a danger to their established way of life.

The White Citizens' Council of Mississippi also supported Beckwith. Organized in July 1954 to oppose the Supreme Court's decision to desegregate the public schools, the council was an immediate success: by October, twenty-five thousand people had paid their dues, including many of the most influential citizens of every community—people who decided that segregation could be maintained within the law. As one historian has noted, "In an atmosphere of unremitting hostility to social change in any form, where law was the servant of white supremacy, white supremacists had little need for lawlessness."[21] The White Citizens' Council became a legitimate means for illegitimate actions: its real use was to channel hatred and sanction violence.

In 1957 the white-supremacy battle was joined by the newly created Mississippi Sovereignty Commission, whose immediate preoccupation was the tense dispute over school desegregation and the civil rights movement—their goal was "state sovereignty," in whatever manner achievable. The commission's aides gathered information on civil rights activists, undermined the work of desegregationists and directed public relations. Spies infiltrated rallies and sit-ins, reported rumours, investigated persons who sponsored voter registration drives and appealed to employers to fire anyone suspected of supporting the civil rights movement. They handed lists of such names over to police. They obstructed blacks when they tried to register for the vote and carried out "actions" in the service of their cause, with special attention to the horror of race mixing. When one white couple thought the young man their daughter was dating might be of mixed race, the commission investigated his lineage, then, during the course of a personal visit, scrupulously examined his fingernails because they were convinced that white people have half moons and blacks do not. Although the boy was not yet of draft age (it was the time of the Vietnam War), the investigators arranged to have him illegally conscripted, should the parents' suspicions turn out to be correct. (He turned out to be of Italian heritage.)

Although the Sovereignty Commission was publicly funded only until 1973, its secret files remained available to legislators and other administrators until February 1988, when the Mississippi ACLU filed a lawsuit alleging that state officials were harassing people engaging in lawful activities. In 1989, the court held that the laws governing the commission were unconstitutional. Only then did the public learn that the Mississippi Sovereignty Commission had tampered with jury selection on behalf of Byron de la Beckwith during his two trials for the murder of Medgar Evers. The district attorney reopened the case, and in 1994 Beckwith was finally convicted. Decades of impunity dissolving in the new Mississippi.

By March 1998, all countersuits against the opening of its files were exhausted, and records documenting eighty-five thousand names of "suspects" were at last released to the media. "When you start to read those files, you realize that what we had was comparable to a police state, even though we had elections," David Ingebretsen, the executive director of the Mississippi ACLU, tells me. "When you learn that the commission was contacting the boards of dentistry and medicine to tell them who should not get a licence to practise, and the state bar regarding who should be admitted, there is really no other word for it. We weren't all racists down here, but the structures of racism smothered us, and people paid a price for speaking out. So very few did, and the Sovereignty Commission and the White Citizens' Council became all-powerful. Ministers were investigated and run out of the state, and teachers were fired. The very idea that white people would want to teach blacks was so improbable to those people that they assumed everyone who was not a white supremacist must be a Communist. Anyway, outsiders were always called 'Communists' or 'agitators.' If you had any political ambition in the South you had to be a segregationist."

Ingebretsen's open-necked shirt and the Elvis Presley puppet on the wall behind his desk provide a light touch and belie the seriousness of his work, but like many Southerners of his age (he is fifty-four in 1998) he had taken part in a social revolution—the civil rights movement—that had brought him face-to-face with the values of his society.

"Segregationism was learned, an acquired taste. I remember well one day when I was six years old, out front with some of the other kids, and an ice-cream truck came. I paid the black kid for the ice cream, and one of my friends said, 'You touched a nigger.' That was news to me, and I guess that's why I never forgot it. You got all this stuff drilled into you by your culture, by the newspapers, the schools, everything.

"I'm ashamed now, but in 1962 I taunted James Meredith [the black student who tried to enrol at the University of Mississippi][22] as he passed before our campus on his way to Ole Miss. But I changed within the space of a year. I was at a relatively progressive college in Jackson, and fortunately I got in with the right group of people and had some very good teachers. For the first time I met people with different views who were allowed to express them. In high school, all non-conforming opinions were suppressed. I remember our civics teachers telling us we were never to talk about segregation or integration."

He had problems with his family when he began to change his views: an uncle did not speak to him for years, and he says his newly liberal ideas also cost him economically. "I became active in the ACLU early on, and I was quoted as saying that black people were more likely to get the death penalty, which was true and still is. I was in real estate at the time and I lost business over that. Now I am 'out' as a liberal, of course, although that's still a dirty word around here, and I usually call myself a moderate." He laughs.

We leave the air-conditioned comfort of his small office and climb into his pickup truck. He wants me to see how Jackson's inner-city blacks live all these decades later. There are a few blocks of wooden shacks, many of them boarded up. Old people are sitting on their front porches fanning themselves; youths loiter on corners in the middle of a school day; a factory sprawls over an entire block spewing dirty smoke; a disco blares music next to family dwellings. I've see worse urban poverty, in Mexico, in India; on the other hand, this is the richest nation in the world. We leave the ghetto, then pass the white corner house that once belonged to my cousin, Perry Nussbaum. After the bombing, he and Arene packed up and left Jackson forever.

Now I am headed for the old Delta—the eye of the civil rights hurricane and before that, a century and a half of African-American history: an ancient locale of cotton-and-slave mystique where I will begin my search to understand why the tragedy of American slavery has so resolutely refused to go away. The Delta fans out for three hundred flat, treeless kilometres from the banks of the Mississippi River over the northwest quadrant of the state, and the topsoil, laid down by centuries of flooding, is so perfect that people thought planting cotton was worth the risk of malaria. Pioneer farmers brought their slaves to the Delta in the early nineteenth century, and after the Civil War, the slaves became sharecroppers on the same rich plantations, staying on as tenant families. But freedom did not mean advancement. I'd been surprised to learn that it was the 1970s before an African American reached even the level of foreman: the first was John Warner, from the town of Rayville, who had started as a water boy in 1937.[23]

History in the Delta is multilayered. The Delta is the birthplace of the blues, the famous rhythmic songs of black slave and sharecropper origin that were sung in the cotton fields and by the men in chain gangs. It lies at the heart of African-American Christianity, where the preacher and his Sunday congregation rocked, swayed, shouted and sang the soon-to-be-famous spirituals that spread from the South. In the 1960s, the Delta was at the centre of the struggle for civil rights—*and* white supremacy. Byron de la Beckwith came from the Delta.

Now it is the late 1990s, and I am perched high in a rented van on my way to an election rally, more than three decades after the U.S. Supreme Court passed the Voting Rights Act of 1965. My destination is Mayersville, a village that flanks the Mississippi River. The power that came with the right to vote was supposed to thrust African Americans into the mainstream: hundreds of people in the South had been killed in the struggle to claim their civic due. What, I wonder, does voting mean to the people of the old Delta all these years later? Has it changed the pattern of their lives?

The highway out of Jackson descends gradually into the Delta lowland, and metaphorically into another world, as the broad, well-kept American freeway narrows into smaller and smaller roads. I pass through Yazoo, a town whose frontier roots are still visible, where a plaque in front of the bank informs passersby that this community, and presumably this bank, raised money after the Civil War for the battle-ravaged, suddenly slaveless cotton planters.

The main street of town recedes in the rear-view mirror, and now the terrain stretches flat as far as the eye can see. From time to time, lovely "big houses"—once the manor homes of the slave masters—dot the horizon. And then the *casus belli*: the cotton fields. In the days of the Old South, this territory was known as the richest cotton-farming area in the world.

It is fall harvest time, and the ripe white balls are exploding from their pods all along the dark stalks, but there are no human pickers bent over from the waist moving up and down the rows. Instead, combines crawl through the fields, collecting and depositing the white fluff into cages. The road—now two-lane and rural—is lined with rectangular cotton bales clamped down with plastic and netting, each one numbered. I drive past an even older incarnation of the mythic region: an ancient cypress swamp, where dank waters eddy around drowned-looking forked trees, and white egrets stand and wait, then catfish ponds where the preposterously flat-faced, whiskered creatures are bred.

I miss my turn and mistakenly veer into a tiny hamlet. The road has degenerated into dry clay that clouds the air with red dust; cotton tufts that fled the fields on a breath of wind lie trapped in the grasses alongside. I stop to ask directions, find the main road again, then finally I am there: Mayersville, at the river limit of the Delta, once a seat of huge cotton wealth and now a village of dirt streets and a few straggly habitations abutting the levee, where slaves were transported up and down to New Orleans and places in between.

This was once a town of substance, with a hotel, a laundry, ten stores and the best dry-goods shop for dresses next to Memphis's. The county had more slaves per owner than any other place in the United States, and the small number of local white denizens lived as a planter aristocracy. Later, I am told about a son of this class who, never having learned to dress himself, set out for the University of Mississippi with his black servant. In the eccentric ways of the Old South and its so-called peculiar institution, so marked by violence and paternalism, the slave or servant (I never did learn whether this happened before or after Emancipation, which says a great deal about the law's impact in these parts) was also a companion and "friend." The two of them roomed together during the entire university career of the young cotton aristocrat, who, according to the story, never did learn to tie his shoelaces.

The election rally is being held on a summer-parched baseball field. The candidate for Chancery Court judge is the sitting incumbent: an atractive black woman named Vicky Roach Barnes. About thirty-five people (including at least a dozen non-voting children) sit on benches and fan themselves under an awning in the impossibly intense midday heat, waiting for the promised free picnic. An overweight white man in an apron and straw hat sweats over a barbecue; he is Robert Monty, a former state senator, who has donated both the food and his services as chef.

This is old-style electioneering: voters being seduced with hot dogs, plates of chili and free T-shirts that say "Vote for Vicky." I find myself in the hut that's serving as a makeshift kitchen, pouring grape juice for a crowd of enthusiastic children lined up outside. Standing beside me is a long-suffering disk jockey who is sweating profusely as he talks a steady stream of disk-jockey babble and plays ear-splitting rap music for the cause. I wonder about the strains of a political campaign that must bring the candidate to a remote settlement such as this for the sake of a couple of dozen potential votes. The food is served, and Robert Monty disappears from sight. I find him leaning in a half faint against the side of the kitchen hut, trying to recover from the heat.

Who are these people, and how many of them will vote for Vicky? Will they vote at all? And if not, what does that say about the dream that Martin Luther King Jr. died for? Their families have been in the Delta since time immemorial, they tell me. The commander of the Union troops, William Tecumseh Sherman, had promised their slave ancestors "forty acres and a mule" with which to start their lives as free people. The promise was later rescinded by the Southern-born president Andrew

Johnson, who succeeded Abraham Lincoln. So most of the freed slaves stayed right here, where they and their parents were born. They worked the same properties as sharecroppers—as poor as dirt. Few could read or write: it was a crime to teach a slave, since literacy might incite revolt.

Vicky Barnes's campaign manager, Dorwin Shields, tells me that most of the people milling around the baseball field are still illiterate. They had poor schooling, or no schooling, or school for only part of the year, because children were always needed in the cotton fields. Now the combines harvest the crop, and the only work around is in catfish farming or at the medium-security prison that looms adjacent to the baseball field. Everyone else is on welfare or pensions of one sort or another. This, too, is a residue of slavery: free, yes, but not from ignorance and dependence.

Some people are trying very hard. Dorwin Shields is fifty-two, but his taut body and energetic manner suggest a much younger man. He has already run the election campaigns of eight black candidates, including that of the former U.S. Agriculture secretary Mike Espy, who first took office in 1993, and he is old enough to remember the civil rights battles with clarity. In 1963, the Ku Klux Klan burned a cross near his parents' house in Vicksburg, just down the highway—a staunch stronghold of white supremacy that was a major battlefield of the Civil War. He remembers that when Martin Luther King came to town, only one church would welcome him. There were threats of arson and bombs, and the Klan paraded up and down the streets, but the church took a vote and decided to open its doors anyway and, in the way of the religious South, let God decide the outcome. He went to hear King speak: "He encouraged us to register for the vote and not to be afraid because we had the Lord on our side. I have such deep convictions about the work he did and about the people who died during that era," he says.

Registering people for the vote, then getting them out at election time, has been his obsession, but he tells me that he has become discouraged in recent years, because, although he is in Mayersville with Judge Barnes, handing out T-shirts and glad-handing the tiny constituency, he believes that his dream of African-American participation in the broadest sense is becoming increasingly elusive. From experience he knows that only 20 or 25 per cent of eligible voters will bother casting their ballot. "It is disheartening to realize that in the United States of America, the greatest democracy on the surface of the earth, people do not cherish the right and the privilege of that ballot. Blacks should be out in numbers because people literally gave their lives for this right, but we have become apathetic. Maybe we think we have overcome, but we have certainly *not* overcome, and we have a long way to go when we do not understand the power of the ballot."

He is starting to declaim emotionally into my tape recorder as though he were on the hustings, but the avalanche of feeling also has a personal source. "This will sound far-fetched," he says, "but I am an engineer. I have an advanced degree from Tennessee State University."

Why is this far-fetched, I wonder. I have no reason to doubt that he is a highly educated professional. So he explains. In 1964, because the race laws of Mississippi prohibited him from attending a state university, the state government, in an extraordinarily convoluted scheme, paid for his education elsewhere. It was, he says, common practice at the time, after every effort had been made to dissuade the black student from pursuing an education by telling him or her that university studies were beyond the ability of a black person. Blacks had the right to attend college like anyone else, if they had the qualifications, but Mississippi did not have to educate them in its schools.

He went anyway, because he sensed the bitterness of his father's curtailed life. "My father worked as a porter for thirty-eight years, but he was not respected. When we went to the butcher, he would have to step aside so that white people could place their orders. He would tell us, 'Get an education and perhaps someday you can change this.'"

Dorwin has worked for the past nineteen years for an international engineering company located in Vicksburg, but he is currently in the process of suing his employers for refusing to promote him past a glass ceiling no black person in his firm has ever penetrated. He speaks for a long time about his lawsuit, and I listen carefully, because what he seems really to be talking about, beyond the details of the case, is his underlying grief. "I am paid well, but blacks are still not allowed to assume the top jobs in industry here. I supervise projects worth many millions of dollars. I recently said to the man responsible, 'I know I am the best qualified person here and that my record has been excellent.' He looked me in the eye and said, 'Well, that's just the way it is.' Maybe some blacks are satisfied with the status quo, but I believe in justice. I can't let it go." He looks as though he is about to cry.

Feelings of injustice have propelled him into the backrooms of politics, and his belief in democracy and the ballot box as a way out of inequality are as profoundly American as the racism that drove him there. But despair has chiselled deep grooves: "Look around here," he says, waving towards the handful of prospective voters munching on free hot dogs and dancing happily to the music. "Either they don't vote at all, or if they do, some of them still have the slave mentality. Whatever the owner says, they agree to. If they're told to vote for a certain candidate, a lot of them will do it."

"Would an apology for slavery make any difference at this stage?" I ask.

He laughs. "I don't want an apology personally. I just want to be treated as an equal in this society. But I'll sure as heck take that forty acres and a mule!"

With this joke he recovers his campaign manager persona. I watch him bound into the centre of the baseball field, grab hold of the ever-smiling Vicky Barnes and raise her arm in a triumphant victory salute.

There is a small commotion: Unita Blackwell, the mayor, has arrived with her mother. She is tall and imposing in a red-and-white striped dress and clearly loved in Mayersville as a woman of the people. Blackwell has built housing units, brought in clean water and sewage treatment and put gravel on some roads; before that, only white people had gravel. She is also a veteran of the civil rights movement. In 1964, when the activist Stokely Carmichael brought the drive for voter registration to the poverty-stricken black communities of Issaquena County, Unita, who was picking cotton for $3 a day, volunteered to register—or try to. When a circuit clerk refused her application, her life in politics began. (In response to the drives, Mississippi authorities thought up far-fetched impediments, including asking undereducated or illiterate people to interpret complex clauses of the U.S. Constitution.) Blackwell started by organizing her community, and in 1976 she became the first black woman ever elected in the state of Mississippi.

She takes me to her little house just off the baseball field. It has one main room, with a couch, a chair, a table and a hall that leads off to the bathroom and bedrooms—and, happily, air conditioning. She and her mother offer me a small plate of packaged bacon rinds, a Southern specialty. After days of fried chicken, fried fish, fried pickles, fried potatoes, fried okra and fried hamburgers, I pass.

Unita folds her long legs under the couch. She is slim and beautiful—and direct. "To enter politics was different for black people. It was out of necessity," she says. "In the Delta here, we had nothing, but they said that if you registered for the vote and voted you could get things to make your life better. The Constitution says this and that about being equal—

I learned that in school—but here we didn't ever have the opportunities."

She was born on a "small plantation place" called Lulu, just north of Mayersville, where the local children went to school only two or three months of the year, and she would have remained illiterate and hopeless if it hadn't been for the ancient mother who now sits beside her. Blackwell's mother could neither read nor write, but she was determined that her daughters would learn. Unita and her sister were sent to live with their grandmother just across the Mississippi River, in Arkansas. Most of the women in the Arkansas "big house" went out to the fields to pick cotton, but the grandmother, who was the domestic in charge of the interior, made sure the girls went to school. Grandmother could read a little herself "because she cooked for the boss." In antebellum days the "house Negro" sat at the top of the slave pyramid, a position that sometimes included privileges such as literacy, and the tradition of relative learning in the hierarchy of servants continued.

I presume that Unita Blackwell is working hardest for her constituents on the economic front, but she makes it clear she thinks this is a prejudice on my part. Yes, she says, she does try to find employment in the army for some of the young men, but as far as she is concerned, the most important legacy of the civil rights movement for black people in the Mississippi Delta is psychological: to reinstate pride in African-American history. "If we can bring back what happened to Harriet Tubman and Frederick Douglass and all those other people, if we can instill how important what they did was for our freedom . . . *that*'s what's important. The teaching of black history is essential and so neglected. Where did we fit in? We *were* a part of the world! When they found the skeleton of this black woman that is one million years old—you know, they think that we all have her DNA, every one of us on earth—that kind of thing assures a lot of people that they are okay too." My own thoughts trail back to Atlanta and the Memorial Hall quotation from Martin Luther King Jr.: "We blacks also have a soul." And the banner spread across the chest of the marcher declaring "I am a man."

"First we wanted integration, but only because we wanted *books* for our children," she continues. "It had nothing to do with going to school with white children; that was not what it was about. But now, when we pull back and say we want to educate our children differently, they say we are racist! We can't be! There's no way any of us can be racist, because we didn't have the power of the system and we still don't. It's who has the power in the system that counts when you're talking about racism."

I have heard this self-serving argument many times, and it incenses me. Racism is hatred for others based on inborn group characteristics, no matter who expresses it. Yes, the powerful can feel this kind of antipathy, but so can the powerless, as twentieth-century European history has amply revealed. But she has already moved on, caught up in her passionate harangue: "We went to jail, we marched, we did all these things, then a few people got good jobs and a few things. A few more of us had a chance to finish school—not the best schools, but we finished. Then some people got good jobs and a few material things. So they showed them to us on the TV to show that we blacks have made it, and a few people like me stood up and screamed, 'That is not true!' Most of us still keep coming back to nothing. So we end up talking about economic development, saying white people's words, just because a few got into a situation where they could buy a car and have a decent house. They could even move to where the white people were, or decide not to. They had that choice. But how many people did not make it to that level? You know, in the past we always had people who had status, the preachers and the schoolteachers and the postman and so on. They lived in the community. So finally they could move out, and now who's left in what America calls 'the ghetto'? The ones that moved out can say, 'I'm better because I don't live in the ghetto.' They can say, 'The reason the others don't make it is because they don't want nothing.' Then they show how they have made it by marrying a white woman."

Her bitterness fills the small room; neither her mother nor I speak. "So my first priority," she continues, "is for us to learn who we are, and the second is to make sure whites understand who we are. But I need to know who I am first because I think that if people know who they are, they cannot be put down, not if they know that they are human beings and that they make a contribution to the world. Now the scientists find that it is just the colour of the skin and the texture of the hair that is the difference between races, because in evolution your body changes over time, depending on where you are. I mean, the skin of human beings lightened in northern places where it is colder. So I say I could go to Chicago and stay a long time and get a little bit lighter!" Her face softens and she laughs out loud at her joke.

Her mother is smiling proudly. "Are you Mrs. Blackwell?" I ask her.

"How could she be!" Unita shoots back fiercely. I am taken aback—until it occurs to me that assuming Unita's mother might have the same name as her daughter—in other words, my feminist, mainstream surmise that Unita, though married and a parent, might have kept her birth name—is seen as one more cultural bias. Here in Mayersville, Mississippi—black, self-conscious and layered with history—my comment has been interpreted to mean that Unita is an unmarried mother. There is, hanging in the air, an implicit assumption about *my* racism. For a moment we look at one another from across a chasm. I forgot momentarily that I am white and the people here are black. I stand reminded.

The mother's name is Bradley. Mrs. Virdia Mae Bradley. She is eighty-four years old, with a firm handshake, the same direct, intelligent gaze as her daughter and a broad, toothless smile. How much has changed here? It is true that thirty years ago there would not have been a black incumbent judge running in Chancery Court elections, nor would there have been a black woman mayor in Mayersville, but in the former slave lands of the Mississippi Delta, there is still not money for dentures.

After three decades, Martin Luther King's dream of integration into the mainstream of society has been rejected by a leader who started her political life by signing up black voters. Tony Hall's suggested apology for slavery—an idea that springs directly from the ideals of the American Creed—evokes cynical laughter from Dorwin Shields, a man who is suing his employer for discrimination. Yet the Creed of equality remains everyone's birthright, and almost two hundred and fifty years after the Reverend Peter Fontaine wrote his equivocal letter about the "moral impossibility" of living without slaves, an African-American woman will claim it as her own—in full, ironic awareness of myth and right:

> *I have come to you tonite as an equal . . .*
> *pulling my history with bruised heels,*
> *beckoning to the illusion of America.*[24]

I plan to go to Charleston, South Carolina, the city blacks call the "Ellis Island[25] of slavery," the port of entry for the bound captives from Africa, the place where the story began. In this city of origin, the descendants of the Low Country plantation slaves may have something more to tell me about the impasse in black-white reconciliation.

A striking thing about antebellum Charleston—and this quality can still be felt in the city—was its aristocratic hauteur. On a foundation of slave labour, the planters became a leisure class of gentlemen and ladies whose wealth enabled them to lead lives of refined consumption and princely demeanour, and they built themselves mansions in the city to demonstrate their status and to accommodate the seasons of society. From the earliest days, Charlestonians were known for their "generous hospitality and noble bearing."[26]

The guide on a conducted bus tour of the city takes care to emphasize this patrician history. We drive along leafy avenues, past the nineteenth-century town house of one aristocrat (a red-brick fortress-like structure with a tower) whose friendly architect refused fees because, as the guide explains, gentlemen did not work for money. Then there's the Martin House, built in 1830 and fronted by magnificent Corinthian columns as well as a split, curved outside staircase whose two sides wrap around a central landing: gentlemen on the right, ladies on the left, so the men would not be in a position to observe the ladies' ankles. The estates were built to maximize air circulation before air conditioning was invented. The homes were protected from intruders by high brick walls or hand-forged wrought-iron gates.

The contained exhibitionism of these immense properties signals the enormity of the wealth that slavery brought the elite of the American South. The floor plan of one estate is forty thousand square feet (thirty-seven hundred square metres), and marble for the ballroom was imported from Italy. Fathers built town houses for daughters and sons when they married and willed them cooks, butlers, housekeepers, laundresses, seamstresses, footmen, coachmen and chamber- and nursery maids to maintain their new holdings. Many families also held property in the Carolinian Up Country, where they went to escape the fierce summer heat and the ever-present threat of malaria on the swampy coast. Whenever possible, plantation and town homes, together with all other assets, including slaves, were transferred intact from generation to generation to uphold the influence of the family. And slave holding was the measure of that influence; although only 10 per cent of the 274,563 inhabitants of South Carolina owned chattels in 1850, and of these only 1,471 possessed fifty or more, the planting gentry ruled public life almost without interruption until the end of the nineteenth century, well beyond the strife of the Civil War.[27]

The tour guide is circumspect about the slaves. When obliged to mention their existence as the obvious backbone of this lavish world, he carefully describes them as "servants" and calls the shacks where they lived at the back of the big house "dependencies." We pass by the old slave market without hearing a word about its origin, except to learn that there are bargains to be found in the shops there. We visitors are all white and either foreign or from outside the South. It's the old story: there's an elephant in the salon, but we're too polite to notice.

She does not want me to use her real name, so I shall call her Sandra. She is full-bodied and warm, with an unguarded, expressive face. It is evening, fast becoming night, and a cooling breeze brushes across my skin, bringing welcome relief. We—Sandra, Maxine, my old friend from Toronto, who now lives here, and I—are sitting on the darkened veranda of an elegant nineteenth-century Charleston house. The veranda, which is on the second floor, overlooking a private garden that is hidden from the street, was built to accommodate a large family seeking relief from the heat. To get here, we have climbed a broad stairway that sweeps past a downstairs sitting room with a large marble fireplace. Today, the building houses the Charleston branch of a cultural preservation society. Sandra is assistant to the co-ordinator: her job is to attract people from diverse backgrounds to conferences in the city. But the building itself was once the town house of a rich slave-owning planter family, and that history makes Sandra physically uncomfortable.

She was born in Charleston in 1952, during the era of the Jim Crow laws. Her parents divorced when she was ten, but she says she was blessed to have been raised by a mother with strong values and a sense of self-worth, who encouraged her to seize opportunities. Sandra's mother had a child-care business that made quite a bit of money, so when the white schools were forced to open their doors to blacks, Sandra was sent to a private Catholic institution. At first she was spat upon, and later she was subjected to curious questions about her hair, and how it happened that her family could afford such a school (the only blacks most of the children there had seen were domestics), but Sandra's warmth invited friendship (she says with a laugh that she was voted Miss Congeniality), and she eventually became the first African American in her city to participate in a cultural-exchange program that took her and a group of white students to Europe.

What amazed her was the music: rhythm and blues was popular in Europe then, and in the discos, everyone wanted to see her dance. And all the people with brown skin, especially in southern Italy—they were as dark as she was! She had never imagined there might be dark-skinned people outside the United States.

Later, she spent many years in Los Angeles, working in the film business for Home Box Office, but her mother fell sick and Sandra returned to Charleston to take care of her. The adjustment to Charleston after Los Angeles, a city that hummed with energy, where she had had a career at the cutting edge of the next century, had been arduous, because she had hardly thought about slavery before. Coming home after all these years, she found something in the atmosphere of Charleston that frightened her.

As we sit on the elegant old veranda, the overhead lights turn on in the narrow street beneath us, and cars and passersby cast mysterious crooked shadows across the building on the other side. To my eyes, the city is intriguing and lovely—filled with the relics of its history, but to Sandra, Charleston in the 1990s feels like a throwback to a time when her people were slaves.

"Everyone is very happy here," she says softly. "The whites are very happy because the blacks still know their place, and there is not the terrible violence that exists in other cities. And the blacks *are* very much in their place here, in the most subservient ways. I am finding that the older people are still very insecure about where the boundaries are with whites.

"I had a happy childhood here. African Americans owned restaurants and stores, so even though you were excluded from certain things, you had a community. In the sixties and seventies I saw black Charlestonians come together and fight discrimination on all levels. But there is none of that anymore. No one even speaks about injustice. They just accept it. And the racism is deep, very deep. I have two degrees, and I had trouble finding this low-level, minimum-wage job. And I am the only black person I know in this kind of community work."

It is dark now, and I can barely make out the contours of her face as we sit side by side, but her words speak of tense wonder at the strange feel of her birthplace so many years after the terrible times ended. "There is a frightening sense of oldness here," she says, almost whispering. "I'd say that Charleston reminds me of a plantation, or of how I imagine plantation life: the white people doing well, enjoying the luxuries and the fun aspects of the city, and the black people trying to make it from day to day with little other than their church life as recreation. Because 'culture' here is seen as white. Go to a concert; you will not see a black face, because people do not feel comfortable there. If they do go—as I did once—they will be stared at by the whites and *also* criticized by blacks for 'trying to be white.' What I'm trying to say, in a way that may be hard for you to grasp, is that there is still a sort of slave mentality in this city. I can feel it in my bones."

Coming home awakened other atavistic memories. Sandra is convinced that the streets of the city and the rooms of the mansion where she works harbour ghosts. She looks at me hesitantly, possibly to determine my level of scepticism, before confiding that the spirits of the slaves who once lived in this house are still present. Her environment in Los Angeles was bright and new, but this place is haunted by the moans of slave ancestors. When she first returned, she had a temporary job in the old Exchange Building next to the port, which was the place where the slaves were brought. There is, she says, a dungeon in the basement that tourists never see. She couldn't stay in the place and quit after just a few days.

The past feels too close, too menacing and too unmediated. Ancestral memory hovers in the shadows of her city.

On March 4, 1865, one thousand black children descended upon the first Charleston school ever to welcome their presence. The Civil War had reached a bloody close, the Southern Confederates had lost and a Northerner named James Redpath had been appointed superintendent of public education in the city. Much of the funding for the revised Charleston school system came from the American Missionary Association (AMA), an organization that helped prepare freed slaves for a life in society. In 1868, the AMA supported and staffed the Avery Institute on Bull Street, which was founded as a centre for teacher training and a high school for advanced students. (Most teachers and students came from the "free person of colour" class and had already received a basic education.)

The academic standards of the Avery Institute were high, and its graduates eventually taught all over the state, once blacks were allowed to do so. (Until the 1930s, only whites could teach in most South Carolina locales, even in the black schools.) Eventually the Avery was incorporated into the College of Charleston and became a major archival repository for local African-American history.[28] When the PBS network needed materials relating to South Carolina for a televised series on slavery, the Avery was where its researchers headed.

The Avery is mounting an exhibition on slavery, and I have an appointment with the archivist and curator, Sherman Pyatt. I walk up elegant broad stairs: the Bull Street building is another of Charleston's lovely old mansions. Pyatt is waiting: he is a dignified-looking man of forty or so, with a rather formal manner. This is the first major exhibition on the subject ever presented in Charleston, he says, and the point the museum wants to stress is that slavery was a planned, structured business. "It would have been easy for us to present just a room full of shackles and other devices—we have tons of them, and we do show some—but we wanted to go deeper and to do it as objectively as possible."

Upstairs in the gallery, the business of slavery couldn't have been plainer. The shackles are there—leg irons in different sizes for adults and children, an anklet with a key and numbered slave tags worn by individuals who were hired out by their masters. There are ship manifests detailing incoming cargo marked "herbs, spices and slaves," and papers indicating slave ownership: one document lists expenditures and income, including the sale of a female slave for 140 pounds sterling, and an insurance policy for $1,100 taken out on two females. There is also a small wooden chair, which has been included in the exhibition to help the visitor understand relationships: though built for an adult, it was child-size, because a slave's chair was never to be as high as a white person's chair. A slave looked up. I think about Alexis de Tocqueville's insight into the crafting of the slave persona: he noted that slave owners had forged regulations of an "intellectual" nature to erode self-esteem and secure their power.

A propped-up copy of the *Illustrated London News* depicts the Charleston slave market in 1856. In this scene, the slaves are being sold behind the Custom House, and the transaction is invisible from the street. "By 1856," Pyatt explains, "the debate over slavery was so heated that some owners did not want to be seen doing this. There was a sense that it was not right. It didn't stop them, because the economy was more important, but many people were starting to worry about it."

What I'm getting is the "basic tour," but I have a sense that Pyatt might say more under less formal circumstances, so I ask for another meeting. Two days later, I am back at the institute, and this time we sit alone in a quiet room. Now he tells me that to have curated this exhibition on slavery is a personal milestone in his life—that of recovering black history, understanding it in the context of its times and seeing it as an integral part of the American experience: the same quest Unita Blackwell had described so passionately.

But what is "history" in the 1990s? Pyatt and I both know that the discipline—once understood as a pristine, value-free repository of unarguable truth—has become a battleground of competing claims and that the push to insert the black story into the mainstream represents certain pockets of self-interest. Important material is being uncovered, he says, including the realization that in the years following Emancipation, the long-suppressed intellectual energies of many former slaves had exploded into creativity. But underpinning the emerging black narratives is the desire to salvage pride. "Afrocentric" history is looking for ways to reconnect American blacks with Africa in order to counter the entrenched, often subliminal, belief that the "dark continent" had produced little of value, and that African Americans have been "civilized" in America. (At the extreme reaches of this logic, slavery can be viewed as a benevolent institution.)

But if traditional Western history often denigrated Africa, Afrocentric history romanticized it hopelessly. Egypt was posited as the black rootstock of Western civilization and African philosophers were said to have predated the ancient Greeks, while still others claimed that white Europeans had "stolen" African civilization. Established scholarship repudiated these claims on grounds of insufficient or non-existent evidence, but for the purveyors of Afrocentrist revisionist history, working in a climate where all traditional claims of objectivity in scholarship were viewed as suspect, the white historian's response was rooted in bias.

"I want to illuminate the facts of African-American history," Sherman Pyatt tells me. "We have changed the way we name ourselves from 'coloured,' to 'Negro,' to calling ourselves 'black' and 'African American,' and finally we have identified with the continent of Africa. Giving ourselves a base of African-American history and culture works as a foundation to let young people know they can do things they might have been told they can't do—not to let themselves be told they can't become a mathematician or a physician. I think all children in this country have to begin to think more critically about these issues of colour." But he has rejected the distortions, insisting that his exhibition contextualize the institution of slavery on the basis of real evidence. "We are not revisionists," he says, "the Avery Institute is not a political platform, and we look carefully at credentials before we invite speakers to come here. People may not like it, but we present facts. We collect the primary materials and hope people will use them for research."

He thinks he understands what lies beneath the wishful narratives of Afrocentric history. "I have yet to find a psychological study about the impact of the institution of slavery on people," he says in a lowered voice. "About how one who was considered chattel, non-human, had to, and *still* has to, constantly try to convince another group of people that I am human." He has unconsciously switched to the first-person singular. "People sometimes don't understand that when a sportscaster recently said about a black athlete, 'Boy, he runs like a horse,' then referred to the white athlete as intelligent—well, that sends shock waves. I think we haven't *started* to look at the ramifications of dehumanization. You saw the ship's inventory that lists a person like a bag of spices and herbs? There is not a face or mind attached to that. It's a piece of cargo. You know, I think it was [W. E. B.] Du Bois who talked about oneness and twoness, that there is a constant battle within the black person to strive for oneness—oneness meaning that he is human, twoness, that he is perceived as not being totally human. The black person somehow strives to prove that he is human and it is an ongoing battle within. Even today."

Will he talk to me about his personal history? He is educated. Did he come from the mulatto class of "free persons of colour" who emerged from the Civil War with a head start on the others?

"No," he says, there was no privilege in his background. He was raised by three women: his mother, his aunt and his grandmother. They were all domestic workers. His grandfather, who passed away when he was an infant, had been a cook on a riverboat. When Pyatt was a child he sometimes went to work with his grandmother and his mother, to help out in the yard. It was exciting to see how white people lived. They had a brick house with real hardwood floors and wooden stairs. The mistress of the house liked Pyatt; when he got older, she told his mother that she was considering him for a position with the family as a gardener or chauffeur. There is only mild bitterness in his voice: "The white family had two daughters about my age, and it was known that they would go to college. My position was also determined."

Pyatt had plans he didn't talk about then. It was the late 1960s, and there were new opportunities. He became the first person in his family to finish high school: "My mother had quit school in ninth grade, and my grandmother in Grade 2. Children had to come home and work the cotton crops for six months of the year."

"Was it the civil rights movement that gave you a sense of possibilities?" I ask him.

"In a way. But in my community I really didn't know what the word *poverty* meant, because I had no meaningful comparison. I knew that I was sometimes hungry and that when the lights were turned off because you couldn't pay the bill, you used kerosene lamps. But I also knew that there were people in my community who had graduated from black colleges and that their children were saying they were also going to college. I knew a pharmacist who had his own pharmacy, where we would go to get medicine. I knew a plumber who had his own company. I knew a postman, and when I was little I wanted to be like him because of the uniform. I knew the teachers who taught me. They also lived in the community. Then I heard some kids talking about becoming physical therapists. They had some magazines that were mainly about white people, but they exposed me to something different. So, yes, the civil rights movement helped, but I had role models even living in that segregated community."

He completed a bachelor's degree in history at a small black college, then a master's in library science at Indiana College in Bloomington, where he had his first classroom contact with white students. Being with whites was a new experience, "like entering another world and waiting for something to happen, or trying to plan, saying to myself, I have to be at the top of this class because there are going to be people here who expect me to fail. I thought I had to find out who were the students who didn't want me there and keep an eye on them to make sure not to get into the same group for study sessions and seminars. It took me a semester to adjust, but one thing that really helped was leaving South Carolina. I found that there were people of colour at Indiana who spoke Spanish and had some of the same problems I had, as far as being a member of a minority. I found that when I was able to bond with people, the world became bigger, and I no longer felt alone in the same way."

"You're middle class now and a museum archivist. How has this changed your sense of yourself?"

"It is gratifying to work here and bring in the collections about the African-American experience, but when I look at the materials it saddens me terribly to see how black folks in this state and this city have been treated. On the other hand, it's uplifting to see the resilience. People survived. This gives me hope that I can survive too."

I am surprised: "What do you mean?"

"I mean I experienced growing up without being one of the free persons of colour in this city, and going to segregated schools and movie theatres, and sitting at the back of the bus, and not getting an explanation, only being told by my family, 'That's the law.' You learn to live with that: the law. Your family gives you instructions about how to conduct yourself when you go into stores. Everyone knew that if you tried something on you had to buy it, because that store wasn't going to keep those shoes or that piece of clothing if they had touched your skin. You knew that when you went into a store you had to go right to the area you wanted, because as soon as you walked in a clerk would walk behind you constantly, asking what you were looking for. We all went through that, but I look at the materials that come in here and I say, We did not commit suicide or kill folks because of that. It actually surprises me that we haven't had a higher suicide rate."

An educated man of relative wealth, he had left the ghetto, but uneasy feelings still accompanied that move. Unita Blackwell had talked to me about people like Sherman Pyatt—those who made it out, then were held up as evidence of other people's failure—but Pyatt says that for responsible black men, there is no guilt-free escape. "Someone like me moves to the suburbs and gets a better car, but for everyone who does that, two or three people fall by the wayside. And they could be your old neighbours. So there is this gap within the black community between those who have made it to the middle class and those who have not. There is a lot of pressure on professional black people to give volunteer time, and maybe one out of five will read to children in the elementary schools, for instance. But people have their own lives, and a lot say, 'Nobody helped me and I made it.'"

He worked with one boy for several years, and they still keep in touch, but the need, he says, is endless: the ghettos have been stripped of their old leadership—the male professionals who once lived there, then moved away to the suburbs. The move into the middle class did not necessarily derail fear: "I think about the fact that my son may end up in the wrong community when he is driving my car, my middle-class car, and another black boy shoots him." Or, on the other side of the class divide: "I may have a medical practice or be a lawyer, but I still don't know when my son is going to call me late one night to say he has been arrested because he is driving my car. The police have an idea that African Americans should not be in certain kinds of cars because they don't have the money, so they are likely to stop the driver. I have had to prepare my son to handle such things in the same way my family prepared me to go into a department store."

Thinking about our conversation later in the evening, I remember something similar that happened a very long time ago. In fifteenth-century Spain, when society was organized along religious lines, Jews were offered a way of avoiding persecution—by converting to Catholicism. Although there was coercion at the beginning, enhanced opportunity eventually became the major factor in the decision to "move out," so the most talented members of the community left the others behind. But the converts never did assimilate entirely; they were still called Jews by Christians who had trouble accepting them and reviled by their unconverted families and friends, who beseeched them to return "home." African Americans who benefited from the civil rights movement and the sacrifice of leaders such as Martin Luther King Jr. were faced with like dilemmas. They were still "black" in the eyes of the white majority: that hadn't really changed, but the old communal solidarity—bred, in part, by segregation—had been shattered, and they faced rejection from those they had left behind. Tony Hall's would-be apology for slavery couldn't touch this complexity. "Reconciliation" would have to be black-on-black, as well as black-on-white and white-on-black.

I think about Unita Blackwell. There ought to have been a universe between the worries of her depressed community in Mayersville, Mississippi, and that of Sherman Pyatt, M.A., archivist and curator at the renowned Avery Institute in Charleston. But there wasn't. The legacy of slavery and race crossed all lines.

Elayna Shakur, who was born into the middle class, has agreed to meet me, and I take a long taxi ride to her home on a beachside road. These are the flat lowlands that are periodically overwhelmed when the hurricanes blow in from the Atlantic Ocean, the houses that are flooded, the places where people sometimes drown. The big, wide windows of her house open to the sea; the air tastes of salt.

Elayna is exploring a return to "blackness." She is tall and very light skinned, the genetic outcome of a great-great-grandmother who was the daughter of the master and a slave. At Emancipation, this woman loaded her thirteen children on a covered wagon and left the South for Ohio. She had a "house-slave mentality," says Elayna, which means "she imitated the white family." Most of her children were of mixed race. Elayna remembers asking her own mother why great-great-grandmother didn't marry any of the fathers of her children, and that her mother replied, "It just wasn't done." "She didn't explain that it *couldn't* be done."

Striving for white was a characteristic of her family. They lived in a white neighbourhood, and when Elayna's mother brought her future husband home to meet her parents, her father took her aside and said, "We're trying to *lighten* this family, not darken it!" Everyone expressed contempt towards dark-skinned blacks. One day, a visiting aunt told Elayna that what she disliked most about Charleston was the presence of "so many black niggers." Elayna tells me the remark wounded her like a knife. "You must have a lot of conflict," she said to her aunt. "I do," she confessed.

Naturally, the family was also the object of racism. Elayna's father wanted to be an architect, but *his* father said, "Have you ever heard of a coloured architect? Take a commercial course." He did.

When she reached marrying age, Elayna chose a white man; her family had steered her in that direction without ever saying so. He was a minister, someone committed to cross-cultural tolerance, but his congregation did not share his openness, and he lost his job. They moved to Illinois and rented an apartment, but after a week the landlord found out Elayna was black and cancelled the lease. So they moved to a university community, where her husband found a teaching job. She started a branch of the Panel of American Women, which was composed of blacks, whites, Catholics and Jews. For years they met once a week and gave talks about what it felt like to experience prejudice. Elayna says she never actually spoke; she preferred to be the moderator, to stay out of the limelight. Very few people were entirely sure of her origins, and that was the way she wanted it.

Her house feels like a summer cottage from my childhood, and she, inexplicably, feels like an old friend. We sit on the couch, feet propped up on the coffee table, and drink tea together, as she tells me of her odyssey from "white" to "black," and what it means to her memory of race and sense of identity. A Jamaican housekeeper put her in touch with black people by taking her to West Indian events, opening up a universe that had been inaccessible. There, she met a black man who had never wanted to be white. Never had she known such a person. She fell in love with him, or rather, she says, with what he represented. Her marriage to the white minister came to an end.

She and the man went to Canada, where Elayna thought she could leave what she calls "the racist air" of the United States behind. She says that crossing the international border at Windsor was a tangible relief, and that the West Indian community in London, Ontario, helped her learn, or "remember," as she put its, what it was to be a black person. But there were far too many white people in Canada for someone intent on exploring "blackness." She thought she needed to know who she was under all the accumulated layers of her personal history—at home.

A return to the United States was inevitable ("I'm an American; I *had* to find a place here"), but this time she chose Charleston because there were so many dark-skinned people in the city who issued from families that had never interbred with whites. She thought these pure blacks, the ones from the Low Country and the Sea Islands, who sold local baskets and crafts in the marketplace, carried the least bitterness of any blacks she had ever known. They didn't want to be white, and they didn't hate whites because whites wouldn't accept them. When they smiled, Elayna thought they meant it. Although she did not have many white friends in Charleston, Elayna, unlike Sandra, liked the way people of different races interacted here. "People in the South have lived together for centuries, under troubled conditions, yes, but they know each other and there's a graciousness that pervades relationships. I felt more *overt* hostility in Ohio."

She wanted to enter "blackness" as a way of purging herself of family attitudes that had been built, she says, on the rejection of self: "I am learning that the only place I can be at home in America is inside myself," she tells me. On the other hand, the ocean-front neighbourhood she lives in is middle class and all white, and I think that in spite of her stated commitments, this environment may actually feel most familiar to her.

Elayna sees racism in America as a collective weight very few black people are able to throw off, but she thinks she must learn to "forgive" the society that did not nurture her because if she does not the inner conflict will destroy her. "We have to go beyond race without forgetting it; I mean, differences should not be ignored, as in a pretense of colour-blindness; they should be enjoyed as an expression of national diversity. Personally, I would like to be seen as a black woman, perhaps even a beautiful black woman, certainly as a human being in a black body. I can accept my difference now; for example, I no longer desire to have a white lover. I think it is possible to go beyond race and still have a preference about who you wish to be with on an intimate level."

She desperately wants Tony Hall's proposal for a congressional apology to go through, because she is positive it would be symbolically healing for black Americans. "It is so hard to forgive when there has been no apology, and some of us have so much anger buried inside—I know I do. I think an apology would start the process of dissolving our defences. Oprah [Winfrey] once said that until the majority heals enough to know what the minority has gone through in this country, we blacks will not be able to recover."

"Isn't that saying that your recovery depends on whites?"

"Yes, and obviously we can't wait for that to happen. It would help enormously to have an apology, which, after all, is only a recognition that wrongs were done, but we can't wait. I know I can't wait."

The driver pulls up to a storefront on a street near the centre of the city where Elayna's son-in-law has a business. She arranged this meeting for me, to my great delight, because Sherman Evans, who is thirty-five years old, is determined to make his mark on the world, and I had told her I was determined to meet him. Sherman has seized the most potent symbol of Southern history and transformed it into an interracial clothing logo, of all things. The emblem is a version of none other than the Confederate flag, under which battalions of Southerners fought to defend their slave inheritance. Despised by blacks, who see it as the most powerful emblem of their oppression, the flag is still idealized by a remnant of whites who have not forgotten the glory days.

His office at the back of the store is stuffed with clothing samples and FedEx boxes—a sign, I suppose, that he is successfully distributing his wares. He is small in stature, with prematurely greying hair but youthful in every way. Bright-eyed, optimistic and articulate.

Back in 1992, he and his friends were trying to publicize a fledgling rap group they had put together, and they wanted to present themselves candidly as coming from the South. "There is a major stigma about associating oneself with the South, and we wanted to overcome that," he says. "Like, when I went to school in Atlanta one year and I'd ask people where they were from, and the first thing they would say was, 'I was *born* in Michigan, or Detroit, but my family moved here to Atlanta.' Yeah? When? So they'd say, 'Well, I was, like, about two months old.'

"I mean, lots of African Americans are in denial about what happened here in the South, and we wanted to break through that. So we started thinking about it, and we said, 'Hey, those people are right when they say this is Ellis Island for us, so there shouldn't be any shame and we shouldn't want to cut that period of slavery and Jim Crow out of our lives like it didn't happen.'" Then it occurred to Sherman and his partners that after all these decades, *they* might be destined to reconcile the races in America. "We said, 'Let's tell the truth about the past and the way we want to see the future.' So we superimposed the red, green and black African-American colours on the Confederate flag and, wow, it just jumped out. We said, '*This* is our album cover!' It really hit me. You know, this frees us all from being victims or oppressors, because blacks can't go on feeling as if we're owed something and whites can't go on as if they're guilty because of something that happened all those years back. I think of Gandhi when he said, 'Be the change that you want to see.' We named our company NuSouth because that's what we want to be. A whole new way of dealing with the past but looking to the future."

The day they tried to make a demo tape, the would-be rappers were paralysed by shyness, and the company never got off the ground. But Evans and his partners did not despair. They thought about the logo—the transformed Confederate flag—and quickly decided it would look very good on T-shirts and other articles of clothing. Under the "new" flag they added the words "For the sons and daughters of former slaves. For the sons and daughters of former slave owners. Threads that connect us. Words that free us."

Evans was sure he was doing something of historical importance, and he convinced others. Raymond Winbush, the director of race relations at Fisk University in Nashville, Tennessee, compared their logo to the origins of Christianity by claiming that the adoption of a hated symbol by a persecuted people gives them the power to transcend it. "The cross was initially a symbol of oppression for Christians, but Christians adopted that symbol to make it something glorious. The Stars and Bars for blacks is odious, and NuSouth took it and reinvented it," Winbush wrote. NuSouth packaged this heady endorsement with its advertising, since in the United States there may be no stronger ratification than one that appears to capture the approval of Christ himself. Then Sherman went to meet a man in Nashville who had recently erected a monument honouring Major-General Nathan Bedford Forrest, who led Confederate troops at the so-called Massacre of Fort Pillow, Tennessee, where some three hundred black soldiers were put to death after they surrendered.[29] Bedford Forrest was also a founder of the Ku Klux Klan. Evans spent several hours with this individual (he headed a branch of the

League of the South, a states'-rights group that believes the South is still being governed illegally by the federal government) and was impressed, because the man told him that Forrest had initially founded the Klan just after the Civil War to help the families of dead Confederate soldiers. "He said it was a good group that went bad much later and it was the good part he was commemorating. I was glad to hear that."

I interrupt the rapid flow of his talk. "That was enough for you?"

"Well, he was sharing things with me. That was his reality. I wasn't there to debate him. I'm interested in the future. He offered me several million dollars to buy out NuSouth, so I guess he saw the commercial promise. But I turned him down. If I make money, that's good, but I want to do something revolutionary with the message."

So they ran off some promotional T-shirts with the transformed flag pasted on the front, and when a teenage girl wore one of them to school, the principal suspended her because some of the other students complained. "Well, this was a high school where the kids were known for wearing the Confederate flag—the real one—all over their clothing, and where some of the white kids wore shirts that said, 'The original boyz in the hood—KKK' or '100% cotton. You picked it.' Like there was a lot of in-your-face racism in that school, but no one was told to take *those* shirts off. So we really took off because MTV came in, and CNN did a piece, and there was a big debate about whether her human rights had been violated. She wore it again the next day and so did twenty other students we gave shirts to. Beginning of the day, they were all gathered up and taken into the auditorium and threatened with expulsion. Everyone changed the shirts except the first girl—they were all scared—but it was amazing how many other kids supported her indirectly, the whites as well as the blacks. Like people really understood the message."

Sherman and his partners had to ask family and friends for capital investment because the banks were notably leery about the venture: one loan officer asked, "Why should I think you're not going to take this money and buy BMWs and Mercedeses with it?" Later, when they advertised in *GQ*, they received supportive letters from whites and blacks, but also a number of anti-semitic letters from blacks who simply assumed NuSouth was Jewish-owned. "I say dammit, it's really unbelievable," says Sherman. "If people see an ad in a good magazine they somehow assume that blacks aren't clever enough, so someone smarter must be bankrolling us. The anti-semitism told us that some blacks think like that. It's like African Americans think of themselves as the bottom of the food chain and they can't believe someone like me would put ads in *GQ*. I had one guy say to me, 'You're urban, you're street.' So I say, when I was born I was told I was African American, then we were black, then this 'urban' came up, and recently it's 'street.' And I said, 'What is *street*? Can you please tell me that? Doesn't sound good to me! Sounds kinda rough!'" His patter is rat-a-tat, like a stand-up comedian's. "I mean, just because I'm a man of colour doesn't mean I'm *street!* Everyone can wear our stuff! Can only people who have horses wear Polo shirts? People keep saying our competition is restricted to the black community. No! Our competition is Polo and Tommy [Hilfiger]."

Advertising in *GQ*, since it is an upscale publication for men, clashed with stereotypes American blacks had internalized about themselves: first, that the mainstream, high-income world of fashion was "white," and, second, that blacks were turning their backs on their culture by attempting to break through. Highly paid sports stars were one thing—they could make millions—but other worlds were beyond the reach of desire. Such discouragement had not stopped Sherman. Fortunately, he possesses a strong streak of humour and an ingrained sense of self (at one point in our conversation he blurted out, "If I were any happier I'd be twins").

I can't think of another country in the world where the launch of a commercial product might be seen as a metaphor for redemption and transfiguration. "We're a hot brand, we're a sexy brand. Our brand is going to rule the market and *mean* something," he announces to me with his contagious enthusiasm. "Like Nike says, *Just Do It*!"

Like Nike says? Once upon a time, philosophy was written in books and transmitted in learned symposia, but for Sherman Evans, and perhaps for others of his generation, the transformative act is born from smart advertising on behalf of a marketable commodity. In this he is as American as Martha Stewart and Hollywood.

"What is the *message* of Tommy Hilfiger?" he asks me rhetorically as I pack up to leave. "They have none. *Our* message is the most important thing that has happened in the South!"

His hopes for racial reconciliation by means of a message on a T-shirt surprise and delight me, and his enthusiasm does slash through the dense wood separating blacks and whites. On the other hand, his openness is disconcerting: he had met, and liked, a man who honoured the founder of the Ku Klux Klan, and this man had convinced him that he was merely commemorating the early, non-violent days of that racist movement.

Did he know that the Klan had turned ugly within two short years of its founding in 1866? Or that its members sang the following ditty?

No rations have we, but the flesh of man—
And love niggers best, the Ku Klux Klan;
We catch 'em alive and roast 'em whole,
Then hand 'em around with a sharpened pole.

He was not a historian, nor was he inclined to scepticism. Sherman wanted to reconcile race and American history. Even with the Klan that hated him still.

There were plenty of people in the Old South who would have shivered at the thought of a black man altering the sacred Confederate flag, and I was about to meet one of them. He ran a hunting lodge on his old plantation (it had been in the family for nine generations), and he was known to engage his guests in provocative conversation about the truth of the Civil War.

I set out by car to drive the 130 kilometres from Charleston to Broxton Bridge plantation on a two-lane highway bordered by cotton fields. After several false turns and stops to ask directions, I finally find the road into the plantation: a track lined with moss-heavy live oaks that parallel a stream through the cotton fields. The plantation house looms in a darkly shaded vale of ancient overgrown trees.

Gerry Varn comes to the door to meet me. He is one of the tallest men I've ever stood beside—six feet, ten inches. When he puts his arm around his wife, Lib, the top of her head snuggles securely under the canopy of his armpit. They are a strange-looking couple in an isolated place.

The inside of the house smells musty from too many years of subtropical humidity and overworked air conditioning. Water stains blotch the ceiling of the large living room; the walls are covered with cheap wood panelling reminiscent of rec rooms in the 1950s; and braid rugs lie scattered on the wood floor. Deer antlers and stuffed pheasants culled from hunting expeditions decorate the walls and the mantelpiece. There are bunches of antique-looking artificial flowers in vases. Nothing seems to have changed here in at least forty years. The huge original fireplace is still in use, and ceiling fans from another era help circulate the air.

I sit down on a torn, colonial-style couch and am offered a welcome drink of iced tea. Varn sprawls in his chair, his long legs draped in khaki.

He looks at me, smiles and drawls, "Some people say that we are backward because we live the way it used to be in some ways. Well, I enjoy running water as much as you do." I smile back. Had he noticed me taking in the room?

He has a set speech on the Civil War and states' rights and wastes no time before launching into his subject. "When they put this country together, our forefathers really understood what Lord Acton said, that power corrupts and absolute power corrupts absolutely. Those were *fabulous* words. So the founding fathers of the United States of America decided to have a Constitution in order to keep too much power from being in any person's hands—you see, they were well ahead of their time—and they envisioned separation of powers in executive, judicial and legislative branches, and they wanted local self-government." The words pour from him in a well-rehearsed torrent. "And then what happened is that King George did *not* make peace with the United States but made peace with the individual colonies, the individual states, the thirteen different colonies. So that meant that the state was the master and the federal government was the servant. South Carolina was a free, independent and sovereign nation. *Sovereign* means they stood on their own, you know. And then the states decided to get together in order to defend themselves better. You see, here it is—Article 1, Section 8, the preamble to the Constitution. You see that? In Section 8, it lists eighteen things the federal government can do. Believe me, if you can get a copy of the Constitution it will be a real experience for you. It says they can build post offices and roads, take care of our common defence, borrow money on credit, have standards for all the states, you know what I mean? An inch is the same thing for all states, that sort of thing—I can't remember all the others—but all the rest of the powers go back to the states—*all* of them. I personally believe very much in a limited government."

Bizarre as this tirade sounds, he is expressing a familiar (though in his case, exaggerated) political posture; for while the American Creed was infused with Enlightenment values of equality and moral justice, it also embodied unusual attitudes to government that shaped the American political experience from the start. As the political scientist Samuel Huntington once put it, "The values of the Creed are . . . basically anti-government and anti-authority. Whereas other ideologies legitimate established authority and institutions, the American Creed serves to delegitimate any hierarchical, coercive, authoritarian structures, including

American ones. . . .[30] Opposition to power, and suspicion of government as the most dangerous embodiment of power, are the central themes of American political thought."[31]

Varn applied that tenet of American political thinking to his own region and to the War between the States. For him, the Civil War remained a living event, one that might have taken place last week, or last month, perhaps, because in 1865 his own family property had been the site of a battle between Union soldiers and twenty-seven hundred Confederate troops. In a brochure he gives to all his hunting guests, he describes the horrors of that war, how Northerners had sacked and razed the countryside as they passed through, even robbing blacks of food and blankets. He has made a point of including slaves among the victims of the Union troops in order to convince his readers that the Civil War was *not* fought over slavery, despite what everyone else thinks. "The [true] Confederate cause was *against* big government, *for* constitutional government and *for* states' rights," he writes, echoing ideas with a very old pedigree, "and . . . when General Robert E. Lee of the Confederate forces and General Ulysses S. Grant of the Union forces met at Appomattox to arrange the surrender, one of them owned slaves and the other did not. . . . *General Grant* owned three slaves. . . . So we are hard pressed . . . to perpetuate the myth that the primary issue of the war was slavery."

There is no denying the passion of the long, gangly man talking so earnestly into my tape recorder—and occasionally asking me to check whether it is on and working properly. Gerry Varn has a message to deliver to the world, and as it emerges it has various strands, one of which is the notion that the Democratic Party is "socialist." "Socialist means government ownership of everything," he explains helpfully. Another strand is Christian fundamentalism, which he opposes to the putative socialism of the Democratic party: "The Scriptures don't go against the people owning private property, and my thinking is governed by what the Scriptures say." A third strain combines related conspiracy theories, at least one of which is coloured by hoary anti-semitism. Seemingly without connection, he suddenly asks, "Have you ever wondered what role the Rothschilds played in the War between the States?" I admit that I have not. He explains. "You see, the Rothschilds started off as goldsmiths and they got to be so vastly rich that they got to the point where they loaned money to governments. Then they would find two countries next to one another and create a war with some of their agents, then run a lucrative smuggling business with the tacit approval of both sides. They just about bilked Europe and England dry. So Rothschild looked over here at America and thought what a vast country this was—so many wonderful natural resources—and he asked what he could do to get that. There was Mexico on the south and Canada on the north, but Canada didn't have many people, and Mexico wasn't strong. So Rothschild and his agents—J. P. Morgan was his agent over here—just decided to cut the U.S. in half and create a war. It was a real conspiracy."

I inquire about the source of this dazzling news. "Read *The Creature from Jekyll Island* by G. W. Griffin," he says excitedly. "I've been in his house in California. Wonderful fellow, very knowledgeable. It's an exposé of the Federal Reserve system, showing that it is really a cartel. People have insider knowledge and make fortunes."

I am tempted to dismiss him as an isolated crackpot, except that he is beginning to lay out some disturbingly familiar pieces of American extremist ideology, and I am thinking I have stepped into unexpected territory. I had anticipated an encounter with someone who would defend states' rights as the basis for the Civil War, an argument that can be defended by reasonable people as a partial truth; I did not come prepared for a lateral shift into the Word of God, or the socialism of the Democratic Party,[32] or Jewish-banker conspiracies, or government plans to bilk the unsuspecting public. I had recently been reading about the work of the Southern Poverty Law Center (SPLC) in Montgomery, Alabama, in preparation for a visit there. The SPLC, a non-profit, civil rights organization that has successfully sued the Ku Klux Klan for millions of dollars as restitution for attacks on people and property, also gathers intelligence about extremist activities, which is shared with the FBI. In recent years they have stepped up their research on anti-government, anti-semitic, anti-black militias, especially since the 1995 bombing in Oklahoma City in which 168 people died.

I try out a key phrase from the "Patriot movement," which is the all-encompassing name most of these groups give themselves. "Ever heard of the New World Order?" I ask. Varn stops short and looks at me with new interest.

"Well, I'm glad you brought that up," he drawls, then orders his wife to look for a publication he wants me to see. While we wait, he expounds: "Yes, I believe there is a Satanistic movement to keep this New World Order and One World Government going. Been going for years and years—probably started with Satan, I don't really know, I reckon I know as much as the Lord wants me to know. Back in the eighteenth century there were the Illuminati. They were a secret Masonic group set on world domination back in those days. Well, one of their couriers with a satchel attached to his wrist was killed, and when they examined the satchel they found a list of all the group's evil objectives." Varn continues his story until he gets to the truly secret part. Then he asks me to turn off the tape recorder. "You see," he whispers conspiratorially, "the courier had had a woman killed to protect the real objectives of the organization from getting out. It was just like Edward Kennedy and Chappaquiddick—he had her killed." He leans back and narrows his eyes with satisfaction.

The "courier with a satchel" story triggers a memory of my own, because, while researching an earlier book, I had come across a like tale. When the bubonic plague swept Europe in the fourteenth century, King Philip of France accused the Jews of receiving plague poisons from their "grand master" in Toledo and infecting the wells. The poisons were said to have been extracted from venomous scorpions, spiders and toads, which were powdered, then carried all over Europe in leather satchels. When the rumour spread, the Jews were massacred. How odd it seemed to be alive six hundred years later, listening to someone apply "facts" of a similar, premodern nature to the contemporary world. The need to invent, then demonize, an enemy has not diminished.

Lib arrives with the magazine: it is called *The New American*, and this issue, dated September 16, 1996, contains a special report titled "Conspiracy for Global Control." I read it later that evening; it contains advice on how to battle the New World Order and "the Godless Conspiracy seeking to enchain us in world government," as well as a history of the conspiracy and the continuing world domination by Communists. The enforcement wing of this would-be conspiracy are the elites of the United Nations, the Council on Foreign Relations, the Trilateral Commission, the Federal Reserve and of course the international bankers. The outcome of this "one world" they all conspire to bring into being will be something called "internationalism": the end of American sovereignty.

Varn explains that he bought one hundred copies of *The New American* to give to "intelligent people." Proselytizing is clearly his vocation, and stitched into this airtight vision of the world are his religious beliefs. "According to the Book of Revelation, Satan is the beast and the false prophet. Now the beast is the One World Government, and the false prophet is the One World Church," he tells me.

"Are you connected to the Christian Identity Church?" I ask, throwing another element of the Patriot movement into the mix. The Christian Identity Church is a "post-millennial" theology that has identified the year 2000 as the hour of the final Battle of Armageddon. But believers do not think for a moment that God will be content to gather up good Christians on the day of reckoning and happily whisk them into heaven: they consider it their duty to prepare for the Second Coming by fighting a war to cleanse the world of Satan's forces. The Southern Poverty Law Center has marked the Christian Identity Church as dangerous, claiming it has permeated the entire Patriot movement, including the Ku Klux Klan and the militias.

There is a long silence. "Never heard of it," Varn finally replies. "I was born in the Methodist Church, but we left it over the civil rights movement. They were preaching the social gospel rather than salvation. Jesus does not want us to be a political pressure group to try to get legislation passed. Liberalism is taking away from the word of God, and Satan is active in this to destroy the word of God. So we formed our own church and affiliated with the Southern Baptist denomination. We own our own property and we hire our own pastor. This means we can control him to a greater degree."

I ask about the slaves that once lived on this family plantation, and here, too, his ideas reflect another time. The plantation had slaves, he acknowledges, but by the time the Civil War came, slavery was becoming unprofitable. "A lot of people say that when somebody's a slave, they don't have any rights, but they don't really understand. Sometimes slaves would be bought for $1,000 apiece, and when you put that in perspective, $1.00 then is worth 2.5 cents today. So today that slave would be worth $40,000. And isn't it just logical that you're not going to abuse something you paid $40,000 for? You don't pay that much for an automobile, and you certainly don't abuse that! The other thing is, they gave these people free health care. The doctor came and checked them out every thirty days. Now a slave in Russia today—you know, in one of the gulags or something—that is one thing, five or six people in a tiny cell, no heat, sleeping on the floor, but these blacks were very much loved by their masters, like the extended family of the plantation owner. I know that when the plantation owner and his family butchered hogs, everybody, all the family, butchered hogs together. And planting the crops, I mean the gardens and things like that, they all did that together. They showed 'em how to do it, with the latest methods. Let me tell you, the talk about slavery as mean and vicious, that comes from people that don't know what they're talking about. Just like during that time of the civil rights movement, there's a lot of people trying to tell us what to do down here. We were getting along just fine down here, but those instigators wanted to come down and start things up. In earlier days those Northern liberals were the abolitionists. Same kinda people."

"Get this down," he orders, pointing at my tape recorder. "*The South did not own a slave ship*. They were all owned by people up in Rhode Island and Connecticut. So you see how hypocritical those folks really were?"

"Do blacks also think of slavery as benevolent?" I ask him.

"They don't know anything except what the NAACP tells them. You see, the black people are not our enemies. They are citizens, they have a soul just like we do. But they have the NAACP telling them about their heritage. And many of them don't even know who their daddy is!" He laughs out loud. "I'm not interested in their colour, but if someone is involved with the NAACP, they are our enemies. If you check the origin of the NAACP, most of them were Communists.

"I'm not justifying slavery. This is a wonderful country. It's wonderful to have freedom and things like that, and I'm glad they've got freedom now, just like I do. I'm only saying it wasn't that bad, not like Northern liberals say."

What angers him most is the appalling idea that anyone might ever apologize for slavery: "I apologize for things I've done, but I didn't do anything! They wouldn't be Americans if they hadn't been brought over here. They were treated as good as people in the sweatshops up north.

"In my own mind I feel that slavery saved people from being savages. I don't mean any disrespect, but they believed in human sacrifices, pretty horrid things, and they came over here and they were civilized by being involved with the people here who were Christians. If you are a Christian, you'll understand what I'm talking about."

He peers at me sternly, possibly wondering about the limits of my faith; or perhaps he is wondering whether he has gone too far, because he returns to the conspiracies of the New World Order: "I don't know whether I should have laid something so heavy on you if this is the first time you've heard about these things."

I assure him I can take the news.

We leave the house and climb into his pickup truck so he can show me the Civil War battlefield on the property. We drive across the fallow fields, then on to a dirt road with rut tracks, bordered by Southern pines and ancient overarching live oaks. He descends briefly to open a locked wooden gate, and we enter a jungle-like forest of thick trees, primitive ferns and hanging moss. The late-afternoon air is damp-hot and still. We get down from the truck; he reaches inside, takes out a small sickle with a long handle and begins to sweep the ground in front of him as we approach the narrow path into the woods. He says he is looking for poisonous snakes—water moccasins and rattlers—and black widow spiders.

We pick our way along a ridge built by the Confederate soldiers. To the right is a dark cypress swamp where tree trunks splayed like chickens' feet root in a still pool of water. He points to an old swimming hole "where hundreds of baptisms took place": the baptisms of newborns of both races and of adult slaves newly converted to the Christianity of their masters.

In 1865, in this primeval semidarkness of swamp and trailing vines and enervating heat, a crucial battle took place. When the gun dust settled, the Confederate forces of Varn's ancestors lay defeated. Here were the earth fortifications, still visible after all these years, and the graves of his grandfather and great-grandfather: weathered white headstones set into a mat of brown oak leaves that cover the ground.

We retrace our steps, climbing over logs and sinking into a cushion of curled leaves. He says that once he just missed stepping on a snake.

On the drive back to the plantation house, he pulls a small well-thumbed Bible from a pocket beside the driver's seat and reads aloud about the Mark of the Beast from the Book of Revelation. He says that "they" have planted computer chips in people so "we can all be tracked." Part of the international conspiracy to destroy right-thinking Americans.

"I hear some people are stockpiling arms," I murmur cautiously.

He looks at me closely. "Well, that is the day we will all have lost."

In addition to running a hunting lodge and growing a little cotton, he also manufactures fertilizer, "but *not* the kind explosives are made from!" he says, laughing at his joke.

In this remote forest shrine to the Confederate cause, nothing seems impossible.

Gerry Varn does not need to "remember" anything about his country's history, because past and present have not yet diverged. There is nothing to understand, certainly nothing to "reconcile." On Broxton Bridge plantation, the hands of the clock stopped centuries ago.

The black taxi driver who has come to take me to the airport looks familiar. Then I remember his name is Tony, and he's the same fellow who drove me to meet Elayna Shaku last week. Thinking I was a tourist, he was full of laughter and advice. Charleston was the best city in the southeast. He was born here, wouldn't think of living anywhere else. Did I like dancing? Ladies had free entry at a place he could recommend. Did I want to know where the good restaurants were?

This time I tell him that I have come here to explore the memory of slavery and the idea of apology. He swivels around in the driver's seat. His face is no longer jolly; it is filled with anger.

"My uncle Malcolm said the whole country should be put on trial, the whole country." He says this in the slow drawl of the region so that his words about Malcolm X, the original spokesman for Black Power, hang long in the air, like wisps of smoke that refuse to dissipate. "But *I* think the Americans have already apologized with the programs they made to help us. And they apologized through the murder of [J. F.] Kennedy. He paid the price for wanting to help black people. His whole family paid the price.

"But those slavers! They already had the Hebrew Bible and they saw that God told Moses to get his people out of there. So did they think they was God! That they could second-guess the Lord and start slavery again and go to another place and just grab people! That was the biggest kidnapping job in the history of the world!"

Whatever relief he has found has come from religion, he says. "I try to be like Jesus. I don't ask whose fault it is, just what I have contributed to making problems."

This would-be calm contrasts immediately with what he says next: "Young people—there's drugs everywhere. When I was younger, the drugs was only with the middle-class white kids, now it's the blacks, an' most of the leaders are selling drugs for the sake of survival. Like crack cocaine. It's gettin' worse. It's real bad. They can't qualify. There's no jobs here. None. No unions in the South, either—not like the North. Tourism is the only industry. So they see everything on television that they want, but their pockets is empty! And they go to school wearing their pants below their bums almost."

I laugh. "Isn't that's just a kids' style?"

"Why no, it isn't. All they see is sex and violence on the television, and if a girl sees a guy with his pants hangin' down she's gonna get interested."

"Do you vote?" I ask him. I am thinking about my visit to the Delta, and Dorwin Shields's dismay that ordinary people seem to have given up on the democratic promise.

"What's the use?" says Tony. "We elect people, but they're outnumbered in the legislature so they can't get anything through for black people. And in Washington, even if they convince the others, they have to depend on the bureaucracy to apportion the money. And it doesn't happen."

"Do *you* vote?"

"Why, that's a personal question! Oh, no, that's *too* personal!"

I spend some moments thinking about this. After all, I didn't ask *how* he voted, only *if* he voted. Earlier in the conversation he had told me that in the 1960s, he once spent eight days in jail for demonstrating, so he had once been willing to make a sacrifice for the future. Perhaps not voting makes him feel guilty, or maybe he feels not voting is an insult to those who died. It is all conjecture since he does not wish to pursue the subject. Instead he wants to talk about the government: the evil government of the United States.

"I'll tell you, they have satellites going all the time and they know everything about you. They are just storing all the information until they need to use it against you." He points to a building on the street, not a special building, just a place we happen to be passing by. "They can hear what's going on inside those walls. Don't ever think they don't know what you are sayin'."

"But why would they want to do this?" I ask. "What have they got against people?"

"It's like this," he explains: "A government that is born with lies will continue to be dishonest in everything it does."

He is as paranoid as Gerry Varn: he thinks all politicians are liars, a common-enough conceit. But a black man issued from slaves could always discern another dimension to the perceived chicanery of the state. He knows it was founded on "lies," on principles of humanity that had excluded him, and until that credibility gap was reconciled he would never truly feel at home.

The man seated beside me on the plane to Montgomery, Alabama—a tiny, sixteen-seat propeller affair that rattles and loses altitude with every air pocket—is Larry. He is a male nurse returning home from a conference on the East Coast, and in the way of stranger-to-stranger conversations, he tells me he attended a desegregated school from the age of ten, and that because of this exposure, he grew up with a more open attitude towards blacks than his parents' generation. I guess he is about forty. But he admits there is one exception to the general rule of tolerance: "Where the attitudes of the Old South continue, I think, is with interracial couples," he says. "It's happening, you see it more and more, but it's not something people can really get used to." Interracial sex is an old anxiety, I think to myself. In slave days it had happened all the time, as a right of ownership; but afterwards, when relationships emerged or, in our own time, marriages, nothing cut closer to the edge of discomfort for some people.

Larry also worries a lot about the public schools. They are terrible. They have metal detectors at the doors. "Can you believe it that children have been shooting other children?" He shakes his head. "I know of a kid who was afraid to use the toilet. He would sneak out of the school and go to the gas station down the street. It is impossible to learn under those conditions."

Like many other middle-class white parents, Larry and his wife fled the public system, meaning that the desegregated schools of his own childhood have been resegregated once again, this time as black. They used to send their children to private academies, but they, and many of their friends, recently turned off institutional schools altogether. Larry and his wife now teach their children at home. "If I had to put my kids in the public school, I would leave Montgomery for another school district and commute to my job every day. I would *never* put my children in a Montgomery public school."

"Whose responsibility is it to improve the schools?" I ask.

"I don't know. No one does anything."

He wants to present a happier picture, but he seems defensive about being from Alabama, where the nascent civil rights movement first defied the Jim Crow laws three decades ago, and where attacks on non-violent blacks and their white supporters were broadcast around the world. "I'm *surrounded* in my company by blacks who are doing as good a job as I am," he assures me. "It's *completely* different now. But when I go north and people learn I'm from Montgomery, their attitude changes. Blacks get really cold. One man said, 'You don't like us much down there, do you?' I feel really bad because it just isn't true anymore. But there's a kind of shame about being from here." He looks away.

I am in Montgomery to visit the Southern Poverty Law Center, which has waged a fierce attack on one of the ugliest legacies of the slave era: the Ku Klux Klan. It seems to me that the unreconciled past will not be pacified until organizations like the Klan, and its progeny, the Patriot movement—which includes a grab bag of White Power racists, neo-Nazis and other paranoid hate-mongers—have been successfully confronted.

I have come a day early to see the city. From the window of my cab, most of the downtown looks boarded up: businesses that have fled the city core have likely relocated in the suburbs, where wealthier residents can afford to patronize them. There seem to have been attempts at urban restoration, but the revived Victorian structures look like prettied-up debutantes in an abandoned ballroom. Only the state capital building remains imposing: the monumental, white-columned, neo-Grecian seat of the old Confederacy. We pass by the Southern Poverty Law Center: in front is a circular black granite memorial naming forty local activists who died during the civil rights era. Farther on, a downtown street sign marks the spot where Rosa Parks refused to give up her seat on the bus to a white man, thus setting off the Montgomery bus boycott. Another small plaque at the Greyhound Bus station indicates the place where, in May 1961, the young "freedom riders," as they called themselves, were met by a mob of one thousand whites and beaten while the police stood by. I am later told that none of these signs was erected by the city of Montgomery: the marker at the bus station was placed there by the Greyhound company and a private individual, the memorial at the Southern Poverty Law Center by the centre itself and the tribute to Rosa Parks by a local historical society.

Dexter Avenue is home to other ghosts: Court Square was once a place of slave auctions, and a nearby site (now an office building) was the slave-traders' pen. In 1861, the Winter Building was a telegraph central: it was from here that the firing order was sent to Rebel troops at Fort Sumpter, South Carolina, marking the start of the Civil War.

My driver is Jimmie, and today is his fifty-third birthday. In the course of conversation, he tells me that he finished high school, but when it comes time to make out a receipt, I note that he can't write numbers. When he was a teenager, he participated in the famous freedom march from Selma, Alabama, to the steps of the state capitol right here in Montgomery. His parents were afraid for him, what with the attack dogs and people being beaten, but the memory of that day on Dexter Avenue is unforgettable, he says. On March 25, 1965, the entire avenue was jammed with people of all races. Martin Luther King Jr. was there. He tried to get as close as possible, and he remembers King standing on the steps of the capitol, calling for an end to the discriminatory laws. He thinks life is much better for blacks today. "Now you can go wherever you want. It's just like in the North," he says with satisfaction.

"Do you vote?" I ask him.

"Of course!" he replies quickly. "So many people died so we could vote. I *always* vote. But the young people, they don't want to bother. They don't want to work or go to school. There's drugs everywhere and the crime here is real bad."

"What would you change first?" I inquire.

"Jobs and education. There's not enough work and the schools are bad. I raised my children to be hard-working, good people and I'm proud of them. Two are in factory work, one works in a hospital and one is a vice-principal in a school. But things are a lot worse now."

I wish him a happy birthday and get out at my hotel, but I can't get Jimmie out of my mind. I wonder if he remembers that "jobs and education" were also a rallying call a whole generation ago?

At the state capitol, top of Dexter Avenue, I feel the power and privilege that once characterized the South. In February 1861, Jefferson Davis stood beneath the tall columns of the portico to be inaugurated president of the newly formed Confederate States. The Daughters of the Confederacy have placed a bronze star to mark the spot, but change comes slowly here: it was 1996 before the Alabama Historical Association added a plaque indicating that three days after the surrender at Appomattox, a Union cavalry corps had raised the flag of the United States over the capitol and a new regime had begun.

Inside the rotunda is a monument to the Alabama governor George Wallace, he who made his mark by crying "Segregation forever!" to the grateful loyalists who had elected him. Wallace was later paralysed by a would-be assassin's bullet, and he spent the rest of his life in a wheelchair. He also recanted his attachment to racism, but here, inside the atrium of the capitol, there is no evidence of trauma. Here, Wallace will remain whole and unhurt for eternity.

George Wallace circumvented the rules that prevented back-to-back terms as governor by having his wife, Lurleen, run in his place. She, too, has a monument to her memory. It is engraved with the syrupy Elizabeth Barrett Browning sonnet "How Do I Love Thee?" in presumed tribute to her wifely devotion. The guard at his station in the rotunda tells me that Lurleen Wallace was the most popular governor in all of Alabama history, probably because "she died in office."

The painted murals on the domed ceiling portray a lopsided lesson in history. One, titled *Wealth and Leisure Produce the Golden Period of Antebellum Life in Alabama, 1840–1860*, depicts a richly dressed couple on horseback before their white-pillared mansion; another, *Secession and the Confederacy*, represents the inauguration of Jefferson Davis. On the ceiling of this Confederate state capitol, there was no Civil War: the next mural, dated 1874–1930, illustrates black labourers in Birmingham loading bales of cotton for shipment to a mill against a background of blast furnaces meant to represent the post-war industrial South.

The first major building to the left of the capitol as I walk down Dexter Avenue is the Dexter Avenue King Memorial Baptist Church; in other words, the first Confederate legislature is ironically mated with the very church where the second phase of black emancipation began. Martin Luther King Jr. was only twenty-four years old in September 1954, when he arrived here to become pastor. The son of a well-known family in Atlanta (his father was a preacher), he had just completed the course work for a doctorate in theology at Boston University.

King would continue work that had already begun. The push to end Jim Crow segregation had started in earnest a decade earlier, after the Second World War, when African Americans, who had been conscripted into the United States Armed Forces to fight Japan and Germany in the name of democracy and the egalitarian values of the American Creed, returned home with a new awareness of injustice. Overseas they fought with white men their age. They were all Americans, engaged in a single emotionally charged cause, but when they returned to the South, blacks were once again subjected to the humiliating laws that governed every aspect of their public life.

The first signs of change appeared as some pushed to register for the vote, and Montgomery, for example, got its first black police officers. But bus segregation hung on. For many of us watching from afar, the bus boycott came to symbolize the civil rights movement, probably because it was a David and Goliath affair involving a small woman of exceptional courage. In the early 1950s, there were 75,000 whites and 45,999 blacks in Montgomery, and most of the latter used the bus system to get to work. Blacks sat at the back, and if a white person boarded when the vehicle was crowded, they had to give up their places. Some of the drivers were harsh; people who complained were sometimes publicly slapped in the face.

Word about Rosa Parks's defiance of the law on December 1, 1955, spread like wildfire throughout the city, and a hastily called meeting at the Dexter Avenue Baptist Church gave birth to a new group, the Montgomery Improvement Association, which passed a unanimous vote to hold a one-day boycott of the bus system. The next day, five thousand people massed outside the church, shouting to continue the boycott: it was the first time blacks in the city had spoken with a unified voice. Bodyguards were assigned to Dr. King—and with reason: his house was bombed. The Montgomery Improvement Association filed a federal lawsuit against the bus segregation law. Weeks later, King and eighty-eight others were indicted for conspiring to boycott a lawful business. It was all-out war for and against the right to segregate the public facility. The United States Federal Court ruled in favour of the Montgomery Improvement Association lawsuit, and on December 21, 1956, after 381 days of boycott, the segregation of Montgomery city buses came to an end.

In the upstairs sanctuary where Martin Luther King Jr. preached during those tumultuous years, seventeen rows of empty pews line each side of a red-carpeted aisle, and a central pulpit hovers over the ghosts of the old congregation. I sit alone in a back row, on a quiet weekday morning, trying to imagine them: the women in the broad-brimmed flowery hats of the era, the men in their dark Sunday suits. To the side of the pulpit, an organ that may once have resonated to jazzy spirituals is silent. Forty-three years have passed since this congregation and its young leader endorsed the bus boycott—a decision that changed Montgomery and eventually the entire South.

One of the people who sat in these pews was Mrs. Johnnie Carr.[33] She was Rosa Park's closest friend then, and at eighty-seven she is still the president of the Montgomery Improvement Association. Although she was at the centre of the civil rights movement, has been awarded honorary doctorates and recently had an adult health-care centre named in her honour, Johnnie Carr continues to live in the house she has occupied for the past fifty years: a small Southern-gabled home, in an all-black neighbourhood, filled with pictures of her children and grandchildren. When she has shown me every picture and asked about my children, she tells me that when her son, who was one of the first blacks to integrate the Montgomery school system, had trouble, she had to teach him how to hold his own. When he said he could not eat lunch because the white children were staring at him, she advised him to stare back. They practised together, and it worked: when a white student threw his books on the ground and ordered her son to pick them up, he was able to say, "Boy, you'd better pick up George Wallace's books and go home." One day he told his mother that when a black student walked down the hall of his school it was like the Red Sea: the waves parted and everyone stared. But that passed as the children accommodated to the new situation, and he went on to university.

She is small, compact and energetic-looking, with intelligent eyes, white hair and large glasses. Her talent was rewarded: she was a senior manager when she retired from her job with an insurance company, so she had personally benefited from the changes she had helped to bring about. Throughout her long life, she has fought racism in the larger community, just as in the case of her own son.

But she, and her mother before her, saw bitter days. After her father died, leaving four children, they moved to the country, just outside Montgomery, where her mother could grow her own food and sell the surplus from a wagon. Her mother was known as an outstanding baker: the white women would bring her the ingredients and she would make their cakes. "Their children and I would play together, so I was quite old before I found out what segregation was about," she remembers.

"When I was older, I had to pass in front of a white school on my way to the black school, and I remember thinking that here was a school so much closer to where I lived. That is when I started understanding what segregation meant. I began to see that when we went into stores, they would insist on bringing us a footlet to try on a shoe, but they did not do that with whites. If a black woman wanted a hat, she was not allowed to try it on, because they said her hair was oily. I also started noticing that white women were called 'Mrs.' and black women were all called 'Auntie,' 'Auntie Mary,' or whatever, but never addressed as 'Mrs.' the way the white women were."

Doing community work, then joining the NAACP, made her less afraid, and she began to push tentatively in new directions. After she was married, she went with a black friend to apply for a credit card in a Montgomery department store. The saleswoman, whom they both knew, made out the application, and Johnnie's friend wrote her name without an honorific, but Johnnie prefixed her name with *Mrs*. The friend got a credit card within days; Johnnie never got hers. "I crossed a line by daring to call myself Mrs.," she says. "No black woman was allowed to do that.

"Before Rosa just plum refused to obey an unjust law, we tried not to run counter to the law, but we were harassed. Once, around 1950, we had a meeting that included liberal white women—I think it was a prayer meeting—and the police went around and took the car licence numbers of all the white women. Afterwards their husbands were badgered and their businesses were boycotted. There were many, many white people who just wanted people to be people, even then. But they got into trouble."

That Rosa Parks was the one to publicly defy the law and lend her name to a federal lawsuit came as a surprise. Rosa, says Johnnie, was a quiet, shy woman of forty-two. But Johnnie was not surprised by the violence that followed: Dr. King had warned them that "anytime you attack a person in what he has done, you can expect retaliation."

I feel the looming presence of Martin Luther King Jr. throughout my conversation with this woman, who came to know him so well. Johnnie Carr was at the Dexter Avenue Baptist Church the day King was introduced as the new minister. "I was with Rosa and I said, 'He's something else!' We realized that he was different. It was a gift God had given him, and I have not seen another like him," she says.

She still participates in a weekly meeting called the One Montgomery Breakfast, and on the first of every month she takes part in the Friendly Supper Club. Both groups have a membership of blacks and whites, including doctors, teachers, ministers, greeters at Wal-Mart, even a retired general with influence in conservative white circles. The One Montgomery Breakfast, which has been going since 1983, is a forum for discussing what is happening in the community, while the Friendly Supper Club is primarily social: people meet in a suburban cafeteria and talk about everything, from the weather to the cost of corn, over trays of inexpensive food.

Both grew out of an incident that occurred nearby in 1983. A black woman had died of natural causes, and her family came from Detroit for the funeral, but when the police saw their cars with out-of-state licence plates, they decided it was a drug party, burst in the door and killed one of the mourners. The others were arrested and jailed for nine days without charges. "People were very upset, and that is when we organized One Montgomery to discuss community relations," says Johnnie. "We have a long way to go. The Ku Klux Klan is still an issue, even though they don't wear white hoods anymore; now they wear pinstriped suits and sit in offices. We are working to try to keep those people from taking over. For the most part, though, the violence has stopped, and blacks in our city do not have the same fears. In 1955, when the civil rights movement began, there were no black cashiers in the stores and no black tellers in the banks. The biggest jobs were schoolteacher, minister or mail carrier; otherwise, there were no opportunities. You could spend your money anywhere, but you weren't allowed to work there. Now it's different. You know, the word is spreading about our One Montgomery Breakfast, and groups are organizing in other places: there's one in North Carolina called the Giraffe, because they stick their necks out. I guess it is still an act of courage for the races to get together like this, especially socially, but we don't get stared at like we used to."

"Is it possible to overcome the legacy of slavery in this country?" I ask her.

"I do not really think it is possible to overcome racism," she replies after a moment. "It's like the air you breathe here, and you really have to search your heart to say that you're not a racist. We have had many open discussions, and I remember one where someone said, 'Well, I don't have any hatred for anybody.' Then one white man said, 'Well, you know, when I'm driving my car and I see a black man driving an expensive car beside me, well, I look, and I know I shouldn't look at a black person that way just because he is driving a nice car.' So I said, 'You know, if there is a crash, the first thing I hope is that there was not a black person involved because I know the black is not going to get justice.' It becomes something you have to work on with your own self so we can live together as human beings. Not in each other's lap, but in harmony.

"But I do think that we blacks still have a problem with self-esteem that's a legacy from the slavery period, even in a dealing with one another.

It was so designed that when blacks were given the opportunity to work in the big house, it made those blacks feel they were above the others. So we have interblack racism within our own community."

"Would a Congressional apology for slavery help?"

"When it first came out, I didn't really understand what Congressman Tony Hall was getting at. It just felt like words, and actions speak louder than words. Personally, I think it would be better to have some sort of monument. Our Sunday-school lesson last week was about when the children of Israel crossed the Jordan, and they were each told to get a stone and pile them up, and those stones would tell their children and their children's children. This means that there is something to show and some way to remember. Look at what the Southern Poverty Law Center has done. You can go and see the names of people who gave their lives on the monument they put there. People come from all over to see that. So anything that will mark what you have come through is a good idea. I say, if you don't know where you came from, you cannot chart your course."

It is late in the evening and I want to call a taxi, but she insists on driving me back to my hotel. In the car I ask her what events stand out in a lifetime of activism in the cause of human and civil rights. Her reply is simple and beautiful: "To have had three children and to rear them to two women and a man, and to feel blessed that they are doing well with their lives, and that they also contribute to the community," she says without hesitation. "The Lord has been good to me." My eyes brim: I, too, am a mother.

With its electronic gates and a guardhouse stacked floor to ceiling with banks of flickering monitors, the Southern Poverty Law Center (SPLC) on Washington Avenue looks like a modern fortress. And with good reason. The Patriot movement targeted the building and especially its high-profile litigator, Morris Dees. Dees has successfully attacked white supremacists in civil court, including winning a $7 million jury award to the mother of a young black man who was lynched by the Ku Klux Klan in Mobile, Alabama, in 1987. The Klan threatened to kill an African-American male if a local jury dared to acquit a black who was on trial for killing a white, and when the defendant was indeed acquitted, they seized Michael Donald—the first black they saw in the street—slit his throat and hung his body from a tree. (The United Klans of America were bankrupted by this ruling and forced to turn the deed to their headquarters over to Donald's mother.)

In 1988–89, the centre filed a civil suit over the murder of an Ethiopian graduate student in Portland, Oregon, by skinheads wielding baseball bats. The attack was directed by Tom Metzger of California, head of the neo-Nazi White Aryan Resistance. SPLC lawyers argued that Metzger and his organization were as responsible for the killing as the youth gang that physically carried out the attack, and a jury agreed. Metzger's appeal to the United States Supreme Court failed. In July 1998, a jury ordered two Klan groups to pay $37.8 million for the burning of a black church just outside Charleston; and in 1990, Dees secured a $12.5 million award against Metzger for the Portland murder.

Joe Levin, who founded the SPLC with Morris Dees in 1971, is slim and boyish in a typically American way. He offers me a striped candy to suck on, then leans back in his chair and props a sneaker-clad shoe on the arm of his office couch. Like David Ingebretsen in Jackson, he was raised in a staunch segregationist family and continued to share his parents' views until he went to college. There, for the first time, he met people who thought differently, and by the time he entered law school, he was convinced that the prejudices of the people he grew up with could not be justified. The most powerful influence, he tells me, was a fraternity friend who was the editor of the college newspaper and a strong proponent of desegregation. Levin watched as his schoolmate was vilified by the community: "I saw what he had to endure and it changed the way I looked at the world."

His colleague, Jim Carnes, who heads the SPLC's Teaching Tolerance project, is serious and sensitive-looking. I am not surprised to learn that he is a deeply religious man who has secularized many of his commitments. Over lunch in a mid-nineteenth-century house turned restaurant overlooking the broad Alabama River, he speaks openly of his ideals: "For me, religion means universal principles that are expressed in particular ways, and they always transcend whatever differences exist. Those principles are liberty and justice for all." I realize that I am listening to another expression of the American Creed—the original ideals of equality, as expressed in the Bill of Rights, that have been accepted as articles of faith in the minds of many Americans—and I remember a rabbi I once met who told me that every Passover, at the annual celebration of the freeing of the Jews from bondage in Egypt, his family would gather on the porch of their home in Denver, Colorado, and read the Bill of Rights aloud.

The Teaching Tolerance project began in 1991 as an aggressive response to the increasing incidence of hate-related crimes across the United States. Nearly half these offences were being committed by people under the age of twenty-one. The school classroom was the obvious place to combat racism—young children were open to one another—but there were surprisingly few materials available to teachers. The Teaching Tolerance project was designed to close that gap by providing free teaching tools, including a magazine that offered strategies for promoting an acceptance of diversity. The project organizers made videos on America's civil rights movement and the history of intolerance. A half million grateful educators from across the United States put their names on the mailing list.

Like so many of the open-minded whites I was meeting across the South, Jim Carnes cleaves to ideas forged during the civil rights era. "For me, the most important thing was school desegregation. I started school in 1961, which was already seven years after the Supreme Court decision to desegregate, but there wasn't an African American in my school until 1968, when one boy's parents dared to send him. In 1970, when I was in tenth grade, there was a court order to desegregate immediately. There were bomb threats, walkouts, marches on city hall. I was shocked, and I quickly got involved in a student bi-racial committee, which was my first involvement with this issue of fairness. We were grappling with what seemed like stark injustices."

He was born in Columbus, Mississippi, a place he describes as having a "strong regional identity." It was a small market town for an agricultural region, an old cotton seat that used to be one of the wealthiest counties in the United States. Lots of slaves, lots of lovely antebellum houses. Jim Carnes remembers the strong sense of history in his town and the paradoxes: the fact that no one ever mentioned that all the wealth had been built on the backs of slaves. The upstairs balcony of the Methodist church he attended with his family was called "the slave gallery," but no one ever talked about why that might be.

He was close to all four grandparents, who were, he says, conservative and racist, but his own parents had somehow broken free. They were adamantly non-racist, and they raised him that way. One day he asked them how they accounted for their attitudes, given their own upbringing and the environment they lived in, and they both pointed to religion: "They said they saw the contradiction between racism and the faith they believed in."

Carnes thinks an apology for black slavery might be useful as an acknowledgement of the suffering people endured but that a permanent monument would be better; in fact, he sent an opinion piece to *The New York Times* saying this, but the paper didn't run it. "Roughly 100,000 people died because of the institution of slavery, and if any group of people deserves a tangible, eternal monument, it is African Americans. Look at the Mall in Washington; it is *filled* with monuments to different aspects of our history! The Vietnam memorial has made an impact on a generation of Americans, and we have thousands of monuments to soldiers who died in the Civil War. But most slaves don't even have a gravestone. I think symbols and rituals can help a country transcend some of its divisions."

Over and over, Carnes returns to his faith in the American Creed: "I know some people feel that multiculturalism and tolerance education is a futile 'Look what you've done to us' sort of exercise, but as Morris Dees has pointed out, for some mysterious reason the founders of this country were able to envision something universal. They weren't able to enact these realities in their lifetime, but they were able to set them as a national goal, and over the centuries and the generations, we have truly come closer to these ideals. Look at who is eligible to vote! If you examine the history of minority rights in this country, there really has been clear progress. We are definitely moving ahead."

He is right technically: there was major legislative change over the century, but at the turn of a new millennium, could his faith in the future translate into anything more? Or was the church of the American Creed like so many other places of worship where the congregants mouthed words, then went home to Sunday lunch?

On November 10, 1997, President Bill Clinton convened the first-ever White House conference on Hate Crimes, a day-long meeting held in Washington. In an earlier radio address to the nation, he declared, "A hate crime is the embodiment of intolerance. . . . Every time one of these crimes is committed, it creates tension and fear, and tears at the fabric of community life. . . . These are acts of violence against America itself."

The conference was assembled as part of a project called "One America in the 21st Century: The President's Project on Race," which had been launched earlier in the year. It was attended by a host of dignitaries: the president, the vice-president, the attorney-general, the secretary of education, members of Congress, selected state and local officials, 350 leaders of law-enforcement agencies, and the civil rights, anti-violence, youth, education and religious communities. Survivors of hate crimes were slated to be there. Thousands more would participate at more than fifty satellite-linked events across the United States. No one would ever be faulted on the fanfare.

On behalf of the President's Initiative on Race (PIR), a seven-person racially diverse advisory board—headed by the black octogenarian John Hope Franklin, one of America's leading historians—was mandated to tour the country for a year to listen to people's concerns. As part of its deliberations, it was to consider Representative Tony Hall's proposal.

The PIR commissioners went away to do their work, and in September 1998, they presented a report that sank like a stone—disappeared immediately from sight. This was not surprising: the commission's recommendations were breathtaking in their banality, especially the central suggestion that the government create a permanent council on race "in order to promote harmony," a proposal that could have come directly from a Chinese fortune cookie. Yes, there were suggestions regarding health, education, affirmative action and the actions of the criminal justice system with regard to minorities, but they were unaccompanied by a call for legislation. Instead, the board issued a feeble call to the country's leaders asking them "to make racial reconciliation a reality."

According to a report in *The New York Times*, the seven-member board had administrative problems from the beginning, including "continued interference by White House officials who feared the political consequences of its [the PIR's] work."[34] One White House officer who spoke on condition of anonymity said, "He [President Clinton] didn't want to create a commission that sort of went off and did things independently and on its own."

The sort of reaction that had apparently affected the commission's resolve was expressed by the syndicated columnist George F. Will, whom I read in the Charleston *Post and Courier*.[35] He opened with a sarcastic salvo: "Some good news has gone unremarked: The Civil War is over. So is its once invaluable echo, the anachronism impervious to the passage of time, 'the civil rights movement.'" Will called the PIR report "limp"—not because it did not go far enough, but because it went *too* far. His criticisms opened a window into what might be called the "race-fatigued" conservative right, who were tired of all minority claims. He claimed that the commission was unnecessary in the first place because three of the most admired citizens in the United States—Oprah Winfrey, Michael Jordan and Colin Powell—were black and that "most blacks consider themselves middle class" (which may have come as a surprise to his readers of all races). Will also thought the commission had spent too much time in the la-la land of Southern California, "where talk about race is obsessive."

California may have been la-la land to Will, but that state had recently voted down its affirmative-action project, and African-American university registration dropped wherever a similar backtracking had taken place. Affirmative action—a program that expresses the values of the American Creed—was Will's real target; as the political consensus shifted to the right, starting with Ronald Reagan in the 1980s, the liberal ideology that underscored progressive social legislation had gradually fallen into disfavour on grounds that "special dealing," for whatever reason, encouraged a pathology of "victimization" and "entitlement" on the part of the undeserving recipients. Will had no truck with what he called "the racial spoils system of preferences": in his view, if blacks fell behind, it was because of their behaviour, especially high illegitimacy rates.

As I read this article, I was impressed by the author's ability to catch in a few paragraphs most of the arguments currently being mustered against a renewal of minority civil rights. George Will simultaneously influenced *and* followed the thinking of millions of Americans, which is why he was syndicated all over the country.[36]

Although one member of the board of the PIR complained publicly about having been denied the latitude to make strong policy recommendations, the former Mississippi governor William Winter did not. Winter, a lawyer, politician and diplomat of long standing, had served as state governor from 1980 to 1984. During the Second World War and the war in Korea, he was an officer in the infantry, and in the private arena, he had taught at the faculty of law at the University of Mississippi as well as practising his profession and contributing chapters to three books, whose titles indicated the range of his interests: *The History of Mississippi*, *Yesterday's Constitution Today* and *Mississippi Heroes*. In other words, Winter was well connected with the constituency that read George F. Will; he was a respected member of the Mississippi and the American establishments, and his presence on the board of the PIR capped a long, successful career.

I want to meet William Winter, not just because he served on the president's commission. Now in his mid-seventies, he seems to personify the transition from the Old to the New South. I have read about him: he was born on a plantation settled by his great-grandfather in 1834 and worked by slaves. After Emancipation, the slaves had stayed on as tenant farmers, and in Winter's own childhood, some of *their* grandchildren and great-grandchildren were his playmates, until he went away to continue his schooling and they did not. During the Civil War, members of his family were proud Confederate soldiers, and he grew up accepting the segregated world he had inherited, reading Southern patriot literature (adamantly not Faulkner, he once acknowledged) and admiring the old traditions. His family plantation home reflected a world that had not changed in a century or more, yet as governor of Mississippi, he had managed to pass far-reaching legislation in the field of education reform. The transition into twentieth-century modernity on the part of a conservative son of the plantation intrigued me.

We meet in Jackson, in his office at Watkins Ludlam and Stennis, an old-guard law firm with long corridors and doors that swing open to expose richly appointed rooms. His starched white shirt and discreetly patterned silk tie speak of conservatism and good breeding, as people used to say, and he has the firm handshake and practised smile of a seasoned politician. But he also fought battles that changed Mississippi for the better. That he is an intense listener may offer a clue to his success: he would have understood that the South was about to change and known enough to position himself accordingly. He tells me, when I ask, that three experiences marked him forever: the example of his father, a state legislator, and a member of the Mississippi landed gentry, with a reputation for noblesse oblige and fairness; his service in the Second World War, where he met blacks on a desegregated basis for the first time; and having had James Silver, the author of a book called *The Closed Society*, as his history teacher at Ole Miss university. Silver helped Winter frame his emerging ideas about the Southern "system,"[37] and when Silver was fired because he openly supported James Meredith's bid to desegregate Mississippi's establishment college, that, too, had impressed Winter.

In 1967, when he first ran, white Mississippians were in an uproar over the court-imposed injunction to desegregate schools and permit the registration of black voters. The Ku Klux Klan was bombing, burning and lynching; the NAACP was organizing the black South; and Martin Luther King Jr. was at his peak. Winter was considered the most progressive candidate in the running, which was not the best way to gain votes among whites, and he sought the behind-the-scenes support of black electors. But on the public hustings he presented himself as an old-style segregationist, choosing a meeting of the White Citizens' Council to announce: "I was born a segregationist and raised a segregationist. I have always defended this position. I defend it now."[38]

I read this quotation to him in the quiet of his office, more than thirty years after the event. He clears his throat and looks unhappy. "Those may have been weasel words, but I was saying that I defended the system in which I had been reared. I defended it based on the economic facts of life because I think that segregation at one point had a justifying economic factor, not a justifying discriminatory factor, but an economic factor." I am not sure what he means and ask him to clarify. "I mean the economic system was built around the tenant-farmer system, and I don't know what would have supplanted that at that time."

"Didn't people make the same argument in the antebellum period by asking what would supplant slave labour?" I ask.

"That's right," he replies, "and the tenant-farmer system did." A silence drops like a screen between us. I am remembering Peter Fontaine's self-justifying letter, dated 1757, and the compromise on slavery, based on economics, that had wormed its way into the heart of the American enterprise. Winter says, "Let me show you what I was up against." He riffles through a filing cabinet and brings out an old election poster from August 17, 1967. There he is, addressing a crowd of potential voters; four black women sit in the front row. The caption reads: "Are these front-row sitters going to determine the destiny of Mississippi? For the first time in our history we are faced with a large NEGRO MINORITY BLOC VOTE. William Winter's election will insure Negro domination of Mississippi elections for generations to come. WHITE MISSISSIPPI AWAKE."

"Is this what defeated you?"

"Segregation was the only issue in the race."

Winter was elected only after the segregationist battle to maintain separate schools was definitively lost, and then, what he did was revolutionary: he reformed the education system in America's most backward state. Mississippi, in its battle against desegregating the schools, had actually abolished compulsory education. In 1982, Winter's new law made school attendance mandatory to age sixteen and established kindergartens statewide for the first time.

The man who had started life on his family's cotton plantation, where little had changed in a hundred years, who had played with the descendants of slaves in the ways of the Old South and listened to heroic tales of the Confederacy, had transformed himself into a symbol of what he wanted the New South to become. Now he thinks the South is "getting much like the rest of the country," and that, "if anything, attitudes here are perhaps better than in other places because we have lived so closely together and known each other as individuals, even in the framework of segregation." I know he would fiercely reject the extremism of Gerry Varn; still, the indulgence, or noblesse oblige, implicit in his comment about how blacks and whites in the South had always known each other as individuals was a throwback to other times. After all, whites and blacks knew each other the way a duchess "knows" her scullery maid.

But Elayna Shakur chose to live in Charleston because she, too, liked the way whites and blacks related to each other in the South. Not as equals, perhaps, but without the hostility she had experienced in Ohio.

As for the President's Initiative on Race, William Winter was too experienced a politician to take issue with the president's decision to diminish the board's ability to make policy recommendations. "I think we achieved our expectations, which were to open a conversation on race, and I think we laid the basis for what will I hope be a permanent initiative which will continue to have as its mission the elimination of racism in this country. We *did* recommend policy changes. The report is full of policy changes."

"Then why were you criticized?"

"Well, if some people wanted reparations for slavery, that was *totally* unrealistic politically. Nobody on the commission thought that was even worth talking about. As Dr. [John Hope] Franklin said, 'What do I need reparations for? I've done all right. I don't need anybody paying me money.' Let's do reparations by ensuring that the next generation of children get an adequate education whatever their race, have adequate health care and have an adequate place to live. An apology for slavery? That's just words. Completely superficial. That was our attitude."

"Can you tell me about your discussions on the subject?"

There is a silence as he thinks. "Well, I don't recall that we had any wide-ranging discussion on that subject. We did not think this would make much difference. We were debating what we thought were *relevant* subjects, not what happened a hundred years ago. We were looking at the twenty-first century, not the nineteenth century. I do think one of the most counterproductive things black people can do is let themselves wear a burden of victimization on their shoulders, because it reduces their ability to seize the opportunities of the present. I have heard a lot of black people say, 'Let's get on with it. Let's stop wallowing in the sloughs of the past.' I say that to white folks too. 'Let's quit glorifying the past, let's quit refighting the Civil War. Let it lie. Get on with it.'"

Tony Hall's idea for a symbolic apology wasn't even considered by the very committee mandated to bring ideas about racial reconciliation to the president. It was summarily, and contemptuously, dismissed.

Why did the suggestion of a minimal gesture of apology incite such an explosive response, when other acts of national remorse—though noisy and divisive—eventually passed through the gates of public opinion? Why does the tragedy of slavery still penetrate to the core of national identity, eluding resolution? The slaves had to be incorporated into the citizenry after Emancipation: the values of the American Creed dictated that this be so; but an ambiguity over whether blacks were ever included in the liberal dream that they cling to as passionately as other Americans is as old as the Creed itself—since, at the founding of the country, they clearly were not. Perhaps because slavery ended just recently in real terms, the time for healing has been relatively short, given the great harm it caused. A century and a half may seem long in the United States, a new country with a short history, but the slave experience is still accessible and vivid, even if the primary actors are dead. In their youth, older whites such as William Winter knew relatives who had once owned slaves, and older blacks had great-grandparents who were born slaves, so the period is still raw, in spite of its perceived distance.

The most intractable piece of the memory puzzle seems to be a dissociation from obvious connections—an apparent blindness to what sits on the proverbial home doorstep *and* to the attendant ironies. For example, on December 17, 1999, U.S. Secretary of State Madeleine Albright addressed a meeting in Berlin that included senior members of the German government, delegates of German businesses that used slave labour during the Second World War, and representatives of the victims. Speaking on behalf of the United States, she congratulated the German government on its decision to pay 10 billion Deutschmarks in reparations. She said:

> The United States strongly supports your effort to provide a measure of justice to those compelled to endure slave or forced labor. . . . Above all, I pay tribute to those who brought us here by insisting

> that hard questions be asked and answered about accountability for the terrible crimes committed more than half a century ago.
>
> This is the first serious initiative to acknowledge the debt owed to those whose labor was stolen or coerced during that time of outrage and shame. And make no mistake, that debt is huge. For no human being should ever be treated as property, and no person can deny the dignity of another without bringing dishonor upon himself. . . . I hope, and believe, that the people of Germany will support this commitment and recognize its value in further enhancing the respect their nation commands around the world.
>
> Because if I have one message to convey this morning, it is this. This agreement . . . reflects a sense of moral responsibility that is absolutely essential to building the kind of . . . world in which we want our children to grow up. And it is critical to completing the unfinished moral business of the old century, before we enter the new.[39]

Strong words—spoken in support of a nation across the sea. But just one year earlier, Congressman Tony Hall's idea for a symbolic apology to the descendents of America's own slaves had been summarily dismissed by the American president's committee on racial reconciliation.[40]

The ironies of the Creed and the tragedy of "America's most enduring dilemma" live on together in the fissure separating these events.

5

The Beloved Country

Truth and Reconciliation in South Africa

The dawn has come, as it has come for a thousand centuries, never failing.
But when that dawn will come, of our emancipation, from the fear of bondage and the bondage of fear, why, that is a secret.

– ALAN PATON, *Cry, the Beloved Country*

For all that I have done and all that I have failed to do.

– BRENDAN GIRDLER-BROWN,
National Register of Reconciliation, December 1997

ON APRIL 27, 1997, the third anniversary of the peaceful liberation of black South Africans from the bondage known as apartheid, I am in a hotel room in Pretoria, watching a television screen. Thousands of people are waiting expectantly in a remote region of the Northern Cape. Some sing and wave banners; others talk and laugh excitedly. A band plays. And then they sight him. Nelson Mandela is moving slowly towards them in a cart pulled by two donkeys, those most humble of creatures. "He is like Christ entering Jerusalem!" gasps the commentator. His voice is breaking with emotion and contains not a note of irony.

President Mandela is greeted by a twenty-one-gun salute, and the crowd roars with happiness. There is a flypast, then a parade by the South African Defence Forces, their black, white and brown faces a true reflection of the newly sanctioned ideology. The "new South Africa"—suffused with remembered pain and beset with present difficulties—has invented a hopeful new identity: a multiracial Rainbow Nation in the very land where, for centuries, *white* and *citizen* were synonymous.

As if in microcosm, fleeting glimpses of the country-in-transition are markedly visible on this auspicious day: the ecstatic presence of black South Africans rejoicing and the very choice of this locale. The remote town of Upington is a heartland of rural Afrikaner settlement, and Afrikaners invented and sustained apartheid.[1] The town is also known for the trial of the Upington 14, who were sentenced to death for treason in the late 1980s and later reprieved as a goodwill gesture to mark the release of Mandela in February 1990 from his twenty-seven-year incarceration on Robben Island, just off the coast of Cape Town. The white heartland together with the memory of the Upington 14 makes this an ideal place to celebrate the recent birth of democracy. Nelson Mandela uses every public appearance to urge the emotional reconciliation of his deeply wounded countrymen.

The first official words are spoken in Afrikaans—no translation offered. There are eleven official languages in the new South Africa (three words that I hear almost always spoken together), and the preservation of Afrikaans is of deep concern to the Afrikaner minority who peacefully relinquished power, following the advice of their leader, F. W. de Klerk, then woke up to find themselves a politically marginal subgroup. The mostly black audience listens with quiet courtesy to the language of their long oppression, for it was the forced use of Afrikaans as the medium of school instruction that first sparked the riots of Sowetan children back in 1976, riots that marked the beginning of the mutiny the world assumed would end in a bloody conflagration. Black courtesy is a separate piece in the microcosm of South Africa that is unfolding in the town of Upington. Africans call it *ubuntu*, meaning "compassion," or a spirit of humanity. I have heard no public calls for revenge against whites, even as the Truth and Reconciliation Commission (familiarly known as the TRC), which is holding public sessions across the land, hears awful revelations of apartheid-sanctioned atrocities.

Throughout the initial stages of this celebration, Nelson Mandela has stood apart; amid the shouts of joy, he has seemed preoccupied, his eyes focused on a distant place. Now he watches as a carefully selected representative phalanx of the Rainbow Nation takes the microphone, one after the other. A white Catholic bishop brings blessings; a delegate from the Indian community prays to Shiva for the unity of South Africa; a Muslim quotes from the Koran: nations were created to live together, he says, so may we accept our differences and work for justice, free our society of crime and bring into the fold those who would destroy and destabilize our new nation.

This is the first mention of the terrible problems that beset the new country.

A rabbi quotes the murdered Black Consciousness leader, Steve Biko: "We need to physically liberate our people from oppression and free them psychologically from a sense of inferiority." There are telegrams for President Mandela from the provincial premiers. One reads: "We have cried, we have been exiled, we have all suffered with you. Today we remember and cherish our freedom."

It is Nelson Mandela's turn to speak. There is silence as he moves to the microphone, for his step has grown laborious and stiff over the past months, reminding one of his decades in prison and the rapid approach of his eightieth year. He begins in English, the lingua franca of the new nation: "We gather to celebrate three years of freedom with you who fought to bring this to our country." Then on to the pride of his government: the newly minted Constitution. "Our Constitution will become a cornerstone of the new patriotism, a framework for mending the legacy of our divided country, for patriotism means we are committed to being citizens in our new democracy." His every word will seek to consolidate the new pluralist nationalism: for black South Africans, a new era of legal protection and common dignity under the jurisdiction of the highest court has begun. "Our deepest aspirations are enshrined now in the basic law of the land," says the man who brought the peace. Children representing each province step forward to shake his hand, and there are fervent speeches, punctuated with references to unity, peace and the sacrifices of millions. "Thank you, President Nelson Mandela, for leading us to liberation," one woman says gratefully.

The commentator's voice alternates between squeaky excitement and crackling emotion. "How typical of Madiba (South Africans' affectionate name for Mandela)," he cries as the president shakes hands with a boy in a wheelchair. "He is building fatherhood as well as nationhood!"

Yet amid the celebrations and brave expressions of hope, a piece of the unity strategy is missing: only a handful of white faces dot the vast crowd. Even the enthusiastic commentator eventually feels a professional obligation to mention the obvious. He notes that the majority of whites in Upington have chosen not to come. Then he wonders aloud, over the airwaves of South Africa, whether "they have not fully accepted the spirit of reconciliation."

I have come to South Africa to explore the very recent memory of white-over-black oppression and the way the new nation is coping with its immediate past. If the great Enlightenment-founded democracy of the United States has not yet found a workable path through—or even around—the remembrance of slavery and its serious, continuing problems of race, South Africa is making strong efforts right from the start of the transition into another mode of governance; but I'm finding that I have questions, and even more doubts, especially about the Truth and Reconciliation Commission, an institution legislated by the African National Congress (ANC)-led government in 1995 to retrieve the truth about the past by allowing victims of apartheid to relate their stories in public and perpetrators to confess and recant. The purpose of the TRC is to restore memory, following the systematic elimination of the nation's archival record—a destruction that took place through decades of censorship and confiscation of materials; the incarceration and assassination of thousands of activists; and the outright eradication of state records by the governing National Party in an attempt to remove incriminating evidence.[2] The hope is that if the past can be reconstructed through truth and possibly atonement, reconciliation will follow.

A fine and noble plan, but beset, to my mind, with formidable problems. Much of what took place during the decades of apartheid rule was criminal in nature, according to international law; however, the TRC has not been designed as a traditional court able to mete out retributive justice; in fact, it offers permanent amnesty from any future criminal prosecution if the act in question was carried out for "political" reasons—although anyone who chooses not to apply for amnesty, or who applies and is refused, *will* be open to prosecution in criminal court. All the same, I wonder if the former butchers of apartheid might not view the prospect of irreversible amnesty as an invitation to whitewash the past by cynically "confessing" to atrocities, and whether the decision not to prosecute them as war criminals—as was done to their counterparts at the Nuremberg trials and is currently being done in The Hague—might actually be dangerous for the new country, in that some of the victims might conclude that a breach of justice has occurred and seek revenge. Is anything resembling "reconciliation" even possible under such circumstances? The Rainbow Nation is awash in violence and the memory of past atrocity. Will the frightful memories being revived by TRC hearings all over the country make what happened even more difficult to bear?

Across the sea, U.S. Congressman Tony Hall's proposed apology for slavery is being debated at precisely the same time as the TRC holds its inquiries, and it is clear that the institutions of slavery and apartheid had much in common. Although the white masters of South Africa lacked absolute power over the bodies and souls of their underlings, in the way of the American South, their cruelties had a similarly harmful effect upon generations of maltreated non-citizens. Ideas of reconciliation and apology came late to America, and for now they seem to be going nowhere. But by striving to settle the humiliations of yesterday at the very moment blacks are being emancipated into full citizenship, South Africa may have a better chance. Provided that the TRC turns out to be a useful tool.

"The spirit of reconciliation." Generous words from the announcer covering the Mandela event in Upington. But several weeks earlier, as my plane landed at the airport on the eastern flank of Johannesburg and their magnificent suburban homes surged into view, it was easy to see that white South Africans had a complex adjustment ahead. It was an idyllic-looking vista—except that each one of these estates was surrounded by fortress-like walls. My seatmate, a middle-aged Afrikaner businessman returning home from the United States, relaxed visibly. So what if his city was reputed to be the world's most dangerous urban space? Home is home. Or maybe he was relieved at the imminent prospect of losing me and my unwelcome questions. I had already learned that *he* was no racist—some of his best friends were black, Indian and "coloured"—but, he added, there is no point trying to mix people beyond a certain point. "Different cultures have to develop in their own way—for heaven's sake, even the *whites* in South Africa are different from each other! The Afrikaners, the English, the Jews, the Greeks, the Italians—we are all separate and developing in our own way."

"Isn't 'separate development' just a polite euphemism for apartheid?" I asked him. "Surely that didn't work out very well?"

"Well, one group was oppressed," he allowed. "And that was wrong."

All the same, he hated the Truth and Reconciliation Commission. The TRC is "a negative" that harmed people by bringing back memories that are better forgotten. "I don't even look at it anymore! Turn off the television. They let people stand up and say terrible things! We need to move on, that's what we need. Get on with building the economy."

There were two subjects he categorically refused to discuss: one was the actual content of the horror stories emerging from the TRC hearings concerning the murderous activities of the former Security Police and the South African Defence Forces in their battle against the ANC. This information was too painful to listen to on television and certainly not a subject for conversation with a stranger. The other was what happened during his term of military service with the South African Defence Forces on the border of Angola. That experience also needed painful re-evaluation.

"It all makes me feel guilty in some awful way," he said quietly, before pointedly clamping on his headset.

How many people in how many countries have said the same: "We need to move on—get on with building the economy." That's what the members of the President's Initiative on Race decided when they dismissed the idea of a presidential apology for America's slave past. "Let's stop wallowing in the sloughs of the past" was the way the former Mississippi governor William Winter put it. Even if one disagreed, this point of view made more sense in the United States than in South Africa, where oppression ended just yesterday and memory is raw. In South Africa, after three hundred years of racist relations and a half century of brutal white supremacy, the transition from old to new would not be easy. Shutting the book and trying to start afresh—pretending, like the enthusiasts of the French Revolution, that "history" has screeched to a halt and is starting anew—hadn't had much success over the centuries. Sooner or later the papered-over cracks tend to be exposed.

Even if one agreed that the past ought to be aired in some way, history is interpretation as well as fact, and in a territory as divided as South Africa there was bound to be a battle over the official record. The country faced the overwhelming task of having to reinvent itself after a discredited era that had been fully justified by "history," nationalism and a sense of God-given right—and still was, in the privacy of many homes. Whites had to be brought into the new nation in a way that acknowledged the crimes of apartheid without incurring corrosive, collective guilt. I could see that this was proving difficult as I watched Mandela being greeted with joy in the town of Upington by a crowd that conspicuously lacked white faces.

The city of Johannesburg is still divided into distinct racial sectors, including the black township of Soweto, in the southwest, which is home to millions. Unlike other townships, Soweto made it onto the map of South Africa during the apartheid era, but only because of the notorious school riots that took place there in 1976. Elsewhere in the country, a visitor might have driven thousands of kilometres and from the map alone never known there were massive sprawls of unserviced shacks near the familiar metropolises. Officially, they simply did not exist.

Now, the centre of post-apartheid Johannesburg is a crime-infested place where any hapless tourist can be mugged, or worse, in broad daylight. Criminal violence is the most dangerous social problem facing the country, and it is not in the least new: with millions of people formerly penned up in townships and rural reserves romantically called "homelands," every conceivable crime of malice and desperation had taken place. Although apartheid is now officially dead, the habits of violence persist, shored up by an unemployment rate higher than 30 per cent; it has seeped into the white suburbs, terrifying the wealthy and precipitating emigration. Part of the problem has been the police themselves: during apartheid, they defended 12 per cent of the population against all the rest, and they are still untrained in the ways of impartiality. The need to protect the whole of society is a new concept in South Africa.

Across the northern cap of the city stretch the luxurious "white" suburbs I viewed from the air, including Sandton, the wealthiest community in the country. My seatmate confided that except for having lost political power, most white South Africans had not seen their privileged lives change. On arrival, I found this immediately obvious.

Since staying in the city centre has seemed unadvisable for safety reasons, I have reserved a room in a family-owned guest house in Roodepoort, an Afrikaner suburb. The house, when I arrive, is partially hidden from view by a gate and a tangle of flowering tropical vines; a second locked gate protects the door. Crime in this once-restricted whites' paradise is so commonplace that my host tells me she keeps weapons close at hand; she and her husband also carry a gun in their car.

Each lovely residence on the street is encircled by high stone walls topped with additional electrified fencing and barbed wire. Windows have been barred; ferocious-looking guard dogs slaver, bark and hurl themselves at the inside of gates as I walk through the neighbourhood. Large warning signs (illustrated with the image of a shiny black revolver) announce that reprisal will be swift and brutal should anyone be foolish enough to enter without permission. One not-so-funny poster advertises that "trespassers will be eaten."

The white tribe of Roodepoort clearly cleaves together. Although I am a stranger, white people wave as they pass by in their BMWs and Mercedeses, the status cars of choice. Only the black workers refuse to make eye contact. Gardeners prune and plant luxuriant beds of richly hued hibiscus, gardenia and magnolia; maids in starched white aprons congregate outside to gossip in the sunlight. Only once during this walk do I intercept a glance, and it is not friendly. After an initial confusing moment, I think I may understand. In this country of collectivities, where people are either "white," "black," "coloured" or "Indian," and where until recently only whites were legally deemed "South African," I am not an individual capable of holding an independent opinion but merely a member of an oppressor race.

The only place blacks and whites interact is on television, where their behaviour can be contrived. Smiling co-anchors announce the evening's programs, each in his or her own language: English and Zulu; Afrikaans and Xhosa. One evening, I watch a talk show in my hosts' living room; four black and two white musicians are politely discussing a litany of shared complaints, until the white music teacher happens to say she runs a school for children from the townships and has received funding from corporations. "See!" shouts one of the blacks, as the camera records the fracas live. "In this country everything comes down to colour! She has access to funding and we don't!" The white woman stiffens. "I'm an educator—all the children in our program are black." A palpable chill descends on the studio as the host frantically leaps in to change the subject.

The couple that runs the guest house—I'll call them Willie and Rebecca—are fair-skinned, big-boned Afrikaners of Dutch extraction; they remind me of long-gone days. Rebecca makes little butter balls for my breakfast toast, and the plate always comes garnished with a pretty flower. There is much jocular talk about what men and women do best

("Women are good at handling hot platters," says Willie) and numerous questions about my marital life. Rebecca is disappointed that I haven't brought a picture of my house.

They both applaud racial integration, except that they do not want their children to marry someone from another colour group. "That's just natural," explains Willie. "They are so different culturally. Also, it's pretty bad around here," he adds ominously. "They'll kill you for ten rand."

In spite of having opinions at the ready, Willie claims to have no interest in politics, and he emphatically does not watch the televised TRC hearings. He and Rebecca have pulled away from all that and opted to focus their attention on God: they have given up the mainstream Dutch Reformed Church as too secular and retreated into the embrace of charismatic Christianity, as have many of their Afrikaner neighbours and compatriots.

"If we have bad government, God will take care of everything." He smiles reassuringly. "Anyway, all governments feed propaganda to their people. We were told that Communists weren't even human beings and that they were the greatest threat to our country and our well-being." He looks momentarily downcast. He doesn't believe that anymore, so he tries not to think about such things. Fundamentalism has brought relief from the incessant shocks of the past few years: "Don't worry, be happy" is an alternative to puzzling over how it has happened that the powerful Afrikaner world has been turned on its ear so abruptly.

We drive to a Sunday service in an enormous hall attended by thousands of people singing and rocking enthusiastically to electric guitar, drums and trumpet. The slick-looking minister raises his eyes to heaven, looks around the room dramatically, then "heals" the mortally ill, who have lined up for treatment. Willie cries "Hallelujah!" and looks joyful.

Although he doesn't watch the TRC hearings, he is nonetheless informed about the atrocities that are being exposed on a daily basis: the revelations about death squads and killing farms and Third Force arrangements in which apartheid politicians at the highest levels financed and trained Zulu fighters to attack and terrorize the ANC.[3] A high-ranking general recently confessed all in his application for amnesty.

"Tell me," he asks me one evening, leaning forward in anticipation. "Were we that different? After all, look at the Nazis! Then what about the United States? Someone killed *President Kennedy*!"

I like Willie very much; he is a kind man and a good husband and father, and I do not want to be hurtful. I suggest to him that there is a difference between individual violent acts and state-sanctioned violence, just as there is a difference between a society laced with racism and a state that enacts racist laws. As for the Nazis, well, yes, it is true; they may well have been the closest approximation to apartheid in the twentieth century.

Willie is still for what seems a long time. Then he speaks. "Men died for this country," he says quietly, averting his eyes.

All-white, oppressive and colonial in its foundations, Willie's "country" disappeared forever on April 26, 1994, the day a black man was elected president of the new South Africa. It was a land imagined into being, like many others, with potent symbol, cultivated myth and crafted memory—except that the underlying idea of the Afrikaner nation was more radical than most, more relentless and certainly more cruel: a true country of the mind built on an idealized foundation. As W. A. de Klerk, an Afrikaner historian who was villainized for challenging established myth, wrote in 1975: "[Justified power] has consistently been the claim of puritan radicals who believed that they had been called not only to govern, but also to remake society from the roots upwards."[4]

From its beginnings, "Afrikanerdom" stood for a vision of nationhood that excluded other peoples living in the territory, whatever their race. Like the Nazi Party, indeed: Afrikaner nationalism was built on a foundation of the inferior "other."

The white Afrikaners born and bred at the tip of the African continent have been here for three hundred years—since the beginnings of European colonization. The Dutch came first, with their formidable "imperial state" known as the Dutch East India Company. In the wake of the Company trailed a small number of independent settlers: Dutch Calvinist peasants, Low Germans, French Huguenots escaping anti-Protestant oppression and a handful of Britons and Scandinavians. Standing on the decks of their ships, these early migrants to the wilderness of a distant continent were met by an untamed, breathtakingly beautiful shore at the southern port of Cape Town. But they didn't become "Afrikaners" until the eighteenth century, when the Dutch East India Company reluctantly allowed a few independents to establish their own farms. These men and women adopted the name, by which they meant that they were as much the children of Africa as any of the black tribes inhabiting the land. Afrikaners were the descendants of the original European settlers, now collectively converted to the God of Calvin and united by the emerging language of Afrikaans, a hybrid dialect of Dutch, German, French and Malay (the language spoken by the slaves imported by the Company). They lived the life of landed gentry—their farm labour carried out by the "lesser breeds," as they called them—but with only a few hints of the culture their European ancestors had enjoyed.

As I strained to understand historical memory in this nation so remote from Europe and North America, I remembered that although the Enlightenment changed the face of eighteenth-century Europe, catapulting revolutionary notions of equality across timeless landscapes, such ideas were barely known—and distinctly unwelcome—in the southern reaches of the African continent. Isolated from the rest of the world, the estates of the Cape Colony contained no books but the Bible. No general education furrowed the brows of Afrikaner children or disturbed the assurance born of racial and religious certainty. I had also to remember that the justification for white supremacy came bundled together with Calvinism, since according to the doctrine of predestination, the salvation (or damnation) of each of us is preordained. White Christian Afrikaners had no doubts about who was destined to be saved (themselves) and who was not (the native people) and no doubts about which race was superior. Because they were unbaptized, the indigenous peoples were considered to be less than human. (The word *kaffir*—the white South African equivalent of "nigger"—originally meant "unbeliever.") Society was divided by both colour and caste from the start, and the mixed-race offspring of master and slave were rarely freed. Afrikaner beliefs were no more monolithic than those of other groups, but the eighteenth-century Cape, far from being benign, as used to be claimed, was, the historians Richard Elphick and Robert Shell have concluded, "one of the most closed and rigid slave societies so far analysed."[5]

Afrikaner identity was to undergo a further refinement that would become central to the memory myths of the white nation—a shift that came from the loss of Afrikaner power, after the British occupied the Cape at the end of the eighteenth century in their drive to expand their Empire. The British did something unforgivable: in 1833, they abolished slavery. That they replaced slave bondage with a Masters and Servants Ordinance maintaining white control was irrelevant. To abandon slavery was intolerable. Everyone knew whites did *not* work with their hands.

To those reared on selected passages of the Old Testament that were interpreted to justify slavery, the notion that the races might be inherently equal was sacrilege. Without legalized bondage, Afrikaners believed, their superiority and their culture were threatened. Demanding autonomy and physical isolation (the separateness known as "apartheid"), approximately twelve thousand dissatisfied farmers, or Boers, set out in 1835 in tented ox-wagons, hoping to find game and the virgin lands of the interior. They called their historical journey into the hinterland of the southern continent the Great Trek, an experience that would become mythologized as the foundation of the Afrikaner nation.

Anyone wishing to explore the seminal memory-myths of Afrikaner history should head straight for Pretoria, where monuments abound. I do a day trip from Roodepoort. First stop: the restored house of the South African Republic president Paul Kruger, who led the Afrikaners against the British in the Anglo-Boer War at the start of the twentieth century. The brutality of that conflict still rankles—the burning of Afrikaner farms, the deliberate starving of women and children—and the house stands as a perpetual reminder. Next, a taxi ride to the Union Buildings, executive home of the former apartheid government. Vainglorious, self-important, standing auspiciously on the cusp of a hill overlooking the city, this erstwhile seat of Afrikaner power nostalgically mimics imperial Rome or ancient Greece. The building curves forward at both ends, like the arms of a stone mother reaching out to hold and protect, or, in keeping with the Christian foundations of the apartheid state, like Christ encompassing his flock. In the spirit of *ubuntu* that characterizes the black response to whites, no one in the ANC-led government has suggested tearing this place down: in post-Soviet Russia, by contrast, grandiose heads of Lenin were unceremoniously rolling off their pedestals. Finally, few would choose to miss the holy shrine to the heart of Afrikaner nationalism, which also crowns the cap of a hill and also was built to last forever. The Voortrekker Monument houses a sculpted wall frieze that recounts the story of the Great Trek—transformed, sanctified and culminating in the creation of a "people."

If the anniversary celebrated in Upington was a microcosm of the "new" South Africa, here, in stark juxtaposition, is the "old." These are the "countries" the Truth and Reconciliation Commission needs to reconcile.

On the walls of the Voortrekker Monument, the emigration from the Cape Colony into the remote African hinterland is idealized in heroic configuration: bold, stern-featured men stand proud, and fearless women wield rifles with ease, while their wagons protectively encircle the camp against the enemy: the formidable Zulus. A bas-relief portrays the encounter of the two tribes, white and black, in the province of Natal, a confrontation that has been transformed into sublime religious-national myth. The core of the story has two parts. Let us call the first "the Great Deception." On February 6, 1838, the Boer leader, Piet Retief, walked into a trap set by the Zulu king, Dingane. The Boers demanded outright ownership of the land and believed they were in a military position to force acquiescence. Dingane agreed to sign the title deed, then immediately ordered the murder of Retief and his party and attacks on other settlements. Hundreds died, and there was no relief for the embattled Voortrekkers until the following November, when a rescue party arrived.

Part two is "the Divine Intervention." A few hundred white Christians, under the command of Andries Pretorius, routed several thousand Zulus in a decisive victory on December 16, 1838. A miracle was proclaimed, and the now-holy battle site was named Blood River. That this miracle was made possible by the fact that the Boers had guns and used them from a defensive position while the Zulus mostly made do with traditional spears does not undermine the archetypal declaration, a claim that consciously parallels the Old Testament sweep of the ancient Israelites into the Promised Land. The Land of South Africa, like the Land of the Israelites, is bestowed by God—an affirmation no mortal can gainsay.

Attaching God to history is the most powerful nationalism of all. In 1978, almost 150 years after the Great Trek, members of the right-wing Afrikaner Weerstandsbeweging (Afrikaner Resistance Movement) literally tarred and feathered a Pretoria professor for daring to suggest that the victory at Blood River might have been accomplished without God's help.

The beautifully sculpted story of the Great Trek reminds me (and not by chance) of the pictorial narratives of the Bible in medieval churches, for they, too, were designed to uplift the spirit and reinforce communal beliefs; reminds me that sculpted storytelling was also a prominent feature of ancient Greek temples, as anyone who has ever marvelled at the magnificent friezes now in the British Museum in London will recall. The imperial Greeks carved the mythical past of their nation into stone: titanic battles between gods and giants, between Lapiths and centaurs, between the (male) heroes of Greece and the (female) warrior Amazons. The enemy was powerful and worthy, but the forces of light (the Greeks and their god projections) always won, just as here, in the Voortrekker

Monument, other god-infused imperial conquerors rightly defeat their forceful foes.

Below the wall sculpture, a part of the floor has been opened to reveal a lower level where a bronze inscription lies exposed. The words are visible under artificial light: *Ons vir jou, Suid Africa* (We for thee, South Africa). But every December 16, on the anniversary of the victory at Blood River, the sun penetrates an angled shaft in the ceiling, and God's own light illuminates the plaque. God, nature, humankind—history acting in concert. After the Great Trek and the miracle of Blood River, the Afrikaner nation and everything it embarked upon were divinely ordained.

The Voortrekker Monument was inaugurated in 1949 in the wake of the Second World War, just one year after the victory of the National Party under D. F. Malan. More than 250,000 people attended the ceremony, arriving from across the country to pay tribute to their shared mythic origins and to marvel at the massive stone fortress and the wall surrounding it, onto which had been carved sixty-four ox-wagons in a traditional *laager* (the defensive wagon circle used in Boer camps). They gazed in pride at the impressive entrance presided over by a carved head of an African buffalo, the most intelligent, dangerous and unpredictable beast on the continent, especially when cornered. The message is unmistakable: the Afrikaner nation will close ranks and defend itself.

This is—or, more precisely, was—the "country" of my host, Willie.

Segregationist laws were long part of the political landscape; as early as 1913, the Natives Land Act attempted to push black Africans into reserves (largely to eliminate sharecropping, which undermined the master-servant relationship, and to provide a pool of contract labour for the gold mines). Attitudes were already entrenched: whites were horrified by the idea of interracial sex, wanted to see the races separated and were possessive about the vote, but not until the election of the National Party in 1948 was apartheid duly refined. During two succeeding decades, politicians created new legislation on the understanding that non-whites were object-pawns to be moved about to suit their superiors. By the end of the 1950s, the structures of apartheid were in place: non-whites were forcibly removed from large and small centres, loaded onto trucks and dumped in their newly designated "home," which was often a barren field in the middle of the open veld. The Population Registration Act classified everyone by race; the Prohibition of Mixed Marriages Act and the Immorality Act prohibited interracial sexual intercourse; the Bantu Education Act provided for separate education systems, with a spending ratio of about 7 to 1 in favour of white schoolchildren[6] (as Hendrik Verwoerd, then education minister and later prime minister, put it: "There is no place for [black Africans] in the European community above the level of certain forms of labour"); and pass laws required blacks to carry "reference books" containing photographs and information about employment, tax payments, residence and contacts with police.

"Apartheid's beneficiaries put disfavoured racial castes into a zoo of being, [and made themselves] zoo-keeper over the kept," wrote the ANC politician Kader Asmal in 1996, but this was not the understanding of the early architects of apartheid. In 1948, Prime Minister Daniel F. Malan expressed a radically different vision: "The last one hundred years have witnessed a miracle, behind which must lie a divine plan. The history of the Afrikaners reveals a will and a determination which makes one feel that Afrikanerdom is not the work of men but of God," he said.[7]

The social and human costs of a half century of such policies are impossible to measure, although the evidence is clear to the eye, from the sharp gap in living standards between whites and non-whites to the continued existence of black and white residential ghettos; the culture of crime, violence and impunity; and the largely unspoken fear of black retribution that haunts privileged whites. But the social disorder brought about by racial classification is perhaps conveyed most directly by the former government's official Gazette announcements. Since every life opportunity, including the right to vote, own property, attend a decent school and live in a better area depended on the racial grouping to which one had been assigned, people applied to move up in the world, if possible ("trying for white," it was called), or were officially downgraded. So we learn that during 1985,

- 702 "coloureds" became "white"
- 10 "whites" became "coloured"
- 249 "blacks" became "coloured"
- 20 "coloureds" became "black."[8]

What this means is that African children born with lighter skins were sometimes classified as "coloureds" by their parents so they might have access to a better education and a freer life, and that "coloureds" were reclassified as "white" for the same reason. You could lose your child that way. In one famous case, a dark-skinned girl born to a white family and reclassified was so alienated that she rejected—and was rejected by—her parents; eventually, she moved to a black township and assumed a new identity.

Just as the Nazis devised ways of identifying who was and was not a Jew by measuring noses, peering into eyes and examining various physical characteristics, so apartheid officials ran pencils through people's hair on the theory that "black" hair's curliness, even if invisible, would hold the object, while "white" hair would not. Police brandishing tape recorders and binoculars investigated the crime of interracial sexual intercourse, examining bedsheets and hiding police officers under suspect beds. But the pass laws seem to have caused the most anguish. Since the nation's economy depended on a ready pool of cheap black labour, and since blacks were not allowed to live in the white areas where they were employed, whites had to sign the pass books to prove that the bearer was an employee and therefore lawfully present for the period of time he or she was at work. Contract miners were forced to live away from their wives for months and years at a time. (As the policy analyst Stephen Friedman put it when we talked together in his Johannesburg office, "In the U.S. ghettos they have a problem of single-parent families; in this society, it was official policy for forty years to *split* families!") To forget one's pass book, or to refuse to carry it as an act of protest, could, and did, land millions of people in jail: between 1948 and 1985 there were more than twelve million arrests for pass book infringements.

With law books filled with countless regulatory details, it is not surprising that in the name of "separate development," the white tribe eventually legislated the black tribe right out of the "country." Blacks had never been part of the mythic nation, which was white by definition, but in 1974 legislated "apartness" was taken a step further: the very boundaries of South Africa were physically redrawn to exclude the black group areas. The "homelands" were ruled by hereditary chiefs in collaboration with the government at Pretoria, and they had been placed in areas where there was no industry and little viable farming land; nonetheless, the fiction that these poverty-stricken reserves were equal to "South Africa" (which was now officially populated by whites only) persisted. "If our policy is taken to its logical conclusion, there will not be one black man with South African citizenship. Every black man will eventually be accommodated in some independent new state in this honourable way and there will no longer be a moral obligation on this parliament to accommodate these people politically," explained the government minister responsible.

Cut off from "the other," except for structured master-servant relations, and inwardly fearful of retaliation from people being oppressed in their name, some white South Africans rationalized the status quo with nervous imaginings about the lesser creatures they controlled. The unknown life of their black workers back in the group areas, or homelands, produced shuddering visions of witchcraft, animism, primitivism and rampant sexuality. Nowhere are these fears described more sharply than in Nadine Gordimer's 1981 novel, *July's People*. The dreaded apocalypse has finally arrived: the black Communists have come to destroy white capitalist civilization and all white people. A liberal family escapes with their loyal servant, July, to his rural village, a place that was heretofore the stuff of private, dubious conjecture. Slowly, as the weeks pass, they sink into the seemingly unstructured life of the *kraal* homestead—first the children, then the parents, one slippery, irrevocable step at a time. Gordimer conjures a Conradian descent into the heart of darkness; she gives shape to the primal fear of otherness from which no white South African—even the most "liberal," she seems to be saying—is exempt.

Back in Roodepoort, Rebecca tells me her own story. She was born in the 1950s to a rural Afrikaner family in the Orange Free State. The farm was worked by male "natives," and female "natives" looked after the house. Her mother taught her to read the Bible and embroider; her father—a good man—built his blacks mud huts with thatched roofs. "They were so different from us," she confides. "They didn't wash, and really you could smell them when they were near. We thought they didn't like to wash, but now we see that they really didn't have enough water. We also see that they have been westernized and they really want to be like us; we've succeeded in changing them!" She is oblivious to her paternalism: it is as ordinary as the air she breathes. But in the past she was always aware of fear—sexual fear—because the law that prevented the wives of men who worked away from the reserves to move to the cities with their husbands meant that the workers lived in all-male hostels for months, sometimes years, at a time.

Rebecca had seen the sexual assaults. When she and Willie first moved to Johannesburg, they lived across from a hostel where the men slept at night. "Sometimes the men grabbed the black domestics when they walked by; we could hear them screaming. When Willie was out, I was terrified. I just kept the gun pointed at the door!"

Even now, Rebecca's vision extends no further than this, although, like everyone else, she probably knows more about despair and humiliation than she is willing to say. Her experience of the "other" is shot through with racial fear and superiority—the polished exclusions of what she calls "civilization."

For decades, whites—Afrikaners, Greeks, Britons, Jews and Italians—continued to elect the National Party with ever-increasing majorities, as they lived out the final stages of an anachronistic fantasy two centuries after the Enlightenment swept Europe, and one hundred years after the American Civil War. As the title of Marq de Villiers's book on his Afrikaner family brilliantly conveys, this was the "White Tribe Dreaming."

I am searching, now, for the memory of the other "country" that has roots in this soil, and I have made contact with Nkosinathi Biko, the son of the murdered Black Consciousness activist Steve Biko. We will meet this evening. I am curious about what has happened to this son, because the story of his father's life and awful death in police custody reached the entire world, thanks to Biko's friend the newspaper editor Donald Woods, whose book, *Biko*, recounted their growing personal relationship under the hostile surveillance of the security police (they both were eventually put under house arrest); Biko's death (he was transported sixteen hundred kilometres over rough roads on the floor of a police van, bloodied, brain-damaged and in a coma); and the widespread cover-up at the inquest, where it was claimed that he had "gone berserk" and deliberately banged his head against a wall. The magistrate, Marthinus Prins, concluded, then, that no responsibility could be assigned for his death. Biko was already a hero when he was killed in 1977 at age thirty-one. He was intellectual, immensely likable and the first to suggest that the struggle for freedom and interracial peace might be built upon black self-esteem—a radical idea that touched deep chords in South African blacks, who had been called animals for so many years, and around the world, especially in the United States, where African Americans suffered from similar feelings of unworthiness. Many of the blacks I would meet on this journey through South Africa remembered the moment they heard of Biko's death in precisely the same way Americans remember the moment they heard about the death of John F. Kennedy. Several dated their "awakening," as they call it, to that event.

I stand near a "Greek" column in the flamboyantly decorated lobby of the Hyatt Hotel, waiting for Nkosinathi. This unlikely meeting place was his idea; the garish Hyatt is not a place I would choose. Well-dressed couples swish by, some of the women flashing jewels. I doubt that I will have trouble finding him; there are almost no blacks here. Then a small, fine-boned man is standing beside me. We greet each other and sit down to talk on one of the lobby couches, but his demeanour is so retiring, and his voice so quiet, that I must strain to hear him. He is twenty-six, with a degree in economics; he works on the business side of *The Sowetan*, South Africa's largest-circulation daily with a targeted black audience. I suppose I look surprised, because he laughs out loud: "Well, I guess I'm political in my way, but not like my father, because I think blacks will only gain real influence through economic power. Until we reduce poverty and manage to redistribute wealth to some extent, inequality will continue. That's why I went into business."

He was just six years old when his father was murdered, but his memories, he says, are vivid. The family lived in the black township of King William's Town in the Eastern Cape, not far from the port city of East London. Nkosinathi was only three when his father was "banned," or consigned to house arrest, which meant that Biko was always at home. "I know it's selfish, but that's how I got to know him, and I'm grateful, because before he was banned he was an activist and always travelling," he says softly. He sat on his father's lap and listened to the never-ending conversations. Banned people were not allowed to be in the company of more than one person at a time, but many managed to get around that law even as the police surveyed their houses. Nkosinathi remembers that the police often questioned him about what went on inside, and he never knew, because his father always sent him out to buy cigarettes when there was a conversation he was afraid the child might repeat.

He grew up fatherless in that other "country," in a violent township, and he tells me it took a toll. "My township was separated from white South Africa by a kilometre that included a river, and they could not have imagined on one side what was going on the other. Someone would be beaten every day, and every weekend we would bury a youngster. We just knew that Friday was a dangerous day—that was when people were paid, and the day they drank. All weekend we stepped over dead bodies. So now all this is being reported, and whites think that

South Africa is suddenly violent. That's not true. This has been the case for a long time.

"We knew about the security police death squads and the camps they operated, because some of the survivors told us. I knew children who were blindfolded by the police, then taken to a place where they were told to bury bags in the ground. They saw what was in them—limbs of people who had been chopped up—and they came and told us what they saw. These were the things the people on the other side of the river could never have imagined, even in their nightmares. One man in our township was accused of being a spy for the government, and later it turned out he had been tortured by the security police and had provided information about something or other. But the police were tricky: they put this guy in a marked police car and dropped him off in the busiest square of the township. Emotions were running high. The guy was necklaced [putting a person's head through a rubber tire, dousing the tire with gasoline and allowing the person to burn to death]. The police had 'clean' ways of doing things and removing the responsibility from themselves."

There is no apparent bitterness in his voice—strangely, almost no emotion at all. I am embarrassed by the contrast between where we are and his suffering. The Hyatt cocktail lounge is nearby; the laughter is raucous and the music is blaring. "You've just described an unimaginably horrible environment, yet you seem like a gentle person," I blurt out. "How did you protect yourself from becoming hard and violent?"

His reply feels like a blow, although I know he does not intend it this way. "Many of my friends went mad, many became criminals, many became fundamentalist Christians and some, like me, just became numb. I have always called it 'numbness.' I have no other word for it."

"Has nothing softened this for you?"

He is silent for several very long moments. "Yes, I always had one parent to return to, where some of my friends had none, and my mother was a source of strength. I also know that many people died for nothing, but that my father died for something. At his funeral one of his friends said he died for a living cause that was felt across the country. That became my strength."

Steve Biko's son now wants the most ordinary life he can manage, although given the deprivation he experienced in his early years, his desires seem almost extraordinary. He wants a "good family," and the opportunity to give his children what he missed. He wants what was never before possible for a black man: success in a career, a middle-class life and "the chance to kick a football around with my kids." But he admits that before he can achieve the peace of mind he yearns for, he will have to "wriggle away" from his father, as he puts it, and become his own person. And that will hard to do, because the Steve Biko case has been reopened by the TRC, and the family has chosen him as their spokesman. What's more, the twentieth anniversary of Biko's death is fast approaching, and he wants to memorialize the event by making a film about his father and raising money for a charitable foundation to ensure that the memory of Biko will not slide into oblivion as the liberation struggle fades from memory over the years. Only then will his obligation be paid, he says.[9]

He drives me home to Roodepoort, and I bring him into the house to meet Willie and Rebecca, as they have asked me to do. They seem awed to have before them the son of the man whose legendary name symbolizes, like Mandela's, the competing version of their nation's history. Everyone shakes hands, Nkosinathi in his direct and serious way, and Willie with his cheerful ebullience. Rebecca offers tea. Nkosinathi politely declines.

Before he leaves, I bring out a copy of T. R. H. Davenport's standard history of South Africa and show him what Davenport has written about his father. "Steve Biko was as tragic a martyr to the cause of his people's emancipation as any person in the history of South Africa, black or white," writes the renowned historian.[10] Nkosinathi's eyes brim with tears as he copies down the words.

The struggle for black freedom brought a third "country" into being, one effectively created by its white opponents. The one thing that united the diverse liberation groups and their few white allies was the fight against apartheid, and through that conflict a new national identity was forged. In the new South Africa, the battle for freedom, citizenship and dignity is revered—as sacred as the ideology behind the old nation. The Struggle, as it is called, is emerging as a patriotic counterpart to the Great Trek, with its own quasi-religious narrative and its own politically correct historiography.

The African National Congress—propagator and keeper of the new history—has not yet built a memorial to compete with the Voortrekker Monument in Pretoria, but writers with an agenda are already strutting their stuff, including three authors directly associated with the ANC:

Kader Asmal, a government cabinet minister; Louise Asmal; and Ronald Suresh Roberts. Their 1996 book *Reconciliation through Truth* thunders with rage at four decades of suffering, exile, ruined lives and death, while steering readers to a particular view by raising, then "resolving," controversial issues. One of the book's claims is that the use of violence in resisting apartheid was unqualifiedly justified, and that the ANC adopted a strategy of violence back in the 1960s only after all else failed. The ANC's "world-renowned Freedom Charter" was "a global model of inclusive politics," according to the authors; and yes, human rights abuses such as necklacing did occur, but they were a result of "failures in the command"—unlike the actions of apartheid masters, who "rejected civilized norms" and occupied a "different, fundamentally incompatible moral universe." Since *Reconciliation through Truth* seems to have been written to create historical facts on the ground, nothing in the way of explanation, recontextualization or justification for the Struggle—the foundation myth of the new nation—can properly be left to chance.

Ironically, those who perpetrated apartheid also defend the use of violence. In his TRC testimony in June 1997, the former minister of law and order, Adriaan Vlok, admitted to having commanded his men to place "small explosive devices" outside two cinemas showing anti-apartheid movies, and to having made bomb threats to theatres planning to screen *Cry Freedom*, the film based on Donald Woods's biography of Steve Biko. Vlok explained that since fighting the communist onslaught was his first duty as a committed Christian, violence had to be met with violence. Other people have decided that since both sides justified the use of violence on the basis of the "different universes" they inhabited, they were equally guilty—or that they cancelled out each other's guilt. Some defenders of the past regime seem to like this idea: they argue that the battle for and against apartheid was a war and that in wartime soldiers sometimes do regrettable things; in other words, what happened was a morally equivalent conflict between two equal movements of self-determination.

Such relativizing of the ethical underpinnings of the Struggle is offensive to many supporters of the new South Africa, and the Asmal book carefully draws a key distinction between the individual and the collectivity: "The suffering of each individual who died [and] the suffering of that person's innocent family may be comparable [on both sides]. But this cannot obscure the fundamentally different moralities of the causes in which individuals died. The primary root of the whole conflict lies in the very existence of apartheid, which must be held responsible for the consequences of the resistance to it."

The Nazi analogy is pursued throughout *Reconciliation through Truth*. Apartheid is a crime against humanity, according to the definition established at the Nuremberg trials and acknowledged by the United Nations, thereby setting up a direct comparison with the agents of Nazi Germany who were war criminals. The troublesome part is that a book supposedly promoting "reconciliation" uses the Nazi comparison as a weapon with which to bludgeon the old enemy. Although the myths of the "Boer Nation" are dying in the new South Africa, the citizens of that old "country" still live here, and the new history makers will have to involve them in a positive way. To include those who were racist enemies, and are still unfriendly, seems to be the most sensitive task facing the new government. Both Nelson Mandela and Archbishop Desmond Tutu have insisted that if the Rainbow Nation is to work, people outside the newly configured "in-group" must be incorporated culturally and psychologically.

Having been released from the clutches of the censor, the daily media boils with a witches' brew of horror stories as victims tell their stories to the TRC and police and army cadres recant in the hope of amnesty. Dredging up what actually happened over the past half century has meant looking closely at the police and the army, whose members had maintained the apartheid system with criminal acts, including atrocities. The most shocking revelations have concerned a state-authorized, security-police death camp called Vlakplaas, near Pretoria, where, from 1979 to 1993, captured ANC and Pan Africanist Congress (PAC) activists were tortured and "turned" into informers, then made responsible for rounding up their comrades, who were subsequently murdered.

The story was exposed in November 1989 by Dirk Coetzee, a former commander of Vlakplaas. "I was in the heart of the whore," he confessed. "My men and I had to murder political and security opponents of the police and the government. I know the deepest secrets of this unit, which is above the law. I myself am guilty of, or at least accomplice to, several murders."[11] Coetzee escaped to London, where he narrowly dodged an assassination attempt. In 1997, he was back in South Africa—appealing for amnesty.

Another leading player was Eugene de Kock, one of Coetzee's successors at Vlakplaas. In 1996, the South Africa Broadcasting Corporation aired an astonishing documentary about de Kock, a man known to his admiring colleagues as "Prime Evil" (also the name of the film) and to himself as "apartheid's most effective assassin." The footage consists of home movies taken by the police at the farm, as well as interviews with the men, most of whom had been granted immunity from prosecution for testifying against their former boss.

I watched this film on the Canadian Broadcasting Corporation, before I left for South Africa, and I was appalled by the careless brutality of these men. The enemies de Kock and his men disposed of so perfunctorily are not human beings but featureless objects to be crushed as part of an evening's entertainment. The viewer is treated to the grisly sight of a skull de Kock has just split open with a spade.

How did such a man come to be? The brutalization of Eugene de Kock seems to have taken place over a twenty-year period, starting in the former Rhodesia, where he learned to hang "terrorists" upside down from trees and push burning sticks into their anuses; then, in Namibia, where he enjoyed cutting off ears as souvenirs and tying those who were about to die to the wheels of Jeeps; then, finally, as a reward for becoming "a warrior" and a "killing machine," as commander of Vlakplaas, where the partying, drinking and cavorting with strippers only momentarily interrupted the "work" of torture and death. De Kock was not alone, as the documentary makes clear: he was merely the tip of an invisible iceberg.

What motivated these police warriors was the conviction that they were serving their country at the highest level. When Prime Minister P. W. Botha said, "Terrorists must be confronted! We will not talk but fight!" the men of Vlakplaas understood their battle was just. "We were taught to hate," Paul Erasmus, who served under de Kock, tells the camera. "The blacks were satanic and godless, uncivilized and uncontrolled in their impulses. And they were going to swamp us."[12]

I think that I will not comprehend apartheid, or the transition to the new South Africa, or the memory work of the Truth and Reconciliation Commission and its attempts to kickstart a new democracy, until I learn more about these security police, who were the savage arm of the regime. Eugene de Kock is in prison, serving two consecutive life sentences, so seeing him is out of the question. But Dirk Coetzee is at home in Pretoria, waiting nervously to hear the results of his amnesty application for the 1981 murder of the human rights lawyer Griffiths Mxenge, whose body was found with forty stab wounds. I call him on the phone. "Sure, I'll see you," he says. I call a taxi in Roodepoort, and I am there in an hour. His suburban house is barely visible behind thick gates, and three guard dogs howl as I approach. I assume Coetzee has enemies: he is living among his own people—Afrikaners—and some of them must hate him for having "betrayed."

He is fifty-three and fit-looking, with a fringe of a blond brush cut standing up on his head. He leads me into a well-furnished bungalow. We take a turn to the right and enter a study that looks towards the street. He is alone in the house today, and his pale blue eyes nervously scan the room, searching out the corners. Is he always like this, I wonder. His anxiety is disturbing. He tells me he likes to talk to writers; they will carry his story beyond the walls of this house.

He is in a rage against the National Party and its (then) leader, F. W. de Klerk, whom he accuses of stonewalling and lying and pretending ignorance about what was carried out in his name at Vlakplaas and elsewhere. He is furious that the ANC did not come to his aid when it was he who blew the whistle and brought the death-squad edifice crashing down on the roof of apartheid. "*I* am the pioneer of exposing the mighty apartheid regime and the mighty security police," he brags. "*I* fought the system and now I'm out in the cold. I compare myself with all the other guys who were involved and the government ministers. Now they're a part of the new South Africa, in the government of national unity! Ha! Some of these guys who are now part of the South African police force did much worse things than I did! I committed maybe eight or nine murders, but they committed ninety or a hundred. And they are still in the police force! De Kock left the police with a golden handshake of 1.5 million rand and I'm living here in poverty!"

"De Kock's in jail," I remind him.

"He tried to save his ass, but he was too stupid. Saving your ass is what it's all about today, but I didn't do that. I told the truth because I believe we can only bury the past if we know what it is we're burying."

He is already shivering with tension and our conversation has just begun. "The security police were a family, an elite, and we were fighting the enemy of the family because they were supporting the right to vote and freedom of expression and all that. I mean, they were Communists and terrorists and we were the last Christian outpost on the southern tip of Africa, and we had to fight the onslaught. That's what we were taught from the beginning. If you were born into apartheid, it was everywhere, in government and the church and the family, and preached as justified and right. And if there is no independent media and everything is carefully monitored, then there is only one point of view and anyone who differs is crazy."

"*You* were so cruel in the way you killed people."

"Absolutely. It was a war. It was no big thing for me to eliminate the enemy. We abducted them and interrogated them in different ways. We gave them electric shocks or smothered them or hammered them on the head. We shot them, then we put them in a fire of tires and wood and burned them to ashes."

He pauses to peer at me closely. "You know, seven bodies will take about seventy-two hours to burn, but the hands and the feet and the head go more quickly."

"Hmmnn," I say.

"After that, we dumped the ashes into the river, and while the bodies were burning we had a barbecue."

"You *what*?"

"Sure. Every Afrikaner carries a barbecue in the boot of his car at all times. It's part of the culture."

I catch my breath. "Why did you blow the whistle?"

"I was being set up to take the rap for a private hanky-panky [a non-authorized killing], but I also saw it as a chance to make peace with my past. With the lies, all the lies."

He falls silent, and the room grows still; I can hear his breathing and mine. "It's all kind of hard to explain now," he says, turning away.

He refuses to come with me to Vlakplaas, so I hire a car to drive the forty kilometres west out of Pretoria. The road cuts deep through rolling hills and brown winter grass, until it dissolves into a dirt track. My black driver is excited, frightened by our destination, and my own muscles are tightening with dread. I close my eyes.

The Vlakplaas caretaker has only recently returned to South Africa after twenty-five years in Canada, and he says this was the only job he could find. "*Ach*, it was a war! Lots worse goin' on in Rwanda and Zaire," he says dismissively. We climb into his Jeep to visit the grounds. The wheels spin in tire ruts forged not long ago by Coetzee's and de Kock's security police. The African veld is still and beautiful, with rounded grass-carpeted hills stretching into the distance. "Used to be stocked with antelope," says the caretaker. "For their barbecues."

We descend a small hill and stop before a tranquil river, where an old willow tree sways over the water. Its branches shade a large stone fireplace flanked by a barbecue. I remember this spot from the television documentary; it was the site of "shoot and burn" parties: torture the enemy, shoot him in the neck, then throw his corpse on the fire while you guzzle whisky, cavort about half-naked or swing from one side of the river to the other on the rope that still hangs there, as in a child's playground, then gather round for a meal of antelope meat, its savoury aroma accented by the smell of human flesh roasting on the adjacent pit.

The Jeep climbs a hill to a burial site, but only one of the graves is tended by the family of the dead. It is the last resting place of an agent who refused to carry out his grisly duties: Eugene de Kock shot his face off.

We drive over the veld to a complex of buildings. Here is the prison—a set of narrow stalls with chains hanging from hooks; and the administrative buildings, adjoined by a guest house for visiting chiefs and government officials. Here is the bar, the biggest open space in the complex and always well stocked. Next to the bar is the patio: another huge fireplace with another adjoining barbecue. Killing, burning and cooking—all in the name of "Western civilization."

These appalling security police defy comprehension, until I remember an earlier state-authorized outrage. In Nazi Germany, as in South Africa, one part of the population was conditioned to see the other as inherently evil and less than human, meaning that when ordinary men and women received orders to carry out grisly government-sanctioned tasks, they did not have to struggle with their consciences in the usual way: they could kill *without* passion, because they were part of an important, approved enterprise—and because their victims were undeserving. I think these people in Germany and South Africa—and, God knows, in Bosnia and Rwanda—are important, because they reveal something about our human capacity to rationalize extraordinary acts.

The caretaker tells me there is a Police Museum in Pretoria where I may learn more. I decide on the spot to go there.

In the Police Museum on Pretorius Street, the entire history of the apartheid state is introduced through the lens of legalized repression. In North America or Europe these gruesome exhibits of dried blood and replicated gore might have belonged to another century and attracted aficionados of freak shows. Not here. This place speaks of a nightmare that ended just yesterday.

Since we are now in the era of the *new* South Africa, the exhibition begins in a "post-election" room, added on in 1995. There are exhibits of pass books; pictures of Durban Indians protesting forced removals, surrounded by attacking police; photos of the 1960 Sharpeville massacre, when the police panicked and killed sixty-nine of the ten thousand people who were demonstrating against the pass laws (the captions look new: the numbers have likely been updated to reflect the truth about the dead and the wounded). There are pictures and statements about the famous Rivonia trial that sent Nelson Mandela to Robben Island for life; an honest comment about Steve Biko ("He was never found guilty of anything except breaking his banning order"); and the names of eighty other men killed while in police detention. For balance, there are pictures of a bomb explosion set off by Afrikaners in 1990, at the site of the signing that ended the Anglo-Boer War eighty-eight years earlier, and a 1991 riot instigated by two thousand white extremists carrying knives and a flag bearing a version of the swastika.

Though meant to represent the new South Africa, the display is still interpreted through the familiar language of race fear: "The aim [of these enemies] was the violent overthrow of the government, replacing it with a socialist African state in which whites would have no political rights" is the statement on the wall.

The next room features a selection of medieval-style torture equipment: stocks, tongue bridles, body fetters, cat-o'-nine tails and a burlap head sack, as well as horrifying mock-ups of actual murders of blacks and whites, some "political," some not. These are accompanied by glass bottles of pickled intestines, hair and bones. In another display a huge, larger-than-life black man wields an axe over a terrified white couple cringing in a car, while nearby, an entire section is devoted to scenes of an African witch doctor preparing a broth of human tissue. I am surrounded by families with children. Everyone, white and black, stares, mouth agape, at the "primitive" savage.

Another room dedicated to killings of police also features mock-ups of bloodied victims. "Only the murderers know why policemen and women are being murdered in cold blood" is the ominous caption. We encounter a gruesome model of a necklacing victim, then pictures of proud generals receiving medals for "political warfare" and "combatting terrorism."

Finally, in a perfect Disney finale, man's best friend is there to greet us: a stuffed police dog standing in his own case against a background of fluffy pink clouds and misty mountains.

The last case in the last room contains the perfect conclusion to this tacky display of apartheid culture. A pair of sculpted hands holds a Bible that is opened at Matthew 6: 13: "And lead us not into temptation, but deliver us from evil."

"Deliver us from evil." On the way out I stop to talk to a black couple who have just completed the tour. "I could look at this and say it is insulting or wonder about the intentions of the people who put the museum together, but I don't want to allow those feelings of inferiority," says the young man, who turns out to be a law student. "I feel we must look past that. I want to take away something positive from this museum. I want to be able to use it to think about the future of my country."

The new South Africa looking at the old—with a generosity that surprises me. My own thoughts are less kind: I am remembering Barbara Tuchman's revealing book *The March of Folly*,[13] in which she wryly describes different sorts of misgovernment across the ages, including government by "folly or perversity," which she defines as "the pursuit of policy contrary to the self-interest of the constituency or state." Tuchman laid down three criteria for her dark choices: one, the policy in question had to have been seen as counterproductive in its own time; two, a feasible alternative course of action must have been possible; and three, the policy had to have been that of a group, not an individual tyrant and have lasted beyond one political lifetime. Apartheid South Africa was a perfect fit, and nothing in my travels so far had exposed the stupidity that propped up the system more blatantly than this mindless Police Museum. This was, naturally enough, not everyone's view: a recent issue of *Boernews*, after listing the names of real and presumed Communists in the ANC-led government, said: "One thing is sure; we are now ruled by incompetents, and a once proud nation is rapidly becoming a Third World cesspit."[14]

I have arranged to attend a hearing of the Truth and Reconciliation Commission, and in preparation I fly to Cape Town, the seat of the new Parliament and the city where the commission has its offices. The TRC is co-chaired by two illustrious representatives of the would-be Rainbow Nation: one black, one white. Archbishop Desmond Tutu has devoted much of his life to his people's struggle for freedom, and Alex Boraine, the former head of the Methodist Church of South Africa and an erstwhile member of the liberal opposition in the all-white Parliament, also has dedicated his life to fighting apartheid. Both have agreed to interviews, and so has Dullah Omar, the minister of justice. All these meetings were arranged before I left Toronto, and the ease with which I managed to pin down a date with Omar particularly surprised me—cabinet ministers are usually more elusive. However, in a country where most senior politicians were until recently fighters in armed liberation movements, there seems to be considerably less formality. Far from being above the fray, Omar himself nearly fell victim to assassination by poisoning in the mid-1980s: Edward James Gordon (known to his friends as "Peaches") testified to the Harms Commission, a judicial body set up in 1990 to investigate allegations of state complicity in hit squad activity, that his handlers gave him a powder with instructions to sprinkle it over Omar's food to induce a heart attack.

The offices of the TRC are in a nondescript low-rise building on Adderley Street, a main thoroughfare of the city, beside the houses of Parliament and a beautiful public park filled with palms. I am slated to meet Alex Boraine this morning. I am directed to a small waiting area and seated beside a nervous-looking man who keeps checking his camera. He is Mr. Balu from Bangalore, India. He tells me he is travelling the world on a single-man peace mission, and he has come to present his credentials to the famous Desmond Tutu. When the smiling bishop comes out to greet him, Mr. Balu jumps to his feet, asks me to take his picture with the archbishop and immediately asks Tutu for his autograph.

Alex Boraine is tall, friendly and informal, in the South African way. About fifty, I guess. He leads me into his office. Tea and cookies arrive, and he settles comfortably into his couch.

South Africa is one of the most church-going nations on earth, for religion brought solace to perpetrator and victim alike. Since I can count on being asked whether I am a "believer" by people I have just met, I am not surprised to learn that Boraine's commitment to fighting apartheid started with religion. He belongs to that small community of whites who struggled however they could—through the churches, or politics, as far as either was possible. "When I was eighteen or nineteen and trying to understand the Judaeo-Christian heritage and what it meant, I suddenly felt sick about this place and the question became, How the hell can you have a country that is supposed to be so religious when we are living such contradictions? I went to study in the United States and got involved in the civil rights movement—I was so lucky to have that chance—but I kept seeing what was happening there through my own eyes. I had the honour of meeting Martin Luther King Jr., and I said to him, '*Please* come to South Africa.' He said, '*You* have to go back—people like *you* have to do something.' So I came back, and when I found that even within my own church, the Methodist Church, there were all sorts of hypocrisies, I started to speak out. That caused a lot of problems, but there were many black members of the Church who could not speak out and were happy to have a white person express their views to other whites. Because of their support, I almost accidentally was elected head of the South African Methodist Church in 1970." He leans back and laughs.

As Church head, he travelled across the country to Botswana, Swaziland and places in between. He also went to the gold mines, where blacks lived and worked away from their families, to the white-owned farms and to remote homeland areas most white South Africans had never seen. What he saw convinced him to enter politics, to "beard the lion in his den," as he puts it. In 1974, he was elected as a member of the opposition Progressive Party (later called the Progressive Federal Party) from a Cape Town constituency. "When I was campaigning I was asked questions like, 'If you're elected, are you going to open this place to all the *kaffirs* in the country and bring down our standards?' Or, 'Are you going to open the schools to *them*?' I had to say, 'Yes, I want to open up our country,' and this was something conservative whites didn't want to hear. I said, 'What's the alternative? Do you want to fight? Do you want to die? Should more and more of your sons be killed at the borders?' I tried to throw it back at them. I said I thought there was a way forward that would not have to include a conflagration."

He served in Parliament until 1986, when "the military was literally running the country and Parliament had nothing to do. I couldn't stay there. I walked out." By this time, he had also left the Methodist Church—impatient with the "stuffiness, hypocrisy and double standards."

His next step was to create a non-governmental organization called the Institute for a Democratic Alternative for South Africa (IDASA), which was the forerunner of the TRC. He talked with every black leader and many who were in exile outside the country. "Only the Pan Africanist Congress refused to talk—because I'm white." On the other side of the race divide, he was vilified by whites for "betraying the country."

After 1989 and the collapse of communism in Eastern Europe, he began discussions with people in Bulgaria, Poland and the former East

Germany about their attempts to heal the wounds of the past. He began to study what was happening in Argentina, Chile and El Salvador, all of which were wrestling with the same question. In 1992 and 1993, IDASA organized two international conferences on truth commissions with luminaries such as the Polish writer and philosopher Adam Michnik and human rights activists, lawyers and writers from Latin America and Europe. "The questions we kept asking ourselves were, What should we do differently during our period of transition? How should we deal with past human rights violations? Is the Nuremberg model of prosecution and retributive justice right for us? What about lustration [forbidding people found responsible for violations to hold public office]? There were very few educated blacks to fill their shoes. What could be done for people who now felt ashamed about orders they had carried out under the previous regime? How could their lives be restored? What about a general amnesty for *all* the perpetrators of apartheid? Would that help us get started again?"

Victims and violators would have to go on living together when apartheid came to an end, and after hundreds of years of unequal relationship, the problem of how to manage this harmoniously loomed large. The central issue of amnesty was magnified by the presence of the military and security police, who now worried about the prospect of Nuremberg-style war crimes trials. "They brought pressure to bear on the negotiations between Nelson Mandela and F. W. de Klerk," says Boraine. "It was clear that it was going to be hard to get agreement for elections unless they had some security about amnesty. The National Party said that from its perspective, a broad amnesty was in order—you know the sort of thing: with a stroke of the pen, the whole of the past gets written off and 'forgotten.' Of course they wanted this, because how would anyone separate the politicians from the military and the police? The latter were just an arm of the party. But we were asking about the victims. Did one just say, 'Too bad' and move on?

"I talked to Mandela about this late one night. Nuremberg-style war crimes trials were already ruled out. We thought that criminal, retributive justice might gouge even deeper rifts between the races, and there was also a money question: South Africa does not have the resources to support hundreds of lengthy litigations. Mandela agreed that a compromise that included amnesty should be allowed, but only according to specified criteria; he said his intelligence people were giving him a strong message that elements within the military and the police would make an election impossible without certain assurances. Bishop Tutu said publicly that the choice lay between 'justice and ashes.' But I think what saved the amnesty from being overly broad was our concern for the victims, because we decided there would not only be an amnesty committee, but also a human rights violations committee to enable people to come forward and tell their stories and a reparations committee that would provide something small in the way of recompense and comfort. I think we moved at just the right time. I just came back from a conference called 'Beyond Racism,' at Emory University in Atlanta, and it seems so obvious to me that Americans are in denial about their slave history. Did you know there is not one official memorial to slavery in the United States? We moved at the right time, and things are working out well because we are not merely focusing on the perpetrators, as in the criminal justice system. In the criminal justice system, the victim is too often forgotten."

The man who would become justice minister was also involved in the deliberations that preceded the creation of the TRC: Boraine remembers that Dullah Omar was fully committed to some kind of nationwide commission and also that he wanted to call it the Truth Commission. "I suggested Truth and Reconciliation," says Boraine, laughing. "I said, 'Think of Orwell and Huxley!' It's true that the business of who ought to be eligible for amnesty was a bit tricky. We had long discussions about human rights abuses with high-ranking members of the ANC, for example, and they were arguing that since they were fighting a system described as a crime against humanity by the United Nations, they ought to be amnestied and not held responsible, and they were quoting international human rights conventions that say any cause that seeks to combat violent, racist regimes is legitimate. But what they initially failed to see was that these conventions also say that no matter how just the cause, the parties concerned must accept responsibility for the acts they commit. So I said, 'Yes, it can be argued that your cause was just, I have no problem with that; but there is still a question about human rights violations.' I gave them the example. I said, 'If you were facing an armed military convoy seeking to attack you, and if you had planted mines in order to destroy that convoy, and a man comes along in a donkey cart with two little children, and they are blown up, where does responsibility lie? Because there *has* to be responsibility.' Eventually, they did concede this, and several ministers ultimately applied for amnesty. I believe they understood that it would be impossible to create a transparent democracy if they did not include themselves in the process."

Eventually, Boraine was asked to write something specific for Nelson Mandela, spelling out the options for South Africa, and a partial amnesty was adopted as part of the TRC legislation. But amnesty remained a problem for everyone—from those who despaired of seeing men like Dirk Coetzee freely walking the streets to the ANC itself. Only traditional justice, meaning trials conducted according to the rules of evidence, with a promise of punishment for the guilty, could fully uphold the principle of personal responsibility that was the legacy of Nuremberg in international law. To reject the traditional courtroom, with its conclusions about personal responsibility, was to open the door to possible accusations of collective guilt—or collective innocence—which was just as worrying.

The problems Boraine and Mandela confronted that night, as they struggled to set a course for what would become the TRC, were massive in their scope, for apartheid had so distorted the thinking and the behaviour of many whites that the abnormal came, over decades, to seem ordinary. South African judges, for example, had applied parliamentary legislation that was acknowledged internationally as contrary to the common law of nations, and they had done so against a disenfranchised population. The judges who passed death sentences were all white; 95 per cent of the people they sentenced were black. More than one thousand people were hanged between 1975 and 1985, of whom only twenty-two were white, until by the mid-1980s, South Africa had the highest rate of capital punishment in the Western world. How could the new country deal with this past without destroying its professional infrastructure? And what role would amnesty play?

Dullah Omar extends his hand in greeting as I enter his elegant office in the Parliament building. How extraordinary this leap must feel to him: from disenfranchised, second-class citizen (he is of East Indian origin and would therefore have been classified as "coloured") to minister of justice in the government of the ruling party. He is quick to answer when I ask about the issue of amnesty: "Yes, Section 255 of the Interim Constitution provided for amnesty with regard to offences, acts or omissions arising from the conflicts of the past and associated with a political objective. I was concerned about amnesty, but I agreed to it, and we negotiated it as part of a total political settlement. It was something we *had* to agree to. The National Party did not enter negotiations with a view to securing democracy or having elections, and they had to be dislodged from that position. We couldn't tell them, 'We want you to commit political suicide. We are asking you to give up power, after which a new democratically elected regime will take over and charge you with the crimes you committed.' They would never have agreed to elections; therefore, we dealt with amnesty right up front. But I definitely draw a distinction between apartheid and the liberation movements: apartheid was a crime against humanity, while the liberation struggle was a struggle for justice. This is an important moral division, and if we denude the current process of morality, it will be difficult to build South Africa on values that will be recognized by the international community. This means we cannot treat apartheid as though it was the same as the liberation struggle, which is what de Klerk and the National Party want us to do. But that does not mean we were entitled to commit human rights violations, so although we were fighting a just war, we must be willing to allow the TRC to deal with our violations as well as those on the other side. Remember we opposed an across-the-board blanket amnesty, like Argentina after the so-called Dirty War, because the only reason to deal with the past is to help us build a route to a democracy based on human rights and the rule of law for all South Africans—for the very first time. We do not want to encourage a culture of impunity. We want individual accountability. Our criteria for amnesty are related to the motive of the offender: malice, revenge or personal gain do not apply—only acts carried out to obtain a political objective. And the person must make full disclosure, because we are interested in retrieving an accurate record of our country's past."

"How do you choose the commissioners for the TRC?" I ask him. "There don't seem to be many people from the National Party."

"We look for people with a track record in human rights. No one in Germany would expect a former Nazi to be in charge of Holocaust memorials," he returns.

"Mr. Omar, you are the first minister of justice for the new South Africa. What are the major hurdles facing you?"

"My job is to implement the new Constitution, which is a radical break for our country. In the past, South Africa was divided between citizens and non-citizens; Parliament legislated for the citizens, and the sole function of the courts was to apply that law—whether just or unjust, moral or immoral. So the law and the police became instruments of the suppression of human rights. Now the majority can participate in the political life of the country, and we have established the supremacy of the Constitution, with its Bill of Rights, over the rights of Parliament. But having said that, it is the case that everything is just paper: the day after the elections in 1994, when the Interim Constitution became law, there were no institutions to back it up. It is the function of my department to create these institutions."

"How does this country's past impinge upon your job?" I ask him. He remains silent for a moment. I glance around the opulent room—a ministerial office where until recently very different discussions about the legal life of South Africa would have taken place.

Then he looks at me directly and speaks slowly: "We are left with a legacy of the past, and the fact of elections did not mean that white domination has ended. Yes, it is gone on the political level, but in all other respects, it has remained: in social institutions, the economy, education, health, the professions, business, at work—everywhere. Also the values of the apartheid order have remained intact."

"What do you mean?"

"I mean people still behave in a racist manner, and it is these attitudes that have to change, and it is a painful process. We would like to ensure the beginnings of social and economic justice, including institutional transformation in the courts, the police and the army, and we would like to see all groups participate in what we are trying to accomplish. But I must say that the National Party has provided a despicable example to whites during this crucial time. It has both feet stuck in the past, and it has tried to defend apartheid. We have much to do. It is a fact that during apartheid, anti-human attitudes developed, and there is an old culture of violence in this country because of the brutalized conditions under which people lived. Elements of the police still participate in crime. Everywhere there is a culture of impunity."

Back to the offices on Adderley Street, this time to meet Archbishop Tutu. Although I am about to talk with one of the most admired human beings in the world today, I can't get Dullah Omar out of my mind—this man who was the object of a failed assassination and who is now in charge of implementing the constitutional changes that will transform the institutions that held apartheid in place for half a century. I think about his openness and his anger: both legacies, it seems to me, of former powerlessness, when he had less reason to be circumspect than he has today, and when anger was the fuel of war.

"The Rainbow People of God": The phrase was invented by Desmond Tutu, a man who is beloved by blacks and by whites, and who, with

Mandela, did most to effect the "miracle" of peaceful change. To talk of miracles is somehow appropriate when it comes to the famous archbishop, because "the Arch," as he is affectionately called, has consistently used his Christian faith to challenge injustice and put his own life on the line. For more than a decade, he was "public enemy number one," as Nelson Mandela once put it. Tutu and his family were threatened; a bloody monkey foetus was strung up in front of their house. "We are not animals. We are human beings with feelings," he returned, never abandoning his determined stance of non-violence.

Decades earlier, Tutu had warned the apartheid authorities about the potential for horrible redress that waited just around the corner. On May 6, 1976, he wrote to Prime Minister John Vorster "as one human person to another human person, gloriously created in the image of the selfsame God . . . who works inwardly in all of us to change our hearts of stone into hearts of flesh."[15] It was one month before the Soweto uprising that was to mark the end of quiet resistance.

Tutu said, "I am writing to you, Sir, because I have a growing nightmarish fear that unless something drastic is done very soon, then bloodshed and violence are going to happen in South Africa. . . . A people can take only so much and no more. . . ." In his reply, the prime minister dismissed Tutu and suggested he had been manipulated by the white opposition in Parliament.

Tutu turned up at every protest and funeral to preach his message of reason, peace, racial equality and reconciliation. He faced the guns of white police and was arrested more than once. He calmed black riots when he could, in the face of *pangas* (machetes) and spears, and where he could not stop the violence he spoke out in the strongest terms. If the necklacing of suspected collaborators did not stop, he threatened to leave the country: "A culture of violence has taken root in our society. What has gone wrong that we seem to have lost our reverence for life?" A man of deep emotion, he cried publicly at the suffering of his people. He spoke out at the United Nations and mobilized a campaign of international sanctions against his country.

In 1984, when he was accorded the Nobel Peace Prize, Desmond Tutu talked about the source of his strength and his commitment to an equality conferred by God alone. "It is a moral universe we inhabit," he said in his acceptance speech. "Good and right and equity matter in the universe of God."

Tutu's lifelong interest in reconciliation was born from his religious beliefs, or, as he once put it, "God's mission to restore the harmony, the unity, the fellowship, the communion, the community that was there at the beginning. . . ." So the Truth and Reconciliation Commission was, like the rest of his work, a secular offshoot of his theology more than a forum for earthly justice. Tutu expressed his developing ideas in November 1990, at the first conference in thirty years to bring together the leadership of the white Dutch Reformed Church and the anti-apartheid South African churches. He said that the victims of injustice and oppression must be ready to forgive, but that those who had wronged them must also be willing to say, "We have hurt you by uprooting you from your homes, by dumping you in poverty-stricken homeland resettlement camps, by giving your children inferior education, by denying your humanity, by trampling down on your human dignity, and by denying you fundamental rights. We are sorry, forgive us."[16] Then, he added, the wronged must forgive. At the same conference, Tutu opened the possibility of paying reparations: what was taken away must be symbolically returned, he said.

The following day, Professor Willie Jonker, a theologian from the establishment Afrikaner University of Stellenbosch, stood up and said, "I confess before you and before the Lord, not only my own sin and guilt, and my personal responsibility for the political, social, economic and structural wrongs that have been done to many of you and the results from which you and our whole country are still suffering, but vicariously I dare also to do that in the name of the NGK [the white Dutch Reformed Church], of which I am a member, and for the Afrikaans people as a whole."[17]

Something pivotal to reconciliation seemed amiss here: Tutu had declared that "the wronged must forgive," after an apology. He repeated this in reply to Willie Jonker's courageous affirmation, saying, "When confession is made, then those of us who have been wronged must say, 'We forgive you. [Confession] is not cheaply made and the response is not cheaply made.'" But could he dictate collective forgiveness on behalf of others? Can anyone? To forgive is a uniquely personal choice, shaped by the complexities of emotion and event and entirely separate from the act of apology that is supposed to trigger it.

For their part, the white Dutch Reformed leadership did endorse Jonker's apology, citing decisions made at a recent synod. But the black

Dutch Reformed churches rejected Tutu's generic acceptance. Again, the archbishop replied, "I have heard people say that I had no mandate to have accepted a confession on behalf of anybody except myself and I believe that it is right for people to say so. It is the height of presumption for me to have suggested that I was speaking on behalf of anybody . . ., [but] I have been with men like Walter Sisulu and others who have been in jail for twenty-five, twenty-seven years for having the audacity to say they are human. . . . They come out of that experience and they have an incredible capacity to love. They have no bitterness, no longing for revenge, but a deep commitment to renew South Africa. I am humbled as I stand in front of such people. . . . God has brought us to this moment, and I just want to say to you . . ., [and] I speak only for myself, I cannot, when someone says, 'Forgive me,' say, 'I do not.' For then I cannot pray the prayers that we prayed: 'Forgive us, as we forgive.'"

The Rustenburg Declaration, which was adopted later that week, included an extensive section on confession and restitution (though not on collective forgiveness); and in radio interviews Tutu repeated, again and again, that what he opposed was apartheid, not whites: "There are very many good Afrikaners who have tried to work for justice," he told his compatriots. His words melted hearts. What would later be called the Truth and Reconciliation Commission had been conceived, if not yet born.

When he was appointed to co-chair the TRC in November 1995, Tutu said, "I hope that the work of the commission, by opening wounds to cleanse them, will thereby stop them from festering. We cannot be facile and say bygones will be bygones, because they will not be bygones and will return to haunt us. True reconciliation is never cheap, for it is based on forgiveness, which is costly. Forgiveness in turn depends on repentance, which has to be based on an acknowledgement of what was done wrong and therefore on disclosure of the truth. You cannot forgive what you do not know."

Desmond Tutu, small in physical stature and informal, even casual, in manner, is wearing his trademark short-sleeved purple ecclesiastical shirt with a clerical collar. He leads me to an office and indicates that we should sit at a round table in the corner. He prays. I say amen. I remember that he is recuperating from surgery for prostate cancer and think to myself that he looks well. He slouches comfortably and waits.

To date, more than five thousand perpetrators have applied for amnesty, and not surprisingly, this aspect of the process is proving to be the most controversial. Many blacks think apartheid murderers are crying crocodile tears and faking repentance in the hope of being excused. On the other side, the Afrikaans press complains incessantly that the TRC is a "witch hunt" designed to denigrate their people and their history. At a recent meeting in Pretoria, a general attacked the commission and proclaimed he was *proud*, not ashamed, of the work carried out by the infamous security police and South African Defence Forces against Communists and terrorists, who deserved everything they got and more. The audience cheered.

"You've been uncovering the truth about apartheid, but do you think you are effecting reconciliation?" I ask him.

"No one can legislate reconciliation—it can't be obligatory," he replies. "All South Africans have to realize that this is a national project. Everyone has to be involved. It can't be left to one group. I will say with honesty that we are disappointed that there are very few whites at our hearings, if any. It is painful for them. The hardest thing is to say I'm sorry. But whether or not we can accept the general excuse that people did not know what was happening, they must acknowledge that their system was maintained by vicious methods. It is probably true that not everyone knew precise details, but when a Biko dies mysteriously in detention, perhaps people ought to have begun to ask questions, even though it was dangerous to do so."

"Most ordinary people are not brave."

"No, it is true that most people will say, I don't want trouble. Why provoke trouble with people who are omnipotent, and the security police were omnipotent." He is silent for a moment, then he says, "When we see now the sort of things that happened, the things that are coming out at the hearings, some of us keep asking ourselves, How did we survive?"

Clearly he was asking the question of himself. And he answered himself; he survived because he was fortified by faith, because he "knew that God was on the side of all of us who were having a rough time, and that justice would ultimately prevail, that this really is a moral universe and the cause was just."

The whole issue of "just cause" is unmistakably central to the commission, and the question of what might be passed over or excused in the name of the "just struggle" is becoming more and more hazardous to the TRC's reputation for across-the-board fairness. Alex Boraine and Dullah Omar have both made a point of saying that human rights violations committed during the struggle against apartheid cannot be whitewashed because the cause was just. But former ANC freedom fighters, who are now statesmen in suits and ties, are not breaking down the doors of the commission in a rush to confess their misdeeds. It is an open secret that Thabo Mbeki, next in line for the presidency after Mandela, Omar himself, the present minister of justice and just about every other member of the ANC cabinet have tales to tell; in fact, Tutu has already threatened to resign from the commission if the ANC does not ask its members to confess human rights violations and seek amnesty, just like the perpetrators of apartheid. No one is more aware than he that the Rainbow Nation doesn't stand a chance if the central players sabotage their own propaganda for openness and transparency. "Murder is murder, and torture in an ANC camp is still torture, and claiming one's cause is just does not absolve such acts," he reflects as we sit alone together in his office. "In terms of legal amnesty, one act is on the same basis as another. *However*, that does not mean that they must necessarily share the same morality. We may say that the fact of opposing apartheid put people on a higher moral plane than someone who justified and maintained it, but that does not mean that any act committed in a just cause is morally acceptable. Legal equivalence is not moral equivalence."

Tutu applied this same tough logic to another controversial issue: ANC informers. It was being alleged that a number of prominent ANC "Struggle comrades" had actually been government spies and had caused the deaths of their colleagues. There was talk of releasing names and worry that to do so might destabilize the government. Tutu thought the names should be released if an investigation found grounds for accusation and that the present high position of those concerned was not a deterrent: what was hidden today would seep out tomorrow with even greater consequences to the nation.

It was this level of integrity that had won him his worldwide reputation and a Nobel. Unlike General Charles de Gaulle and all Japan's postwar leaders, who hoped to build the future by inducing amnesia about the past, Tutu was determined to "pacify" history, in his words—not with forgetfulness, but with truth.

"What realistic expectations have you for reconciliation between blacks and whites?" I ask him.

He is silent a moment. "Well, we're not doing as well as we hoped, but not as badly as it sometimes appears. I get some—not many—letters from Afrikaners. One woman wanted me to know how much her son suffered from upholding apartheid, by being drafted into the army and what happened to him at the border. She said he later had a nervous breakdown. And you know I receive get-well cards from people who might previously have hoped my illness would dispatch me! So I say, 'If you find the chairman of the TRC acceptable, you must also come to terms with the TRC.' I keep making appeals. I say, 'There is an incredible generosity of spirit on the side of those who have suffered—please, you on the other side, do not take this magnanimity for granted. Please respond with a like generosity.' But most of us like finding excuses and don't handle criticism well. I don't. I like to be liked. It's true that when you are shown to be in the wrong, you need a lot of grace to accept the pain."

I wonder about attitudes now, in this country where everyone was assigned to a group and believed to inherit fixed capacities. "Do you believe in collective guilt, Archbishop?" I ask.

His answer intrigues me: "Human beings live in communities; a solitary human being is a contradiction; so, yes, I believe groups must acknowledge their part in the past through their spokespersons. But that does not remove individual responsibility. Each has to say, 'This is what I did, or what I ought to have done.' And because we can't get at every person, there has to be a kind of symbolic confession and forgiving of one another that happens collectively, reflecting the solidarity each individual has with his group."

The collectivizing of guilt is, to me, a dubious proposition, precisely because it tars everyone, without exception. But Tutu's position reflects this country of categorized racial "entities." Apartheid may have failed as a political and economic system, but the thinking of three hundred years is unlikely to disappear as quickly.

The name Tutu does not speak is that of the man who, at the time of our meeting, is still the leader of the National Party, the man who negotiated the peace with Nelson Mandela and won a Nobel Prize for his efforts. F. W. de Klerk has consistently refused to acknowledge personal responsibility of any kind. The "excesses" of apartheid were due, he has said, to "a few bad eggs" and not to government policy. P. W. Botha has been even more adamant: when eventually brought to trial under the regular justice system for refusing to appear before the TRC, the former president stared down damning new corroborative evidence culled from government archives.[18] Here at last was proof that Botha had

- personally ordered bomb attacks and a "national strategy against the revolutionary onslaught against South Africa," according to which "intimidators must by means of formal and informal policing be neutralised" (a word understood to mean "murdered");
- supervised cabinet ministers' lists of "politically sensitive people" for whom "methods other than detention must be considered";
- authorized assassination squads like that which operated at Vlakplaas;
- actively and deliberately destabilized neighbouring states such as Angola and Mozambique;
- thrown tens of thousands of activists into prison without trial and curtailed civil liberties;
- deliberately turned KwaZulu-Natal into a war zone in which thousands of people had died.

The "Old Crocodile," as he was called, did not deny the evidence; instead, he spoke of "attempts to humiliate me and my people." P. W. Botha said he was not ashamed, nor would he apologize for any of his actions. Now, everyone opposed to the forces of chaos, communism and socialism needed to unite, he added. That fewer than two dozen supporters gathered at the courthouse to wave the old South African flag told its own story. All the same, stonewalling by two former presidents was a serious problem for Desmond Tutu, for without the leadership of the National Party, reconciliation with the Afrikaner community was less and less likely, and without reconciliation, the TRC might be seen to have failed.

But speaking the truth was not something everyone wanted to mess with, even when the possibility of amnesty was dangled before their noses. For F. W. de Klerk, who co-legislated the act that brought the TRC into being, acknowledging personal responsibility would be tantamount to bringing down the historical framework of the Boer nation, which was constructed on the building blocks of group separateness and a divinely approved racial inequality. De Klerk was not prepared to do this, not prepared to condemn the foundations of the old history in favour of the new.

Was it unrealistic of Desmond Tutu to think he might obtain an apology from the men at the top? P. W. Botha was in retirement in a place appropriately named Wilderness, and F. W. de Klerk was currently fighting for his political life. (Unsuccessfully, as it turned out: he later resigned.) ANC politicians might eventually apologize for excesses committed for the sake of their just cause, but a personal apology from anyone representing the National Party would have to be in the name of *in*justice. De Klerk was ready to acknowledge the presence of "a few bad eggs," but not the intrinsic evil of a state structure, headed by himself, that had explicitly sanctioned terror and the depravity of a Vlakplaas in the name of its white electors. This he could not—would not—do. To the end, both living apartheid-era presidents, de Klerk and P. W. Botha, would refuse to seek amnesty. Blacks supported the TRC, but polls indicated that up to 80 per cent of whites did not. De Klerk's and Botha's denials gave tacit permission to many whites to do the same: to reject the new South Africa.

Tutu looks tired, but I have one final question. It is the old clunker, "How do you want to be remembered?"

He remains silent for what seems a long time. "I'd like people to remember that I loved," he says finally.

His emotional reply catches me by surprise. I remember the opening of our conversation when he asked himself how he had survived. I remember that he is being treated for cancer.

My throat tightens. When I say nothing, he speaks again: "I'd like them to remember that I loved. And I cried."

As I leave the building, a parade happens to be passing along Adderley Street, just below the offices of the commission. This week marks the seventy-fifth anniversary of the South African navy, and marching behind the banner of the new South Africa are the young faces of Desmond Tutu's Rainbow Nation. They are black, white and "coloured," and their fellow compatriots, who have lined up along the sides of the road, are applauding them. Marching behind the South Africans are battalions of sailors from all over the world who have docked in the magnificent Cape Town harbour to celebrate this event: they are from Argentina, Brazil, France, India, Pakistan, the United Kingdom, China, the United States, Kenya, Russia and Singapore: South Africa has re-entered the international arena. The nations of the world high-step and bugle-blast their way through old Cape Town, just yards from the original Dutch East India Company Gardens where a discredited and suddenly outdated version of this nation's history began. The future still looks murky—and possibly dangerous—but today, in the streets of the city, Tutu and Mandela's multiracial nation is reality.

I have planned a trip to Lusikisiki in the Eastern Cape, a remote town in a remote corner of the former Transkei "homeland," because the TRC is holding a hearing there. My white acquaintances are vicariously frightened. The Transkei is the place they imagine in their nightmares: one says it was the locale for Nadine Gordimer's *July's People*. The Transkei is where the transient mine workers came from—those fearful men in the same-sex hostels. White people do not visit the Transkei; it is not safe. Tourists have been murdered there—two British women travelling by car in 1992, hacked to pieces; then in 1993, an American girl who was working for a non-governmental organization was also murdered. And the car hijackings on the highway.

I am going anyway, but I have to admit the warnings are taking a toll. I fly to East London to arrange for transportation with local TRC officials going to the hearing. First, I call a commissioner named June. She is a white woman who says she is planning to do the six-hour drive alone and I am welcome to join her.

"Will we be safe?" I ask her.

"Are you a believer?" she replies. "I place my trust in Him, so I have no fear."

Since my faith clearly falls short of hers, I decide to look elsewhere.

I call Jabu, an investigator for the commission. "No worry," he says cheerfully. "I don't think we'll have a problem."

"But can you *guarantee* my safety?" I ask this man whom I have never met. I can hear an embarrassing shrillness in my voice.

"Oh yeah," he says, laughing at me. "No worry."

He picks me up at my hotel, which faces the azure Indian Ocean. I have been watching a school of dolphins swim by, just metres from shore, leaping lazily into the air on their journey. This extraordinarily beautiful corner of the earth's surface at the southern tip of a southern continent is typical; the utter splendour of South Africa can almost make one forget what happened here.

Jabu drives the car east out of town. He is young and black—very handsome, I think to myself—and easy to talk to. He is a policeman (why didn't he tell me this before?) and he works in a township just west of Port Elizabeth in the direction of Cape Town. Steve Biko was tortured to death in the police station of Port Elizabeth. "There *was* no policing in the townships during apartheid," he tells me, "just a war waged on blacks by whites. If the police tortured and murdered, you can imagine how casually others accepted violence. Life was worthless. Violence was an outlet for rage, and now the habits persist. It's our biggest problem."

Because the police were so hated and are still viewed with suspicion, townships like the one near Port Elizabeth have introduced community policing. The residents and the police officers collectively decide what to do with someone who has committed a crime, says Jabu. People co-operate because the ANC politicians come home to the townships and say, "If we don't get the crime problem under control, there will be no foreign investment, and without foreign investment there will be no jobs for your children, even though we now have democracy and Madiba is our president." So now the men and women in Jabu's township conduct citizen arrests.

We cross the Kei River, the former boundary of the Transkei homeland and the former racial divide with white South Africa. Still is, but it's no longer official. The Transkei has always been a black territory, in part because whites did not take up offers of settlement there in the nineteenth century, in part because thousands of blacks expelled from the Cape Colony by apartheid legislation had been dumped there.

The two-lane highway snakes across stunningly beautiful terrain. Villages perch on the cusps of grassy hills that slope into the veld, and there are green tablelands as far as the eye can see. The earth under the Cape aloe trees is red: deep gorges slash the land. Here and there are clusters of traditional village huts: round, mud-baked structures with thatched roofs and cow-dung floors. They are unserviced, says Jabu. Women carry jugs of water from the river, and cholera epidemics are not infrequent. Pit latrines. Subsistence farming. Each family tends a small patch of maize, or "mealies." In his autobiography, Nelson Mandela wrote of childhood and mealies, which have been the staple diet of the poor in this part of the world for as long as memory. Jabu says the mealie plots often do not last out the season. Illiterate and isolated peasants know little about basic crop rotation, and they are often hungry.

Cattle, the traditional wealth for the Xhosa people of the Transkei, are tended in fields by small barefoot boys carrying long sticks, just as Mandela did some seventy years ago, in this very region, where he was born. Sheep, goats and cattle browse along the roadside and occasionally decide to cross. Most cars (including the one I am travelling in) are skimming along at 150 kilometres an hour. South Africa has one of the highest road-death rates in the world, and the probability of colliding with a cow is high.

Women trudge beside the road, carrying loads of firewood on their heads and babies strapped to their backs with blankets, but there are few men of working age. They have gone, says Jabu; they are transient workers in the mines in Johannesburg or unemployed or part of the so-called informal economy—the urban street hawkers and seekers of odd jobs who now populate the cities whites used to call their own. They are also, according to Jabu, who ought to know, the "foot soldiers" in the crime syndicates that have moved in to fill a void in the transitional society.

In the busy market town of Butterworth, people buying and selling sit under the shade of trees. We drive through, and then, on the far side of town, we pass a sprawling squatter camp. The Transkei economy has worsened since the elections of 1994: the hoped-for investment did not materialize, so families that moved to the towns, hoping to find work, are living in patched-together tin and cardboard shacks on the outskirts. Some of these hovels perch on the edge of open garbage dumps. Rifling through the refuse is their occupants' daily living.

The road worsens as the isolation of the territory grows deeper; here, some of the young Xhosa women are still smearing the white sap from the umtiza tree on their faces as adornment. Although I have not seen any other whites in several hours, I have almost forgotten that I am supposed to be afraid. Yes, heads in passing cars sometimes swivel when they catch sight of me, but so what? Just then a pickup truck with a half-dozen girls in the back passes by. One waves, but she is gone before I realize her gesture was obscene.

It is dark when the car bumps over the potholes at the entrance to Lusikisiki. Jabu pulls up in front of a large prosperous-looking house where I have been billeted. Dulcie, the owner, is waiting; she is a small, muscular woman in her forties with a soft voice and a fine-featured face that creases when she smiles. Inside, people hover about the dinner table, waiting for me, I guess, and probably hungry. A large friendly man called Amos, who speaks excellent English (many South African blacks are multilingual, fluent in several native languages, English and sometimes Afrikaans); Zola, Dulcie's twenty-seven-year-old nephew;

another man I never get to know because he speaks not a word and looks shyly into his plate all evening; and the family maid, Poosy.

Dulcie's house is furnished with stuffed Victorian chairs incongruously upholstered with scenes of English country maidens and their comely beaux and a mahogany wall clock that chimes hymns on the hour. These are all relics of eighteenth-century England, or copies, that came, almost certainly, from the old Cape Colony. The impala horns sitting on the television set in stately solitude, like an old TV antenna, look slightly more indigenous to the region. The family's money came from Dulcie's late father, who once owned several prosperous businesses in Lusikisiki. Dulcie tells me that "politics" destroyed most of his livelihood in the 1980s. Because the family supported the government homelands policy, her father was attacked by the ANC in the person of young thugs who demanded they close their shops, on threat of death. They did, with the exception of a general store Dulcie continues to manage in the centre of town.

We are invited to sit down, and I am asked to take a place at the head of the table, opposite Dulcie. Poosy, who seems more like a member of the family than a domestic, serves. The fine dinner of chicken, pumpkin, beans, rice and potatoes followed by stewed peaches is almost certainly in my honour. Later in the week I will learn that my willingness to eat cooked "mealie-pap" with my fingers in the traditional way is deeply important to my hosts. I also glean from Dulcie that I am the first white person ever to enter her home.

Dinner conversation begins, as do most conversations in South Africa, with a lament over crime. This seems to be Zola's favourite subject. "Crime pays. You see how well those people live! *Honest* people around here are starving!" He announces that in the next election he will vote for whichever party promises to bring back the death penalty.

"Including the National Party?" I ask, astonished. "That was the party of apartheid!"

"They had law and order," says Zola. "*That's* what we need most now."

Amos tells me he makes a good living selling life and property insurance, for if there is one thing people need in this crime-ridden society, it is insurance. And prepaid funerals. "This area is bad, bad, bad," he moans, shaking his head. "Cars are hijacked on the roads and the passengers are brutally murdered." I hear once again about the two British women.

"Why is it so bad in this region?" I ask him.

Hunger, unemployment and a long tradition of violence, he replies.

"Will the Truth and Reconciliation Commission help?"

Amos is dubious. He thinks many victims of apartheid want revenge.

Every Sunday, the public television network runs a program about this week's activities of the TRC, and Zola and I settle down in the stuffed chairs to watch. Today the host is discussing the murder of an ANC activist by the security police: the man's body was recently dug up in a field near Durban, where TRC investigators have discovered another killing farm just like Vlakplaas. We are shown old clips of F. W. de Klerk and his police chiefs denying all knowledge about the disappearance of this man, the story being that he escaped from custody. De Klerk's denials about this case, and dozens of others, go back to 1987. "If Mr. de Klerk did not know what was going on in the ranks of his security police, why didn't he?" asks the television host. "The buck stopped with him."

Lies, lies, lies. Every day the papers report denials and fabrications so transparent that I wonder whether the new country can survive the cynicism and jokes they engender. Police lie, politicians lie, people lie to each other and, more important, to themselves. The country is sludge-thick with lies. Apartheid was "separate development"—a benign, reasonable system that somehow fell a little bit short of its kind intentions. South Africa is a country in which no one "knew" what was happening, including the leaders of the government.

The TRC, which was mandated to cut through the murk, is having some success. This week, four young black men have admitted to stoning the mother of one of them to death in front of her other children for supporting the pro-government homeland chief in the Transkei and not the ANC. They are currently serving a jail sentence but applying for amnesty on the grounds that what they did was "political." At the same hearing, two black policemen admitted to torturing a woman by stripping her naked, tying her on her back and pouring some sort of acid on her vagina and thighs.

On it goes. The Rainbow Nation is awash in present violence and the memory of past atrocity, brutalized by a history of deceit and cover-up that reaches into the highest office. Can anything put the past to rest?

March 10, 1997, is a big day for the people of Lusikisiki and the surrounding villages. For the first time they will talk publicly about what happened here during the so-called Peasants' Revolt against the government that took place more than three decades earlier. In this remote backwater of the Transkei, the conflict was not just black against white—that would have been straightforward—but black against black: between those who identified themselves with the emerging, urban-based movements of the African National Congress and the Pan Africanist Congress, with the fight against apartheid, in other words, and rural conservatives like Dulcie's father, who supported the traditional tribal leadership, even though those leaders took orders from the government in Pretoria. In an undefined way, this strife was part of the struggle for and against "modernity." In a backward region where people were unschooled and time moved slowly, as it had since memory began, "foreign" ideas challenged historic allegiances to the hereditary "royal" houses that constituted tribal government. A nationalist freedom struggle with roots in distant cities had sought to superimpose its ends on a conservative, peasant society—with violent results.

The intratribal struggle, in the early 1960s, among the Pondos of the eastern Transkei (the Pondos are a branch of the Xhosas, the most populous, prominent tribe in the country) culminated in burned *kraals*, destroyed livestock, threats to life and violent murder. And the conflict led, in turn, to killings by government forces and the imposition of state emergency measures that included arbitrary arrest, detention without trial, regulations prohibiting free passage within the territory and other restrictive punishments. Sons disappeared in police vans, and mothers begged vainly for information about their fate; husbands were shot for attending meetings that had been declared illegal. Neighbour turned against neighbour, and the cycle of poisoned politics and revenge attacks continued.

The hearings are being held in the largest building in town, a newly constructed teachers' college (a concrete sign of the new government's commitments) that unfortunately does not have electricity. A generator off to the side of the hall gurgles ominously, warning of imminent breakdown. Chairs are lined up in rows, and a single line of police in blue uniforms stands at the back of the room.

It is time to begin, but the participants haven't arrived. Lusikisiki is not easily accessible, and some of people who have agreed to testify are coming from villages hundreds of kilometres away, travelling in vans and on the backs of trucks.

Several hours later, about a hundred middle-aged and elderly people enter the hall. Their shoulders are hunched and their faces are taut with the strain of this exceptional moment. The women wear long, printed cotton skirts of the kind favoured by white women at the end of the last century, sweaters against the winter cold and the patterned head scarves of the Xhosa tribe. The men look uncomfortable in ill-fitting jackets, ties and too-short trousers, and only some of them wear socks with their shoes. Today they will be "interrogated" by other black people, the commissioners of the TRC. "I always thought only white people asked lawyers' questions," a woman says to me later in the day.

We stand as the six commissioners—four men and two women—mount the stage: three human rights lawyers, one of whom helped plan and write the Promotion of National Unity and Reconciliation Act of 1995; two ministers, one of whom fought with the ANC here in the Transkei; and a member of the famous Black Sash movement, the organization of determined white women who demonstrated against apartheid for months and years in front of the Parliament buildings in Pretoria under a shower of abuse. She is June, the woman who invited me to place my life in God's hands by driving here with her. I feel sorry I did not have the chance to talk with her at length during the long drive from East London to Lusikisiki, but since she was relying on her faith to protect both of us, I can't say I regret my decision.

A large poster has been pasted to the wall behind them, and a smaller banner hangs down to the floor. The first says, "TRUTH, THE ROAD TO RECONCILIATION"; the second reads, "Some of the crimes of our past: MURDER, ABDUCTION, TORTURE. One of the crimes of our present: SILENCE. Let's speak out to each other by telling our stories of the past so we can walk the road to reconciliation together." A "truth candle" flickers at the front of the stage.

Everyone sings a Methodist hymn, followed by a prayer: "We pray that our country may be healed so that future generations may live with harmony, peace and progress. . . . We have abused and misused one another. . . . Save us from the chaos of hatred and strife."

A man in the front row is already wiping his eyes.

We sit down. The chairman of the hearing speaks: "This is a special day for the commission. For the first time we will be looking at the battle fought here in the 1960s, which will also clarify what happened here in the 1970s and 1980s. We will touch on issues where people without weapons arose to fight for their rights. Before opening this hearing we took two hundred statements regarding this calamity, this battle for freedom by the Pondo people." He thanks one of the minister-commissioners for asking God for healing.

The TRC has been dealt the awesome task of effecting national healing and making the yearned-for Rainbow Nation a reality, and so far every word uttered in this school hall has been carefully weighted in that direction. As in Upington, the seeds of the new nation are being planted, yet here in Lusikisiki, perhaps more so than in places where the battle lines were divided by race alone, the commissioners need to walk a delicate political tightrope. Some of the people in this room were victims of others here: on one side of the hall are ANC supporters, who fought the former white government and their allies, the local tribal chiefs; on the other side are some of the chiefs and *their* supporters, who fought the ANC. If the TRC is serious about the reconciliation part of its mission, it has to help the ANC make peace with black people it continues to despise as much as, and possibly more than, the white Afrikaner enemy. Blacks who fought with the former government are seen as "traitors" in the same way as whites who fought *their* people—as many writers, academics, humanitarians, leftists and conscience-stricken church-goers did—were "traitors." To break rank with the tribe is often seen as the ultimate sin.

At the same time, the developing foundation-story of the struggle against apartheid has to be nurtured, and any action that appears to legitimize the collaborationist chiefs who took orders from Pretoria will be taboo. With this, an underlying conflict between the Struggle and the Rainbow Nation lies exposed; the Struggle is essentially the story of the ANC, while the Rainbow Nation implies that everyone—*all* blacks and "coloureds" and Indians and whites—must feel reasonably comfortable with the historical narrative. I wonder whether this will be possible, in the end. It will probably take years to tell, but intimations of the emerging national story are becoming apparent in this schoolroom in remote Lusikisiki. The chairman's opening address, for instance, in which he speaks of the "battle for freedom of the Pondo people," and the unarmed who "fought for their rights" includes only one group, and it isn't those who supported the Pretoria-led chiefs.

But TRC hearings are supposed to be about healing wounds, and that, too, is a priority. "We pay our respects to those who died before they could appear today before the Truth and Reconciliation Commission, to each of those who were tortured, murdered and who disappeared without a trace," says the chairman. The names of the dead from this community are read aloud, as the surviving members of their families stand silent before the men and women high on the stage before them, these educated commissioners whose language and skin colour is the same as theirs, these important people who have come to their distant village to listen to them tell their stories at last. A woman shudders visibly and hides her face in her hands.

Three men are called. They mount the stage and seat themselves at the witness table facing the commissioners. One struggles on crutches and must be helped. They stand, and each takes an oath of truth. "This is a great responsibility that you undertake," says the chair. "You will tell the country what happened to you on the day in question."

The day in question was June 6, 1960, when, at nearby Ngquza Hill, two aircraft and a helicopter dropped smoke bombs and tear gas on a crowd of unarmed men, then opened fire without warning, killing eleven and wounding thirty. The victims were ANC supporters; the perpetrators were police.

The witness, Adolphus, a straight-backed, strong-looking man with grey hair, describes his people's grievances against the regime: "We had passes and we had to wear them around our necks. We were against Bantu education [the inferior educational structure assigned to non-whites], and we wanted to be represented in the [regional] Cape Town Parliament. But when we went to the magistrate, he didn't listen to us. We were told we were baboons, and baboons didn't go to Parliament in Cape Town."

At these words, muffled sobs break the silence of the room, for the dehumanizing heart of apartheid has been spoken aloud: the crushing accusation that "the other" is not fully human. Shame and humiliation—wounds to the soul—exposed in a torrent of words.

The story of that long-ago June day tumbles out. "There were people all around us shooting. We didn't know where to hide, we were cornered. After, we carried fifty-eight people to our friend's house. He is here today." The friend is in the hall; he is a dwarf, and his eyes are closed tight as he listens. "We would not go to the hospital because they would come there to get us.

"Some of us who were arrested died of our injuries. We were beaten, we couldn't breathe, we urinated. They hanged my friends. Some who were with me in jail stayed there for eleven years.

"Later, the Boers came to my *kraal*. They burned four of my huts and killed my sheep. They were helped by informers who were on the side of the chief. I was shot in the leg and I am still crippled."

Adolphus fixes the commissioners with a piercing gaze and speaks in a forceful voice that grows louder by the minute, until someone moves his microphone back a distance. He pauses to emphasize his words, he shouts in anger, he lowers his voice so we must strain to hear. Adolphus communicates with the power of the ancient African storyteller whose task it is to transmit the past to new generations.

The commissioners listen, transfixed, and when the witness has finished his statement, they each ask questions. Only June, the white commissioner, needs interpretation from Xhosa into English (she and I are the only people in the room using headphones). There is fumbling as the witness adjusts his set so her questions can be translated. June's need for interpretation highlights her marginality. She is an admirable woman, a liberal activist with impeccable credentials, but she is not a member of the suffering tribe. This hearing is not about or for her—even though she, like everyone here, is a member of the would-be Rainbow Nation.

The generator has failed, as one knew it would, and the catered lunch does not arrive. The hearing adjourns so the commissioners and witnesses can go to Ngquza Hill, where the massacre occurred.

The dirt road worsens until it dissolves into a pair of rain-filled ruts, and we find ourselves in the middle of a field with *kraals* and mealie plots on either side of the car. Young men ride by on horseback; old men wrapped in blankets and carrying staffs stand ramrod straight to watch us pass. People are urinating in the open (there is no plumbing in the region). More small boys with long sticks tending cattle—they look about seven or eight years old, and they are evidently not in school. Children stare at me in consternation from the side of the so-called road. A white face is a rare sight, but a white female face seems deeply perplexing.

The caravan of cars stops at the rim of a hill, and we look down into a glorious valley of green-carpeted bluffs that slope toward a river. The eleven men who were shot from helicopters were at the river. They were corralled, with nowhere to hide from the planes circling above.

The survivors of that long-ago day gather around on the grassy knoll as a minister prays. Truth: we have heard their story spoken on oath. Reconciliation: that is what this trip into the rural hinterland is about. History and memory transformed, transcending the searing remembrance of injustice. The minister lays a wreath. The men close their eyes and hold their hands over their hearts.

A spokesman for their group says, "The men who died are buried in the valley below. We would like to rebury them here at the top, where we have laid this wreath. We would like money to build a memorial to them and to this episode in the liberation struggle of our people."

The chair of the commission replies carefully. He is unable to promise anything, but he will take their request to the TRC. The survivors nod their thanks. The chairman is an imposing man from another world. He represents Nelson Mandela himself, their own Madiba, and he is paying attention to them, the forgotten people of the back country.

"You were forbidden to come here by the authorities because the intent was to obliterate this event from history," the chairman tells them. "You were not allowed even to talk about what occurred here. But truth and memory can never be suppressed. The Truth and Reconciliation Commission will help restore memory so you will be acknowledged for your contribution to the liberation of this country. Then we can move ahead together and rebuild our nation."

The elderly survivors have been granted permission to remember aloud, in public, and they wipe their eyes in gratitude. Illiterate peasants in spruced-up ragged clothing, so far from the mainstream of their nation, still living lives of extreme hardship despite the arrival of democracy; on this day they remember, and the TRC has made it possible.

"Nothing can happen to us now. We are not going to be arrested," a beaming, toothless man informs me. "This is the first time we can speak openly about what happened to us. We are very, very happy."

It is evening before the cortège of cars arrives back at Lusikisiki. Lunch arrives at dinnertime, and the generator still is not fixed. Darkness overcomes the room and crickets in corners take up their evening song. But the "truth candle" continues to burn, and the hearings continue by its flickering light.

Now it is the turn of one of the chiefs. He climbs to the stage, accompanied by a lawyer, the only person to be so represented. A low murmur of contempt sweeps the ANC side of the hall. The lawyer says the chief was maligned and that the accusations against him are untrue. The chief is asked by the commissioners to confirm what is being said in his name. His story did, indeed, sound pat.

"You are not telling us the truth," the chairman says angrily. "If you admit the truth and ask for forgiveness, there will be peace. You were supposed to come here and ask for forgiveness." The chief and his lawyer look taken aback. There is, at this moment, very little "reconciliation" in the room, nor is there any doubt about where the TRC stands regarding the unresolved battles of the Transkei. The TRC does *not* intend to memorialize the history of the "traitors."

Dozens more people climb to the stage to tell their painful tales. Women with stoic faces fashioned from daily struggle and forbearance speak in clear voices of daytime shootings, night arrests, and sons, daughters and husbands who disappeared forever. Some knew their loved ones died in custody or after summary trials; others never had any news at all. One woman was refused permission to attend her child's funeral because the pass laws were in effect and she did not have papers for that area. She, like many others, asks the commission to find her child's "bones" and bring them home for reburial in the family. She, like many others, says she would forgive the perpetrators if they would only come forward and express regret. And show her where her son's remains lie.

Some people use this one-time opportunity to request education for their children—those youngsters tending the cattle, who, like their parents, are not learning to read and write. They lean towards the commissioners, pleading, their faces drawn with intensity. There may never be another chance to ask Madiba's representatives for help. Other people produce detailed shopping lists that send ripples of laughter through the audience. "I was the chair of the ANC in my village," announces one man, "and now that the ANC is in power I need help. I want a real house with clean water, a bathroom and electricity." These were ordinary expectations in most places, including all of white South Africa, but tantamount to asking for the moon in the Transkei. One woman finishes her story with a plaintive cry: "The government has done nothing for me. I want President Mandela to come here and honour the women of the Struggle."

The chairman concludes the hearing with a stock patriotic speech intended to link individual grief with the newly cast history of the nation. "Your children sacrificed their lives as heroes," he tells the mothers. "But they would not have been willing to do so if you had not brought them up to want to liberate their people. These children were precious to the organization, and all South Africa salutes them. Please put your hearts at rest. Their blood watered the plants of liberation."

The banality of this trite, generic accolade to the parents of murdered children appalls me. The mother who has just testified and is still on stage looks stunned at having relived her very personal tragedy just moments before. The social worker (who is present at every hearing) leans forward and lays a hand on her shoulder.

Did this woman really bring up her son to "liberate his people"? Or did she plead with him to stay out of politics and save his life? She does not say. Her son was dead at age eighteen—that's what matters to her. Maybe the public "salute" conferred upon him today will help, and maybe it will not. At the very least, her child's miserable end was noted at this event. At the very least, he has been remembered.

Far from the drama of Lusikisiki were many people, both black and white, who worried about impunity, who thought that the fine phrases of reconciliation were not enough, and that amnesty for criminals was nothing more than justice denied. The Steve Biko and Griffiths Mxenge families had tried to fight the TRC on grounds that amnesty eliminated the possibility of redress in criminal or civil courts, but the Constitutional Court had upheld the process. (There was some satisfaction for the Bikos: the killer of Steve Biko was later denied amnesty.)

A victims' support group called Kulamani (Zulu for "speaking out") was adamant in its opposition. I meet two of the women in their one-room office in Johannesburg. They speak quietly and their faces are blotched with pain. The son of one of them was killed by police in 1988, when he was seventeen. His mother shows me a school picture: her child was a student activist, and the Soweto police had been taunting him for months. One day, one of them pulled him into a laneway and put a bullet in his head.

"I would like justice to be done," she tells me in a whisper. "I cannot get it out of my mind. Now I have so many sicknesses. How could I forgive them? Even if they came forward and said they are regretting what they did?"

Kulamani was formed in late 1994 to help women. That year, there were three or four funerals a week in Soweto, and when a woman's son died, the others attended the funeral to offer her support. Since it was mostly men who disappeared, women and children were left without money or work. Kulamani tried to help.

When the TRC opened hearings, Kulamani assisted people who wanted to make a submission, but the women tell me that most people were still afraid—afraid they would be killed by the police if they pointed a finger—yes, killed by police in the *new* South Africa. The TRC could offer protection only when the witness was actually involved in a hearing.

"Would it have been better *not* to have a Truth and Reconciliation Commission?" I ask them.

"We were happy about the idea, but now we are hopeless that all the cases will really get investigated," says the woman whose son was killed. "Maybe at the end the government will say, 'Okay, we'll build a monument, or take your children to school, or give you some money.'

"But what we need is to find out the truth about what happened to our children. Maybe if we find the truth we will find peace in our hearts."

Shame. Many whites are feeling it. How easy it was to enjoy the privileges of pale skin colour by rationalizing the inherent inferiority of the primitive "other," by closing one's eyes to what was *almost* out of sight, pushed away into townships and "homelands." In any case, to stand firm against the pressure to conform to ideology would have required great personal courage: people who took the risk were attacked as Communists, shunned by the group, sometimes banned from practising their professions, imprisoned, forced to seek exile or murdered.

Some assuage shame by helping their servants, like the university professor I meet near Durban who put his gardener through university. Others express open relief that the web in which they were trapped has come apart: "I can breathe more easily now," says Eldon Wait, a professor of philosophy. When Wait hitchhiked in France in the 1970s, people told him they would not have picked him up if they had known he was South African, and once, in Germany, on learning of Eldon's origins, the driver suddenly confessed that he had been a member of the SS. "The two of us off-loaded our guilt," Eldon recalls.

A graduate student tells me he and his friends are "furious" at their parents, and a Dutch Reformed minister (who is writing a novel to exorcise his shame) admits that his children are furious at *him*. He also confides that "late at night, after a few drinks, people say Nelson Mandela couldn't really be a black. They think his skin is sort of yellowish, so he must be a 'coloured'—you know, with white blood."

But only one Afrikaner carries the competing versions of South African history within his person. Willie Verwoerd, a man with a famous, or infamous, last name, is only thirty-two years old, but his prematurely old face is already lined with anxiety. He is the grandson of Hendrik Verwoerd, the architect of apartheid. He is also an active member of the ANC and a commissioner for the TRC.

He tells me he is engaged in a long process of "coming home to myself," as he puts it—of trying to overcome the overwhelming sense of shame that derives, he says, from his family, his ethnicity and his religious background. "Coming home" means learning to accept that he is who he is: "a white Afrikaner, a Christian and a Verwoerd."

Like many white dissenters, Willie first understood the world differently when he left South Africa to study. Between 1986 and 1990, he lived in Holland, where he wrote a graduate thesis on his grandfather's term as prime minister. What he discovered led him to reject everything his grandfather had stood for and to join the ANC; he exchanged the old South Africa for the new.

The Verwoerd family reacted with fury; Willie's father, the son of Hendrik, broke off all relations. "They knew I was moving to the left of the white political spectrum, but there was a big difference between that and joining what they saw as a black-power organization of terrorists and Communists that was intent, as they saw it, on destroying white South Africa. There was also a strong religious connotation: Communists are atheists. My father often uses the image of the prodigal son."

More than anyone, Willie Verwoerd understands the pain of "reconciliation" personally. "I can accept responsibility but not personal guilt for belonging to an oppressor group. I have felt deep shame, and in some ways I look for opportunities to acknowledge this, because I believe hardened identities can be altered once you 'come home' to yourself and overcome denial and anger and blaming the other. I find it difficult to see how anybody can be involved in peace building between groups if they still carry a whole load of anger in themselves."

We are in a small café in the centre of Cape Town, and he must shout to make himself heard over the lunchtime din. I think of the perilously heavy burden this frail-looking man carries. He makes me remember Nkosinathi Biko, who is shouldering the weight of his martyred father's murder because he feels driven by the need to commemorate the life that changed South Africa for the better. Verwoerd is less lucky: the weight he carries—the name *he* bears—is that of the man who drastically changed South Africa for the worse. Willie Verwoerd is the last person I see before I leave Cape Town and South Africa in May 1997. He embodies in his person the wrenching change.

After my return home to Toronto, the professions that were once the glue of apartheid society came under the glare of the TRC spotlight. The legal bar and the judiciary, for example. What the "old" judiciary now had to wrestle with was the moral component of their role: the fact that they had applied the law in a racist state that had excluded the majority of its population from citizenship. The judiciary, as a whole, failed to turn up at the TRC hearings, preferring to send in written briefs, and when the commission delivered its final report in October 1998, it judged the profession harshly: "The Commission deplores and regrets the almost complete failure of the magistracy to respond to the Commission's invitation, the more so considering the previous lack of formal independence of magistrates and their dismal record as servants of the Apartheid state in the past. They and the country lost an opportunity to examine their role in the transition from oppression to democracy."[19]

Problems of reconciliation also enveloped the country's doctors: they too carried responsibility for having collaborated. No exact equivalent to Dr. Mengele practised medicine in South Africa, but seventy political prisoners died in detention from gross medical neglect, or, like Steve Biko, from complicity on the part of a physician. (When the Medical Association of South Africa [MASA] refused to investigate Biko's death in 1977, or cancel the membership of Benjamin Tucker, one of Biko's doctors, several members resigned and the association was forced to withdraw from the World Medical Association. But it was 1985 before a group of outraged doctors took their association to court. Only then was there a formal inquiry into the Biko case, in which Dr. Tucker was found guilty of "disgraceful conduct," and his colleague Dr. Ivor Lang of "improper conduct").

Victims told the TRC about medical abuses: one doctor had allegedly advised police to force-feed a detainee with porridge to make it look as though he had suffocated; another had refused treatment to a torture victim vomiting blood because "he would die anyway." (The man lived to tell his tale.) Many doctors had falsified medical records. Although there was no legislation obliging physicians to treat whites and non-whites separately, the profession had independently instituted its own rules. (In 1995, the medical association apologized for its complicity, but without specifying what it was apologizing for or undertaking to investigate the details.)

Some reasons for breaching medical ethics were obvious: doctors (like lawyers and judges) were members of a society built on race and fear, and in their isolation white South Africans had constructed a shared world view in which human rights violations of all kinds were justified. In its final report, the TRC found that MASA had failed in dozens of ways:

from permitting the establishment of segregated and unequal facilities to the lack of equal medical training for black doctors. District surgeons had failed to record complaints and evidence of torture and failed to take steps to report or halt abuse. Doctors, under the leadership of the surgeon general, had been directly involved in the development of chemical and biological weapons to be used against individuals. The list of connivances was long.

The commission appendixed to its findings the Hippocratic Oath; the Declaration of Geneva, in which physicians pledge their lives to the service of humanity; and the Declaration of Tokyo, which states: "The doctor shall not countenance, condone or participate in the practice of torture or other forms of cruel, inhuman or degrading procedures . . ."[20]

There were other hearings examining the close relationship between business and apartheid and hearings to explore the ways in which the media reflected and shaped public opinion. The horrors leaking from the hidden crannies of the "old" country were hard to bear—but few were prepared for the mad scientists of the Centre for Scientific and Industrial Research who tried to develop a pill that would "turn whites into blacks" so that whites could infiltrate the ranks of the enemy. Scientists at the Roodeplaats Research Laboratories near Pretoria, a wing of the military's chemical and biological warfare division, worked on poisons that would kill, cause cancer and promote sterility in men. They produced poisoned T-shirts designed to maim or kill the wearer through absorption of poison into the bloodstream. (A poisoned T-shirt was given by security police to the five-year-old daughter of Donald Woods, the author of *Biko*. She survived.)

There was no way to understand any of this except as the outcome of long-term social conditioning. Donald Woods's comment on the doctors who handled Steve Biko was true for most perpetrators from the professions. Woods said, "Although not consciously cruel, they are men whose consciences have been so drastically warped by their society that they are capable, through their negligence, of committing acts of extreme inhumanity. Dr. Lang knew about the leg irons, but he did not appear shocked by their existence . . . [T]he casual and minimal treatment of black prisoners was normal."[21]

In May 1997, as the deadline for amnesty applications loomed, president-in-waiting Thabo Mbeki, Dullah Omar and most other members of the ANC cabinet, as well as hundreds of other veterans of the Struggle, joined the rush to apply. (On the opposing side, neither P. W. Botha nor F. W. de Klerk put their names forward; most amnesty confessions came from the apartheid police.) Getting Mbeki and his fellows to take this step was an important victory for Desmond Tutu, for if the governing ANC had insisted on exempting its members from the very body it had legislated into being, and if it had continued to pretend that only the apartheid state had committed human rights abuses, he had warned he would resign. And rightly so: the TRC would have been a laughing-stock inside and outside the country.

In its testimony to the commission, the ANC took responsibility for five hundred bombings over eleven years and for having planted land mines. They conceded that they could have taken a stronger stand against the practice of necklacing so-called traitors. They admitted to torturing and executing dissidents and spies and raping female officers in the guerrilla-training camps. But there was no retreat from the morality of their "just war" against apartheid.

The request for amnesty by people now in power was critical to the credibility of the TRC, but just as the commissioners at the Lusikisiki hearings I had attended were perfectly (though indirectly) clear about what side they were on when confronted with a conflict between those who supported the Struggle and those who had collaborated with the chiefs and government, now another branch of the commission showed its bias. In November 1997, the amnesty committee declared a blanket amnesty for thirty-seven top leaders of the ANC, including Thabo Mbeki and five cabinet members, without public hearings and without indicating what crimes they had committed. The opposition parties crowed that TRC partiality had finally been exposed.

Desmond Tutu had a major problem, and in January 1998, the commission asked for a Supreme Court ruling. The amnesty committee was independent. Had it acted within the legal guidelines of the commission itself?

"No," said the court the following May, overturning the blanket amnesties.

In October 1998, just before the commission released its long-awaited report, the ANC requested meetings with Tutu and Boraine concerning several of its leaders who had been served notice of possible detrimental findings.

To its credit, the TRC refused, but the new South Africa was at the wire. The ANC's anger was not simply about naming names; it was about creating history, about the Struggle and the role it would play in the future narrative of South Africa; it was about whether human rights abusers on the ANC side were going to be formally linked with abusers from the apartheid fold, about whether the Truth and Reconciliation Commission would finish by "casting the same shadow between freedom fighters and apartheid masters." It was about moral equivalence.

The report was due to be released on Thursday, October 29, 1998. On Wednesday, the ANC went to court to force the commission to deal with its concerns beforehand. So did F. W. de Klerk: he handed over more than two thousand pages of documentation to a judge, showing why *his* name should be removed from the commission account.

At 9:55 A.M. on October 29, the judge ruled against the ANC. But de Klerk won: the sheer immensity of the documentation he had deposited with the court could not be handled before the report's scheduled release.

Tutu was devastated. "It is with very great reluctance indeed that I have agreed . . . not to finalize our finding in relation to de Klerk at this stage," he said in a public statement. "It upsets me deeply. We have been scrupulously fair to de Klerk, and we reject the contention that we have engaged in a vendetta against him."

October 29, 1998. As Bishop Tutu prepares to formally hand over the report of the Truth and Reconciliation Commission to President Nelson Mandela, hardly anyone is happy. Both the ANC and F. W. de Klerk appear self-serving, not to say devious. The National Party, the Inkatha Freedom Party and the Freedom Front have already sent their regrets; they will not be present at this historic occasion, and each accuses the commission of bias—against them. Up to fifteen people have been successful in having their names removed from the list of those implicated in human rights abuses: some hadn't had the requisite advance notice; others had convinced the TRC that "mistakes had been made."

Archbishop Tutu calls for a silent prayer for the victims of apartheid, then he launches an offensive, laying out facts in defence of his beleaguered commission and in the name of future history. "This report contains more than just accounts of findings against perpetrators," he says. "It seeks to give as complete a picture as possible of the gross human rights violations that occurred as a result of the conflict of the past. It provides a setting against which to understand our past; it gives insight into the perspectives of those who supported apartheid and [those who] opposed it."

Tutu tells his audience of dignitaries that the report will make proposals "about how we can cultivate a culture of human rights and structures to ensure the atrocities of the past do not recur . . . and how to advance the process of healing and reconciliation of our traumatized and wounded nation." He says that the Truth and Reconciliation Commission is only one small piece in the puzzle and that it is up to all South Africans to commit themselves to the welfare of all South Africans, not just to their own group. By accepting the report, "we will have looked the beast in the eye; we will have come to terms with our horrendous past and it will no longer keep us hostage."

Nelson Mandela tries to set a stately tone and to rise above the actions of his own ANC: "I take this opportunity to accept this report as it is, with all its imperfections, as an aid that the TRC has given us to help reconcile and build our nation," he says.

For ex-freedom fighters and ex-apartheid enforcers both—indeed, for the entire country—this is a family affair, and not least for Nelson Mandela himself. Among those officially cited for gross human rights abuses is his former wife, Winnie.

In its final report, the TRC found that apartheid in South Africa was "a crime against humanity," as defined by the International War Crimes Tribunal at Nuremberg and later codified by the United Nations. "From the late 1970s, senior politicians—as well as police, intelligence and defence force leaders—developed a strategy to deal with opposition to the government. This entailed, among other actions, the unlawful killing, within and beyond South Africa, of people whom they perceived as posing a significant challenge to the state's authority. . . . The predominant portion of gross human rights violations was committed by the former state through its security and law enforcement agencies." Former president P. W. Botha received special condemnation: "By virtue of his position as head of state and chairperson of the State Security Council, he contributed to and facilitated a climate in which . . .gross violations of human rights did occur, and as such is accountable for such violations." Black liberation groups, including the ANC, were cited for similar breaches, notably the Inkatha Freedom Party leader (and national home affairs minister in the current government), Mangosuthu Buthelezi. From the Sharpeville Massacre of 1960 until the transitional election of 1994, South Africans lived within a culture of human rights abuse: "To a greater or lesser extent, this touches all major role-players who were party to the conflict that enveloped South Africa," said the report. "Where amnesty has not been sought or has been denied, prosecution should be considered. Under no circumstances should the government allow an undifferentiated blanket amnesty to wash the past away."

No blanket amnesty—Archbishop Tutu's most passionate recommendation or, perhaps, plea. He knew the government would be pressured to forgive and forget now that the TRC had finished its appointed task; on the other hand, victims, and those born into the families of victims over the decades of apartheid rule, would be unlikely to let a general amnesty happen without the strongest protest. Nor were they likely to "forget." Not in this land where a force as powerful as the TRC had held sway during the transition from police state to democracy.

Now that the commission has formally completed its work,[22] how will the new South Africa remember its past? Was there "moral equivalence" between enemies? Equivalence was what many whites on the ex-apartheid right had always claimed: they said they were fighting their *own* "just war" against international communism. Equivalence was what the ANC feared would be the commission's conclusion: a judgment that would find its way into the history books.

A decision in favour of moral equivalence was always unlikely—nor did it happen. An editorial in the Johannesburg *Mail and Guardian* hit a resonant chord: "No equivalence was ever suggested between the violence and immorality of the apartheid regime and the activities of the liberation movements. That the ANC, as a consequence of the war against apartheid, committed human rights abuses in its own detention camps and killed unarmed civilians, is something we imagined it had already accepted with humility and acknowledged with regret. The only thing that put the ANC on the same moral level as former president F. W. de Klerk was its attempt to gag the report." The editors acknowledged Bishop Tutu's declaration that the TRC was only one piece in the work of creating a new South Africa. "The process of national healing, uncovering the truth and even prosecuting the offenders must go on," they said; the Truth and Reconciliation Commission had performed an "extraordinary service" for the country.[23]

Many of the whites who disagreed with the process and the conclusions had already left the country by the time the commission presented its report. To abandon beliefs inculcated over a lifetime, and the lifetimes of parents and grandparents, was not possible for everyone; nor would all those with the means to leave choose to remain in a land where the violence might now include them.

The justice minister, Dullah Omar, expressed high hopes when we met in Cape Town, calling for the creation of a human rights culture, accountability, racial reconciliation and victim rights, but at this writing, only the smallest steps have been taken. Despite these efforts, there are more murders per population in South Africa than anywhere else in the world; torture is reportedly still a tool of police investigations; blacks remain undereducated and poor (although a small middle class is emerging); whites still live in affluence; victims complain that the TRC opened wounds without adequately addressing their needs; and the country is as racialized as any on earth—including the racism of black against black. (In January 2000, the newly appointed national police commissioner called his female subordinate a "chimpanzee," echoing the white-against-black insults of yesteryear.)

Underscoring these problems are even deeper concerns, the most important of which is accountability. The TRC report held P. W. Botha "accountable" for gross violations of human rights and called for his prosecution in the criminal justice system for having refused a subpoena to appear before the commission. But had Botha and F. W. de Klerk chosen to apply for amnesty, the men at the top of the apartheid pinnacle might have been formally exonerated—that is to say, never made accountable in any way. It is unlikely that either De Klerk or Botha will ever be indicted under the South African criminal justice system, which is a pity, but the possibility that they might have been amnestied seems strikingly inappropriate, given the leadership role they played. Although it is true that only a small percentage of people who applied for amnesty have been successful (at the end of 1999, just 568 out of 7,142 applications, with 815 cases still pending, the rest having been withdrawn for various reasons), the dilemma of amnesty versus accountability remains unresolved. Worse still, since the perpetrator's abusive act had to have been conducted with a political motive in mind in order to qualify for amnesty, the familiar "I was only obeying [political] orders" rationale seems to have reappeared on the international scene. Struck down at Nuremberg, it has re-entered through the back door of a new, semilegal process.

Liability also seems disturbingly one-sided. Although the regulations for amnesty specifically called for an admission of individual responsibility for particular acts, the leadership of the ANC had originally applied as a group—and been amnestied as a group—a decision that Archbishop Tutu decried and sent to the Supreme Court for arbitration. When the ANC lost the court case in May 1998, they reapplied, again as a group, to the amnesty committee, but in April 1999, the new collective application was simply dismissed. The committee said: "An act, omission, or offence must be the subject matter of an application, [and since] none of the applicants had been involved in any individual action for which they would be required to seek amnesty, [their application] did not comply with the requirements of the act." Why the ANC application did not "comply with the act" the second time around, when the same leadership had initially been offered a blanket amnesty, is unclear.

I ask Archbishop Tutu about this when we meet again in a Toronto hotel, in February 2000, after he has received an honorary degree from the University of Toronto. Almost three years have passed since our first conversation, and I am startled by how unwell he now looks; he has recently undergone another operation for cancer. Ever open, as is his way, he indicates that he was disturbed by the ANC joint amnesty application—and by the results. "Their motive was good," he insists. "They wanted to show their support for the commission and to indicate that they accepted collective responsibility for policies that led to abuses. But I do wish that more people in the leadership had requested amnesty for specific acts, such as ordering people to plant land mines or to carry out bombings. Their application was a laudable moral act, but it ended up blowing up in our faces." I am taken aback by the directness of this statement. I remember that across-the-board fairness was, and is, the cornerstone of Tutu's vision, and that he has had to fight the ANC every inch of the way on this matter—from their exculpatory claims of a "just war" to their attempt to prevent the commission from naming names in its final report.

Forgiveness—so important to Archbishop Tutu—presents another complication, and a true story nicely illustrates the point. A security policeman named Gideon Nieuwoudt went to the Port Elizabeth home of a man he had confessed to murdering to ask the family for forgiveness. Instead of hugs and thanks, the victim's son clobbered him on the head with a flower vase. There is something refreshing in this tale, because, after all the seriousness, it brings home a central truth: no matter how sincere the apology, forgiveness is never automatic, nor can it happen collectively. Forgiveness can be bestowed only by the victim, or the victim's descendants, by choice. And reconciliation may or may not follow.

The list of problems is endless, but somehow, in spite of major criticisms, South Africa's Truth and Reconciliation Commission transcended its failures and inadequacies. Archbishop Tutu held firm on a crucial test, distinguishing between the morality of a "just war" against apartheid and the illegal means that were used to wage it. Human rights abuses are unjust, regardless of who carries them out or to what end. And there is something else, something very new: the TRC appears to have successfully drawn a line between the old and the new South Africa at a crucial transitional time. The recovery of the past and the obscured fate of many individuals emerged almost immediately after the events from the mouths of the perpetrators themselves. Not even the staunchest pro-apartheid supporter disputes that these events happened.

To have achieved this, if only this, is a triumph for the nation seeking to be born.

In December 1997, long before the TRC hearings came to an end, Mary Burton, a commissioner and a former member of Black Sash, called for a national "register" of reconciliation, to give voice to ordinary South Africans—not only those who actively participated in apartheid oppression, but those who were silent bystanders. "The register [is] in response to a deep wish for reconciliation in the hearts of many South Africans . . . who want to demonstrate in some symbolic way their commitment to a new kind of future . . ." she said. People were invited to write to the TRC, or to post their responses on the Internet.

Several hundred of them turned to the Internet, including many who had left their homeland, and some of their comments are deeply moving:

I am an Afrikaner who was grossly misled by my peers. I was led to believe that all was well both in the Christian and worldly sense. I now realize that this was not so and I will do all in my power to make amends for the wrongs of the past and ensure that those who follow me will be exposed differently. – *Ulrich Swart*

It is with deep regret that I reflect on my past. It is with deep sorrow that I acknowledge my complicity as a white South African. And it is with

immeasurable guilt that I assume responsibility for my role in our shameful past. I cannot say "I did not know." I can only say I chose not to know. I chose the safety of my own family over my moral duty to my compatriots. . . . I raised and educated my children with privilege, whilst those around me were deprived. I am so deeply sorry! And the opportunity to express this regret and offer apology does not unburden me . . . [but] allows me to reach even further into my soul to express the remorse that I feel. It impels me to continue to seek in my own small way to help repair the damage to our people and our land caused not only by "perpetrators" but also by us, the bystanders, in the tragedy of our past. . . ."
– *Dr. Merle Friedman*

As a black man who grew up in Soweto, inhaled the tear gas and was *sjambokked* often by the SADF [South African Defence Forces] and men (brutes?) of de Kock's ilk, including many other horrors, I remain angry and very bitter. But having observed the rancour (if not hatred) of blacks towards whites in America during my short stay as a student, I can't help but beg, please let us save South Africa. Although I battle to forgive my white compatriots, the need to forgive and help build our country remains another level of the struggle. . . . Good enough reason to make me stay put here at home . . . Africa. – *Bereng B. Mtimkulu*

To my daughters: I wish to apologize for the fact that I did not do more to give you a better country than the one I inherited from my parents. . . . To any South African, or southern African, who may have been affected by my not questioning my participation in the SADF in 1973, I wish to express my deepest regret. . . . I pledge myself to fighting racism and oppression, both overt and covert, wherever and whenever I encounter it in my daily life. I pledge myself to do all I can to heal the wounds and rebuild this country so that our grandchildren will never experience the fear and hatred of the apartheid era. – *Andrew Scholtz*

I am very aware of my ancestry. I descend from Krotoa whose people watched van Riebeeck come ashore in Table Bay in 1652. I descend from Swiss, Dutch and German mercenaries, soldiers of the Dutch East India Company, who came to the Cape because it offered them more opportunities for advancement than their homes in Europe ever could. I descend from Huguenot refugees who came to the Cape to escape religious persecution and social degradation in seventeenth-century

France. I descend from slave women, like Angela van Bengale, brought to the Cape to serve in van Riebeeck's fort, or Eva van de Caap, born at the Cape of unknown parentage towards the end of the eighteenth century. I descend from an Englishman who, following the first British occupation, settled in Cape Town in 1797.

And my ancestry has taught me, as nothing else can teach me, that our external appearance means nothing. We are all able to be good and kind and filled with love, and we are all able to be brutal and cruel and filled with hatred. I do not believe that all those who suffered discrimination under the policy of apartheid are virtuous. I do not believe that all those who lived silently enjoying the fruits of apartheid are evil. Not many people are cut from heroic cloth. We allow the mythmakers to rewrite the truth of our ancestry. We allow party hacks to sit on the judicial bench. We allow psychopaths to commit murder in the name of "law and order." We betray ourselves and our country. . . .

I confess that I took the easy road of silence. . . . I am deeply sorry about, and bitterly regret, the damage done to my fellow South Africans. I ask—without any right to be heard—that the new South Africa learn from its past.—*Andries William de Villiers*

War, Memory and Identity

6

Who Will Own the Holocaust?

> *We are still incapable—due to the short distance in time between us and those events—of understanding the significance of all that we have lived through and suffered. . . . It is simply impossible yet to draw conclusions . . . but the image of the Holocaust will dominate.*
>
> – GERSHOM SCHOLEM, 1989

"YOU SHOULD BE *ashamed* of yourself!" calls out the woman in the second row after I have finished giving a lecture on Daniel Goldhagen's controversial new book, *Hitler's Willing Executioners*. I am standing before an audience in my home city of Toronto. The subject of my talk has been advertised as "History, Memory and the Burden of Guilt."

The room falls abruptly silent as every head swivels to stare at her, then swings back towards me expectantly. The woman, heavy-set and pushing elderly, is flushed with anger. I too am suddenly flushed—with surprise. I had already reviewed the book in a large-circulation newspaper before the invitation to speak arrived on my desk, and although I knew emotions were running high as far as Goldhagen was concerned, it hadn't occurred to me that criticism might be interpreted as a sign of moral turpitude.

I apologize for having unwittingly caused hurt and state my deep respect for people who survived a horror I can barely imagine. All the same, I had been invited to talk about my ideas, and they had come to hear them.

A man jumps to his feet to defend me, at which point a verbal free-for-all breaks out in the hall. Members of the audience shake their fists and shout at one another from across the room, attacking or defending my views and my right to express them. Since my presence is clearly marginal to what is going on, I sit down and marvel at the event.

What had I done to provoke such outrage? I had described the thesis of the Goldhagen book: the notion that ordinary Germans were "willing executioners" during the Holocaust, people who killed with zealous enthusiasm because they had been conditioned to desire the murder of Jews. Goldhagen called this collective urge to destruction "eliminationist anti-semitism." I had said that while I agreed that Germans were conditioned over centuries to reject the Jewish minority living in their midst (initially on religious grounds) and that this was undoubtedly a major factor during the decades leading up to the Holocaust, I thought Goldhagen had exaggerated his views beyond credibility while maligning just about everyone who had ever written about the subject. Finally, I had held up examples of Goldhagen's inflammatory language and suggested that he had missed the essence of what Primo Levi once called the "grey zone" of human affairs, described by the historian Christopher Browning as that foggy universe of mixed motives, conflicting emotions, personal priorities, reluctant choices, opportunism and accommodation, all wedded, when convenient, to self-deception and denial. I thought that by marshalling his research into an overly narrow narrative, painted without nuance in black and white, the author had missed the human complexity and the ordinariness of racism. All in all, it had been a straightforward talk, and I had perhaps naïvely expected the usual kind of open debate.

Out of that night's uproar, two remarks have remained with me. The first came from a man at the back of the room, who said, the hurt audible in his voice, "In thirty years you can give a talk like this. When we are all dead. But while we live you have no right to talk to us like this." The other came from a person who exclaimed, "We don't *need* history! We were *there*! What you said is just dry linguistics!"

How was I to decipher the violence of this reaction? What I eventually had to accept was that for some survivors of the Holocaust, the only acceptable response to the tragedy they endured is commemoration—and its complement, commemorative history. From this optic, *Hitler's Willing Executioners* is a model of correct history, perhaps because its scholarly footnotes appear to justify visceral hatred towards the nation that committed crimes of imponderable magnitude. My analysis did not fit that approved model and was unwelcome to many in this group. An affront—an attack on identity.

Daniel Goldhagen's book was but the latest in a string of controversial works seeking to explain who, or perhaps *what*, was a Nazi, starting with the philosopher and political scientist Hannah Arendt's famous reports on the 1961 trial of Adolf Eichmann, first published in *The New Yorker*, then later in book form as *Eichmann in Jerusalem: A Report on the Banality of Evil*. Arendt thought Eichmann was unimaginative, ordinary and unthinking: not stupid, as such, but utterly lacking in judgment. She concluded that given the inverted moral world he inhabited, his conscience had ceased to function in any recognizable way. Arendt surprised even herself in adopting this view: before going to the trial, she had subscribed to the prevailing opinion that Eichmann (and his fellows) were beyond comprehension, monstrous exceptions to humanity. Why, he was "not even sinister!" she wrote to her husband, Heinrich Blücher, on April 15, 1961.

The "exception to humanity" theory was an attractive piece of populist demonology that Daniel Goldhagen had revived, then extended beyond the Nazi leadership to the German population at large. Perhaps my critique of this thesis, and my suggestion that Germans are people like any other, myself included, with the capacity to be corrupted by incessant propaganda, had been construed as an insult. I wasn't sure. What did seem certain was that I had misunderstood the unspoken rules of discourse when addressing survivors of the Holocaust. A powerful orthodoxy with quasi-religious tenets has emerged, and by challenging one of its recently adopted expressions, a new book with a cherished thesis, I had committed a blasphemy of sorts: a heresy. Like all religions, the survivor religion had boundaries that were not to be transgressed.

In retrospect, I think that I should have been less surprised. In the late 1980s, I attended a lecture by Raul Hilberg, whose seminal book, *The Destruction of the European Jews* (1961), marked the beginning of contemporary Holocaust investigations. Recently reprinted, the book finally reached the broad audience it deserved. During his presentation, Hilberg happened to say that new research indicated that the number of Jews murdered during the Hitler years was closer to five million than to six million. Anger erupted in that room too: the figure six million mattered. Some people jumped to their feet and said that by altering an important symbol of commemoration, Hilberg was an accomplice to Holocaust denial, especially since one of the most notorious of the so-called revisionist books was titled *The Myth of the Six Million*, and another, *Did Six Million Die?*

Hilberg looked annoyed; he had heard it all before and he was not about to back down. Such objections were motivated by politics, he said later, and he neither wrote nor lectured to make political points.[1]

He had already aroused controversy with the initial publication of his book when he questioned the role of the Jewish Councils of Elders, organizations put in place by Adolf Eichmann in Nazi-occupied territories in order to inventory the Jews' property and expedite the deportations. The ghetto leaders had co-operated with their oppressors, including drawing up deportation lists, in the pathetic hope that conditions might improve if *they* were in control. What actually happened at the end of the railway line was rumoured but not clear; whisperings about mass murder were denounced as impossible; and those who spread the truth were sometimes called "insane." Although most of the Jewish Council elders and their families were deported with the last convoys when their usefulness came to an end, the debate over what they knew and the assistance they offered to the Nazis lived after them.

Fiery disputes about the ghetto leaders were matched by the hot-button subject of Jewish wartime resistance. Everyone had heard the stories about passive victims who walked to their death; indeed, the origin of this description could be traced to the Palestine Yishuv, as the original community was called before the creation of the state of Israel, where the archetypal "new Jew," the native-born *sabra* whose existence was removed in fact and by design from the boundaries of a tainted Europe, had sculpted an altered Jewish self in opposition to the so-called ghetto Jew. The *sabra* was active and physical, in supposed contrast with the presumed passive intellectuals of the pre-war Continent. ("The younger generation's psychological distance from the Holocaust was apparent in their lack of interest in anything . . . that had to do with the old Jewish world that had been destroyed. . . ," wrote the historian Anita Shapira.[2])

In Europe there was, naturally, Jewish resistance of sorts. Among those who escaped the deportations, many had fought bravely as partisans, sometimes in Jewish bands, sometimes with Poles or others. The men and women who had waged the uneven, hopeless battle in the Warsaw Ghetto on April 19, 1943, were courageous in the face of impossible odds. But in the 1960s, Raul Hilberg, the historian of record, concluded that Jewish resistance was on the whole "negligible," and resultant German casualties "almost nil." More dangerously, he dared to explain this state of affairs by reference to the long millennia of Jewish history itself. Hilberg wrote that vertical structures of communal authority, such as the ghetto councils, were deeply rooted in the experience of the Diaspora, and that the small, powerless Jewish communities had always depended upon leaders at the apex of the pyramid whose job it was to seek protection from the rulers of the day, be they king or caliph. He argued that the Nazis understood and exploited this traditional alignment, and by slipping into the familiar organizational fold, the Jews effectively precluded the possibility of widespread rebellion. He pointed out that when resistance did take place, those who led the uprising had first to challenge the ghetto leaders themselves, as in Warsaw, where the first action of resistance was directed against the Jewish Council.

Hilberg's conclusions about resistance, or the lack of it, were decidedly unpopular, and in November 1962, a first salvo in the struggle to shape remembrance appeared in the pages of *Commentary* magazine. The article, by Oscar Handlin, a Harvard specialist in immigration who had won the 1952 Pulitzer Prize for history, was titled "Jewish Resistance to the Nazis." Handlin allowed that there had been collaboration, but he argued that it had happened everywhere in Europe, and that the attitude of the Jews themselves "had no effect on the extent of the catastrophe." This was the usual stuff of historical disagreement (although the Holocaust was not Handlin's field). But what was infinitely more startling was his religious terminology: Oscar Handlin called Hilberg's interpretations an "impiety." He said that Hilberg was "defaming the dead."

I meet Raul Hilberg in April 1999 at his home in Burlington, Vermont, where he is living in retirement from the state university where he taught history for forty years. He is in his early seventies. His mouth is etched with deep creases, and his speech carries a bitter, ironic edge after a lifetime of unending controversy over his work. His backyard looks out into a woodland, which has deer, he concedes, when I question him. He is not interested in nature: "That's for the grandchildren." At the forefront of his concerns is his reputation and his legacy, and after almost forty years, he is still consumed with anger at Oscar Handlin for having trespassed the boundaries of scholarly legitimacy by bringing the equivalent of a religious curse to what should have been a discussion between professionals. Not that he doesn't understand Handlin's impulse to protect reputations—or the search for comfort. "I was looking for resistance every time I opened a new page of documents," he tells me. "*I* also wanted the comfort. But the evidence just wasn't there. On the other hand, there were plenty of legends about resistance, even during the war, because the Jewish leadership wanted to suggest the Jews were fighting—for many reasons. For one thing, the Allies were actively looking for anti-Nazi resistance because it could be used to gauge the extent of German strength and could have military implications, but the Germans countered all resistance with collaborators and that nullified however little there was."

Hilberg is also a survivor of the Holocaust, although he was never interned in a camp. He was born in Vienna in 1926 and was lucky enough to escape to the United States in 1940 with his parents (the relatives who stayed in Europe were less fortunate). His personal background has made the reaction to his life's work even more painful, and he has just recently uncovered information that will likely reduce his popularity even further among the commemorators: the *pièce de résistance* of Jewish pride, the battle of the Warsaw Ghetto, was itself an exaggeration of fact, he says. "Since I revise my text continually, I decided to revisit the ghetto battle because I thought I had not fully grasped it, and in this case I had relied entirely on Jewish sources. But current research in Europe is very advanced, and they go straight to the archives. In Germany, historians have been looking at an enormous amount of testimony from the trials of SS men and police who fought in that battle, and what I have learned from these sources is that the famous tank that was supposedly put out of action on the first day of the uprising actually had no cannon. It was a training tank. That means that as far as resistance is concerned, I have been attacked for almost four decades for what I had actually overestimated."

That Hilberg has used German documents as a basis for most of his work—over and above survivor testimony—has also been a source of criticism in some quarters, the implication being that some German accounts are biased while those of the survivors are not. Here again, Hilberg gives not an inch, his claim being that no one can grasp this event fully without studying it through the accounts of the perpetrator nation. "It was always clear to me that I was going to write the story of the Holocaust through the eyes of the Germans because that was the only way," he says, "and it was imperative to start with the Nuremberg war crimes trials documents. I did use survivor testimony, but I also had to acknowledge that the Jewish view of what was happening was extremely limited. How far do you see when you are boxed into a ghetto or a camp? A few hundred yards? Also, one has to bear in mind that most Jews are not interested in the details of the Holocaust as a historical process. The Holocaust has been incorporated as an important element of Jewish memory, but memory is not history as the 'footnoters' like myself understand it, and that is sometimes resented."

Hannah Arendt's conclusions about Adolf Eichmann's "banality" also crystallized into enduring controversy. Others may have hoped to see Bluebeard in the dock, she wrote, but for her the horror lay in the fact that "there were so many like him, and that the many were neither perverted nor sadistic . . . [but] terribly and terrifyingly normal." She was one of the first to refute the "monster theory" of less-than-human Nazis (however, if *banal* meant "common," there was much to argue with: among the defendants at Nuremberg were eight jurists and a university professor). Using Hilberg as her source, Arendt also wrote about the Jewish Councils of Elders that operated under Nazi jurisdiction, concluding from the trial testimony that "without Jewish help in administrative and police work . . . there would have been either complete chaos or an impossibly severe drain on German manpower." And she was pitiless when she wrote: "To a Jew, this role of the Jewish leaders in the destruction of their own people is undoubtedly the darkest chapter of the whole dark story. . . ."

Like Hilberg, Arendt was excoriated for having impugned the integrity of the Jewish people. In a postscript to a later edition of *Eichmann in Jerusalem* she spoke bitterly about the controversy, noting that elements of "the Jewish Establishment" were trying to justify the wartime leadership by citing all the commendable services they had rendered. On the other side of the controversy, Arendt's critics feared that anti-semites would point to her document as evidence that the Jews were no less guilty than others for what happened.

Starting with Arendt and Hilberg, the need to commemorate the dead and the experience of those who had survived what Elie Wiesel has called "the night of the soul" clashed with the equally serious need to seek out and interpret historical fact, wherever the search might lead. And by the 1960s, these positions were at loggerheads in the emerging struggle for post-Holocaust Jewish identity.

Perhaps Hilberg and Arendt were on the scene too soon. Perhaps the stakes were too high. In the epigraph to his sad, bitter autobiography (tellingly called *The Politics of Memory*), Hilberg quotes H. G. Adler: "History without tragedy does not exist, and knowledge is better and more wholesome than ignorance." But he also admits that he had "underestimated the importance of myths and placed too much reliance on soberness. I had not reminded myself enough of Franz Neumann's words: 'This is too much to take.'"[3]

The Jews remember their history as they are enjoined to do by their ancient texts. The ultra-Orthodox remember that the Messiah will arrive at the end of days and that Jews are commanded to prepare for that joyful event; Jewish humanists remember the biblical prophets and their insistence that responsible men and women must try to make the world a better place for all peoples; the religious nationalists living in their barricaded Israeli settlements also remember—they have no doubt that the soil on which they have built their homes is the Land, a realization of God's ancient promise to his people; secular Zionists remember their faith in the values of physical labour, productivity, communal sharing and a defended homeland. The kibbutz farms have been changing as new generations abandon their parents' and grandparents' idealized fervour, but the collective memory of Israel as refuge and homeland continues to permeate the entirety of Israeli society.

But in Israel and elsewhere, no memory is more powerful than that of the Holocaust, and at its core lies the belief that the Jews were deserted by the world. This conviction took root during the Eichmann trial as people looked back for the first time, then swelled into hollows of fear as Israelis listened to their radios during the buildup to the 1967 war with Egypt and heard the mobs in Cairo calling for their death. At that moment, the younger generation finally understood the Holocaust; at that moment, their contempt for the survivors, the "ghetto Jews" from Europe who now lived in their midst, was transformed into respect.

In the late 1970s, a survey conducted in Israel revealed that the suffering of the Jewish people during the Holocaust had become the central rationale for Israel's right to exist, overcoming the earlier view that

Jews had a historic stake in the land the Zionist pioneers had claimed through settlement and acts of self-defence.[4] The Israeli pollster Hanoch Smith put it best: "Both generations in Israel believe that the Western powers did nothing to save the Jews during the war. This is a powerful indictment and it has a strong influence on the way Israelis act and think. The point is that people here start with the belief and it colours what they see."[5]

The locus of Holocaust memory was, and is, located in Jerusalem, at the famous Yad Vashem memorial. Mandated by parliament in 1953, the museum describes itself as a "commemorative" site that houses "the collective memory of the Jewish people." "Yad Vashem is the monument of a nation's grief," said the illustrious Abba Eban, Israel's former ambassador to the United Nations, ambassador to the United States and vice-president of the UN General Assembly, as well as foreign minister of Israel. "It gives moving testimony to the unparalleled violence which afflicted the Jewish people at the hands of the Nazi Germany, leaving a vast legacy of death and suffering in its wake. Yad Vashem is therefore one of the most significant landmarks in the moral history of mankind [and] merits the reverence and support of free people everywhere."[6]

A moral landmark and a commemorative site—without question. One and a half million visitors arrive annually on what must be called a pilgrimage, including heads of state. Yad Vashem houses the world's largest archive on the Holocaust, including more than fifty million pages of documents and hundreds of thousands of photographs and films, as well as the most important library on Holocaust research. Its message about memory is explicit: visitors are to be instructed about "the uniqueness of the Holocaust and its universal lessons."[7]

The continuity of Jewish historical memory is reflected in a quotation from the testament of Elkhanan Elkes, leader of the Jewish Council of Kovno (Kaunas), Lithuania, which spreads in large type across the Yad Vashem site on the World Wide Web: "Remember . . . that which Amalek did to us; remember everything, do not forget for the rest of your lives, and pass on as a holy testament to the coming generations that the Germans killed, slaughtered and murdered us . . ."[8]

According to this view, the Holocaust was a singular episode in the long saga of misfortune and redemption that has comprised traditional Jewish consciousness: some people have argued that historical memory is the key to Judaism itself.[9] The Torah urges the reader to remember the Jewish past: the Book of Exodus demands that Jews "remember this day, on which you went free from Egypt, the house of bondage, how the Lord freed you from it with a mighty hand."[10] Certain ultra-Orthodox believers date their calendar from the destruction of the Second Temple in Jerusalem in A.D. 70. From within this long tradition, Elkhanan Elkes had assimilated Amalek, the founder of a tribe hostile to the ancient Israelites, with the Hitlerian assault: a synthesis of biblical tale and twentieth-century reality. *Now Amalek came and fought with Israel in Rephidim. . . .*

And Moses said to Joshua, "Choose us some men and go out, fight with Amalek. . . .

And so it was, when Moses held up his hand, that Israel prevailed; and when he let down his hand, Amalek prevailed.[11]

Yad Vashem had adopted the ancient view that time-anchored events and biblical story dissolved into one continuous saga of catastrophe and recovery. Amalek begat Hamen who begat . . . King Ferdinand of Spain (he who expelled the Jews) begat Hitler, who begat . . . One trembled, for the enemies were many. In this familiar synthesis, historical fact dissolved into religion.

With this quotation, the museum also affirmed its commitment to the revindication of the Jewish people—*when* they kept their hand raised in the way of the new Israel—and to the ultimate defeat of the eternal foe. "*God said to Moses: Write this remembrance in the book . . . that I will surely erase the memory of Amalek from under the heavens.*"[12]

I was affected by Yad Vashem when I first visited in the mid-1980s;[13] the photographs on the walls raised difficult questions in my mind about the psychology of hatred, just as they did, years later, in the Topography of Terror museum in Berlin: the perpetrators smiling as they stand over their trophy victims—so grotesque and perplexing. I was grateful for the emphasis on gentile rescuers: noble human beings with the strength to resist the brutal onslaught of propaganda and the courage to put themselves at risk. And I was deeply distressed to realize that although I was at the biggest Holocaust registry in the world, I was unable to trace the members of my own lost family because my parents, both second-generation Canadians, were unsure of our relatives' first names. As my daughter, Michelle, and I stood helplessly before the impatient finger-drumming archivist, our unknown murdered relatives slid back into the dense fog of oblivion from which we had hoped to rescue them. They were lost to me, my parents, my siblings, my children and to all who would be born to us; in this place of names, where every identifiable death had been retrieved from the abyss of anonymity, they were lost to memory itself.

It is now a truism (although it didn't used to be) that every rendition of history inevitably distorts because it is the product of an individual researcher's choices, emphases and point of view. This is not to adopt the postmodern view that there can be no "truth" in history—a stance that can reduce inquiry to subjectivity and meaninglessness—but to acknowledge that when historians comb through the detritus of the past for an approximation of reality, they must ultimately express their findings in a form far removed from the "booming, buzzing confusion" (to quote William James) of once-contemporaneous life. A museum may simplify history even further by its choices of what to emphasize and by the necessity of a linear narrative that inevitably flattens the layers of complexity.

So there were significant choices to be made at Yad Vashem, as at any museum: choices that would shape the way the story would be understood long after the survivors all were gone.

In constructing its narrative of the Holocaust, Yad Vashem stressed familiar themes, but it did not suggest that any part of its presentation might have been subject to ongoing debate. When I visited, the very first item in the exhibition introduced the still-raw subject of wartime abandonment: the conviction that the Allies knowingly stood by while the Jews of Europe were being destroyed. There was evidence for this view, from speeches in the U.S. Congress to the infamous voyage of the *St. Louis*, the ship that left Hamburg on May 13, 1939, and whose Jewish-German passengers were rejected all along the Atlantic coast of North America, from Cuba to Canada, before being forced to return to Europe where many were rounded up by the Nazis and killed. But the core of resentment centred on what had happened, or, rather, *not* happened, at the Auschwitz death camp, and the first picture to greet the visitor to Yad Vashem was a huge blow-up of an aerial reconnaissance photo of the Auschwitz-Birkenau complex taken by the U.S. Air Force on August 25, 1944. The newly arrived transport train is clearly visible against a grainy background, and so is its newly discharged human cargo: thin black lines of people in queues for the selection process. The black line forks: one part snakes to the right, towards the gas chamber, which also is clearly visible.

The day I was there, the tour guide described the picture to a group of American tourists: he said the Allies knew about Auschwitz and had chosen not to save the Jews. An older man retorted angrily, "We were fighting the war *with* the Allies, *against* the Nazis!"

"The United States did not enter the war to help the Jews," the guide replied evenly. "It knew about Auschwitz and never helped the Jews."

That was the end of the discussion, but the question of why the United States did not bomb Auschwitz was not as clear-cut as Yad Vashem and its guide were suggesting. The museum's point of view may have originated with an article by the historian David Wyman that first appeared in the May 1978 issue of *Commentary* magazine, and later turned into a sensationally successful book titled *The Abandonment of the Jews: Americans and Holocaust, 1941–1945*.[14] Wyman argued that the air force could have wiped out rail lines and gas chambers if the commanders had wanted to. But they didn't care enough.

Such claims were hotly debated, especially the suggestion of "not caring" that hinted at anti-semitism. But there were other views: Raul Hilberg had written that although the Jewish proposals to bomb the railways lines, crematoria and gas chambers had come at the last minute, and were presented in an unco-ordinated manner, fundamentally "bombing was an idea whose time had not come. . . . The Jewish leaders were not accustomed to thinking about rescue in terms of physical force, and Allied strategists could not conceive of force for the purpose of rescue."[15] Others noted that for Americans the war was not about European Jews but about revenging Japan's attack on Pearl Harbor and Japanese atrocities committed against American POWs. In a book titled *The Myth of Rescue*,[16] William Rubinstein argues that it was impossible for the democracies to save significant numbers of Jews and that historians who maintain otherwise have misunderstood the situation in Nazi-occupied Europe. But this contention has recently begun to crumble: in 1999, British records, which were intended to be closed until 2021, were released under the Open Government Initiative, revealing that Anthony Eden, Britain's wartime foreign secretary, rejected a 1944 proposal from the United States to repatriate Germans from South America in return for the release of thousands of captive Jews carrying South American passports who were still in Nazi-occupied countries. Eden was afraid the freed Jews would immigrate to Palestine and create problems for Britain.

The man responsible for advising whether or not to bomb continued to defend his choice long after the war. In the mid-1980s, sometime around his ninetieth birthday, the former U.S. assistant secretary of war John J. McCloy told Benjamin Ferencz, an American lawyer who had prosecuted the Einsatzgruppen death squads at the Nuremberg trials, that he thought bombing railway tracks was an inefficient way to stop the trains transporting humans because another, loaded with new rails, would be on the spot within a day. He also said that bombing the crematoria and gas chambers ran the risk of hitting inmates, which would have been a political as well as a human disaster—and that neither option was going to end the war faster.

"McCloy did not deny his personal involvement in the decision, but he reaffirmed that he thought it was the right one, even in retrospect," recalled Ferencz when we met in Montreal in February 1999. "He continued to believe that it was wiser to concentrate on targets that were likely to win the war quickly." Ferencz offered to arrange a television program where McCloy could explain himself, but McCloy declined. "He said he was not prepared to try to defend himself in that way. He obviously did not think it would be useful," said Ferencz.

Perhaps he should have presented his case publicly, given the high level of emotion now swirling about the choice he made so many decades earlier, although one can understand the reluctance of a ninety-year-old to revisit a strategic military decision that was now a raging controversy.

One reason for the immense success of David Wyman's article and book was simple timing: the *Commentary* piece was published at the close of the Vietnam War, just as the Holocaust began to intrude upon the consciousness of Americans. As perceptions changed and the destruction of the Jews of Europe came to dominate other images of the Second World War, so history was increasingly revisited from the vantage point of new sensibilities, and the failure to bomb Auschwitz became a crucial symbol of American wartime indifference. Some Holocaust survivors and historians argued that a recognition of Allied interest in the ongoing murder of the Jews *would* have mattered to the Nazis, especially to Himmler, who was hoping to negotiate a separate peace with the West from May 1944. Others claimed, along with McCloy, that bombing would have made things worse, while many more sided with Wyman's thesis that the Allies simply didn't care about the Jews.

David Luebke, a former historian with the U.S. Holocaust Memorial Museum in Washington, has suggested that the incendiary discussion of the non-bombing of Auschwitz has eclipsed other issues, such as, for example, the restrictive immigration polices of the 1930s and early 1940s that prevented trapped European Jews from finding refuge in the United States and Canada, because it is easier "to cope with helplessness after the fact if you can convince yourself that mendacity, not circumstance, produced it."[17] Nothing, he implies, is more distressing than helplessness.

There was, and still has been, no resolution to the debate, but given the emerging centrality of the abandonment thesis to Holocaust memory and the need to adopt a clear storyline, Yad Vashem decided to assign the aerial photo of Auschwitz feature billing without a hint of the controversy surrounding the subject.

In 1948, the state of Israel was voted into being by the international community, at least in part as a response to the Holocaust. And since Zionism was a political and restorative vision within the framework of Judaism—a secular religion of sorts, an alternative to the eternal waiting for the Messiah—there was little doubt that Israel's Holocaust memorial museum would have something to say about the historical conjunction between the Jewish catastrophe and the new state.

It did, of course—by way of a striking conclusion. At the end of the tour, one steps onto a broad outdoor terrace dominated by a large bronze sculpture: the work of the Yugoslav artist Nandor Glid. Stylized human figures caught on stylized barbed wire hang in various postures of agony, yet this encounter with a beautifully rendered, artistic abstraction helps one to leave the emotionally jolting experience of the exhibition behind. Even greater meaning lies just beyond this work. Viewed through the angled hollows of the sculpture rise the hills of Jerusalem, where rooftops glint in the sunlight: a statement of life and renewal that leaves the darkness of the museum story behind.

Only afterwards did I question the pointedness of this narrative. It is true that all historical museums set out to inform by their choice of artifacts, by the written interpretations that accompany them and sometimes by the architecture of the museum space itself, but given the magnitude and the horror of the Holocaust, I would have welcomed a choice of "exits"—including the possibility of no resolution. Although redemption through the birth of the Jewish state was a soothing balm in the aftermath of the Holocaust, to affirm the Jewish homeland on the ashes of the dead cemented the bond between Jewish victimization and the political state, overshadowing the history of the early Zionist movement that had been moving in the direction of international recognition for a Jewish state on strictly political grounds for decades before the Final Solution. And it sacralized the Holocaust as a quasi-religious event that included the biblical tale of Amalek. Furthermore, if the state of Israel was literally born out of the Holocaust, and if the Jewish people were redeemed by the birth of the state, as Yad Vashem metaphorically declared, then the death of more than five million Jews was a prelude, and mysteriously necessary, to that redemption.

This conclusion disturbed me—and I wasn't alone. As Robert Alter, a scholar of Hebrew literature, put it almost two decades ago, "Only by violent wrenching can the destruction of European Jewry be 'justified' as the first stage in the birth of the state of Israel. The only real exodus from the camps was in smoke."[18]

He was neither the first, nor would he be the last, to express this concern: there have been many responses and counter-responses over the years. Against this complex background, I began to think that everyone, Jew and gentile, must try to sift through the implications of the Holocaust alone, in the recesses of the heart—without political or religious directives.

Every Israeli knows the living history of the Holocaust: it is taught in every school and remembered at every turn. The casual stroller on almost any city street is likely to encounter park benches and gardens dedicated to the victims or, should he or she undertake a trip out of town, an entire forest planted in their memory. Kibbutz settlements and other communities remember the dead as heroes or martyrs or both. In a real sense, the entire country is a memorial to the past and a tribute to the present.

But there is far less knowledge in the United States, where the majority of Jews now live. A survey by the American Jewish Committee conducted in 1994 indicated that Americans of all ages knew surprisingly little about Second World War events in general, far less than the British, the French and the Germans.[19] (Germans, not surprisingly, were the best informed.) Although 95 per cent of Americans had heard the word *Holocaust*, and 85 per cent said they knew what it referred to, their knowledge was rudimentary. Only one out of four people had information about the basic facts: that Jews were persecuted by Germans (or Nazis). (Knowledge of history was not an American strength: 41 per cent of respondents said they knew "only a little," or "nothing" about the civil rights movement that had unfolded in their own country.)

No surprise: the more education people had, the more history they knew, either from school studies or from their general reading of books, magazines and newspapers. Socio-economic status made a difference and was in turn related to education and to the amount of information that individuals sought out in their daily lives: 85 per cent of people with college degrees had the basics of what the researchers called "knowledge" about the Holocaust.

In spite of widespread ignorance, 76 per cent of Americans thought the Holocaust contained "lessons" that were relevant to the present day. This does seem paradoxical, but these numbers included thousands (if not millions) of uninformed citizens who possessed what the surveyors called "emotional knowledge": people who had assimilated the idea that the Holocaust was a bad thing that should never be repeated, without knowing much about the details. Americans believed, as always, in a better future, in a *morally* better future. That was their civil religion. And if something called the Holocaust had denied familiar-sounding rights and freedoms, they were dutifully opposed.

It was this national optimism that made it possible to create a major museum to the Holocaust at the heart of the American nation, a museum that was not without terrible problems in the conceiving but whose lessons could stand for American beliefs—for a future of democracy and continued liberty. But the American planners had specific priorities. American soldiers had liberated the death camps in 1945, they had been among the first to see the survivor inmates and the mountainous heaps of the dead, and American lawyers and judges had played a leading role at the Nuremberg trials. This meaningful involvement would allow the planners to transform a vaguely apprehended catastrophe that had once engulfed a people far from their shores into an event that held contemporary meaning for their own diverse population, with special reference to American history and American core values. It meant that the so-called lessons of the Holocaust—inferences people might draw for the vigilant maintenance of democracy, equality, civil rights and the other liberal values the United States professed—could be seen to have special meaning.

In the immediate post-war years, there had been almost no talk about the "catastrophe" (the word *Holocaust* had not yet been invented), least of all by those who had lived through it. "Let's get on with things" was the general credo. Survivors arriving in North America in the late 1940s and 1950s were derided as "greenies" or "DPs" (displaced persons) with funny accents. They didn't want to discuss their experience, and neither did anyone else; in fact, new arrivals were frequently warned not to frighten Americans and Canadians with their strange tales of horror. Then, as now, the focus was on the future, not the past: the same cast of mind that would blunt African-American attempts to raise historical awareness about slavery half a century later.

I had had my own experience with this mentality. In the early 1970s, I submitted an article to a Canadian Jewish affairs magazine about having accidentally stumbled upon the ruins of Natzweiler-Struthof in the Vosges Mountains a decade earlier. The editor sent it back with a note saying his readers would not be interested in such things.

Television finally made the difference: in April 1978, NBC broadcast the miniseries *Holocaust* to an astonishing 120 million people, and for the first time, packaged information about what the author Lucy Davidowicz called "the war against the Jews" reached a wide audience. Some people thought the story of genocide was trivialized by being popularized in this way: the English professor Alvin Rosenfeld said portraying Nazism as amusement was a moral scandal, while the Holocaust scholar Lawrence Langer thought the lightness of the film was in direct opposition to the reality of the events it was supposedly portraying.[20] Others argued that *Holocaust* opened the eyes of ordinary folk all over the world to some idea of what had taken place during their own lifetime. Knowledge, they said, was to be preferred over "indifference, silence, and . . . [the] shunning of survivors."[21]

Opinions aside, the results of the 1994 American Jewish Committee survey were clear: whatever modicum of knowledge Americans possessed came primarily from films and television.[22]

In the 1950s, *The Diary of Anne Frank* had become a perennial hit, both as a book and as a Broadway production. Anne's story contains no unseemly horror, and her bloodless, off-stage demise is upliftingly redeemed by her famous child-like statement: "In spite of everything, I still believe that people are really good at heart." (I played her myself in an amateur production when I was fifteen, and I well remember how I and the audience responded to both the character and the drama with cathartic tears.) Thinking back, I cannot recall an American portrayal of the Holocaust written for a mass audience that does not end on an inspiring note, from William Styron's *Sophie's Choice* to Steven Spielberg's phenomenally popular film *Schindler's List*.[23] About *Schindler's List*, a film that tells an epic tale of battle between a good German, who saves Jews, and an evil German, who is intent on killing them (the good guy wins, of course), the French filmmaker Claude Lanzmann, the author and director of the eight-hour documentary *Shoah*, complained, "To tell the story of the Holocaust through a German who saved Jews can only lead to a distortion of the truth, because for the overwhelming majority of Jews things like this did not happen."[24]

Lanzmann was right—truth matters. It is unlikely that *Shoah* could have been made in Hollywood, since the American way tends not to include staring into the abyss. But a niggling question remained: Would a cross-section of North Americans attend a "show"—movie, or television, or theatre—about the Holocaust that provided no emotional shelter for the audience? Or a museum?

In November 1978, U.S. president Jimmy Carter founded the President's Commission on the Holocaust (its very creation confirmed Carter's belief that the Holocaust could represent broad American concerns). The object was to bring into being an institution that would inform and educate. But what kind of museum could possibly integrate the specificity of the Jewish tragedy and the presumed universality of its "lessons"? Affirmative endings with an emphasis on justice and human dignity were expected, but the right to life, liberty and the pursuit of happiness was not exactly in tune with Auschwitz. Feel-goodism bordering on easy sentimentality presented a risk.

In his book *Preserving History: The Struggle to Create America's Holocaust Museum*, Edward T. Linenthal tells of the battle to build the unprecedented museum to memory that was eventually erected on the Washington Mall, the symbolic centre of the nation. President Jimmy Carter was a deeply religious Christian who believed in universality, meaning that if the proposed Holocaust museum was to find a home on the Mall, the broad spectrum of Nazi crimes against a wide range of peoples would need to be represented, not just the tragedy of the Jews. But Elie Wiesel was chairman of the commission when it began its work in 1978, and he had his own ideas.

For two decades, Elie Wiesel, author, lecturer and explorer of the dark soul of survival, had occupied centre stage in the struggle to fight oblivion. Unlike Primo Levi, the gifted Italian author whose post-Auschwitz suffering led to his suicide in 1987, or the philosopher Jean Améry, an Austrian-Jewish survivor who also ended his life long after the war, Wiesel had survived survival. He spoke from inside the abyss to those who suffered from despair and to the rest of the world, which had rewarded him with the Nobel Peace Prize in 1986.

He was born in 1928 in the village of Sighet, Romania, near the border with Ukraine. It was a tiny Jewish community imbued with Hasidism, or Jewish Pietism, a popular movement that emerged in eighteenth-century Poland to counteract what some thought were the overly rational, overly legalistic patterns of Jewish scholarship and the empty formalism of ritual. Hasidism was emotional rather than intellectual: it emphasized mysticism, prayer, personal devotion and the telling of moral tales, and its rabbis were more than simple teachers. They approximated holiness in unfamiliar ways. They were charismatic. They had received "sparks from heaven," which meant they could sometimes intercede with God on behalf of the faithful.

Without rejecting faith or tradition, Hasidism encouraged its followers to seek God's presence in the world in a direct, intimate way. The lowest of the low could experience God, provided they reached out with an open heart.

It is important to know this about Wiesel's background because his response to the Holocaust grew directly from his religious views, and because he has been so influential in shaping contemporary Holocaust remembrance. "I spent most of my time talking to God, more than to people. He was my partner, my friend, my teacher, my king, my sovereign, and I was so crazily religious that nothing else mattered," Wiesel recollected about his childhood in Romania during an interview in June 1996.[25] More than a decade before this conversation, Wiesel had argued that the collapse of religious norms in Germany was a direct cause of the Holocaust.[26]

He also seems to have been the first to apply the word *holocaust* to the murder of the Jews. In the Septuagint, the ancient Greek translation of the Bible, the adjective *holokaustos* is used to describe the wholly burnt offering in which the entire animal is sacrificed to God. Wiesel had been working on a biblical commentary, writing about the intended sacrifice of Isaac by his father, Abraham: he knew the biblical Hebrew word *olah*, which also meant "burnt offering." "I thought the word *holocaust* was good," he told an interviewer. "Fire and so on. The word had so many implications. . . . In the Bible, it was the son who almost died, but, in our [family] . . . , it was the father who died, not the son."[27]

The resonant, capitalized word *Holocaust* soon became a prism through which to recast the searing memory of the ghettos, the deportations, the death camps, the gassings and the ovens; indeed, the orthodoxy that came to surround these events—the notion that the murdered Jews were sacrificed martyrs; that to stray from what was deemed to be the proper representation of their deaths was blasphemy; and that to speak critically about the leaders of the ghetto Jewish Councils and the historical traditions of Jewish political leadership, for example, as Hilberg and Arendt had done, was an impiety that defamed the dead, sprang from this religious evaluation of a historical event. The Hebrew word *shoah* (as in the Lanzmann film) means "catastrophe"—a stark, unembroidered description of the mid-century genocide, but the Greek-derived word *holocaust* redirected memory into the sanctioned sphere of Jewish metahistorical myth where Bible, pogrom and remembrance fused into one. "The Holocaust is a sacred subject," explained Wiesel in 1973. "One should take off one's shoes when entering its domain; one should tremble each time one pronounces the word."[28]

Trembling before the presumed-to-be sacred would have been difficult for the diverse members of the President's Commission on the Holocaust as they struggled to piece together a museum that would work for everyone. The commission was composed of Jews and gentiles alike, most of whom were practical-minded men and women, yet Elie Wiesel, the chairman, was the world voice of Holocaust memory. The stage was set for a renewed conflict between secular historians and those in the Wiesel mode who had adopted a religious interpretation of events; between social scientists and curators and those who thought it was effectively impossible to represent what was inherently holy and inexplicable. Finding a common language of discourse was a problem in itself, let alone agreeing upon an overarching philosophy.

There were lengthy discussions over the proposed architecture of the building, the kinds of artifacts to be collected and displayed, what to emphasize in the museum and what to downplay, but nowhere was the dissonance between these differing approaches more visible than in the debate over whether the Holocaust is unique in human history, or in the discussions surrounding how Jews and other victims of the Nazis were to be represented. Numbers became crucial to the battle. There were approximately five million non-Jewish victims of the Nazis. Did that mean there were eleven million victims of the Holocaust?

Many Jews worried about the possibility of losing Jewish specificity—and with reason: in July 1979, the commissioners travelled to

Holocaust sites in Europe, where they were disturbed by the apparent disappearance of the memory of Jewish victims as Jews. Murdered Jews had been posthumously transformed into "Poles" (although during their lifetime, and for centuries preceding, Jews in Poland had been objects of exclusion and anti-semitism). Some of the commissioners thought Auschwitz was a tacky tourist site featuring souvenirs, refreshment stands and tour buses. At Babi Yar, near Kiev, the thirty-three thousand Jews who were massacred there by an Einsatzgruppe killing squad during a two-day orgy in September 1941 were recalled only as non-specific victims of fascism. Had they gone to France, the commissioners would have learned that Jews had died for the sake of their native land (*Morts pour la France*) like supposed soldiers on a battlefield, or discovered that they were not mentioned at all, as in Alain Resnais's seminal film about deportation, *Night and Fog*.[29]

When Wiesel presented the commissioners' *Report* to President Carter on September 27, 1979, the document's conclusions bore the stamp of his commitments, as well as his eloquent prose and that of the deputy director of the commission, Michael Berenbaum: "Our central focus was memory—our own and that of the victims during a time of unprecedented evil and suffering," stated the *Report*. "That was the Holocaust, an era we must remember not only because of the dead; it is too late for them. Not only because of the survivors; it may even be too late for them. Our remembering is an act of generosity, aimed at saving men and women from apathy to evil, if not from evil itself. . . . Not to remember the dead now would mean to become accomplices to their murderers."[30]

Wiesel did not back away from the most contentious question that had faced the commission: "Whom are we to remember?" he asked rhetorically. "Mr. President . . . millions of innocent civilians were tragically killed by the Nazis. They must be remembered. However, there exists a moral imperative for special emphasis on the six million Jews. While not all victims were Jews, all Jews were victims, destined for annihilation solely because they were born Jewish. . . . [The Holocaust] is essentially Jewish, yet its interpretation is universal."

The powerful claim for uniqueness was constructed on the argument that although there have been unspeakable massacres throughout history, including under Joseph Stalin, no other group of people was killed because of who they were, as opposed to what they had presumably done. Others may have been murdered as so-called enemies of the state or for a variety of confabulated reasons, but only the Jews were objects of genocide, as defined in this way. Perhaps the German historian Eberhard Jäckel put this view best at the height of the Historians' Debate in 1987 when he wrote: "The Nationalist Socialist murder of the Jews was unequalled because never before has a State, with the authority of its responsible leaders, decided and announced the total killing of a certain group of people, including the old, the women, the children, the infants, and turned this decision into fact with the use of all the possible instruments of power available to the State."[31] The point, according to the German philosopher Jürgen Habermas, was that "[in Auschwitz] one touched on something which represents the deep layer of solidarity among all that wear a human face; notwithstanding all the usual acts of beastliness of human history, the integrity of this common layer had been taken for granted. . . . Auschwitz has changed the basis of the continuity of the conditions of life within history."[32]

In other words, a profound human taboo was transgressed.

Throughout the long process of constructing a museum to memory (the Holocaust Museum did not officially open until 1993), there were challenges and questions about the meaning of "uniqueness." What about the Gypsies, or Roma-Sinti, as they were more properly called? Were they not a group of people murdered simply because of who they were? What about Turkey's massacre of more than a million Armenians in 1915? This latter attack had preceded the Nazi era and was therefore not integral to the period of the Holocaust per se, but Hitler's decision to eliminate the Jews was explicitly influenced by the indifference of the world to that bloodbath. He had said so openly: "Who today remembers the Armenians?" he retorted when his ministers voiced fears about international opposition.

Not only had the Turkish government never apologized, but it continued to deny that a genocide had occurred. Even in the 1990s, Turkey lobbied to prevent the Armenian story from being included in the museum displays, including threatening consequences should the president of the United States mention the Armenian connection in his planned speech about the Holocaust memorial. (Carter came up with a compromise that headed off trouble.) Ironically, Israel also refused to acknowledge the genocidal nature of the Armenian slaughter: Israel had a strategic relationship with Turkey.

Few reputable historians were about to deny that what had happened to the Armenian community was an act of genocide according to one of the two definitions of the term originally coined by jurist Raphael Lemkin in 1943. Lemkin spoke of "genocide" as the planned annihilation of a people, but he also described it as a progressive process, as a "co-ordinated plan of different actions aiming at the destruction of the essential foundations of the life of national groups, with the aim of annihilating the groups themselves." The Armenian-American community wanted recognition of its history, but some members of council worried that including the Armenian story might open the door to recognizing other tragedies, such as the ravages of Pol Pot in Cambodia, or the massacres of North American Indians. The question was, Who is "in" and who is "out"? Where were the boundaries to be drawn?

According to Edward Linenthal, the Roma-Sinti did not figure in the commission's thinking until the mid-1980s, when persons from that community began to complain that they too had been victims of genocide, and that they should have a seat on the council determining the future shape of the museum. Wiesel and other council members assured the Roma-Sinti representatives that their absence to that point was an oversight and that they would be included. (They were, in 1987, but the delegate was still so angry that he immediately charged the council with "overt racism" for its previous inattention to his community.) Relations did improve over the years, and the council and the museum staff were careful to include the poorly known Roma-Sinti story in the museum narrative.

Polish and Ukrainian Americans also fought for inclusion—in discussions that were exceptionally harrowing for Jewish survivors, who were upset at the prospect of sharing Holocaust memorial space with national groups, some of whose members had collaborated with the Nazis in their destruction. Although Poles and Slavs were marked as *Untermenschen* and destroyed in the millions, and although they might eventually have been designated for all-out genocidal slaughter, no blanket decision was ever taken, possibly because the war ended before things reached that point.[33] All the same, Auschwitz was geographically located in Poland, and it had been the main concentration camp for the occupied Polish territories, the Polish underground and the Polish intelligentsia. Two generations of Poles had memorialized Auschwitz as Catholics, just as generations of Jews memorialized it as Jews. The death camp had emerged as a shared memory space where both groups remembered the past and tried to understand the present. Given this interlocking history, much of it painful, it is not surprising that there were bitter battles on the Holocaust Museum planning committee—in spite of goodwill and general civility.

Some scholars of the Holocaust were uncomfortable with the trans-historical implications of "uniqueness." In his book *The Holocaust in History*, Michael Marrus suggests that it might be more to the point to claim that the Holocaust was unprecedented. "With this we are on more familiar historical terrain [although] to be sure we are speaking in relative terms," he wrote. "No event occurs without antecedents, and few would assert that there were no preceding instances of massacre or anti-Jewish persecution that bear a relationship to the murder of European Jewry. The real question is: How much of a break with the past is this particular event?"[34]

Raul Hilberg was even more direct when we met at his home in Burlington. "For me the Holocaust was a vast, single event, but I am never going to use the word *unique* because I recognize that when one starts breaking it into pieces, which is my trade, one finds completely recognizable, ordinary ingredients that are common to other situations, such as Rwanda or Cambodia and possibly many others I have not examined. In the final analysis, it depends whether we want to emphasize the commonality with other events, or the holistic totality—in which case the Holocaust stands by itself. But I consider the latter perilous. Do we want one Rwanda after the other? You know, when a group of Tutsis sits around and watches a neighbouring village burn, when they say, 'Well, that's them, it's not going to happen to us,' they are repeating the history of the Dutch Jews who, when they heard about the Holocaust in Poland, said, 'This is the Netherlands; it can never happen here.' They are also repeating the words of the Germans in 1096 when they heard what the crusaders were doing in France. It is staggering to draw that line through the centuries and look at the sameness of language. You have to say, 'Wait a minute, what's going on? Should we not look at this? Of course we should.' The alternative is to see the Holocaust as outside of history, as not part of anything. And it is impossible to learn from something that is so apart."

On April 22, 1993, the day the Holocaust Museum finally opened, there were ironies aplenty. Another catastrophe was unfolding in Europe, this time in Bosnia, although Western governments had taken care not to use the *genocide* word, which might compel them to intercede according to the UN Charter, the Geneva Conventions and the Genocide

Convention of 1948, all of which had come into being as a result of the Holocaust.

Bill Clinton, by then president of the United States, officiated at the dedication. During the election campaign of 1992, he had solemnly declared that American air power would intervene to end the Bosnian conflict. Nothing happened. Now, as helpless civilians were again being slaughtered across the sea, the president gravely intoned, "Never again," instantly stripping the pregnant words of their moral meaning. The late Croatian president Franjo Tudjman also was present, he who was party, at that moment, to the ruthless ethnic massacres taking place in Bosnia, he who had cast persistent public doubt on the historical truth of the Holocaust. Back in 1988, Tudjman had written: "The estimated loss of up to six million [Jewish] dead is founded . . . on exaggerated data in the postwar reckoning of war crimes and on the squaring of accounts with the defeated."[35] (His personal calculations suggested to him that approximately 900,000 Jews might have perished during the Second World War.)

"Tudjman's presence in the midst of survivors is a disgrace," fumed Elie Wiesel, the only person to call attention to the tragedy currently unfolding in Bosnia. "As a Jew I am saying that we must to something to stop the bloodshed in that country," he said to President Clinton before the assembled microphones. "People fight one another and children die. Why? Something, anything, must be done." Clinton was not amused, but he should not have been surprised: Elie Wiesel had written almost identical words about the Holocaust thirty years earlier, in a *Commentary* article on the Eichmann trial. ("Someone should have stopped it. There must have been something they could have done!")[36] And it was Elie Wiesel, the survivor, who had dared to confront Ronald Reagan in 1985 as the president prepared to travel to West Germany to stand beside Chancellor Kohl at the military cemetery of Bitburg, where Waffen-SS soldiers were also buried. No president in post-war America had made the need for a Holocaust museum more transparently clear than Reagan, whose ahistorical understanding of reconciliation involved "putting the past behind him," as he expressed it, without a just appreciation of who was who or what they should be remembered for. It was moral confusion of this kind that had made a museum to teach the "lessons" of the Holocaust necessary.

Eight years and two presidents later, Wiesel continued on with his prepared text. He said, "We have learned that though the Holocaust was principally a Jewish tragedy, its implications are universal. . . . We have learned that whatever happens to one community, ultimately affects all others."

But had "we" really learned anything at all, I asked myself when I read his words. A museum to the memory of the Holocaust was, and is, a wonderful thing, but if it cannot affect foreign policy at the moment of its dedication, when a new genocide is raging, there are grounds for despair.

"When Sarajevo was surrounded in April 1992, I couldn't work for a week. I said to myself, How the hell can we be building a museum when the same thing is happening over there? We blame people everywhere for not doing anything during the Holocaust and we are just sitting here!" Now director of education, Joan Ringelheim had been on staff at the museum since 1989, starting as head of research. When she arrived on the planning committee, the storyline for the exhibition had already been decided upon: her job was to find the appropriate secondary sources for the designers of each segment. Later on, she produced a section called "Voices from Auschwitz" by editing 130 interviews with survivors and weaving them into a rich quilt of storytelling.

Ringelheim's father lost his entire family in the Holocaust, and she was deeply, personally, involved, but the tension she experienced in April 1992 was too much. "I thought about quitting, but what then?" she says as we talk in her Washington office. "I asked myself, What do I have the power to do?"

In 1996, she was invited to Sarajevo to give a lecture about the U.S. Holocaust Memorial Museum. She tells me she felt unnerved: what could she possibly say to Bosnians who were suffering while she and other Americans were building a museum to an earlier human disaster? While her government dithered and did nothing to help? She went anyway—talked about memory and survival and whether, finally, it does any good to remember when people seem never to learn.

"Does that question still trouble you?" I ask her quietly as we talk together in her Washington office.

"I ask myself that all the time," she replies. "I have only one answer, and it doesn't really bring much comfort, and that is that it is impossible to live without memory; it is the only way we can live. Hannah Arendt once said something about stories. You tell them, you repeat them, because you don't know what the effect will be. Because you don't know whether people learn or not, you have to keep doing it—just in case they do."

She used to be a philosophy teacher, but against the background of her father's survival and the loss of the rest of his family, there was only one thing she wanted to teach: racism and anti-semitism. "It was also because I grew up in this country in the 1950s and 1960s and saw what happened here with the life-and-death struggle for civil rights. All of it came together in my mind. In 1968, I made up an undergraduate college course called 'Prejudice and Oppression.' We read books on ethics, the philosophy of language, the philosophy of history and the psychology of the prejudiced personality—and I have to say that I have often felt strange working here at the Holocaust Museum when there is not a memorial to slavery in this country. At one time, I hoped that the fact that we exist would push that idea into the forefront. But that hasn't happened."

Her office is filled with the works of Hannah Arendt. "Why is she so important to you?" I ask.

"When I first read Arendt—it was her *New Yorker* piece on Eichmann in Jerusalem in 1963—I was furious at her, like all sorts of other people. But it must have been 1974 or 1975 when a friend said, 'I don't know why you are not rereading her. She is the only twentieth-century philosopher the centre of whose work is the Holocaust.' I had never thought about that. I started reading her, then I began teaching her. I became completely captivated—everything she writes fills the empty space. She is like a mystery writer; I never know quite where she is going. She has a huge richness."

I look at this woman I have just met as at an old friend: I too have been captivated by Arendt's probing explorations of history and prejudice.

Between 1993 and 1999, over eleven million people visited the Holocaust Memorial Museum, including thirty-one thousand school tours. Most were under fifty—born after the war. Although many people initially made special trips to Washington, by the end of the decade the museum was on the itinerary of ordinary tourists who happened to be visiting the capital, the vast majority of whom were non-Jews.

It is hard to imagine anyone entering this powerful place without adequate preparation, for the Holocaust Museum is, without a doubt, one of the most disturbing galleries in the world. It is also one of the most magnificently realized, from its unsettling architecture to the immediacy of the information and emotion it conveys. The architecture is especially remarkable when one considers the conditions under which the architect was working: how, for example, was any professional to design a building meant to represent what Elie Wiesel called the unrepresentable?

After visiting the Auschwitz death camp, James Ingo Freed decided that his design would have to be "expressive of the event,"[37] but he was not without reservations. In an interview with *Assemblage* magazine, he acknowledged his problem: "I have to make a building that allows for horror, sadness. I don't know if you can make a building that does this, if you can make an architecture of sensibility." Somehow he succeeded. The result is a self-contained, textured environment of raw materials—brick, steel beams, glass, concrete—and a design that bewilders as we are led into surprising dead-end angles that require us to stop and question where the next step will lead—just as the victims of Nazi terror were disoriented by incoherence and disruption at every turn. The architectural critic Jim Murphy has called Freed's work "the most emotionally powerful architectural event most of us will ever experience."

In the name of memory, the Holocaust Museum is carrying me closer to the awful nature of the experience than most museums would attempt, or desire. ("I've heard people on the street saying, 'I'm going to the Holocaust,'" Joan Ringelheim had complained. "They're *not* going to the Holocaust, they are going to a museum!") A guide offers me a card with the name of a real person of my own sex and information about what happened to her. I am being asked to identify at a vicarious, personal level. I enter a bare steel elevator of a style common in Germany around 1940: it removes me from the everyday world of the main-floor lobby and deposits me in a dimly lit place in front of videos depicting the encounter of American soldiers with Dachau in April 1945. The ceiling here is low and oppressive. It is very quiet. Although there seem to be hundreds of people in this place, there is little noise other than the sounds of shuffling feet as I move through angled, jagged space.

The displays are contextualized with the architecture; the immediacy is startling. To begin with, the "closeness" to the event. At the groundbreaking ceremony on October 16, 1985, the soil of the Washington Mall was ritualistically mixed with soil brought from concentration camps, so the site itself was "sanctified" with an authentic reminder of the dead. Cobblestones from the original Warsaw Ghetto pave a section of the museum floor, and under a light sits the milk can in which young Emmanuel Ringelblum buried his extraordinary archives of ghetto life (the can was preserved to resemble the way it looked when first excavated from the streets of the city in 1950). Faded, striped concentration-camp uniforms of all sizes, donated by survivors, hang behind a gated prison-like fence.

A bridge connects to another part of the exhibition. Isolated spotlights beam from the ceiling; there is a looming suggestion of watchtowers. This astonishing architect has built a facsimile of a Nazi concentration camp at the heart of America. Then another room, where a cast of the original door of the Lódz ghetto hospital graphically illustrates an accompanying written description: I am informed that on September 1, 1942, all the patients were pulled out through this very door and deported.

An original stained-glass window from the synagogue in Kraków lines part of one wall, near the wrought-iron gate to the old Jewish cemetery in Tarnów, southern Poland. Finally, I stare at one of the carts that carried away the bodies of people who died overnight of disease and starvation at Theresienstadt.

On the floor lie pieces of the railway track that once led into the Treblinka camp near Warsaw, where an estimated 750,000 people were murdered between July 1942 and October 1943. And on these tracks stands a German freight car of the type that was used for human transports. The path of the museum visit leads the visitor into and through the rail car (although it is possible to detour around this experience). I steel myself to enter this symbolically evocative space. Inside is still air and quiet emptiness: open-ended, porous, poised for imaginative understanding. Here, disconnected for a moment, I pause at the heart of the genocidal process: the transport of millions of people from a known world to oblivion.

All these artifacts were collected in Europe by alert museum personnel—located in remote places, dug up or donated by established memory sites such as Auschwitz. Some of the material caused problems for those survivors who subscribed to the idea that the Holocaust is atemporal and holy. From the State Museum at Auschwitz came a mountain of objects, among them toothbrushes, suitcases marked with the names of their owners, shoes (the stylishly strapped women's shoes from the 1940s piled haphazardly with the rest are a startling reminder of the sophisticated life their owners once lived), discarded Zyklon-B cans (another difficult sight) and umbrellas. But Joan Ringelheim had told me that nothing caused more turmoil among staff and council members than nine kilograms of human hair. (Hair shorn from victims was sold to German factories for fifty pfennigs a kilo to make socks for U-boat crews and industrial felt, among other things, and when Auschwitz was liberated by the Russians, they found seven thousand kilos stockpiled for future use.) Some people thought the hair and its uses exposed the utter dehumanization of the victims, but there was concern about the boundaries of acceptable taste, especially about displaying relics from what were once living bodies outside the place where the deed was done—that is, Auschwitz itself. Expressions like "defilement," "an offence to the dead" and "inherent sacredness" found new voice. Others, including many survivors, disagreed. A Jewish religious authority offered his assurance that hair, as such, was never "alive," in that it had never contained living human cells. Ringelheim argued that a display of hair would bring needed attention to what had happened to women.[38]

"Initially I didn't want anything taken from the site, but then I thought that if we were going to do it, we should do it right," she told me when we spoke together in her office. She recalled the committee meeting of February 13, 1990, as "volatile" and "horrific." "One of the women survivors said, 'I don't want to go in there and see my own mother's hair!' Someone else screamed at her, 'It doesn't matter what you think! This exhibition is not for you or for me, but for the public!' There were about twenty-five or thirty people present and the room was pounding with emotion. A man said, 'Well, we wouldn't show a rape and this is like a rape.' That was when I joined in. I think I screamed something like, 'Every woman in this room knows what the difference is between getting their hair shaved and a rape!' It was just too vile. I remember saying that I didn't think the hair should have been taken out of Auschwitz or any historical site, but since it was here, no picture could substitute for the real thing. I said, 'It's not insulting, it's disgusting, but the whole Holocaust is disgusting, so if you want to portray it honestly, this will be an important part of what people remember.'"

There was a vote and the decision was to display the hair, but then, said Ringelheim, something strange happened: two female survivors went privately to the director, and the decision to exhibit the hair was quietly reversed. (The museum now displays a picture of the hair.) Almost a decade later, she still wasn't sure why the hair issue became so terribly volatile, but she did think it was an example of the moral authority of the survivors over everyone who had not shared that experience of pain, be they historians, curators or even rabbinical authorities.

After the hair incident, great care was necessary, for it had been made clear that mistakes in judgment would not be simple errors but a desecration of memory. No one put this more clearly than Menachem Rosensaft, the founding chairman of the International Network of Children of Jewish Holocaust Survivors, when he warned, "Anyone who casts aspersions on their [the victims'] memory somehow participates retroactively in their murder."[39] Since such defamation could be unintentional, everyone involved in planning and implementation was implicitly enjoined to watch themselves carefully lest they inadvertently assassinate the dead a second time.

I don't appreciate such censoring threats, but I do understand the hostility. Listening to Joan Ringelheim, then walking through the museum, I, too, have mixed feelings about displaying artifacts from Auschwitz. I know rationally that there would be no museums anywhere in the world if objects were not removed from their original environments, but remnants from the murder of millions cast a special shadow. I remember how angrily I reacted to two of the museums I visited in Germany: the "Jewish Section" of the museum of Rothenburg ob der Tauber, where old gravestones were exhibits and the "Holocaust" referred to a medieval pogrom; and the strange collection in the Protestant church of Jebenhausen, where neighbours had collected the religious and personal objects that lay scattered over the road after a Nazi roundup of the local Jews and made a "museum" of them, with curatorial explanations. There may be no other way to salvage memory after the fact, but some artifacts do seem more questionable than others.

In the Holocaust Museum, as in Yad Vashem, the aerial photo of the Auschwitz installations and the Allied decision not to bomb once again receive prominent billing. The last lines of the display text (in which the assistant secretary of war John J. McCloy is faulted) ground the memory firmly: "At the very least [bombing] would have demonstrated Allied concern about the fate of the Jews."

The memory to be retained is that America abandoned the Jews of Europe.

During the museum planning stages, Jewish wartime resistance was once again a touchy topic. Menachem Rosensaft thought that the idea that Jews had gone "like sheep to the slaughter" was a calumny in the ever-expanding category of defiling the dead. Heated debate was inevitable. How to define *resistance*? Conventional wisdom held it to be physical rebellion, as in the Warsaw Ghetto or among the partisans, but it was always possible to include "spiritual" resistance. Was prayer resistance? Was managing to remember the sabbath while in Auschwitz resistance? Were brave, possibly dangerous, acts of unselfishness, such as sharing a morsel of bread, resistance? Many had argued that the latter *were* acts of resistance, including the Israeli historian Yehuda Bauer, who wrote that resistance is "any *group* action consciously taken in opposition to known or surmised laws, actions, or intentions directed against the Jews by the Germans and their supporters."[40]

The debate has not been resolved, but I note that the Holocaust Museum has downplayed unsafe subjects. "If the museum was uncontroversial when it opened, I think it was because we did not tackle most of the disputes in a contentious way," explained Ringelheim. "We could have taken a tack that would fit one community's interests over another, but we did it in a more distanced way. And I think it was the right decision."

The story of the Warsaw uprising is appropriately present (the rebellion gets an entire wall), as are other instances of resistance, but Ringelheim's "survivor voices" in the audio theatre are notably low-key. The men and women whose stories intertwine and overlap speak about brutality, fright, hunger, exhaustion, squalor and the terror of separation. Their responses are recognizably human, not unrecognizably heroic; their focus is on the everlasting need to bear witness.

The sensitive topic of collaboration is also passed over lightly. A relatively small section describes the quandary of the Nazi-installed ghetto leaders and explains their involvement. Since it would have been grossly inappropriate to use language that identified these elders with the murderous partnership of a certain number of Estonians, Ukrainians, Lithuanians and other occupied Eastern Europeans who voluntarily joined the SS in its massive killing operations, the perilous *c* word is never used in the museum displays. The Eastern Europeans are described as "accomplices," and the text and Nazi-photographed films of their contribution to the German enterprise are screened behind a low wooden barrier that offers the visitor the choice of forgoing that part of the exhibition.

A section on one wall details the suffering of the Poles. Homosexuals, until recently underresearched in Holocaust studies, are also given their due. The Armenian genocide gets a mention. No one has been entirely left out, although constituencies may well have been displeased at the wall space they managed to obtain.

Finally, since this is an American museum on the Washington Mall, the exhibition ends, as it began, with the role of U.S. liberators. With videos and testimonials. And walls upon walls covered with the names of Righteous Gentiles who took great personal risks. (By 2000, sixteen thousand such persons had been honoured by Yad Vashem.) It is proper to esteem these men and women of character, but in doing so the U.S. Holocaust Memorial Museum has, like Yad Vashem, shifted the collective memory of the "catastrophe" (*shoah*)—a plain, undoctored word—to one that favours heroism. Is this one more triumph of a "feel-good ending"? Sixteen thousand rescuers? Out of how many hundreds of million people in the countries of Nazi-occupied Europe?

The background thinking is apparent in a form letter soliciting funds for museum membership, an American institution appealing to Americans in upbeat, Hollywood-hyped language: "Finally, when breaking hearts can bear it no longer, visitors will emerge into the light—into a celebration of resistance, rebirth, and renewal for the survivors—whether they remained in Europe, or as so many did, went to Israel or America to rebuild their lives. And having witnessed the nightmare of evil, the great American monuments to democracy that surround each departing visitor will take on new meaning, as will the ideal for which they stand."[41]

Like Yad Vashem, the U.S. Holocaust Memorial Museum directs the visitor to understand the event it portrays in an acceptably politicized manner: this is the "happy ending" that will enable Americans to leave one of the world's most demanding exhibitions without losing faith in the future. The planners have been successful: on exiting, 90 per cent of people replying to a questionnaire have given the museum an eight- to ten-point rating on a scale of ten. Fifty per cent have ranked their visit ten out of ten.

Would an exhibit devoted to the dark night of the Holocaust have attracted such praise if it did not meet American cultural needs, I ask myself. A question to speculate on—for historical memory is shaped from just such choices.

Near the exit I see a book of visitors' comments. A teenage girl is signing in. I line up behind her and look at what she has written. In a large, childlike, loopy handwriting she wrote: "Is this planet doomed? Is everyone mean? What will happen? Is everybody evil? Can we at least stop fighting each other? Who knows all the answers to my questions? Who knows . . ." Her dots trail off into despair.

As I leave the building, I see her sitting on a step, bent over, with her head hanging down between her knees. I want to protect her, but something stops me from approaching. Although I am decades older and far more informed, I wonder what I can possibly say to ease this moment of her encounter with history. Her grief is not an irrational response.

The sunlight, the bracing air of this February day and every step I take back into the welcome bustle of contemporary Washington reminds me that more than fifty years have passed and that the century that witnessed the horror I have just "visited" is almost done. But the sorrow of the child on the steps stays with me. I think to myself that attributions of "holiness" and the claim that the past is "unrepresentable" and the private domain of those who survived lead away from understanding, and that understanding is the road this child, and her generation, needs to travel. I think to myself that the "lessons" of the Holocaust are, first of all, historical—having to do with the Jews—but then also universal, having to do with the impulse to genocide. What happens to human beings when they are subjected to propaganda that consistently dehumanizes an "enemy"? What happens when the highest authorities and elites of a land call for the persecution of a minority? What happens when law is "illegal" in a moral sense, as the Nuremberg Tribunal declared? What happens when good people say and do nothing?

I think that to try to understand—however tentatively, however gropingly—is a part of my own continuing quest.

7

The Furies of War Revisit Europe

Yugoslavia and Bosnia

Lying is a form of our patriotism and is evidence of our innate intelligence. We lie in a creative, imaginative and inventive way.

– DOBRICA ĆOSIĆ, president of the Federal Republic of Yugoslavia, 1992–93

Belgrade

THERE IS NO BETTER PLACE to wonder about the questions that underlie the Holocaust or the way national identity can be reshaped by the unscrupulous than Belgrade on the eve of the twenty-first century. Belgrade: the fiefdom of President Slobodan Milošević. My trip there starts badly—in the Yugoslav embassy in Paris. I have the requisite invitation, from the Belgrade branch of PEN, as it happens, but the visa does not come easily. In late 1997 foreign writers are not quite *personae non gratae*—they are not being expelled, beaten, imprisoned or threatened with death, as will happen later, when the war in Kosovo breaks out, but they are apparently not quite welcome either.

The embassy of the Federal Republic of Yugoslavia—that is, Serbia and Montenegro—is a world apart. One Alice in Wonderland step through an inconspicuous door and Paris, with its delightful obsessions (were the croissants fresh enough? buttery enough? what year was that excellent Bordeaux?), is left behind. One enters a large, bare, smoke-filled room furnished with two or three rickety wooden chairs. Hardly useful, hardly necessary. Everyone is standing in long, patient lines staring at a counter where busy officials stamp documents and wait to use the one available typewriter. Outside the embassy stroll self-conscious, elegant Parisians of both sexes; inside are hunched men with faces leathered by exposure to a mountain climate and old-looking women in head scarves with anxiety creasing their foreheads. I guess they are all trying to get "home," or somewhere near there. Bosnian Serbs. Refugees. People unable, or perhaps unwilling, to return to their communities after the 1995 Dayton Peace Accords theoretically made this possible. People looking for sanctuary in Serbia.

I immediately recall Ryszard Kapuściński's book *Imperium* and his vivid descriptions of the long lines of people who wait, without end, without complaint, everywhere in the former Soviet Union. No one thinks to demur. To whom, or to what, would they protest? The state and its representatives live on an unreachable planet. "That's life," they say with a sigh.

The old capital of Belgrade creaks under the weight of its misery, bleak in the November light, with an all-pervasive, bone-chilling greyness that bores under every surface. The walls of downtown buildings have cracked with neglect and darkened with the grime of decades. Ancient streetcars rattle down the centre of main streets, carrying a crush of pasty-faced passengers. Gridlocked traffic everywhere: frustrated drivers honking aggressively, driving on the wrong side of the road.

A bearded young man with only one leg sits on a square of cardboard on the sidewalk, begging for pennies. His eyes are blank, as though someone has pulled plastic wrap across them. No one gives him money or pays the slightest attention to his plight. Was he mobilized into the Yugoslav army and wounded, I wonder. Had he volunteered to avenge the presumed humiliations of Serbian history on behalf of the very people who pass him without so much as a glance?

"Wanna change money, wanna change money?" whisper shadowy men at street corners as I walk by. The only currency that matters is the German mark, and the standard exchange rate is to be found not at the banks but on the black market. Even financial institutions are rumoured to obtain part of their foreign reserves after hours in dimly lit places.

There are, however, exceptions to the crumbling decline. Here and there a woman with proud bearing draped in an expensive fur coat, or a shiny Mercedes or BMW honking away in the traffic. But the very richest of the new rich are the nation's First Family: Slobodan Milošević, his wife, Mirjana, and their son, Marko. Marko is a pugnacious, gun-toting young tycoon who owns Serbia's largest discotheque, a soccer team, a bakery-patisserie chain and race cars, as well as controlling a large slice of the country's black market, which includes just about everything else, especially the lucrative trade in cigarette smuggling. His father's iron hand on power has made him virtually invulnerable to criticism. In 1996, Marko filed charges against the *Srpska reč* newspaper for a series of articles describing his shady activities (a Belgrade court would find the paper culpable and impose a fine of approximately $US15,000—payable to Marko. The average monthly salary in the country is $100).[1]

Besides the carnage, the main outcome of the war in Bosnia has been smuggling, theft and profiteering: the homes of the murdered or "cleansed" were looted, drug protection rackets have flourished, and Marko's specialty, cigarette smuggling, is said to be the biggest "business" in ex-Yugoslavia. Hardly surprising. Almost everyone chain-smokes. On the streets of Belgrade, the most visible commerce is a multitude of tiny round kiosks selling cigarettes and chewing gum. Cigarettes are addictive, so they may be a necessity to most of the population, but to chew gum is a Western-style luxury. Suitably expensive with no nutrition, a fleeting pleasure, a sudden hit of sugar on taste buds. Gum is perfectly useless, therefore a welcome show of status. I remember the stories from post-war Japan: the silvery gum wrappers that summoned up a universe of luxury and "democracy" in the minds of children. Will chewing gum figure in the future literature of Serbia? Perhaps as a symbol of impossible excess and bitter inequality in a post-Communist society where misery reigns.

My hotel, the Excelsior, may once have been worth the 100 German marks posted for foreigners (the rate for nationals is 50 marks), but those days are long gone. The wood panelling has fallen off the walls of my room; the toilet runs continuously; the management cuts the heat off at night, in spite of the early winter cold; and the permanently dented mattress has been slept on by too many overweight guests. The city's food shortages are evident in the dining room downstairs. Travelling through Yugoslavia in 1937, Rebecca West wrote in her book *Black Lamb and Grey Falcon* that the Belgrade cuisine was one of the world's most satisfying: risottos, soups and stews "made luxurious by urban lavishness of supply and a Turkish tradition of subtle and positive flavour." No longer. Most of what appears on the restaurant menu is unavailable—the waiter shrugs with a sad, apologetic smile. "That's all right," I say, shrugging back, as we both turn towards a table of drunken young men from Montenegro who have begun to bellow their country's national anthem with patriotic abandon.

Another early observation: the old habits of surveillance and secrecy run deep. My Belgrade contact refuses to leave a message with the clerk at the front desk about my interviews. Just in case, he says. And when a visitor arrives at the hotel for a meeting, and I request a room, the manager insists on meeting her first. "I'm so and so," he says to her, extending his hand expectantly. She smiles and does not reply.

There are several names on the list of those who connived to bring about the most recent outbreak of ethnic nationalism in ex-Yugoslavia, and they include all the political leaders: Slobodan Milošević of Serbia, Franjo Tudjman of Croatia, Alija Izetbegović of Bosnia and Herzegovina and Radovan Karadžić, the leader of the Bosnian Serbs. But outside the theatre of daily politics, one man is identified to me above all others, throughout the territories. He is a writer and a national icon; his work is taught to millions of schoolchildren; he is a power-broker, a former political figurehead, an intellectual in the European tradition of public figures with ideas to argue, an erstwhile dissident from the Tito regime who managed to remain relatively safe.

Dobrica Ćosić is his name.

Ćosić rarely accepts interviews, but he claims to like the subject of my book and has agreed to meet me. In preparation I read and ask questions.

"His hands are deep in blood," says Drinka Gojković, a Belgrade translator.

"They should try him at The Hague," mutters Slavo Šantić, a Bosnian Serb columnist for *Oslobodjenje*, the famous Sarajevo newspaper that stayed open during the siege. Šantić accuses Ćosić of "crimes against humanity" for having revived the old idea of Greater Serbia and whipped his compatriots into a fever of ethnic hatred.

"He's a con artist," spits out Miloš Vasić, a founder of the independent Belgrade weekly *Vreme*. *Vreme* is respected internationally. It was to Vasić that the American and European media turned for a reliable take on the war in Bosnia.

No one has anything good to say about the role Ćosić played except the admirer who has arranged our meeting. He tells me Ćosić is known as "the Father of the Nation."

On the surface, Dobrica Ćosić had been a fierce supporter of Josip Broz Tito and his Partisans; he and Tito were personal friends for more than twenty years. But what bothered him to the point of speaking out was the old "nationalities question" Tito had tried so hard to subdue, especially the issue of the Albanians in Kosovo. Kosovo was a remote, backward province of two million people tucked away in a southern corner of Yugoslavia on the border of Albania. It was the poorest region in the country, possibly in all of Europe, with the exception of neighbouring Albania. Not much of a vacation spot for Serbs or any other Yugoslavs. The special place Kosovo held in Serb religious and national life made it more of an abstraction than a locale anyone would want to visit, unless they were on a pilgrimage to the holy sites.

Tito was a practical man who understood the potential for ethnic conflict, especially in Kosovo. The Kosovo Albanians were a majority in that province *and* they were ethnically different: they were not Slavs. Furthermore, they were proudly Muslim, a constant reminder to Serbs that the hated Ottoman Turks had once defeated their Christian land.

Tito had promoted "Brotherhood and Unity" as the watchword of his regime—and made sure there was always jail space available for people who suggested otherwise. At the same time, given their worrisome numbers, he had shrewdly allowed Kosovo Albanians a degree of autonomy from the start. In 1945, he declared Kosovo an "autonomous region" and granted nominal authority to the Albanians, although the important posts were reserved for Serbs. Independent governance was increased marginally in the late 1960s, culminating with a new university in Priština in 1969. Then in 1974, Tito created a new constitution in which Kosovo was allowed special status as an independent region within the Serb Republic, with its own vote in the Yugoslav presidency.

Dobrica Ćosić, who was already nationally famous, took offence at Tito's decision to reduce Serb control over Kosovo. And said so. Their friendship ended. In 1968 he was punished, purged from the League of Communists of Yugoslavia—for "nationalism."

The Kosovo Albanians were more successful at creating their own ethnic identity than at managing their economy. Continuing backwardness in rural areas translated into a high birth rate over the years (among both Serbs and Albanians, but more so among Albanians), and by the late 1960s the struggle for limited resources led to civil unrest, which was promptly suppressed by Serbia. Serbs were migrating out, most of them heading for Belgrade:[2] between 1961 and 1981 their numbers dropped from 18.4 to 13.2 per cent of the total population of Kosovo, while in absolute terms the Albanian population doubled. However, none of these demographic changes was "news" until Tito died, and the Serbian press began to claim that Kosovo Albanians were forcing Serbs to leave. What these attacks revealed more than anything was that only Tito had kept Yugoslavia from flying into fragments.

As in other Communist countries where speech was controlled, writing in Tito's Serbia became a political act, and according to Juraj Martinović, a literary historian I was to meet later on in Sarajevo, Ćosić's novels struck forgotten chords in the hearts of his readers: he gathered the loose strands of Serbian identity—those unbound tendrils that had escaped incorporation into "Yugoslavism"—and reconnected them with the old nation. The style of Ćosić's romantic works had once been common to all of Europe, stretching back to the national liberation movements of the nineteenth century, but the genre had long been archaic in the West, at least since the post–First World War modernists rejected sentimentality and heroics.

No such literary shift had taken place in Serbia. In Ćosić's first novel, *The Commissar*, written just after the Second World War, the tragic hero is a nationalist Serb peasant, a Chetnik, who cannot bring himself to leave his land although he knows he will be executed by Tito's Partisans the moment they find him. Rooted in the soil of his ancestors, this symbolic incarnation of "Serbness" will die rather than survive in a world where the soul of the Serbian nation has been defeated. In another of his works, *The Sun Is Far Away*, the Partisans command the tragic hero to leave his village (he is a peasant, once again bound to the

Serb earth) to fight the Nazis. Eventually the young man is executed for violating Communist ideals: for caring too much for family and land.

Ćosić's literary career had long fused writing and politics, but he did not come into his own politically until after Tito's death in 1980. What happened to Yugoslavia after the Leader died has been described in dozens of recent books, and what they say in essence is this: Tito had prepared no successor; Yugoslavia was left "headless" by its president for life. The Communist bloc was imploding, and the economy was collapsing. Titoism was quickly losing its hold.

Everyone talked of democracy in those early post-Tito days, but what was the meaning of that word in a country that had not known freedom of speech or thought? Where the population had been conditioned for generations to do what the Leader said and not ask questions? What if everything communism had taught for forty years was a lie, including the history drilled into schoolchildren and their children after them? On the other hand, what was "truth" in a place where whatever the Leader said had happened, perforce had happened, historical accuracy notwithstanding?

Tito's myths were not unlike those of the supposedly all-encompassing French Resistance that similarly became the ideological basis for postwar France, except that in Communist Yugoslavia, the heroic stories could not be openly challenged. Like the French, Tito had found it convenient to deny, for the sake of Brotherhood and Unity, that something approximating civil war had racked the land: to deny that many thousands of Serbs had collaborated with the Nazis and fought with the SS *against* the Partisans. But in the 1990s, new research (archival, from outside Serbia) suggested that the leap from fascist collaboration to Communist insurgency actually took place in the wink of Tito's eye.[3] In 1944, he offered amnesty in return for nationalist support, Chetnik support: a tempting offer, since a Nazi defeat looked imminent, and cooperation with the Partisans came packaged with a promise of guaranteed rehabilitation once the war was over. Tito's amnesty strategy was so successful that the Serbian Partisan movement grew almost tenfold during the twelve-month period ending in late 1944.

That Serbia had opportunely joined the Allied cause for the last six months of the war also contributed to myths of universal anti-Nazi resistance that were transformed into "history." The universal anti-Nazi part was especially useful: it was trotted out by the Serbs during the

1999 NATO air campaign against Serbia over new ethnic atrocities being committed in Kosovo.

Lies. Big ones, little ones. What, for example, is truer than a map? Maps tell us where we are. Where "here" is positioned relative to "there." I have seen maps all over the world that don't quite lie but like to tell people that they live at the epicentre of things. My old school maps showed the vast reaches of Canadian lakes and forest as the central presence in an otherwise fairly inconsequential geography. (Russia occupied a small space somewhere "over there.") My favourite is a map I chanced upon in New Zealand that situated that tiny island at the centre of the world. You would have to look down from space to excise politics from cartography.

But exaggeration is not the same as an outright removal of the deemed lesser parts, as in the former East Berlin, where school maps obliterated the western part of the city. Drew a blank. It simply did not exist.

Lies. Big ones, little ones. In her book *The Culture of Lies*, the Croatian author Dubravka Ugrešic writes: "It seems that this culture of lies is something that the small nations of Yugoslavia created long ago, learning to live with it and reinforcing it to this day. Lying—just like dying—has become a natural state, a norm of behaviour, liars are normal citizens." She continues: "If one [wished to] give credit to Dobrica Ćosić . . . it must be for his remark: 'Lying is an aspect of our patriotism and confirmation of our innate intelligence.' In these lands every lie becomes a truth in the end."[4]

Actually, Dobrica Ćosić was even more original. He said, "Lying is an aspect of our patriotism and confirmation of our innate intelligence. We lie in a creative, imaginative and inventive way."

During the Cold War, writer dissidents from behind the Iron Curtain were happily appropriated by the West as partners in the struggle against communism, as imprisoned consciences who yearned for Western-style democratic pluralism. Many did: one thinks immediately of Václav Havel and the Polish writer Adam Michnik, to name just two. Dobrica Ćosić, on the other hand, did not.

By 1983, he had published the first volley in his dissident attack on Yugoslav communism.[5] But he was not calling for pluralism. Ćosić's thesis was the contrary of Tito's, which had been to promote ethnic multiculturalism, then enforce it with an iron fist. Ćosić said that under the federation that Tito had put in place, Serbs were persecuted by

Yugoslavia's other ethnic groups. Serbs gave and gave and were stabbed in the back. They had even lost control over holy Kosovo.

Dobrica Ćosić was sixty years old when Tito died. He had a long literary record and the status of maturity. He was a famous dissident and an influential member of the Serbian Association of Writers, as well as the Yugoslav Association of Writers.

This is how the dissidence of the Serb intellectuals evolved. In 1981, one year after Tito's death, the Association of Serbian Writers became front-line fighters for free speech by resisting the suppression of a collection of poems critical of Tito. Writer members set up the Francuska 7 tribunal (named after the Belgrade street where meetings were held), which became synonymous with the free expression of critical views. Then the association shifted direction.[6] At a series of evenings called "On Kosovo—For Kosovo," the subject was no longer freedom of speech but "the defence of Serbs." There were impassioned discussions on "Serbophobia," "Serbs outside Serbia," "Serbian cultural space" and something dubbed "The White Plague" (the negative population growth among Serbs).

Ćosić argued strongly in favour of free speech, for without the repeal of Tito-era legislation prohibiting attacks on other ethnic groups it would be impossible to rally popular support for his emerging agenda, which was the right to a Greater Serbia—a right of dominance based on ancient claims to Kosovo and grievances against Kosovar Albanians as well as hatred for Croats, dating, most recently, from the Second World War. His speech to the "On Kosovo—For Kosovo" forum, which was reprinted in the respected literary journal *Knjiz˘evne novine*,[7] reduced the difficulties facing Yugoslavia after the death of Tito to the problems of Serbs alone. Kosovo was crucial for Serbia's "fate," he explained, because it epitomized the problems Serbs faced throughout the federation. The "crisis" in Kosovo proved that Yugoslavia had already collapsed: since "the minority population [was allowed] to terrorize the majority ethnic group and to use persecution to take over their territory," the "misuse of autonomy" in order to create "an ethnically pure Albanian territory" had to be stopped.

Others at the forum spoke in a racist vein, including Pavle Ivić, a well-known professor of linguistics, who emphasized the "Afro-Asian" birth rate among Albanians. At a subsequent meeting to which writers from both Serbia and Kosovo were invited, Milan Komnenić, then of the Serbian Association of Writers, was even more outspoken. In response to an Albanian writer who pleaded for a more rational discussion of the facts, he replied, "You can talk forever. I don't believe a thing you say. . . . Let me remind you that the modern world knows of no greater atrocities per capita than in Kosovo. Perhaps you believe you will become a cultured people through violence. We thought otherwise. We left a trace of spirit behind us, not a [spirit] of wild animals. You consider our essence to be a myth. You are sick from history-destroying aggression and we from historical melancholy."

"Essence," "spirit," "historical melancholy." The romantic language of the nineteenth century was being reborn after forty years in the wilderness of "dialectics," "determinism" and "historical materialism."

In January 1986, two hundred Serb intellectuals, led by Dobrica Ćosić, signed the seminal "Memorandum of the Serbian Academy of Arts and Sciences." The memorandum depicted Serbs as the most oppressed group in Yugoslavia and accused Kosovo Albanians of raping Serb women, beating nuns and perpetrating "genocide" through a deliberate policy of high population growth. Albanian autonomy (though inconsequential in terms of real power) was called a "national treason" and an anti-Serb plot. No evidence sustained any of these terrible accusations, and the facts told another story. According to readily available police records, the incidence of rape in Kosovo was proportionately less than in Serbia proper, with only one recorded rape of a Serb by an Albanian.

The memorandum also claimed that Serbs did not have their own state because Tito had suppressed the "national question." The only solution was "the territorial unity of the Serbian people," which must come about because "the establishment of the full, national integrity of the Serbian people, regardless of which republic or province it inhabits, is its historic and democratic right."[8]

How was this "right" to "the territorial unity of the Serbian people" to be achieved against the will of Croats and Muslims in the other Yugoslav republics except through "ethnic cleansing"? The intellectuals who signed the memorandum and gave speeches at meetings of the Writers Association did not address this question publicly. It was enough to describe their goals as "democracy."

This was not a new call. There had been an almost identical movement for Greater Serbia in the 1930s, which also included the would-be expulsion of Muslim Albanians from Kosovo. The author of this earlier program, a dark brooding man named Vasa Čubrilović, was a member of the same nationalist-resistance group that had carried out the assassination of Archduke Franz Ferdinand in Sarajevo in 1914. In a famous paper titled "The Expulsion of the Albanians," he argued that Yugoslavia would find political stability by colonizing other lands and by expelling certain nationalities from the country. The word "cleansing" appeared prominently throughout.

Though fascism was fashionable across Europe in the 1930s, the arrival of Tito and the Communist Partisans had brought Mr. Čubrilović's plans to a sudden end.

To be revived fifty years later in the memorandum.

The memorandum was leaked to the press. It caused a sensation; and by 1987, an ambitious apparatchik named Slobodan Milošević, with an eye to the future, had fastened on Ćosić's nationalist ideas. With Yugoslavia disintegrating, Titoism dying and debilitating poverty rampant everywhere, "the Serb nation" was an attractive—and distracting—hook to hang power on. An old reading of Serbia's history was being revived for new service.

As a token of his gratitude to Dobrica Ćosić and as a sign of his need for a reputable intellectual basis for the nation's new nationalist agenda, Slobodan Milošević made Ćosić president of the Federal Republic of Yugoslavia in 1992. For one year only. Milošević unceremoniously impeached Ćosić in 1993.

However, Ćosić's influence ranged wider than formal politics. During the war in Bosnia (which began in 1992, the same year Ćosić ascended to the presidency), officials of the UN High Commission for Refugees (UNHCR) reported that whenever the government-controlled Serb media began to speak of "genocide," "ethnic cleansing," "mass rape" and "cultural destruction"—language that was first publicized by Ćosić and his followers in the Memorandum of the Serbian Academy—Serb militias in the area understood they were to begin the "cleansing" of non-Serbs. UNHCR said that by monitoring broadcasts, they were often able to predict where the next attacks would take place.

The famous writer rises from his chair, narrows his eyes to a squint and stares at me pugnaciously. At seventy-six he is still solid-looking, even stocky. With a shock of thick white hair. What precisely do I want to discuss? Have I been properly informed that talk of politics is off limits?

"Of course," I say. "What interests me is national identity. And the way countries choose to remember their history."

"Ah," he replies, his face relaxing into a smile. "That is *precisely* my subject."

Dobrica Ćosić's office is located in the architecturally majestic (if rundown) Serbian Academy of Sciences, and to reach his room my interpreter and I have climbed a wide, curved staircase flanked by marble busts of austere-looking former academy presidents. My interpreter is a young man from the Democratic Centre, a non-governmental organization that has become a small political party of the opposition. The centre is trying to promote the importance of free media, tolerant interethnic relations and other mainstays of Western civil society, but it is locked in an internecine conflict with other opposition groups, which has rendered all of them impotent. My translator evaded the draft and spent the Bosnian war years in Prague, where he was a student. Then he came home, he said, to try to effect change.

I notice with some curiosity that his hands tremble as he makes notes to himself before translating Ćosić's replies.

I address my interlocutor: "You are one of the major interpreters of this country. What do you see when you examine the history of your country?"

He looks serious and sad. "I see that human fate has two characteristics: first, one's family environment, and second, the larger history of the nation. In the twentieth century, historical destiny was the crucial one in determining what would happen because we live in an environment where history is alive and still happening today.

"This is also true for other places that have not developed a sufficient sense of nationhood. If our past history is alive and unresolved, it is because we have not developed our own national state. It is because we have not developed a sufficient sense of nationhood to fulfil our destiny."

He speaks a sentence, then waves at the interpreter to translate.

"Why is the nation-state, as you conceive of it, necessary?"

He laughs. "I don't mean nation-state in the ethnic sense but as a civic society, the way states were created all over Europe. We just started a century later than Europe. We were delayed by the Turkish Empire, the Austro-Hungarian Empire, then the Germans, then communism.

"But we do not want to *exclude* the multi-ethnic community. In the war we have just come through, we fought for one state—one unified state of the southern Slav nations. The nation-state does not have to mean an ethnic or cleansed state, the way the Croats meant it! Serbian society should, and does, strive for a multi-ethnic state. There has always been a place for other cultures. In the First and Second World Wars, Serbia fought for a multi-ethnic state to unify all the southern Slavs, and even in the war we have just fought, we fought for one unified state of the southern Slav nations."

Given his speeches and writings, which are available on the record, and the quite different meaning of "Greater Serbia" that he has ceaselessly promoted for almost fifteen years, I find it difficult to know what to make of this response. Except to remember his own words about the "patriotic creative lie." On the other hand he has acknowledged that Serbia actually fought in Bosnia—unlike his president, Slobodan Milošević, who is on record as denying any Serb involvement in that war: an astonishing prevarication dutifully propagated by the media.

"Historians say, from the evidence, that Serbia had a very *strong* position in the Yugoslav Federation, but you deny this."

"Ha!" He laughs. "Serbia had the most important geographical position and we were the largest population, but we did not have the most important role."

"Please help me understand what happened in this country after Tito's death. Why did you argue that Serb history and destiny were threatened?"

He begins to speak in firm tones. After a moment, the interpreter tells me he is not answering the question.

I try again. "In 1987, you made speeches in which you claimed that Serbia was threatened by its neighbours in the federation. What were your grounds?"

"Yes, it was threatened," he replies, "but indirectly. Since the 1970s when Kosovo became a semi-autonomous region [constitutionally], Serbs from inner Serbia did not have the same rights. The only point I wanted to make was that Serbs from inner Serbia should have the same rights as others in their common state."

"Since you are interested in history and identity, it must concern you when the past is manipulated for political purposes. Did that happen here?"

His eyes begin to narrow again. "Generally speaking, Serbian history is pro-liberation and pro-democratic, but some politicians and other leaders did misuse the past."

"Were your own writings and speeches used or misused?"

"Certainly not! There is not a sentence or a word that is not democratic in any of my twenty books."

"All the same, you are surely aware that many people draw a straight line between your public utterances in the late 1980s and the subsequent war in Bosnia. Do you acknowledge any connection between your work and the growth of a less innocent nationalism in this country?"

He is silent. Then he smiles. "Even Christianity, a religion of love, has sometimes provoked hatred. But Jesus Christ cannot be held responsible for the Inquisition."

I turn to the interpreter, unsure of what I have heard. He nods at me wordlessly.

Ćosić observes this communication. "Not that I am comparing myself to Christ," he adds quickly.

"What are the consequences now that the war in Bosnia is over?"

"They are deep and tragic. In spite of all the blood that was shed for a unified state, we are left without a Fatherland. As a nation we are ruined."

"What future do you see for your country, Mr. Ćosić?"

"Only darkness."[9]

On April 24, 1987, Slobodan Milošević travelled to Kosovo to lay claim to the Serb heartland. When Albanian police used truncheons to disperse the crowds of Serbs waiting to communicate their grievances, he uttered a sentence that made him famous. He said, "From now on, no one has the right to beat you. . . . You are suffering from injustice and humiliation. It was never in the spirit of the Serbian and Montenegrin peoples to withdraw in the face of difficulties, to demobilize itself when it should fight."

Deliberately provocative words. Two years later, however, Milošević did something even more dramatic. He returned to Kosovo, but this time his destination was Kosovo-of-the-mind, the abstract place of myth and memory that was transfigured long ago into the birthplace of a holy nation, into "Serb Jerusalem."

On June 28, 1989, he stood on a large decorated podium to commemorate the anniversary of a famous battle in the year 1389 when Lazar, mighty prince of the Serbs, was allegedly beheaded by the invading Ottoman Turks. (What actually occurred during this battle has been lost in the mists of time.) It was a routine military encounter for the era, including the beheading (if beheading there was), but exceptionally bitter in its consequences, for the Ottoman victory was adopted by the mythmakers of history as the central event that brought medieval Serb independence to an end. The debacle in medieval Kosovo also provided the starting point for something else that was new and ominous: a propaganda war between the Serb Orthodox Church and Islam. Although the reality of everyday life under the Ottomans was multicultural and generally accommodating (including allowing the continued presence of Serb monasteries, for example), a largely fabricated chronicle of ancient rivalries was nurtured in Serb sermon and lore as part of a nineteenth-century nationalist awakening.

On that day in Kosovo in June 1989, one million Serbs waited to hear Slobodan Milošević speak—that is, almost the entire Kosovo Serb population. The podium on which Milošević stood was decorated with a large backdrop of red peonies (symbols of the revered blood of the "martyrs" of 1389) and twinned portraits of Milošević and Prince Lazar, both "saviours" of the Serb nation. Past and present dissolving into one. And history and literature, too. Along with their posters of Milošević, many people were carrying portraits of a nineteenth-century prince bishop of Montenegro, a writer of national epics known as Njegoš.

To read Petar Petrović Njegoš's most famous work, the verse drama known as *The Mountain Wreath*,[10] is to glimpse the dangerous blurring of presumed historical event and nationalist fantasy that was to mark Serbia in the 1980s and 1990s. Njegoš's story about a Serb attack on Muslim Slavs in Montenegro during the early eighteenth century was either a conflation of several events or altogether fabricated from imaginative cloth, since no such happening was noted in contemporary historical sources.

Throughout *The Mountain Wreath*, Muslims are called "Turks" in order to emphasize their supposed identity shift following a conversion to Islam. The word *cleansing* makes a repeated appearance, as does the timeless, racist canard that people defined as "other" smell different from ordinary folk. In *The Mountain Wreath* the chorus chants, "The high mountains reek with the stench of non-Christians," a protagonist mutters darkly about the murder of Prince Lazar and the horrors of Islam, and the massacre of the Muslims takes place at Christmas—as a religious blood rite of Serb nationhood. At least since the time of

Njegoš, Serbs had been invited to think of the Ottoman Turks as "Christ killers," as the destroyers of the prince who incarnated their nation and therefore as the destroyers of their essential selves. It was easy to extend this label to the so-called descendants of the Turks: those who had converted to the religion of the occupier.

As Slobodan Milošević played the lead role in a concocted medieval pageant tying the mythologized past to the mythologized present, his overwrought Serb compatriots literally disinterred the bones of Prince Lazar and paraded them about the grounds. He who had died while trying to defend his subjects had been linked with that other saviour, Jesus Christ, and before long, the prince was endowed with an entourage of twelve disciples, a Last Supper and a Judas figure who betrays him.

Prince Lazar was "resurrected" on that June day. And the Serb nation that "died" with him six hundred years ago was symbolically reborn.

Dobrica Ćosić may have been a prime mover in Serbia's most recent return to its "destiny," but he was not alone in recasting history. Someone suggests I meet Klara Mandić, a woman who became a celebrity during the heady days of the late 1980s when "Greater Serbia" was heating Belgrade to a boiling pitch and playing the history card was the fastest route to fame.

It was no accident that Ćosić mentioned Croatia in our conversation—mentioned it as an ethnic-cleansing state, as opposed to Serbia, which was a proponent of multi-ethnic pluralism. Aside from Kosovo and the purported genocidal tendencies of the Albanians, the psychological preparation for war focused on Croatia. With Tito and his Brotherhood and Unity strictures out of the way, it was possible to reopen old Second World War wounds that had never healed, especially the death of many thousands (the numbers were vastly disputed) of Serbs and Jews who perished in the notorious Jasenovac concentration camp. Collapsing a half century of post-war reconciliation (or the appearance of reconciliation), the nationalists had conflated contemporary Croats with wartime Ustaše "Nazis."

The memory of Croatian fascist atrocities was not limited to Serbs; it lingered in the minds of other nationals who also remembered the camps and the slaughter. What *was* new was the contemporary suggestion that all Croats had been, and still were, Nazis and that they were still intent on destroying Serbs.[11]

And Jews. This was where Klara Mandić came into the picture. Before the notion of Greater Serbia was revived, she was an ordinary woman—a Belgrade dentist, as it happens. Then her ancestry helped propel her into the limelight. Because she was a Jewish survivor of the Holocaust who had been raised by a Serb-Orthodox family after her parents were deported, her concerns were double-edged. On the one hand, she was tormented by the murder of her family; on the other, she was convinced that Croats still harboured genocidal intentions and were drawing up plans for the imminent annihilation of Serbs. Mandić had come to the conclusion that contemporary Croats were "Nazis," and contemporary Serbs were "Jews"—on the verge of new destruction. But the genocide of the "Jews" would never happen twice, she declared triumphantly to the press. This time the victims must attack their enemies *before* it was too late.

She built her case by arguing the familiar Tito line: all Serbs were anti-fascist Partisans during the war. Only now, with Tito dead and the taboos against inter-ethnic calumny lifted, thanks to free speech, she could also claim the converse: that all Croats were pro-fascists. Having established these first terms, she then conjured up the Holocaust to describe what the Nazi Croats had visited upon their Serb victims in the early 1990s—their Serb/Jewish victims.

In order to make the Serbs-are-Jews formula work, Mandić had to insist that there had been no Serb collaboration in the wartime extermination of Jews living in Serbia. This argument would have been hard to make in an open society where facts will eventually become known; however, since the myths of the post-war period claimed that Serbs loved and had protected the Jews, and since there were almost no Jewish survivors to gainsay the tale, her task was considerably easier.

Ninety-four per cent of Serbia's Jews were murdered during the war years, most by the Nazis, and among the 6 per cent who survived, many were rescued by compassionate Serbs, such as the family that had adopted Klara Mandić.[12] But homegrown anti-semitism had a real two hundred-year-old history, reaching back to the end of Turkish rule. Yes, the *end* of Turkish rule. The cruelties of the Ottomans were legion, but religious oppression was not foremost among them. The hated Ottoman Empire had accepted religious diversity in its occupied lands, provided that people paid their taxes and were obedient to the ruler. It was the new Serbian state that had brought change. Jews were expelled from the interior of Serbia and obliged to live in Belgrade or leave the country. A British diplomat who visited the Belgrade Jewish community in 1871 described several hundred people "literally starving [by] being deprived by law of earning their subsistence."[13]

In the 1930s, emerging fascism was reflected in the media's support for Serb ethnic purity. By 1935, a pro-Nazi political party called Zbor was on the move, and the Serb Orthodox Church was producing rabidly anti-semitic articles drawn directly from Nazi texts.[14] By 1940, the Jews of Serbia were prevented from enrolling in universities and high schools and prohibited from producing or distributing food.

After the German occupation in 1941, the collaborationist press declared that Serbs should take it upon themselves to exterminate the Jews,[15] and the military arm of Zbor captured, and delivered, Jewish fugitives to the Gestapo. There was method to this: the Germans had ordered that for every one of their men killed, one hundred Serbs would die, and Jews and Gypsies helped fill these quotas. The ultra-nationalist Chetniks gave over both Jews and Partisans (fascist ideology claimed Jews and Communists were one and the same) and murdered in their own distinctive manner: by torturing, mutilating and slitting throats. The bestiality that marked the Bosnian and Kosovo wars had a precedent in this earlier ethnic cleansing.

Little if any of this was known to the post-war Serbian public. "History" under Tito was written by Tito. "Lying is an aspect of our patriotism," explained Dobrica Ćosić.

Klara Mandić might have remained an intriguing footnote if she had not helped divert international attempts to intervene in the war in Bosnia—the kind of efforts that did eventually push the Western nations to intercede in Kosovo a few years later. For example, one might have reasonably expected Jews, who did know something about genocide, to have been the first to speak out against ethnic cleansing, and had they done so they might have exercised a powerful moral influence. For this reason, targeting then mitigating Jewish opinion was a priority for Serb nationalists who believed (as stated in the Krajina Serb parliament in 1992) in "the vast Jewish influence worldwide."[16] As a Jew, Mandić was an invaluable propagandist.

"There *is* no anti-semitism in Serbia, nor has there *ever* been any because Serbs simply do not know how to hate. I live here and *nobody* from another country is going to tell me what I know!" she declares as we sip tea in the dining room of a dingy Belgrade hotel. Klara is old-fashioned glamorous. As she speaks, she fluffs up her blond curls and fixes me with dramatically made up steely blue eyes. Her rhinestone earrings glitter in the overhead light, and not one but two oversize Stars of David on gold chains nestle in her cleavage.

Klara Mandić is a celebrity, and the waiters know it. They hover about her like thrilled groupies as she jokes and smiles magnanimously. True, her star has faded more than a little since the abysmal failure of the war for Greater Serbia, but fame, even diminished fame, is a tonic.

She seized her chance after Tito died, she tells me. "I suggested to Serb and Jewish intellectuals that we publicize the truth that Serbs had never in their history engaged in anti-semitism," and in 1987, along with ten high-profile members of the Serbian Academy of Sciences, including Dobrica Ćosić, she created the Serb-Jewish Friendship Society. Slobodan Milošević gave his personal blessings, and up to three thousand people attended public meetings.

"Why was the Serbian Academy of Sciences interested in this?" I ask her.

"They always had a good opinion of Israel and the Jews, and this was their first chance to show it," she replies, fixing me with her blue gaze.

Perhaps it was also important to establish a connection with Israel in order to shore up sympathy for Serbs as old and *new* victims of Croat-Nazis. There were Croatian survivors of the Holocaust in Israel who could attest to the brutality of the wartime Ustaše, but almost no one from Serbia since just about all the Jews there had been exterminated. As Serbia geared up for new war, the story that the Serbs had been the saviours of the Jews was given wide circulation. Israel was the very best place to campaign.

Like many half-truths, Mandić's vision of Nazis intent on murdering Serb-Jews in present-day Croatia was a fantasy constructed upon a basis of reality. Serbs had reacted against Croatia's declaration of independence from the Yugoslav Federation in 1991 by sending the Milošević-commanded Yugoslav army into the Serb-dominated Krajina area of Croatia and "cleansing" the region of non-Serbs in the name of Greater Serbia. But Croatia had retaliated with Operation Storm in 1995, recapturing the Krajina and killing hundreds of people. In August of that year, at least 100,000 Croatian Serbs (the numbers are disputed) packed up and abandoned their homes in the Krajina, where they had lived for centuries, and in just four days streamed down the road towards Belgrade in their cars, on their tractors and on foot.

The evacuation was orderly—so orderly that what lay behind it is still disputed at this writing. Some claim that Slobodan Milošević planned the exodus for the propaganda boost it would provide; others accuse the late Franjo Tudjman of massive ethnic cleansing. Both scenarios may be true.[17] In any event, approximately six hundred Croatian Serb civilians who refused to leave the Krajina were brutally murdered by Croatian soldiers.

Klara has added her own twist to these events. "I knew the destiny of Jews and Serbs in Croatia," she tells me in a low voice. "The Serbs living in Croatia knew that one day the Croats would stop being so polite. They knew their destiny. So they started to fight to defend themselves. Anyone can say what they like, but this was my Jewish optic on the Serbian problems because I will *never* allow *anyone* in this life to take me or my children as Jews or as Serbs anywhere again. I am ready to fight!"

She bangs on the table. The waiters look alarmed.

Klara didn't just talk about her convictions. Radovan Karadžić was a "loved, respected friend" (reputed to have been a lover) and an honoured member of her Serbian-Jewish Friendship Society. Klara "understood what he was doing during the war," and to prove this she went to the Bosnian front lines to shore up the morale of Radovan's "boys." Once, during one of the many peace conferences, she and Radovan were together in London, watching the news on CNN. She remembers that Radovan sat in silence for two hours, chain-smoking cigarettes. Then he turned to her and said, "If I were not the leader of the Bosnian Serbs, if I did not know the truth, I would weep to see the destiny of the Serbs. This [the news report] is how you manipulate the minds of people through the media."

"I will never forget that fantastic sentence," she sighs.

"But he has been accused of genocide by the International Tribunal at The Hague," I say to her. "As a Holocaust survivor, what do you think of your friend?"

"I was not there. How do we know what happened? Should he be a war criminal and that Ustaše Tudjman not? For me, Radovan will never be a criminal. A lot of things did happen, I know that, but they were outside the supervision of Radovan. They were done by uncontrolled forces.

"Besides, who speaks about other ethnic cleansing? Right after the Second World War Croatia wanted to be cleansed of Serbs. It took them fifty years, but they did it. And what about the United States? They fought a bloody war in Vietnam and I do not remember that the president was accused of being a war criminal! I ask you, *who* has the *right* to make accusations against *anyone!*"

The campaign to co-opt Jewish opinion fired volleys from several quarters. First, the Memorandum of the Academy of Science declared that Serbs had the same right to a holy "Promised Land" (in Kosovo) as the Jews, based on their genocidal suffering. Then the Serbian author and politician Vuk Drašković wrote an open letter to Israeli writers claiming "every foot" of Kosovo as "Jerusalem," and that Serbs were "the thirteenth lost, and most unfortunate, tribe of Israel."[18]

Serbs were no longer merely like the Jews, they *were* the Jews.

With support from Slobodan Milošević, Klara Mandić organized Serbian Week in Israel to promote business, culture and tourism. In 1990, 440 Serbs and 10 Jews flew from Belgrade to Tel Aviv. That so few Jews accompanied the group reflected the opposition of the Jewish community to the Serbian-Jewish Friendship Society. The group denied that Jews were being persecuted in Croatia.

The delegation to Tel Aviv was scheduled to visit Yad Vashem, after which the Serbs hoped to create their own book of memory with the names of their own victims of (Croat, and now Albanian) genocide. Klara also hoped to build a commemorative monument in Belgrade to the genocide of Serbs.

In February 1992, she was invited to visit several Jewish communities in the United States and Canada. One of the stories she repeated on that trip concerned an old Jewish woman living in Croatia whom Klara claimed had been murdered and mutilated by Croats, but what her audiences did not know was that eyewitnesses to the killing had expressly stated that the woman in question was not Jewish, nor was she killed by Croats. She was a Catholic Croat killed by the Serbs during the "cleansing" of the Krajina in 1991. Before she released this story to the North American Jewish press in early 1992, Klara was approached by the Federation of Jewish Communities of Yugoslavia. They demanded that she stop representing the elderly Croat woman as a Jew. She refused.

I question her over the teacups. "You went on a lecture tour in North America and talked about a woman you claimed was the first Jewish victim of Croats. Yet you knew that story was false."

She sighs. "All I know is that the people from the village where this happened came to the Serbian-Jewish Friendship Society with the story and I had no reason not to believe it."

"Do you still believe it?"

"Absolutely. I was not present and neither were any of the people who have criticized me! Now I am finished talking about that!"

The strength of her appeal in Israel and North America came not only from the memory of wartime Ustaše atrocities that was deliberately confounded with the present, or from stories of Serbs protecting Jews, but also from a conjured-up image of "fanatic" Bosnian Muslims bent on anti-Serb/Jewish *jihad*. Given the long duration of the Arab-Israeli conflict and the fear of Islamic extremism, it was useful to paint the mostly secular Bosnians in this frightening light. The tactic worked well. In a scholarly paper on the subject of Israel and the Bosnian war, the political philosopher Daniel Kofman quotes the wide range of Israeli opinion makers who latched on to a thesis that corroborated their prejudices and accentuated their fears. Among these, none was more direct than the former Jerusalem mayor Teddy Kollek. Asked by a reporter from *The Boston Globe* why Israel must retain control over Jerusalem, Kollek replied, "Deep down in Arab philosophy is the conquest by war and not a peaceful conquest. . . . I'm convinced of that. They don't want East Jerusalem. Look, they still want Granada and Cordoba and half of Spain. . . . 'The *Dawlet el Islam*, the land of Islam that we once ruled, we will rule again.' You can observe that again about Bosnia. That is basic Islam."[19]

The habits of totalitarianism. Half-truths stretched until they are transformed into lies. History contorted or imagined to fit the designs of politics. "In these lands, every lie becomes a truth in the end," Dubravka Ugrešic wrote in *The Culture of Lies*. Or, as the famous Yugoslav dissident and author Milovan Djilas once said, "The hardest thing about being a Communist is trying to predict the past."

At the Hotel Excelsior one evening, I happen to turn on the television. Slobodan Milošević leads the news report. He is on a trade mission in

China and in conversation with a very young-looking Chinese official. The president's face fills the screen for fifteen minutes—I'm looking at my watch. No cutaways, no long shots, just a talking head whose words are being paraphrased by an announcer doing a voice-over. For another eight minutes we observe a montage of stills of Chinese-language newspapers, presumably announcing the visit.

Next item on the news: Milošević is giving a speech that is also being broadcast in what seems to be its entirety. The audience claps warmly. The president smiles, shakes hands all around, then delivers a second speech during an "interview" with a female reporter. She hunches forward in tense deference as she listens. She does not speak.

This is the state-controlled media telling the 95 per cent of the population that tunes in what it wants them to hear. During the buildup to war in Croatia and Bosnia, the Serb leadership made sure that everyone got the message about the murderous Croat Ustašes and the genocidal Albanians in Kosovo. There was no escape, and that included peasants living in remote mountain valleys who were forced to pay for a television subscription that came bundled together with their electricity bill. Miloš Vasić of *Vreme* later told me one pig farmer had tried to sue the government. "My pigs don't watch television!" the man complained helplessly.

Vasić said Slobodan Milošević did not actually ban the independent media (although he did later on, during the NATO air campaign and afterwards, by overriding freedom of information provisions in the law). Instead, he denied financial subventions to privately run publications and broadcasters and made their advertising rates on state television prohibitive. (Pro-regime papers advertised free.) Some independents could not afford professional reporting; if they insisted, the cost to consumers rose beyond the means of most people. So an alternative media was available but barely accessible.

I meet Miloš Vasić at the Excelsior, in a room provided by the ever-curious manager. His fatigue-heavy face broadcasts every minute of his fifty years. He orders a double espresso with a shot of slivovitz on the side, both of which he downs in a gulp.

He has spent years in moral protest against the tawdriness of his world, a commitment that has entailed sacrifices. "My wife gave me the Sarajevo ultimatum," he mumbles, his head enveloped in a cloud of cigarette smoke. "It goes like this: the wife and kids have escaped to Amsterdam or Oslo, and she says, 'Okay, you asshole, either you come here and join us or I want a divorce. I'm still young, you know.' So most of the husbands don't go, because during the siege of Sarajevo it was considered shameful to leave. So that's what happened to me, but here in Belgrade."

It happened because Vasić's wife (his latest; he has had several) had a Muslim last name. That she was born and bred in Belgrade didn't help—she had to leave for her safety. "If I had a dollar for every threatening call we received, I'd be a rich man," he mutters. He wouldn't leave *Vreme*.

Vasić started the newsmagazine (which was based on *Time* and *Newsweek*) in 1990 with funds provided by a private supporter with an interest in human rights. That was when Yugoslavia was still nominally intact and the new Milošević regime had other concerns. When the government did come after *Vreme* in 1991, it was already too late: the publication was the most quoted Yugoslav source outside the country.

Vreme had people in the field in Croatia and Bosnia from the beginning. "We saw it all. We knew about the concentration camps early on and the fact that people were being buried two or three times when their bodies washed to the surface during ground melt. We saw our obligation as countering the official media. For instance, television would show a dismembered body and say, 'Look what the Croats did!' So I spoke to a military surgeon whom I trust who said that judging from appearances, that was a picture of someone who had been hit by an explosive like a land mine or a mortar. Then a priest came on television carrying a little yellow skull and said, 'This is a Serb child killed by Croats.' Judging from its colour, the doctor thought the skull had to be least fifty years old and had probably come from an anatomical exhibit. It was absurd. Belgrade television showed piles of mutilated bodies and said they were Serbs, and Croats showed the same pictures of the same bodies and said they were Croats. Then it turned out the film came from German television and they had *no* idea what 'type' the victims were. Just victims. That's the thing that is not repeated often enough. The most endangered 'ethnic group' was unarmed civilians, whatever their so-called nationality. *They* were the victims. And the aggressor was whoever was attacking them."

The role of the Serb intelligentsia in the buildup to war was "one of the greatest disappointments of my life," he says. And the man he points to with bitter hatred is Dobrica Ćosić, whom he describes as "utterly despicable." "It was *he* who started the whole thing as an attempt to realize his half-baked intellectual and artistic dreams. You have to understand that what was left over from the Communist state was the total obedience of the intellectuals—God, I hate that word! So when the bugle sounded, they were there to serve—to prod people with their warmongering, their speeches and their jingoism. The disfiguration of the sciences, especially the human sciences, was a major force. The same lazy, half-baked scientists and journalists, the same untalented poets, the same superficial and half-literate fiction writers joined the Serbian national cause with as little sincerity as they had joined the Communist cause before that. You have a whole parasitic social class that just changed one ideology for another. Where was the 'history' in their nationalism, you ask? There was none. It was just old-style propaganda."

Our conversation comes to a halt. All I can think is that I want to offer him another shot of slivovitz.

"I am ashamed," he says finally.

"Ashamed as a Serb?"

"No. I'm ashamed as someone who has been living with all these people for decades. If you want to know, my answer is that I am ashamed as a human being. I worked in Germany in the 1970s and I remember spending nights talking about guilt and shame. I still think the very idea of collective guilt is wrong and unfair. On the other hand, history sometimes hangs over us in terrible ways."

There are other sufferers. One is Borka Pavićević, once a famous dramaturge and now director of the ironically named Centre for Cultural Decontamination. Another is her husband, Nikola Barović, one of ex-Yugoslavia's most prominent human rights lawyers.

Borka's Centre for Cultural Decontamination is located in an old courtyard next to the German embassy, where a line of depressed-looking people hoping to get out of Serbia stretches several blocks. Slobodan Milošević can pretend what he likes: the inheritors of Prince Lazar and the glorious Serb nation are voting with their feet.

Borka's courtyard is Belgrade dingy, Belgrade grey. Sagging, cracked concrete walls and piles of rubble. I walk up a set of exterior stairs attached to one of the buildings to a small office, where she is waiting. Her greying hair is pulled back from her forehead. She comes towards me to shake my hand, and it seems to me that her solid body carries with it the weight of her great distress.

We sit down at a table in a room where several other people are working (one is trying vainly to establish an Internet connection, which strikes me as a metaphor for the deep isolation of this country). Borka tells me that for thirty years Belgrade was a centre of European theatre;

others have said that she was its heart. She travelled constantly throughout Yugoslavia. Theatre was part of the glue that held the Yugoslav nationalities together, and Tito's way operated here as elsewhere: the staff of every production included representatives of all the ethnicities.

Her parents had a summer house on the Croatian Adriatic, but now that beautiful coast has been lost to her; Croatia is another country. This particular loss—one that is mentioned to me in sorrow by many people in land-locked Serbia and Bosnia—is one among many. "Belgrade was a centre of culture and common values. So now we ask, What right did these people have to destroy our history and the value system we lived with?"

She is talking about her generation's "history," the ethos she had been raised with: the post–Second World War shift into Titoism that preceded the current wrenching back to an even earlier time. Her voice grows angry and gravelly, roughened by cigarettes and rage; it rises until she is shouting into the room. The space feels too small to contain the immensity of her passion. "The entire process of this war was to use history to destroy history—to destroy memory! Can you imagine what children will read in a few years in the schools about what happened here? Will they read anything at all? Yugoslavia was in Europe. Now we are outside Europe. We fought a medieval war. What does a war for territory mean in the modern world? Did the majority here really care about a few Serbs living peacefully in Croatia?

"Anyone can create a quarrel where there are people with different backgrounds. I can do it in my theatre in five minutes if I want to. If a Serb in a Bosnian village is angry about a cow, and if he is armed and has three times the equipment, of course he can kill his Muslim neighbour! You start the propaganda, and prejudice grows until people are contaminated. You ask someone why he cannot live with his neighbour and you realize finally that he has *heard* that he cannot live with his neighbour. He has been listening to patriotic songs and hearing our 'intellectuals' talking about 1389 or some goddamned *insane* thing. And now we have four million exiled people and I don't know how many dead. And for what? For this crazy idea of Greater Serbia these power-mongers have killed our country! Killed our past!"

She lights a cigarette from the stub of the one squeezed between her fingers and waves her hand in a gesture of contempt, fury, rage, impotence. A pained silence ensues. She gulps for air. "What people here have learned is *criminality*. Human beings have the best and the worst in them, and if you emphasize the worst, you end up with war. So what happens now? People push and hit each other in the bus, and everyone says, 'Oh well, he was wounded in Vukovar,' or someone steals something and people say, 'Oh well, it's not much compared with all those corpses.' Then they say to themselves, Why should *I* not steal a car?' And they do. You know, the process of degeneration is not all that visible; it's an emotional thing, and it happens step by step, but you will see how aggressively people are behaving in the streets. It comes from hiding from the truth. Either you face what happened here or you do not. If you face it, you will be called a traitor, or a hater of the Serb people, or crazy, and most people don't want that kind of trouble. You must somehow find a place of comfort in order to go on living. And if your leader goes on television and says there was no war here, and even if there was a war somewhere else, of course Serbia was not involved, and therefore you are not guilty. It is easier not to think too hard and not to have to take responsibility. It is certainly not pleasant to hear yourself called a traitor or crazy on television, as I have. But it is also true. There *is* real craziness here."

I listen to her closely, watch her with sympathy, and remember another passage in Ryszard Kapuściński's *Imperium*. The author is in a desolate outpost in Siberia called Magadan that once was the site of a concentration camp where millions of Stalin's captives died. He too is thinking about books, two of them to be precise, both written by inmates of that appalling place. One is by a proud German Communist who is convinced that he has landed in an irrational, insane locale. Communism is still an excellent idea—it's just the camp in Magadan that is an aberration. The other book was written by a native Russian who is an anti-Communist. He, on the contrary, understands everything that is happening as part of the natural order, like the wind or the rain, and that to rebel is senseless. Kapuściński contrasts the Westerner's "Cartesian rationalism" with the Russian's fatalism.

Borka is in the rationalist tradition. She is well travelled outside Serbia. She thinks for herself. She yearns to be in "Europe."

Like the others in the tiny, fractious anti-Milošević opposition, she is a member of that minute constituency that reads *Vreme*. But in the end it is the Dobrica Ćosićs and the Klara Mandićs of the land who are heard.

Borka's theatre group, the Centre for Cultural Decontamination, performs dramas she hopes will inform through analogy. Talking politics in code; it is the old way. One performance took place on a bus the actors had cleaned up for the occasion, in order to shock people into seeing how filthy, decrepit and smelly their city-owned vehicles were, with implications about the quality of their lives. The company also acted *Macbeth*, a play about the overweening will to power. The centre is Borka's revenge. She was forced to resign as director of the Yugoslav National Theatre after she refused to dismiss all the Muslims from her staff. Her redress is to hold up a mirror to society.

Her husband understands that although much has changed since the days of Tito, much more has remained the same. Nikola Barović's eyes brim with humour, and he misses nothing. A Belgrade lawyer cannot afford to ignore a word or gesture or to fumble any of his own, since defending people who are deemed guilty the moment they are accused depends almost entirely on counsel's wit. Certainly not on any evidence he or she might bring to bear on the case, he says.

He defended political dissidents during the Tito era: people charged, for example, with "spreading hostile propaganda." This crime against the state was largely directed at writers, of course, but ordinary people also could be caught. A joke with political overtones whispered to a "friend" at a party could get you seven to twelve years in jail. The pertinent legislation was adopted from Article 58 in the Soviet Union, "The one that helped get rid of the opposition and fill up Siberia!" Nikola says with a laugh. Laughter is clearly his favourite recourse.

Since the accused is already guilty ("otherwise, why would he be charged?"), Barović and his colleagues may rely on creating a public scandal so intense that the government will consider reducing the sentence or even dropping the case from sheer embarrassment. A lawyer has to demonstrate that his or her client has friends elsewhere, but in order for that to happen, the international press has to pick up the story. Since all the foreign embassies are located in Belgrade, lawyers like Barović try to have their cases heard there.

Because he had worked throughout the former Yugoslavia, Barović found he could continue at least some of his activities under the new national regimes. During the Bosnian war, he travelled from place to place, often under dangerous conditions. Now, in the post-war period, his clients are deserters from the military, prisoners of war and minorities: Serbs in Croatia, and Croats in Serbia.

"You cannot count on the law here. Cases look formally correct, but the court is just an arm of the state. The 'spreading hostile propaganda' law doesn't exist anymore,[20] but if you happen to read that a local court has accused someone of 'armed rebellion,' or 'organizing a criminal group' or 'war crimes,' you can assume that that person is almost certainly innocent. The accused is always from the minority community—you will never find a Serb accused of war crimes in Serbia, or a Croat accused of war crimes in Croatia, unless it's for show.

"In the whole of ex-Yugoslavia, I have not encountered one case where the accused was really guilty. The accused are the victims, usually refugees trying to return to their homes under the terms of the Dayton Accords. It is the so-called witnesses who are usually the perpetrators of the crime in question. This is one of the ways they have come up with for keeping the refugees from returning and making sure that ethnic cleansing becomes a permanent reality."

Black humour has helped him understand the uses of language in the coded world he lives in: the layers of meaning that float about like screens of wispy cigarette smoke. "Uncontrolled forces" is one of his favourite codes, meaning those small groups of anonymous men who allegedly committed massacres and other unspeakable acts outside the command of a military or political leadership.

"It's a matter of the time frame one is operating in. You see, if someone goes to the police station one morning and says, 'Last night half the houses in my village were blown up,' the chief of police will write it all down dutifully. But he will never find the perpetrators—all of whom are members of 'uncontrolled forces'—because these people do not exist during the daytime, when he is the police chief. They exist only at night. Because they *are* the police, perhaps the chief himself, and other representatives of the regime. You remember that American story *The Three Faces of Eve* about the schizophrenic woman with three personalities? Well, we call the 'uncontrolled forces' 'Eve groups.' Naturally not one of them has ever been seen anywhere in ex-Yugoslavia."

Should they be arrested by NATO peacekeeping forces, the true perpetrators of an atrocity might find themselves whisked away to be tried at the United Nations International Criminal Tribunal for the Former Yugoslavia at The Hague. But members of ethnic minorities who are accused locally of having committed war crimes—even if falsely, as Barović claims—still need lawyers to defend them, and the only legal recourse is tactical, says Nikola, now as before.

"You have to pretend the law can help, so all you can do is push. You make a lot of noise, you petition the government, you indicate that you know what went on and what has been shoved under the carpet. But you have formidable opposition because the prosecutor himself may be an 'uncontrolled force' in that area. And almost all judges will convict—because they are commanded to do so by the state. I knew only three in the whole of ex-Yugoslavia with the integrity and the courage to be independent, and one was attacked and seriously wounded—by 'uncontrolled forces,' of course. There was one judge, a woman, who had the courage to find seventeen peasants not guilty in separate cases. They were all accused of war crimes, genocide, armed rebellion and so on, and they were all ethnic minorities in the region where they lived. Can you imagine just how deeply innocent a person has to be to decide to stay where he is living when a hostile government comes into control? Say it's Republika Srpska and you are a Croat or a Muslim?"

Barović has faced danger. Not long before, he had been physically attacked on a television set by the bodyguard of Vojislav Šešelj, the leader of the ultranationalist Serbian Radical Party, which is part of the ruling coalition led by the Socialist Party of President Slobodan Milošević, and leader of the paramilitary forces known as the White Eagles, which had committed widespread atrocities against Muslim civilians during the Bosnian war. In spite of his personal, hands-on experience with crime, Šešelj has a doctorate of law from the University of Sarajevo, and, like Dobrica Ćosić, he was a human rights dissident in the 1980s, before turning to nationalism. (Later on, Šešelj was appointed deputy prime minister of Serbia, in the same way Ćosić was briefly president of the Federal Republic of Yugoslavia.)[21]

"We had been together on a panel, and I was talking about Croats in Belgrade who had been forced out of their apartments. These people had lived in Belgrade for four generations, and now they were being pushed into the streets. After the program, Šešelj's bodyguard came back into the studio and punched me on the nose, broke it. There was a big public scandal—Šešelj told the media I had slipped on a banana peel!—but it didn't matter and it won't change anything. The government wants those Croats out of Belgrade, so even if the court decides they can stay, the police will not enforce the court's judgment. Nothing counts here except the will of the regime."

Barović stops talking rather abruptly.

"How do you function in this climate, personally?"

A wry smile crosses his face and he laughs out loud. "You carry on. You protect as many as you can, especially when you know the person is innocent. Sometimes you are lucky. If your client is a soldier, he may be exchanged, if he's not killed. But I don't trust any of the local governments. Civilians were the real target of this war for all the regimes and they still are. Every time one person from a Bosnian village is accused, others will refuse to return."

"Is the ethnic cleansing conclusive, then?"

"Probably, yes."

Drinka Gojković had written a carefully researched report on how the Association of Serbian Writers contributed to the rise of ethnic nationalism. She did this alone, out of moral outrage. Her work was even published as part of a project detailing the rise of Serbian nationalism within institutions, and the book was freely available in the bookstores. That Drinka's work was available was irrelevant. No one had money to buy books. Nor did they seem to care. The executive of the Writers' Association barely bothered to respond to her attack. They didn't have to; there was no publicity, and no one was paying attention. So the public discussion she had hoped to stimulate did not take place.

We meet at the Excelsior. She has fine lines drawn across a once-beautiful face, and like Miloš Vasić, Borka Pavićević and Nikola Barović, she speaks with a directness that has evolved, perhaps, as a protest against obfuscation. She too mourns for the world Tito built. It was "real and natural," she says.

Because Tito had kept the "nationalities question" at bay for almost half a century, most people under the age of fifty or sixty identified themselves as Yugoslavs and not as members of an ethnic group. "Yugoslavia was really the only solution for this part of the world," she says sadly, "and now we are sitting on dynamite again. You know, it's not hard for power-mongers to turn people against each other in a society where everyone is accustomed to being ruled from above. Even today we do not have a large picture of what happened in the war in Bosnia, like how many military units were sent there and what they did. We only know that Serbs did some bad things, but so did everyone else. So it is all relativized and nothing matters anymore. Just the need to feed one's family. No one is accountable. And the worst thing has been seeing Slobodan Milošević, an accused war criminal, negotiating with the West. Nothing has seemed a greater betrayal by nations supposedly committed to human rights. Why should we talk about Serbian responsibility for the Bosnian war when the whole world takes this bloodied man as a partner?"

"Impunity leads to injustice," I say sympathetically.

"Oh!" She laughs heartily, and her face lights up. "There is *definitely* no justice!"

Her cynical mirth, this terrible despair—I'm suddenly overcome, embarrassed, by my own privileged life, by the fact of being here as an observer, with the option to leave when I wish. Such unbidden thoughts unexpectedly call into question my book-in-progress, premised, as it is, on this mode of observation. I pull myself back with a start. I am recoiling from the core of what it is to be a writer: to watch, to ask, to elicit a response, to empathize, to weigh, to judge—feeling momentarily overwhelmed by doubts that I shall strive to shake away, if only for now. I am not the first to experience the ambiguity of the role in the face of true suffering.

How right she was about Slobodan Milošević and the West. It was years before serious initiatives to stop the appalling crimes against civilians in Bosnia were undertaken. By then, 250,000 people were dead and more than two million had been displaced. The brutal rapes of women of all ages, carried out as a genocidal Orwellian attempt to destroy the future of the "race" in question by producing infants of another "blood"; the herding of men into barbarous concentration camps, such as Omarska, near the town of Prijedor, where Muslims were slaughtered by their Serb guards—camps such as the world had not seen since the pictures from Auschwitz and Dachau sent shock waves across continents in the immediate aftermath of the Second World War; the UN "safe haven" at Srebrenica, where Bosnian Serb forces massacred up to eight thousand Muslim men and boys over twelve days in July 1995—these events and others, even when exposed in the Western press, starting with the report by *New York Newsday*'s Roy Gutman, who recounted the horror of Omarska, on August 2, 1992, were rationalized as the "ancient rivalries" of faraway peoples. During the intervening years, dozens of books and articles had tried retrospectively to explain the failure of the West in Bosnia—and in Rwanda, where 800,000 Tutsis of both sexes and all ages were slaughtered by extremist Hutus in a ninety-day rampage in spring 1994. Through it all, Slobodan Milošević remained the chief negotiator with the West on the subject of Bosnia. No wonder Drinka and the others felt betrayed.

Not until "this bloodied man," as Drinka called him, moved his troops into Kosovo to begin a new round of ethnic cleansing, this time of the hated Kosovo Albanians, would Western patience run out, when, in March 1999, NATO began bombing to stop the assault, basing its act on the UN Charter, in which member countries had committed themselves to "promote and encourage respect for human rights."[22] During these dizzying eleven weeks of passionate, conflicting opinion about whether the bombing raids against Serbia were justified; about the limits of state sovereignty in the face of flagrant human rights abuses; about duties, obligations and the kaleidoscope of international interests, I would be deeply affected by the words of one man who had seen it all before. He was Marek Edelman, the last surviving member of the doomed uprising in the Warsaw Ghetto.

On April 5, 1999, this old survivor of the Holocaust, who was still living in Lódz, Poland, published an open appeal to President Bill Clinton, President Jacques Chirac, Prime Minister Tony Blair, Chancellor Gerhard Schroeder, Javier Solana, secretary general of NATO, and to the governments of the nineteen members of NATO. He wrote:

> The decision of the member states of NATO to initiate a bombing campaign to save the people of Kosovo will change the nature of the world. For the first time in history, war is not being waged to conquer power or territory, or to defend economic interests, but for humanitarian reasons.
>
> During the time of Second World War, in the Warsaw Ghetto I was a witness to genocide. The leaders of the Free World, President Roosevelt and Prime Minister Churchill, didn't know how to stop it. They proclaimed that once the war was over, all men, whatever their race, religion, nationality or ethnic group would reconquer their equality and live in peace, instead of being hunted down like animals. [But] when the war ended and democracy had triumphed, those in whose name the struggle had been fought were no longer there to enjoy the peace. . . ."[23]

I heard the resonant echo of his words, spoken on behalf of the millions of silent dead, those who are remembered in Jerusalem, Washington, Amsterdam, Berlin, Paris and Toronto, to mention those capitals where I have personally visited memorials, as well as in hundreds of other places. The anguish of Germans fifty years later, and the French, as they recently convicted one of their own, remain evidence enough of the psychological outcome of allowing atrocity into the world without protest.

Miloš and I have spent many hours together; he is my sometime guide and money-changer, has accompanied me to interviews, even helped translate on one occasion. His girlfriend, Gordana, has come along too: once they took me to a park on a hill overlooking the Danube River that cuts through the city, this river of myth and celebration, wending its way across the lands of Eastern Europe to the Black Sea. Miloš and Gordana are both twenty-one years old, and in their rootlessness and monochromatic flat despair lies evidence of ruin: the social and psychological destruction of young people grown to adulthood during a decade of hate speech, war-mongering and rumours of unfathomable atrocities committed by their own. Gordana is tall, intelligent, beautiful: a student of Albanian. (Her uncle told her this would be a useful language for a career in translation.) She yearns to be hip and modern, "Western," and in her mind this means only one thing: consumerism. "Do you like *things?*" she asks me as we walk along a street lined with small barren shops.

"Things?"

"Yes, you know, *things*—stuff you can buy?"

Gordana keeps disappearing into doorways, then running to catch up with Miloš and me, triumphantly clutching new knick-knacks she has purchased. One is a gift to me: a candle to celebrate her saint's day.

But the pervasive cynicism has touched her too. She "knows" that something as crucial as the historical record (whatever it might be, she isn't sure anymore) has been bent and tampered with in order to make war, and this has made her sceptical about the very possibility of truthful discourse. "I don't believe in recorded history anywhere in the world," she says with a toss of her head. "It's all lies everywhere."

To lose trust in history is to be set adrift in a floating, detached present, and this is precisely where Gordana lives: on a bleak, unmoored island.

But Miloš is experiencing even greater difficulty. His father is a journalist who was on the Bosnian front lines. He privately told Miloš that their people, Serbs, had started the war, and Miloš compared this trusted, first-hand information with the lies that continue to fill the airwaves. He was just fourteen years old when Slobodan Milošević went to Kosovo to orate over the disinterred bones of Prince Lazar and fifteen when the fighting began. His entire adolescence was marked by confusion and emotional distress.

Miloš also tries to escape but not through consumerism. He reads foreign literature and goes to the movies, up to three a day. "I don't like the world," he confides to me. Even the remote possibility of a job with the independent radio station B92 frightens him because it would connect him with "the news."

I rarely see Miloš eat, even though I buy him food. I suspect drugs. He seems to live on cigarettes. One evening he begins to tell me haltingly and earnestly that he wants to understand the meaning of responsibility. What "the personal" means. He says he wants to study philosophy. "No one here takes any responsibility for what has happened." His voice has dropped to a whisper. "They blame everyone else, or they say it was just the political leaders. Everyone thinks they are nothing and powerless. But they have their own power in themselves, whether they accept it or not. Don't they? Doesn't that make them responsible?"

Such big thoughts. Remarkable thoughts in a culture that has devoted unlimited resources to controlling opinion.

Nikola Barović had talked to me about the predicament of the young. He said, "When they were out demonstrating against the regime a year or so ago they looked like kids in Berlin or Paris or anywhere. Hopeful, with bright faces. But that failed, and now they know there is nothing for them here. They can't leave either. No one has money." Then he added, "We all know that Serbs are the new Nazis of Europe for having started the Bosnian war and that one day we will have to explain what happened here. That thought is daunting for a lot of good people."

His honesty filled me with sadness—for him and for the other "good people." Where Klara Mandić was happy to assign the Nazi stigma to Croats, he was incorporating it, appropriating it as his own. I remembered the tortured Germans I had met and wondered, as I listened to him speak, about the fate of the generations to come.

Bosnia

Although no one, these days, travels after dark in a car with Sarajevo licence plates that mark them as Muslims or friends of Muslims, there were so many delays in leaving Belgrade that it is night as we drive into the mountains of Bosnia. Drinka has arranged this lift on my behalf, and I am grateful, since the bus from Belgrade to Sarajevo is not a reliable option, I have been told. Sometimes it runs, sometimes it doesn't. My fellow passengers—a lawyer, a literature professor and the former manager of a large enterprise (they are all returning home to Sarajevo from Belgrade after attending the first inter-ethnic conference on war refugees in the former Yugoslavia)—have decided, as far is this is possible, to bypass presumed hostile territory. Our route is therefore a circuitous one—via Croatia, where we drive through the ghostly, deserted Krajina; across the Sava River on a dubious makeshift barge that carries our car and several others; then through western Bosnia, in order to miss the whole of Republika Srpska. This detour is intended to avoid encountering unfriendly posses, but the vehicle keeps breaking down and we are delayed interminably, frighteningly, on deserted unlit roads. Bosnians are armed, and killings and other inter-ethnic attacks are still frequent, in spite of the Dayton Accords. Vehicles have been stoned in recent weeks in many places. There are land mines.

The atmosphere in the car is strained: I have brought food for everyone, but during the entire nine-hour trip all but one are too tense to eat.

It is very dark and I don't have a map to indicate exactly where we are until the car headlights illuminate a wooden sign for the town of Tuzla, which was, like Sarajevo, a "special" city where Muslims, Croats and Serbs had lived together familiarly and in peace; then another sign for Mostar, where the beautiful, sixteenth-century Stari Most (Old Bridge) was deliberately bombed to pieces on November 9, 1993, the anniversary of Kristallnacht. I realize with a start that we are in southwestern Bosnia-Herzegovina, and we will have to double back to Sarajevo. Mostar, which used to be a popular tourist destination, was once populated by Muslims, Croats and Serbs, but the large Croat majority "cleansed" their former neighbours, and now half the population is gone—either dead or living somewhere else as refugees. I recently read that those who stayed here, or were resettled in the city as refugees from elsewhere, live in either the Croat or Muslim parts of the city and dare not step over the "border" that stretches across the bombed-out centre of town.

Our headlights sweep across a signpost for Sarajevo. We are climbing fast now. Snow is piled along the sides of the road and hill, and shadows loom in the dark. We drive through unlit mountain villages, past abandoned houses with roofs gone and windows smashed. "I don't know why there was so much fighting here," says Boro, the former business manager, somewhat forlornly. "Just neighbours killing neighbours."

Someone is flagging us down. A huge bonfire burns yellow-red at the roadside several metres away. Whoever is stopping us is also trying to stave off the freezing night.

My heart is pounding; we are all very still. But, relief—it is NATO Stabilization Force (SFOR) troops warning us that the bomb-damaged bridge ahead is washed out and closed.

We drive on in silence until we are on the ridge of a mountain overlooking the dark valley of Sarajevo.

Two scenes play across my mind. They are both from television footage about the war.

Scene One: In the hills above Sarajevo, the Serb warriors are roasting a pig on a spit and singing lustily, "Oh, Turkish daughter, our priests will soon baptize you. Oh, Sarajevo in the valley, the Serbs have encircled you. . . ." One of them plays the *gusle*, a traditional, one-stringed, bowed instrument. The haunting sounds it produces are distinctly Eastern—one might even say "Turkish."

"*We* own this country," Radovan Karadžić is saying to Edouard Limonov, the famous Russian poet who has come here of his own volition, as together they cast their eyes over the destroyed rooftops of Sarajevo. "The Turks defeated us in 1389 and some of the Serbs here converted to Islam. They're the successors to the Turks, but *we* own this country. The world must understand that we are not besieging Sarajevo, but reclaiming Serb territory."

Radovan is in an expansive mood, and as the red light on the BBC camera moves closer to his face, he confides a revealing little story. Twenty years ago he was writing premonitory poems about this very war in Sarajevo, he tells Limonov. Couldn't help it, the words just came out that way. "It was a prediction that sometimes frightens me," he explains with a shrug and a helpless smile.

The camera zooms into the streets below. A middle-aged woman is rushing across the road, clutching a plastic bag

There's a machine gun propped up on the site, with its barrel pointed towards the city. It's picnic-casual on the hill. No one pays any attention as Edouard Limonov approaches the gun and runs his hand along its surface with evident curiosity. He bends down from the waist and peers into the sights. Then pulls the trigger. *Rat-tat-tat-tat*, *rat-tat-tat-tat*, in quick succession. Limonov is thrilled. Smirking with boyish pleasure.

Scene Two: He is about twenty-three years old, with dark, prison-shorn hair clipped close to his skull. Hunched forward on a stool, head bent to his chest, he waits to be questioned. He does not raise his head when he replies, but rolls his eyes upward in their sockets and squints at the camera through hooded lids. His expression is lifeless, his voice flat.

"They taught us how to do it. They showed us how to hold a pig down by digging our knee into its back, then how to cut deep across its throat. That was for practice. Then we were ready."

One day he slaughtered six people, every one of whom he knew personally. On another day, he and two others—his father and his uncle—came across four children and two women hiding in a cellar. "The old woman was so scared, she gave us gold and German marks. We said, don't worry, but then we killed them anyway. Afterwards we found five litres of brandy in the house and drank it all. Then we threw the bodies in trucks."

His eyes roll down in their sockets. He is motionless, except to flick ashes from his cigarette.

"Did you do it from fear or because you liked it?"

"They said they would kill me if I said no."

"Did anyone refuse?"

"No."

"What is your future?"

"I want to die."

It is too late to call Ferida Duraković, my Sarajevo contact, so I accept an invitation to stay in Boro's extra room. The driver lets us off in front of a destroyed apartment building near the airport, where the heaviest fighting took place. Damaged, darkened, here and there a light where people have moved back or are occupying the abandoned homes of others. We are suddenly accosted by a guard with a gun. Boro fumbles for his pass.

The building is pitch-dark inside and the elevators don't work. Boro insists on carrying both our bags up ten flights of stairs, and he arrives at his door exhausted. His apartment was spared during the siege, but the windows shattered the day a bomb exploded in the living room of his neighbours just across the hall. Two years after the fragile peace of Dayton, his household water is still rationed. The bathroom is stacked with pots and brimming basins. His wife is in the United States, visiting their daughter and her husband; they escaped when it was still possible, with their parents' blessing. Boro says he misses his daughter, especially now that she has a child he has never seen. But she will not return; he wouldn't want her to.

In the early light of the next day he tells me his full name: Boro Pandurević. For twenty-five years, he worked for a successful import-export company, most recently as managing director. For the six years preceding the war he represented his firm in Lahore, Pakistan, then he returned, mistakenly, in September 1991. The information he received from the Yugoslav embassy in Pakistan was spotty, much too spotty.

He is Serb, but, like his extended family—a mix of Serbs, Croats and Muslims—he thinks of himself as Yugoslav. He had always lived peacefully in what was a predominantly Muslim area of the city, but when he returned in 1991 there was already violence in the streets—surprising violence, he says. By spring 1992, there were barricades at intersections and directives urging Serbs to escape the city. Boro and his wife chose to stay. "I had travelled and seen what refugees are reduced to," he says. "We decided we would stay here. If we had to, we would die where we were born."

He is a strong-looking man of about sixty with a straight back and a manner that suggests someone accustomed to taking charge. But the veneer of that remaining strength is wearing thin. He walks me to the window. We look out at a bleak wall pitted with shell holes and wires dangling through the frames of blown-out windows across the alley. "I decided that if there was no hope I would jump," he says flatly. "I thought of it many times. I still do."

For three months they lived in the basement shelter, along with the other inhabitants of the building. One person was delegated to run the sniper fire and get water from a nearby stream, another to reach the airport when food supplies arrived. Upstairs, their apartments were looted by marauding gangs.

Then, every day was a challenge to stay alive. But the present is worse, because he can see no future. He used to be relatively wealthy, with a monthly salary of more than 1,000 Deutschmarks; but when his savings evaporated from the bank he was reduced to 30 DM a month. With this, he helps support nine people: his elderly mother and her sister; one of his own sisters, who escaped to Belgrade with her two children and cannot come back because the municipality of Sarajevo is refusing to authorize the return of Serbs to their apartments, which are now being lived in by Muslim refugees from elsewhere in Bosnia; his brother-in-law, who is still in Sarajevo and cannot survive on his income; another sister, who has been in a refugee camp for four years; plus his wife and himself. He has a temporary job with an international human rights agency, but his contract is coming to an end and he has no prospects, except for consulting work, which he is trying to create from home in his free time. "There is an appearance of normality in Sarajevo now, but it is an illusion," he tells me. "People are working for the international community, but their jobs will come to an end like mine and then there will be nothing."

"Do you understand how it happened that apparently normal people were able to commit atrocities?" I ask him.

He pauses a long time, then answers slowly. "Power-seeking people with no scruples saw an opportunity to seize control. Children in the streets were given guns and knives and taught to kill. After a while, if a Muslim wanted to kill a Serb, or a Serb wanted to kill a Muslim, no one cared. So it came about that people of other ethnicities were not considered human, even when they had once been personal friends."

Serbs had a mythologized history powerful enough to justify war, but the inhabitants of Sarajevo had their own unifying myths that the fighting had called into question, and these two "histories" could not have been more different. While Serbs dreamed (with interludes, including the Tito years) of territorial repatriation and revenge against the evil Turks, the myths of Sarajevo reflected the Yugoslav ideology of Brotherhood and Unity. Sarajevans had profoundly assimilated the proclamations of Tito; there was hardly a family in the city that did not include more than one so-called ethnicity.

Andras Riedlmayer of Harvard University, a specialist in the art and culture of Bosnia and co-founder of the Bosnia Action Coalition, which has been working to rebuild the destroyed cultural heritage of the region, told me about one of Sarajevo's favourite parables: the movie *Valter*, which was made during the Tito era. The film features an anti-Nazi resistance hero, who is based in Sarajevo. The Germans try vainly to pierce the mystery of his identity, but they never succeed, for Valter turns out to be every Sarajevan. During the siege of the city in 1992–95, the myth of "Valter" made a new appearance, as people identified the drama of the resistance film with current realities.

But Sarajevo's tradition of multiculturalism stretched far beyond the twentieth century. The Ottoman Turks had tolerated religious pluralism in return for loyalty and taxes, and for hundreds of years, Serb

Orthodox and Croat Roman Catholic churches had cohabited next to mosques and synagogues, for the Jews, too, were welcomed in Sarajevo after their expulsion from Spain in 1492. Sarajevo under the Ottomans seemed to me to have been remarkably like medieval Córdoba under the rule of the Arab caliphs before the Catholic Church successfully imposed religious homogeneity or "purity"—a development that led to the eventual banishment of non-Catholics from the country and an Inquisition to examine the practices of converts to the faith. Like the Córdobans of old, multi-ethnic Sarajevans took immense pride in their multicultured city.

But Sarajevo happened to be located in the Balkans, with all the complexity encompassed by that geography, and there was, in addition to the good times, a history of tension that may have been forgotten by its passionate "Yugoslav" citizens. Although medieval Sarajevans had maintained a common language and their Slav identity after the Ottoman occupation, high-level Bosnian Muslims grew powerful under the feudal-militaristic regime, while the poor in the surrounding hills—Christian peasants, but some Muslims, as well—worked the landed estates. Serb Christians were never "slaves" of the Ottomans, as Serb propaganda would have it, but they were not preferred, either: the Ottomans favoured the converted without persecuting those who chose to keep the faith. So it is entirely possible that the hatred of Serbs for "Turks" (insofar as such hatred actually existed before the appearance of nationalist mythmakers in the nineteenth century) may have been based as much on centuries of economic resentment as on religion and doctored legends about Prince Lazar.

After the Austrians arrived in 1878, bringing Ottoman rule to an end, the new nationalism grew stronger. Thirty-six years later, the event with the most devastating implications for the twentieth century would take place in Sarajevo: the murder of Archduke Franz Ferdinand, heir to the Austrian emperor Franz Joseph, on June 29, 1914. The assassin was Gavrilo Princip, a member of a Bosnian Serb nationalist movement, and the outcome was the First World War. Princip's ideological progeny could be found in prominent Serb circles until they were suppressed by Tito at the end of the Second World War, but like Pandora's Furies, they had merely been pushed out of sight.

All this suggested that when Sarajevans who survived the siege of the 1990s longed for the easy co-existence they said had always characterized their city, they might have been adding a comforting dollop of selectivity to the historical mix; the fact that their once-lovely capital is and always was located in the tinderbox of the Balkans had meant invasion, occupation, partition and nationalist tensions. Yugoslav Brotherhood and Unity was a recent invention, albeit with authentic echos, but in this part of the world no one idea could hope to encompass the tangled skein of the whole.

The drive into the centre of Sarajevo is riveting. Half-destroyed buildings line both sides of the road, and plastic sheeting stretches across the broken windows of individual apartments. My taxi driver's face is hideously burned and grafted.

The downtown streets are Sunday quiet, but every building is pockmarked with dozens to hundreds of shell holes. I stop to look in the window of a bookstore. The titles seem to speak of new realities: the Koran, *The Islamic Declaration*, by Alija Izetbegović, *The Genocide of the Muslims*, *The Croatian Genocide of Bosnia* and a nostalgic picture book about beautiful Sarajevo.

The graffiti on the walls of buildings also express new truths—like the blunt, black-lettered English-language scribble "NO FUTURE" and the one-word question "WHY?" The same three letters someone had scrawled on the Berlin Wall. Still, humour has not entirely died. A fierce Serb nationalist has scratched "THIS IS SERBIA" on the post office wall, to which a local wit replied, "IT'S THE POST OFFICE, YOU IDIOT."

The downtown Park Café contributes to an illusion of normality. Rows of cream cakes sit under glass, and two whirring espresso machines suffuse the room with the rich aroma of Bosnian coffee. There are recessed pot lights, mirrors and music. The atmosphere seems positively joyous.

A group of teenage girls giggles happily, showing one another pictures in the way of adolescents everywhere, but coffee drinkers over the age of twenty look unlike café patrons in other places. Most are single men with faces grey with fatigue. They sit alone, smoking. The loneliness of the man opposite me is palpable. He has a soft face and deep circles under his eyes. He may be thirty or fifty—it is impossible to tell. His hands lie limp in his lap, and his shoulders slouch forward as he looks blankly out the window at a passing cavalcade of white trucks with the logo of the United Nations. Is he one among the thousands of Muslim refugees who have come to Sarajevo because they are unable to return to their "ethnically cleansed" communities? Is he a Sarajevan who survived the siege and now lives with dreadful uncertainty? Has he lost members of his family? The music and lights of the Park Café seem to mock his numbing sorrow.

The poet Ferida Duraković has arranged my meetings in the city, but first we walk. We pass the intersection called Sniper's Alley, where she and others crept across the street under the supposed protection of a UN armoured personnel carrier, while the international press huddled together behind a corner building, cameras ready. "They were waiting for me to get killed," she says casually, without any apparent bitterness. On to the central marketplace, where sixty-eight people were massacred in February 1994 when a massive shell exploded in their midst. This internationally televised event aroused so much indignation around the world that reluctant nations were finally embarrassed into negotiating the first well-monitored ceasefire of the siege. We climb a hill to a main locus of the killing: the Serb-held residential quarter of Grbavica. Here are grand old houses in the Austro-Hungarian style with curved balconies now twisted, burned and deserted. There are crushed cars and the rusted frames of building foundations, sandbags still piled high in what used to be first-floor windows and an old Jewish cemetery that cannot be visited because it is seeded with land mines.

Sarajevans tread daily on an underground city of the dead. Next to the Olympic Stadium (a physical reminder of happier days), there are hundreds, perhaps thousands, of Muslim headstones. We watch a woman and her three children lay flowers on not one but two adjacent graves. The dead—they number 10,615—have been buried in parks and behind houses. Hardly an open space that has not been appropriated to accommodate them.

That afternoon I visit the celebrated Turkish marketplace, where mosques with graceful minarets and low-slung wooden shops with red-tile roofs line narrow walkways. An ancient water fountain is still in use, coffee houses beckon and the *tap-tap* of coppersmiths hammering out the traditional, long-spouted coffee pots and tiny cups rings though the lanes like the distant clamour of tiny cymbals. As dusk falls, hundreds of lights illuminate the minarets like small stars. A muezzin circling the top of a steeple high above the darkening street calls out his haunting summons, and when he has finished, another man perched in a neighbouring minaret takes up the chant, his lean body silhouetted in the shadowy evening light. Time stands still in this ancient place; the memory of war dissolves.

A few blocks away, higher once-sturdy buildings display their wounds and bullet holes, but even here it is possible to experience the grace of the famed city. The ruined Jewish cultural centre sits close to the Croat Roman Catholic cathedral, which is close to the Serb Orthodox church, which is, in turn, close to the mosques. East and West had met and married here, lived together not without quarrels but like an old household, accommodating one another and never separating. The beauty of curved balconies, the wall sculptures decorating a destroyed facade that now stand alone in the bombed shell of a once-elegant house, the ancient stone steps that lead mysteriously to another street level—all these offer a fleeting glimpse of what used to be, the way an aged, ravaged face will occasionally reveal a passing hint of remembered beauty.

Ferida is thirty-nine, lithe and dark-haired, and she speaks excellent English at a hurried pace. Nominally a Muslim (although she says she never attends a mosque and thinks of herself as a secular Yugoslav), she is the only Sarajevan I have met whose face is not chalk grey with depression.

When war broke out in spring 1992, she was living with her parents and her grandmother. No one in the family had ever noticed that their house straddled some kind of "border" between Muslims and Serbs. Neighbours had been . . . well, neighbours. When the shelling started in April—paramilitaries firing from one "side" of the street to the other—Ferida's senile grandmother returned abruptly to her senses and began to talk obsessively about the two world wars she had lived through. The old woman clung to Ferida: "Will it happen again?" she asked her constantly. Ferida took charge of the family. One night, during a lull in the shelling, the four of them crept away to her brother and sister, who resided in the centre of the city.

They all lived on the ninth floor of a high-rise apartment without drinking water and with almost no food. Again, Ferida designated herself the family anchor. "I remember all this as though on a movie screen, so I can make it as remote as possible," she tells me. "It was strange and horrible, and sometimes even funny. We had almost no money, so I tried to recover all my debts from my friends, and sometimes I was even successful! I also hired myself out to foreign journalists. I was their fixer, their guide, their interpreter and they paid me and introduced me to other foreigners who had money. Black-market food was impossibly expensive—believe me, there were lots of crooks getting rich. There still are. You can see them driving around here in their BMWs. A kilo of sugar was 70 German marks, the same amount of salt cost 20 marks and coffee was 120 marks. So we ate macaroni and some beans. I walked for two hours to get five litres of water, and of course I couldn't go there in a straight line. A ridiculous illusion, I know, but I had my lucky routes where I felt I would be safe.

"I often thought I was in the middle of a postmodern literary cataclysm. For example, the international community sent rat poison, and suddenly the streets were filled with dead rats. It was futuristic, surrealistic, those sickening piles of rats and the city in ruins and the shelling all around and the expectation that one might die at any moment. It was so crazy that I actually found myself laughing out loud."

Ferida's mother had lived through the Second World War, but in her own house, where she could grow food in the garden. Since then, she always had a garden. During the Sarajevo siege, she would disappear every few days without a word to anyone and make her way through the dangerous streets to the family home, then return to the apartment, clutching a handful of vegetables. Her father's suffering was of a different sort. He had fought with the Partisans, and afterwards he had been a member of the Yugoslav militia. That involved arresting and prosecuting people—mostly nationalists who had fought against the Communists. Her father had never talked much about this, but now he spoke of nothing else. "He felt a terrible sense of betrayal," says Ferida. "He couldn't believe that the Yugoslav People's Army had taken the side of Serbs and was killing Muslims. He was sure the men doing the shooting and the shelling *must* all be paramilitaries and not regulars. He was also terrified that the sons of people he had brought to trial wanted revenge and were coming after him. No one was hunting him—he was a old man—but his fear was dreadful."

An appalling sense of betrayal has corroded the hearts of the people who had placed their faith in Tito's multicultural values; and among them are the members of Circle 99, a group of authors, journalists and academics. The heartbroken members of Circle 99 hold conferences and draft earnest statements, and now they are welcoming like-minded friends from Belgrade. Simply to meet the Belgradians is reassuring, a sign that ethnic hatred has not infected friendships. Ferida takes me to their office, a joint space that is shared with PEN (the Circle 99 writers are members of both organizations). It is a large room on an upstairs floor of a bullet-marked building, with a desk, a couch and a few chairs. The Belgradians have just arrived, and there is much hugging and laughter. I recognize some of them; they came to the hotel in Belgrade to say goodbye to the men I travelled with to Sarajevo; they had all been at the same inter-ethnic conference on war refugees. Now I am an "old friend"—entitled to hug, which I do. Someone shows me their English-language journal called *99: A Review of Free Thought*. It is the spring 1997 issue—titled "Sarajevo?"—and it contains sober reflections on the politics of the war and a declaration "for a free and unified Sarajevo." Another article describes the "special symbol of the city—the presence . . . of four religions and their [contiguous] places of worship." Still another describes the "urbicide" of Sarajevo and "the killing of its soul." There are several "In Memoriam" pages naming the dead, and many poems, poorly translated, but haunting. Like these lines by Josip Osti:

In that city, my first love is living and dying
In the city that does not resemble itself anymore.
Where the shooting never stops
In the street that has lost its name . . .
In the flat with neither doors nor windows
Sitting by a dead, cold stove . . .
She cares not
whether it is night or day . . .
In that city my first love is living and dying.
My mother, whose tragic fate,
like the fate of my native city
Is indelibly tattooed on my heart.

With ethnically based "entities" in place across Bosnia following the terms of the Dayton Accords, and millions of refugees unable, or afraid, to go home, the easy cohabitation of the past seemed to be gone forever, but some people were trying to reconstruct civil society in practical ways. One of the most promising was the Soros Media Center, supported by the U.S. financier and philanthropist George Soros's Open Society Institute, which had been training journalists since 1995. It would not be easy to reform the old sycophantic practices: journalism had long been an arm of government, and journalists either censored themselves or were punished by laws against "hostile propaganda," meaning anything the regime judged inappropriate. Such habits had not ended with the death of Tito, for if one thing had emerged with utter clarity, it was the poisonous, propaganda-inspired role the media across ex-Yugoslav had played in the buildup to war.

Ferida and I visit the media centre in Oslobodjenje (Liberation) Square, beside the Serb Orthodox church. Rows of television monitors blink patterns of light, and there are several simulated studios, with banks of controls. The goal of the program, says Boro Kontić, the thin, harried-looking director, is to develop standards of journalism that will serve "as a cornerstone of democracy." "When we started, our most serious problem was the lack of experienced journalists: almost 60 per cent were between fifteen and twenty-five years old, because so many of the others had left the country as refugees. In some towns in Bosnia and Herzegovina, almost 90 per cent of the journalists were new to the profession; they had only started working with the beginning of the war."

In 1996, the BBC School of Journalism joined in, providing courses for radio and television journalists, and the Soros Media Center began inviting students from all over Bosnia and Herzegovina, including the Serb Republic, and some from Serbia proper, to train in their programs. Other workshops were directed by Agence France Presse and Press Now, Amsterdam. Guest speakers included Susan Sontag and Noel Malcolm, the author of *A Short History of Bosnia*. That young journalists from different ethnicities were coming together to study ethics, critical objectivity and the mandatory use of more than one source for a news story was encouraging—if the money for the program lasted. A professional press corps could not prevent powerful demagogues from abusing both past and present to manipulate public opinion, but properly trained journalists could expose the process and establish bunkers against propaganda.

If the Soros Media Center was good news, the bad news was that serious mental illness was debilitating the residents of the city. Ferida takes me to meet Dr. Ismet Cerić, the head of psychiatry at the Sarajevo Hospital, a building that sits on a small hill, just across the road from the mass graveyard beside the Olympic Stadium. Dr. Cerić appears to be a feeling man; he also laughs a lot, using his natural humour, I guess, as a consolation to himself, and probably to others. He tells me that suicides rates are climbing now, two years after the end of the fighting. "You can see many pathologically disturbed people on the streets, lots of full-blown psychosis and depression. Almost everyone is suffering from stress-related disorders, including the professionals, including myself," he says. "That is what makes this situation so unusual. People have shattered identities. They think things ought to be as they were before the war, but nothing can ever be the same. It is hard to explain what happened to people's minds during this trauma when there was no real or emotional protection for an exceptionally long period of time." He tells me he used to be vastly overweight, but he lost fifty or sixty pounds from stress.

Dr. Cerić and his colleagues consulted internationally and came to the conclusion that there will be psychological trauma in the Sarajevan population for generations to come. "Like the children and grandchildren of the people who survived the Holocaust," he says.

Suicide on people's minds. I had asked Boro Pandurević how this had come to happen among friends and neighbours. Knowing that Dr. Cerić had been a colleague of Dr. Radovan Karadžić—psychiatrist, as well as poet—for seventeen years, I ask him as well.

"Was Radovan Karadžić crazy?"

"Unfortunately not. He was an ordinary family man and a very ordinary psychiatrist, certainly not brilliant. And, I may add, a terrible poet."

"One can sometimes recognize tendencies to manipulate others."

"There was nothing. Often you can see the development of a person with problems from their troubled childhood onward. But a so-called normal person can surprise you at any time."

"So he didn't fit any psychiatric personality type?"

"No. He was completely ordinary. You know, everyone smiled when Hitler began with just a few colleagues, and it was the same with Radovan. Before all this, he was absolutely without political ambition. After the end of communism, he joined the environmental movement because he hated political parties. That's what he told me. But he changed his mind after a few months and became leader of the Bosnian Serbs. Even though he didn't like the Serbs."

"Pardon? He didn't like the Serbs?"

"Not at all. He often told me Serbs were untrustworthy, primitive peasants. Most of his friends were Muslims."

"So he engaged in groupthink even then?"

"Yes. This is the big problem."

In the middle of the siege, Ferida had found herself taking stock of her life in a stark, new way. It was 1995. She was thirty-six and single. Even if she survived, she thought to herself, it was impossible to imagine a future. She, too, considered suicide fleetingly. Then she stopped and asked herself the only question that mattered: What do I want from life, why should I survive? The answer, when it came, surprised even her. She wanted a child.

"To want a child was to choose life, to choose survival," she tells me one day, in a soft voice, as we sit together in a small café.

A friend and sometime lover agreed to be the father, and their daughter, Farah, was born in 1996. "She is everything to me," says Ferida. "I have discovered that I am happy to be alive."

A lump of emotion rises in my throat. I raise my coffee cup in a tribute to her courage. "*L'chaim*," I say. "To life."

On this, my last day in Sarajevo, I hire a young writer with a car to take me to a smaller place where, he says, ethnic reintegration looks possible. I am assured that the "cleansed," now-Croat town of Vitez, an hour or so northwest of Sarajevo, is safe.

The highway is virtually empty—no cars, no people, just burned-out houses along the roadside. Damir tells me he was on the Sarajevo front line for two years opposite Serbs who had been his school friends and neighbours. He survived emotionally by distancing himself from reality, by entering into his observer-writer self and pretending he was watching a play. But his war is not yet over: "It can only truly end when it ends in our heads. When we can face each other again. That has not happened."

We stop at the entrance to what used to be the Muslim village of Ahmići, on the outskirts of Vitez. On April 16, 1993, Croats from Vitez shot, burned or otherwise butchered 120 men women and children here in one of the most grisly massacres of the war. Every building was demolished, including two mosques. We turn off the main road and drive in. "No, don't get out!" he warns. "Land mines."

There is one rudimentary street lined with the shells of several destroyed houses, but the most disturbing sight is the wreckage of a smashed mosque: its beautiful, multicoloured minaret has been lopped off and is lying across the road. I take a few pictures through the car window and we turn around to leave. This means pulling onto the shoulder. What is he doing? Are there not mines? Holding my breath, staring transfixedly at the mud, I barely notice the car coming towards us, or that the driver has waved at Damir to stop. The man rolls down his window. He looks like a thug.

"Sarajevo *Turks*! We should kill you!" I do not need to know the language to understand what he is saying. In my confusion I wonder how he knows where we are from. Now I remember—the car licence plates.

"Who is *she!*" He jabs his index finger in my direction.

"A writer from Canada. She wanted to see this place."

He is staring at me with a look of hatred. I take out my passport and hold it up. He reaches forward, I pull back.

"She'll give you her business card," says Damir quickly, translating for me.

"Who sent you here? Alija [Izetbegović, then Bosniak president of Bosnia-Herzegovina]?" asks the man. He pokes at the air again. "Did she take pictures?"

"No," lies Damir.

Another car has pulled up behind us, licence plates from Vitez. The thug looks thoughtful.

"Get out of here, shits! If I see you again, I'll kill you!"

I had wanted to get a sense of what things were like outside Sarajevo two years after "peace" and I have done so, more directly than I might have intended. How ironic. At the end of my voyage into dismembered Yugoslavia, I am hearing again about "Turks"—except that safe distance has collapsed and I am now one of "them." *Turk* is a code word calculated to make the tribal blood rise. "Turks" are the abstract, imagined enemy, the historical "other," a confabulated, mythologized creation of evil nurtured over dark centuries, keeping passions alive. The past—bloated, allegorized and unrecognizable—honed into a weapon of war.

Is There Justice?

8

New Genocide, New Trials

The Legacy of Nuremberg

There will be justice when the living know the suffering of the dead.

– *The Three Lives of Lucie Cabrol*

THANKS TO the British regiment of the UN Protection Force (UNPROFOR), which entered Ahmići on April 22, 1993, to check on rumours of catastrophe, the massacre in the tiny village where 356 Bosniaks and 87 Croats once lived together was exceptionally well documented. The tape made by the BBC war correspondent Martin Bell displayed the charred bodies of an adult and a child on the stairs of a burned house and the carbonized remains of four women and children who had tried to hide in the basement. Every Bosniak home was razed to the ground, but not one Croat house was harmed and there were no Croat deaths.

Thirteen months have passed since I was threatened in the destroyed village, and I have come to Holland to hear what had actually happened there. I am in The Hague, to be precise, a dour and proper city with a history of worthy internationalism since the seventeenth century, when it became a centre of diplomacy and a refuge for persecuted minorities such as French Protestants and Portuguese Jews. The International Court of Justice is located here and so is the United Nations International

Criminal Tribunal for the Former Yugoslavia (ICTY), where atrocities from the Bosnian war are being investigated by panels of robed judges in a solemn process designed to add justice to diplomacy.

The physical appearance of the tribunal evokes little of the idealism and optimism embodied in such an undertaking. The exterior is sterile and functional, the security guards look bored, a pale yellow reception hall features dirt smudges over much of its wall surface and a nylon palm tree in a corner stands forlorn and self-conscious in this chilly northern clime.

Yet upstairs in Courtroom Three, a dramatic story is unfolding.

I seat myself behind the wall-to-wall pane of bulletproof glass that separates the spectators from the participants. There are just four of us on this side of the barrier, in a room built to accommodate at least one hundred. Two women smile and wave at the defendants (who turn out to be their husbands); the other visitor is a young law student from England. A fair trial in the British-Continental tradition is a tedious process that bogs down in the detail of evidence, and barring news of a sensation in the offing, the press will show up only at the beginning and the end.

The case is "Kupreškić and Others." Six men accused of crimes against humanity and violations of the laws of war, accused of persecuting the inhabitants of Ahmići on ethnic or religious grounds and "cleansing" them from the area. They sit at tables, under the watchful eyes of their guards: two brothers, Zoran and Mirjan Kupreškić; their cousin Vlatko Kupreškić; and their friends Drago Josipović, Dragan Papić and Vladimir Šantić. They range in age from thirty-one to forty-four, and most of them lived or worked in Ahmići. They were friendly with the people they are accused of killing; Vlatko Kupreškić drank coffee at the home of a Muslim neighbour the night before the attack. All six have pleaded not guilty to a total of thirty-eight charges.

I anxiously study their faces, looking for the man who threatened to kill me on the half-paved road just past the toppled minaret of the mosque. I eliminate five of them; the other does look familiar, but were I a witness on the stand, I think I could only guess. All six have gaunt, cell-greyed faces; they are dressed in suits, and they have brushed their hair neatly for the occasion. It occurs to me that the features of hatred look different when composed.

Earlier in this trial, several of the survivors testified. The first was Sakib Ahmić, discovered by a member of the UN Commission on Human Rights in the nearby city of Zenica, where he was in hospital recovering from burns. He told the court that Zoran and Mirjan Kupreškić entered his house on the morning of April 16 and killed his son, his daughter-in-law and their two children, the youngest of whom was three months old.

The next witness that day was Abdul Ahmić. Everyone in his family—father, mother and three young sisters—had been murdered. Abdul himself was "executed" with a shot to the head, but he survived because the bullet entered his left cheek and miraculously exited from the right, without harming bones or vital organs.

A third witness, Esad Rizvanović, had sought refuge in Ahmići in the summer of 1992, after having been "cleansed" by the Serbs in Prijedor. He identified the first shots on April 16 as emanating from the part of the village where the Kupreškićs lived.

Finally, a group of widows, sisters and daughters arrived in Courtroom Three. They said they were wakened early in the morning of April 16 by powerful explosions. Their Croat neighbours broke into their homes and forced them out, then set their houses on fire and killed their husbands and sons. One woman told the court she had pleaded with two Croat neighbours to spare her fourteen-year-old son. "Not Amir, not Amir!" she begged them. But they killed Amir and her husband and her father before her eyes. Then they threw pails of a liquid they were carrying on the furniture and set off explosives. A daughter told how her mother had died trying to save her: they were running from the village, running past the house of the Kupreškićs. The daughter fell, wounded, and when her mother, who was ahead of her, turned back to help, she was picked off by a sniper bullet.

"We were good neighbours. . . . We had a good life," said one of the women before she stepped down from the witness stand. "But they betrayed us."

Payam Akhavan, the member of the UN Commission on Human Rights who discovered Sakib Ahmić, returned to the stand to testify that he had questioned the political and military leaders of the Bosnian Croats in the region of the Lašva Valley, Dario Kordić, Tihomir Blaškić and Mario Čerkez, all of whom were later arrested and sent to The Hague for trial. Kordić's explanation for the Ahmići massacre, Akhavan reported, was that the Muslims had slaughtered their own people "in order to gain international sympathy."

A publicity stunt, in other words. This, I remembered, was the same explanation the Serbs had put out in February 1994 after the shelling of the central marketplace in Sarajevo in which sixty-eight people were killed and two hundred were wounded.

Dario Kordić was honoured for his actions by the Croatian president, Franjo Tudjman. He received:

- The Order of Prince Branimir with Neckband, for "particular merits in advancing the international position and prestige of the Republic of Croatia and its relations with other countries"
- The Order of Nikola Šubić Zrinski "for a heroic deed in the war"
- The Order of Petar Zrinski and Fra Krsto Frankopan with Silver Braid, "for contributions to the maintenance and development of the Croatian state-forming idea, and the establishment and betterment of the sovereign state of Croatia"

Blaškić was similarly rewarded. He was promoted to the rank of general in 1995 *after* his indictment by the International Criminal Tribunal.

I watch from behind my bulletproof screen as a witness for the defence is being cross-examined. The prosecutor is trying to prove that the three Kupreškićs were active members of the Croatian Defence Council (HVO) on April 16, 1993, the day of the massacre. The witness, a former HVO commander in the nearby town of Vitez, agrees from the documentation being held up before him that they were. A defence lawyer takes over. She wants to establish that there was a military battle of equals going on in the entire Vitez region of the Lašva Valley and that Bosniaks were attacking Croats just as Croats were attacking Bosniaks. This would imply that what happened at Ahmići was part of an ongoing armed war, not the slaughter of helpless civilians. She asks the witness about a bomb that fell on Croat children in a Vitez playground. That was the most terrible sight I have ever seen, replies the witness—body parts hanging from trees. It was so awful that the TV stations would not accept the pictures for broadcast. The defence lawyer probes the pre-war relationships among the "ethnicities" in the area. Did the witness associate with his Muslim neighbours before the outbreak of hostilities? Oh yes, and afterwards, too, he replies with a hopeful smile. During the events under question, he and his wife shielded a Bosniak family from Vitez by hiding their children "in the cupboard under the bed." "I do not wish to boast but I also supplied flour and oil and sugar and medicine and cigarettes to the Muslim detainees who were being held in the town cinema," he adds. "There were hundreds of examples of Croats doing the same. We were just human beings helping other human beings under very difficult circumstances."

Some of the accused men slouch at their tables in frustration or in real or affected boredom; another is writing voluminous notes. I watch them with close curiosity. I think about the ravished village, the minaret lying on the ground, the land mines still seeded along the roadside, the ghostly destroyed homes. Neighbour set upon neighbour: the "good life" of Tito's multi-ethnic Yugoslavia gone forever.

How does this happen? It is the question that has been running through my mind throughout. I think about Boro Pandurević's reply, when I asked him, and that of Dr. Ismet Cerić. They had both said more or less the same thing: that when an identifiable group is demonized, and the humanity of the individuals within it is purposely erased, anything can happen—without conscience or qualms.

I am beginning to feel crushed by the barrage of words spoken here: anxious words, words pronounced in a strong or faltering voice, words hoping to be heard outside these walls. This is the international community, as represented by this court, attempting to confront the consequences of what it had allowed to happen by not intervening in the Bosnian war in time, trying to pull from the jumble of disparate remembrances a judgment that may help reconcile the parties. Black-robed lawyers and judges doing their job. Doing what they can.

But it is after the fact and therefore second-best. Amir, just fourteen, is dead, and so are all the others: the baby of three months, the mother who turned back to save her daughter and the children in the Vitez playground. The war of genocidal "ethnic cleansing" could have been stopped before they were killed. The proceedings of this court are depressing—but they are, at least, an attack on the scourge of impunity.[1]

The ICTY was created on May 25, 1993—just one month after the atrocities at Ahmići, as it happens. It was born from Resolution 827 of the UN Security Council, and based on Chapter VII of the UN Charter, the section that empowers the United Nations to order military force, create agencies relating to the maintenance of international peace and security and override national sovereignty if necessary. The ICTY was the first judiciary to be created by the United Nations (the Nuremberg and Tokyo tribunals were the products of a victorious wartime coalition). It was to be a temporary institution, mandated to prosecute four types of offences committed in the former Yugoslavia since 1991, offences that had been on the international humanitarian law books for half a century but largely ignored. These were crimes against humanity, including genocide, the most serious perversion of civilization ever defined by legal code; violations of the laws or customs of war; and so-called grave breaches of the four Geneva Conventions of 1949.

Following the thinking of the jurist Raphael Lemkin, genocide was defined in 1948 as "acts committed with the intent to destroy, in whole or in part, a national, ethnic, racial or religious group," while other crimes against humanity concerned offences such as murder, enslavement, deportation, rape and torture committed during armed conflict and directed against a civilian population. The next category—violations of the laws of war and the Geneva Conventions—included the wanton destruction of cities, towns or villages, or any devastation not justified by military necessity, and wilful damage done to institutions dedicated to religion and education, the arts and sciences, historic monuments and works of art. Most of these laws came into being after the Second World War and the Holocaust, which was the most far-reaching assault on a helpless civilian population the world had known, but they had lain dormant during the long decades of the Cold War when no country on either side of the Iron Curtain was willing, or able, to alienate its block leadership.

In the debates leading up to the creation of international tribunals for the former Yugoslavia, then Rwanda, the African nation where ethnic hatred had inspired a ninety-day slaughter of mind-numbing proportions in 1994 and where few disputed the occurrence of genocide, the phrase "the lessons of Nuremberg" was heard as often as "the lessons of the Holocaust." Although such "lessons" were the backbone of Holocaust studies courses offered in a few countries, primarily Germany, the United States and Canada, they had been infrequently heeded. Pol Pot had carried out a genocidal massacre of 1.7 million Cambodians in the 1970s, almost 20 per cent of the population; more than 50 million "enemies of the people" had been dispatched in the former Soviet Union between 1918 and 1958; ethnic Kurds had been massacred; the world had knowingly ignored an open call-to-genocide broadcast over Rwandan air waves; and no country had come to the aid of the Muslim minority in Bosnia before thousands were annihilated, mostly by Serbs. Not until 1999, when a similar pattern of Serb atrocities was resumed in Kosovo, this time against Muslim Albanians, did the member countries of NATO choose to intervene. Perhaps because the debate over the abandonment of Europe's Jews during the Second World War was growing louder by the day, there was for the very first time an attempt to rescue a persecuted minority within the boundaries of a presumably sovereign state.

But this is to jump ahead too far in what became a deeply divisive debate over the limits of sovereignty at the end of the twentieth century. At the beginning of the process that led to the decision to confront impunity by creating the ICTY in 1993 was the Allied International Military Tribunal at Nuremberg and the seminal trials of Nazi leaders. Nuremberg had changed the world.

I spent many weeks reading about the Nuremberg Tribunal before I left for The Hague, and the subject felt close and personal—because "Nuremberg" has been on my mind since the beginning of my quest into the how, and the why, of racism, and the way we construct historical memory, as well as the role of courtrooms and judicial proceedings in helping to reconcile the past. When I was very young, "Nuremberg" consumed my thoughts, as I struggled to overcome the trauma of my visit to Natzweiler-Struthof. The film *Judgment at Nuremberg* was playing in the movie houses of Paris; I went to see it repeatedly, only to leave in the middle, when it overwhelmed me. More recently, when I was in Nuremberg to attend the conference on the Holocaust and the opening of the exhibition by Adolf Frankl, I visited the courtroom where the trials took place. It was a strange experience, because the pictures from the trials—the notorious defendants seated in two rows behind their defence lawyers, and the prosecutors and the judges representing the victorious nations—are now so familiar that to step inside the courtroom, so pregnant with meaning for both Germans and their former enemies, is to understand that one has inadvertently stumbled into an intimately apprehended place. A guard unlocked the door for me. Inside, the room was silent, still and haunted by ghosts, like the church where Martin Luther King Jr. once preached in Montgomery, Alabama. My companion that day was Dirk Kuhl, whose father, an SS camp commandant, had been hanged as a war criminal. He belonged to that generation of sons and daughters of Nazis whose innocent lives had been blighted by their parents' crimes. Like Niklas Frank and Martin Bormann Jr., he had spent his entire adult life trying to atone. Dirk was also in Nuremberg to attend the conference on the Holocaust, and he, too, was taken aback by the "familiarity" of the famous courtroom, which he had never seen before. He told me that in his mind, what took place here was Act One: the beginning of the attempt to penetrate the core of Nazism in the immediate aftermath of the war.

But the Nuremberg trials almost did not happen. When rumoured reports of atrocities first filtered through in 1942, the initial desire of both the British and the Americans was crass retribution—the summary execution of the leading Nazis—while the French and the Soviets preferred formal trials. (Stalin had already set a pattern of political show trials in motion and may have planned to pursue this with the Nazis.) Eventually, the Americans and the British thought revenge killings might not look well in the history books and began to lobby for Western-style procedures of courtroom justice as a better option. Robert H. Jackson, the future chief prosecutor for the tribunal, argued that "to free [the prisoners] without a trial would mock the dead and make cynics of the living."[2] The Allies, in other words, ought not to follow the example of Hitler in denying the protection of the law to their enemies.

Justice Jackson expressed this notion forcefully in his opening address to the Nuremberg Tribunal on November 20, 1945. "That four great nations flushed with victory and stung with injury stay the hand of vengeance and voluntarily submit their captive enemies to the judgment of the law is one of the most significant tributes that Power has ever paid to reason," he said.[3]

Three months before, on August 8, 1945, representatives of France, Britain, the Soviet Union and the United States had met to sign the London Agreement, which defined the principles that were to govern the trials of the major Nazi war criminals. It was a moment of sober reckoning and rejoicing—and (in retrospect) great irony: only two days before, the United States had dropped the world's first atomic bomb on Hiroshima and on August 9 it would drop another one on Nagasaki. As for the Soviets, Joseph Stalin had long been disposing of real and imagined enemies by the millions in the camps of the gulag and through the destruction of the peasant class in Ukraine from 1930 to 1937, during which ten million men, women and children were starved to death. So

Nuremberg was indeed victors' justice, as later charged. That, however, did not make its accomplishments unjust.[4]

Among the Allies, there was a sense of unbridled optimism when the Nuremberg trials opened on November 20, 1945.[5] Hitler was dead, but most of the highest-ranking members of his entourage were in the prisoners' dock, including Hermann Goering and Hans Frank. Justice Jackson's opening address, in which he expressed a post-Enlightenment yearning for reason and justice as the appropriate redressers of war crimes, articulated the mood of liberal hope. "The wrongs which we seek to condemn have been so calculated, so malignant, and so devastating that civilization cannot tolerate their being ignored," he said. "The real complaining party at [the] bar is Civilization. In all our countries it is still a struggling and imperfect thing. . . . Civilization asks whether the law is so laggard as to be utterly helpless to deal with crimes of this magnitude by criminals of this magnitude. It does not expect that you [the tribunal] can make war impossible. It does expect that your juridical action will put the forms of international law, its precepts, its prohibitions and, most of all, its sanctions, on the side of peace."[6]

Of the original twenty-two defendants,[7] twelve were eventually sentenced to death by hanging, seven were sentenced to various terms in prison, while three were freed. (Martin Bormann was tried and convicted *in absentia*.) And although certain verdicts have remained controversial—for example, the hanging of Julius Streicher for having incited genocide, although his role was non-military,[8] and the lifelong imprisonment of Rudolf Hess in Spandau prison—these groundbreaking trials set precedents. The "principles of Nuremberg" reflected the ideals of the Charter of the fledgling United Nations; and although the "lessons" of the Nuremberg legal experiment may have been ignored by that institution during the decades of the Cold War, the law that emerged from these trials remained on the books—to be revived with the creation of the ICTY in The Hague.

Nuremberg altered the way the twentieth century judged world events, and prime among its newly minted principles was the idea of personal liability under international criminal law. Although individuals were already responsible in their own national precincts for whatever crimes they were accused of, before the era of Nuremberg, only states were held liable for transgressing the international laws of war; and states were seen to be supreme, sovereign and—most important—

capable of protecting their elites by establishing immunities from prosecution. The Nuremberg Tribunal overturned this status quo by indicting individuals who participated in the commission or planning of a war crime, whether foot soldiers, commanders up the line or heads of state—a judgment that provided the basis for the Tokyo Trials in Japan, for thousands of future trials of German soldiers, politicians and civilians, such as doctors and business people who had contributed their expertise to the criminal project, and for later trials: of Adolf Eichmann in 1961, Klaus Barbie in 1987, Paul Touvier in 1994, Maurice Papon in 1997 and the judgment of the British Law Lords denying immunity to Augusto Pinochet in 1999, according to which the general was refused permission to return immediately to Chile. "Crimes against international law are committed by men, not by abstract entities, and only by punishing individuals who commit such crimes can the provisions of international law be enforced" was the way the Nuremberg Tribunal put it at the close of its proceedings in 1946.

The second "principle" of Nuremberg grappled with the tricky subject of "superior orders." This defence had been the mainstay of the German legal team, and no one on either side was foolish enough to suggest that obeying orders was not fundamental to military life. If soldiers did not obey their superiors, there would be no discipline, and without discipline they might as well pack up and go home. But Nuremberg presumed a code of universally understood morality that superseded the word of a military corporal barking out commands or, in the case of the Nazi civil service, murderous orders spewed out through the hierarchy of a faceless bureaucracy. The tribunal decided that a court confronted with the plea of "superior orders" in a case involving war crimes needed to pay serious attention, especially in the sentencing, but that "the true test . . . is not the existence of the order, but whether moral choice is in fact possible." In other words, members of armed forces could not escape liability if in obeying orders they committed acts that violated the rules of warfare and transgressed universal standards of human behaviour. "Individuals have international duties which transcend the national obligations of obedience imposed by the individual State," concluded the tribunal. The ultimate allegiance of a soldier is to humanity.

The judgments of Nuremberg have never ceased to be controversial, and at the far end of the spectrum, refuting the court has become a favourite weapon in the arsenal of those who deny the Holocaust and defend Nazism.[9] More defensibly, a heated debate about "victors' justice" has persisted, and it would be senseless to deny that the tribunal was an instance of victors judging the vanquished. But if the principles of Nuremberg have endured, and they have, it is likely because the trials were conducted according to accepted standards of due process and seen to be so—even in Germany, where the defeated population had only to observe that three of the defendants were acquitted even though the prosecution had argued forcefully for convictions.

Another powerful criticism is that the indictments at Nuremberg were based on law that did not exist before that time. The long-standing maxim *Nullum crimen, nulla poena, sine lege*, based on the proposition that no one can be punished for something that was not deemed criminal at the time of the act, was argued at length before the court by the German defence lawyers, and there was truth to their claim, since "crimes against humanity" had never before been articulated as such. However, the common and criminal law of nations had long outlawed the sort of acts that were being defined as crimes against humanity, and there were precedents in international law itself, even if formal legislation had never been codified. The response of the Nuremberg Tribunal was that "the law of war is to be found not only in treaties but in the customs and practices of states which gradually obtain universal recognition, and from the general principles of justice. . . . This law is not static, but by continual adaptation follows the needs of a world that is changing."

There were blatant hypocrisies and major mistakes: some of the war crimes under judgment at Nuremberg and Tokyo had been mirrored by the Allies themselves—the nuclear bombing of Hiroshima and Nagasaki, for example, and the deliberate firebombings of Dresden and Tokyo, the most densely populated region on earth. Victors' justice entailed serious shortcomings. Realpolitik was never absent from the scene. Yet alongside these indisputable shortcomings, the legislation established at the Nuremberg trials, and the principles they enunciated, have been understood as a milestone in the quest for human rights and accountability. In line with the usual contradictions humanity is noted for, the century that carried out and witnessed atrocities previously thought unimaginable was simultaneously capable of creating new tools of deterrence and punishment.

By punishing those who had transgressed boundaries, to use a suitably religious term, the Nuremberg trials helped restore the equilibrium of liberal values; in other words, by stressing universally understood moral law that transcended the jurisdiction of the individual state, the tribunal helped to revive social commitments that had been distorted by war. This would have been especially important for German society, it has seemed to me, where ethical prohibitions against murder and other violations had been inverted through Nazi re-education; a society that had led Hannah Arendt to conclude that one of its architects, Adolf Eichmann, was "banal" because his conscience had simply ceased to function in the inverted moral world he inhabited. By reminding both victor and vanquished of "transgression," the Nuremberg court helped human beings reconnect with one another in a shared moral universe. By eliciting the details of who did what to whom through the medium of courtroom testimony and seized Nazi documents, the trial process helped people who had lived through the chaos of war to understand the structure of the recent Nazi past, then to draw conclusions.

Show trials have a justifiably bad name, but Nuremberg was a political trial in the most exemplary sense, a point skilfully demonstrated by the late American political scientist Judith Shklar. Nuremberg, in her opinion, served to "reinforce dormant legal consciousness" among Germans and to frame the future direction of society.[10] In this scenario, the trials can be seen as a physical divide between past and future—and a bridge that reconnects everyone involved. The mountains of factual evidence available to the prosecution also helped. The U.S. chief prosecutor, Robert Jackson, said that the proof of atrocities was so solid and detailed that "there can be no responsible denial of these crimes in the future, and no tradition of martyrdom of the Nazi leadership can arise among informed people." Jackson's words *responsible* and *informed* are as true today as they were then: the disturbing denial movement that emerged in the decades that followed has remained marginal and is universally discredited.

But the Nuremberg trials also permitted ordinary Germans to distance themselves from the reality that the Nazi ethos had penetrated their entire society. Not all Germans were "willing executioners," as Daniel Goldhagen exaggeratedly claims, nor were they poisoned by an "eliminationist" anti-semitism that directed them to approve of mass murder. But every adult was to some degree a bystander, in that no rational person with eyes and ears could have missed what was happening—first, in terms of the discriminatory legislation, then when their Jewish neighbours began to disappear. Psychological distancing of the sort Nuremberg wittingly or unwittingly encouraged did allow the growth of a post-war historiography in which Hitler and a handful of henchmen were depicted as isolated monsters who appeared out of nowhere to impose their views on a resistant populace, a view that is thankfully disappearing. But that same distancing also made it easier for Germans to take back their liberal past, in the belief that they had never abandoned it.

Show trials have been used for vastly different purposes. Stalin's legal spectacles were meant to instil fear—to impress his subjects with the need for absolute obedience. Hundreds of years earlier, the trials of the Spanish Inquisition had had precisely the same intent: they were designed as public extravaganzas in which the powerful inquisitor meted out God's justice, while terrified sinners were paraded through town streets. Executions were frequently carried out in public, deliberately adding to the terror. The line between exemplary show trial and state propaganda is still a fine one. During the trial of Adolf Eichmann in Jerusalem, the prosecutor Gideon Hausner had in mind a case built less on what Eichmann did than on what the Jews had suffered. He wanted to raise questions of apparently greater import than the guilt or innocence of one man, questions such as, How could such a thing have happened? What role did the Allies play in the Jewish tragedy? Why the Jews? Or, for that matter, Why the Germans? There was much discussion about lessons for future generations. Eventually, the only question the court rightly agreed to address was that of Eichmann's personal guilt, but there was powerful (and understandable) pressure to use the defendant as a stand-in for all Nazi crimes.

The Klaus Barbie trial was another example of the fine line. Barbie's return to France in 1983 opened a floodgate of impassioned analysis about France's recent history and the purpose of his prospective trial, little of which had anything to do with law, guilt or innocence. Within days, Barbie and his trial became a metaphor for the past, present and future of France and sometimes for the entire world. The issues he was seen to symbolize were all-encompassing, the most prevalent being the wish to publicly condemn the underlying ideology of Nazism, including its inheritance, which was identified as the victims of the Irish Troubles, the suffering of Vietnamese and Guatemalan peasants and the terror of Russian intellectuals imprisoned in state mental hospitals, among other things. One commentator thought all ideologies of both the left and the right should be put on trial; another thought the case ought to be about what happens when democracies give up before a totalitarian system; still others insisted that the purpose of the trial was to expose Holocaust deniers, several of whom were French.

Something similar took place when Maurice Papon was tried for complicity in crimes against humanity. Crowded into the dock with the former deputy prefect of Bordeaux were, among others issues, the fate of the Jewish people, the activities of the French Resistance and the history of French misrepresentation about the war and the Collaboration.

Although all these trials had educational "show" purposes that stretched well beyond the realm of the law, they did settle down to the subject at hand: the guilt or innocence of one man. All of them upheld the rule established at Nuremberg decades earlier: laws passed by sovereign nations that are contrary to the precepts of universal rights and morality are not to be obeyed and that to do so is no defence. All of them established new case law that would become useful in the future. They were "shows," yes, but conducted with due process. As at Nuremberg, whatever lessons emerged could be drawn directly from the evidence.

In each case, the "show" attacked and put on trial those who had derailed the train of liberal Enlightenment values from its two hundred-year-old track.

Assaults on civilians have existed since the beginning of recorded time, and they've been debated for just as long. It is hard to read the passionate dialogue in Thucydides' *Peloponnesian War*, from the fifth century B.C., without a shudder as the author describes the still-familiar realpolitik alternatives being offered to the Melians by the Athenians, as the former plead for the right to remain neutral in the battle between Athens and Sparta:

- **Athenians**: *You know as well as we do that . . . justice depends on the quality of power to compel, and that the strong do what they have the power to do and the weak accept what they must.*
- **Melians**: *Since you force us to leave justice out of the account and confine ourselves to self-interest, it is useful that you should not destroy a principle that is to the general good of all men—namely . . . that there should be such a thing as fair play and just dealing. . . .*
- **Athenians**: *This is no fair fight, with honour on one side and shame on the other. It is rather a question of saving your lives and not resisting those who are far too strong for you. . . . Our opinion of the gods*

> *and our knowledge of men lead us to conclude that it is a general and necessary law of nature to rule wherever one can. This is not a law that we made ourselves, nor were we the first to act upon it. We found it already in existence, and we shall leave it to exist forever among those who come after us.*

When the Melians refused to join the battle, the Athenians went in "under the command of Philocrates, the son of Demeas," and "put to death all the men of military age whom they took, and sold the women and children as slaves."

There are examples from every era, but the story of the First Crusade—and its aftermath—is cheeringly revealing of our own. In July 1099, the exhausted knights reached holy Jerusalem, where they laid siege to the city and proceeded to slaughter every Muslim and Jew they came across: men, women and children. But in July 1999, more than two thousand Christians from Europe and North America descended upon Jerusalem to *apologize* to every Muslim and Jew they happened to encounter in the streets.

It took several thousand years before two worldwide wars, universal communications and a genocide carried out with the tools of twentieth-century technology transported atrocities that had been committed in sometimes faraway places to the centre of the international stage. Nuremberg was the first major attempt by outside powers to add courtroom justice to more conventional efforts to reconcile the wartorn past.

The creation of the International Criminal Tribunal for the Former Yugoslavia (and soon afterwards, the International Criminal Tribunal for Rwanda [ICTR]) was the second attempt, but the ICTY lacked what Nuremberg possessed even before the courtroom jousting began: jail cells filled with top Nazis awaiting trial and mountains of seized documents. Although there could be no legitimate discrediting of the ICTY on grounds of *ex post facto* law, as at Nuremberg, or victors' justice, since no one ever effectively "won" the war in Bosnia, the new tribunal faced difficult hurdles. First, the political ambiguity of the very international community that created the court to begin with. The Charter of the United Nations and the Declaration of Human Rights (based on the Nuremberg Principles) authorized the trials of war criminals, as at Nuremberg, but the indicted still had to be arrested, and nations were loath to do this for fear of imperiling the fragile Bosnian ceasefire.

Second, Slobodan Milošević, who had instigated the war for Greater Serbia in ex-Yugoslavia, as well as the later ethnic cleansing of Albanians in Kosovo, was the point person for international peace negotiations, both for the Dayton Accords and for attempts to negotiate a halt to attacks on civilians in Kosovo—a leadership role that had appalled Drinka Gojković and other Belgrade democrats. Western nations, especially the United States, held reams of classified information on Milošević's criminal activities, but in order to indict the Serb leader, the chief prosecutor of the ICTY would need watertight evidence. As long as Slobodan Milošević was seen as the key peace broker, that information might be slow in coming.

When NATO's air campaign against ethnic cleansing in Kosovo officially catapulted Milošević into the camp of U.S.-designated "rogue" leaders, an indictment by the chief prosecutor was no longer seen as a hindrance to peace. On May 27, 1999, Louise Arbour, then the ICTY prosecutor-in-chief, did cite Milošević for crimes against humanity, establishing a precedent: never before had the sitting leader of a sovereign country been so charged. However, other ICTY indictees—such as Radovan Karadžić; Ratko Mladić, the architect of the massacre at Srebrenica; and Željko Ražnjatović, known as Arkan, whose paramilitary forces were responsible for some of the worst atrocities committed against civilians—either roamed freely and gave self-congratulatory interviews to the Western media (as did Arkan), or kept out of sight. (Arkan, a warlord of drug running and smuggling, was shot dead in the lobby of Belgrade's Inter-Continental hotel in January 2000.) The ICTY had in its cells some of the lesser perpetrators of the Bosnian catastrophe, such as the Kupreškićs and their friends. Higher up the line, it held the Bosnian Croat general Tihomir Blaškić, the man in charge of the larger Lašva Valley enterprise that had included the massacre at Ahmići.[11] But it seemed clear that if the politicians and military men at the top of the command chain were not indicted, apprehended and tried, the little guys would be seen as scapegoats for their grisly bosses.

The situation was altogether different at Nuremberg. Although thousands of cogs in the Nazi wheel escaped prosecution immediately after the war, the International Military Tribunal captured the public imagination because it successfully carried out a judicial purge at the top of the Nazi enterprise and because it reinstated principles of liberal rights in such a way that victors and vanquished alike could reconnect in a commitment to joint values, as happened when the Nuremberg

Principles were incorporated into the ideals of the fledgling United Nations in 1948 when the General Assembly passed the Universal Declaration of Human Rights. If the only perpetrators the ICTY managed to prosecute were foot soldiers, the tribunal would be hard-pressed to fulfil its other role, which was to rebalance the social pendulum and deter future war crimes by attacking criminal impunity.

The fault lay less with the ICTY than with the ambivalence and dual purposes of the nations that gave birth to the tribunal. Trying war crimes was important in principle, but negotiating the peace was more important, even if this meant supping with a devil named Milošević. Immersing myself in news and commentary before going to The Hague, I found the approach short-sighted. The political dilemma was, and is, real, but the larger question of whether peace without justice can hold over the long term looms ominously. Without the rebalancing brought about by public trials, or by the spectacle of a truth commission that is designed to expose the reality of what has happened and elicit public statements of remorse, as in post-apartheid South Africa, for example, it is harder to strike a visible break with the past.

There is no statute of limitations on memory. Or on crimes against humanity, as Eichmann, Barbie, Touvier, Papon and Pinochet learned. Negotiating a peace that does not grapple with impunity for war crimes is certain to be risky.

By most accounts, Louise Arbour was doing a fine job in one of the world's most difficult postings. Outside Croatia and Serbia, both of which were repeatedly called upon to deliver indicted nationals to The Hague, there were few serious detractors. Arbour thought the escalating rhetoric coming from those countries about the bias and illegality of the tribunal was actually a good sign, an indication that they were growing afraid. She had warned her staff to expect worse still.

It hadn't been easy to find someone to act as chief prosecutor for the two international criminal courts (in The Hague and in Arusha, Tanzania, where the Rwanda tribunal was located) who would satisfy all concerned on the Security Council. Although the statute of the ICTY was adopted by the council in May 1993 (the Rwanda tribunal was voted into existence in November 1994), it took another fourteen months to agree on the first candidate: Richard Goldstone, a respected South African judge and lawyer and a member of that country's Constitutional Court, was appointed on July 8, 1994. He had established an international reputation by heading a 1991 commission of inquiry on Third Force activities in South Africa, in which he implicated the National Party government in a network of murderous strategies involving the South Africa police and elements in the Zulu-based Inkatha Freedom Party. He had been recommended for the ICTY job by Nelson Mandela, which meant he was acceptable to everyone. When Goldstone returned to South Africa in 1996, he suggested Louise Arbour as his successor.

Just as Richard Goldstone represented the new South Africa, an eminently respectable place on the international stage, so Louise Arbour represented Canada, a country known for peacekeeping and peace initiatives. Before her appointment to The Hague on October 1, 1996, she had shone as a professor of criminal law at Osgoode Hall in Toronto, one of Canada's prominent law faculties, and as a judge on the Ontario Court of Appeal. Arbour had a reputation for caring about civil rights, including women's rights. And she was known to be tenacious *and* diplomatic, qualities that do not always cohabit with ease.

Yesterday, I watched the trial of the Kupreškić brothers and their friends, and this morning I have an appointment with Louise Arbour. I thought I would have more trouble getting this interview, since she is surely one of the busiest people on earth and probably one of the most harried. Surprisingly, I was scheduled in without problems, and now I am about to meet her. I feel uncharacteristically nervous—a little overwhelmed by her job description, I think.

She is down-to-earth friendly, almost breezy in her manner, a woman of early middle age with an easy laugh and half glasses perched precariously at the end of her nose, whose relaxed style belies the toughness that is a bottom-line prerequisite for this post. We sit together at a small round table near the door of her office and chat for a moment about mutual friends in Toronto.

"Do I think about Nuremberg?" She laughs in response to my question. "I think about Nuremberg *every* day! The images constantly come to mind. I don't know whether the people at Nuremberg had a sense that they were rooting themselves right in the middle of the twentieth century as probably its most significant event. Maybe they did. I certainly don't compare myself in any way with the giants of that court like Telford Taylor or Robert Jackson. It's the technical things I think about, and sometimes I'm so envious. Just think of it! They had *every* defendant in custody and the ones they didn't have, like Martin

Bormann, they tried *in absentia*. They had no appeals. They applied capital punishment. I am not saying I would approve of, or even want, all these things, but it made their job a heck of a lot easier. They had every document; they had the demobilized German army of thousands, including sophisticated intelligence officers; they had translators by the zillions. Can you imagine? The comparison would be if I had control of SFOR [the UN Stabilization Force] so I could sit there in the theatre and be both prosecutor and general with the army in charge. I could dispatch people right, left and centre!" The chief prosecutor of Nuremberg's first successor tribunal laughs aloud at the thought of such ease of operations.

Her job is a thousand times harder, what with SFOR refusing to arrest the top indicted war criminals in Bosnia, President Franjo Tudjman practising non-compliance in Croatia[12] and Slobodan Milošević outright refusing the jurisdiction of the ICTY, even as Serb forces cut a new killing swath through Kosovo. But one accomplishment has made her proud. Under the prosecutorial regime of Richard Goldstone, a perception had taken root that the ICTY was entitled only to the co-operation of states in carrying out its mandate. Arbour read the founding statute of the tribunal under Chapter VII of the UN Charter differently: to mean compliance. "It became clear to me that you cannot run a criminal justice system on a voluntary charitable basis. Our statute says that all states shall co-operate with the prosecutor and that all states shall *comply* with the orders of the court in its requests for assistance. For example, we believed Croatia held critical evidence. We made many requests for documents, and when they were not forthcoming we applied for a subpoena against the state and against the minister of defence personally. Croatia didn't budge. So we litigated. And we won the principle that we are entitled to order states to comply with this tribunal."

This precedent was central to the operations of the ICTY, but even with compliance established in law, what was a prosecutor-in-chief to do about a man like Slobodan Milošević, who openly flouted the tribunal's jurisdiction?

Her priorities are clear, as she likes to point out in every interview she gives. The obstacles she faces in the political arena are maddening, but she does not plan to limit her indictments to the little guys: she will go right to the top of the command chain, if she can—when sufficient evidence is released or uncovered. She says, with notable bravado, that concessions made on the political front have nothing to do with her mandate, which has been defined by the Security Council. Her message that there is no statute of limitations for war crimes and crimes against humanity is directed at Milošević, Karadžić, Mladić and company. The ICTY is independent of the political process, she says.

She is impressive, but I wonder what backup lies, unused, behind her forceful words. "What punishments for non-compliance with the tribunal are there in the international arsenal beyond reprimands followed by economic sanctions?" I ask her. After all, the latter are already in place against Serbia.

"The buck stops with the Security Council," she replies, partly dodging the question. "That's where we finally have to go to denounce non-compliance. They created us. Either they are going to back us up or they are spending a lot of good money for nothing.

"But I am not pessimistic. The leadership of the former Yugoslavia know they have more reason to worry about us than we have about them, and the chance of obstructionism closing us down is zero, in my opinion. Our budget was increased at a time when UN programs were being slashed. Here we have this newborn experiment in criminal justice backed up by the 185 member states of the United Nations. There are twelve hundred people working here. I don't think the UN would be making this kind of commitment if they felt we were in jeopardy." All the same, she can't wait forever, she says. "I just don't think the peace process can afford to have justice lag too far behind."

Justice in the wake of atrocity. Hundreds of thousands of victims and survivors. Displaced, mangled people with shattered psyches. In Sarajevo, Dr. Cerić said it would take generations to sluice the pain from memory. At Nuremberg, the few who sat in the prisoners' dock symbolized the criminality of the regime they had incarnated—but their numbers had been small.

"Whatever success you achieve with your indictments, you will only be able to try a tiny percentage of the people who committed atrocities," I say to Arbour. "Can that ever suffice?"

"In a sense, no," she replies, "because for most of the victims, the people we are most interested in, the leaders, are only abstractions. They never knew them. The man whose daughter was raped and killed in a camp has in his mind the person who did it, but he is not the one we are likely to prosecute. I have to say there is an anonymity in the number of victims that is overwhelming, and in that sense the perpetrators have won. They took away the lives of their victims, that was the easy part, but they also took their identity, their humanity. We either pull them out of the grave—and even then there are many we can never identify—or we do not even pull them out of their graves because we do not have the resources. It is our strong belief that every one of these victims counts, yet having said this, I am the first to concede that the ICTY is not a commission for missing persons. So in the sense that we cannot attend to every victim, the perpetrators have won. They didn't just want deaths but wanted to destroy religion, ethnicity, family membership, everything that made their enemies human."

Her strong voice cracks almost imperceptibly.

"When I met Archbishop Tutu, he did not entirely reject the idea of collective guilt," I persist. "He said that individuals were responsible for their actions, but that groups also had to acknowledge their part in the past, through their spokespersons. Given the thousands of anonymous dead in the Balkans and the thousands of perpetrators you will never see in this court, do you agree with him?"

She thinks I am asking about the proposal for a Balkan Truth and Reconciliation Commission *à la* South Africa that was recently put forward by the U.S. Institute of Peace and approved by her predecessor, Goldstone, and she hastens to say she thinks the timing for such a process is premature, that a Bosnian TRC would interfere with the search for evidence at a criminal standard, and that such a commission would in all likelihood lead to an attempt at rewriting history by the ethnicities concerned since, unlike in South Africa, there was as yet no real will to live together in Bosnia without outside enforcement by SFOR troops. Which is not to say, she points out, that she does not believe in the usefulness of amnesty under certain circumstances, especially when the crimes in question go back so far that the frailties of human memory make convictions under the strict standards of criminal law hard to come by. But this is another subject altogether, one that opens up the problem of prosecuting war crimes dating back to the Holocaust, for example, which Arbour clearly believes puts the traditional criminal system, with its reliance on identification and memory, under strain.

I ask her again about collective guilt: does she agree with Archbishop Desmond Tutu that *groups* have to acknowledge their role in the past? "Let me say that I understand the concept of rejecting collective guilt," she replies. "It is a rejection that is at the core of what we do here: by personalizing individual responsibility, we help diffuse the stigma on a whole nation or ethnic group. But I don't think it is as straightforward as I did before I started this work. I think that having a clear demarcation between the individual and the collectivity, or the group, works reasonably well when the perpetrators who are being tried in court are somewhat distinct from the group, and the group can distance itself from that person. Take our first case, Dušan Tadić. It was possible for the Bosnian Serb community to say he is not us, he is a war criminal. But that becomes more difficult when you move up the chain of command, say with Radovan Karadžić. We have become aware of this during discussions about what would happen if there was a move to arrest him, because ultimately, when you get to the head of state, there is a fusion of the community with that individual. They may have elected the person or supported him throughout his misdeeds, often with open eyes. Even if they did not know every crime by name, they heard the rhetoric of hate and supported it. So as we move higher up the chain, there is more and more resistance, because the people we are calling war criminals are still heroes to their community, and the personal guilt of such people may be perceived as an expression of collective guilt.

"In our tribunal, we look only at personal criminal responsibility in a very tightly defined, narrow way and we demand proof beyond a reasonable doubt about the involvement of the individual. We do not have a mandate to establish the moral responsibility of those who saw things happen and did nothing, including people who might have had the capa-city to stop the process and did nothing. But we have to be careful in thinking that just because we focus on individual criminal guilt we therefore absolve the community. The old distinctions are too simplistic when we move up the chain of command and witness the merging of the collectivity into the personae of these charismatic political and military leaders."

I think she is brave and outspoken to say this, because the subject of collective guilt is usually anathema to lawyers and judges, and to many other people too. The very question is likely to call forth a quick, dismissive reply about the basis of the Western legal system being individual responsibility before the law. What she has said does not refute this in any way; she has simply dared to explore the issue further. I think the parallels with Germany are striking. The Nuremberg trials allowed Germans to distance themselves from the Nazis, even though there unquestionably was what Arbour has just called "the merging of the collectivity" into the persona of Adolf Hitler. The process of distancing permitted people to recover their pre-Nazi moral roots and move on, but it had also led to a distorted historiography that pinpointed a tiny number of major perpetrators and ignored the rest, including the bystanders. The shifts that took place in Germany over the decades—from the accusations of the young against "the fathers," starting around 1968, to the conflicted, diffused guilt of the 1980s and 1990s, to the collective indictment of Daniel Goldhagen's *Hitler's Willing Executioners* in 1996—were, perhaps, one result of a too narrowly focused trial process. Germans cried "Enough!" from time to time, but the problem of the perpetrators and the collectivity was still present in German culture.

Was there a viable alternative? At the ICTY, as at Nuremberg and all other traditional criminal trials, what Arbour called "the standard of proof" was key. Archbishop Desmond Tutu's Truth and Reconciliation Commission, because it was not traditional retributive justice, could include questions of communal responsibility if it wanted to. No one would go to jail in South Africa for confessing the truth of what had happened; or for implicating the political leadership of the apartheid era, for that matter; or for claiming that whites had profitted from the absolute power they held over blacks. On the contrary, the refusal to come forward to confess one's past acts opened the door to a real trial in the real justice system. The extraordinary governing idea in South Africa was that clearing the air by admitting crimes was a necessary first step in restoring trust and reconciling the bitterness.

But what would, or could, reconcile the bitter past in Bosnia and Kosovo after the hideous butcheries of the 1990s? Would traditional criminal justice, with its high standards of proof, be sufficient, even if the ICTY did eventually arrest and try the perpetrators at the top? Could such trials reinforce even a glimmering of "dormant legal consciousness" in a region of the world that had known only totalitarian governments that devised their own self-serving laws? Could ethnic communities accept the guilt of their leaders without feeling collectively incriminated, as Louise Arbour wondered aloud? And to what degree *were* people incriminated by having adopted the course set by their leadership?

Would there be a hiatus of decades, as in post-war Germany and France, until the next generation began to ask what daddy and granddaddy did during the dark *fin-de-siècle* days? The Belgrade lawyer Nikola Barović had hinted as much when he told me that one day, Serbs would have to accept the implications of what was done in their name. I wonder, as I sit in Louise Arbour's office in The Hague, whether new child sufferers in the mode of Niklas Frank and Martin Bormann Jr. are stumbling through the rubble of the Balkans, and whether those who survived "ethnic cleansing" would seek revenge one day? Or would they, like many who had lived through the Holocaust, find recourse in suicide, as was already happening in Sarajevo?

So many questions without answers.

The good news—and there was some—was that fifty years after Nuremberg the ICTY, through its trials, was creating new law to serve the future. In the past, international laws and treaties had bowed before sovereignty, even though international law, by its very existence, implied limits to state law. (As the legal scholar Anthony D'Amato has pointed out, without limits to sovereignty, "international law"—that is, transnational legislation—would be meaningless, even as a concept.)[13]

International law used to limit itself to relationships between states, but Nuremberg changed history by making personal criminal responsibility a central tenet of the law—by making it harder for individuals to hide behind a shield called "the nation." In theory, that is; none of this mattered during the Cold War, when both East and West demanded loyalty from their satellites.

Why, then, after all the intervening decades, did the United Nations decide to create Nuremberg's daughters in The Hague and in Arusha? Michael Scharf, who was attorney-adviser for UN Affairs at the U.S. State Department in the early 1990s, tells the story in his book *Balkan Justice*.[14] In 1992, the Serbs were carrying out their Bosnia campaign of ethnic cleansing in full view of the international media, and the nightly sights of televised horror were increasingly embarrassing for the politicians who were carefully avoiding intervening militarily in the Bosnian catastrophe. (Scharf is scathing in his appraisal of the United Nations' failure to halt the atrocities.) Action—any action—was urgently needed.

On October 6, 1992, the UN Security Council adopted Resolution 780, which became the 780 Commission. Its mandate was "to make recommendations for further appropriate steps." When the commission presented its interim report to the secretary general in February 1993, it provided the first definition of ethnic cleansing—*cleansing*, the word that had appeared in Serb chronicles going back to Njegos, finally, formally, explained. In the dry terminology of the report, it was "rendering an area wholly homogeneous by using force or intimidation to remove persons of given groups from the area." The commission also concluded that ethnic cleansing came under the definition of crimes against humanity, war crimes and genocide as defined at Nuremberg, then later in the Genocide Convention. (Reading this, I thought that to include genocide in the definition was a dubious judgment, since cleansing did not include targeting a group for total destruction, which was a criterion.)

But why choose a Nuremberg-style tribunal rather than bring the war to a forceful military close? After all, criminal impunity on an international scale was, and is, as old as humanity. The Nuremberg Tribunal may have altered international law long ago, but it was followed by a string of atrocities that were effectively ignored by the United Nations, including the "disappearances" of thousands of civilians in Argentina, Chile, El Salvador and Guatemala, to name just a few. There was no new Nuremberg to address these abuses. The Cold War was over, but what incentive was there to remember Nuremberg now?

I ask Louise Arbour this question. "It may be that there has been a gradual increase in respect for the law in the leading democracies," she says. "The leading Western democracies have seen their criminal systems expand and become more sophisticated, with more respect for individual rights, and I think this shift has translated into a willingness to set up international courts. Also, a new, younger leadership with these priorities has come on the scene in the West; they arrived at the same time as atrocities in ex-Yugoslavia and Rwanda began to demonstrate unequivocally that what the world thought would never happen again after the Holocaust *was* happening again—right before their eyes, and the eyes of the generation that did not experience the Second World War firsthand but had received the legacy that it would never happen again.

"So the Holocaust was a factor, without a doubt. What was happening in Bosnia was not of the same magnitude, but it was getting there, and the question—the test—was, Are we going to let it happen again? I have to say honestly that if Rwanda had happened first, I'm not sure there would have been a tribunal for that country. Where were we when the Khmer Rouge was committing atrocities? It happened because the Balkans were in Europe and too frighteningly close to the history of the two great conflicts of the twentieth century; what was taking place right in Europe's face was rattling its memory, if not its conscience.

"To answer your question about why this has happened *now*, I think we have to think about what was going on at the Security Council. It was paralyzed during the Cold War, but the Balkans and Rwanda erupted just when people were beginning to hope that the council could once again manage conflict and secure peace. The council was really at its wits' end about what to do. It had passed zillions of resolutions, none of which were doing any good, and traditional peacekeeping missions were not working; they hadn't prevented a Srebrenica from happening. Really, I don't think anyone thought international justice would solve problems overnight—justice alone will never bring peace to our planet—but it was clearly worth a try. So, you see, a lot of different factors came into play."

One of the most powerful voices in favour of an international criminal tribunal was that of Madeleine Albright, then U.S. ambassador to the United Nations. "There is an echo in this chamber today," she said on February 22, 1993, the day the resolution to establish the ICTY was debated. "The Nuremberg Principles have been reaffirmed. We have preserved the long-neglected compact made by the community of civilized nations forty-eight years ago in San Francisco to create the United Nations and enforce the Nuremberg Principles. The lesson that we are all accountable to international law may have finally taken hold in our collective memory."[15]

The Holocaust was the catalyst for the creation of the Nuremberg Principles, but in February 1993 Madeleine Albright was still four years from acknowledging that she was herself of Jewish origin, and a survivor, as well. Her Czech parents had converted to Roman Catholicism before the war, trying to avert disaster by changing their identity. They had escaped with their daughter to Britain, returned to Prague after 1945, then escaped once again, this time from the Communists, to the United States, where they reinvented themselves as Americans and never hinted at their Jewishness. In a studied American way, they let go of the past, lived in the present and planned for a better future. Albright herself converted to Episcopalianism when she married.

Her parents never spoke about who they used to be or the fate of their lost relatives, which was not unusual behaviour even among people who survived the death camps. She travelled to Prague several times and visited its Jewish memorials without alluding to her personal history.[16]

Then, in July 1997, she finally spoke openly, in the old synagogue of Prague, about the family whose names were engraved there, on the memorial wall to the deported dead, repeating the convictions that had underscored her speech at the United Nations four years earlier: "I have always felt that my life story is also the story of the evil of totalitarianism and the turbulence of twentieth-century Europe," she said. "To the many . . . facets that make up who I am, I now add the knowledge that my grandparents and members of my family perished in the worst catastrophe in human history. . . . The evil of the Holocaust has an even more personal meaning for me, and I feel an even greater determination to ensure that it will never be forgotten. . . . Identity," she added, "is a complex compilation of influences and experiences."

Identity. Memory. Forgetfulness. Dissimulation. Reinvention. And always the searing presence of the Holocaust. The threads that snaked through the cloth of the twentieth century were visible in individuals like Albright, whose lives were the product of the turbulence, and within the collectivity of nations themselves, as they sought to shape the past and invent the future.

Once the ICTY and the ICTR were established in The Hague and Arusha, Tanzania, respectively, and once trials began to take place, international criminal law as set down at Nuremberg, Tokyo and in the aftermath of the Second World War expanded with new life. By April 2000, the ICTY had indicted ninety-three people and completed sixteen trials, although twenty-seven of the indicted were still at large, including big-name suspects: Milošević, Karadžić and Mladić. The Arusha court had indicted fifty-two people, rendered verdicts against seven accused and mandated the detention of forty-six suspects. Important suspects. The Rwanda court held former cabinet members, local politicians, religious leaders, military brass, senior media personalities and top government administrators, many of whom had fled to Europe and other African countries. The unambiguous defeat of the Hutu rebels made the arrest and handover of indicted criminals easier than at The Hague.

On September 2, 1998, the ICTR made legal history by finding a former Rwandan mayor, Jean Paul Akayesu, guilty of genocide—of having intended to destroy the Tutsi people—as well as other crimes. The mayor was judged "individually and criminally guilty" of inciting townspeople to commit genocide, of ordering the murders of intellectuals and of personally participating in murder. He was also found guilty of rape, which was judged, for the first time, to be an act of genocide when committed with the intent of destroying the targeted group by producing children with the blood of the victorious group.

Two days after the verdict against Akayesu, the ICTR court also found the former Rwandan prime minister Jean Kambanda guilty of genocide and sentenced him to life imprisonment. Kambanda had pleaded guilty to the charge: he was the first person in history ever to do so. He and Akayesu also became the first persons to be judged guilty under the 1948 Genocide Convention.

The plea and subsequent conviction of Kambanda, the most important political leader in the country, startled Rwandans by demonstrating that the genocide was planned and carried out at the very highest level, including the military, which came under the command of the prime minister. The man at the top was guilty of orchestrating a massacre of his own nationals. Suddenly a fully contoured picture of what had taken place in their country swam into focus for Rwandans themselves.

At the time of my visit, the president of the ICTY was the distinguished American jurist and federal judge Gabrielle Kirk McDonald, a woman with a reputation in her own country for open-mindedness.[17] The president is broadly responsible for the organization (including the Office of the Prosecutor): her job is to preside over the Appeals Chamber and conduct the plenary meetings—but most important, to interject the needs of the ICTY and the ICTR into the political agenda of the UN Security Council.

When Arbour and I have finished talking, I am conducted to McDonald's office on the next floor. How extraordinary, I think to myself, that this international tribunal is currently headed by two women: ten years ago, I doubt whether this would have been possible, yet today, hardly anyone seems to notice. Although her job, like Louise Arbour's, is one of the toughest on the international scene, McDonald's manner, when we meet, is disarmingly casual—friendly in an inimitable American way. Her office holds reminders of things she wants to keep at the forefront of her thoughts—for example, two blow-up photos placed side by side on one of the walls. The first picture is of a very old, poverty-stricken Bosnian woman, who gazes past the camera with an expression I recognize for having seen it many times before: utter despair and abandoned hope. The woman's eyes are sunk deep in her skull, their regard trained on a distant, unreachable place. The other picture is also of a woman. She is wearing a Muslim head scarf and sitting on the ground in some sort of temporary shelter with her belongings tied in a sack beside her. Unlike her wall companion's, her look is unflinching and defiant, straight at the camera. She is still in touch, still able to feel something other than hopelessness. Perhaps it is hatred.

On the shelves across the room sit pictures of McDonald's two adult children, both of them very far away from her now. They border Telford Taylor's memoir, *The Anatomy of the Nuremberg Trials*, and *Crusaders in the Courts: How a Dedicated Band of Lawyers Fought for the Civil Rights Revolution*, a work by McDonald's mentor, the Columbia law professor Jack Greenberg, who was the director of the NAACP Legal Defense and Educational Fund from 1961 until 1984.

The presidency of the UN tribunal was the direct outcome of a lifetime commitment to human rights, for Gabrielle Kirk McDonald had known race hatred first-hand. Her father worked on the railroad in Minnesota (where she was born in 1943), then sold insurance; her mother was an editor with Prentice-Hall. Their experiences, coupled with her own, had pushed her into the civil rights movement and law studies in the 1960s.

She tells me, as we sit in the "living room" area of her large office, that her mother had been half white, and looked white, meaning that things that might have been hidden under different circumstances were often blatant. Like the time her mother stepped into a New York taxicab to have the driver apologize for "the stink" because "some niggers just got out." Or the afternoon she took nine-year-old Gabrielle to have her hair cut while she went shopping and came back to find her daughter sitting alone in the waiting area just as she had left her. Or the fight Gabrielle herself took on as a strong-minded eight-year-old when the landlord made it clear he did not want a black child living in his New York City building.

She did not abandon the struggle for rights, and now she is president of the ICTY in The Hague. In December 1998, in a speech in Madrid to the assembled members of the Peace Implementation Council of the United Nations, she mollified no one. She said, "The problem of non-co-operation looms larger than ever. . . . The authorities of the Republika Srpska and the government of the Federal Republic of Yugoslavia persist in refusing to arrest and transfer indictees on their territory to the tribunal. . . . The Prosecutor believes that more than twenty-five indicted individuals remain at liberty [in Republika Srpska]. . . .

"The obstructionism of the government of the Federal Republic of Yugoslavia has far-reaching consequences for our ability to discharge our mandate . . . [and] is blatantly violating international law. . . . I urge you: end this obstructionism now. Failure to do so will imperil all of the tribunal's work to date . . ."[18]

"I was so frustrated in Madrid, you should have heard me!" she fumes just weeks after this event. "The way the diplomats approach these problems! They are given five minutes to speak and they spend the first minute saying how wonderful it is to be there and how lovely the poinsettias look. But I had recently been on a trip to Rwanda and seen the aftermath of genocide with my own eyes. I thought the officials would ask me to lay a ceremonial wreath, but I was taken to a site that was formerly a school and it was full of skeletons of all sizes. They were leaving them there in preparation for creating a museum. I was overwhelmed. When I left they asked me to sign the guest book and I wrote, 'How can people do this to one another? How can the survivors go on? What do any of us tell our children?'

"We walked up a steep hill and an official offered me his arm. I took his hand. It was so soft. He was so kind and gentle. I said to myself, What was this hand doing during all of this? I was there because I hoped we could make a difference in people's lives, and of course the legal issues are important and really very intriguing. But I think a lot about those people. How can they go forward? How do they live with themselves? How do you get over the memory of seeing your mother slaughtered? How do you get over the memory of slaughtering someone yourself?"

The president of the world's first international criminal court since Nuremberg falls abruptly silent as she struggles with her own memories.

"In Madrid you said that obstructionism can imperil all your work. Do you still want to go that far?" I ask her.

"Sure. Imperil does not mean destroy. The problem is that we are an international criminal-judicial institution but without the powers that such institutions have in domestic situations, and that means without the power to compel. We can request co-operation, we can demand compliance, but we do not have a police force. For that we are entirely dependent on the international community, but there we are faced with the politics of maintaining a balance between international world order and state sovereignty. You know, we've already seen a move towards giving up some sovereignty in order to maintain world order with the creation of the UN and the Geneva and Genocide Conventions. There's been a realization that we all live in this world together, and what goes on in my state *is* the business of other states because what goes on internally can affect the right of others to live peacefully and the peace of the world itself. So when Yugoslavia thumbs its nose at the ICTY, it is not at us but at the United Nations, which established us under the Charter. If they get away with it, it sets a very bad example."

The see-saw of state sovereignty versus international criminal and humanitarian law has not yet reached stable equilibrium and is unlikely to do so anytime soon, but when I went to The Hague in early 1999, there were powerful signs that the current tilt was in favour of international law. Augusto Pinochet, for example. He was the former dictator of Chile who decreed immunity for himself after 55 per cent of Chileans voted against him in a referendum, in 1988, that was supposed to authorize a continuation of what he liked to call his "authoritarian democracy."

Pinochet seized power on September 11, 1973, by overthrowing the elected government of Salvador Allende in a coup that killed Allende as well as other leaders of leftist organizations. Five thousand people would be murdered or "disappeared" by the military junta that was to rule Chile for seventeen years. One hundred thousand people either escaped from the country or were expelled.[19]

Allende was hated by the Chilean monied classes for understandable reasons: he expropriated their large estates for peasant co-operatives and supported policies of large wage increases in industry. When he nationalized all U.S.-owned copper companies whose mines had been developed with U.S. capital and technology in the early years of the century and were still lucrative, he made an implacable enemy of the United States and its president, Richard Nixon. Henry Kissinger, then U.S. secretary of state, openly stated American intentions after Allende's election in 1970 when he said, "I don't see why we need to stand by and watch a country go Communist due to the irresponsibility of its people."[20]

During his seventeen years of power as head of a military government, Augusto Pinochet introduced two kinds of policies. One was economic: by applying the new supply-side economics well in advance of any other nation in Latin America, he created wealth and a powerful middle class. The other was terror: the killing and the torture of men and women who opposed him and the policies of his regime were described as part of the war on communism, as necessary for the unfolding of an orderly society.

In March 1978, the Pinochet regime produced an amnesty law, forgiving everyone who had committed a crime from the day of the military coup, and for a while Chileans, including those in exile, believed in the "ethical imperative" that was said to motivate the new law. The wording of the "imperative" was as familiar as the impulse behind it: forgetfulness in the service of national reconciliation. "To strengthen the ties that bind Chile as a nation, [and] leave behind hatred that has no meaning today, [while] fostering all measures that consolidate the reunification of all Chileans."[21]

General Pinochet's enemies soon understood that they were not the intended beneficiaries of the new law: when the courts began to apply the legislation, it became clear that the amnesty the general had in mind was meant to aid the perpetrators of crimes committed in the name of his regime. Civil courts declared themselves unable to deal with cases concerning "disappeared" persons. They transferred their files to the military courts, which promptly applied the amnesty law and closed the cases. The amnesty was a gift by the regime to its agents.[22]

Under the terms of his 1980 constitution, Pinochet established a lifetime seat in the senate for any past president who had served a term of at least six years, and in 1990 he decided to take up his own offer. That was two years after he held a referendum on whether to extend his "authoritarian democracy." And failed. In his seventies, and possibly feeling his age, he stepped aside and was replaced by Patricio Aylwin—who was elected: the famous "transition to democracy" was under way. But Pinochet arranged to stay on as head of the all-important armed forces, until March 1998, when he opted to be sworn in as a senator for life with legal immunity from prosecution for any human rights abuses that had occurred during his tenure.[23]

The actual swearing-in ceremony could not have been much of a party for the general, since thousands of people demonstrated against him, the police lobbed tear gas, opposition politicians paraded about carrying photographs of people known to be executed or "disappeared" (including a picture poster of Salvador Allende), a fistfight broke out in the senate chamber and visitors heckled and shouted, both for and against. "Murderer!" they screamed. Or "Long live Pinochet!" That day tanks rolled and water cannons sprayed neighbourhoods. More than five hundred people were arrested all over the country. It was a sharp reminder of earlier violence.

Pinochet loved England and "Englishness" (like others in the conservative upper classes of Chile, he was known to break his daily routine for tea and scones), and on their many trips to London he and his wife, Lucia, frolicked like delighted tourists.[24] They visited Madame

Tussaud's wax museum, stood in line to visit Windsor Castle. When he wasn't shopping for rockets and other armaments, Pinochet sampled delicacies at Fortnum and Mason and purchased fine Egyptian-cotton shirts at Harrods. He usually stopped by for tea and conversation with his friend the baroness Margaret Thatcher, to whom he frequently sent flowers and chocolates. The two had been excellent friends since 1982, when Pinochet supported Thatcher during the Falkland Islands War with Argentina.

Margaret Thatcher was a great admirer of General Pinochet's "economic miracle"; in fact, as prime minister she once sent an adviser to Chile for six months to study the general's accomplishments. Pinochet's mastery of massive 150 per cent inflation and other economic evils—made possible by a ruthless suppression of the political opposition—opened the way for right-leaning democratic governments such as those of Britain and the United States, for whom monetarism and anti-communism were closely linked ideologies, "not to know" the details of what was taking place in Pinochet's Chile and to maximize their support under the cover-all of "the fight against communism." The deaths, the disappearances, the track-down assassinations of opponents in other lands, the covert assistance of the Central Intelligence Agency (a widely known "secret" that was finally confirmed in June 1999, when the U.S. government released thousands of formerly classified documents proving direct governmental support and detailing its intimate knowledge of the killings of Chileans)—all could be denied or glossed over in the name of the new prosperity and the so-called national reconciliation of the Chilean people.

As the years passed, memory itself was subverted—except among Pinochet's victims. As the possibility of political change receded, many people lost interest. Tomás Moulian, a Chilean professor of sociology, put it this way: "The most calculated expression of forgetting is depoliticization."[25]

But times had changed since the days of the Falkland War. Britain had Tony Blair, a new prime minister from the Labour side of the House, and since 1988, a new Criminal Justice Act that adopted international jurisdiction in the case of torture. Section 134(1) of this legislation stated: "A public official or person acting in an official capacity, whatever his nationality, commits the offence of torture if in the United Kingdom or elsewhere he intentionally inflicts severe pain or suffering on another in the performance or purported performance of his official duties." In plain language, torture carried out, or ordered by, an official became an offence under British law, wherever the act was committed.

General Pinochet must have known that since 1996, a Spanish judge named Baltasar Garzón had been investigating the fate of hundreds of Spaniards who disappeared during the Latin American "dirty wars" of the 1970s, despite the amnesties the leaders had conferred upon themselves and their associates. In Argentina, between twenty and thirty thousand people were tortured, killed or "disappeared" between 1976 and 1983. This brutal era of dictatorship was best summed up by General Ibérico Saint Jean, the military commander of Buenos Aires, when he said, "First we will kill all the subversives, then we will kill their collaborators, then their sympathizers, then those who remain indifferent and finally the indecisive."[26]

Victims of disappearances included suspected terrorists and "subversives"—the latter being anyone who espoused Marxist, Communist, or Liberation Theology ideologies and/or worked with the poor or in labour unions; or students who belonged to political organizations—or were thought to belong; or journalists, lawyers, academics and psychiatrists. Among the victims were pregnant women and small children, many of whom were given to other families to raise. Babies born in captivity were handed over to men and women close to the military.

After the return of democracy to Argentina in 1983, a national commission reported on what took place, and criminal procedures were instigated against many of those responsible. But when several of the leaders were sentenced to jail terms, the still-powerful military staged armed mutinies, and a cowed government passed two amnesty laws stopping most of the investigations and prosecutions. Finally, even those who had been convicted were pardoned by President Carlos Menem in 1990.[27] At the same time, Menem passed new laws making it impossible to try anyone else.

Using tools of international criminal law derived from Nuremberg and after, as well as complementary Spanish law, Judge Garzón had been trying to reindict, rearrest and retry the Argentine leadership.[28] He had already issued an international arrest warrant against former Argentine military president Leopoldo Galtieri, whom he accused of responsibility for atrocities committed under his command. Argentine authorities were refusing to co-operate, but the arrest warrant did inhibit Galtieri's leaving his country.

Other nations had also been trying to prosecute Argentines abroad; Spain was merely the most successful. The Italian League for the Rights and Liberation of People started criminal procedures in the early 1980s in the names of "disappeared" Italian citizens. (These were abandoned after Argentina returned to democracy and began to prosecute the military but restarted after President Menem's amnesty laws in 1990.) France prosecuted and convicted the Argentine Navy captain Alfredo Astiz *in absentia* for the murder of two French nuns. (Argentina refused to extradite him.) With these precedents, human rights activists began a series of meetings with jurists, lawyers and prosecutors that led to criminal charges against members of the Chilean and Argentine military in Spain.

At first, few people took Baltasar Garzón seriously. The young judge had made a reputation for pursuing corrupt politicians, drug lords and arms dealers in Spain, but now, by pitting himself against Pinochet, he was boldly prying open the era of terror in Latin America in a way no one else had dared. In 1996, when he began his investigations, the UN courts in The Hague and Arusha were already breathing new life into international criminal law—certainly an encouragement to the ambitious magistrate from a country whose nationals had been murdered across the sea. The decision of the Spanish government to support him also helped, by marking another success in the effort to establish international criminal jurisdiction for crimes against humanity, war crimes and genocide when nations refuse to indict their citizens and run their own trials.

Was Augusto Pinochet unaware that Judge Garzón was investigating his purported leadership of Operation Condor, a collaboration among the Southern Cone military dictatorships in the persecution of leftists? Operation Condor was organized by the head of the Chilean National Intelligence Directorate (DINA) as a means of exchanging intelligence that would lead to the elimination of communism and the defence of Christian society. Dozens of Chileans, Uruguayans, Paraguayans, Brazilians and Bolivians who had sought refuge in Argentina, for example, were arrested or "disappeared" by their own national agents operating in that country.

Did the general not know that in April 1996, the Union of Progressive Prosecutors had filed a complaint against him and other members of the Chilean military for genocide, terrorism and crimes against humanity? Or that a private criminal charge was brought that same year by the Salvador Allende Foundation, which was joined by Izquierda Unida (the United Left) and thousands of Chilean citizens—people whose memory of persecution was not in the least diminished as they gazed daily at mantel-top pictures of their murdered children?

Pinochet knew, but he felt safe enough in his cloak of self-designated immunity not to care, secure enough to travel to London for back surgery. Indignation over human rights violations only bored him, as he did not hesitate to tell the American journalist Jon Lee Anderson who interviewed him for *The New Yorker* magazine on September 25 and 26, 1998. "Let's put an end to the lawsuits," he complained. "There's more than 800 of them. They always go back to the same thing, the same thing." The general believed in letting the past settle quietly. "It is best to remain silent and to forget. . . . And forgetting does not occur by opening cases [and] putting people in jail," he said prophetically on September 13, 1995. "FORGET, this is the word, and for this to occur, both sides have to forget and continue working."

Pinochet was recovering from his surgery in a London clinic when he was arrested on an international warrant from Judge Garzón on October 16, 1998. Two crucial things had happened in just a few days: first, when they heard that Pinochet had left Chile and was in England, Izquierda Unida asked the Spanish court to charge the general for the disappearance and kidnappings of named people and to question him about his role in Operation Condor. Second, another group representing the relatives of victims had formally asked that Pinochet be charged with genocide and torture. Judge Garzón accepted these requests and ordered Pinochet's arrest. On November 6, he requested the general's extradition to Spain.

In his internationally publicized ruling Judge Garzón found that the military leaders of Argentina, Chile and others had collaborated in Operation Condor and that General Pinochet gave orders for the execution, torture, kidnapping and "disappearance" of Chileans, as well as people in different countries. He found that an armed military organization was created to institutionalize a terrorist regime that had carried out the systematic elimination of members of national groups.

Garzón's legal bases had many threads, but the most important were those currently being revived in The Hague and in Rwanda: the requirement for international co-operation in the detection, arrest, extradition and punishment of persons guilty of war crimes and crimes against humanity.

Pinochet was held under house arrest in a mansion just outside London. On March 24, 1999, England's highest court reduced the charges that could be brought against him, by limiting the time frame during which his offences might be considered to 1988 and later—1988 being the year torture carried out elsewhere became a crime punishable in Britain. But the Law Lords also ruled that the general had to stay in England and face possible extradition to Spain. That decision was a slap in the face to the former Conservative prime minister Margaret Thatcher, who had befriended Pinochet, admired his works, ignored his crimes and ceaselessly clamoured for his release. But in March 2000, the British home secretary, Jack Straw, released Pinochet, stating that a team of British doctors had declared him unfit to stand trial. He immediately fled back to Chile.

With or without an extradition, the decision to reject arguments of sovereign immunity and self-serving amnesties in cases of crimes against humanity was another step along the road to international criminal justice. Pinochet made a fatal mistake when he left Chile for England; heads of states, past or present, are not immune—as Slobodan Milošević was to discover when he, too, was indicted for crimes against humanity by the tribunal at The Hague, and as Hissène Habré, the former dictator of Chad, discovered, on February 3, 2000, when he was indicted on charges of torture by a judge in Dakar, Senegal, where he lived in exile. The case against Habré was inspired by the "no safe haven" provision of the 1984 UN Convention Against Torture, which Senegal ratified in 1986, and directly by the Pinochet precedent.

Behind these men, and others like them, were thousands of victims who had experienced assaults upon the innermost core of the self, and surrounding them in an expanding radius were their families: parents, children, and now, after twenty years or more, their grandchildren. The survivors did not forget. Nor did they forgive in the face of flagrant impunity.

"Can anyone explain why Alejandro was sentenced to die without a trial? Why were his remains buried clandestinely in Army property? Why were his detention, murder and burial concealed for 15 years? *Who* is responsible . . . ?" asked one grieving relative in Argentina.[29]

Who, indeed. That was the question international criminal law now sought to answer when heads of state or nations chose the path of forgetfulness.

"Justice alone will never bring peace to our planet," Louise Arbour had said. But as the chief prosecutor for the two international criminal courts for the former Yugoslavia and Rwanda, she knew all about the poison of impunity. With Nuremberg on her mind, she knew the symbolic role a court of justice had played in positioning Germany to move forward after the Second World War. Her predecessor, Richard Goldstone, had voiced the same convictions when we met in Paris in the fall of 1997. "Justice being done and being seen to be done is the difference between lasting peace and an intermission between hostilities" was the way he put it then.

Goldstone and Arbour both believed that if the temporary, ad hoc UN tribunals they had headed were to have any long-term importance, they needed to evolve into a permanent international criminal court with the capacity to investigate and deliver justice to persons who commit the most serious violations of international humanitarian law—namely, war crimes, crimes against humanity and genocide. Take Pinochet and the Argentine generals who were so generously amnestied by their new government after a tenuous democracy took hold. Had such a court already existed on the international stage, one judge (Baltasar Garzón) in one nation (Spain) would not have had to take on the extraordinary task of investigating the criminal acts of the leaders of other countries when the countries themselves proved unwilling to undertake legal action.

The idea for a permanent international criminal court was born long ago, with the Nuremberg trials and the newly created United Nations, then disappeared during the next half century except in barely noticed appeals from a handful of human rights activists.[30] But when the Cold War ended, and the impasse between two superpowers dissolved, the dream that once was relegated to a never-never land of unworkable fancy returned to the realm of reality. In 1993, the atrocities of the Bosnian war finally galvanized the United Nations to do something on the justice front by creating the ICTY and the ICTR. In 1994, human rights groups like No Peace Without Justice and other non-governmental organizations began to lobby the UN for a permanent court. An estimated fourteen million civilians had died in war-related deaths since Nuremberg, and the recourse of sanctions, embargoes and, eventually, collective military force had proved insufficient. With the new face of war increasingly ethnic in character and directed against defenceless civilians, a permanent criminal court began to look like a useful next step.[31]

In 1995, the United Nations dusted off the old draft Statute for an International Criminal Court that had been prepared in its early days, and planned for six preparatory committee meetings over the next two years to allow governments to debate the complicated political and legal issues that would be involved in creating a permanent court. NGOs and international lawyers (both of which became increasingly important to the process as lobbyists and experts) met with governments regionally. In June 1998, representatives of more than 150 countries gathered in Rome for a historic conference convened by the United Nations. On July 17, they voted 120 to 7, with 21 abstentions, in favour of a new statute to create an international criminal court of justice that would be known as the International Criminal Court, the ICC.

With its 13 parts and 128 articles dealing with the creation of the court and its relationship to the United Nations, the new statute was a challenge even to the lawyers. It outlined the crimes that would come within the court's jurisdiction (initially, they would be war crimes, genocide and crimes against humanity); principles of criminal law drawn from different legal systems; the structure of the court and the qualifications and independence of judges; the rights of suspects; trial proceedings, and penalties, appeals and enforcement, to name just a few. The statute would remain open for signature by all states until December 31, 2000. Sixty countries needed to ratify their signatures by an act of parliament, but if this happened according to plan, the Court could begin operating by 2005.

Ominously, the United States was one of the countries that voted against the court. It was in poor company: among the others opposed were some of the world's most notorious violators of human rights: Algeria, China, Libya and America's nemesis, Iraq. And Israel, whose Jewish population had been the object of humanity's worst genocide. (The balance there was tipped by Arab nations that fought to include a paragraph defining the transfer of civilians into the Occupied Territories as a war crime—a move meant to enable the prosecution of Israeli government leaders for allowing Jewish settlers into the area.)

As the single remaining world power after the Cold War, the Americans insisted on their right to use force internationally, when necessary, and complained that their military would be subject to politically motivated accusations. U.S. delegates to the Rome conference tried to pass an amendment that would have forced every proposed case before the ICC to be approved by the UN Security Council, where the United

States has a veto. They also raised suspicions about the power of a completely independent chief prosecutor, suggesting that he or she also should be controlled by the Security Council. Lawyers arguing against the United States pointed out that the statute already controlled the prosecutor to a significant degree and that politically sensitive prosecutions could be halted by the Security Council, even if the council did not hold the sole key to their prior authorization.[32]

Louise Arbour was scathing on the subject when I raised it during our meeting in The Hague. "You can never create a solid institution if you start with the premise that it will be run by corrupt and idiotic people," she told me. "You must start with the assumption that it will be run by intelligent, dedicated, ethical people, and then make sure that happens and that there are mechanisms—checks and balances—to impeach or otherwise remove the prosecutor. You start with a clear idea of what such a court should look like, then create a selection process that is likely to yield what you want, which must be a prosecutor with the capacity to initiate investigations *ex officio*. So that it is not just a political game. All other suggestions, like referrals by the Security Council and so on, are profoundly political. The Security Council is a political organ, and states *never* accuse each other in good faith. What you would have is Iraq accusing the U.S. and vice versa. We could sit down and write the script right now. There's this image out there of a mighty prosecutor—a Master of the Universe. I said to the Americans, *I wish! In my dreams!* There are about one hundred professionals in the Office of the Prosecutor. They are prosecutors, military analysts, investigators, criminal analysts—very smart people, very ethical—and they come at senior levels with a long tradition in their own countries. If they viewed me as some kind of political puppet, they would resign in protest. The assumption is that you would not only have this corrupt Master of the Universe in the job, but that he or she would manage to silence all these other people. If I said, 'Get me an indictment on Milošević and I don't care if you have the evidence,' they would walk out. What is this? It is a convenient Orwellian fantasy to hide the fact that some states do not want to have such a court."

She was angry, but the chief U.S. negotiator, David Scheffer, continued to sound threatening over the months that followed the ICC meeting in Rome. While stating his government's support for the principle of an international criminal court, he also said, "We have a competent legal system in the United States and that system is capable of handling these issues where U.S. citizens are involved."[33] He added, "We have chosen to work within the process, although if we find in the months ahead that this doesn't work, all-out opposition clearly is an option we would have to consider."[34]

The other problem for the Americans was the bugbear of the 1990s: national sovereignty. However, war crimes, crimes against humanity and genocide—the offences that would occupy the new ICC—already transcended the laws of individual nations. Were the Nuremberg Principles to be discarded or watered down because the world's most powerful nation wanted a special deal?

Whether or not the United States succeeded in obstructing or weakening the ICC, the current road bent away from sovereignty in cases of crimes against humanity and war crimes. Augusto Pinochet was served with a warrant and arrested less than four months after the Rome conference. His lawyers, and other friends of the general, argued that the section of the UN Charter based on the sovereign equality between nations prevented Spain from intervening;[34] however, the Spanish parliament had determined that the Charter article in question was not juridical in its intent, and that Spain was exercising its own sovereignty vis-à-vis international crimes. The founding idea for an international criminal court was based on the conviction, already established in law, that leaders with the power to shelter themselves through amnesties and immunities should be answerable to humanity itself.

For half a century, one man never abandoned the campaign for a permanent international criminal court. Benjamin Ferencz, the confidant of the late assistant secretary of war John J. McCloy—the man who took the decision not to bomb Auschwitz—had been a young prosecutor at the Nuremberg trials. It was he who tried twenty-two leading members of the infamous Einsatzgruppen mobile "elimination units" that murdered more than a million Jews. He had also played a central role in negotiating German restitution agreements to compensate victims of Nazi persecution.

Ferencz came to prominence again fifty years later, during the Rome Conference. He was a historic figure, a man of passion and fervour, and a speech he made to the assembled delegates on the second day was quoted everywhere: "I have come to Rome to speak for those who cannot speak: the silent victims of monstrous evil deeds. The only authorization I have comes from my heart: I have spent a long life in pursuit of peace and justice. . . . If we care and dare enough, an international criminal court, the missing link in the world legal order, is within our grasp," he said.[36]

How right he was to speak in the name of the tortured and the dead in a hall filled with lawyers, negotiators and diplomats who had come to thrash out the concept of a permanent court. When Gabrielle Kirk McDonald pleaded over the poinsettias in Madrid, she, too, spoke from her heart, as a woman who had been inspired by the struggle for black civil rights in her country and risen, against the odds, to become president of the ICTY in The Hague. Like her, Benjamin Ferencz had been marked forever—in his case, by an encounter with the perpetrators of genocide.

I contact him though the Justice Watch Discussion List on the Internet, and we arrange to meet in Montreal, where he is slated to receive an award at an upcoming conference titled "Hate, Genocide and Human Rights Fifty Years Later: What Have We Learned? What Must We Do?" organized by Irwin Cotler, a professor of international humanitarian law at McGill University and a renowned crusader for human rights in his own country and elsewhere.

The meeting, at the McGill Faculty of Law, has attracted a distinguished assembly of jurists, parliamentarians, diplomats, human rights activists and community leaders that include Richard Goldstone of South Africa; Harold Koh, assistant U.S. secretary of state for human rights, democracy and labor; David Scheffer; and Philippe Kirsch, the chairman of the Rome Conference to establish an International Criminal Court. (Louise Arbour was slated to come, but the Serbs have begun their attack on Kosovo, and she is at the border, trying unsuccessfully to get in.)

Ferencz is a tiny, aged man of seventy-nine who has clung to a dream; he is as wiry as a taut spring, funny and self-deprecating. "I'm running out of years," he tells his audience as he reflects on decades of obscurity that included writing books about a possible international court. "Never lose hope. Trust your common sense, and if something stinks, say so! You'll be called a fool, and no one will read your books. Then your time will come. When you're old and grey they'll give you a prize you can't carry!"

They laugh appreciatively. Ferencz holds up a (heavy) plaque that has been engraved in his honour.

When the presentation is over, we share muddy cafeteria coffee in Styrofoam cups and he tells me about the days that changed his life. He was born to an immigrant family from Romania and raised in the slums of New York City's Hell's Kitchen, one of the toughest neighbourhoods in the United States. ("That's where I was introduced to crime and the law. I saw that the cops were corrupt, so I became a lawyer.") He volunteered for the army, but hated the robot obedience his superiors demanded.

He was twenty-three years old when he rolled into Europe with the D-Day invasion on June 6, 1944, and entered Germany with the first wave of U.S. troops. Since he was a newly graduated lawyer and had some notion about war crimes (to support himself during law school he had done research for Sheldon Glueck, a leading criminologist from Harvard), he was quickly extricated from his battalion and assigned to General George Patton's headquarters. There he was labelled a war crimes expert and told to set up the investigative division.

The "war crimes division" consisted of Ferencz and one other soldier who was also a young lawyer. Their first job was to investigate the murder of American flyers who had been shot down over Germany, then (if they were still alive) killed by mobs of local townsfolk. That meant digging up the bodies with shovels or getting the locals to do the job. Ferencz and his colleague took written testimony with the help of interpreters, and if twenty people said the same thing, they assumed they knew what had happened, even if the rest lied. Ferencz would try to arrest the person responsible, or get the names of family members or witnesses. Then he would return to his headquarters to write a report.

This rudimentary research formed the basis for the first war crimes trials held by the U.S. Army, in Dachau, in May 1945. Ferencz hammered up a sign: "Third Army War Crimes Trials." But he was disgusted by what took place. "The trials were held by military officers, most of whom were drunk most of the time. They didn't know what it was about. There were no lawyers for the accused. Kangaroo courts. These guys were shell-shocked and couldn't have cared less." Ferencz left the officers to their distasteful business, knowing their prisoners didn't have a chance. A map on his wall told him where the American troops were moving. He caught up with them and entered what were later known as "concentration camps" with the first wave.

What he experienced when he stepped inside Buchenwald and Mauthausen burned itself into his memory: piles of bodies being incinerated, the odour of human flesh being cooked. Emaciated inmates with blank faces. But he had a job to do; he was looking for documentary evidence. "I would tell the U.S. commander, 'I'm here from General

Patton's headquarters and I want everything sealed—no one in and no one out.' I collected what was there: files, archives, the death books, the lists of all the camp guards who had been there. They became the basis for indictments and convictions. Only later did I understand that what I saw there traumatized me for life. Now psychiatry has a name for it: post-traumatic stress disorder. It created a sickness in me, a compulsion. I never stopped after what I saw there. I don't know if it's good or bad, or if I'm just plain crazy!"

Not long afterwards, he met Brigadier-General Telford Taylor, who was about to become chief counsel for war crimes. Taylor asked Ferencz to join him. The young man agreed and soon found himself head of the Berlin branch of Taylor's office, with a staff of fifty people. The Nazis had left their archives intact. Ferencz and his associates, along with a number of German-Jewish refugees who knew the language and something about Nazi structures, went through ten million Nazi Party records, the foreign ministry files and whatever was left from SS ledgers. Then they hit proverbial gold. Ferencz smiles with pleasure in the telling. "One of my researchers found the entire Einsatzgruppen files in the basement of the Gestapo building. There were three or four loose-leaf folders with daily reports from the front. The Einsatzgruppen assignment was the first cold-blooded genocidal slaughter of the war, and they reported that they killed every Jew, Gypsy and opponent of the Nazis they could get their hands on. They had listed their own units and the commanding officers, the times, the places and the numbers killed. I did my tabulations on a little adding machine with one finger—until I passed a million. Then, when they said a town was cleansed of Jews, I put down the number one. It could have been a thousand, but after a million I sure had my case. I took a sampling and flew down to Nuremberg. 'Telford,' I said, 'We have to put on another trial.' He said, 'Yes, but we have a limited budget.' So I said, 'We can't let these guys go free. I'll do it.' And that's how I became chief prosecutor of the Einsatzgruppen case."

The trials of twenty-two leaders of the four Einsatzgruppen (units A, B, C and D) shaped Ferencz's future commitments in yet another way. These were all educated military men, volunteers to the genocidal task. The leading defendant, Otto Ohlendorf, head of Einsatzgruppe D from June 1941 until June 1942, held a Ph.D. and was a devoted family man with five children. He was thirty-eight years old, and he had joined the Nazi Party as a young radical of eighteen.

What struck Ferencz was the lack of remorse among the plaintiffs. And their pathetic lies. The evidence collected in Berlin established the facts as soon as the trials began, and thereafter none of the accused disputed the activities of the Einsatzgruppen. What they did deny was their own particular involvement. One said he had been on leave to attend his grandmother's funeral, and when he returned to the front he learned that terrible things had happened without his authorization. Another claimed he was sick in the infirmary when his men went berserk, out of control. (When Ferencz had their homes searched, he found letters to their wives, bragging about the mass slaughter of Jews.) Sometimes the defendants proudly exaggerated the numbers of murdered dead while simultaneously denying their own participation. Only Otto Ohlendorf calmly and collectedly told the whole truth, in detail, including killing procedures. His unit successfully "liquidated" (his word) ninety thousand people. He was present. He gave the orders.

"When Ohlendorf was sentenced to hang, I went down to his cell to see him," says Ferencz. "I thought maybe he wanted to write to his wife or his children or something. I said, 'Herr Ohlendorf, is there anything you would like to tell me?' He looked at me and said, and I quote, 'The Jews in America will suffer for what you have done to me.'"

Ohlendorf's testimony confirmed, in Ferencz's mind, the need for a permanent international court based on the Nuremberg Principles of accountability, a court whose jurisdiction would extend beyond the sovereignty of every state, whatever its law. Because the rule of law can be depraved.

The testimony is still disturbing:

Ohlendorf: I led the Einsatzgruppe, and therefore I had the task of seeing how the Einsatzkommandos executed the orders [they] received.

Ludwig Babel (counsel for the SS): But did you have no scruples in regard to the execution of these orders?

Ohlendorf: Yes, of course.

Babel: And how is it that they were carried out regardless of these scruples?

Ohlendorf: Because to me it is inconceivable that a subordinate leader should not carry out orders given by the leaders of the state.

Babel: This is your opinion. But this must have been not only your point of view but also the point of view of the majority of the people involved. Didn't some of the men appointed to execute these orders ask you to be relieved of such tasks?

Ohlendorf: I cannot remember any one concrete case. I excluded some whom I did not consider emotionally suitable for executing these tasks and I sent some of them home.

Babel: Was the legality of the orders explained to those people under false pretenses?

Ohlendorf: I do not understand your question; since the order was issued by the superior authorities, the question of legality could not arise in the minds of these individuals, for they had sworn obedience to the people who had issued the orders.[37]

Ferencz and I return to the conference hall to hear the keynote address by the renowned Canadian judge Rosalie Abella, a smart, accessible woman who has sent a gust of fresh air into the stuffy chambers of the Canadian judiciary. She greets her friends, for this conference is, above all, a meeting of colleagues, then launches into her subject, which turns out to be the Holocaust. Abella is the child of survivors, and she, too, speaks from the heart. Her Polish-Jewish parents survived, although most members of their families had not. Neither did her brother, then two and a half years old. She was born in 1946 in Stuttgart, where her lawyer father set up the system of legal services for Displaced Persons at the request of the Americans. She says that she grew up with a passion for justice and a commitment to Nuremberg and its offspring, which includes the United Nations Charter and the Genocide Convention of 1948.

Now she is in her fifties and beset with sadness at the dearth of constructive outrage when atrocities occur. Because, however important they may have been, the Nuremberg trials were nothing but an after-the-fact judicial response to a genocide that should have been stopped. "We still have not learned the most important lesson of all—to try to prevent the abuses in the first place," she says. "We have not finished connecting history's dots. All over the world, in the name of religion, domestic sovereignty, national interest, economic exigency or sheer arrogance, men, women and children are being slaughtered, abused, imprisoned, terrorized and exploited. With impunity."

The audience looks momentarily stunned by her directness and emotion. I am filled with admiration. In my mind, I replay my encounter with Gabrielle Kirk McDonald in The Hague, remember that injustice propelled her into civil rights activism and the study of law, and how despairing she felt when she went to Rwanda and was shown a schoolhouse filled with human skeletons. I think about the convergence of my own passions with those of both these women. Where, I wonder, was the outrage when Hutus massacred 800,000 ethnic Tutsis of both sexes and all ages in Rwanda? Well, outrage can be exhausting; outrage can require one to act. I suppose it was easier for television-jaded populations to switch off their sets and mutter about ancient tribal hatreds, thus allowing their elected leaderships to do nothing—as happened in the early days of the Bosnian war before film from the market bombing of Sarajevo shocked even the most cynical.

The atrium of the building where the conference is being held is strikingly minimalist in design, with full-length windows, white tile floors, black steel pillars and a layered white ceiling from which hangs an array of stylish spotlights. Dramatic and rich. The reception tables are set with smoked-salmon canapés and excellent wines.

But the white walls display a jarring exhibition by the photographer Robert Lyons. Large portraits from Rwanda. The faces of the killers, men and women. Many stare off-camera into a deep, distant place, like the woman in the picture on the wall of Gabrielle Kirk Mcdonald's office. The look in their dulled sunken eyes is recognizable; it is the set expression of people who have witnessed the inhuman or done things so terrible that they can no longer connect with the world. One portrait is of a woman named Ancille Mukaminega who confessed to killing her own children. She is Hutu, the children's father was Tutsi, and she was given the choice of killing them herself or being killed with them.

A few months after Rosalie Abella's speech, for the first time in known history, an international armed intervention was initiated, in Kosovo, with the stated goal of saving a civilian population from ethnic atrocity. The trigger was two-fold: the massacre of forty Kosovar civilians in the village of Račak, by the Yugoslav army, on January 15, 1999; and the failure of peace negotiations in Rambouillet, then Paris, in March. Serbian president Slobodan Milošević did not understand that there had been changes since he agented the peace in Dayton in 1996. Human rights lobbies that came into being during the Bosnian war were better organized and vocal; the public was more informed: dozens of books had been written about specific events, such as the murder of between seven and eight thousand men at Srebrenica;[38] there had been a shift to the liberal centre on the international political front, with Tony Blair elected prime minister in the United Kingdom and Gerhard Schroeder in Germany; the ICTY had better support and funding; and the 1998 Rome Conference had transported Ben Ferencz's dream of a permanent international criminal court into the realm of possibility. The environment had changed under Milošević's nose, so that when the Rambouillet talks failed, an armed intervention that had seemed impossible during the earlier Bosnian debacle was now entirely feasible.

NATO's air campaign succeeded in stopping Slobodan Milošević, but at a huge public relations cost, since there were civilian casualities in Serbia proper (between 488 and 527 according to the respected NGO Human Rights Watch; between 1,200 and 5,700 according to the Yugoslav media); and for the rest of 1999 and into the following year, strange alliances of unlikely bedfellows ceaselessly chipped away at NATO's credibility. In North America, the old Left (or what remained of it) linked arms with neo-conservatives: the former historically hated NATO and "U.S. imperialism," while the latter opposed intervention on grounds of Serb national sovereignty (fearing an erosion there might precipitate an erosion at home), and cited a lack of political and economic interests in the region. In Europe, the United States and Canada, some of the media highlighted conspiracy theories suggesting that NATO and the Kosovo Liberation Army had deliberately left the villagers exposed in order to justify the bombings. Everyone was "spinning" their version of events—until the longstanding reality of Serb oppression of Muslim Albanians in Kosovo seemed to dissolve in a quagmire of relativized guilt where everyone was equally responsible, and where unfathomable "ancient hatreds" were, once again, put forward as a reason for neutrality. It was reasonable to raise questions about the conduct of the intervention—but as the French daily *Le Monde* pointed out in an article on the way the story was being covered, "So-called 'disinterested objective journalism' is the new name for a philosophy of history that refuses to identify a situation of oppression and injustice, that finds excuses to absolve the persecutors, in the name of state sovereignty, of whatever acts of barbarism are permitted in their name, . . . [that finds excuses] to grant inviolable legality to the powers in place, whatever they may represent, and [grants] nothing to the right of people to resist those who subjugate them."[39]

What was indisputable, in spite of the rhetoric, was that Serb forces had committed serious crimes in Kosovo before the NATO intervention, and had a plan for massive ethnic cleansing, to be co-ordinated by the Yugoslav army, Serbian police and paramilitary forces. As Balkans specialist Noel Malcolm pointed out in *The Spectator* in late 1999,[40] thousands of civilians were murdered (by May 2000, the ICTY had estimated that the final number was close to five thousand), 800,000 people were expelled into neighbouring countries; and more than sixty thousand homes, and hundreds of mosques and historic buildings, were destroyed. Because there were doubts over whether refugees were, perhaps, fleeing NATO bombs rather than the forces of Milošević, the respected American Association for the Advancement of Science (AAAS) undertook a statistical study of the data. In May 2000 they reported that "only a small fraction of Kosovar Albanians fled Kosovo as a direct result of NATO bombing raids," and that the massive flight was the result of a deliberate Yugoslav policy of "cleansing."[41]

Did NATO's air campaign against Serbia signal a change in the traditional laissez-faire behaviour of the great powers? It would take years to tell, but the decision to intervene militarily in the affairs of Serbia, a sovereign country, did suggest the prospect—remote, perhaps, but possible—that the century of genocide might be giving way to a changed world view in which international human rights were finally accorded greater value. Although the anarchy that emerged in Kosovo in the months after NATO forced an end to the conflict was appalling—furious Kosovars exacting revenge on the remaining Serbs, in spite of the presence of United Nations peacekeepers—and although the prospects for a return to multi-ethnic society continue to look dismal at this writing, these developments do not diminish the importance of an intervention on the part of the international community that made it possible for hundreds of thousands of Kosovar refugees to return home and loosened Serbia's grasp on Kosovo. Fittingly, the ICTY is also extending its investigations to crimes committed by the Kosovo Liberation Army (KLA).

On the other hand, a justified invervention does not condone abuses, if they occurred, and old concerns about "victors' justice" have been reawakened. Human Rights Watch has called for an independent commission to investigate possible violations, and an international effort, headed by Noam Chomsky and Canadian law professor Michael Mandel, accuses sixty-eight Western leaders of having committed "flagrant violations of international law" during the air campaign over Serbia.

Once charges such as these have been levelled, they must be looked into; in late 1999, the Mandel file was placed in the hands of Carla Del

Ponte, who had replaced Louise Arbour as chief prosecutor at The Hague in September of that year;[42] but she was immediately called to account by the United States. The White House issued a blunt statement saying: "We point out that NATO fully followed the laws of armed conflict in training, targeting and operations involving Kosovo, and that NATO undertook extraordinary efforts to minimize collateral damage. Any inquiry into the conduct of its pilots would be completely unjustified."[43] Rear Admiral Craig Quigley, a Pentagon spokesman, defended NATO personnel and suggested there was no reason for an inquiry: "We're darn sure we followed the laws of armed conflict for anything and everything in Kosovo," he said categorically (if colloquially).[44]

Del Ponte responded furiously when questioned about what U.S. Senator Jesse Helms triumphantly called her "backpedalling." "'Backpedalling' is an ugly word. And it is not my way of working. I pedal only forwards," she told a journalist from the London-based Institute for War and Peace Reporting. "I have just received a preliminary report on the documentation. . . In the meantime, I am waiting for the second report and an analysis. . . [Then] I will take a decision on whether or not I must open an investigation."[45]

In June 2000, Del Ponte declined to investigate—meaning that corrosive doubts about possible war crimes and breaches of human rights would persist. No one had addressed this issue more clearly than Telford Taylor in his book, *The Anatomy of the Nuremberg Trials*: "There is no moral or legal basis for immunizing victorious nations from scrutiny," he wrote prophetically. "The laws of war are not a one-way street."[46] Alex Boraine had made the same point about the ANC and amnesty when he argued that human rights violations can occur, and must be addressed, even when the cause is just.

The long road from the Nuremberg trials stopped abruptly when the Cold War began, then started again at century's end. It saw the invention of distinct landmarks along the way: conventions to strengthen international human rights and criminal law; war crimes trials in Germany, Israel, France, Britain and elsewhere; and finally the creation of ad hoc United Nations tribunals in The Hague and Rwanda. It saw a return to the idea of a permanent international criminal court that now seemed possible, if not inevitable, in spite of problems in its definition, and a continuing, world-shaking debate about the limits of national sovereignty. It saw the arrest of a dictator who was foolish enough to leave his home territory, and the first-ever indictment of a sitting political leader for war crimes. Although Pinochet was successful in his quest to avoid extradition and prosecution in Spain, a new message had been delivered to the tyrants, and would-be tyrants, of the world.

But Rosalie Abella's words rang in my ears. "Nuremberg," she said, quoting Elie Wiesel, "is the story of those who did the killing. . . . Nuremberg is also the story of those who did nothing."

Not just the perpetrators of the twentieth-century catastrophes, but the bystanders who watched it happen.

For justice is only a response to evil after evil is done. A necessary, but never fulfilling, recompense.

Coda

In the Wake of Memory and Forgetfulness

THE STORIES OF COUNTRIES are much like the stories of our own lives: filamented, partly illusory and threaded through with remembered fact and fantasy. They are, as the author and political scientist Benedict Anderson has suggested, "Imagined Communities."[1]

Yet after three years of travel to the places of this book—the stricken lands of unresolved event, as I think of them now—I am impressed by how fiercely people will fight to chronicle their personal and collective experience in the face of an official history that has been falsified. I met such people everywhere. I met them in Japan, where the former Nagasaki mayor Hitoshi Motoshima had risked his life to speak out against the ambiguous leadership role played by the late Emperor Hirohito during the Second World War, and where the nuclear-bomb survivor Dr. Kōsō Matsuo struggles impotently with his conscience over his government's stubborn refusal to acknowledge the fact of the 1937 massacre in Nanking. I met them in France, where a fabricated story of widespread heroic resistance camouflaged the French contribution to the Final Solution and submerged the extent of the tragedy of its Jewish citizens—and where Michel Slitinsky laboured in obscurity for twenty-five years to discover the truth about what had happened to his family in

Bordeaux. I met them in Germany, where a new generation has risen up in anger against silence and dissimulation; where children of Nazi perpetrators still suffer—and where, at the deepest level, an entire society remains indelibly marked by twelve years of Nazi rule in the middle of the twentieth century. That period is, it appears, impossible to assimilate or explain away but to Germany's great credit it is now memorialized and taught in the schools. I met them in the United States; there, those who fight to be heard are mostly, but not all, black Americans striving to surmount the legacy of their country's slave past, a legacy that has not been dislodged by the enlightened democratic ideology that is the foundation of their country, leaving a lacuna that affects American culture in visible ways. I met such people in South Africa, where a powerful need to know the truth about what happened during the decades of apartheid rule led to the Truth and Reconciliation Commission, in the belief that the past must be an open book if the nation is to make the transition to full democracy. Finally, I met them in the former Yugoslavia, where the people who flailed against what passed for history were, to my mind, the saddest and most cynical of all. Serbs who knew what had been done in their names slashed their swords through the insubstantial air. Where lying is described as "a form of our patriotism and . . . evidence of our innate intelligence," in the words of the Belgrade writer Dobrica Ćosić, "truth in history" is a meaningless phrase, even at the most basic level of factual event. What matters is the way that the past—however it is conceived—can be bent to serve the present. Although twentieth-century totalitarian cultures perfected the art of the controlled historical lie, in varying degrees, the *desire* to shape the way history is remembered is universal, and as true of any of the other countries I visited as it is of present-day Serbia.

Beyond contemporary postmodern theorizing about what we can "know" and what is "true" lies the bedrock of the historical record. And when that record is tampered with—and Serbia is a good example—there are, it seems to me, two responses. One is the desire to fight back, as so many have done. The other is despair and disorientation. I shall never forget Miloš and Gordana and their matter-of-fact conviction that everything they read and heard was a public lie, or Miloš's halting questions about personal accountability—a concept so alien to the only culture he had known—or his fear of life itself. Nor will I forget Drinka Gojković's tale of the role "dissident" intellectuals played in the hysteria of renewed Serb nationalism, or her painstakingly researched book that gathers dust on the shelves of bookstores because hopelessness and penury have flattened the desire to care. Or the screaming voice of Borka Pavićević, or the self-preserving cynical laughter of her husband, Nikola Barović.

The number of ways we shape historical memory is, I now believe, surprisingly limited, ranging from outright lies and denial, as in Serbia and Japan, through judicious mythmaking, as in France, to benign or deliberate negligence, as in the United States, to attempts to confront and possibly right the past, as in South Africa. And the memory of the Second World War, which sits implacably at the heart of the twentieth century, refusing to be displaced, contains almost every style of coping. Although the worldwide wars of the past century were separated by two decades, the second came in the psychological wake of the first. The century of global conflict that opened with the shock of the Great War, which was (and has remained) devastating—physically, culturally and socially—shook loose nineteenth-century ideas about progress in human nature, the belief that moral improvement would parallel the developments of technology. After that loss there were fewer moorings and fewer certainties—and new kinds of equivocation.

Possibly because Emperor Hirohito was never charged with war crimes under the rubric of command responsibility, and possibly because a secret immunity deal was struck with Dr. Shirō Ishii in return for his data on biological warfare (meaning that the details of his horrific experimentation on human beings in occupied Manchuria did not emerge during the Tokyo Trials), life in Japan carried on under an imposed democratic constitution. But the personal guilt of old soldiers eventually penetrated the traditional screens that had been carefully positioned to block out the memory of war (except for approved commemorations of the nuclear attacks on Hiroshima and Nagasaki). Not until the emperor died, and the haunted men began to confess, did visible shades of grey appear on the black-and-white tableau of Japanese memory. An established culture of impunity that sanctifies designated war criminals made it considerably easier for the Japanese to dismiss the Tokyo Trials as the imposition of foreign "un-Japanese values" than for the Germans to dismiss Nuremberg. And easier to deny the macabre events of their war using the education of children as a springboard for dissimulation.

Germany, the perpetrator state at the heart of Europe, had fewer choices when it came to the construction of Second World War memory, since the Nuremberg Tribunal had confirmed the facts beyond any reasonable doubt. Fifty years later, the continuing debate in that country is about *degrees* of national guilt (compared with Soviet guilt, for example), about what part of the population carries the blame and how long they must expect to make apologies and amends. Unlike in Japan, it is not about denial.

As for the idea that "France" resided in London during the war, General Charles de Gaulle seems to have succeeded in his unlikely myth-making for one understandable reason. After an initial flourish of rough justice, during which the most visible pro-Nazi collaborators were summarily dispatched, the rest of the population was more than pleased to accept the designation of *résistant* in the hope that thousands of other equivocal acts would never see the light of day. And, for the most part, they did not: a half century passed before Maurice Papon, an ordinary bureaucrat in the service of Vichy and Marshal Pétain, assumed his seat in a Bordeaux courtroom.

If distortions and lies about the past seem to have a limited lifespan, it may be (although this may alarm the cynical) because of something as primary as shame. Shame and the need to confess seem to be universal traits: the Catholic Church understood this centuries ago when it instituted the confessional, and in our (largely) post-religious age, secular sufferers may lie on an analyst's couch or (in the United States) compete to appear on a tell-all talk show. But whatever techniques people or cultures adopt, the presence of shame seems to offer evidence for what the International Military Tribunal at Nuremberg established in law so long ago: that there are universally understood principles of just behaviour, deriving perhaps from the spiritual underpinnings of human society, that override the laws of nations when those laws direct soldiers and citizens to engage in anti-human acts.

Such ideas used to belong in the realm of theology, and they still have a cross-over in the minds of some people; for example, in a speech to the Parliament of Canada on April 29, 1999, the Czech president, Vacláv Havel (himself a superlative example of what was *right* with the twentieth century), said that such universal standards make sense "only in the perspective of the infinite and the eternal. . . . If we did not sense this, or subconsciously assume it, there would be some things that we could never do."[2] It is unclear whether the men (and they were all men) of the Nuremberg Tribunal had God in mind when they invented new international humanitarian and criminal law, but even without the Eternal, millions of post-religious denizens of contemporary Western societies might willingly affirm the existence of universal standards based on post-Enlightenment ideals of civil society. Or on the more pragmatic grounds of a tacit Rousseauian social contract in which we abandon our right to behave in certain narcissistic ways in the expectation that our neighbour will do the same. (Perhaps we refrain from running him down with the electric lawnmower because he has walked on our grass, hoping he has conditioned himself to obey similar restraints. Not very godly, but a reasonably useful covenant for living in society.)

The most pernicious aspect of unresolved shame is that it visits itself upon the innocent. The lives of many children of Nazi perpetrators were effectively ruined as they found themselves forced to disown once-beloved parents or to incorporate the memory of them differently, as Martin Bormann Jr. has somehow managed to do with his notorious father. Denial, anger and shame rose to the surface in South Africa as apartheid withered and died. Like Martin Bormann Jr., Willie Verwoerd has to live on with a tarnished name. He had internalized the goals of "truth and reconciliation" and committed himself to work for Archbishop Tutu's commission; he was trying "to come home to [himself]," as he put it—to accept his unerasable identity as "a white Afrikaner, a Christian and a Verwoerd."

The legacy of shame can be found twisting through the generations in other places. In the United States, 135 years after Abraham Lincoln's famous Emancipation Proclamation of 1863, the scion of a South Carolina slave-owning family broke the dense silence and published a book about the old family business and about his blood kindred, both black and white. I went to hear Edward Ball lecture at the University of Toronto. He talked about the rift his work had created among his white relatives and the threats he had received on radio talk shows from black callers. He said, "I feel like a projection screen for people's feelings about race and the memory of slavery."

His Toronto audience was made up of white expatriate Americans, some of whom had family ties to slavery: many had come to participate vicariously in the expiation and said so. It was also made up of blacks, all of whom had old ties to slavery. They, too, wanted to participate vicariously. Some were descended from families that had been enslaved in South Carolina and thought they might actually be "Balls." In its review of *Slaves in the Family*,[3] *The Village Voice* wrote: "Ball breaks hundreds of years of silence from white people. . . ."[4] The *Chattanooga Times*, a southern paper, wrote of "how the legacy of an evil institution still resonates in the collective memories of black and white Americans." One man's remorse inching open closed doors.

And finally, as I write these words in the aftermath of the slaughter in Kosovo in which thousands of civilians were destroyed, there are reports of shamed Yugoslav soldiers beginning to confess. The *Chicago Tribune* published a story on July 7, 1999, just days after the end of the conflict, quoting one Corporal Radovan Milićević who was haunted by images he could not banish from memory. Milićević was forty-one and a research engineer in private life. Nothing in his experience, he said, had prepared him for the horror he became a part of.

Miloš Vasić, of the Belgrade weekly *Vreme*, said he was "ashamed as a human being" over Serb ethnic cleansing in Bosnia. Not as a Serb, or a Yugoslav, but as a human being. His pained, resonant words echo in other places, in the cadences of different languages.

Perhaps lies and inventions about history are inevitably exposed because the leaders who propagate such fables fail to understand something visceral and primary: that ordinary people will remember, even when they are ordered not to; that the victims—including their children and eventually their grandchildren—will not disappear, although they may be traumatized and cowed for many years. The Chinese diaspora in the United States and Canada finally felt secure enough as new citizens of pluralist societies to initiate public lobbying over the 1937 Rape of Nanking, and by doing so, they brought a poorly known event to world attention and seriously embarrassed official Japan. Going public over things that happened long ago also encouraged a few brave Korean and Philippine "comfort women" to speak out, although they had to overcome cultural shame in order to do so: only 20 per cent had survived the ordeal of sexual slavery, and to acknowledge what took place was difficult for these now-elderly women. It took the Japanese-Canadian community forty years to overcome their silent shame and successfully demand apology and damages from the Canadian government for their internment during the Second World War. They were awarded $291 million as reparations in 1988, the same year President Ronald Reagan compensated Japanese Americans. None of these people had forgotten. Victims never forget.

When he was eight years old, Serge Klarsfeld saw his father ripped away from the family by the Nazis as he and his mother hid, trembling, behind a false wall in the closet of their Nice apartment. "Help! *Au secours!* We are French citizens!" his father cried, voicing the Enlightenment promise of inclusiveness and religious tolerance. Decades later, Klarsfeld and his German-born wife, Beate, were responsible for reviving the public memory of Jewish deportations from France and for the series of French trials that began with Klaus Barbie and ended with Maurice Papon.

Jewish victims of the Holocaust were silent for many years; if they did try to speak, they were barely listened to. But Elie Wiesel, who was but one among many, successfully rallied an entire generation of Jews *and* gentiles until the Holocaust came to symbolize the war in large measure—and *holocaust* became one of the most overused words in the late-twentieth-century lexicon.

And when the Argentine president Carlos Menem declared an irrevocable pardon for people who had engaged in "Dirty War" crimes, a short chain of events blocked the oblivion he desired. The first was family. For twenty years the mothers of "disappeared" children have paraded around the Plaza de Mayo in central Buenos Aires, on the same day every week, carrying picture posters of their missing sons and daughters and demanding justice. Other victims began to bring lawsuits outside the country. And the establishment of ad hoc international courts for ex-Yugoslavia and Rwanda by the United Nations in The Hague and in Tanzania encouraged a young judge in Spain to apply the same principles of international law to Argentina and Chile at the highest political levels and to accept petitions from injured parties in both those countries.

Because the experience of having been victimized travels through the generations, carrying calls for justice or revenge or both, victims will necessarily outlast—and outnumber—the leadership that lies about what happened to them or tries to deny their suffering.

In the end, their stories are known.

What pushes people on is impunity: the rankling, intolerable fact that those who commit murder and other atrocities get away with it and sometimes dare to say the crime never took place. The erasing of personal as well as public history.

Serge Klarsfeld told me that impunity was what kept him going in his search for Klaus Barbie in Bolivia, where Barbie had lived for almost forty years. What outraged him was the realization that many of the men and women who had committed terrible crimes went on to bear children and lead successful lives while their victims lay dead in the ground.

Impunity is what lay behind the story of an ordinary woman in Argentina, recounted to me by the Canadian writer Alberto Manguel. During the Dirty War, he told me, the oldest daughter of the family, who was about twenty, and a former classmate of his in Buenos Aires, was shot in the street for her reputed political involvement. Her brother, who was seventeen, was arrested by the security forces. Days later, his mutilated body was stuffed into a bag and deposited on his mother's doorstep. This woman happened to know the man responsible for her son's arrest, just as many other Argentines had a personal acquaintance with their persecutors, and for years after the election of Carlos Menem she lived in the hope of an arrest and the possibility of justice. On the day Menem announced his final, irrevocable pardon, she happened to be shopping in her local supermarket. The man who had taken her son was shopping too. He smiled pleasantly and said, "Good morning, señora."

The woman returned to her home and took her life.

An environment of impunity, together with public apathy, encourages the initially hesitant. As Elie Wiesel wrote in his report to the President's Commission on the Holocaust, "Still, the killers could not be sure. In the beginning they made one move and waited. Only when there was no reaction did they make another move, and still another. From racial laws to medieval decrees, from illegal expulsions to the establishment of ghettos and then to the invention of death camps, the killers carried out their plans only when they realized that the outside world simply did not care. . . ."

Fifty years after the Nazis, impunity also laid the groundwork for one of history's most brutal massacres. Before the bloodbath in Rwanda, Radio Télévision Libre des Milles Collines, a Hutu-operated radio station, transmitted poisonous anti-Tutsi propaganda urging its listeners to genocide. The international community knew about this and stood by. At approximately the same time, the Serbian president, Slobodan Milošević, was able to observe the parallel lack of Western resolve in Bosnia and understand the implied message that he could disregard UN resolutions and blustering threats. Doubly, as it happened: Milošević not only got away with ethnic cleansing, he became the point person for peace negotiations in the region. That he went on to perpetrate ethnic cleansing in Kosovo before the dead in Bosnia had been exhumed from their graves, and with precisely the same pattern of atrocities, was a clear signal that he understood the bluff—or thought he had. His 1999 indictment for war crimes was a belated blow against the impunity he enjoyed for so long, but until he is transported to The Hague, exemption will rule the day.

The moral, psychological and political issues are tangled and complex. For example, impunity is often legitimized by amnesty, and amnesty is a time-honoured tool for moving on after difficult times, especially in the wake of civil wars or when there is no clear winner to a conflict. On such occasions, amnesty is often described as an act of generosity on the part of the victors, and because it looks like the political expression of Christian forgiveness, it may appear even more attractive at first glance. There are often supposed economic reasons for indulging in amnesties. President Menem of Argentina may have been intimidated when the powerful Argentine military took exception to the conviction and imprisonment of some of its members for crimes committed during the Dirty War, but he also had in mind the need to jump-start the economy of his ravaged country as well as the need to create new democratic institutions. In Argentina, as well as in Chile and other Latin American countries emerging from military dictatorships, amnesty for past wrongs has often been depicted as an easy restart button.

"Starting again" has a long tradition in France (when the 1789 Revolutionaries threw out the standard calendar, they merrily drew up another one starting with "Year One"), and the need for amnesty loomed especially large after the Second World War. Many of the reasons that were put forward sounded right at the time, just as they did decades later in Argentina: peace, reconstruction, the transition to democracy and a sincere hope for reconciliation among erstwhile enemies. What could be more desirable?

These goals are important—too important to dismiss—and if it really is a route to their realization, amnesty cannot be easily rejected. But amnesty cannot be counted on to bring long-term peace and reconciliation. The decision of the French National Assembly to push the murky business of 1940–1944 into the back closet of history with a far-reaching amnesty law failed in the long term because unacknowledged criminal acts do not quietly disappear into the ether of the past; on the contrary, they frequently reverberate ever more loudly as the years go by. The sight of known murderers walking in the streets and shopping in supermarkets can only be corrosive. Can anyone imagine amnesty as a workable "solution" for Germany at the end of the Second World War?

Because it is often a legal underpinning to impunity, amnesty is, in the deepest sense, unjust. Unjust to the victims. Unjust to societies where appalling crimes have been committed. And, strangely enough, unjust to the perpetrators themselves, in that by tacitly condoning a criminal act, amnesty stands in the way of the personal and social rebalancing that can be brought about by acknowledgment and penalty. Although amnesty is an apparently easy solution that looks good and feels familiar (partly because of its ostensible Christian pedigree) and seems promising in the short term, it only papers over the past. Pandora's untamed Furies have been known to wait, forever if necessary, for their next release. Until history opens the box again.

Accountability is, it now seems to me, the key. Without it, the reinvented wartorn countries I visited seem headed for further trouble. With accountability come facts about the past and possibly an acknowledgment of wrongdoing, but most important, accountability is a way of separating the ill-favoured past from the present and perhaps a stepping stone to something akin to justice. In countries where accountability takes the shape of trials within the legal system, these need to be conducted with the strictest guarantees of defence counsel, cross-examination and timeliness, because any perception of bias inevitably maintains the very links with the past that such trials are supposed to sever. Nikola Barović's description of skewed trial procedures throughout the former Yugoslavia was cynical, perversely funny and unforgettable; as an arm of the all-pervasive state, the courts were useless as tools of justice, accountability or reconciliation. (In March 2000, the European Union acknowledged the travesty by placing on its list of *personae non gratae* fifty-four judges, magistrates and prosecutors from Serbia who had been prominent in government prosecutions of independent media and opposition politicians.)

Because "truth" and "reconciliation" do not add up to justice in any recognizable sense, South Africa ran a certain risk by holding a Truth and Reconciliation Commission, with its emphasis on confession, amnesty and hoped-for racial forgiveness. The families of Steve Biko and the murdered Durban lawyer Griffith Mxenge understood that amnesty and justice are incompatible when they tried, and failed, to curtail the commission in the South African courts. In thousands of less high-profile cases, confessing butchers were amnestied because their acts were judged to have had a political motivation. Desmond Tutu argued to me that standing up and confessing before the country is punishment in itself, which is true to a point, but it is not punishment in the usual sense. Is it enough that the infamous Dirk Coetzee blew the whistle, so to speak, on the strange, government-sponsored, semi-cannibalistic environment of Vlakplaas? One imagines he plans to stay far away from places where he might happen upon Griffith Mxenge's surviving relatives.

It will take years, perhaps a generation, to know the long-term results of the South African experiment, but Brandon Hamber, a psychologist at the Centre for the Study of Violence and Reconciliation in Johannesburg, told me that the TRC process had made it possible for a "middle-road between the polemics of prosecution and blanket amnesty" to emerge.[5]

But the TRC was far from satisfying, as Hamber acknowledged when he pointed out that the commission had exposed only some of the truth about apartheid and that it had emphasized some truths over others. For example, he said, violence between the ANC and the Inkatha Freedom Party took more than fifteen thousand lives between 1990 and 1994, but the TRC investigations had concentrated on *state* violence. I thought that focus made sense: the state held ultimate power, and state-authorized violence will always inhabit a category all its own, wherever it occurs. But still, there was a contest and a trade-off. Systemic violence in apartheid South Africa was a densely complicated affair with tendrils that reached into dark places, but the TRC, given its limited time frame, needed to be simple, centred and (one must add) politically careful in its decisions.

Yet the major achievements of the commission are plain to see, and the most important of these has been the swift establishing of fact, even if partial. What actually happened during the apartheid years will be part of an authentic historical record, even if it is not the complete story. The TRC may have tried to be a court of truth *and* a metaphor for social transformation—two possibly incompatible aims—but in spite of its lapses and failures, it was a strikingly bold effort to overcome the chasm of race and class hatred after decades of oppression and a long civil war.

It is impossible to argue with the suggestion that a Nuremberg-style court of justice would have brought renewed violence to South Africa, because the hypothesis was never tested, and it is conceivable that allowing one side to try the other side for war crimes or crimes against humanity would have been a disaster. Still, at the end of Tutu's brave effort, the lines of Nuremberg justice seem clearer—and possibly more permanent. The formalities of trials and due process were sobering and instructive. They put out the message that justice, even partial "victors' justice," remains possible after a debased past.

The Nuremberg court cracked opened a new era in international law, then languished for decades, but at the start of the twenty-first century it is possible to hope that the United Nations courts for the former Yugoslavia and Rwanda might also help end a dark epoch. Glimmerings of transition could be seen in Rwanda, when Prime Minister Jean Kambanda pleaded guilty to genocide, and in the arrest of General Pinochet outside the borders of his country. Within this emerging culture of international justice, a permanent multinational criminal court would offer even greater hope. The very prospect of a trial beyond their national borders might give pause to future tyrants.

"Out of timber so crooked as that from which man is made, nothing entirely straight can be built," wrote the eighteenth-century German philosopher Immanuel Kant. There will inevitably be future tyrants—future incarnations of Augusto Pinochet, Slobodan Milošević, and even Adolf Hitler—if the past is an indicator of the future. Many sense this. Writing in the *Bangkok Post* on July 14, 1999, James Hightower, a U.S. defence consultant, related the story of a woman whose relatives were killed by the Khmer Rouge after the death of Pol Pot. Informed that the leader had not personally done the deed, she merely shook her head sadly and said, "There are many Pol Pots."

Hightower was struck by her fatalism and by the futility of trying to combat the demon of genocide. He wrote of "the mirage of justice," of "floundering attempts to achieve accountability in Cambodia," of the convictions in Rwanda that were, he said, of "little weight balanced against the anguish of millions," of the graves being uncovered in Kosovo and of what he called the "grotesque malevolence" we see around us. He wrote of the falsity of fixing entire responsibility on individual "monsters" such as Pol Pot and Slobodan Milošević. And of the endemic problem of dehumanizing "the other" so that anything—absolutely anything—can be inflicted on the presumed-to-be inhuman enemy.

I sympathize with his grief and agree with almost every word—except his implied premise that since crimes against humanity are overwhelming, hopefulness is a luxury one should leave to Pollyanna. I was reminded of a letter George Orwell once wrote to Arthur Koestler, during the blackness of 1944: "It is possible that man's major problems will never be resolved," he said in despairing recognition. Then, unable to endure the implications of his own words, he immediately added: "It's unthinkable! Who is there who dares to look at the world today and say to himself, 'It will always be like this, even in a million years. . . ?'"[6]

Orwell's words were much on my mind as I travelled through once ravaged lands. Especially his subsequent rejoinder to himself as he struggled with the meaning of his thoughts. "Perhaps the choice before man is not always a choice of evils," he continued in his letter to Koestler. "Perhaps even the aim of Socialism is not to make the world perfect, but to make it better."[7]

To conclude that partial victories may be the ultimate achievement possible cannot have been easy for an early-twentieth-century utopian such as George Orwell. He had lowered his impossible expectations.

The tricky question of guilt—individual guilt, collective guilt, guilt passed down through the generations—was also much on my mind. Like Louise Arbour before she went to The Hague, I started this quest with clear-cut ideas about the unfairness of the "guilt tarbrush." Although the subject of my book—the historical memory of nations—dictated that I look at groups as well as individuals, I believed—and still believe—that collective guilt is intolerant and discriminatory; it smears entire peoples and leads to generalizations and racism, a point I made to my audience of Holocaust survivors when I disagreed with Daniel Goldhagen's thesis about "Germans." The entire system of Western justice is based on individual responsibility before the law, and when that wavers—as it began to do during the early days of the trial of Adolf Eichmann, for example, when dozens of peripheral questions about why the Holocaust had happened were asked, and during the run-up to the trial of Klaus Barbie, when the same marginal subjects were raised—justice can be subverted. (Barbie tried to use *tu quoque* [you too] arguments to relativize his own deeds). Both of these cases did refocus on the guilt or innocence of the accused, but outside the courtroom there were—and are—disquieting dilemmas. When Louise Arbour talked to me about the psychological fusion of the community with the personality of the leader—she was thinking specifically about Bosnian Serbs and Radovan Karadžić—she opened the door to a question that includes, but also transcends, the courtroom: how would the collectivity react to the trial of their leader for war crimes they had passively acquiesced to? The Nuremberg prosecution had allowed ordinary Germans to distance themselves from the so-called monsters in the dock, but would the result have been more complicated had Hitler been on trial in that famous courtroom? Two post-war generations of Germans still suffer from the knowledge that Hitler "belonged" to them and they "belonged" to him: Karl Jaspers's assertion that there is a difference between "guilt," for which there is only individual culpability, and "communal responsibility," for crimes that could not have been committed without a collective looking-away, has never been resolved.

Many of the people I met were troubled by feelings of associated guilt. Miloš Vasić thought the idea of collective guilt was "wrong and unfair," but, he added poignantly, "history sometimes hangs over us in terrible ways." Archbishop Tutu said that because human beings live in communities, groups must acknowledge their part in the past, through their spokespersons, in a symbolic confession of wrongdoing. The distressed young woman I encountered in the synagogue in Berlin had dreamed that she had been chosen to make amends to the Jews on behalf of her family. In the tiny community of Friedrichstadt, Karl Michelsohn, a veteran of the Hitler Youth and the Wehrmacht, was restoring dignity to the dead by chronicling the lives of his murdered townsfolk.

Some people respond with denial and counteraccusations; I met them too. But broad questions about personal guilt, collective responsibility and the inherent complicity of passively standing by when appalling crimes are being perpetrated seem to be emerging like unexploded land mines that have washed to the surface after a torrential rain. And for the first time in history, we seem all to be indirectly involved—thanks to television technology. When people innocently turn on their sets and see unmediated, uncontextualized pictures of atrocity and suffering sandwiched between ads for beer or mutual funds, they are, like it or not, transformed into complicit bystanders. I am reminded of a documentary that was broadcast on the South Africa Broadcasting Corporation (SABC) in January 2000 (later rebroadcast on CNN and CBC), said to be unlike anything ever shown before on television. *Sierra Leone: Out of Africa* opens with a fearful scene: a young man, suspected to be a rebel, pleads for his life on the ravaged streets of the city: "I am a woodcutter," he tells the soldiers standing over him with guns. "I only came to find fish for us to cook. Don't you people know me?" The men threatening him were, in other words, acquaintances (like Vlatko Kupreškić, who drank coffee with his Muslim neighbour in Ahmići the night before he attacked and killed most of the family). But pleas are useless. A soldier shoots the young man point-blank and he dies before the eyes of the viewers—a gruesome atrocity filmed by Sorious Samura, a Sierra Leonean documentarist so deeply pained by the effects of civil war on his country that he wants the situation known internationally. At the same time, he now asks himself whether the presence of the camera may actually have provoked the killing. Claire Robertson, an SABC editor, said she went through "a long night of the soul" before deciding to broadcast the film. She said television must tread a fine line between showing the reality of war and exposing audiences to unnecessary horror, and that she and her colleagues eventually decided that viewers had the right to "witness history."[8]

But witnesses incur responsibilities, as anyone who has ever seen a traffic accident and had to go to court to testify, knows. In the new world of globally televised war crimes, the defence of "not knowing," or neutrality, will dissolve for everyone. To be a witness or bystander is not a value-free choice but, inadvertently, a moral position; and in this sense the "guilt" of people who live with the memory of crimes committed by members of their families, or communities, has been unwittingly extended to everyone who watches appalling pictures on the news. Western nations finally took action in Bosnia and Kosovo only after millions of people had viewed the marketplace in Sarajevo where a massacre had occurred. Military intervention to stop crimes against humanity and genocide, and international courts to deter and punish, may partly be compensation for the guilt we feel—an antidote to world-wide television programming that has transformed us into involuntary voyeurs and bystanders.

Besides being a source of the problem *and* a reason for human rights initiatives, the democracy of global information is influencing history and memory in other ways. Of the various efforts to reinvent a nation after difficult times—all of them flawed, all of them incomplete, all of them trapped in contradictions—the least successful seems to be the outright telling of lies about the past, but this oldest of strategies may become less possible in the twenty-first century as the Internet cracks open the most iron-clad of containers. Knowledge, including historical knowledge, can no longer be sealed off in quite the same way by political leaders whose strategy is to shape opinion through censorship and propaganda.

At the end of this journey, it seems to me that reconciling the long shadows cast by the uneasy past may ultimately depend on elements so basic that they bring to mind a simple Slav proverb I once came across and never forgot: Eat bread and salt and speak the truth. They are the recovery of fact, public accountability and the instituting of fair trials of one sort or another, to help mark ends and beginnings and to return the moral compass as close to the centre as possible. The demand for politically expedient solutions will always be present; for the sake of social harmony and perceived stability, responsible citizens are often expected to put away the past and never to speak publicly about what happened or who was responsible. But seen through a long lens, peacemaking founded on "forgetting" appears to have a limited lifespan.

There are other ways. In the deep place where memory lives, simple actions can speak of a national commitment to turn the historical page: official acknowledgments; apologies, if necessary; memorials to the victims; restitution; permanent museums that tell a factual story; the teaching of schoolchildren about the origins of hatred. All potent, symbolic acts.

But even then. . . .

The Germans call it *Vergangenheitsbewältigung*: mastering, or overcoming, the past. A lofty ideal that is doomed to failure, not just because of the immensity of Nazi crimes. For the past, it seems, can never be overcome. It lurks forever in memory. It loiters in cemeteries. It shelters behind beautifully painted movable screens.

The past can only be managed. With remembrance. With accountability. With justice—however frail, however inadequate, however imperfect.

Notes

1: The Stone of Sisyphus: Germany

1 *Dateline*, NBC, 17 September 1997.

2 In 1998, the Canadian government announced the allocation of a three-year budget of $46.8 million for its War Crimes Program, including more than $11 million for Second World War cases.

3 Erna Paris, *The End of Days* (Toronto: Lester Publishing, 1995; Buffalo: Prometheus Books, 1995), chapter 16ff.

4 Hannah Arendt, *The Origins of Totalitarianism* (New York: Harcourt Brace, 1951), 11.

5 During his tenure as mayor, Klaus Schütz instigated the idea of inviting Berlin Holocaust survivors in exile back to the city as guests, an idea that was subsequently adopted by other German municipalities.

6 Within this second generation, a fringe minority carried the passionate rejection of Nazi-perpetrator parents to extremes—to left, rather than to right-wing terrorism—that were as horrific as anything they opposed. Their activities brought former chancellor Helmut Schmidt's government to the brink of collapse and made it easy for conservatives to condemn the youth movement for change and to ignore demands for the recovery of repressed Nazi memory.

7 *Topography of Terror, Gestapo, SS and Reichssicherheitshauptamt on the "Prinz-Albrecht-Terrain": A Documentation*, ed. Reinhard Rürup, trans. Werner T. Angress (Berlin: Verlag Willmuth Arenhövel, 1989), 208.

8 Ibid.

9 Cited in *Topography* (above, n7), 214.

10 Ibid., 216.

11 For a full translation see Geoffrey Hartman, ed., *Bitburg in Moral and Political Perspective* (Bloomington: Indiana University Press, 1986), 262ff.

12 Jennifer Golub, American Jewish Committee, *Working Papers on Anti-Semitism*, "Current German Attitudes Towards Jews and Other Minorities," 1994.

13 Wolfgang Lenz, e-mail correspondence, August 20, 1997.

14 *The Revolution* (1849) in *Richard Wagner's Prose Works*, 1892–99, trans. W. A. Ellis, cited in Paul Rose, *Revolutionary Antisemitism in Germany from Kant to Wagner* (Princeton: Princeton University Press, 1990), 360.

15 Dan Bar-On, *Fear and Hope: Three Generations of the Holocaust* (Cambridge, Mass.: Harvard University Press, 1995).

16 The death of Martin Bormann was long disputed in some quarters, and "sightings" were frequently reported. In 1998, his remains were positively identified through DNA testing, and in August 1999, the German government quietly disposed of his cremated ashes at sea.

17 Peter Sichrovsky, *Born Guilty: Children of Nazi Families*, trans. Jean Steinberg (New York: Basic Books, 1988).

18 Annick Cojean, "Les Mémoires de la Shoah," *Le Monde*, 28 April 1995.

19 Niklas Frank, *In the Shadow of the Reich*, trans. Arthur S. Wensinger with Carole Clew-Hoey (New York: Knopf, 1991), 5.

20 Raul Hilberg, *The Destruction of the European Jews* (New York: Holmes & Meier, 1985), 69.

21 Frank (above, n20), 136–37.

22 Ibid., 265.

23 Telford Taylor, *The Anatomy of the Nuremberg Trials* (New York: Knopf, 1992), 539.

24 Ibid.

25 TV5, 14 October 1997.

26 Charles S. Maier, *The Unmasterable Past: History, Holocaust, and German National Identity* (Cambridge, Mass.: Harvard University Press, 1988), 15.

27 Jürgen Habermas, "The Theory of Communicative Action," 1981, cited in Maier (above, n26), 57.

28 Ibid., 59.

29 In June 2000, Nolte was awarded the Konrad Adenauer Prize for literature. On accepting, he argued that Hitler's anti-semitism was "rational" because Nazism was anti-Bolshevik and the Jews supported "Bolshevism." A new uproar broke out, echoing the "Historian's Debate" of the 1980s.

30 Raul Hilberg, 21 March 1985, cited in Hartman (above, n11), xiii.

31 Ibid., 19.

32 Cojean (above, n18).

33 Ibid.

2: Through a Glass Darkly: France

1 Erna Paris, *L'Affaire Barbie: Analyse d'un mal français* (Paris: Editions Ramsay, 1985).

2 For the historical background to this chapter, and the connections between the trial of Klaus Barbie and that of Maurice Papon, I have relied on my own previous research for Erna Paris, *Unhealed Wounds: France and the Klaus Barbie Affair* (Toronto: Methuen, 1985; New York: Grove Press, 1985).

3 Cited in Serge Klarsfeld, *Memorial to the Jews Deported from France, 1942–1944* (New York: Beate Klarsfeld Foundation, 1983), 332.

4 *Le Monde* (Paris) 10 December 1997.

5 Paris (above, n2).

6 Ibid., 61.

7 Ibid., 228.

8 Michael R. Marrus and Robert O. Paxton, *Vichy France and the Jews* (New York: Basic Books, 1981).

9 Pierre Péan, *Une Jeunesse française* (Paris: Fayard, 1994).

10 Television interview, 12 September 1994.

11 Jean Bassompierre, cited in Paris, *Unhealed Wounds* (above n2), 87.

12 André Halimi, *La Délation sous l'occupation* (Paris: Alain Moreau, 1983), Introduction.

13 Ibid.

14 Cardinal Suhard.

15 Seventy-six thousand were deported; 3,000 returned.

16 Jacques Duquesne, *Les Catholiques français sous l'Occupation* (Paris: Grasset, 1966).

17 *Le Point*, 1 November 1997.

18 *Le Canard enchaîné*, 6 May 1981.

19 BBC, 22 October 1997.

20 *Le Monde*, 1 October 1997.

21 Ibid.

22 Nuremberg Charter.

23 Michel Debré, Georges Pompidou and Maurice Couve de Murville.

24 Roger-Samuel Bloch.

25 Commission report of 15 December 1981.

26 Pierre Pujo, *L'Action française hebdo*, 30 October–5 November 1997.

27 In January 1999, the Front National split into the Front National–Mouvement National (FN–MN). Supporters of Le Pen and his rival, Bruno Mégret, clashed violently over the following months, and the parties lost favour with

the public. Their combined vote for the European elections in June 1999 was 8.97 per cent (5.69 per cent for Le Pen, 3.28 per cent for Mégret) compared with 10.52 per cent for the Front National in 1994, 15 per cent for Le Pen in the French presidential elections of 1995 and 14.94 per cent in the parliamentary elections of 1997.

28 National Union of Uniformed Police Officers, 7 October 1997.

29 Henri Amouroux, *Pour en finir avec Vichy: les oublis de la mémoire* (Paris: Laffont, 1997).

30 Henry Rousso, *Le Syndrome de Vichy: de 1944 à nos jours* (Paris: Seuil, 1990).

31 Maurice Papon, with Michel Bergès, *La Vérité n'intéressait personne* (Paris: François-Xavier de Guibert, 1999).

32 Robert O. Paxton, "The Trial of Maurice Papon," *The New York Review of Books*, 16 December 1999.

3: Erasing History: Pretense and Oblivion in Japan

1 Chronicles of Japan (*Nihongi*), completed in 697 A.D.

2 Ruth Benedict, *The Chrysanthemum and the Sword: Patterns of Japanese Culture* (Cleveland: Meridian Books, 1969), 24.

3 *Mainichi Shinbun* (Osaka), 9 February 1938.

4 Cited in "Japanese Imperialism and the Massacre in Nanking," by Gao Xingzu, Wu Shimin, Hu Yungong and Cha Ruizhen, trans. Robert B. Gray, 1996, *China News Digest*, 1995.

5 *The Rape of Nanking: An Undeniable History in Photographs* (Chicago: Innovative Publishing Group, 1996) claims 369, 366 dead. I have used a lower figure estimated by the legal scholar R. John Pritchard in Peter Calvocoressi, Guy Wint and John Pritchard, *Total War: The Causes and Courses of the Second World War*, 2nd rev. ed. (London: Viking; New York: Pantheon, 1989).

6 Harold John Timperley, *What War Means: the Japanese Terror in China, a documentary record* (London: V. Gollancz, 1938).

7 W. G. Beasley, *The Rise of Modern Japan: Political, Economic and Social Change Since 1850* (New York: St. Martin's Press, 1995), 18.

8 Sheldon Harris, *Factories of Death: Japanese Biological Warfare 1932–45 and the American Cover-Up* (London and New York: Roultedge, 1994). Harris's primary source was Peter Williams and David Wallace, *Unit 731: Japan's Secret Biological Warfare in World War II* (London: Hodder and Stoughton, 1982).

9 Major-General Kawashima Kiyoshi, ibid., 55.

10 Testimony at the Khabarovsk Trial in the Soviet Union, 1949.

11 Harris (above, n8), 66–67.

12 *The New York Times*, 4 March 1999.

13 Australia, Canada, China, France, Great Britain, India, the Netherlands, New Zealand, the Philippines, the Soviet Union and the United States.

14 Cited in Noam Chomsky, *Year 501* (Boston: South End Press, 1993), Chapter 10.

15 The story of the American cover-up of Japanese biological warfare research on humans and the protection of Shirō Ishii has been widely told since the 1980s, most recently by Sheldon Harris and Nicholas D. Kristof, "Japan Confronting Gruesome War Atrocity," *The New York Times*, 17 March 1995.

16 *San Francisco Examiner*, 1 December 1996.

17 Cited in Harris (above, n8), 190.

18 This article was posted on TheHistoryNet, the World Wide Web, September 1996, two years after the U.S. publication of Harris, *Factories of Death*.

19 Yamamoto Shichihei, *Every Gentleman*, March 1972.

20 Suzuki Akira, *Every Gentleman*, April 1972.

21 Robert Lepage's *Seven Streams of the River Ota* was first performed at the Edinburgh Festival, September 1994.

22 *Asiaweek*, 14 March 1997.

23 *The New York Times*, 22 January 1997.

24 Ibid.

25 Statement at Tokyo conference, International Citizens' Forum of War Crimes and Redress—Seeking Reconciliation and Peace for the Twenty-First Century, 10–12 December 1999.

26 Cited on Yoshiyuki Masaki's Web site.

27 *China News Digest* Web site.

28 Foreigners in Nanking were actually helpful in several ways, including attempts to create a safety zone during the brutalities and helping refugees to escape.

29 *New York Times Magazine*, 2 July 1995.

30 Iris Chang, *The Rape of Nanking, The Forgotten Holocaust of World War II* (New York: Basic Books, 1997).

31 Given the notorious unreliability of the Internet, I did a check on Masaki with Gillian Griffiths, a British television producer with whom he had worked as a researcher and interpreter.

32 Prime Minister Murayama's apology was on 15 August 1995.

33 *The New York Times*, 22 April 1999.

34 Ibid.

4: The Shadow of Slavery: The United States

1 March on Washington, D.C., 28 August 1963.

2 Ulrich B. Philips, *American Negro Slavery* (New York, 1918).

3 Kenneth M. Stampp, *The Peculiar Institution* (New York: Knopf, 1956; Vintage Books edition, 1989).

4 Cited in Stampp (above, n3), 245.

5 Finally proved by DNA testing in 1998.

6 Benjamin Franklin, September 17, 1787, cited in *Africans in America*, Part 2, *The Constitution*, www.pbs.org.

7 Sol Cohen, ed., *Education in the United States: A Documentary History*, Vol. I (New York: Random House, 1974), cited in *Africans in America*, Part 2: 1750–1805, PBS, 1998.

8 Dr. Samuel Cartwright, "Diseases and Peculiarities of the Negro Race," *DeBow's Review*, New Orleans, January–February 1862.

9 Yale University, 10 October 1997.

10 National Advisory Commission on Civil Disorders, 1968.

11 House Concurrent Resolution 96, 12 June 1997.

12 March 1998. Many thought the Vatican document did not go far enough in assigning responsibility.

13 Tony Hall, 18 June 1997.

14 Brent Staples, *The New York Times*, 21 July 1997.

15 *The New York Times*, 1 April 1998.

16 Thomas Sowell, "Apologize for What? More on Phony Black History," (Thomas Sowell Resources on the Web).

17 March on Washington, D.C., 28 August 1963.

18 Eudora Welty, *One Writer's Beginnings* (Boston: Harvard University Press, 1984).

19 There were 534 between 1882 and 1952.

20 Cited in John Dittmer, *Local People: The Struggle for Civil Rights in Mississippi* (Urbana: University of Illinois Press, 1994), 467.

21 Neil McMillen, ibid., 46.

22 On 30 September 1962, a mob rioted over Meredith's (eventually successful) attempt to enrol at the University of Mississippi. Two people died and 160 were injured. Twenty-three thousand federal troops were required to restore the peace.

23 Susan Roach, "Willing to Take a Risk: Working in the Delta," The Mississippi Delta Cultural and Historical Background, 1991: 6–7

24 Sonia Sanchez, "homegirls & handgrenades" in Norrece T. Jones Jr., *Mechanisms of Control and Strategies of Resistance in Antebellum South Carolina*

(Middletown, Conn.: Wesleyan University Press, University Press of New England, 1990).

25 Hundreds of thousands of immigrants to the United States first disembarked from ships on this piece of land in New York City harbour.

26 Rosser H. Taylor, *Ante-Bellum South Carolina: A Social and Cultural History* (Chapel Hill: University of North Carolina Press, 1942), 37.

27 The interruption was the period of Reconstruction (1865–77) when, for a short period, blacks exercised political power.

28 The Avery holds about 135 primary manuscript collections covering South Carolina and the Low Country.

29 The date was 12 April 1864.

30 Samuel P. Huntington, *American Politics: The Promise of Disharmony* (Cambridge, Mass.: Harvard University Press, 1981), 4.

31 Ibid., 33.

32 Having been pushed to the right by the Newt Gingrich Republican "revolution," President Bill Clinton was viewed in Europe as the most right-wing sitting leader in the Western world.

33 Johnnie is her given name.

34 "President's Advisory Board on Race Produces Modest Report," *The New York Times*, 18 September 1998.

35 *Post Examiner* (Charleston), 28 September 1998.

36 At this writing, an eye-opening indication of current American ideology and its reflection in language can be found in the thesaurus sold with the word-processing program Microsoft Word 6. A check of pre-packaged synonyms for *right-wing* turned up just two: "conservative" and "old-fashioned." The nine synonyms for *left-wing* included "extreme," "radical," "fanatic," "fringe" and "extremist."

37 "The system" was a euphemism for segregation, just as "our peculiar institution" was a euphemism for slavery.

38 John Dittmer, *Local People: The Struggle for Civil Rights in Mississippi* (Urbana: University of Illinois Press, 1994), 417.

39 U.S. Department of State, Office of the Spokesman (Berlin, Germany), 17 December 1999.

40 Tony Hall did not give up. He reintroduced his resolution on June 19, 2000, saying that the PIR had blocked debate of his earlier proposal. "Apology for Slavery Resolution of 2000," House Concurrent Resolution 356.

5: The Beloved Country: Truth and Reconciliation in South Africa

1 Segregation was codified after the election of the National Party in 1948, but discrimination and segregation existed long before then.

2 TRC final report, Vol. 1, chapter 8, October 1998.

3 These revelations were first exposed in 1991 by the Goldstone Commission into Third Force activities. Political identities are as complex in Kwa-Zulu/Natal as elsewhere, but the base support for the Inkatha Freedom Party (IPF) was predominantly Zulu.

4 W. A. de Klerk, *The Puritans in Africa: A Story of Afrikanerdom* (Middlesex, England: Rex Collings Ltd., 1975).

5 Richard Elphick and Robert Shell, "Intergroup Relations, 1652–1795," in *The Shaping of South African Society, 1652–1840*, ed. Richard Elphick and Hermann Giliomee, 2d ed. (Middletown, Conn.: Wesleyan University Press, 1989), 214.

6 Raphael de Kadt, J. W. Fedderke and J. Luiz, "Uneducating South Africa: A 1910–1993 Legacy," ERSA (Econometrics Southern Africa), University of the Witwatersrand, 1999.

7 Kader Asmal, Louise Asmal and Robert Suresh Roberts, *Reconciliation through Truth: A Reckoning of Apartheid's Criminal Governance* (Johannesburg: David Philip Publishing, 1996), 31.

8 Ibid., 28–29.

9 Thanks to Donald Woods and others, including Denzel Washington, Peter Gabriel, Richard Attenborough and Ken Follett, a bronze statue of Biko was unveiled in front of the East London town hall by Nelson Mandela on the twentieth anniversary of Biko's murder.

10 T. R. H. Davenport, *South Africa: A Modern History* (Toronto: University of Toronto Press, 1977), 393.

11 *Die Vrye Weekblad*, story by Jacques Pauw, 26 January 1990.

12 Quoted in documentary film, *Prime Evil*.

13 Barbara Tuchman, *The March of Folly* (New York: Ballantine Books, 1984).

14 *Boernews*, 3 February 1997.

15 Desmond Tutu, *The Rainbow People of God* (New York: Doubleday, 1994), 6.

16 Ibid., 222.

17 Ibid.

18 Botha was convicted of refusing to appear before the TRC on 21 August 1998 and sentenced to a fine of 10,000 rand or twelve months in jail, but his appeal was upheld on "technical grounds" on 1 June 1999.

19 TRC, final report, Vol. 4, chapter 4.

20 Ibid., chapter 5.

21 Donald Woods, *Biko*, 3d ed. (New York: Henry Holt, 1991), 231.

22 The amnesty committee continued its work in order to clear the backlog.

23 *Mail and Guardian* (Johannesburg), 29 October 1998.

6: Who Will Own the Holocaust?

1 Author's interview with Raul Hilberg, Burlington, Vermont, April 1999.

2 Alvin Rosenfeld, ed. "Holocaust and World War II as elements of the Yishuv Psyche until 1948," in *Thinking about the Holocaust After Half a Century* (Bloomington: Indiana University Press, 1997).

3 Raul Hilberg, *The Politics of Memory* (Chicago: Ivan R. Dee, 1996), 128.

4 Charles S. Liebman and Eliezer Don-Yehiya, cited in David Arnow, "Victors, Not Victims: Attributing Israel's existence to Holocaust perpetuates a myth that keeps us from taking control of our own destiny," *Reform Judaism Magazine*, February 1999.

5 Erna Paris, *The Garden and the Gun: A Journey Inside Israel* (Toronto: Lester & Orpen Dennys, 1988; Chatham, Mass.: Semaphore Press, 1991).

6 www.yad-vashem.org.

7 Ibid.

8 Ibid.

9 Yosef Hayim Yerushalmi, for one.

10 Exodus 13:3.

11 Exodus 17.

12 Ibid.

13 Paris (above, n5), 148.

14 David Wyman, *The Abandonment of the Jews: Americans and Holocaust, 1941–1945* (New York: Random House, 1984).

15 Raul Hilberg, *The Destruction of the European Jews* (Chicago: Quadrangle Books, 1961; New York: Holmes & Meier, 1985), 324.

16 William Rubinstein, *The Myth of Rescue* (London and New York: Routledge, 1997).

17 Cited in Edward T. Linenthal, *Preserving Memory: The Struggle to Create America's Holocaust Museum* (New York: Penguin, 1995), 223.

18 "Deformations of the Holocaust," *Commentary* 71 (February 1981): 48–54.

19 Initial statistics were compiled in 1993 by the American Jewish Committee, but problems with the wording of some survey questions led to an AJC-commissioned follow-up by the National Opinion Research Center of the

University of Chicago in 1994. Tom W. Smith, "Holocaust Denial: What the Survey Data Reveal," Working Papers on Contemporary Anti-Semitism, The American Jewish Committee, Institute of Human Relations, 1995.

20 Cited in Judith E. Doneson, "Holocaust Revisited: A Catalyst for Memory or Trivialization?", *Annals*, AAPSS, 548 (November 1996).

21 Irving Greenberg, cited in Linenthal, *Preserving Memory*, 12.

22 Jennifer Golub and Renae Cohen, "What Do Americans Know about the Holocaust?" Working Papers on Contemporary Anti-Semitism, The American Jewish Committee, Institute of Human Relations, 1995. Table 15a, 56.

23 For an interesting discussion on this subject, see Alvin Rosenfeld, "The Americanization of the Holocaust" in Alvin Rosenfeld, ed., *Thinking about the Holocaust After Half a Century* (Bloomington: Indiana University Press, 1997).

24 Ibid., 141.

25 Interview with Elie Wiesel, Sun Valley, Idaho, 29 June 1996.

26 Report of the chairman of the President's Commission on the Holocaust, 27 September 1979.

27 Wiesel interview, 29 June 1996.

28 Cited in Irving Abrahamson, ed., *Against Silence: The Voice and Vision of Eli Wiesel* (New York: Holocaust Library, 1985), Vol. 1, 30.

29 This situation began to change in the early 1980s.

30 Linenthal (above, n21), 35.

31 Cited in Saul Friedlander, "The Shoah in Present Historical Consciousness," in *Memory, History, and the Extermination of the Jews of Europe* (Bloomington: Indiana University Press, 1993), 50.

32 Ibid., 49.

33 Hilberg, cited in Linenthal, 120.

34 Michael R. Marrus, *The Holocaust in History* (Toronto: Lester & Orpen Dennys, 1987), 20.

35 Franjo Tudjman, *Bespuca povijesne zbiljnosti* (Horrors of War: historical truth and philosophy), Zagreb, 1989.

36 Elie Wiesel, "Eichmann's Victims and the Unheard Testimony," *Commentary*, December 1961.

37 Linenthal, 88.

38 Ibid., 210–16.

39 Ibid., 110.

40 Yehuda Bauer, *They Chose Life: Jewish Resistance in the Holocaust*, 1973, cited in Marrus (above, n34), 137. Italics in the original.

41 Solicitation letter by Miles Lerman, chairman, United States Holocaust Museum, cited in Rosenfeld (above, n23), 127.

7: The Furies of War Revisit Europe: Yugoslavia and Bosnia

1 Associated Press, 29 January 1999.

2 Andrei Simić, *The Peasant Urbanites: A Study of Rural-Urban Mobility in Serbia* (New York: Seminar Press, 1973).

3 Philip J. Cohen, *Serbia's Secret War: Propaganda and the Deceit of History* (College Station: Texas A&M University Press, 1996).

4 Dubravka Ugrešić, *The Culture of Lies* (London: Weidenfeld & Nicolson, 1998).

5 Dobrica Ćosić, "Reality and Possibility," cited in Christopher Bennett, *Yugoslavia's Bloody Collapse: Causes, Course, and Consequences* (New York: New York University Press, 1995), 80.

6 Drinka Gojković, "The Birth of Nationalism from the Spirit of Democracy: The Association of Writers of Serbia and the War," English language unpublished manuscript.

7 Ibid.

8 Cited in Norman Cigar, "The Serbo-Croatian War, 1991," in Stjepan G. Meštrović, *Genocide After Emotion: The Postemotional Balkan War* (New York: Routledge, 1996), 55ff.

9 Author's interview with Dobrica Ćosić, 21 November 1997.

10 Petar Petrović Njegoš, *The Mountain Wreath*, trans. D. Mrkich (Ottawa: Commoners's Publishing, 1985).

11 Cohen (above, n3) indicates that the Ustaše (unlike the Serb Chetniks) did not enjoy broad acceptance within the local population, and that the Nazis themselves estimated Croat support for the Ustaše at about 2 to 6 per cent, 106.

12 Mandić's family was deported from Italy. Her father was a Jew from Serbia.

13 Cohen, 66.

14 Cited in Cohen, 72.

15 *Naśa borba* and *Obnova*.

16 *Danas*, 10 March 1992, cited in Daniel Kofman, "The Mediterranean Connection: Israel and the War in Bosnia," *Journal of Mediterranean Studies* 6, no 2 (1996).

17 Nalini Lasiewicz of the Lasiewicz Foundation claims to have seen flyers that were dropped in the area by Serb authorities telling them to leave, and that refugees reported being ordered to evacuate; e-mail correspondence, 8 July 1999.

18 Vuk Drašković's letter of 17 December 1985, cited in Cohen, 116.

19 *The Boston Globe*, 29 November 1992, cited in Kofman (above, n16).

20 In 1998, the Milošević government revived an old law named "spreading false information."

21 Šešelj's appointment took place in mid-March 1998.

22 Article 1, paragraph 3. For a discussion of the place of the UN Charter in justifying the NATO invasion of Yugoslavia see Anthony D'Amato, *U.N. Law Reports*, ed. John Carey, May 1999.

23 *Gazeta Wyborcza*, 5 April 1999.

8: New Genocide, New Trials: The Legacy of Nuremberg

1 On 14 January 2000, all the accused in the "Kupreškić and Others" case were convicted and sentenced to terms of up to twenty-five years in prison, with the exception of Dragan Papić, who was acquitted for lack of sufficient evidence. The presiding judge, Antonio Cassese, said, "Indisputably, what happened on April 16, 1993, in Ahmići has gone down in history as comprising one of the most vicious illustrations of man's inhumanity to man."

2 Cited in Taylor, *The Anatomy of the Nuremberg Trials*, 53.

3 Ibid., 167. An earlier instance of international criminal justice took place in the period immediately preceding The Hague Peace Conference of 1899, which set out the conventions referred to as the Law of The Hague: cf R. John Pritchard, "International Humanitarian Intervention and Establishment of an International Jurisdiction Over Crimes against Humanity: The National & International Military Trials on Crete in 1898," *International Humanitarian Law: Origins, Challenges, and Prospects*, John Carey and R. John Pritchard eds. (Lampeter, Lewiston and Queenston: Robert M. W. Kempner Collegium/The Edwin Mellen Press, 2000), 1–81.

4 There are dozens of authoritative accounts of pre-Nuremberg negotiations. My principal sources are Taylor (above n2) and Mark A. Bland, "An Analysis of the United Nations International Tribunal to Adjudicate War Crimes Committed in the Former Yugoslavia: Parallels, Problems, Prospects," *Global Legal Studies Journal* 11 (1999).

5 Some early meetings took place in Berlin, starting 18 October 1945.

6 Cited in Taylor, 167, 171–72.

7 Robert Ley committed suicide in prison and Gustav Krupp was found unfit to stand trial.

8 The prosecution claimed that through his publication, *Der Stürmer*, Streicher deliberately created a psychological environment of hatred that conditioned his readers to rationalize and ultimately accept the destruction of the Jews. He was charged with having helped create and propagate the "master race doctrine" as a new religion.

9 Cf apologias for Nazism such as Carlos Porter, *Not Guilty at Nuremberg* (Hull: The Heretical Press, 1998) and publications of the Institute for Historical Review and *The Journal of Historical Review*.

10 Judith Shklar, *Legalism: Law, Morals, and Political Trials* (Cambridge, Mass.: Harvard University Press, 1986).

11 On March 3, 2000, the ICTY found General Tihomir Blaškić guilty on nineteen of twenty counts of crimes against humanity, grave breaches of the Geneva Conventions, and violations of the laws or customs of war committed in central Bosnia from 1992 to 1994. He was sentenced to forty-five years imprisonment, the longest sentence yet handed down by the tribunal. The ruling also found that the Bosnian Croat war in Bosnia and Herzegovina was directed by the late president of Croatia, Franjo Tudjman.

12 The government of President Stipe Mesić, who succeeded Franjo Tudjman, is far friendlier to the ICTY. In May 2000, the new president of the tribunal, Claude Jorda, visited Croatia, and on 17 May 2000 he wrote Mesić thanking him for his forthright co-operation. On 26 May 2000 Croatia joined NATO's "Partnership for Peace."

13 International Justice Watch Internet Discussion List.

14 Michael Scharf, *Balkan Justice* (Durham, S.C.: Carolina Academic Press, 1997).

15 Ibid., 54.

16 Michael Dobbs, *Madeleine Albright: A 20th-century Odyssey* (New York: Henry Holt, 1999). Dobbs revealed in 1997 that Albright was Jewish and claimed that she had known she was Jewish at least since 1967.

17 Gabrielle Kirk McDonald left the post in December 1999 and was replaced by Judge Claude Jorda of France.

18 McDonald's speech in Madrid was 15 December 1998.

19 *El Pais* (Madrid), 11 December 1998. Indictment against Augusto Pinochet Ugarte, 10 December 1998.

20 Derechos Human Rights, Chile (www.derechoschile.com).

21 Ibid.

22 Ibid.

23 In May 2000, the Santiago Court of Appeals voted to strip General Pinochet of his immunity, opening the door to a prosecution in Chile.

24 *Financial Times* (London), 19 October 1998.

25 Derechos Human Rights (Chile).

26 Derechos Human Rights.

27 Prosecutions had been taking place in Argentina against human rights violations that occurred during the Dirty War.

28 Garzón argued that what took place in Argentina was a genocide based on national status—that people were persecuted for not approximating what the military leadership thought an Argentine should be. There were related arguments of religious persecution; for example, Argentine Jews were targeted for special persecution.

29 Elisabeth Lira, *Utopías de fin de siglo: verdad, justicia y reconciliación*, 1995, cited Derechos Human Rights.

30 Shortly after the creation of the United Nations, the UN International Law Commission (ILC) was mandated to codify the Nuremberg principles and prepare a draft statute to create an International Criminal Court.

31 The ICC would not be retroactive.

32 John L. Washburn, co-chair of the Washington Working Group for the International Criminal Court and many others.

33 Cited in *The Washington Post*, 26 February 1999.

34 Ibid.

35 UN Charter, Article 2, Section 1.

36 Benjamin Ferencz, 16 June 1998.

37 Taylor, 248.

38 According to the International Red Cross in Sarajevo, 7,414 people from Srebrenica are missing, almost all males; 1,650 dead bodies have been discovered, of which only 60 have been identified at this writing. *Het Parool*, (Amsterdam), 1 August 1999. My thanks to Erna Rijsdijk for the citation and translation.

39 "Un voile révisionniste jeté sur le Kosovo", *Le Monde*, 3 May 2000.

40 *The Spectator* (London), 4 December 1999.

41 Patrick Ball, "Policy or Panic? The flight of Ethnic Albanians from Kosovo, March–May 1999", AAAS, May 2000.

42 Arbour returned to Canada to take up a position on the Supreme Court.

43 *The Washington Times*, 30 December 1999.

44 Ibid.

45 *Tribunal Update* 161 (24–29 January 2000).

46 Taylor, 641.

Coda

1 Benedict Anderson, *Imagined Communities: Reflections on the Origin and Spread of Nationalism* (London: Verso, 1983).

2 Cited in *The New York Review of Books*, 19 June 1999.

3 Edward Ball, *Slaves in the Family* (New York: Farrar, Straus and Giroux, Inc., 1998).

4 *The Village Voice*, 12 December 1998.

5 Brandon Hamber, "Remembering to Forget: Issues to Consider when Establishing Structures for Dealing with the Past," in *Past Imperfect: Dealing with the Past in Northern Ireland and Societies in Transition*, Brandon Hamber, ed. (Londonderry: INCORE, 1998), 56.

6 September 1944. George Orwell, Sonia Orwell and Ian Angus, eds., *The Collected Essays, Journalism and Letters of George Orwell*, vol. 3, (1943–1945), (New York: Harcourt, Brace and World, 1968), 234ff.

7 Ibid.

8 Corinna Schuler, "The Ethics of Airing Horrors of War," *The Christian Science Monitor*, 27 January 2000. The documentary was rebroadcast by CNN and CBC in February 2000 as *Cry Freetown*.

Index

A NOTE ON THE AUTHOR

Erna Paris is the author of five critically acclaimed books including: *Unhealed Wounds: France and the Klaus Barbie Affair* (1985); *The Garden and the Gun: A Journey Inside Israel* (1988); and most recently *The End of Days: A Story of Tolerance, Tyranny and the Expulsion of the Jews from Spain* (1995), which won the 1996 National Jewish Book Award for History. She lives in Toronto.